THE END OF JUSTICE

WHY AMERICA IS THE MOST INCARCERATED COUNTRY IN THE WORLD

James Bowers Johnson

Published 2016

The End of Justice

Table Of Contents

For Cory, Heather, Timothy, and Emma
What do I always say? "*Trust Daddy! Trust Poppy!*"

I would like to acknowledge

my mother and father for giving me life,

my children who gave my life distinction, and

my niece, Maddie, who gave me timely joy.

I praise my Creator for truth and the

inherent value of tribulation and perseverance.

Romans 5: 3-5

DEDICATION

This book is dedicated to the innocent men and women who have suffered throughout the ages in unimaginable ways, those who are innocent and currently behind bars in local, state, and federal jails and prisons in America and those who will be unjustly imprisoned in the future.

AUTHOR'S NOTE

As you will soon learn, this book is in large measure about titles, titles of those who exercise authority over people, places, and things. Since my theme is ultimately about freedom contrasted with America's imprisonment epidemic, an epidemic which exists because of the arrogance of governing institutions and the officials that operate them, I was certain the title to this work would have been Institutional Arrogance, Ignorance, Apathy, and Fear—Four Reasons America is the Most Incarcerated Country in the World. However, I received many opinions that this title was too *academic*. Some argued ignorant, apathetic, and fearful Americans would not be enticed to read a work with such a clinical appellation. So, after much deliberation, I chose The End of Justice.

The End of Justice is appropriate as it establishes the conclusiveness of the book's theme. If we as Americans are *satisfied* with the fact that the "justice" system sends innocent men and women to prison, we have arrived NOT at an ideal, but at ignominy. We have arrived at the end of an American excellence once embraced by our forbearers. In fact, since justice is so integral to the perpetuation of a grounded and respectable culture, we may conclude the jailing of the innocent in a rather ubiquitous and perfunctory manner epitomizes the end of a once free and noble people. An end of justice reflects and is the end of freedom itself.

Regardless of the title of this book, be mindful that the arrogance of America's governing institutions and the resulting high incarceration rate are a direct result of the ignorance, apathy. and fear of the American people.

DISCLAIMER

This book does not dispense legal advice and should not, in any manner, be perceived as such. If you want legal advice, if you want the increased possibility that you will cop a plea, pay a fine, or go to prison, contact a lawyer.

Please note, any and all citations for the United States Code and the Code of Federal Regulations were taken from the federal prison "law library" computer system while I was incarcerated. I attribute all citations as property of the "United States" Government or its respective agencies. These citations were current at the time of research and were only changed by adding emphasis as indicated by italics, bold, underlining, brackets, and quotation marks.

ACKNOWLEDGMENTS

The End of Justice was written during the most difficult of times, a time when I was ripped from my family, and four years were stolen from me and my children. Ironically, then, I must acknowledge that, but for the depraved indifference of those actors involved in the game of court, be it Judge Norman Moon, Assistant United States Attorney C. Patrick Hogeboom, IRS Agents Nicholas Pompei and Robert Biggs, Federal Public Defenders Randy V. Cargill and Andrea Harris, and the countless minor players within the entire judicial and penal systems, those in the trenches who serve at the behest of those with titles, I would not have acquired the experience and vast knowledge of what is "American justice." I would not fully appreciate that America is a conquered country, where the innocent suffer indignation at the hands of the arrogant.

I acknowledge:

- My children Cory, Heather, Timothy, and Emma for their courage and willingness to "Trust Daddy." Their loss was great and so unnecessary.
- My mother who provided support in several ways while I was both unjustly incarcerated and upon my release. She was instrumental with the editing of this work. I am grateful.
- My father, for his moral support. He passed away years before the trial. He was incensed that Timothy Geithner cheated on his taxes and was appointed as the 75th Secretary of the Treasury rather than serve a prison sentence.
- My sister Holly for her support before, during, and after prison. She was a firsthand witness to "justice" exacted at trial.
- P. Morrill for her financial, moral, and legal support. She is a true friend.
- F and C Heisey for their support over the years. With their generosity, I was able to type this manuscript while imprisoned.
- M. Secrist for allowing me to use his home as my office.
- L. Batista and O. Carter for their friendship and support.
- The innocent men I met in prison. I am grateful for their time and willingness to share. They know all too well of the ugliness of the justice system. They know those on the outside are imprisoned behind the bars of ignorance, apathy, and fear.
- R. McKee, D. Beckerman, D. Thody and T. Brehmer for reading The End of Justice and providing their constructive criticism. Thank you.
- D. Pruss for the time and effort he expended to create illustrations for this book.
- D. Parson, R. McKee, B. Erbst, and J.R. for their financial support. They provided typewriter ribbons, copy cards, coffee, and postage. Without their selfless contributions, The End of Justice would not have left the perimeter of the fourteen-foot prison fence.
- L. Brehmer for his financial support.
- Mr. Wagner for the cover & illustrations: www.freelancer.com/u/wagner1012.html.

Prologue

Truth has no friends. Truth *needs* no friends.

Truth takes solace in the company of its own light and the companionship of its cousins—knowledge, understanding, and wisdom. Truth may delight in the occasional explorations of men who seek its bounty; yet few ever reach its domain.

Truth is a frontier infrequently probed and rarely conquered. Like the Antarctic, outer space, and the vast ocean depths, truth exists—but it is rarely seen. There is no clear path to truth. Few ever reach its core. Why? Is truth elusive? Is it unattainable? Is the trek so arduous that men shy from the effort? Most certainly not. With perseverance and the mettle of souls intrepid enough to leave the comfort of their frail existence, the essence of truth may be reached.

The rare man will assess life and reckon a path for truth. Those who would never consider the journey will inevitably disparage and criticize. Such is human nature. Little do naysayers comprehend that truth and justice are indispensable for humanity. Champions are vital to bridge the divide between timidity and courage, uncertainty and change, complacency, and resolve. May men heed the noble calling to those beacons of light on distant horizons, beacons of truth which remind mankind that satisfaction with mediocrity is not acceptable.

If not for those valiant souls who venture beyond the realm of denial, lies would subdue as easily as an eastern wind compels tall grass to genuflect. May truth be ascertained and fully known. May truth inspire those who dare to prevent carnage from the absence of truth.

Obedience to truth is the singular trait through which its light will pierce darkness. We beckon those who are willing. Come, valiant champions! Run the race of solitary and solemn reckoning. Come, valiant champions! Obediently follow the rays of illumination into the abyss. Come, valiant champions! Grasp the essence of truth and bring it to our collective conscience. Come!

Make the daring trek into the untamed and unknown. Battle towards victory or defeat. Regardless of the outcome, humanity is indebted to your sacrifice. May the scars which mar your body, the anguish which sears your psyche, and the tumult which shapes your soul serve as a testament of a life that shunned the conventional. May history sing your praises and forever memorialize your pursuit of excellence and insatiable thirst for truth.

Now, consider the import of truth and then weigh the significance of the following response from the Social Security Administration to a query from an American.

TEH2A
OX1355

November 12, 2003

Number 109
8370 West Cheyenne Avenue
Las Vegas, Nevada 89129

Dear [redacted]:

This is in response to your letter about the law requiring an individual to obtain a Social Security number (SSN).

The Social Security Act does not require a person to have a Social Security number to live and work in the United States, nor does it require a Social Security number simply for the purpose of having one. However, if someone works without a Social Security number, we cannot properly credit the earnings for the work performed, and the worker may lose any potential entitlement to Social Security benefits.

Other laws require people to have and use Social Security numbers for specific purposes. For example, the Internal Revenue Code (26 U.S.C. 6109 (a)) and applicable regulations (26 CFR 301.6109-l(d)) require a person to get and use a Social Security number on tax documents and to furnish the number to any other person or institution (such as an employer or a bank) that is required to provide the Internal Revenue Service (IRS) information about payments to that person. There are penalties for failure to do so. The IRS also requires employers to report Social Security numbers with employees' earnings. In addition, people filing tax returns for taxable years after December 31, 1994, generally must include the Social Security number of each dependent.

The Privacy Act regulates the use of Social Security numbers by government agencies. They may require a Social Security number only if a law or regulation either orders or authorizes them to do so. Agencies are required to disclose the authorizing law or regulation. If the request has no legal basis, the person may refuse to provide the number and still receive the agency's services. However, the law does not apply to private sector organizations. Such an organization can refuse its services to anyone who does not provide the number on request.

If you have further questions, you may contact the Las Vegas office at 5460 West Sahara Avenue, Las Vegas, Nevada 89146 (telephone 702-248-8717) or call our toll-free number, 1-800-772-1213. Our representatives there will be glad to help you. For general information about the Social Security program, you can access *Social Security Online*, our Web site on the Internet, at <http://www.socialsecurity.gov>.

We hope you find this information helpful.

Sincerely,

Annie White

Annie White

"Would you tell me, please, which way I ought to go from here?"
"That depends a good deal on where you want to get to."
"I don't much care where-"
"Then it doesn't matter which way you go." **Lewis Carroll, Alice in Wonderland**

CAVEAT EMPTOR (BUYER BEWARE)

The foregoing letter from the Social Security Administration (SSA) should raise several questions. One query may be: Is it true? Is one able to live and work in the United States without a Social Security Number (SSN)? Those who are not inclined to believe so will never appreciate true freedom. For freedom begins with the clarity of truth, confidence of the mind, and the yearning of the heart. Absent truth, it matters not which way one goes. Any path will lead to the same destination, a destination that does not require independent thought. Why? Without clarity of truth, a yearning heart and independent thought, ignorance, apathy, and fear will always be one's constant companions.

The End of Justice takes a particular and uncommon path which is not for the feeble. This book will challenge you to not only read but understand what is otherwise unorthodox. If you did not know that obtaining an SSN is not required by law, that you are not required to them for your children, then allow the SSA letter to serve as a shot across the bow, to stop you from reflexively believing all you were and are told. Clearly, all hospital employees who told all uninformed Americans they had to get an SSN for their newborn were not truthful.

What else do you believe that is not the truth? Moreover, does it matter that what you currently accept as "truth" is inconsistent with reality? When we weigh the significance of justice in America, we cannot be cavalier with our discernment. We must reconcile that America, with only 5% of the world's population, has almost 25% of the imprisoned. Do you believe that all Americans in prison deserve to be there?

If your answer is in the affirmative, please put this book down and continue your blind journey as you ask others where you *ought to go from here* because you don't much care *where you want to get to*, for, it *doesn't matter which way you go*.

However, if you question the number of criminal convictions, be prepared to take off the shackles that bind you. Be prepared to move beyond your own ignorance, apathy, and fear. Be prepared to defeat the destructive influence of institutional arrogance.

The words "people of the United States" and "citizens" are synonymous terms, and mean the same thing. They both describe the political body who, according to our republican institutions, form the sovereignty, and who hold the power and conduct the government through their representatives. They are what we familiarly call the "sovereign people," and every citizen is one of this people, and a constituent member of this sovereignty...
Boyd v State of Nebraska, 142 US 135 (1892)

Knowledge and Power

As one who takes exceptions to clichés, I disagree that "knowledge is power." I believe what one does with knowledge makes knowledge powerful. Many in positions of authority are not knowledgeable or, if they are, they use knowledge for ignoble ends. Regrettably, people all too frequently give credence to those with titles. Titles represent the appearance of knowledge. People tend to believe those in positions of authority *know*; otherwise, they would not be there. Whether a teacher, congressman, or doctor, we naturally conclude each is competent. Yet, when any of them performs without complete understanding and we are unaware of this fact, they still have their titles, and we continue to perceive them as credible. One with a title may hide his incomplete understanding behind the very system he serves while and we blindly trust the system.

It is not until students fail standardized tests, the government runs another annual deficit, or the wrong medicine is prescribed that we recognize that those with titles are as unaware or ineffective as the results indicate. Surprisingly, with few exceptions of true accountability, the system continues to perform with the same mediocrity. The ineffective teacher gets tenure, the career congressman blames partisan politics and medical malpractice insurance pays for the doctor's mistake. Such is life on a spinning plane where titles convey greater significance than deserved.

The End of Justice is a book about titles. It discusses a serious topic—the criminalizing of America. America has acquired its own title as the most incarcerated country in the world. This title is not by happenstance. We are not a more immoral people than any other. Thus, to understand how and why we are aggressively imprisoned, we must appreciate the motives of those with titles. Those with titles are an unfortunate reason America has acquired such an unworthy distinction.

The gravity of our incarceration rate is probably the most credible indicator that America's fate is all but certain. In a very practical sense, there are two conclusions to be drawn. One, our high rate of imprisonment reflects the beginning of the end of our republic. Or two, the criminalizing of our culture *is* the end, with the beginning having occurred some fifty or more years ago. Regardless, the ominous implication of America's ignoble title is as sobering as it is real.

This book is a limited attempt to, even if only anecdotally, substantiate and justify how and why we face such a demise. Without a scientific basis, this book is an effort to draw upon the innate sense of equity that lies within the hearts and minds of the common man. For, with the title of *common man*, we have no ax to grind or promise to fulfill. We have no system to support or behind which we may hide. We are accountable to our conscience and fair sense of right and wrong. We may be honest and vulnerable. We may observe with a common man's perspective. With a sense of fair play, we determine what is just or not. We don't need someone with a title to tell us what or how to think. Moreover, our individual assessment is not subject to motivations that malign inherent decency, civility, and balance.

Often the power associated with titles is an impairment to sound judgment. The ego is consumed with power and allows arrogance to gain a foothold. As a result, discretion is abused. Arrogance, when manifested within the institutions of the legal system, obscures and frustrates any initiative that was once christened with a true and just intent. The legal system, for example, should be concerned with justice. Is there any other intent? With arrogance, justice is secondary to the conviction and incarceration of innocent men. When justice is compromised, we are no more than a conquered people.

I completed the rough draft of The End of Justice in federal prison when a man handed me a letter written by Bernard Kerik, a foremost expert in the corrections industry. Kerik spent his professional life managing jails and prisons in America. His curriculum vita is replete with awards which reflect his expertise and accomplishments. His assistance on behalf of the United States and foreign countries earned him a reputation of distinction.

Kerik sent his letter to the United States Attorney General, the U. S. Sentencing Commission, and members of Congress. Ironically, Kerik wrote this correspondence with the title of *federal prisoner*. Notably—and to his credit—Kerik admits to not having fully understood the real problems within our incarceration system *until* he became a convict. It was when he was subject to the penal system that he appreciated the magnitude and repercussions of the process. It took his own imprisonment for this key player to understand that he was wrong.

I applaud Kerik for his attempt to determine the cause of America's shameful condition. He should be commended for his willingness to articulate the cause of our most significant plight. If anything, Kerik was able to peek from behind the institutional arrogance which shielded him from understanding the depth and breadth of the problems he fostered. Unfortunately, and Kerik is likely big enough to appreciate this observation, he may have shed some light on this topic, but he does not comprehend its true nature. This is not a negative reflection upon Kerik. He is, has been, and will always be part of the system. He views the problem from the vantage point of the judicial and penal process.

While this may appear to be an indictment against Kerik, such is not my intent. I merely invite him to consider that, regardless of his public service and time in prison, he views America's incarceration rate from a limited perspective. While Kerik cites symptoms which affect our country, he fails to grasp the root cause. If he understood the cause, he would not be speaking to the power players with titles; he would speak to the American people. Instead, he has written to the *titled* elite, spoken before CPAC (Conservative Political Action Conference), and appealed to governors and political hopefuls. This may be good, but these political operatives are no different. They only lack the time behind bars. They are a part of the system. They created the problem and are reluctant to solve it. These operatives will continue to be a part of the problem in the future. Kerik's efforts to ameliorate what is now an industry in America—prisons are big business—are better spent determining the true cause and sharing the truth with fellow citizens. This would be the best use of his time and insight.

Undoubtedly, Kerik appreciates the gravity of the problem. In his correspondence he states, "the system is in dire need of repair."[1] I, however, would suggest the current system needs to be *replaced* to a large extent. At a minimum, we need a regulator on a system which operated fine before the increase in the number of incarcerations. Ideally, those who caused and/or encouraged the present crisis should be replaced. Kerik typifies this notion, as do many public servants. This is evident by his words, "I have learned that most of what I thought to be true is not just reality."[2] He then offers that public officials

[1] Bernard Kerik, *U. S. CRIMINAL JUSTICE SYSTEM IN DIRE NEED OF REPAIR*, June 2011

[2] Ibid.

"just don't know what the prison system is really like."[3] This underscores that ignorance is part of the root cause. Kerik never moves beyond ignorance and hints that officials have no reason to care, if only because they are unaware. What he fails to realize is those who created the problem did so out of arrogance. Arrogance is the reason those with titles do not care. Arrogance is the root cause he never addresses. Why? Kerik may be too close to the problem. He has not examined how institutional arrogance became such an influence.

Kerik continues his letter by citing officials like Supreme Court Justice Anthony Kennedy who, in 2003, stated the sentencing guidelines were "unwise and unjust."[4] Kerik is shocked that the problems exist and are worse than a decade ago. He suggests, once again, "our legislators and the American public do not care about a problem they do not know exists."[5] This is too facile a conclusion. To suggest lawmakers are not cognizant of the problem is unacceptable. Certainly, those elected officials with seniority are aware. This speaks to the arrogance which encouraged the situation in the first place.

Kerik misses the mark. He suggests an "out of sight/out of mind"[6] syndrome. While he is correct in some respects, the degree of comfort which insulates America and the people's fear of government are what need to be addressed and exposed. Even if people fully appreciated the injustices of the system, they would care no more than legislators. Kerik suggests "unless they see it for themselves—either personally or through eye opening discourse—they will not act."[7] Yet, may I suggest people will not act until they are affected personally—and even then, it is questionable. Absent a true sense of community, why would there be an individual or collective call to right the wrongs within the legal system? Furthermore, would the people have the mettle to see it through?

When referencing non-violent drug offenders, Kerik offers that "families and communities have failed them."[8] If this is so, we must ask why it would be any different if families and communities knew. How would change be realized? Wouldn't these groups potentially be equally disengaged? Many a family and community member is in prison unjustly with no resolution. Kerik, especially with his influence, must reconcile with the ignorance, apathy, and fear of the American people as equally as he confronts the ignorance, apathy, and arrogance of those with titles who operate government institutions.

Consider Kerik's words:

> *In all the years I spent in the correctional field, I never focused on the collateral damage to the offender, their families and, more so, to our society and country. My principal focus was the care, custody and control of the inmate population, ensuring that the prisoners received the programs and services they were supposed to receive according to state and federal minimum standards. When I thought of incarceration costs, my only concern was the incarceration cost to house a prisoner within our system.*[9]

This was the extent of his perspective as a public official. His "only concern"[10] was the incarceration cost and minimum standards, not families or society. Kerik's limited perspective epitomized ignorance, apathy, and arrogance of those in authority with titles.

To Kerik's credit, he ties in the concern of over-criminalization by federal

---

[3] Ibid.
[4] Ibid.
[5] Ibid
[6] Ibid.
[7] Ibid.
[8] Ibid.
[9] Ibid.
[10] Ibid.

prosecutors who are increasingly "investigating and criminally prosecuting people for what was once civil, administrative, and regulatory conduct."[11] However, Kerik doesn't go far enough. He only brushes up against the central concern that speaks to the issue of "mass incarceration."[12] Judges, prosecutors, and defense attorneys represent the legal system and all its flaws. They operate behind the arrogance which perpetuates the likelihood the problem will not go away anytime soon. Their decisions and actions are unchecked. Consequently, they become unaccountable.

In the past, Kerik, by operating the prisons, was on par with the prosecutor. He viewed the process for what it represented and gave it his full support. Now with the title of *convict*, with a fresh perspective, he will remain in support of the system as long as he fails to appreciate why the government is able to make criminals out of the innocent. Mr. Kerik suggests: "It is time to consider a way to give these men a second chance...a real second chance."[13] Yet, instead of seeking to give men a second chance, why not prevent ever sending them to a place they do not belong? Kerik must consider this point. If he did, and injustices were resolved, he would have no need to appropriately assess that these "people who should not be in prison are rotting away." Kerik makes a worthy observation.

> *The flaws, failures and inadequacies of the system are overwhelming. From within the system, I can see them clearly. I also know they can be fixed.*[14]

As a prisoner, Kerik became one in the trenches. He articulated his sense of the injustice that is "American justice." He must go further. He cites that the federal prison population went from 25,000 in 1980 to approximately 210,000 in 2011.[15] This is an epidemic which does not require change, but a comprehensive systemic elimination. If those in prison serve only ten percent of their sentences, this does not solve the problem. Placing them on home confinement continues the pattern while giving the appearance of change. Unless federal jurisdiction in our lives is challenged, until the government complies with the limits of the Constitution, we are subject to the unacceptable.

Kerik appropriately suggests possible solutions that would reduce the length of sentences. He states, "without these changes and more, the U. S. prison system will continue to grow in staggering numbers."[16] He draws upon the words of former House Speaker Newt Gingrich: "the effects of rampant incarceration in recent years have been devastating for families, neighborhoods and civil society."[17] Yet, Kerik states Gingrich has no idea from the "outside looking in."[18] Good for Kerik; but he must convince those with titles that they are culpable. This is the point. Kerik states:

> *We have allowed our criminal justice system to devolve into one that lacks fairness, mercy and compassion, and seems to pride itself on over criminalization, conviction, mass incarceration and the destruction of humanity. Sentences are too long, punishment too harsh, and true rehabilitation is non-existent. If Congress and the American people could witness what I have since my incarceration, there would be anger, there would be outrage, and there would be change. No one in their right mind*

[11] Ibid.
[12] Ibid.
[13] Ibid.
[14] Ibid.
[15] Ibid.
[16] Ibid.
[17] Ibid.
[18] Ibid.

would allow this system to continue as it is today.[19]

As passionate as Kerik is, as correct as his incomplete assessment may be, even if most Americans knew of this injustice, it would and will continue. We need only look at the fiasco of federal spending that has gone on for decades and has "incarcerated" all Americans and future generations into an inescapable financial prison. We allow this abuse to persist unabated. What should we expect from a people affected by ignorance, apathy, fear, and officials who are equally so—and arrogant?

While Kerik may be effective at managing prisons, we need more than an incomplete opinion as to how to change the system. Kerik deserves credit for expressing a thought which warrants attention. If politicians are "tough on crime" because their constituents applaud this posture, if the electorate wants aggressive criminal enforcement, the establishment is granted a license to achieve this aim. The intense effort expended on *perceived* crimes equals what we expect for true crimes. Those who operate the legal system no longer exercise discretion that is just. Defendants and their families are adversely affected by this regrettable dynamic. Pointedly, how the situation occurs to people affects how they perform. Unless someone speaks with an eye to the future, as to what may be, to the exclusion of what presently is, the audience will be limited to only those affected. Few will act for change.

It is past time for Americans to weigh the individual components of the legal system. With insight from Kerik and those who have been criminalized, we may learn how each facet contributes to injustice. We may understand why America is heavily incarcerated. However, given the influence of the *system*, we should not take comfort that those who operate it can or will offer solutions. Here is the overarching concern. At some point, whether we have thirty, forty, or fifty percent of the world's incarcerated; we must accept that America has been and is subdued. The rate of twenty-five percent reflects this benchmark.

Kerik has served his country as an insider with a title. Since he hopes to expose a national crisis, he deserves our attention and appreciation. We should heed his dire warnings for what they are—indicators. America may cease to be the essence of freedom. Rather, it has become the land of the imprisoned. We would do well to couple Kerik's ominous assessment with the root cause, our ignorance, apathy, fear, and arrogance.

Any number of convicts has acquired a healthy understanding of the true nature of the judicial system. They may not be able to articulate the particulars, but the gnawing sense of injustice is overwhelming. We, thankfully, have a public servant in Kerik, who senses the same gnawing. His overview of what he experienced is consistent with countless others. His conclusions can do nothing but underscore the thesis of <u>The End of Justice</u>. May this message alter the presumptions of all Americans. With a new understanding and a resolve to seek credible remedies with a resurgent courage, we may humble an army of arrogant public officials who have the known or unknown intent to conquer a nation.

If man employs titles and abuses corresponding powers to defeat justice, injustice will reign. Such abuse of discretion will ensure America retains its ignominious title as the land of the imprisoned—likely the last phase culminating in the end of a once great, powerful, and free country. The easiest country to conquer is one which rots from within. May this book encourage a revelation of the truth that exposes a rather foreboding present and future.

<u>The End of Justice</u> encourages the belief that institutional arrogance exists because

[19] Ibid.

of the ignorance, apathy, and fear of the American people. When people take comfort in the use of titles and the subsequent abuse of discretion and rarely challenge the result, we have both an intended and unintended consequence—the unflattering conditioning of the body public. Society will gravitate to a rather common acceptance of a title, term, or concept which fills a void. When the void is filled, the conversation may continue, but only with a limited perspective.

Consider the following. Americans believe they have *constitutional rights*. Yet, from where does this expression originate, except largely in the vernacular? Judges may use this broad term to articulate the rights of the people, but are these rights not natural rights or unalienable rights? We certainly do not get rights from the Federal Constitution. The Constitution serves the purpose of restricting the Federal Government. The Constitution *constitutes* the government. We would be justified to refer to *constitutional constraints* which bind the federal authority. The government is bound by the language which *constitutes* its existence. While the Bill of Rights expresses the fundamental rights of the people antecedent to the creation of the government, we may rest assured the federal authority was not to encroach upon them. This is why the language of the Constitution states, for example, the Second Amendment "shall not be infringed."[20] The emphasis is on what the government cannot do—a constitutional constraint.

When we casually fill the void without the least degree of enlightenment, we limit our possible understanding. The title "constitutional rights" skews any conversation from the outset. The people accept what should have been rejected and do not embrace what was not proffered—the truth. Those with influence exacerbate the problem when they prey upon the ignorance of the people. They abuse their powers with a "discretion" that robs people of their liberty. We would be well served to conclude that their power exceeds preordained constitutional constraints.

Consider another example. We universally accept that all Americans are "United States citizens." Yet, few understand the historical relevance of the term. We do not know that not everyone was or is a "United States citizen," which suggests there may be more than one definition. Once again, the *term* fills a void, and we loosely embrace an application of a title which lacks the scrutiny it deserves. We may agree that, as citizens of one of the fifty States of the Union, which comprise the united States of America, we are by default "United States Citizens," as in one of the citizens of one of all the States. Past Supreme Court decisions express that one may be a citizen of a state and not be a United States citizen. The latter is a separate and distinct person from the former. Each is a separate and distinct title. Who, then, is a "U. S. citizen?"

As may be plainly seen, those in authority with titles, those who abuse discretion, may and do use the divide between ignorance and understanding as an unjust advantage. This realization acquires greater significance when we delve into multiple definitions of a single term within the United States Code (USC). These definitions are not the generally accepted ones we would otherwise readily accept in our everyday use of language. Yes, our preconceived notions of a definition fill a void with what is not true. This revelation should compel us to question the titles and terms we use and how and why our present frame of reference is incorrect.

The following example reflects the nature of this concern. The definition of "Non-Federal Government" and "Federal Government" are in essence the same.

19 USC Section 2155 - Information and advice from public and private sectors:
(m) "NON-FEDERAL GOVERNMENT" DEFINED As used in this section, the

[20] Amendment II, The Constitution of the United States

term "non-Federal government" means—
(1) any State, territory, or possession of the United States, or the District of Columbia, or any political subdivision thereof; or
(2) any agency or instrumentality of any entity described in paragraph (1)

47 USC Section 224 – Pole Attachments
(a) DEFINITIONS As used in this section:
(2) The term "Federal Government" means the government of the United States or any agency or instrumentality thereof.

Given the above definitions, we, as common folk, unschooled in the legal realm, would have never considered that "non-federal" is "federal." We can plainly see that legal terms or titles serve an intended purpose we would not have imagined. Naturally, we readily embrace that anything and everything which is not federal is non-federal, just as we accept that we are "United States citizens" with "constitutional rights."

We are unaware because we supposedly already *know*. Honestly, why determine what a "United States citizen" or "non-federal government" means when we presume to know? Why consider the alternative to a constitutional right when we would not question our understanding in the first place? Such a posture results in and reflects disbelief and culminates in our broad acquiescence that all laws must apply to all people. This is true since those with titles presumptively exercise the proper power to enforce them. Yes, we fill the void, again, with our own incomplete or incorrect presumption.

Having established that we may not know, just as Bernard Kerik realized he had no understanding of the incarceration system, we will move forward with a simple tactic. We will presume—and this is important—we are "United States citizens," and "United States" means exactly what we currently accept, while "State" means nothing more than some generic definition which fills the void. These uninitiated and unchallenged representations are as the titles imply. However, once we read any law and the corresponding definition of the above terms and realize they do not apply to Americans, we will have established a point of departure from ignorance and entered knowledge.

If we reconsider how we view any given topic and defy any prior understanding, we become enlightened. The "knowledge is power" mantra becomes relevant. Knowledge may give the appearance of power; yet, what is done with knowledge is paramount. We have the possibility of eradicating the ignorance, apathy, and fear which afflicts the American people. With a new understanding, we may reverse the accelerated growth of the prison industry over the last thirty years. We can defeat the institutional arrogance which has led to our demise.

This, my fellow Americans, would be powerful.

You may be whatever you resolve to be. **General Thomas "Stonewall" Jackson**

The Path of Least Resistance

Anyone who observes cattle in a pasture may notice several things. One, the cattle generally stay as a herd. Two, cattle travel in a pattern. Three, occasionally, some may wander away from the herd. This is life. This is what cattle do. Largely driven by forces within their nature, they follow a routine and seldom deviate. There is no need to change.

The paths in the pasture tell their story. These routes usually track along the perimeter of the fence and depart at certain junctures that lead to other destinations, whether a pond, salt blocks, or hay bales. When the day is done, a lone path typically leads back to shelter. Yes, cattle lead a rather simple and mindless existence. This existence is reflected in the path. The path, which is worn and packed by constant trudging of hooves, is a solitary one. There is no other path to the left or right. Cattle typically don't travel side by side. They follow, one after the other. Following is easy. There is no risk. When they enter the pasture daily, they do what is known. They follow the path and each other. No leader is required. There is no thought or challenge, no need for daring resolve or ingenuity. No single one calculates a shorter or easier path. They simply trace the steps of those before them.

Hence, when cattle follow their predecessors, they fulfill their destiny. They stare at the back end of the one in front and infrequently benefit by happenstance. Those leading may block the wind or the sun's rays which ease above the horizon. Those that follow also suffer the repercussions. Those in front may relieve their bowels and bladders while in motion. Cattle do not realize the positive or negative. They just follow.

If we consider why the path is where it is, we can reach transparent conclusions. The fence which surrounds the pasture serves as a barrier. The path can be no further than just inside. Not that the cattle use the fence as a guide, it is a guide, nonetheless. The fence contains and the path becomes. The location of the path, then, is not because it is the easiest and most practical route; it is formed by virtue of constraint. The cattle may go no further than what is permitted.

The few paths that branch off exist for a reason. There is a need to satisfy. A pond is water source. A hay bale provides food. No fence is required. Instinct serves to direct and restrict movement. Such is the nature of cattle. These adjacent paths are no different than the one along the fence.

An observer of a large herd grazing in the pasture may perceive disorder. As cattle meander loosely, there is the appearance of randomness. Yet, the herd, after exercising a communal rite of feeding, as if obediently and with order, complies instinctively within the constraints of its environment. The ennui and ritual of following renews.

There are lessons gleaned by observing cattle and the pasture. The pasture reflects nature, a microcosm of life. It is a representation of a world of patterns. The pasture symbolizes inherent order within seeming disorder. The pasture demonstrates the predominance of group think and reactive compliance. The ant hill is no different. The beehive is the same. The venues and boundaries may vary. However, within apparent chaos, there is rhyme and reason; there is order.

Human nature is not dissimilar. If a thousand people were placed at the base of a massive hill and told to climb to the top, it would appear chaotic. With their ascent, a few might consider the route they would take, but they would be the exception. Most would place one foot in front of the other and proceed. Those behind would naturally follow. Those in the lead would negotiate any obstacles. A rock might divert the path to the left, a hole may impede to the right. A steep incline would force a forty-five-degree trek for a short distance. In the end, 990 may scale the hill and arrive at the top. Not surprisingly, the hill would likely not have one, two, or three different paths but, perhaps, seven paths marked by downtrodden grass.

With their descent, the people would likely follow the same paths. Through past efforts which did not involve much consideration, and given the limitations of the hill, the way to proceed would be clear. This does not mean an eighth or ninth path wouldn't be created. But, invariably, over time the seven to nine paths would diminish to possibly four, or those that would be the easiest to traverse. From a random ascent and descent, humanity establishes order.

Those who never made the initial journey may have been unwilling or unable. Twenty who made the climb may have been mavericks. Those who plotted their own way would likely be the most efficient, but not the ones others followed. Their paths might be the most arduous and invigorating and, therefore, traveled by them alone. The rest of the climbers would not reap the bounty of their decisions or choices. The experience of the twenty would be unique. We may conclude, then, that most would not challenge the conventional. The balance would simply follow the masses. Such is the nature of man.

If we survey history, we may draw a correlation of humanity's journey through time and the climb up the hill. Parameters like the fence in the pasture, or the rock and hole upon the hill exist. Some parameters are seen; others are not. Time is the ultimate barrier. Influence by those with authority is another.

What is seen are laws, decrees, and written rules which guide—right or wrong—to an intended or unintended objective. As with the 990 who scaled the hill, most know nothing and do nothing but conform. Most care for little more than to comply. Most are too fearful to do otherwise. As such, the well-worn path is sufficient. This is the sad truth. The human experience is rather limited. Yet, there are those who refuse to follow. They are iconoclasts, the unconventional. For any number of reasons, they defy the norm and venture into the unknown. Invariably, they suffer the consequences. They experience the unexpected and endure the unfortunate. Regardless, and because of their intrepid posture, their paths are ones of distinction.

If we consider the administration of justice throughout history, we perceive a pasture, the ant hill, a beehive, a massive hill. We see order out of chaos. Ironically, the order is not always for the cause of the truth and justice. The parameters of justice are used for ignoble ends. The innocent are condemned. Just as cattle are controlled and eventually ushered through the gates of the slaughterhouse, man suffers. As honey is taken from the hives of the most industrious insects, the lives and property of men are seized.

Time represents the massive hill. Billions upon billions of souls have negotiated this hill. They have and still follow the sundry paths laid before them. The most traveled paths have been winnowed down from the many to the definite. One such path is *justice*, off which forks a path for *injustice*. Those who willingly, or by force, travel the latter, they endure the worst. They experience man's inhumanity to man.

The benefit of history rests in our ability to distinguish the repercussions of unjust acts. Regrettably, the disadvantage is the damage already wrought. Yet, with hindsight, we can appreciate past cause and effect. We can perceive the unspoken and unwritten controls used to achieve the dubious by those with titles. For those who are willing to question the past, such insight illuminates the unjust or exposes what is not true. There are countless examples which have worn a dreary rut through the ages. Men and women have suffered needlessly which underscores the refrain of man's inhumanity to man. Notables, such as Jesus of Nazareth, Joan of Arc, John Bunyan, Gandhi, and Mandela are but a few who were courageous. Their solitary sojourn defied the norm for which they made the ultimate sacrifice. Humanity would be wise to recognize their contributions. If these intrepid warriors accomplished anything, they exposed the dark side of human nature.

Those who view the hill from a distance may see the paths that line its terrain. Those who observe history notice the paths that shaped human thought and behavior. The discerning will parlay their observations and distinguish the injustice and inhumanity of today. It exists. The nature of man is no different now than yesterday or even a thousand years ago. Man will do good. He will do evil. He will seek to control. Parameters will be established. The masses will follow. The path will lead the unsuspecting to what will be. Those who veer to the left or to the right and refuse to follow will chart their own course and likely suffer the consequences.

This book discusses a number of legal cases and men who suffered terribly. Their stories were but a foreshadowing of the present. Each example is an explanation of innocent people who forged their own way. As a result, they were dragged down to the path of injustice. Josh Hus, Galileo, Giles Corey, and Arlon Jones contended with what is irreconcilable. We, by retrospection, would do them, ourselves, and our progeny a great service to understand their travails in the context of man's present and future.

America is the most incarcerated country in the world. There are definitive reasons for this ignominious distinction. The institutional arrogance of every component of the legal system and government is culpable. There is little humility demonstrated by public servants. Officials abuse their discretion and the innocent suffer. There are three fundamental elements which give rise to such arrogance—the ignorance, apathy, and fear of the American people. This theme will be reinforced time and again. The people follow. Out of ignorance, comfort, and anxiety, they comply and never venture beyond the worn path of conformity. By default, officials with titles have license to regulate beyond their authority. It is then that institutional arrogance is born.

Live your life in such a manner that you will be killed. **Roger Smith**

Perspective

Upon my unjust incarceration as a federal prisoner, I received a letter from a friend in which he stated I was a *common criminal*. I was humbled. I asked myself questions. Why do men malign? Why do we limit understanding and exclude what is unknown? Why did my friend judge me? What did I know that he did not?

I began a search for truth regarding the income tax laws some twenty years ago that culminated in my imprisonment. I am innocent of the charges for which I was convicted. As an innocent man, my intentions were just, and my objectives were transparent. Yet, if only because I was in prison, others considered me to be no more than a common criminal. My friend's candid characterization did not detract from my beliefs. Rather, I was determined to appreciate how and why he concluded so. My intent was to understand and, quite possibly, influence his perspective.

Sages throughout history have cautioned against judging. God proclaimed this wisdom. What does one do in the absence of judging? The answer is to seek knowledge, understanding, wisdom, and truth. If the tongue is quick to destroy—and it is—then reflection anchored in understanding prevents unwarranted conclusions. Restraint reflects wisdom, wisdom grounded in discernment. I accepted my friend's label. I was not angered. I did not retaliate. I weighed his observation. I had no intent to seek agreement. I simply wanted to contribute to the conversation. I concluded that if my friend would consider what was previously unthinkable, my objective would be achieved.

As it stands, America is in peril, more so than at any point in history. With only five percent of the world's population, America has almost *twenty-five* percent of the prison population. This is unthinkable. Yet, there is hope. We can alter this dynamic with healthy and non-judgmental dialogue. The alternative is ominous for our future. We ill-serve ourselves and any cause when we fail to understand and then blindly judge. America is and has been excessively criminalized. Our neighbors are becoming common criminals at an alarming rate. Why? The system makes them so. We, an unsuspecting people, are oblivious to this regrettable truth. If we distinguish between our perception of freedom and the reality of our expanding prisons, we may realize the former is no longer and the latter must end. Our future will become more austere unless we reconcile with three dire conditions—our own ignorance, apathy, and fear. The difference of my perspective and that of my friend is caused by these conditions. If we remedy each condition, we avail ourselves to the possibility of understanding. Otherwise, not only will our prison problem persist, but we will also ensure the demise of our diminishing freedom and further create an atmosphere of judgment.

It is axiomatic that man will not believe what he is unable to accept. In psychology this is known as cognitive dissonance. Overcoming insurmountable disbelief is no small task. Such an act requires knowledge and courage. Ultimately, though, we need a healthy regard for the truth and a willingness to relinquish what is comfortable.

Man doesn't want to be uncomfortable. Man tends to maintain what is known and to exclude what is not. We don't typically embrace unnecessary circumstances. However, if we accept that circumstances are what they are and nothing more, we may appreciate that being comfortable is crippling. Knowing and understanding, if derived by experience, are paramount if one is to be uncomfortable. Experience is the path to wisdom and truth. If we know the truth, circumstances become less consequential. For example, ultimately, it doesn't matter if I am *uncomfortable* and in prison instead of at home with my family. *In the context of life and the pursuit of a greater purpose, the truth alone matters.*

Consider this question. Does it matter whether one lives on the beautiful beaches of Hawaii rather than the golden plains of Kansas? One may prefer the ocean to the prairie. One may be comfortable in Kauai and uncomfortable in Topeka. Yet, these are but circumstances. Whether wading in temperate waters or in the throes of tornadoes, what matters most is relevant. We should not prevent knowing through experience simply for the disbelief that life is not as we expect. Cognitive dissonance should not impede life and the manifestation of truth. Living in Hawaii or Kansas is not unlike distinguishing between what is hot or cold. We don't know cold unless we experience hot. Either may be uncomfortable. Experience, then, overcomes cognitive dissonance. Experience begets knowledge, which begets understanding and, ideally, wisdom. Each is gained through discomfort. This is the nature of experience.

I refer to the concept of cognitive dissonance for the inhibitor it is. Human nature balks at possibility because of disbelief, which underscores another axiom. We don't know that we don't know. Not knowing is ignorance. Ignorance is a crevasse that will not be bridged unless we are willing to experience and understand. This willingness requires that we relinquish what we currently believe to be true. We should dispense with limitations and perceptions which bind our minds and hearts. We should shun what makes us tractable. Docility prevents knowing and understanding. It fosters ignorance.

Ignorance may be acceptable to most and is a sad indictment. However, ignorance is not as troubling as its first cousin, apathy. One may care that he is ignorant. He may seek knowledge but lack the means to acquire it. If so, he could at least ask questions. Questions are the hallmark of initiative. Questions establish a point of departure whereby the unknown becomes known. Those who are apathetic won't bother to question. Apathy repels experience and returns one to the demise of being comfortable. Ignorant or not, being apathetic is an unenviable state. An indifferent mind and heart are the antithesis of hope. Moreover, deliberate or not, indifference is our nemesis. Apathy serves no constructive purpose and underscores the influence of ignorance. Apathy is ignorance coupled with resignation.

Apathy is eclipsed in severity by fear. Fear is the great immobilizer. Fear is the pervasive and often unwavering influence which reduces the mighty into submissive and timid souls. Fear emasculates the bravest of intentions. The most knowledgeable and fervent, when cloaked in fear, become inconsequential. The repercussions of fear are far reaching. It is safer to remain in comfort than to cower in the presence of others or oneself. Fear is infectious to those susceptible and scarring to one's sense of purpose and being.

Ignorance, apathy, and fear are the greatest detractors to understanding. These dire conditions *encourage comfort* and discourage experience. Each frustrates questioning. Each serve as the mortar which solidifies the foundation of lies and subsequent judgment. Consider your life. Where do ignorance, apathy and fear dominate? How does each destroy? There is no escape from them. How we relate to these conditions affects how we relate to ourselves and one another. Our response to these crippling conditions can be, quite frankly, life-changing, life-denying, and life-defying.

This brings us back to the letter from my friend. Before I considered his judgment that I was a common criminal, I had to appreciate how he related to ignorance, apathy, and fear. He did not know what I understood. He did not care to know. He was fearful of the reasons for my plight. He admitted to an unhealthy dread of the powers that opposed me. I don't blame him. As a result, I didn't judge him for judging me. While I do not agree with his conclusion, I did not find fault. My understanding of ignorance, apathy, and fear allows me to relate to a friend who condemned in ignorance, apathy, and fear. I did not listen to him through the filter of my prejudices. I did not read his letter with expectations. To project or to expect would discredit him and our relationship. From his vantage point, he understands my situation. It is *his* understanding. He views my actions and decisions through a filter which distorts and limits. He travels an all-too-common path. His values are not misplaced; rather, they are misapplied to me.

My conviction and imprisonment are a result of my principles. These principles are unchangeable. My friend may share these principles, but he does so with different priorities. If he judges without knowing my principles, he fails to understand me and my search for truth. The result is disharmony. We must change this dynamic. We must replace criticism with comprehension and reach harmony. I am not suggesting that we agree to agree or disagree. How we relate and appreciate the context of conversations to the exclusion of judgment is important. This may not always be an attainable goal; yet we should make the attempt. When others offer an explanation, we should listen and willingly suspend our disbelief. To the extent we are willing and able, we should set aside reservations and entertain possibility. Some conversations are too important not to have. Whether in marriages, families, friendships, business, or life in general, conversations must occur. The reasons for my unjust incarceration are worthy of a conversation. Whether accepted or not, the implications for my demise affect all Americans.

Like my friend, we are all critics. Given the consequences of my decisions, I will share with those who will listen. I will explain how and why the cost of ignorance, apathy, and fear are far too high. Most may choose to live in comfort. Most may choose to be ignorant and apathetic. Fear may prevail by happenstance or conditioning. Eventually, though, the cost of all three becomes staggering and unconscionable. At some point we must reconcile that our beliefs are incongruous with what is true. We must consider that we do not know that we do not know. If we venture beyond the boundaries of ignorance and enter the orbit of truth, if we exhume our satisfied existence from the clutches of apathy, if we overcome the fear that entombs our hearts and minds and enslaves our souls, the world of possibility arises. Those who are willing become accountable to truth and, consequently, confront what is uncomfortable.

Meaningful experiences will lead to truth and a life of purpose. If we as individuals or as a society embrace what is counterintuitive, we may see the errors of the past, accept the truth, and arrest the urge to judge in the future. My incarceration and the jailing of thousands, which just fifty years ago would have been unthinkable, are illustrative of why understanding, resolve, and courage are vital. Without these traits, we naively claim America is the freest country in the world. However, the illusion of freedom and the highest rate of imprisonment does not equal a sum of anything positive. The import of this thought may not be overstated.

To defeat the influence of ignorance, apathy, and fear, we must understand the inherent machinations of the legal system. When we realize how it operates, we will know our ignorance, apathy, and fear contribute to the imprisonment of fellow citizens. As we examine the judicial process with specific cases, we will more fully appreciate how men are found to be guilty because of the system itself. This realization should propel us to explore the innocence of supposedly guilty criminals. For, if we readily accept the guilt of a man simply for the fact that he went through the legal process, we should consider his innocence because he endured that same legal process. Most of us have not considered this perspective. How could we? What exists is unthinkable and intolerable.

To adequately assess why so many Americans are behind bars, we must define *legal process*. For our purposes, the term shall mean and include the electorate—the voters who elect lawmakers, legislators who create laws, grand juries that issue indictments, investigators who collect evidence, prosecutors who bring charges and try cases, defense lawyers who contend for the accused, witnesses and evidence, juries that hear cases and render verdicts, probation offices and Pre-Sentence Investigation (PSI) Reports which recommend sentences and, finally, judges who administer the judicial proceedings and pass sentences. By exploring the legal system, we may see that it has become what we did not know and what was never intended. If we grant convicted men some latitude and suspend our tendency to label them as common criminals, we may reject the conclusions of a system designed to reach judgments of guilt.

Each component of the legal process has a direct impact on and can affect every case and verdict. If we broaden our awareness of each component, we will likely view our current perceptions of the legal process as overly simplistic and wholly unfounded. This may lead to an appreciation that we have no idea what people have suffered from a judicial system we once believed to be just.

With any court case we should dignify that if something looks like a duck, walks like a duck, and quacks like a duck, then it must be a duck. What simply is must be as it is. If we exercise transparency, we may grant many common criminals the benefit of the doubt. We may conclude they are innocent because they were not proven to be guilty. Hopefully, we will cross the threshold of our own ignorance, apathy, and fear and enter the domain of truth. This would render impotent our propensity to pass judgment. This will lead to the harmony that is lacking in a culture detached from truth.

One critical thought will surface. One fundamental principle will cry out. The cry may be nothing more than subconscious thought that something is not right. This fundamental principle is integrity. The something that is not right is a lack of integrity.

Integrity is the unassailable quality which adheres to virtue with an inseparable bond. Truth will not prevail when integrity is absent. Justice will not reign when integrity does not. Justice is not justice without integrity. A judge who lacks integrity is not a judge. A prosecutor who executes his office and powers without integrity is not a prosecutor. A defense lawyer who does not zealously defend his client is without integrity. If a man, office, or concept claim to be genuine without integrity, they are not. When integrity is found wanting, a court of law is nothing more than a court of lawlessness.

Integrity has two important meanings. Integrity is honor, forthrightness, or a noble and unflappable stand for what is true and right. Second, integrity is completeness and wholeness, as in fully functioning. When someone is without honor he is without integrity. When he is incomplete, when he has failed to do something, he is without integrity. A judge is without honor and is incomplete when he operates his court in a manner that is inconsistent with an ethical, moral, and just intent. He lacks integrity. The judge is no different than a wheel with broken spokes. The wheel is not whole or functional. A judicial system with prosecutors who knowingly mislead and distort the truth is not whole. Both the wheel and the judicial system lack integrity. Both are broken. Integrity is essential to life and the conduct of affairs among men. Against the backdrop of ignorance, apathy, and fear, whether we acknowledge it or not, integrity is marginalized if not summarily dismissed. Noteworthy, those who are *comfortable* likely discount the primacy of integrity.

Consider this illustration. When a man travels across a bridge every day, he doesn't question the structural soundness of the bridge, its integrity. Yet, as time passes, he notices cracks in its pylons. Does integrity become important? Not likely. He sees the cracks, but he crosses anyway. The bridge still appears to be whole and functional. The man presumes the structure will bear the weight of his body. The cracks, as he perceives them, do not pose an imminent threat. In fact, the man would be inconvenienced if he had to find a different route.

Now, consider that this man does business with a local grocer. He has done so for five years. He trusts the grocer. However, when the man receives incorrect change three times in one month, he questions the grocer's integrity. Why? The impact from the grocer's lack of integrity is immediate and personal. The man's loss is uncomfortable. He is guarded. He distrusts. The relevance of integrity becomes a priority.

Integrity is lacking in both illustrations. However, the man is more intimately affected by the grocer than the bridge. The man is still able to cross the bridge unharmed. The cracks are insignificant compared to the immediate and tangible loss with the grocer. Notably, a parallel exists with the judicial system. If the man were the defendant in a court case and the judge and prosecutor were the grocers, he would distrust the system. If the man is merely another American unaffected by the legal arena, the dynamics change. He passes the court without reservations. He knows of the cracks in the foundation of the judiciary, but they are of no consequence to him. He is far from the cracks and their implications.

Unfortunately, the bridge analogy reflects our cultural awareness. We may notice the cracks in the justice system. However, since we are unaffected, we don't question. We presume the best, rarely imagining the worst. This is what is comfortable. We are not vested personally with any immediate loss. There is no need to experience discomfort. We reject this possibility. It is easier to remain unaware and indifferent. Amid apathy and fear, integrity is insignificant if we are not directly harmed. Here is an obvious question. How would we know justice is sacrificed because of a lack of integrity unless we were adversely affected? Most of us have little involvement with the courts. And if we do, the interaction is generally limited to formalities.

We ignore what is flawed and willingly accept that the justice system and all its components are whole. We don't presume, much less know, that authorities compromise justice and short the people. We assume a just outcome. If our perceptions remain unchallenged and we conclude unwittingly that the legal system is sound, we accept America's incarceration rate as credible. The supposition is that Americans are a more immoral and corrupt people meriting the ignominious distinction as a country of criminals.

The irony is that a free and moral people do not require laws. An immoral people would, by necessity, require laws, laws they would violate. Or a docile and disengaged people would not notice countless and unnecessary laws which lead to verdicts of guilt. Regardless, the number of (or the need for) laws is a barometer of less freedom.

Our institutions and authorities do not achieve their purpose when operated without integrity and anything accomplished outside the intended purpose is a lie. For example, the instant the courts deny an innocent man a just remedy, justice becomes a perversion. A lie is born the moment integrity is found wanting. Unfortunately, since we are disengaged, we accept and believe the lie. We believe every man in prison deserves such punishment. However, as we scrutinize each component of the legal system, as we assess how justice is achieved, we will confront a compelling contrast. This contrast should inspire us to understand what is fundamentally wrong. If not, the wisdom of Edmond Burke will ring true. He said when "good men… do nothing" evil will prevail.[21] Restoring integrity may be the saving grace which enlightens us to secure what once was and may be again—the pursuit of truth and justice.

Integrity is powered by principles. Principles are universal laws which govern the conduct of the virtuous. Without principles, or when principles are compromised, integrity suffers. As with spokes of a wheel, principles are the substance and strength which ensure

---

[21] https://www.goodreads.com/author/quotes/17142.Edmund_Burke

a man, office, or concept are sound. Otherwise, a man who lacks principles lacks integrity. A man who strikes a woman is not a man with either principle or integrity. A man who lies to his wife is the same. The husband is not whole. He is the reason the marriage is incomplete. The local grocer who randomly cheats his customers is neither principled nor with integrity. Once patrons realize his deceit, his business will suffer. The prosecutor who abuses his power is unprincipled. Once this is understood, people will distrust the man and his office. When an innocent man is unjustly convicted and adds to the highest incarceration rate in the world, the institution of justice will not and should not be trusted.

The prosecutor may excuse his decisions and conduct as acceptable simply because the rules of the court permit. The grocer may rationalize that his customers steal from him, notwithstanding he is a subset of a larger community where principles should be congruent with a greater moral fabric. However, the principles which govern the affairs of men should transcend the conduct of the grocer and prosecutor.

The rules of court allow what most would consider inexcusable. We expect what should be even if we are unaware of the questionable conduct from the government, its officials, and any component of the legal apparatus. We should expect fundamental principles to remain constant and consistent and integrity to serve as the cornerstone of the judicial system. And when we find integrity lacking, we should demand its restoration.

The law of gravity is a principle which remains constant and consistent. It is integral with the universe. We should expect justice within our courts would be the same. Freedom and liberty must not be sacrificed. Justice must not be corrupted. Officials should not remain in office when their actions violate what is sacred. We should intercede when unjust motives assault the rights of the people. We should demand that principles be honored, and authorities dignify their actions or suffer the consequences. Our failure to hold officials accountable proves we are unaccountable and without integrity.

America's culture has morphed from one with a *healthy distrust* of the government to an *unhealthy trust* and dependence upon government. The reason is simple; government dominates virtually every aspect of our lives. Its dominance of the national psyche is undisputed. Consequently, we accept without question what is done by or in the name of the government. When a friend labels another as a *common criminal* with little understanding, this parallels his acceptance of government sanctioned conclusions simply because the judiciary decrees it so. This happens at all levels of government regardless of the subject matter. Former Secretary of Defense Robert McNamara stated on national news before his death that the Gulf of Tonkin incident in Vietnam never occurred. Yes, America committed itself to an armed conflict for a lie, constructed by design. Former President George W. Bush asserted Iraq's President Saddam Hussein had "yellowcake" uranium from Niger as justification for invading Iraq. His claims were never substantiated. In both cases, integrity was absent, and Americans suffered the consequences. Consider that many of those incarcerated are innocent. Yet, we blindly accept their guilt, just as we blindly send our sons and daughters to foreign conflicts without just cause.

I accept my friend's assertion that I am a common criminal. This motivates me to educate those who are influenced by ignorance, apathy, and fear. I am moved to defeat the lies and overcome cognitive dissonance. May we unsettle our individual and collective sense of comfort. With unwavering perseverance, pursuit of principles, and restoration of integrity, fueled by knowledge, engagement, and courage, we may become a critically discerning people again and reap the bounty of the justice we richly deserve.

In every government on earth is some trace of human weakness, some germ of corruption and degeneracy, which cunning will discover and wickedness insensibly open, cultivate and improve. Every government degenerates when trusted to the rulers of the people alone. The people themselves therefore are its only safe depositories. And to render them safe, their minds must be improved to a certain degree. **Thomas Jefferson**

Context

I once had a friend, Eric, who had a unique ability. He called it *slow eye.* He was able to see the imperceptible. For example, he could "see" the stitches on a fastball. We were at a golf course where he critiqued my swing. *Slow-eye* enabled him to see how my wrists were positioned when I made impact with the ball. Of course, Eric knew my mistake based upon where the ball landed or what it did. This would be obvious for those who know golf. Looking at the end result, however, was not the essence of slow-eye. While many can tell what was done incorrectly based upon the ball's trajectory, few will see which of the many components of the swing caused a poor shot.

A ball which fades to the right is likely the result of an open club face. Determining the cause of the open face is where Eric's ability proved beneficial. He saw my mistake and offered solutions. He told me what I did not know and could not see. Eric knew what a proper golf swing entailed. He golfed. His muscles, mind, and instincts knew what the body should do. His experience was essential to his knowledge and gave him context. Eric shared his knowledge with others. He was not intimidated by the complexity of golf. He was confident, complete, and whole with golf. His mastery represented integrity. His ability and integrity were the reasons why I deferred to his wisdom. Since he golfed and exercised his ability to see, he had credibility.

Some have suggested that I have an ability—to distill the essence of a broad or detailed representation to its integral truth. Some call it discernment. As a child, I was sensitive to the macro perspective without the need to immerse myself in the minutiae. With experience, knowledge and understanding this ability proved credible.

Consider an example. I grew up in the Catholic faith. As a small child, I had questions and doubted this religion. I sensed Catholicism was incongruent with what I discerned to be a fundamental spiritual truth. I knew the facts of this faith. I understood its dogma. Yet, at a very young age, what I discerned was inconsistent with these teachings. I instinctively rejected what was without integrity. I did not accept, as an illustration, that the Pope was a holy man and without sin. I did not accept the centrality of Mary, the mother of Jesus or the role of the saints as protectors. I eventually rejected these propositions. To me, these precepts defied what was transparent and, therefore, lacked integrity. In the end, I rejected what was generally embraced by other Catholics.

While the example of religion may be a poor choice, it will serve a purpose. Religion is a sensitive topic, no less than meting out justice in American courts. Please understand, I am not suggesting Catholics are wrong. Not all Catholics believe as I was taught. The point is that we should challenge what we are taught as it concerns American justice and discern the truth. We should learn from those with direct experience.

Just as Eric observed, I observed. I discerned what was true by noting the general and specific within the judicial system. While many may distill the essence of a dynamic or situation, the extent to which this ability is developed becomes relevant. There is a difference between abilities used and those neglected, or those never employed. A man may have slow-eye and not use it. He may not know about golf. If so, he is not one with whom I would rely upon for an analysis of my swing. A Buddhist may have the ability to discern, but I would not seek his counsel about Catholicism. Yet, I would not exclude a man who knows baseball or a Buddhist from relating with me about sports or faith. I would not dismiss their contributions or the possibility of what could be if each were willing and teachable. This is an important point. If we shared what we knew and were open to what we did not know, we would benefit.

This discussion is on par with an examination of life. How we relate to and with each other and concepts is the difference between a life of possibility and a limited existence. We may question and observe until we realize what is true is not what we thought. Those who discern what is either wrong, incomplete, or unknown are likely to determine what is credible. Those who believe the Pope is infallible do not and may not consider other possibilities. They may not consider that their belief is inconsistent with truth. To understand the truth, they must be willing to reject what they *know* and consider another perspective. This is not easy. Firm beliefs and an unwillingness to weigh options are a challenge. If I dismissed Eric's ability and observations, I would not have benefitted. I would have practiced an incorrect golf swing. This would have culminated in limited understanding, growth, and effectiveness. My golf swing would not have been whole or one of possibility.

If we don't break through the familiar for what is just beyond, little will change. We will remain comfortable with an idea, situation, or way of existing and deny ourselves what is within reach. The ability to discern, while it has led me to a life of challenges, has also brought me foursquare with distinct truths. My unjust incarceration was a result of my own discernment. Furthermore, because I was imprisoned, I have been able to acquire a clear representation of the utter injustice of the justice system that I would never have appreciated otherwise. The irony is that serving a federal prison sentence liberated me. Had I remained *free*, that is outside of prison, and comfortable, and compliant within a scripted world which appears real, I would believe as most do. I would believe a lie.

What is credible and true is not necessarily readily perceptible. In my pursuit of truth, I experienced what was extremely uncomfortable. I stepped beyond the ordinary and defied the bounds of ignorance. I wanted to know. More importantly, I could not relinquish what I discerned to be true. The only impediment to knowing the truth was raw intimidation, whether self-imposed or imposed by others.

There are reasons why understanding truth is difficult. Being comfortable, which is desirable, precludes knowing. Why? The comfortable is perceived as reality. Second, indifference, which is a by-product of comfort, rejects possibility. Possibility requires effort and change. Finally, intimidation inhibits one from accepting what is credible.

Consider the following illustration. Suppose a father and mother notice a lump on their child's throat. Such a revelation would instill fear in any parent. The lump, which is not normal, is unsettling. The parents want to solve the problem. They want their child to be healthy. As they await the diagnosis, they must contend with not knowing truth.

The point at which the doctor reveals his assessment is noteworthy. The father may want to know regardless. He wants to apply solutions. The mother may cringe with fear of confronting what has been and is still unknown. Why? The consequences may be devastating. Will their child die? Is the problem curable? What are the repercussions from any operation? Will their finances and insurance cover the costs? Will their child receive the care he requires? Even though truth will be offered, they may not accept it. They may wrestle with disbelief. What was once a normal and healthy child, what was once a comfortable and happy home, what was once a hopeful future is no more. Fear may never fade as disbelief becomes entrenched. Both fear and disbelief manifest a new existence.

How one views life is vital to living life—to being *alive*. If I ignored Eric's observations and refused to correct my golf swing, I would not improve. I would remain comfortable with what is incomplete. The same applies to the perspective about the Pope. I could have blindly accepted that the most powerful man in the Catholic Church is holy and without sin. This may have been comfortable, but it would have limited the possibility of knowing. My spiritual life would have been constrained within the myopic, a belief represented as truth by those with authority (titles) over me. If I followed this *truth*, I would have remained unaware and uninitiated within a world that made me compliant and satisfied. Finally, the unfortunate news that a child suffers an incurable malady may be denied. But this denial does not make the ailment any less real. Rejecting or disbelieving what is true prevents experiences and understanding. Reluctance to accept uncomfortable circumstance keeps a truth-based life at bay. Life is not one of integrity. It is incomplete.

What is one to do? How does a discerning man reconcile a lie when he encounters the truth? The answer may not seem apparent; but it is obvious, nonetheless. He accepts truth as paramount and the repercussions as circumstantial. He evolves into an understanding which conquers ignorance. He acts with volition and subdues indifference. He embraces courage and conquers fear. Why? Truth matters; all else is secondary. As an innocent man, I want to live undeterred by limitations that reduce life to a lie. The incarceration of my body does not make the truth any less true. To the contrary, being courageous in the face of the undesirable is defining. Truth is elevated to the importance it deserves. Defeating fear leads to change. When we do not equivocate, we cross the threshold of resignation and into the possibility of being without pretense.

Being courageous beyond circumstances empowers man to live in truth. When I chose to be courageous, I learned about the entire lie which, conversely, revealed the entire truth. The lie was perpetrated for an unjust aim. When I learned the truth, I was drawn, even within prison, to what was credible and possible.

If we accept and believe a lie, we are not being. Rather, we exist. *Being* encompasses a world of possibility, truth, and wholeness. Existing equates to resignation, deception, and incompleteness. Ask yourself the following questions. Do you believe a lie? Do you deceive yourself? Are you afraid to test what you *know*? Are you willing to consider alternatives? Are you willing to sacrifice to live in truth and with integrity? If you understand the lie, what price would you pay to effect change? Would you risk a prison term? Would you risk death? Would you stand for truth until you were killed by those who wanted to prevent the influence of your actions? These are not rhetorical questions. We have the choice to embrace what may be or relegate our lives to what is not.

When I wrote the words to this chapter, it was December 25, 2013. I was in a federal prison in Ohio. My two small children were in Florida sleeping. They woke to a joyous Christmas morning without their father. We had not spoken, written, or seen each other in over a year. A marriage was unduly harmed by an eight-year federal investigation. As a father and husband, I stood for truth most refuse to see. The cost was staggering. Did it have to be this way? No. The marriage could have and should have remained. Our children should have had both parents involved in their lives. They should have had visits with and access to their father. But, in the face of a lie, possibility is absent.

The alternative anchored in truth would have a distinct and divergent effect. If my wife saw my efforts as noble and with integrity, she would have drawn closer to me. She would have honored a man for the just cause and hopeful change he sought. Our children would have witnessed a man with the character to persevere with a hope that their future would not be mired in a greater lie. My journey is no different than any other struggle in life. What is worth the loss of a marriage or parent? Do men and women fight in wars in foreign countries which do not directly involve credible American interests? Yes. Do men risk their lives performing dangerous jobs and tempt the future of their children without a father? Yes.

At the risk of sounding insensitive, the consequences of any fight for truth are circumstantial. Many may magnanimously weigh the eventual aftermath and decide the battle is or was entirely unnecessary. Yet, through what perspective? Through the lens of veracity or deceit? Let's reduce this to the ridiculous. If a man wanted to improve his golf swing, he would be willing to listen and learn. If a man sought a greater spiritual truth, he would consider the unknown and acknowledge falsehoods. To be with purpose with a dying child, a father would courageously embrace truth. He would be with himself, his grieving wife and his son in every sense of the word.

We have a serious challenge as the most imprisoned country in the world. Pause and weigh the implications of this fact. America, supposedly the land of the free and the home of the brave, imprisons more of its citizens than any other country. This should conflict with your perception and presumptions of truth. Ask the obvious. Why do we have more men and women behind bars than China, Russia, India, Japan, or Mexico? How did this happen? This fact should spur other queries. We should challenge what we gratuitously conclude to be true. Is the judicial system just? Are we such an immoral people whereby a higher rate of incarceration is justified? Could there be underlying motives for this disparity? If so, what are they? Why do we not know of such influences?

What is the truth? Do we care to know? Or are we content with the belief that America is free? Are we content with the belief that those in prison deserve to be there? Are we satisfied that America is the most morally bankrupt country? Or are we willing to suspend disbelief, defy the comfort we seek, and learn that what we know is not true?

If these questions have not jarred your thinking, perhaps some candor is needed. Consider that we, the people, are the reason America is heavily regulated and excessively imprisoned. We are the reason governing authorities have such an overwhelming influence and oppressive control of our lives. We are the reason our children and grandchildren will inherit a more austere and less free future. The reasons for these assertions are simple. We don't know that we don't know. We are comfortable not knowing. We are satisfied with complacency. We care only for what is convenient. We are content with what we *know* and are unwilling and incapable of moving beyond that knowledge. Finally, we are afraid to unsettle our lives for what contradicts our perceived *truth*.

Consequently, we live in fear. We cannot and will not challenge the norm; we would have to sacrifice too much. We are reluctant to challenge any governing authority with truth, or have truth be known. Fear is our constant companion. We may not see fear in our walks, but a companion it is. Fear governs our thoughts and actions and relegates our sense of being to a refuge of disbelief. Our being, our ability to be alive, to be a life, to manifest a purpose for a more noble cause, is wrapped within the perceived protection that only disbelief offers.

Do you disagree? If so, I shall escalate the level of candor. First, we don't care that innocent men and women are imprisoned at a ghastly rate. Why? It does not affect us and prevents us from not only considering the state of our judicial system but prevents us from asking questions. We don't care to know. Second, we would not entertain the implications of our rate of imprisonment until we were personally affected. Even then, we would simply comply with the overbearing demands of the authorities—those with the titles. Why? We lack the fight or the resolve to apprehend beyond compliance. We are of the ilk that cooperates to effectuate the least costly outcome for ourselves and those within our immediate comfort zone.

We should not take this personally. It is human nature to escape the imposing for that of self-preservation. Why? In our culture, we have a low expectation for community. Why? We have a low regard for ourselves. Why? We have a low regard for truth. Knowing truth is unsettling. Truth requires commitment and sacrifice, which involves communal interests and, yes, integrity.

A life manifested by and for the sole aim of self is a life oblivious to macro pronouncements which portend an ominous fate for self and the greater community. Here is the great irony. Our unwillingness to sacrifice self for the greater good is injurious to ourselves and society. When such sacrifice occurs, there is no confusion. When people of character persevere into truth, we benefit. Their efforts defeat fear and apathy, an apathy sourced in ignorance.

If we categorically reject these concepts, we are unwilling and unable to look beyond ourselves and reconcile a desperate need in this country. We have a problem which will not be solved unless good people acknowledge the crisis. Those willing to suspend disbelief will accept the foregoing observations. Otherwise, we are destined to a rather foreboding future.

Most would agree there is something terribly wrong with our country. Yet, few can articulate the root causes. Some causes are ignorance, apathy, and fear. We have an obligation to understand how these root causes affect the legal system—for we must cure this common and crippling disease, not just the symptoms. To dismiss the disease, the core of our demise, would be folly. America's high incarceration rate is found in the disease of ignorance, apathy, and fear of the people. These contagions prevent us from toppling the resultant arrogance of the institutions which control our lives and country. We are imprisoned at such a high rate, not for the *crimes* committed, but for the system that ensures these convictions. The system thrives because we don't. We blindly accept and allow what we would never permit because we don't and won't dignify truth.

The import of this message is critical. I will relentlessly restate it. I will do exactly what crafty lawyers accomplish in court. I will tell you what you need to know. I will then tell you what I told you. And finally, I will restate what was said. We must challenge what we perceive to be truth. We must confront the reasons why institutional arrogance prevails with such a destructive and pervasive influence. Man has been subjected to and controlled by governing authorities since the beginning of time. The use and abuse of force, both physical and written, has reduced man to submission or volitional compliance. There is little difference now than the days of self-righteous kings, dictators, and rulers who exercised power by fiat.

Consider the American Revolution. King George was determined to prevail with arrogant indifference against the claims and clamoring of Americans who sought the dignity of free men. When the monarch refused, the people appealed to their natural aspirations—freedom at all costs. Curiously, only about two percent of the people were the impetus for the revolution which secured our now waning freedom. Most people were uninformed, compliant, and fearful or loyal to the crown. A minority were the enlightened stalwarts who yearned for what was noble. They had the courage to fight rather than suffer the indignities of an imperial empire. They were beholden to the cause of freedom at the cost of their lives, fortunes, and sacred honor. They led with a mighty resolve buttressed by solutions.

Where are we today? Does the United States Government function within the context of its original mandate? Do we enjoy and covet freedom secured by our predecessors? Or are we a submissive and compliant people no longer bothered by sideshows such as truth, principles, integrity, and freedom? If the state of our Union is reflected by both the number of laws and Americans in prison, we lack the context of our glorious past. We lack the resolve to restore our freedom. The fact that America is overly criminalized more so than any other people on earth is not a problem as much as it is an indicator. As certain as the sun will rise, ignominy will fall upon a nation which is detached from its principled past, disengaged with the present, and vexed about its future. Yet, history reflects that a defiant people will rightfully correct the ills that plague them.

There must be an awakening. At some point we must recognize that what is discomforting should not be comfortable. We must realize that we accept lies not for their origins, but our susceptibility to believe them. We don't have to believe lies or their sources. We may know truth and offer solutions to those willing to listen. Undoubtedly, those who govern in our *best interests* have no desire to deviate from their course.

We no longer have a country where freedom reigns. To appreciate this fact, many of us must suffer at the hands of the system and its inherent deception. It will happen. Some of those reading these words will lose their freedom. They will be imprisoned. If you become one of the system's victims, you will wonder what occurred. You will be confused. Regrettably, you will have no answers. An ignorant, apathetic, and fearful man has no answers. If you are not directly or personally affected, it will happen to a family member, friend, or acquaintance. As such, although indirect, you will be affected whether you realize it or not. Ignorance is blind and oblivious to what could be known.

There is a salient thought expressed by a notorious Native American, Chief Joseph of Seattle, who said that what we do to the web of life we do to ourselves. Perhaps more importantly, what we fail to do is equally destructive. We affect life and ourselves when we do nothing. Unfortunately, we don't know to do something. When nothing constructive or of value is forthcoming, it represents and is a travesty. The sacrifice of those who sought truth and opposed injustice reveals one inescapable conclusion. We need men and woman who will sound the clarion call for truth. The will to coalesce with a resolve and courage to right the wrongs which affect our present and future is crucial. Do not ignore the insight gained by those who are discerning. Do not relinquish the truth, a truth neither seen nor understood by many. We must accept our responsibility to seek and discern truth and then share that truth.

Truth matters and it belongs to everyone. Thankfully, the light of truth defeats the darkness of the lie. This can be no more aptly expressed than to consider that those unjustly imprisoned—the innocent—know the truth. When confined within prison compounds surrounded by fourteen-foot fences topped with rolls of concertina wire, they don't see this stark perimeter. They know truth that allows them to see the glorious and brilliant orange sun rise above the horizon. They see the same tranquil red orb drop to the west. Yes, for these *prisoners* the truth rises and sets as it lights the day's path. For them, the lie is not a factor. They understand that truth blinds from view what is irrelevant, the circumstances which would otherwise bewilder and defeat. They are indebted that truth is the apex of their being and relegates all else as secondary.

America's high incarceration rate is a macro indicator which forewarns an unsuspecting people of current and future challenges. A lack of knowledge, subsequent indifference, and inaction from trepidation is the intent of those who *govern* a compliant people who offer negligible resistance. As such, we must embrace truth that should not and cannot be denied. If we accept the possibility that new perspectives are required, if we accept that our preconceived notions are wrong, then we know solutions are needed. We need solutions anchored in experience that accentuate understanding rather than prevailing ignorance.

This leads us back to the discussion about Eric and his slow-eye ability. The solutions we seek are likely sourced within the experiences and abilities of those who have traveled where so many have not. They not only appreciate what is wrong, they observed where the problems occurred. Here is a comparison. I would no sooner ask lawyers or judges why there is a lack of truth and justice throughout the legal system than I would a Buddhist about Catholicism, or a baseball coach about my golf swing. The officers of the court, or any official involved within the legal system, play a game, a process, a controlled gig that is separate and distinct from what is real.

The legal process has rules. It has a referee who has a support staff to enforce the rules. Like chess, pieces of the game of court are moved about as the action unfolds. There is a deliberate orchestration of efforts by opposing players who exercise strategies and tactics tied to specific motives which shape the conclusion. What transpires is dissimilar with what would be deemed credible. Those involved with the game of court know this racket—a racket which has little to do with justice. A judge does not *overrule* his own private affairs in the same manner he does his court. A prosecutor does not *object* with a man on the street in the manner he would in court. He does not *appeal* what is unsatisfactory with his private relations as he would in the legal realm. Why? In life, he contends with reality. There is no pretense. Life is not form over substance. The legal process is a fiction, a world unto itself. The actors within this fiction are unable, unwilling, or deliberately indifferent. They do not observe what injuries are caused within or by their game of court. Just as I am unable to see my own mistakes with my golf swing, they are limited. In like manner, these men and women are blind to their own deficiencies.

We need only observe a prosecutor in his private life and then professionally. He plays the role of two separate characters. He believes in the role he portrays in court. He *must* believe to win the game. When done acting, he exits the doors of the court, descends the step, and lives as a private citizen. He is not the same man. This dynamic should trouble Americans.

Some may argue that lawyers and judges know the game of court as Eric knows golf. I would agree. Allow me to make an important distinction. As stated previously, I would not ask a judge why there is a lack of truth and justice in court. Rather, concerning his *game of court*, I would ask him what is wrong with a particular facet performed by a given player. If I were a lawyer, prosecutor, or bailiff, I would ask the judge how I could improve my performance, my role. Like Eric, if the judge exercised his ability, if he observed, he would discern. He would analyze my legal briefs or critique my arguments to a jury. He would emphasize the elements of a crime or how to effectively select jurors who would likely support my position. The judge would help me improve my game of court as Eric does with golf.

There is another distinction to weigh. The judge and those players immersed in the fiction of court are not necessarily vested in the genuine pursuit of justice. A prosecutor, blinded by a linear perspective, is not altruistic about truth and justice. Both the judge and prosecutor are controlled within the contrived just as anyone who plays Checkers, Chess, or golf. It is the game and how it is played that determines the results, as in who wins and who loses. The Professional Golf Association could easily change the rules of the sport it governs and alter golf beyond what is currently known. The same is true for the producer of any game. If any game were changed beyond the original representation, we would need new rules. This is no different for the legal system.

The rules of court have resulted in what is not reflective of the past. One could argue that justice, true justice, justice anchored in truth, justice once pursued by the players within the game of court, is no longer manifested. With a disproportionate share of the world's prison population, observers of the game, especially the innocent who are imprisoned, question the outcome. Even passive observers may conclude that the lack of justice has more to do with the game, its players and its rules than truth. Heed this observation. America must reconcile the loss of truth and justice. Here is the salient question: Who can articulate the game of court and discern what is flawed? Who can assess what is wrong and when it occurs? We don't want just any critic who is able to see results and determine the problems.

As with the golf shot that fades to the right, where many may conclude the club face was open, we want to know the source of the mistake. We should seek to understand how and why the mistake occurred in the game of court. We should ascertain how the incarceration rate jumped from three percent of the world's imprisoned in 1963, with a recorded 217, 283 state and federal prisoners nationally[22], to the twenty-two percent of the global population we have today.[23] We must know why there is such a disparity between the total in prisoners then and some 2.2 million prisoners today.[24] There is a great need for those like Eric within the game of court, those who may explain their experiences and understanding. Their discernment will explain the loss of both truth and justice. There should be no mistake; some who are not directly involved in court know the game, nonetheless. They understand. They have credibility. They know how and why justice was not achieved. As Eric was able to observe the mistakes of a man's golf swing, these observers may attest to the ailments of the legal system. Who are these observers?

When I was an officer in the United States Army, I learned an invaluable lesson. As a Company Commander, I learned that those at the lowest level within my command, the privates and specialists in the trenches, knew the problems which affected the unit. They were the silent, those who experienced, observed, and discerned. They were even willing to offer solutions. Private Jones knew what needed fixing. He knew how and when problems arose. The irony is that the First Sergeant and Platoon Sergeants did not necessarily know. They were playing the game of soldier by their rules and my rules. We could not see everything. We were too immersed in the game and less concerned with what was credible and true.

Perhaps surprisingly to those who may not have considered this thought, those subjected to the game of court, those forced to endure the rules, those at the mercy of a system that defied justice, were the defendants themselves. Defendants experienced, and, if they had or exercised the ability to observe, discerned what was wrong. The defendants who became inmates because of how the system was played know how and why justice and truth were and are excluded. They understand that the fiction of court had little correlation with life. Not only are discerning inmates a credible source, their spouses, families, and friends are too. Those with an intimate awareness of the game will share that court is not what they ever imagined. For, courts are not concerned with truth and justice.

My sister, who is an attorney, and presently a federal administrative law judge, observed my trial. She realized the game of court had little to do with justice or truth. With her discernment, as with select inmates, she became a credible source. She saw the cracks in the foundation of the judiciary. She was in many ways directly affected. She suffered the loss of her brother for four years. She was no longer comfortable with her own ignorance and apathy. She may not have feared the court process, given her prior experience, yet she began to realize what *she did not know.* She, like innocent inmates, could not reconcile the results. My sister and innocent inmates were once comfortable believing the legal system was solely concerned with truth and justice. Ironically, they once feared a process they never understood. What a difference experience makes.

---

[22] http://www.bjs.gov/content/pub/pdf/p2581.pdf

[23] https://en.wikipedia.org/wiki/United_States_incarceration_rate

[24] https://en.wikipedia.org/wiki/Incarceration in the United States

Referring to Eric, we see a parallel. The experiences of both my sister and unjustly convicted inmates offer context. Just as Eric golfed, they *played* the game of court. As with Eric, they were no longer intimidated by the complexity or difficulty of the game. Their experience and observations represent a mastery of sorts and integrity. Consequently, they no longer believe a lie. Their preconceived notions of the legal system are no longer credible. Truth, which was elusive, is now transparent. When my sister saw and heard a federal agent testify falsely on the stand, she was rudely confronted with truth. Since she was directly involved with the event about which the agent testified, she could not reconcile his statements with what she knew to be true. This was not a matter of a bias toward a brother or prejudice to an interpretation. Her twenty years in the legal profession, which included years as a prosecutor and defense lawyer in the Navy, validated her concerns. The game of court was not about truth or justice.

My sister's observations were relevant since she confirmed the same discernment of inmates who had similar experiences. Many of us suffer from cognitive dissonance and are unwilling to consider the observations of even *select* inmates. Most of the horror stories which could be weighed would be rejected because of disbelief. Though inmates experienced what was uncomfortable, we are unlikely to grant them credence within our world of comfort. Even my sister's testimony would not influence our incredulity. We see a biased sister and disgruntled inmates, common criminals who lack integrity.

Here is the irony. Those of us who perceive Eric as credible do so for several reasons. He mastered golf. He has a skill that he exercises. He observes what is wrong, the imperceptible, and compares it with what he knows. Why are discerning inmates or even my sister not viewed the same? As stated before, we accept lies not because of their origin, but for our susceptibility to believe them. Thus, we reject truth, not for its origin, but for our unwillingness to accept it. Just as we deceive and believe in deception, we deceive ourselves and disbelieve truth. In both regards, we affect the web of life.

Perhaps when the day is done, when a decade has passed, when a generation has moved on, when a century or an era enters the annals of history, our progeny will objectively determine the errors of our current conclusions. As with the end of slavery, the folly of the Salem Witch Trials, the condemnation of those who believed the sun was the center of the solar system, we may reflect with humility at the transparent causes for America's prison problem, a rate which defies reason. We may question why we never listened to those defendants with experience in the trenches, within the courts or in prison cells, those who observed the effects of the rules of the game of court, who eventually acquired understanding. Our progeny may understand why inmates who once feared the legal system do so no longer. Why? They have integrity. They know the court and all its sundry components are not as we falsely and naively believe. They know truth and will not relinquish it at any cost. The balance of us remains satisfied viewing the process from afar. We are comfortable with our lack of knowledge, resolve, and courage. Our ignorance, apathy, and fear remain, as will the cracks in the foundation of the judiciary.

Such is a life without integrity and principles. We dismiss the unacceptable as tolerable; we are not personally vested. We follow the same path and far removed from the cracks in the foundation, a path which includes the unwillingness to listen. Listening would require us to consider what is unknown. It would require that we understand the discernment of others, even those we hold in disdain—common criminals. Listening would be uncomfortable. It may even require that we experience and be alive, to be a *life*. It is far easier to remain ignorant, apathetic, and fearful. It is far easier to exist within and with a lie. It takes effort to be in a world of truth and possibility that is uncomfortable.

The Folly of Human Nature

JOHN HUS

Year: 1414
Occupation: Catholic Priest
Marital Status: Not Married
Children: None
Criminal History: None
Spiritual Beliefs: Catholic
Age: 32
Education: Educated, Rector of University of Prague
Summary: Hus was a maverick in the Catholic Church who espoused reform with its doctrine and clergy. He was a supporter of John Wycliffe and the Protestant Reformation.

THE PARTICULARS

Original Charge: Heresy
Final Charge: Heresy
Trial: Yes
Verdict: Guilty
Plea: No
Sentence: Death—burned at the stake
Appeal: No
Summary: Hus was excommunicated for heresy. After a trial before church officials, Hus was found guilty of supporting and promoting beliefs that contradicted church dogma.

THE CASE OF JOHN HUS

John Hus was a Catholic priest known for his fiery sermons and attacks on the morals of the clergy. His teachings reflected the Protestant Reformation. He supported some of John Wycliffe's beliefs. For example, Hus condemned the practice of selling indulgences by the church to fund the crusades. His vocal nature and candor attracted proponents and opponents. When he became Rector of the University of Prague, the German teachers and students rebelled. They fostered the belief that Hus was a heretic. Hus was ordered to cease preaching for reform. When Hus refused, the church excommunicated him.

Pope John XXIII issued a papal bull concerning a separate issue which Hus repudiated. Consequently, Cardinal Degli Stephaneschi excommunicated Hus again, which placed Prague under a church interdict. Hus deferred and left the city. In 1414, the Catholic Church convened a council at Constance to settle what was known as the Papal Schism. Only after he was assured of his safety, Hus decided to attend. However, he was brutally imprisoned and accused of supporting the beliefs of John Wycliffe. Hus demanded that he be able to defend his positions. He appeared before three hearings that were far from impartial and based largely upon fabricated charges. Most of the "evidence" used for his "prosecution" was a distortion of his beliefs. John Hus was found guilty of heresy. He was burned alive at the stake on July 6, 1415.

Galileo Galilei

Year: 1632
Occupation: Astronomer, Physicist, Mathematician
Marital Status: Not married
Children: 3
Spiritual Beliefs: Catholic
Age: 70
Education: College
Summary: Galileo, an astronomer and scientist, was an advocate for scientific discovery.

The Particulars

Original Charge: Failure to disclose; violating an edict
Final Charge: Failure to disclose; violating an edict
Trial: Yes—Inquisition of the Church
Verdict: Guilty
Plea: No
Sentence: Life Imprisonment
Appeal: No
Summary: Galileo, accused of failing to disclose a papal order and violating an edict, defended himself. He was found guilty and sentenced to life imprisonment.

The Case of Galileo Galilei

In 1613, Galileo openly supported the Copernican Theory, the belief that the sun is the center of the universe. His position was opposed by priests and educators. In a letter to Benedetto Castelli, a Benedictine monk, Galileo maintained that scripture should not be imposed against science. This letter only agitated the church authority. The Castelli letter was forwarded to Rome for consideration by The Inquisition. Galileo began to fear for his safety and the virtuous and unfettered pursuit of scientific discovery.

In 1615, Galileo proclaimed his support for the theory developed by Copernicus. This angered Pope Paul V. The Pope established a commission to study the issue. The commission concluded that this theory was incongruent with the scripture and possibly heretical. In 1616, the Pope conferred with Cardinal Bellarmine who warned Galileo to abandon his position or suffer the consequences. Galileo complied.

When Galileo's friend, Maffeo Barberini, became Pope Urban VIII, Galileo asked him to rescind the edict of 1616. Urban refused. Yet, he permitted Galileo to compare both systems. As a result, Galileo wrote Dialogue Concerning the Two Chief World Systems in 1632. Five months later, Galileo was ordered to appear before The Inquisition. He was accused of failing to disclose to Urban VIII an order never to teach the Copernican Theory.

Urban VIII was indignant. Galileo, however, asserted that his recent work was approved by the Pope and the printing was sanctioned by a license received from the church. At trial, Galileo produced an affidavit from Cardinal Bellarmine attesting that there was no order, but a warning for Galileo not to hold the belief or promote the theory.

Galileo argued that he abided by the warning and knew of no order. He was forced to admit that he violated the edict and was sentenced to life imprisonment. The punishment was read at the universities and his books were banned. When supporters sought a pardon, Galileo claimed that pardons were for the guilty. He said accusers use wrongful condemnations of the innocent to justify their agenda. Authorities portray the crime for what it is not to persuade those who may do the same.

GILES COREY

Year: 1692
Occupation: Landowner/farmer
Marital Status: Yes
Children: 1
Criminal History: Yes, unrelated to witchcraft
Spiritual Beliefs: Unknown
Age: 81
Education: Unknown
Summary: Giles Corey was accused of being a witch. He refused to enter a plea of guilt or innocence during the Salem Witch Trials.

THE PARTICULARS

Original Charge: Witchcraft
Final Charge: Witchcraft
Trial: No
Verdict: None
Plea: No
Sentence: Death
Appeal: None
Summary: Giles Corey was charged with witchcraft and for being a witch. He was asked to enter a plea of guilt or innocence. He refused. Without a plea, he couldn't be tried. He was pressed with weight with the expectation that he would be forced to do so. He refused.

THE CASE OF GILES COREY

In 1692, Salem, Massachusetts was overwhelmed with accusations of witchcraft. Many people believed in witches. When several young girls began to exhibit peculiar behavior, people became hypersensitive. The hysteria grew when the girls accused others of witchcraft. These accusations were filtered through a special court convened without discerned judgment and fundamental oversight.

The authorities arrested the accused, which included prominent citizens. Hundreds were imprisoned and the infamous Salem Witch Trials began. Men and women were convicted and hanged for being witches.

When Giles Corey refused to plead to his guilt or innocence, he was pressed. English law allowed for this practice. Regrettably, people were too fearful to renounce what was sensational. They feared that they might be accused of the same charges.

Corey was placed on the ground and a board was put on top of his naked body. Men then lifted large rocks onto the board. Even the sheriff stood upon him. Corey eventually died after asking that more weight be placed upon him. He never entered a plea of guilt or innocence. He died days later from this legal punishment.

The ordeal in Salem lasted a year. When the Boston clergy made an appeal to Governor William Phips, he disbanded the special court. Some of those involved in the proceedings admitted their errors. Judge Samuel Sewall was forthcoming. He confessed publicly that he exercised poor judgment.

HAYWOOD PATTERSON AND THE "SCOTTSBORO BOYS"

Year: 1931
Occupation: None
Marital Status: Not married
Children: None
Criminal History: Unknown, likely none
Spiritual Beliefs: Unknown
Age: 12-17
Education: Unknown, likely very little
Summary: A group of nine black boys were on a railroad line hopping train cars. After a verbal altercation with two white girls, the boys were accused of rape.

THE PARTICULARS

Original Charge: Rape
Final Charge: Rape
Trial: Yes
Verdict: Guilty
Plea: No
Sentence: Eight of the nine were sentenced to death
Appeal: Yes
Summary: In racially charged Alabama, the Scottsboro Boys were convicted of rape and sentenced to death. The United States Supreme Court, however, overturned the convictions. Yet, Alabama pursued the charges over subsequent years.

THE CASE OF THE SCOTTSBORO BOYS

On March 31, 1931, nine black boys in Alabama were indicted for raping two white girls. The boys and girls were separately hopping train cars. A verbal fight ensued which led to rape allegations. However, two doctors responsible for examining the alleged victims determined there was no evidence of a crime. After a trial, eight of the nine boys were convicted and sentenced to death. However, liberal and powerful interests from the north intervened. The case was appealed and eventually heard before the Supreme Court. In Powell v Alabama 287 U. S. 45 (1932), the court, on grounds of ineffective assistance of counsel, overturned the convictions.

Alabama officials were determined to prosecute the boys again. As a result, only one of the boys was sentenced to death. Four others were convicted and sentenced to serve 75-99 years in prison. The charges against the remaining boys were dropped. In later years, the boy facing death had his sentence commuted to life in prison. The others were released over time by the parole board. Noteworthy is, during the second trial, one of the rape victims recanted. She acknowledged that her allegations were not true. The jury convicted the boys anyway. The judge, however, exercised his prerogative and ordered a new trial. When the third trial netted the same result, the Supreme Court intervened again. Since the jury was improperly selected (no blacks were permitted to serve as jurors), the lower court decision was overturned.

Arlon Jones

Year: 1940 (approximately)
Occupation: Unknown
Marital Status: Married
Children: 2
Criminal History: Unknown, likely none
Spiritual Beliefs: Unknown
Age: 45 (estimated)
Education: Unknown; likely very little
Summary: Arlon Jones was a simple man who loved his wife and family dearly. In a time of need, he did what he probably would never have done. He stole food to feed his family.

The Particulars

Original Charge: Cattle rustling
Actual Charge: Cattle rustling
Trial: Yes
Verdict: Guilty
Plea: No
Sentence: Life in prison
Appeal: No
Summary: Arlon Jones was accused of killing a heifer owned by a nearby farmer and stealing the meat. After a trial, he was found guilty and sentenced to life in prison.

The Case of Arlon Jones

In or around 1940, a man named Arlon Jones (pseudonym) needed to feed his family. He had a wife, who was a paraplegic, and two small children. They lived together in Piedmont, Virginia.

As the story goes, Jones went to a nearby ranch owned by a wealthy neighbor. Under the cover of darkness, Jones slaughtered a heifer and stole the meat, apparently not at all concerned with the trail of blood he left behind. Jones was charged with cattle rustling and the case went to trial. He was found guilty and sentenced to life in prison. The judge enforced a dated law which permitted the harsh punishment.

The balance of the story, which would not have been common knowledge, is revealing. The wealthy rancher was a close friend of the judge. They were hunting partners. The rancher used his relationship to ensure that Jones received a harsh punishment. The judge obliged his friend's request. When some eighteen years passed and Jones was eligible for parole, the rancher was just as involved. He effectively assured that parole was denied.

It is presumed Jones died in a state penitentiary in Richmond, Virginia.

ELIZABETH RAMIREZ

Year: 1997
Occupation: Unknown
Marital Status: Unknown
Children: Unknown
Spiritual Beliefs: Unknown
Age: 23
Education: Unknown
Summary: Elizabeth Ramirez became known recently when her case was highlighted in the national press. A Texas convict, she claimed her innocence of a sex crime against her nieces.

THE PARTICULARS

Original Charge: Sexual Assault
Actual Charge: Sexual Assault
Trial: Yes
Verdict: Guilty
Plea: No
Sentence: 37.5 years
Appeal: Unknown
Summary: Elizabeth Ramirez was accused of sexually assaulting her nieces, seven and nine years old. After a trial by jury, she was found guilty and sentenced to thirty-seven- and one-half years in prison. With a new Texas law challenging forensic evidence, she was to be released on bail with the hope of establishing her innocence.

THE CASE OF ELIZABETH RAMIREZ

In 1997, Elizabeth Ramirez was sentenced to 37.5 years in prison. She was found guilty of sexually assaulting her nieces. To this day Ramirez states that she never committed this heinous act. According to a November 15, 2013, Wall Street Journal article by Nathan Koppel, Dr. Nancy Kellogg, a pediatrician, was a key witness. Kellogg provided testimony used to convict Ramirez. Kellogg now rejects her conclusions.

After sixteen years in prison, the case against Ramirez took a different turn. The forensic evidence used in the trial became suspect. According to a 2009 report, "The National Academy of Sciences… concluded that no forensic method, with the exception of DNA analysis, has been proved to reliably allow crime-scene evidence to be linked to a particular suspect."[25] As Koppel explains, "a Texas law specifically allows people convicted of crimes to bring fresh appeals by claiming that new science contradicts evidence in past trials."[26] Ramirez took advantage of this new law. Kellogg "conceded recently that evolving scientific standards have discredited her trial testimony that an alleged victim had exhibited physical signs of an assault."[27] Kellogg asserted, "new medical standards by the American Academy of Pediatrics contradict her conclusion that the victim exhibited signs of an internal injury."[28]

---

[25] Nathan Koppel, *On Trial: Evidence Gathering* (The Wall Street Journal, November 16-17, 2013), p. A3
[26] Ibid.
[27] Ibid.
[28] Ibid.

Propitious smiles of heaven can never be expected on a nation that disregards the eternal rules of order and right which heaven itself has ordained. **George Washington, First Inaugural Address**

American Justice—Guilty or Innocent

The preceding cases are about people who experienced *justice* over the prior centuries. These examples give us context. From a macro perspective, we can see the paths these men and women traveled, routes that forked in a direction divergent to the journey taken by the rest of humanity. We also see those who were dragged down the path of *justice*. They had no choice but to endure what was compelled. None of these victims experienced what was comfortable; and none deserved the label or punishment associated with the alleged crime.

As we view history from safety and reach *reasonable* conclusions, we may appreciate the principles, truth, and integrity which motivated these intrepid souls through the thick of their struggles. Appropriately, with an historical perspective, the influences of ignorance, apathy, and fear do not hinder our judgment. Why? We, as readers of dated cases, are unaffected by the cracks and flaws in humanity. We are unaffected by those unjustly harmed by people with titles who exercised power, just as we are unaffected by the system used to enforce a past and unjust process or objective. We are reading history as it was.

Ironically, and quite unfortunately, we remain as unaffected with equal examples of injustice today. Comfort becomes a priority. Ignorance, apathy, and fear blind us to the wrongs that occur in and around us daily. And, if we are not blinded, we do nothing still.

When I was a child, I witnessed two older boys take a younger boy's winter coat. I sat in the car and watched. I was angered as the strong took advantage of the weak. For my unwillingness to act, I saw myself as weak. I was small and certainly no match for the power the victim faced. However, I could have done something—anything. Yet, I never entered the fray. As much as I desired to stand with the stranger, the oppressed, I never left the comfort of the car. I never ventured down the path that would have righted a wrong.

The cases which follow are examples of *justice* in the present. There are literally thousands of men and women like them who suffer at the expense of a system we do not understand. Regrettably, it will be those in the distant future who will look back with a degree of objectivity and note the carnage dispensed by what we currently refer to as *American justice*.

Ken Wahler

Year: 2011
Occupation: Programmer
Marital Status: Married
Children: 2
Criminal History: None
Spiritual Beliefs: Christian
Age: 45
Education: College
Summary: Ken is smart and successful. He retired at an early age; but he still enjoyed business.

The Particulars

Original Charge: Trespassing onto a private server
Actual Charge: Trespassing onto a private server
Trial: No
Verdict: Guilty
Plea: Yes
Sentence: 36 months
Appeal: No
Summary: Ken sold a software program to a company. After the sale was finalized, he accessed the server and downloaded a file. He was arrested and charged for this *crime*.

The Case of Ken Wahler

Ken, a successful businessman, retired by the time he was thirty years old. With the advent of the internet, he became a programmer. At one point, he contracted with a company which requested that he develop a software program. Ken agreed. After time passed, the company asked him to transfer the coding outright. Ken refused. He cited ownership of the technology. He stated that the contract reflected a license agreement to lease the technology, while he retained exclusive ownership rights. The company sued.

Ken prevailed in court and kept control of his intellectual property. Unless the terms of the agreement stipulate, this is standard procedure in the software industry. Yet, Ken took stock of all that transpired and determined that his clients were unscrupulous. Even his attorney encouraged him to end the business relationship. The judge, who adjudicated the civil suit, even intimated that the plaintiffs were of questionable character.

Ken reached an agreement to sell his technology. Within twenty-four hours after finalizing the sale Ken logged onto the server. The username and password remained the same. He accessed the files and downloaded a document which was not sensitive or proprietary. He did nothing to disrupt or destroy the programming. However, it was this act, this crime, that precipitated his conviction as a felon.

When the new owners were notified of the intrusion, they retrieved the IP address and determined that Ken was the intruder. They called an FBI agent with whom they were familiar and reported the crime. A SWAT team raided Ken's house. To the horror of his wife and children, age ten and eight, gun toting agents used a battering ram and swarmed their house. Their singular aim was to arrest an unsuspecting Ken Wahler.

Ken hired a top-notch lawyer. Yet, it was not long before he knew he had to make one of two decisions; risk a trial and a stiff sentence or accept a plea with leniency. Without ill intent, he knew he accessed a server which he no longer owned. He knew he would lose at trial. He accepted a plea and was sentenced to thirty-six months as a felon.

Butch Richardson

Year: 2011
Occupation: School Superintendent
Marital Status: Married
Children: Yes
Criminal History: None
Spiritual Beliefs: Christian
Age: 65
Education: Doctorate
Summary: Butch was a respected educator. After three decades serving students and families in his community, Butch reached professional satisfaction as the Superintendent.

The Particulars

Original Charge: Misappropriation/theft of government funds
Actual Charge: Misappropriation/theft of government funds
Trial: Yes
Verdict: Guilty
Plea: No
Sentence: 36 months
Appeal: No
Summary: After a formal complaint by disgruntled parents, the government audited and investigated his business. He was charged with two crimes. He contested both and lost.

The Case of Butch Richardson

Nestled among the fertile farmlands of Lancaster County, Pennsylvania, schools are filled with children and educators. Butch Richardson was familiar with their rigors and routine. He was an educator. He spent his entire adult life influencing the minds of youth and teachers alike. Butch was knowledgeable and effective. He pursued his education until he received his doctorate. His most recent position was as Superintendent for the surrounding counties. He had reached personal and professional accomplishment and satisfaction.

In Pennsylvania, the role of Superintendent is served in a private capacity. Butch was not employed directly by the school system. He operated his own business, as a consultant, if you will. While he was compensated with funds from the school system, he was his own boss.

Butch was an important figure in his community. He was involved in policy decisions and engaged both civic leaders and citizens. Given his responsibilities, exposure to the public was expected and dissension was, at times, inherent.

Butch's problems began because of local politics. Those who disagreed with his policy decisions did what was petty and indignant. Some cried foul and accused him of wrongdoing, specifically, misappropriation of government funds. The fact that he was a private consultant did not limit the probe. The aftermath of the investigation ended with two telling charges. First, Butch was accused of sending nine personal packages to his daughter with the use of a postal meter in his office. Second, he was accused of failing to take personal leave when he attended events that were part of his profession. His crimes centered on the misuse or theft of government funds. These two allegations were the net result of a full audit of his business.

Butch was incensed with the vitriol associated with local politics. He secured legal counsel and decided to fight the charges. When the government offered him a plea agreement, he flatly refused. He was not willing to endure an unjust punishment. Moreover, since the alleged crimes involved government funds, he risked the possibility of losing his retirement account and pension. He was not willing to lose his livelihood for those who disagreed with his positions and leveled specious claims.

Butch assessed his situation. He conceded that, although he ran his own business, he should not have used his office or postal meter and business funds to send personal correspondence. It was not a business expense. So, he volunteered to reimburse the $100.00 expended to ship the packages.

He also offered to pay for the days he attended professional functions without taking leave. He still disagreed that he had committed a crime in this regard. He attended functions sanctioned by the school board or those events affiliated with his profession. For example, he participated in a golf tournament sponsored by the school system. He paid for the entrance fee as a business expense and attended in his professional capacity. As a fundraiser for the schools, it was an opportunity to network. He golfed as a professional obligation.

When the authorities rejected his offer to reimburse the costs for the mailings and personal leave, Butch fought the charges in court. With no criminal record, he believed a jury would discern justly. The jurors, however, determined that Butch was guilty of both counts. He was sentenced to three years in prison as a convicted felon. He lost his significant retirement account and his annual pension.

David Ingalls

Year: 2012
Occupation: None (SSI disability)
Marital Status: Widower
Children: Stepchildren
Criminal History: Yes
Spiritual Beliefs: Christian
Age: 55
Education: Did not finish school
Summary: A giant of a man physically, with a simple mind, David lived a lonely life after his wife's death.

The Particulars

Original Charge: Conspiracy, negotiating stolen checks
Actual Charge: Conspiracy, negotiating stolen checks
Trial: No
Verdict: Guilty
Plea: Yes
Sentence: 36 months
Appeal: No
Summary: In an effort to earn some money, David agreed to help a friend cash some checks. It was a mistake that cost him his freedom.

The Case of David Ingalls

Among the rolling mountains of Johnson City, Tennessee, David Ingalls coped with life like many indigent people. He survived on $770.00 a month from a SSI disability check. He received SSI, in part, for his inability to make sound decisions. Meanwhile, unemployed, and about to lose his home to foreclosure, David looked for work. As fate would have it, David decided to earn some extra money helping an acquaintance. This unwise decision cost him three years of his life.

David knew a man named Jesse. Jesse had a girlfriend, Amanda. One day David saw Jesse and Amanda on the city bus. The following day, Amanda called David and asked if he would do them a favor. They needed to cash three checks. Jesse agreed to pay him $100.00. David was interested. He needed the money.

To his credit, David asked Amanda why they could not cash the checks themselves. She explained that Wal-Mart had a limit to the number of checks which could be cashed within a week. Her answer was simple and logical, which David accepted as truthful. He agreed to help.

The following day, Jesse and Amanda drove David to Abington, Virginia. As confirmation of David's inability to make sound decisions, when he crossed the Virginia border, he violated the conditions of probation for a prior conviction. David was not permitted to leave the State without permission from his probation officer.

When they arrived at Wal-Mart, David asked the cashier if the checks were legal. She responded in the affirmative. David asked two more times before he gave her the instruments. The cashier took the checks made payable to David, which totaled just over $400.00. David received the cash in return and gave the total to Jesse, less $100. They then returned to Tennessee. The next day, Amanda called David and asked if he would be willing to cash three more checks. He said no.

The checks were blank and belonged to COMDATA, a company which serves the trucking industry. Jesse had hundreds of these checks. They were stolen and he was illegally cashing them. The Federal Government arrested Jesse and Amanda and those who volunteered to cash the checks. David was arrested as well.

The court appointed an outside attorney to represent David. Lawyers in private practice have an obligation to serve as public defenders. While David was behind bars, his lawyer met with the U. S. Attorney. He then met with David for a fifteen-minute conversation. During this discussion, his lawyer went over a thirty-page plea agreement. He told David that he had two choices. He could risk a stiff sentence at trial from a guilty verdict or accept a plea and a reduced prison term.

David was overwhelmed. He faced punishment for a crime he believed he did not commit. He told his lawyer he did nothing wrong. He mentioned his disability and expressed his inability to make wise decisions. However, as far as David was concerned, his attorney did not listen. At the end of fifteen minutes, David was *influenced* to sign the plea agreement which included a prison term of thirty-six months. He believed that he was pressured and made yet another poor choice.

Krister Everston

Year: 2003
Occupation: Inventor
Marital Status: Unknown
Children: Unknown
Criminal History: No
Spiritual Beliefs: Unknown
Age: Unknown
Education: Unknown
Summary: Krister was an inventor developing clean energy cells.

The Particulars

Original Charge: Failing to affix label to a mailed package
Actual Charge: Failing to affix label to a mailed package
Trial: Yes
Verdict: Not guilty
Plea: No
Sentence: None
Appeal: N/A
Summary: The government charged Krister for failing to affix a warning label to a package that contained hazardous materials. He fought the charges and won. However, additional charges were filed and led to his conviction and imprisonment.

The Case of Krister Everston

Krister Everston is an inventor. At the time of his arrest, he was developing technology for a clean energy cell (battery). The Federal Government accused him of mailing a package through the postal system that lacked the required warning label for the contents it contained, supplies associated with his technology. For this he was charged criminally. He refused a plea agreement and fought the charges. As his own legal representative, Krister prevailed and was acquitted by a jury.

Unconscionably, and seemingly without justification, the federal authorities filed additional charges against Krister. With his time and effort spent fighting the first charges, he neglected his work. His material, supplies and invention remained untouched. The U. S. Attorney charged him for abandoning material, as if he created an environment hazard. As with the first trial, Krister defended himself. Regrettably, the result was different. He was found guilty and served almost two years in prison.

John Williams

Year: 2011
Occupation: Pastor
Marital Status: Married
Children: 4
Criminal History: None
Spiritual Beliefs: Christian
Age: 60
Education: Doctorate
Summary: John is a quiet and strong man with a profound faith in God. He lives simply and devotes his time to his wife and family.

The Particulars

Original Charge: Possession of a firearm at an airport
Actual Charge: Possession of a firearm at an airport
Trial: No
Verdict: Guilty
Plea: Yes
Sentence: 6 months of probation
Appeal: No
Summary: John forgot he had a pistol in his luggage. When the authorities detected it at the airport, he was arrested and charged. He accepted a plea rather than risk a sentence.

The Case of John Williams

The tranquil Blue Ridge Mountains are home to the picturesque Shenandoah Valley. It is also home for a pastor transplanted from Iowa. On a vacation to visit his family, John encountered the force of federal power which changed his perspective of life.

One morning John packed his suitcase and made his way to the airport. Rather forgetfully, he packed more than he realized. Within his luggage was a pistol. He failed to remove it from a separate pocket after a recent local trip. For this mistake, he would suffer the consequences. When the firearm was detected at the security checkpoint, John was detained and questioned. This mild-mannered and unassuming pastor confronted the unknown—the federal bureaucracy and subsequent criminal charges.

John disavowed knowing the pistol was in his possession. He explained that he left it inadvertently. His answers and explanations, as well as an admission of an innocent mistake, made no difference. He was charged with possession of a firearm at an airport.

John hired an attorney. Like other defendants, he had two choices, face a trial and punishment if found guilty or accept a plea and leniency. He made the obvious decision. John couldn't argue that he did not break the law. If he chose a trial by jury, he could only hope the jurors would understand his absentminded mistake. His attorney encouraged him not to take the risk. John accepted the plea and a reduced sentence. He served six months of probation and no prison time.

George Norris

Year: 2003
Occupation: Retired/small business owner
Marital Status: Married
Children: Yes
Criminal History: None
Spiritual Beliefs: Christian
Age: 67
Education: Unknown
Summary: George was a content and retired man who settled into a routine that included his passion for orchids. For him, life was good.

The Particulars

Original Charge: Buying/selling illegal orchids
Actual Charge: Buying/selling illegal orchids
Trial: No
Verdict: Guilty
Plea: Yes
Sentences: 24 months
Appeal: No
Summary: George was charged with buying and selling illegal orchids. He did no such thing. Improper paperwork led to his conviction and a two year federal prison sentence.

The Case of George Norris

There is great anticipation with retirement from the daily struggles associated with work. In the great state of Texas, George Norris eased into retirement and enjoyed leisure with his wife, children, and grandchildren. He also immersed himself in his passion for orchids. His love of this unique flower increased his stature among orchid aficionados. He created a following. With his knowledge and experience, he started a small home-based business. He cultivated orchids, developed contacts with foreign growers and sold plants to an increasing clientele. Ironically, doing what he loved would be his undoing.

For what should have been a routine transaction, George made an unexpectedly devastating purchase, if only for how it was perceived by the Federal Government. Quite simply, George bought an orchid from a known and established overseas supplier. George did not realize the supplier failed to send the proper paperwork with this shipment. With international imports, the details and documents required by the federal agencies are often overwhelming and incomprehensible. The missing credentials for this shipment, which should have been easily excused, precipitated the unimaginable.

On an ordinary day for the Norris couple, they had unexpected intruders. Agents of the U. S. Fish and Wildlife Service raided their home. With weapons drawn, federal agents busted through the doors. Once George and his wife, Kathy, were subdued and their property secured, the agents rifled through their papers and possessions. The couple had no idea why the government was there or what the agents were seeking. According to the Washington Times, in October of 2003, Kathy Norris was still unaware of the reasons for the home invasion. Court officials told her, "You don't need to know. You can't know."[29]

George hired an attorney from the surrounding county. This lawyer was out of his league, however. He knew little to nothing about international treaties, imports, environmental law, or federal prosecutions. When George and his attorney met with the authorities, the U. S. Attorney asked George to become an informant and snitch on his suppliers and dealers. George could not comprehend this request. He was not involved with illegal activity. He refused to compromise innocent colleagues and clients.

Eventually, George fired his attorney and hired one with the commensurate experience to fight the charges. He was determined to pose a strong defense and to clear his name. Regrettably, time and expense compelled George to make a difficult decision. He accepted a plea of guilt for a crime he never committed. He spent nearly two years in prison for what amounted to a clerical mistake involving the purchase of a legal orchid.

DAN MCGINNIS

Year: 2010
Occupation: Writer
Marital Status: Divorced
Children: No
Criminal History: Yes
Spiritual Beliefs: Unknown
Age: 50
Education: College
Summary: Dan lived a quiet life as a writer and reporter.

THE PARTICULARS

Original Charge: Writing bad checks
Actual Charge: Writing bad checks
Trial: No
Verdict: Guilty
Plea: Yes
Sentence: 24 months
Appeal: No
Summary: When Dan received a check with insufficient funds from a friend, he unknowingly wrote two checks that bounced. He would spend two years in jail for this crime.

THE CASE OF DAN MCGINNIS

On the outskirts of the Christian conservative bastion of Lynchburg, Virginia, where Jerry Falwell staked his claim, Dan McGinnis learned firsthand that forgiveness and mercy are not universal virtues. As a white-collar professional, a successful writer and reporter, Dan was charged with writing two bad checks. The first check bounced when a check he received from his roommate had insufficient funds. Consequently, when Dan's first check was dishonored, the second one was deficient as well.

Dan went to the owner of the first business. He explained the situation and offered

[29] http://www.washingtontimes.com/news/2009/oct/05/criminalizing-everyone/?page=all

to cover the amount and any associated fees. The owner refused and stated that the matter was already in the control of the local prosecutor. Enough time had lapsed; the crime had been reported. Not surprisingly, the second business owner gave Dan the same response.

Dan did the only logical thing possible. He spoke directly with the prosecutor and explained the situation. Dan offered to cover the checks and any fines. The prosecutor refused. So Dan hired an attorney and, like so many other defendants, chose the lesser of two evils. His attorney advised him that he would likely lose at trial and receive a severe sentence. Dan did not want to risk an unwarranted prison term. He accepted a plea agreement with a sentence of twenty-four months.

Dan had a prior criminal charge which was resolved prior to writing these checks. He did not disclose the details and I did not inquire. It was not necessary. The punishment served satisfied whatever crime he committed. If the charge was like the current crime, it would validate the absurdity of prosecution. Moreover, if his sentence of two years for the current crime, which was harsh, was tied to his prior sentence, this would reflect the unfairness of the system.

Ron Webb

Year: 2011
Occupation: Mechanic
Marital Status: Married
Children: 3
Criminal History: None
Spiritual Beliefs: Christian
Age: 62
Education: High School
Summary: Ron lived a quiet life in his humble home. He operated his own mechanic shop on his property. He loved his wife, children, grandchildren, and motorcycles.

The Particulars

Original Charge: Selling prescription drugs/conspiracy
Actual Charge: Selling prescription drugs/conspiracy
Trial: No
Verdict: Guilty
Plea: Yes
Sentence: 24 months
Appeal: No
Summary: Ron was arrested for selling prescription medicine. He was innocent. Yet, to escape the prospects of a ten-year prison sentence, he accepted a plea.

The Case of Ron Webb

In his humble country home in Amherst, Virginia, Ron Webb enjoyed solitude and a simple life. Rarely did anyone visit except family. His wife, though, had an infrequent visitor with whom Ron had no dealings. This person would cause Ron trouble.

Ron's wife had a prescription for pain pills, which she rarely used. Occasionally she sold these pills to an acquaintance named Andy, who was not Ron's friend. Ron had nothing to do with Andy or the medication. The money from the transaction, $10.00 per capsule, belonged to his wife. It was that simple. What Ron did not realize is, as the owner of his home, he was liable for his wife's illegal acts; at least this is what he was told.

Andy had been under investigation and was soon arrested for operating a meth lab.

As is common for those apprehended, the prosecution offered Andy a conditional plea agreement and a reduced sentence. Andy had to divulge his clients and suppliers. He became a snitch which assured him of leniency. His list included Ron's wife as a supplier.

Andy wore a wire and went to Ron's home. He met with Ron's wife and made the purchase. As fate would have it, Andy confronted Ron about the pain pills, something he had not done in the past. He had no reason to do so. Ron responded with his matter-of-fact country style. "I have nothing to do with those pain pills." An armed SWAT team raided Ron's home. He and his wife were arrested for conspiracy and selling a controlled substance. With no criminal record, Ron faced jail time and loss of money.

Ron hired an attorney and dealt with all that unfolds with any criminal charge. After preliminary formalities, he reconciled with one of two options. Ron could endure a trial and a stiff prison sentence if found guilty or agree to a plea agreement and leniency. Ron was terrified of the thought of spending up to ten years in prison. He accepted the government's offer of twenty-four months for a crime he never committed. Ron's wife was found guilty, as she accepted a plea agreement and received a prison sentence as well.

In the United States, sovereignty resides in the people... the Congress cannot invoke sovereign power of the People to override their will as thus declared. ***Perry v. U. S., 294 US 356 (1886)***

Critical Analysis

These eight men have several things in common. They are human and fallible. They made mistakes or happened to be in the way when others made mistakes. They were unexpectedly caught within a web from which they could not extract themselves. They are Americans at the disposal of a system of justice as flawed as any in the world. They suffered loss of time, money, and freedom for accusations or actions which could easily have been excused or remedied. In the end, they were labeled as common criminals. Each, except for John, was among the vast number of incarcerated in America's jails and prisons.

How did we get here? How does a country, which espouses justice, exact such a toll upon its countrymen? We know the components of the legal system. How does each contribute to our high rate of incarceration? What are the solutions? How do we return to the treasured principles of justice and equity?

The answers are not simple if only because the truth is hard to understand or accept. The truth is only gained by honest appraisal which, today, is a rare commodity. When truth and understanding are acquired, when solutions are found, we must have the will to change what is flawed. More importantly, if we make the changes, we must be resolute and eradicate the injustices that reign and prevent them from recurring.

With any unknown issue, we must investigate and determine the facts. With facts, we may sense the nuances and appreciate what is occurring. Subsequently, we form sound perceptions which further influence our understanding. We do this instinctively, whether dealing with family, spouses, children, colleagues, or neighbors.

In the last eight cases, we have the facts from the defendants. We, however, are without the *facts* from the prosecutors. This is by design. Simply stated, there is no reason to understand the government's perspective. Why? If a reasonable man can honestly articulate a cogent explanation as to why he is not guilty of a crime, why would we give credence to the government? This is a vital reason the justice system is flawed. If the government must fabricate its version of the facts, or if the prosecutor must ignore his own honest assessment of the crime, we have less reason to consider his argument.

Consider an example. If at any point the prosecutor in the Norris case knew, to whatever degree, that the issue was missing paperwork and not the sale of illegal orchids, and he never acknowledged this fundamental truth, why would anyone dignify his words or perspective? Any principled prosecutor would cease to prosecute or imprison an innocent man for a clerical mistake.

Thus, we shall proceed with the premise that none of these men were guilty of the alleged crimes and examine how the components of the legal system contributed to their incarceration. With what we know, we may project that ignorance, apathy, and arrogance on behalf of the government and ignorance, apathy, and fear of the people are major reasons for the verdicts in each case.

To begin, we will consider the people—the electorate. The electorate has an incumbent civic responsibility to be informed. If the people are not informed, they are disengaged. If the people are disengaged, they surrender any practical claim to their freedom. Lack of civic involvement is a cause, not a symptom, of the disease which strikes at and defeats justice. Our individual and collective malaise allows an undetected and overbearing power to strip away any remaining vestiges of the people's natural rights and freedom. Our disengagement is evident daily. If only with anecdotal examples, we hear of investigations and guilty verdicts. We note, if only subconsciously, that the system *works*, and *truth* and *justice* prevail. This is the extent of our participation.

We rarely go to court to observe. Court is an unknown arena. It is imposing because of our lack of familiarity. We respect the court and bestow homage to it as an established institution. Through our passive posture, we grant the courts and its players a pass as virtuous and just. We rarely question those with titles, those with the power to influence with impunity.

We apply the same respect to state and federal legislators and members of the executive branch. We afford them and the institutions they operate with a deference that is absent the scrutiny they deserve. We fail to note that these representatives are just as unaware once elected as they were before they ran for office. We, by default, superimpose a level of knowledge and understanding upon them that they lack. Frankly, the positions people hold and the titles they carry do not make them. Yet, we behave as if they do. And, regrettably, the power they possess tends to blind their moral compass or disproportionately inflate their actual roles into what should not be.

This sweeping generalization is not without merit. Crucial to our discussion is that officials within the White House, Senate, House of Representatives, Governor's Mansions, state legislatures, prosecutors' offices, investigative agencies, and the courts often breach the constraints of their authority under the guise of *discretion*. Since accountability is lacking when the people are disinterested and disengaged, the creators and enforcers of law are less likely to mind their masters. More importantly, when we fear any of those officials and institutions, we consign ourselves to the status we rightly deserve—controlled and conquered.

State and federal legislatures write laws ad nauseam. If we don't know of these laws, we cannot and will not prevent or reverse them. As a result, laws, which are incongruous with written constitutions or the will of the people, remain, as do these elected representatives. For example, there is a dated law on the books in a State which prohibits citizens from buying chocolate on Sunday. Illinois passed a law in 2011 limiting the number of cats per home to four. The Federal Government recently passed a law requiring citizens to buy health insurance or pay a penalty. If we don't know or don't care to know about these laws, or if we are too intimidated to challenge them, the system is unaccountable, and we are unaccountable.

When crimes or matters of law enter the courts, our lack of accountability persists for the same reasons. When citizens are found guilty of buying chocolate on Sunday, having five cats, or for selling illegal orchids, we have no one to blame but ourselves. A system which operates unabated is a system that morphs into what was never intended.

Former U. S. Attorney General Richard Thornburg expressed the essence of the overreaching of government. He stated, "Those of us concerned about this subject share a common goal, to have criminal statutes that punish actual criminal acts and do not seek to criminalize conduct that is dealt with by the seeking of regulatory and civil remedies."[30] Stephen Saltsburg, a law professor at George Washington University said the Norris and Everston cases "illustrate about as well as you can illustrate the overreach of federal criminal law."[31] Both Thornburg and Saltsburg directly suggest that the distinction between what is criminal and what is not has been blurred or obliterated. The system has become what was never intended. Our liberties will not endure if this onslaught continues

---

[30] Ibid.

[31] Ibid.

unchecked. Let there be no misunderstanding—innocent Americans are incarcerated for nothing less than the failure of the electorate to hold lawmakers and courts accountable.

Our current judicial crisis speaks to the adage that we reap what is sown. Ignorance, apathy, and fear are the seeds which give rise to the injustice that wraps itself around our freedom with a fatal chokehold. Timothy Lynch, from the CATO Institute, called for a "clean line between lawful conduct and unlawful conduct."[32] He is correct. As citizens who retain the ultimate sovereign power in our republic, we must distinguish that line. We must draw the distinction between our resolve and resignation. Otherwise, the lack of clarity of what is criminal and what is not will reduce us to a state of impotence.

The ability to draw any proper line requires us to be accountable. When we are accountable, we may then call for restraint. Absent the exercise of civic virtue, we concede to the confusion between good and evil, right and wrong, lawful and unlawful, truth and fiction. One of the reasons I grant such latitude to my friend's conclusion that I am a common criminal is because of my own personal knowledge and experience. I see a distinction of those proper lines; he does not. He imagines what he wishes within a narrow scope of ill-informed thought which provides no distinction and no accountability. He provides only judgment while our culture continues to collapse. He will not accept the definitive—I did not commit a crime—and he will not understand until he is accountable. Only then will he know the legal system is complicit with forcing a right into a wrong. Only then will he alter his perspective.

If my friend appreciated how or why David Ingalls became a prisoner, which had nothing to with the law, he might understand the system lacks equity and is unjust. These insights would dispel judgments borne out of ignorance. We must conclude that there are flaws within our legal process. There are reprehensible and regrettable verdicts One such example is a man who was charged with murder. He was imprisoned for thirty years, which was a life sentence because of his age. He never stopped pleading his innocence. His wife remained loyal and never forsook him. When DNA tests absolved him of any wrong, he was released from prison in Alaska. A second example is a man charged and sentenced for a rape he never committed. He was a college student with a promising career as a professional basketball player. After serving five years of his sentence, the *victim* had a crisis of conscience and admitted to fabricating the story.

Even with clearly defined laws, these two men and their families suffered needlessly from a system that exacted justice that was anything but just. Do situations like these occur? Yes. Should they? No. These men illustrate our need to prevent injustice. We should be ever vigilant and love our neighbor, which requires that we hold ourselves accountable first and foremost.

The State and Federal Governments are governed by constitutions which constrain their powers. These documents, which account for the legislative, executive, and judicial branches, serve as chains which restrict these political bodies from encroaching upon the rights of the people. Lawmakers should create laws in keeping with established legislative constraints. Executives and their agencies are expected to enforce laws as written. Government should govern in a manner consistent with these constraints. The judiciary renders decisions concerning questions of law by referring to the Constitution. Judges should interpret the laws in conformance with the Constitution—and no more.

We have a rather linear flow, and all three branches serve as a check and balance and ensure that unconstitutional laws or ill-conceived laws are minimized. Yet, life is not as black and white. Rather, nuances within legislation, enforcement, and interpretation

---

[32] Ibid.

exist. Even worse, all three branches coalesce, whether by design or happenstance, to engineer an agenda or outcome.

Referring to the eight cases in question, let's assess the crimes allegedly committed. We may realize these cases reflect outcomes which involve the participation of all branches that eventually coalesce within the venue of court. With this assessment as voters, to whom lawmakers and executives are accountable, we may further appreciate what occurs within the courts. This may provide insight as to how and why non-criminal acts and mistakes are prosecuted.

One of our conclusions may be that this linear process, whereby the three branches of the government are controlled by the Constitution, is generally sound. However, we may discover two other results without realizing the degree to which they exist. First, the latitude of discretion exercised by lawmakers is too vast. Second, the enforcement of laws by the executive branch is fraught with misjudgment, overzealous application, and strident indiscretion. The same holds true for judges who take liberties with their actions and decisions. Out of ignorance, apathy, and arrogance, each branch acts counter to the Constitution and adversely affects the rendering of verdicts and punishment.

THE ELECTORATE

The first demonstration of any discretion within the legal system should be made by the electorate. Voters elect lawmakers to office. If voters elect men and women who are ignorant, apathetic, or arrogant, the potential for questionable laws becomes an ever-present concern. If we elect executives who are the same, the enforcement of laws becomes problematic. Even the judiciary is not immune from exercising a lack of discretion. The first two branches, it may be said, are controlled by the *discernment* of the judiciary. Thus, if the electorate were more discriminating of those elected to office, the people would be better served.

The legal realm may be viewed as a mathematical formula. The more laws created the more crimes will be committed. The telling aspect is that the increase of crimes is not necessarily for the abundance of laws, but for the manifold interpretations by the scads of officials with the titles and authority to decide if laws are violated. There can be no doubt those elected or hired into office have a significant impact upon the justice system. Voter indiscretion serves as an exponential multiplier of systemic indiscretion.

Let's refer to this dynamic as "The Ten Commandment Rule." If our culture had only ten laws, few crimes would occur. Few laws would suffer the varied distortions of interpretation by those in authority. This mindset begins with the intent of the people. If we elect those who exercise restraint, we will have a less controlling government. However, if we elect and hire those with the intention to define and refine our existence ad infinitum, we, the people, would be culpable for the immeasurable number of unnecessary laws and resultant *crimes*.

A book by Lynn Powell, Framing Innocence, is an excellent critique of how authorities and the legal system exploited the power of discretion bestowed by the electorate. A law created by Ohio legislators and enforced by the executive branch enabled those with the commensurate arrogance to charge a woman with what was not true. The story is a perfect portrayal of all that is wrong with justice in America. It demonstrates that the practice of arbitrary judgment can and does destroy a person's life. This *discretion* must originate somewhere. That somewhere is with the people. The abuse of power must fall upon those who are able to influence the situation from the outset or exercise the influence to change how the process is handled.

As in Powell's example, the enforcement of a law may lead to a travesty when the *discretion* of those elected may be wholly inconsistent with "community standards,"[33] according to Powell. She states, "nevertheless, human beings with biases, ambitions and personal histories filled every position from policeman to prosecutor, from social worker to judge and jury, all sorts of people who might find..."[34] the discretion to impugn the innocent. Indeed, the problems of indiscretion will persist if voters do not check the arrogance of those who hold titles and use power to justify errant abuse of authority without merit.

With our own discretion we shall proceed with the notion that the eight men were not guilty of a crime. This is in keeping with the claim that we are innocent until proven guilty. Then we will examine these cases *without* considering the laws that were supposedly violated. While one may cry foul for such an approach, consider that the laws are not essential for this exercise. We need only refer to the men convicted of murder and rape who were later proved to be innocent. The laws were available for their convictions.

One of the conclusions we may draw is that factors other than the law are the reasons innocent people are found guilty. For our benefit, questions become more important than the law. Questions will strike at the heart of the motives of the elected and appointed officials involved and their exercise of *discretion* to prosecute *crimes*.

Let's ask if these eight men committed a crime. That is, did they injure anyone, or did they meet an official's negligible threshold for what amounts to a violation of mere words, black ink on white paper? The second question: Did these men have malicious intent to harm, wound, disrupt, steal, lie, or otherwise threaten society and the fabric of goodwill that clothes a man's interactions with his fellow citizens? There is a third question. Was there harm or injury other than what was done to another's person or property for which these men must be held to account? Furthermore, could any *injury* be satisfied in a manner befitting how civil men *reconcile* an obligation owed?

These questions are important. If a law is enforced solely for a loss suffered, the loss may be satisfied without unjust punishment, especially when malicious intent is lacking. We are a culture driven with inflexibility, spite, revenge, political calculations, and agendas. We shun any sense of equity and decency. The result is the imprisonment of men who were never given the benefit of the doubt by those in power.

Let's bring some accountability to ourselves, as the electorate, by answering these three questions for the preceding eight cases.

1. Did the men commit the crime?
2. Did they have malicious intent?
3. Was there an injured party?

As a vote, regardless of your education, understanding, and experience, try to draw upon your innate sense of equity, your sense of right and wrong. As expressed by Thornburg and Saltsburg, assess whether non-criminal behavior was gratuitously criminalized. Weigh the circumstances and facts and discern if each man deserved the punishment he received. Our accountability to the justice system as voters, coupled with principles, creeds, and beliefs that govern our relationships between men, is essential if we are to receive and achieve justice.

Ken Wahler—Computer Programmer

1. No. Ken did not commit a crime. He made a mistake. Just as one cuts across another's lawn, he accessed a server that belonged to him a day earlier.

[33] Lynn Powell, *Framing Innocence* (The New Press, 2010), p. 134

[34] Ibid., p. 16

2. Ken had no malicious intent.
3. There was no injured party.

Butch Richardson—Superintendent of Schools

1. Butch did not commit a crime. He made a mistake when he sent personal mail from his business, which was his own accounting issue.
2. He had no malicious intent.
3. There was no injured party and he offered to pay for his personal expenditures.

David Ingalls—Check Cashing

1. David did not commit a crime. He exercised poor judgment.
2. He had no malicious intent when he erred by cashing, as verified by the cashier, what were legitimate checks.
3. David could not have injured the company. He was a victim of the scheme. As a victim, he sought to refund the full amount.

Krister Everston—Mailing Label

1. Krister did not commit a crime.
2. He had no malicious intent.
3. There was no injured party.

John Williams—Gun at Airport

1. John failed to exercise good judgment. He did not commit a crime.
2. He had no malicious intent.
3. There was no injured party.

George Norris—Sale of Orchids

1. George did not commit a crime.
2. He had no malicious intent.
3. There was no injured party.

Dan McGinnis—Bounced Checks

1. Dan did not commit a crime
2. He had no malicious intent.
3. While there were injured parties, he, too, was affected by extraordinary circumstances. He attempted to cover the loss to the respective businesses.

Ron Webb—Prescription Medicine

1. Ron did not commit a crime. He did not sell prescription medicine.
2. He could not have had malicious intent.
3. There could not have been an injured party.

If you agree with these answers, even remotely, you recognize America's problem. Even without knowing the prosecutor's perspective or the language of the law, we sense that these eight men suffered from excessive authority and rampant indiscretion. We sense a need to understand why the innocent are criminalized.

It has been said that life is not a dress rehearsal. We have but one life to live within sundry circumstances that compel us to respond to the degree we are able. Life, therefore, can be tenuous. Those who do not value life, those who violate the life, liberty, and property of others, should be held accountable. We should not condone deliberate harm. We should also prevent harm caused by the legal system. We should be equally intolerant of the abuse of power that results in the senseless destruction of lives. George Norris, for example, should never have been subjected to the atrocious experience he endured.

I am suggesting, rather forcefully, that our lack accountability as the electorate results in public officials who destroy lives without ample cause. While officials may be reluctant to agree, we will explore why this supposition is well founded. Ignorance, apathy, and arrogance underscore how and why officials are neglectful and exercise authority unconscionably. Public employees, whether elected, appointed, or hired—be it a prosecutor, policeman, or a building inspection official—have varied knowledge, experience, and motivation. They do not necessarily perform their responsibilities as they should. For example, not all city building officials read their codes and protocol or properly exercise their powers.

Consider this example. I once observed a city inspection official who briefed an audience of landlords about a new rental inspection ordinance. He showed various pictures of apartments that were "messy," as he described them. He referred landlords to the housekeeping skills of tenants. He stated these conditions were not acceptable and would cause the property to fail inspection. The landlords laughed in disbelief. Not only was the inspection official ignorant of the code, but his discretion also perverted his powers to enforce the ordinance. He presumed to enforce what was never intended and what could never be.

In another example, a Zoning Administrator for the same city had a disagreement with a business owner concerning the use of a table outside of an establishment. The zoning official required the owner to submit a "permit" to use the table on the sidewalk, something she was never required to do for the previous ten years. This, therefore, amounted to a rather simple civil matter. So, the zoning official went to see the owner directly. However, before he went, he called the police. Unbelievably, two policemen accompanied this zoning tsar. As luck would have it, the local press was on hand to "conveniently" memorialize the event on the front page of the only local newspaper. In retrospect, the police chief admitted that the use of the police officers was an abuse of his personnel and department and an indiscretion by the zoning official.

These two illustrations are but small representations of what happens every day across America. Local, state, and federal officials misuse their positions and authority. Why? Either they are unaware of the policies which restrict the scope of their offices and duties, or they are ignorant of the proper use of power, and, thus, exceed their authority.

Apathy with the enforcement of laws or public office is just as prevalent, if not a greater problem. Officials become comfortable. When comfortable, they become careless. They neglect their positions. They abuse their titles. They become indifferent when people are complacent. Had I not, as a local citizen, spoken directly to the police chief about the use of his office for what was not a criminal matter with the zoning official, he may not have accounted for this mistake. Clearly, the zoning official was indifferent as to what was just and proper, and certainly not indifferent about creating a powerful impression of himself and his office through the local media. Such indifference often culminates in rogue officials who disregard the proper parameters of their authority.

Apathy is overshadowed by arrogance. When officials have a sense of infallibility and entitlement with their powers and positions, a pernicious and predatory posture prevails upon an unsuspecting people. It is axiomatic that power corrupts, and absolute power corrupts absolutely. Undeniably, there are officials who operate as if they are immune from wrongdoing. This mentality is, in part, why citizens distrust and fear those in authority. This constant and often unseen sense of entitlement breeds contempt and disenfranchises citizens.

People experience the overreach of leaders who exceed their authority, often done behind the guise of policy or position. It does not matter that such acts are cloaked in language promoting the "greater public good," or whatever line being sold to the public. It doesn't matter that an unaware populace does not see or understand such misuse or abuse of power. The result is the same. Officials who are comfortable with a heightened sense of arrogance contradict the virtues of public service and, in the process, affect the life, liberty, and property. The Zoning Administrator reflects a disdainful posture of one who, out of arrogance, had no regard for his office, policy, and the dignity of a private business.

There is arrogant abuse of power with these eight cases. To fully appreciate how such arrogance contributes to our national imprisonment dilemma, we must view the actions of the officials involved. We, as members of the electorate, must view these cases with a greater degree of engagement and discernment. We can no longer be passive observers. If we care to distinguish how the enforcement of laws is contrary to what was intended, we must be critical with our observations. We must know when officials take liberties that morally or ethically malign the integrity of society. When officials take liberties, there is cause for fear.

Consider one important aspect. There are literally tens and hundreds of thousands—even millions—of officials at all levels of government in America, many of whom err daily when exercising their authority. The implications of such errors are often unnoticed, but the collective short-term and long-term impact is significant. Vigilance is essential if we intend to curb the effects.

THE LEGISLATURE

A society free from the constant presence of needless laws would be a society free from the misuse or abuse of discretion from the creation and enforcement of those laws. Indiscretion is a driving force in the criminalizing of America. From the creation of laws, we are saddled with the machinations and maligned judgment of lawmakers who legislate to a fault. Legislators would serve constituents by asking:

1. Is the law needed?
2. Upon what grounds is the law justified? Do we have jurisdiction?
3. What is the intended purpose of the law?
4. What are the repercussions for the misapplication of the law?

Given the reach of the legislative branch, one would think lawmakers would extrapolate the subsequent toll of their *discretionary* creation of statutes and the impact of such laws upon the electorate. The obvious implication is, given the literally thousands of *law enforcement* personnel across any given jurisdiction, the potential for harm is great. A reasonable conclusion would be that the actual law has less to do with a crime than the judgment of those who enforce or prosecute those laws. Consequently, indiscretion is a common denominator with every miscarriage of justice. Note that, according to Merriam-Webster's Dictionary and Thesaurus, 2007 edition, the definition of discretion is "individual choice or judgment" or "power of free decision or latitude of choice."

THE INVESTIGATION

There are subtle and obvious indiscretions in the eight cases which reflect a culture of arrogance. These indiscretions began with agents who investigated the *crime*. The conduct of the investigators and collection of evidence can be and most often is suspect to some small degree. The repercussions from the investigation are critical to any verdict of guilt. If the integrity of these agents or process is tainted, the integrity of the prosecution is compromised. Pointedly, if the facts that are *true* become what are not we have the genesis of a lie. This can be nothing but the antithesis of justice from the start.

We must conclude that an investigation occurred in each of these eight cases. The integrity of each case may be gauged by questioning how and why the investigation was performed. From a layman's perspective with a non-legal frame of reference, let's ask:

1. Was there a need for an investigation?
2. How was the investigation conducted?
3. What was the objective?

These simple queries allow us to assess whether the officials complied with or were interested in conducting a legitimate inquiry. Therefore, we must be mindful of the relationship and interchange between the prosecutor and the investigator. To what extent does the prosecutor exert influence in the investigation? We know each component of the legal system is influenced by ulterior motives. These motives affect the process and conclusions. Answer the foregoing questions for each case.

Ken Wahler—Computer Programmer

1. Yes, there was a need for an investigation.
2. The probe was conducted as if Ken were a criminal.
3. The investigators intended to secure charges regardless of the facts.

Butch Richardson—Superintendent of Schools

1. Yes, there was a need for an investigation.
2. The probe was conducted with great intensity, as if Butch were a criminal.
3. The objective was to charge him with anything.

David Ingalls—Check Cashing

1. Yes, there was a need for an investigation.
2. The agents collected facts which indicated the possibility David was involved.
3. The objective was to arrest those associated with the scam with disregard for David's probable innocence.

Krister Everston—Mailing Label

1. There was no need for an investigation.
2. Agents pursued the claim that he failed to place a label on a package as if it could not have been a simple mistake.
3. The objective was to build a case to justify charges.

John Williams—Gun at Airport

1. Yes, there was cause for an investigation.
2. Given the crime, John was treated as if he were a man with questionable motives, which was not unreasonable.
3. The objective was to justify charges.

George Norris—Sale of Orchids

1. Yes, there was a need for an investigation.

2. It was conducted with austere rigidity, as if Norris committed a crime.
3. The objective was to make a case that Norris sold illegal orchids.

Dan McGinnis—Bounced Checks

1. Yes, there was a need for an investigation.
2. The probe was conducted as if Dan were a criminal.
3. The intent was to charge him even after he explained the circumstances.

Ron Webb—Prescription Medicine

1. Yes, there was a need for an investigation.
2. It was handled rigorously, as if Ron were guilty.
3. The objective was to apprehend those involved with the meth lab without weighing the possibility of ensnaring those who were clearly not involved.

A reasonable man would want the investigators to execute their responsibilities with professionalism and with the intent to solve crimes and catch bad guys. Yet, a reasonable man would want to prevent those same officials from criminalizing anyone outside the *criminal* scope of the law. Agents should exercise discernment and discretion and check their tendency to secure trophy charges.

Examine the Norris Case. Those who conducted the raid were from the United States Fish and Wildlife Service. They count fish and track deer! Now with police powers, these federal agents stormed the Norris' humble abode brandishing arms. What were their psychological motives? They wanted to do well and serve with distinction. Yet, in a bizarre twist, those who deal with *Nemo, Bambi, and Thumper* conducted a terrorist assault against a peaceful and God-fearing, retired couple. At the risk of sounding extreme, did the agents get a rush charging into the tranquil living room of these innocent elderly Americans?

Police are motivated by the execution of such militant tactics. Like the days of playing cops and robbers in their youth, the chance to appeal to their base nature was a tempting and heady experience. Those who would besmirch this characterization have turned a blind eye to human nature and the militarization of civilian police forces. The George Norris case and the baseless charges represented an opportunity for government-sanctioned and trained agents to exert thug-like behavior as they terrorized an old man for ordering and selling legal flowers.

If we distinguish between noble civil service and the overzealous and heavy-handed tactics used in the Norris case, we have the answers to the three questions. We may even conclude, after an initial query, that there was no need for a full-blown investigation. We can determine that the intent was to manufacture and force false accusations into court.

THE PROSECUTOR

In each of the eight cases, the prosecutor eventually received the due diligence of the investigative agents who collected the *evidence*. The prosecutor was responsible for warrants, charges, and indictments. This is a critical moment in any case. The discretion that the prosecutor exercises unduly influence the lives of the suspect and his loved ones. The implications are huge. We know the prosecutor is affected by ignorance, apathy, and arrogance, as well as with his psychological and emotional motives. All these factors—and more—influence his perception of the facts. The prosecutor is a critical node in the legal system. He ensures that those who have injured life, liberty, and property are held accountable. He has a vital and necessary responsibility. Yet, he ill-serves people and society when the innocent are wrongly charged contrary to the letter and spirit of the law.

A prosecutor who knowingly applies *facts* and *evidence* which he knows loosely represent what is true, or if he crafts a *story* with *facts* that are reasonably doubtful, but gives the case the appearance of legitimacy, he injures the public. The injury may not be realized for some time. When the repercussions are manifested and people learn the innocent are incarcerated because of dubious prosecutorial intent, they understand that the misuse and abuse of power is a greater crime than the one supposedly committed.

At a minimum, shouldn't the prosecutor err on the side of caution when deciding a course of action when the *crime* is non-violent with no injured party? Should he not restrain any compunction to proceed if he has doubt as to the guilt of the accused? We would expect him to be responsible to the public trust and less cavalier when prosecuting men who neither committed nor intended to commit crimes. If the prosecutor ignores this proper and prudent restraint, if he seeks convictions or guilty pleas regardless of his doubts, he does not dignify his power and the best interests of the public. The prosecutor should charge those who committed criminal acts and dismiss those who have not. With such awesome responsibility, if the prosecutor is influenced by arrogance and personal agendas, he sacrifices sound discretion for what is ultimately untenable.

As a practical matter, the office of the prosecutor is where all roads connect concerning the enforcement of law within the courts. He has the law, evidence, and witnesses. He has the collusion of the investigators. He has the use of the press to further his efforts whether his intentions are wholesome or not. As an additional tool, he has the attorney who represents the accused. The defense lawyer is a direct route to a conviction and factors into the prosecutor's plans. He has access to the defendant and a plea.

Consider three questions as they apply to the prosecution for the eight cases, as the prosecutor *investigates* and determines whether or how to proceed.

1. Was there a need for a prosecution?
2. How was the prosecution conducted?
3. What was the intent of the prosecution?

Leveling charges against anyone is a weighty proposition—at least it *should* be—and is even more so if one is not a criminal. As we answer these three questions, we should be respectful of the prosecutor's powers and wary of any misplaced or misguided judgment. As lay people, with an insufficient understanding of his perception of the case, we may conclude whether something is a duck or not. Ultimately, we want to know how and why the prosecutor contributes to the criminalizing of those within his jurisdiction.

Ken Wahler—Computer Programmer

1. There was no need to prosecute Ken.
2. The prosecution was pursued is if Ken were a criminal.
3. The intent was to secure a conviction at all costs.

Butch Richardson—Superintendent of Schools

1. There was no need to prosecute Butch.
2. The prosecution was pursued as if Butch were a criminal.
3. The intent was to secure a conviction at all costs.

David Ingalls—Check Cashing

1. There was no need to prosecute David.
2. The prosecutor pursued David as if he were a criminal and not one of the victims.
3. The intent was to convict him at all costs.

Krister Everston—Mailing Labels

1. There was no need to prosecute Krister.
2. The prosecutor pursued Krister as a criminal.
3. The intent was to convict at all costs.

John Williams—Gun at Airport

1. There was no need to prosecute John.
2. The prosecution was pursued as if John were criminal.
3. While leniency was granted, the intent was to convict.

George Norris—Sale of Orchids

1. There was no need to prosecute George.
2. The prosecutor pursued George as if he were a criminal.
3. The intent was to secure a conviction at all costs.

Dan McGinnis—Bounced Checks

1. There was no need to prosecute Dan.
2. The prosecution was pursued as if he were a criminal regardless of the circumstances and Dan's offer to cover the checks.
3. The intent was to secure a conviction.

Ron Webb—Prescription Medicine

1. There was no need to prosecute Ron.
2. The prosecutor pursued Ron as a criminal and ignored the facts of his innocence.
3. The intent was to prosecute Ron at all costs.

Close examination of these eight cases from the prosecutor's perspective illustrates that he has the latitude to move a case forward with either reasonable or unreasonable intent. Any of these men could easily have been freed from the specter of criminal charges and the loss of time, freedom, and money—not to mention needless suffering.

THE DEFENSE LAWYER

If people expect defense lawyers to counter the impact of such prosecutorial power, the system is twice as unjust. Although the discovery process provides the defense with the *evidence*, the innocent defendant is in a reactive mode. He is at the mercy of unwarranted and unsubstantiated assertions backed by the full force of government. With the added burden of the rules, protocol, and procedures of court, the defendant faces insurmountable odds. His challenges are compounded if his defense lawyer operates with restraint and questionable motives. Otherwise, well-intentioned attorneys who zealously defend their clients must overcome what is the prosecutor's version of the facts and the system itself.

We must apply similar questions asked of the prosecution to the defense lawyers. This requires us to speculate as to how ignorance, apathy, and arrogance influence their decisions. We must also include psychological and emotional objectives and how these affect their judgment and performance.

There are some discouraging revelations to consider at this juncture. First, the defense lawyer is unable to remotely match the driving force of the prosecution. He does not have equal time, resources, or power. Second, the legal system encourages that defense lawyers aid and abet its flawed process. Defense attorneys reconcile that the pressure and odds are geared for convictions, and they default to this expectation. Pleas are a common staple which the legal system grows. Defense lawyers help reap the harvest. Finally, the judicial process is without self-correcting remedies or adequate oversight to prevent errant indiscretions and injustice. Defendants raise the white flag of surrender and agree to those plea agreements delivered by defense lawyers.

Most of these eight men resigned their fate to a system that is not wholly concerned with truth and justice. Most of them gave up the quest for exoneration and vindication. We must conclude that their defense lawyers, rightly or wrongly, were complicit with their capitulation.

Every defense lawyer has varying degrees of knowledge and experience. A lack of either quality directly influences the outcome of the case. Public defenders, those who work for the government and defend the accused, have a reputation for not being as aggressive or knowledgeable as private attorneys. Private attorneys, invariably, specialize in particular areas of law, but the cost to retain them is prohibitively high. Defaulting to a public defender may be a matter of necessity. Regardless of who represents the defendant, though, the task of mounting a defense against the government is formidable.

Defense lawyers are affected by apathy as well. Many are overworked. They lack staffing and resources to adequately manage cases. Even private attorneys experience the constant grind of caseloads that inevitably impact their performance. They are not immune from being desensitized. Indifference is often a direct result of a routine that is as mundane as any other vocation. Lawyers, as a practical matter, are only able to expend a limited amount of time preparing for each case. These factors affect their motivation, attitude, and performance, all of which contribute to an increase in convictions.

The issue of arrogance is equally applicable to defense lawyers. When clients become just another name and number, another part of a routine job, when the defense lawyer's *strategy* complies with or completes the established expectation of guilt and a conviction rate of over 98%, arrogance *must* play a role. This arrogance is revealed when we consider the defense lawyer's motives. Does he want a victory? Does he seek truth and justice? Is his goal simply financial? Does he covet his time and, therefore, prepare less? Does he, as a result, push his clients to plead? Courts are saturated with cases. To think defense lawyers are not encouraged to seek pleas is naïve. Whatever the motivations, we must acknowledge how defense lawyers are influenced—to whatever degree—by arrogance and, therefore, complicit with an unjust system.

Consider the following questions:

1. Was there a need for a rigorous and complete defense?
2. How was the defense conducted?
3. What was the intent of the defense lawyer?

Ken Wahler—Computer Programmer

1. There was a need to defend Ken.
2. The defense was conducted to convict Ken.
3. While his lawyer may have wanted Ken to prevail, he encouraged a plea.

Butch Richardson—Superintendent of Schools

1. There was a need to defend him vigorously and completely.

2. The defense was conducted to fight the charges.
3. The lawyer's intent was to win at Butch's request; yet he advised Butch to plead.

David Ingalls—Check Cashing

1. There was a need to defend David rigorously and completely.
2. The defense was conducted to convict.
3. The lawyer's intent was to get rid of his client.

Krister Everston—Mailing Label

1. There was a need to defend against the charges.
2. Krister defended himself.
3. His intent was to win.

John Williams—Gun at Airport

1. There was a need to provide a defense.
2. The defense was conducted to ensure a conviction.
3. Making the best out of a bad situation, the lawyer secured a conviction.

George Norris—Sale of Orchids

1. There was a need to defend George rigorously and completely.
2. The defense was conducted at George's behest to beat the charges.
3. The lawyer's intent was to defend; though he advised George to plead.

Dan McGinnis—Bounced Checks

1. There was a need to defend Dan.
2. The defense was conducted to ensure a conviction.
3. The lawyer's intent was to convince his client to settle for less than his innocence.

Ron Webb—Prescription Medicine

1. There was a need for a rigorous and complete defense.
2. The defense was conducted as if Ron could not win.
3. The lawyer's intent was to convict by encouraging Ron to settle with a plea.

Do you sense the limits the legal system imposes upon defense lawyers and defendants? The frequency of lawyers convincing clients to plead for less time in prison is a sobering thought. Defense advocates concede defeat if only because the system is unbeatable. The irony is that those who are adamant about their innocence are threatened with harsher sentences for fighting the case in court. We must conclude that defense lawyers are an inherent part of the problem. They are grafted into the process solely to offer solutions which free courts of excess demands and provide easy victories for prosecutors. This is troubling. Defense lawyers do not view a case from the outset as worthy of battling for those defendants who are clearly not common criminals.

We must not lose sight of the notion that people prefer comfort over discomfort. If the innocent stand for principles against a system that is unforgiving (an uncomfortable prospect) yet acquiesce at the thought of a stiffer sentence (also uncomfortable), truth and principles are sacrificed. This reality, by its very nature, reflects a flaw within the system which cannot be denied. A process that discourages the assertion of the truth is indefensible. The justice system becomes the *injustice* system.

Should defense lawyers be blamed for their role? Are they to blame for their lack of fortitude? Would it be a fair to conclude that defense lawyers serve the best interests of court and not their clients? We must conclude that each of the seven lawyers involved in the above cases conducted their own appraisal and rejected an acquittal as a possible. They viewed it as impractical to even vie for victory. As distasteful as this may sound, with plea offers, these defense lawyers sought confessions of guilt. This end says it all.

THE GRAND JURY AND TRIAL JURY

Since most Americans do not have an appreciation for either the generalizations or specifics of the legal process, let's pause and reflect upon one important observation. While most people avoid discomfort, we learn and grow during times of testing. A tree does not establish a strong root system unless tested by the winds. These eight cases, which served as tornadoes in the lives of these men, should also serve as strong winds that shake our minds and hearts. The reality that justice is not what we expect should unsettle us. If this is the case, let us reappraise our trust of the government and assess our level of ignorance, apathy, and fear.

Most Americans believe the pinnacle of our justice system is the jury. The jury represents a *discerning* body which deliberates to a just conclusion. The jury is the noble institution which ensures those charged with a crime will receive objective consideration of the facts and a balanced judgment of guilt or innocence.

This perception of the jury, in most cases, could not be further from the truth. Sadly, we are quite comfortable with our incomplete understanding. We take satisfaction simply knowing the jury *works*. It matters little that the jury is unable and inadequate to do complete justice. In fact, we rarely consider, and most would never know, that the jury and grand jury were designed to hold the prosecutor, judge, defendant, and law accountable. In particular, the grand jury was employed to prevent the abuse of prosecutors since they allege charges against the people. Such is not the case today.

Once again, our greatest impediment is our failure to know that we do not know. If we knew how the grand jury and jury were designed to function or what they were to accomplish, we would compare and contrast this historical context with our current reality. We must, therefore, conclude that those who serve as jurors are woefully unaware and unwittingly complicit with the incarceration of innocent men. Jurors are told their responsibility is to determine the *facts*. They are told the judge will provide the *law*. As *peers* of the defendant, jurors hear evidence and ascertain what they believe are the facts based upon competing versions from the prosecution and defense. The jury's perception of the facts is then weighed against the law to determine guilt or innocence. This is what is accomplished by the jury. Their role is limited in scope. Any generalized conclusion about the legal system must include the notion that the jury is the cause of the greatest injustice.

The following illustration describes a practical application of the jury's role. Suppose authorities in Illinois charged a man for having five cats. The defendant hired a lawyer who investigated and had his client consider a plea agreement offered by the prosecution, just as we saw in other cases. This is the standard operating procedure. Yet, suppose the defendant refused the plea and the case went before a jury. The jurors were informed that the facts centered on whether the defendant had more than four cats. The judge underscored that while jurors determined the facts, he would give them the law. Once the prosecution and defense alleged potentially dueling facts, the jurors would deliberate until they determined the man's guilt or innocence.

The prosecution presented its version, complete with pictures and testimony, that the defendant had five cats. The defense argued that one cat belonged to a relative who was on vacation. The jury, after receiving the facts and jury instructions, learned the law. The judge told them that a person may not have more than four cats. Based upon the facts and the law the jury found the man guilty as charged. If we accept what we are told or what we know as truth, this is the extent of the jury's role. It is rather simplistic; not much is involved. Since we do not know otherwise, we accept the constraints of the jury's role. We are ignorant and we may not care to know any differently. Finally, we may be too fearful to challenge the rather entrenched and limited role of the jury.

Given the element of apathy, we must recognize that jurors often find serving on a jury to be an inconvenience, a disruption to a comfortable life. Their psychological and emotional motives are critical, which often includes the tendency to quickly dispense with their responsibilities. Did the defendant have five cats? Yes. Is he guilty? Yes. Okay, let's go home.

Consider the premise that the role of the jury is far more significant. What if we understood the jury to be the defining component of the legal system and truth mattered and principles reigned—and the deliberations of jurors had tremendous implications? Would these thoughts influence jurors and their motivation to serve? Yes, very likely. What if they understood that they were the ultimate *checks and balances* put in place to keep prosecutors and judges at bay?

There is an association which educates people about the proper role of the jury. The Fully Informed Jury Association teaches that the jury is a powerful body in our republican form of government and instrumental for defendants and society. The jury is critical to prevent abuses that are pervasive today. In fact, the jury has often been referred to as the fourth branch of government. Having the proper understanding of the jury's role would not only defeat ignorance but encourage us out of a state of apathy. We would be emboldened to no longer fear public officials or government institutions. Defendants would no longer be found guilty because of a controlled and rigged process. One of the main purposes and functions of the jury is to not only judge the facts, but the law as well. If we know why jurors should and may judge the law, we may appreciate not only the power of the jury, but that of the electorate.

We will tackle this notion rather simply. The electorate elects lawmakers. Lawmakers create laws. They know laws will impact the people they serve, citizens who serve as jurors. If jurors knew they could pass judgment upon the very laws passed by their representatives they would satisfy an important objective. They could and would reject bad laws. Repudiating laws would send a clear message to lawmakers that certain laws are unacceptable and should be reviewed, revised, and removed. If lawmakers realized jurors knew that citizens could invalidate laws, lawmakers would be reluctant to pass questionable statutes. This concept of invalidating bad law is known as jury nullification. One of the defining purposes of the jury is to pass judgment on the law and nullify those which should not be. The jury, the fourth branch of government, was to be the ultimate checks and balances, a powerful and discriminating body that rejected what was antithetical to federal and state constitutions, our conscience, and sense of justice.

Consider the following quotes:

The jury has an unalienable right to judge both the law as well as the fact in controversy.—**John Jay, 1st Chief Justice, United States Supreme Court, 1789**

The jury has the right to determine both the law and the facts.—**Samuel Chase, United States Supreme Court Justice, 1796, Signer of the Declaration of Independence**

The jury has the power to bring a verdict in the teeth of both law and fact.—**Oliver Wendell Holmes, United States Supreme Court Justice, 1902**

> *The constitutions of most of our States assert that all power is inherent in the people; that they may exercise it by themselves, in all cases to which they think themselves competent (as in electing their functionaries executive and legislative, and deciding by a jury of themselves, both fact and law, in all judiciary cases in which any fact is involved)....*—**Thomas Jefferson, Letter to John Cartwright, June 5, 1824, "The Thomas Jefferson Papers," Library of Congress**

We can plainly see the founding fathers and luminaries of former times believed juries had an essential role in criminal actions as the "conscience of the community."

Refer to the Illinois cat illustration. We understand how and why juries are integral to expressing the "conscience of the community," the legal process, and a republican form of government. Was the defendant legally guilty of having more than four cats? (Did he *literally* violate the law?) Yes. Were the jurors able to consider that the law was unwarranted? Not according to the judge. The judge specifically told the jurors that he alone would tell them the law. The implications are huge. The jurors must accept the law as the judge represents and written as the lawmakers intended. However, since we know jurors may nullify bad law, the entire dynamic changes.

Is there a law in Illinois which states one may not have more than four cats? Yes. Is the law unsound on its face? Many would agree the law is unacceptable. By virtue of the power vested in the jury, it may determine that the law is untenable and find the defendant not guilty as a result. Without this power, the people are subjected to laws that can never be nullified. Unless the laws are eventually changed or expunged, we suffer under and from a body of laws which should not have been written. Ask yourself if a country drowning in laws was our founding fathers' intent.

The jury, both the grand jury and the trial jury, was designed to serve as a ballot box of sorts, a means of voting against laws and expressing a lack of confidence to lawmakers, who may be decent people, who should be retained in office, yet who do not appreciate what laws are unacceptable. The jury is essential to the preservation of our freedoms. The jury is the final discriminator that regulates the entire lawmaking and legal system. The jury is the final arbiter, the conscience of the people, which says "Enough!"

We need only ask one question. How do we, the people, currently reject bad law? The answer—we don't! No other party will censure laws that should not be. Do lawmakers routinely erase laws from the books? Courts may compel the revision of laws, but to what end? The jury is the only practical means to reject laws. Consider this thought: if a man were charged for buying chocolate on Sunday would you convict him? Would you find him guilty of buying a candy bar after church? Should we accept that he is guilty simply because the legislators wrote the law, and the judge stated the law? We already know the facts. As jurors, our responsibilities, as currently represented, would not be that involved. Wouldn't it make sense to question and exercise the discretion that a law is intolerable?

Understanding the proper role of the jury is empowering. It liberates jurors from ignorance and lifts them into enlightenment. Jurors are bestowed with power to determine how lawmakers are performing. This power to discern is enough to eradicate apathy and vanquish fear. Who would not be courageous and resolved knowing they could ensure justice and truth in a system which avoids both? The jury is the most powerful and solemn position within the court system. With the exercise of this authority, there would be no reason to fear.

If we hold the legal system and authorities accountable for their actions and decisions, we may determine, with confidence, that thousands are unjustly charged, convicted, and sentenced and imprisoned for violating laws that should never have been written and enacted. This is the *discretion* that is so desperately needed. The alternative is the scheme currently employed with its net result—the most incarcerated people in the world. Our legal process is unforgiving and rather foreboding for our future. Our form of government never included a jury that would passively accept the law as written.

One juror is all that is needed to defeat laws that deserve nullification. One juror alone would free a defendant from an unforgiving system bound to find him guilty. One fully informed juror may educate himself and other jurors of the power they possess.

Another thought is that jurors are to be *peers*. What is a peer? This is not a small concern. When our country was founded, communities were smaller and more intimate. People knew each other. People knew of a man's character, history, and family. When jurors deliberated about the law and facts, they did so with the defendant in mind. The jurors were generally as well informed of the law as was the defendant. They were peers or equals in understanding. If a man were charged with a crime that dealt with an issue of which jurors knew little, would they be peers? For example, if a juror did not have a basic understanding of the Constitution, would he be a peer to a defendant who did?

Consider the term peer in our present day. What is a peer? Peers are simply jurors taken from within the community. That's it! Weigh the ramifications of this thought. Today is not the past. The practice of the past has little significance with our current legal system. Presently, one is excused from serving as a juror if he knows the defendant. We no longer consider that a juror who knows a man would be able to better assess whether the defendant had the intent to commit the crime. We also preclude the idea that a juror may exercise his good conscience and sound judgment simply because he knows the defendant.

A final factor affects which jurors is jury instructions. These are often complicated rules which limit, define, and control how the jury determines guilt or innocence. These lengthy and technical rules involve terms and definitions which provide constraints and overbearing structure. These instructions are often tedious and overwhelm lay people unaccustomed with the law. With what is already a difficult position, men and women must perform mental gymnastics to satisfy court mandates.

There can be little dispute that jury instructions affect the jury. Jurors are affected by psychological and emotional objectives as well. Jury instructions serve to further frustrate jurors to make decisions out of expediency, confusion, and resignation. Trials are often very technical and last days and sometimes weeks or months. The patience, endurance, and intellectual stamina of jurors are taxed to the detriment of healthy deliberation. It is tempting to take the easy path which often leads to verdicts of guilt.

The function of the jury exists, but its essence is no longer. The change has not been for the better. One may see the value of having a true *peer* in the jury, one who is informed and not overwhelmed with the responsibility and instructions. These factors influence the eventual outcome of a trial.

If all eight cases were tried before a jury, we could forecast that the end results would have been guilty verdicts. Six men did not seek a jury trial. Why? *Because of the jury and the judgment that was expected.* Consider this thought. Of the two who went to trial, Butch and Krister, each had to consider waiving the jury out of prudence.

Having discussed not only how the jury operates, but how it should operate, we see more plainly how the system discourages and even prevents a just outcome. Most people and defendants don't perceive these distinctions. We are products of our educational system and a culture that is complacent. We don't question and would not even know to challenge the role of the jury. Butch and Krister were undoubtedly affected by the totality of the demands and constraints placed upon the jurors. We must reconcile that one of the main reasons the government has a 98% conviction rate is a result of how the jury is controlled, or more appropriately, how it is not operated.

Consider the grand jury. The prosecutor presented the grand jury rather grave charges in all eight cases. He captivated the jurors with hard *facts* as he perceived them—his portrayal of the *truth*. He asked this august body to grant him the latitude to prosecute in the interests of the public trust. Not once were the jurors truly asked to challenge his assertions. Not once were they either asked or did they voluntarily question the facts and the law. More importantly, as these eight defendants lived their lives, not even knowing the grand jury was meeting secretly, the jurors approved a life-altering event without the benefit of these men offering a rebuttal. These eight men were ruined financially, physically, emotionally, and otherwise. We already know the ending of their stories, endings that were a direct result of either the trial jury or the plea process. Now we know that the beginning of the entire judicial process is no different. It is a process wanting in principle and integrity.

Given the significance of the grand jury and trial jury, there are three questions that should be answered. If each juror genuinely assessed the facts, challenged the government's position, and resolved their own doubt—if they challenged the law—would their decision to indict or convict be any different? Would *you* indict or convict any of these eight men? Here are three questions:

1. Did the suspect violate a law resulting in a loss of life, liberty, or property?
2. Did the suspect have malicious intent?
3. Is the law consistent with an objective standard that reflects the "conscience of the community" and warrants criminal prosecution?

In other words, would *you* object if each man were prosecuted as a criminal? Would the people condone this outcome?

Consider these questions for each of these eight cases. Discern whether as a juror you would have voted to either indict or convict. If the jurors exercised their powers and answered these questions intelligently and truthfully, any number of prosecutors' requests and assertions before the grand juries or trial juries would have been summarily rejected.

The six men who capitulated and did not request a jury trial were *tried by a jury*. There can be no dismissing that, given how the jury functions, each man pleaded guilty to *avoid a jury* and an even stiffer prison sentence. The defense lawyers explained to each defendant the downside of exercising the jury option. Part of the explanation included how the jury determines the facts and is spoon fed the law. By changing this controlled process, if the jury functioned as it should or could, most of the suffering experienced by these eight would have never occurred. Most of the injustice would have been prevented.

As it stands, the grand jury denies few requests for indictments. These eight cases prove questionable cases are brought before a grand jury and requests for indictments are approved. The criminalizing of America exists because a grand jury does not exercise discretion as the gatekeeper it is. For Ron, David, George, Krister, Ken, Butch, John, and Dan, the role of the grand jury was no trivial matter. The start of each travesty began with grand jurors who were not fully informed. Not only did jurors fail to exercise legitimate powers, but they also reflexively accepted as true what prosecutors proffered.

Imagine a room of grand jurors appointed to this elevated position, meeting secretly to be briefed by a prosecutor. Any number of people would be enamored with this title and opportunity. Imagine the U. S. Attorney lauding them for their willingness to fulfill such an awesome civic responsibility, as he commends them for the tough decisions they would make. These unsuspecting jurors would be *primed to discern* in favor of an indictment. Consider that the three questions we asked were and are not a part of their discretionary latitude. For, the jurors do not even know to ask or answer these queries.

THE JUDGE

The judge is a key player in this gamesmanship. How a judge performs has a direct and indirect impact on the outcome. As we weigh his influence, consider these fundamentals. First, the judge is *the court*. While many define the courthouse or the courtroom as the court, it is the person sitting in the capacity as the Jurist—the Judge. Second, the court process is governed by established rules and procedures. The judge and lawyers are bound by these restrictions. For example, the Federal Rules of Civil Procedure and the Federal Rules of Criminal Procedure limit how legal business is conducted. We may consider them as the rules of the game. Since judges are nothing more than referees, an official administrator of the judicial process, he is to abide by these rules and ensure that lawyers comply. The role of the judge, quite simply, is to ensure justice. From a common man's perspective, with no more than a basic high school civics education, the role of the judge is restrained and straightforward. However, judges, as with any other party, are influenced by ignorance, apathy, and arrogance and the ever present psychological and emotional motives.

Judges are not unlike prosecutors and defense lawyers with varying differences and distinctions. Some are liberal, others conservative. Some are personable and agreeable; others are rigid and uninviting. Some may be less engaged with court proceedings and allow each side some latitude while others may strictly control all that occurs. There are any number of variables that affect the temperament and decisions of judges. They may become desensitized and, by design, render rulings knowing the defendant is unlikely to prevail in court or on appeal. Such a posture would demonstrate that they are governed more by indifference than principles.

A judge will not likely impugn his court with decisions that are clearly inconsistent with the rules; yet they may deny what is a rule of court that should be upheld. The subtleties of how they *apply* rules may accomplish the intent of either supporting the prosecution or defense. It would be naïve to deny that varying stripes and colors of judges do not unduly influence cases. While these jurists are elected or appointed based upon their experience or judicial temperament, they are not infallible. Even the canons of judicial ethics which govern their conduct are violated. There are issues with judges that are never revealed and adversely affect the defendant.

Most people view court with the respect they believe it deserves. They perceive it as an institution with a noble end. This respect may be too deferential as a practical matter. Even lawyers fail to hold judges accountable for indiscretions or blatant judicial misconduct. It would be unwise not to entertain the possibility that court actions and decisions are a significant part of what ails the legal system. The bottom line is that the influence exercised by judges directly impacts verdicts and sentences.

Consider a seemingly trivial example which is anything but. In the final case we will review, the prosecution requested, and the court granted a venue that was over three hours from the defendant's home. The rules of court, however, stipulate that the most convenient court for the defendant is the proper venue. The court closest to the accused was less than an hour away. Undoubtedly, the prosecutor presented information to the court knowing the approved venue would provide the greatest inconvenience for the defendant. The judge, meanwhile, had ample information to ensure that the proper venue was selected. Yet, the judge made his decision with apparent indifference.

Why did the prosecutor engineer and the judge make this ruling? Perhaps the intent was to further frustrate the efforts of the defendant who had to spend time, money, and effort to travel, thereby further diminishing his support network and flexibility to prepare for his case. There is no doubt the prosecutor made the request with dubious intent and the court ignored the clear language of its own rule.

Since most of the eight defendants accepted pleas, the judges in most of the cases were not too involved. However, there is one example when the judge was bound by a plea agreement but was uncomfortable with the result. According to Ron Webb, the judge in his case did not think Ron deserved the sentence negotiated through the plea offer. The judge encouraged Ron's lawyer to prepare a sentencing reduction request in a year. This example illustrates the constraints of court rules and the potential benefit to a defendant.

We must suspend disbelief and recognize a court's ability to abuse its discretion as well. The judge's attitude in Webb's case is an anomaly. Most judges are indifferent or purposely caustic. Consider the judge in the Norris case. George Norris decided against a trial and accepted a plea, to which he stated, "I hated that, I absolutely hated that."[35] Quite telling, the judge gave him some advice at sentencing:

> *Life sometimes presents us with lemons. Sometimes we grow lemons ourselves. But as long as we are walking the face of the earth, our responsibility is to take those lemons and use the gifts God has given us to turn lemons into lemonade.*[36]

Even if the judge's intentions were remotely sincere, which appears unlikely, he demonstrated how detached he was to the carnage that the law, the prosecutor, and the court brought into George's life. He was an innocent man wrongly charged and unjustifiably sentenced by a prose spouting judge who waxed philosophical as to how George should handle this adversity. This judge was far too comfortable in his position of power to know or care how arrogantly his words were perceived by others.

In our analysis of judges, given the prominence of this position, we must return to the lofty concerns of the law. From a non-legal perspective what would we expect the judge to weigh? Consider the following questions:

1. Did the defendant violate the law?
2. Did he have malicious intent?
3. Was there a victim who suffered a loss of life, liberty, or property?
4. Did lawmakers intend for the law to be applied in this manner?
5. Was the process handled judiciously and fairly? Was the defendant treated fairly?
6. Were the ends of justice served?

These questions speak to a paramount concern. If there is a tendency for *injustice* to thrive, we must seek safeguards. We need remedies to protect innocent people or non-criminals from incarceration. If there are no preventative measures in place from the beginning and throughout the judicial process, we want to know that the judge will ensure justice and not foster injustice. If not, for this is the reason these questions were suggested, if the judge does not ward off wrongs or if he caters to wrongs, we are without recourse within the legal system.

There is no party more concerned about the answers to these six questions than the defendant. Butch and Krister labored through a jury trial. Would it be unreasonable to conclude that had the judge answered these queries honestly each man would have been set free? What does it say about a system if the judge is without or does not exercise the power to prevent injustices within the judicial process?

---

[35] www.heritage.org/research/reports/2009/07/the-unlikely-orchid-smuggler-a-case-study-in-overcriminalization

[36] Ibid.

THE DEFENDANT

The defendant would be wise to observe his central role with an array of parties circling, directing, and either forcing or enforcing the rules and process. He either accepts or counters what he perceives. He would be well-served to examine himself as he endures the pressure. He must weigh his principles as he is compelled to decide his own fate.

History is replete with examples of men and women who weathered forces of judgment to their eventual incarceration or death. John Hus, a martyr for his faith, was burned at the stake. John Bunyon was imprisoned for twelve years for preaching without a license. Nelson Mandela was imprisoned for twenty years for his principles. Defendants of today are no different. They battle with integrity for truth. Though their efforts may never reach the renown of iconic heroes, their fortitude, often manifested by happenstance, is a testament to their strength and their fight for what is right and just.

If a defendant eventually equivocates in the thick of adversity, is he wrong? Are his principles no longer true and worthy of the highest consideration? Why or why not? We should not dismiss the six of the eight men who resigned to defeat. They, too, were influenced by fear. They knew relatively nothing of the rigors and forces ahead. They knew nothing of the unjust and arduous process that included the complicity of their own defense counsel. When these defendants realized they would not and could not prevail, they relented. They had no other options. Their fate became more important than the truth. This is not a criticism. It is an expression of a reality, however unfortunate and repugnant. Defendants operate out of fear to salvage the best possible scenario to the exclusion of the worst. We have the psychological and emotional motives of these defendants as they concede to the unthinkable. Their decisions are borne out of self-preservation, as a means of instinctive survival rather than a heartfelt appeal for truth. This is an indictment against the entire legal system.

Defendants like Butch and Krister who chose the path less traveled were noble and courageous. They remained true to their principles. Regardless of the outcome, they refused to concede defeat. This is a testament to their integrity. Are they martyrs? Perhaps. Even this title is not important. Their courage and perseverance is a reflection of their innocence given the ruthless nature of the process. Those who willingly wage war when there is no other recourse deserve our respect. For, if good men do nothing change will never occur. While men such as George Norris and Krister Everston suffered unimaginably, their loss will serve as an example of what is destroying our country. Meanwhile, those who chose to accept a plea rather than receive double or triple the sentence are just as worthy of distinction. We cannot discount the hopes of men who desire to rescue any semblance of their former lives in the best interests of their families.

Defendants who do not fight to the bitter or better end may prevail against nothing—while defendants who do fight to the bitter or better end prevail against ignorance, apathy, and fear. In the latter scenario, truth reigns and arrogance is vanquished. Even if these men are imprisoned, the result is nevertheless virtuous. In due time, the singular or cumulative effects of each innocent person's efforts will lead to scrutiny and discernment desperately needed. For their valiant contributions, may we sing our praises for their willingness to fight and sacrifice.

History by apprising them of the past will enable them to judge the future; it will avail them of the experience of other times and other nations; it will qualify them as judges of the actions and designs of men; it will enable them to know ambition under every disguise it may assume, and, knowing it, defeat its views. **Thomas Jefferson**

The Four Corners of Justice

Let us hope those who do not understand the state of *American justice* will be awakened. There is no antidote to this disease other than the hard and uncomfortable truth. May we come to know how the innocent become fodder for an unrelenting process fueled by nothing other than ignorance, apathy, fear, and arrogance. Only by knowing will we restore sound psychological and emotional constructs for our culture with the noble intent to secure justice for all. May we yearn for what is equitable. May we understand and, as a result, love our neighbors without undue judgment. May we hold ourselves accountable as we hold public officials accountable.

The truth may be known. As referenced earlier, questions are the hallmark of initiative. Let us ask questions. Let us engage in conversations with the intent to broaden our knowledge. What follows is a list of questions which may be applied to each of the ten components of the legal system. They serve as a benchmark for further queries. What we do with the answers gleaned from our observations is important. To effect change we must act on our understanding. As a practical exercise, we will assess our present understanding quantitatively. Measuring our observations will allow us to substantiate what is otherwise a subjective representation that lures us to a presumptive conclusion that justice has been reached. These questions will assist us with a measurement exercise with what is known as *The Four Corners of Justice* diagram.

Defendant:

1. Was a crime committed?
2. Was there malicious intent?
3. Did a victim suffer loss of life, liberty, or property?

Electorate:

1. Does the electorate know of the laws used to charge the people with crimes?
2. Does the electorate know how government acquires jurisdiction?
3. Does the electorate know how officials gratuitously enforce laws?

Lawmakers:

1. Is the law enforced as lawmakers intended?
2. Do lawmakers know of constitutional constraints which limit legislative power?
3. Are lawmakers creating laws enforced as crimes that are not criminal in nature?

Investigators:

1. Do investigators exceed their authority?
2. Do investigators hold prosecutors accountable for their abuse of power? Do prosecutors misuse or abuse the authority of investigators?
3. Is an excessive length of time to investigate an abuse of power?

Prosecutor:

1. Did the prosecutor abuse his discretion or the authority of his office?
2. Did he deliberately misuse or distort the spirit and intent of the law?
3. What are his psychological and emotional motivations?

4. Did he compromise the public trust for his own personal gain?
5. Did he consider the possibility that the defendant is innocent?
6. Should the prosecutor have the latitude to lessen a charge in order to secure a conviction?

Grand Jury:

1. Do the grand jurors know the full extent of their authority? Or are they a mere rubberstamp of approval for requests for indictments?
2. To what extent do grand jurors challenge the credibility of the charges?
3. Do grand jurors challenge whether there is a victim or a loss?
4. Do they question the possible innocence of the accused?
5. Are they judging both the facts and the law?

Witnesses/Co-defendants:

1. Should witnesses be forced to snitch regardless of the cost?
2. Should the plea agreement for a witness be disclosed to the jury?
3. Should the psychological and emotional motives of a witness be considered?

Defense Lawyers:

1. Is the defense beholden to anyone or anything before the interests of his client?
2. Should it matter to the defense lawyer if his client did not commit a crime?
3. To what extent should the rules and mechanics of the legal process relegate the truth and merits of a righteous defense as less than consequential?

Jury:

1. Do jurors know the full extent of their authority?
2. Should the jury determine both the facts and the law?
3. Should jurors question if there is a victim or a loss?
4. Should jurors have a fundamental understanding of the Constitution, government, and basic civics before serving?

Judges:

1. Is the judge fair and impartial?
2. To what extent does a judge hold prosecutors and defense lawyers accountable for indiscretion, abuse of power, or *illegality* affecting the interests of the defendant?
3. Does or should a judge sentence a defendant in the absence of a victim or loss?
4. Does a judge's prejudice influence his decisions or actions?
5. What is the judge's motivation psychologically and emotionally?
6. Should the judge have more discretion with passing sentences?
7. Does the Pre-Sentence Investigation Report represent a fair punishment?

THE FOUR CORNERS OF JUSTICE

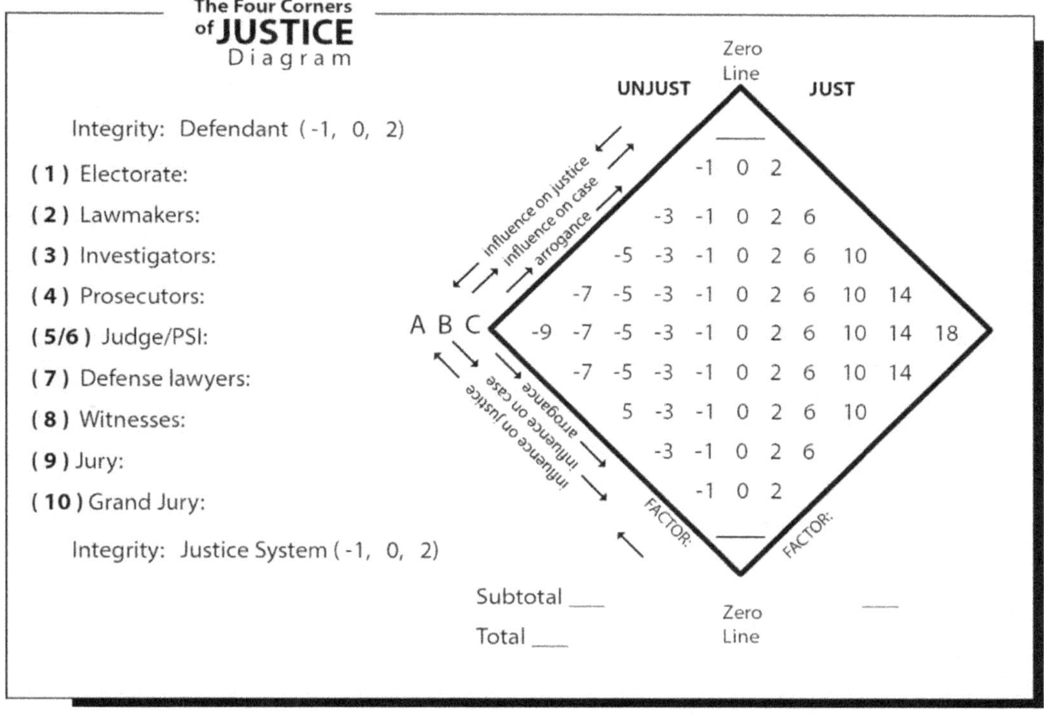

1. *If the American people were knowledgeable, engaged, and courageous, the line which reflects "A" (above) would represent the proper flow of power that would ensure justice, beginning with the "Electorate" and the "Grand Jury" at the top and bottom of the list, respectively, and flowing downward and upward, respectively, toward the judge. If the people exercised their power, they would guard against injustice. They would apply the requisite pressure to ensure that each component within the legal system defeated what is potentially unjust. Each component would ensure accountability to the truth. Ultimately, given the limitations of court, the judicial process would reflect a virtuous and wholesome intent of the people and proper enforcement of law.*
2. *Since Americans are not knowledgeable, engaged, and courageous, line "B" represents the inverse effect we currently have in our judicial system. Beginning with the court, prosecutor, and defense lawyer, since they do not respect the power of the people (a people who no longer respect their own power), these components unduly influence the outcome of cases. They have little accountability. The power of the judicial process flows from the center of the list out toward the electorate and the grand jury. Is there any wonder the people, as represented by components (1) and (10), stand in unjustified awe of officials and a system that preys upon people's ignorance, apathy, and fear?*
3. *As a result of the flow of power as represented by "B," the arrogance of the institution of justice, line "C," reigns supreme. Arrogance prevails because the people do not.*

With various questions we posed earlier that would potentially hold each of the ten components of the judicial process accountable to the end of justice, weigh the import of the *Four Corners of the Justice* diagram. This diagram will allow us to qualify and quantify a *score* for any given case. However, before we examine the particulars of how this score is achieved, it is worth noting why it is significant.

People, as discussed earlier, simply presume an outcome is just. We take it for granted that the system accomplishes what was intended. However, we are not able to substantiate these conclusions. Rather, the result is subjective and undefined. There is no *measurement* of the system that verifies the *justice* attained in any given case. Consequently, we don't know if the justice is, in fact, justice or injustice. We don't examine the process, akin to using the ability of slow eye, to understand how each component of the judicial process is either assisting or defeating the end of justice. Not knowing if or how the judicial process is or is not accountable to justice breeds the lack of accountability which ensures America's ignominious title as most incarcerated country in the world. With a scoring method for any case, we may hold ourselves accountable to what is not justice and afford ourselves the possibility of achieving what may be justice.

The Four Corners of Justice (FCOJ) diagram has the ten components of the legal system listed on the left-hand side. Noteworthy, the component at the top, the electorate, and the component at the bottom, the grand jury, are the elements reflective of the people—the source of power in our republic. From the electorate, there is a progression of increased control over a legal case from the lawmakers, investigators, and prosecutors until we reach the judge in the middle of the list. This progression reflects a flow of power from the general, the people, to the specific, the court. Likewise, the flow is the same for the bottom half of the components from the grand jury to the jury, witnesses, and defense lawyers until the judge is reached. The flow of power is from the general to the specific. This flow will become extremely relevant as we further analyze how and why the FCOJ diagram functions.

The corresponding numbers to the right of the components reflect the potential influence each element has on a case. Those components, which may have a greater impact upon other components or the case in general, have a wider range. Compare the electorate with a range of "-1, 0, 2" and the range of the investigators of "-5, -3, -1, 0, 2, 6, 10." The wider ranges do not suggest one component is any more or less important than another. It merely reflects that the electorate will have less of a direct impact on the outcome than the investigators who are intimately involved.

Consider the following example. The prosecutor has a tremendous amount of power. If he abuses this power, he can adversely influence the equal, if not more important, role of the grand jury. If the grand jury knew the full extent of its power, it would challenge the prosecutor's representations and deny the possibility of a wrongful indictment. As it stands, prosecutors unduly influence the grand jury and, therefore, the balance of the case. Consequently, the prosecution is given a wider scoring range which aptly reflects this potential influence.

Given its role of electing and re-electing lawmakers, the electorate is perhaps the most powerful but underrealized aspect of the legal process. This component has an exact, but far-removed influence in a case. Lawmakers may—knowingly or not—fail to exercise their authority with the creation or proper enforcement of laws. Lawmakers have a greater potential to influence a case than the electorate and, thus, its range of scoring is greater.

We see that the FCOJ diagram attributes more significance to certain components that have a direct impact on the rendering of verdicts. The remaining components, while fundamentally more powerful within the concept of justice, are more indirect. Yet, these latter components are not fully exercised. These less influential components underscore the subsequent impact of ignorance, apathy, and fear, while heightening the dominance of institutional arrogance.

Consider an illustration. Most of us would tend to minimize the relevance of a witness compared to that of a prosecutor or a judge. However, if a witness honored the truth and refused to equivocate to threats, coercion, or duress, he would be unaffected by those in authority. Regrettably, the prosecutor can manipulate and directly influence a witness. When the witness caves and agrees to a conspiracy charge in exchange for leniency, the prosecutor heavily influences the case. Any positive benefit that would have been gained by the defendant from the testimony of the witness is effectively destroyed.

The result is telling. The jury sees a witness who agrees with or confirms a prosecutor's assertions. The jury does not see that the witness was unduly prejudiced by the government and the truth was defeated. The jury, which is far more powerful potentially than the prosecutor, is influenced by both the witness and the prosecutor. This cascading effect of arrogance maligns truth and justice.

We no longer have the supremacy and inherent power of the people. We no longer have a philosophy that true crimes are limited to loss of life, liberty, or property. We have the inversion. Consider this possibility. The arbitrary and sweeping influence of the judicial branch affects the executive branch, which includes the prosecutor. The arbitrary and sweeping influence of the executive branch affects the legislative branch, the creators of law. The arbitrary and sweeping influence of the legislative branch affects the power, sovereignty, and freedom of the people. Institutional arrogance exists only because of the ignorance, apathy, and fear of the people, the source of power that is the electorate and the grand jury. Obviously, if both the electorate and the grand jury were effectively employed, this inversion would be limited if not negated outright.

JUST AND UNJUST

Given the dominance of institutional arrogance, there is a greater possibility each of the ten components will have a negative rather than a neutral or positive impact on a case. For this reason, the point value on the left side of the FCOJ diagram, the UNJUST reflects leniency, while the right, the JUST, is weighted. This scoring approach proves a point. If the legal system is truly biased against defendants, we would expect the scores to reflect this conclusion. We would expect there to be negative scores on the left side of the neutral or *Zero Line*. Remember, our supposition, in part, is that the conduct and operation of the legal process is why America is the most imprisoned country. To preclude any unjust bias, the value of any positive benefit received by the defendant through any of the ten components is increased. Weighted scores on the JUST side of the diagram counter any negative scores, akin to grading on a curve.

If the legal system operated in accord with truth, with the sole intent to seek justice, a case would be scored from top to bottom along the center of the diagram, the *Zero Line*. Impartiality and integrity would never deviate to the left of this distinct barrier; it would not be possible or permitted. Only because of injustice and dubious motives, a score would score exist to the left of the Zero Line. For example, if a lawyer does not adequately defend a client, the points must naturally decrease to reflect an injustice and prejudice. A negative score would be appropriate, but entirely unnecessary. Conversely, if the defense lawyer goes above and beyond on behalf of his client (which should happen as a matter of course), the reverse is true. The lawyer seeks truth and justice, and this would result in a weighted score to the right of the Zero Line.

At the conclusion of a case, with a just system, there would be no scores on the UNJUST side of the diagram. We would expect the judicial process to track along the center or err on the side of caution, with the defendant receiving the benefit of any superlative performance and scores on the JUST side of the diagram. Any possibility of the justice system being unjust would result in more scores and points to the left. The total on each side of the diagram would tell the tale. Any grand total in the negative side greater than the total for the positive would confirm the errors and arrogance of the judicial system.

FACTOR

There is a second score which tracks with the individual ratings of the ten components of the legal system. This score is called the Factor. There are two scores for the Factor—one for the left side of the diagram and one for the right. The Factor is simply the number of scores of the ten components that occur on either side of the Zero Line. The Factor provides some balance and context for cases that have a high or low score on either side. For example, if only three components are scored on a given side, this would reflect differently than if seven components made up the total number of scores on the other side. Additionally, since the numbers on the right are weighted, a higher total score with a low Factor would be telling.

INTEGRITY

The third and final score that comprises the FCOJ diagram is the assessment of the Integrity of both the judicial process and the defendant. This score is independent of the two sets of scores which rate the ten components. The Integrity scores are located at the top and bottom of the diagram and serve as an overall reflection as to whether each is consistent with truth and justice. The significance of this score is simple and powerful. While one could easily cite it as unfair, since there are ten parts of the legal system and only one defendant, to do so would be to dismiss an expectation that the judicial process is just. If one component were to impugn the entire judicial system, it would, like a bad apple, spoil or taint the whole. Moreover, since the life and liberty of a defendant is dependent upon a virtuous process, the legal system must be scored as one. In the end, we would expect this score to validate the total of the points assessed for the ten components and the number for the Factor on either side of the Zero Line.

With the explanation of the three scoring elements of the FCOJ diagram, it should be apparent that this comprehensive assessment of the judicial process and the defendant, given the particulars of the case, is not merely concerned with justice and injustice. These scores enable us to shun our tendency to accept that the outcome of some unknown case is JUST simply for the fact that it was adjudicated through the *justice* system. The FCOJ scores give *substance* to an otherwise unappreciated process that yields an all-too-often outcome which is not challenged and subjected to scrutiny. Such antipathy and disengagement with the judicial system may end with the efforts of the FCOJ method.

The FCOJ diagram invites us to look inwardly. The FCOJ snapshot should jar our mental and emotional constructs. Forced to reconcile with the existence of a negative score, we must consider who we are and who we are not. When we see a score to the left of the Zero Line, we should ask how and why not only of the legal system, but of ourselves. Do we seek justice and truth? Do we love our neighbors? Those who are innocent and incarcerated are our neighbors. Moreover, any one of us could fall prey to a similar fate. We could be the ones searching for understanding and compassion as defendants.

Not only is the FCOJ a viable means of measuring justice and injustice, the FCOJ is a call for accountability. To be held accountable means that we should account for questions such as:

1. Do the people hold themselves accountable for laws that should not be written?
2. Do we hold lawmakers accountable for creating such laws?
3. Are credible laws enforced with discretion and fairness?
4. Are we so fearful that we may not account for laws which should not be enforced?

We, as the electorate, would serve the interests of society if we asked and sought accountability from each of the ten components of the legal system. Those who work for and within these components are no different than us. Consider elected officials. What do they know when they decide to run for office? They know nothing more than we do. They have their opinions and passions. More importantly, who do they become? With newfound power and a lack of accountability are they arbitrarily hawkish on crime and criminals and, therefore, gratuitously lump non-criminals in the same class?

Imagine the value of asking questions of all ten components. We gain context and clarity with the FCOJ diagram. We can quantify and qualify a case and the operation of the judicial system.

The FCOJ diagram reflects the outcome of a case. It reflects not one, but all ten elements of the process, a system that supposedly reaches JUST conclusions. It reflects ten individuals or parties, the application of their power, and their psychological and emotional motives. The FCOJ diagram represents the accidental and purposeful weaving that each component injects into a conclusion which, if reflected negatively as a score, depicts the regrettable state of the justice system and our culture and is, in fact, a revelation of the hearts and minds of the people.

As we put the FCOJ diagram to practical use, step back and ponder the scope of our problem once more. We did not acquire most of the global prison population by accident. Furthermore, the rate of incarceration will not be reduced by accident. Any case that even hints of injustice implicates the core disease of ignorance, apathy, and fear of the American people. Each implicates the arrogance of officials necessary for injustice to prevail.

We will apply the FCOJ diagram to the cases discussed earlier and acquire a sense of the repercussions of the judicial system, a process that is underappreciated, much less qualified and quantified with any reasonable means of measurement. With our results, we can then imagine such injustice occurring repeatedly everyday throughout America.

THE FOUR CORNERS OF JUSTICE—JOHN HUS

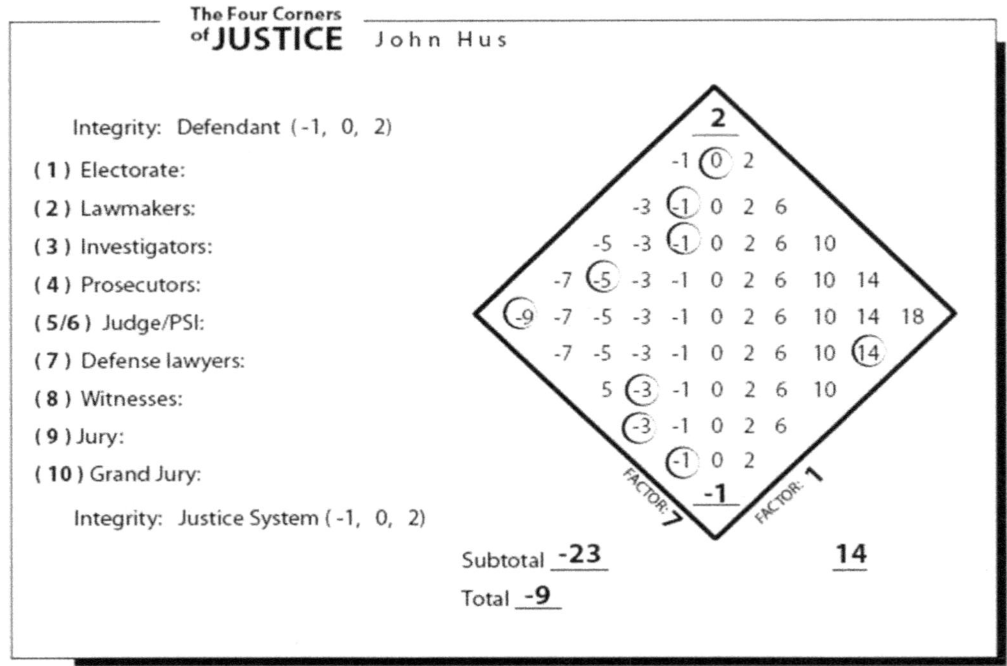

ANALYSIS OF JOHN HUS

If guilty of anything, John Hus was guilty of a desire to account for the injustices of the Catholic Church and the moral turpitude of the clergy. While he may have rebelled against church theology and attempted to change its doctrine, this did not make him a criminal.

The Catholic Church served as lawmakers, investigators, prosecutor, judge, grand jury, and jury. The church even served as the witness. For the crime of heresy, which had as sweeping an application as conspiracy charges in America today, Hus was charged for failing to conform. He did not voluntarily comply with church dogma.

As a priest with a following, the church did not want his message or sense of dissent to spread. Whether genuine or not, the offer to grant Hus safe passage to Constance allowed the church to solve its problem. As with any rebel who continues his passionate appeal for truth and reform, the authorities had to silence him. His demise would serve as an example to others who might dare to thwart church laws and officials.

According to historical accounts, we know the hearing was anything but impartial. The church had every reason to distort Hus' views. As we see in modern cases, the church never intended to give the defendant an opportunity to prevail. The authorities could not allow anyone to press for the change of immutable church doctrine—doctrine not subject to challenge in the first instance.

FOUR CORNERS OF JUSTICE SCORE—JOHN HUS

- Lawmakers (the Church): -1 It is one thing to decree church doctrine as absolute; it is quite another to stifle the ability and a priest's wherewithal to question church authority.
- Investigators (the Church): -1

- Prosecutor (the Church): -5 The Church's deliberate distortion of the defendant's views was a base practice that was as perfected in the year 1414 as it is by the Federal Government today. The motives of men in power and the ploys of prosecutors are both telling and sobering in any given era of history.
- Judge (the Church): -9 If we could give a worse score, we would. The punishment of death by burning at the stake was evil. The execution of Hus, who had the courage to challenge the powers-that-be and injustices of the church, served as a deterrent for anyone with similar boldness.
- Witness (the Church): -3 Note the power of a witness regardless of the period in history. Those in authority have the irrepressible inclination to rely upon and use those who can influence a case. The Catholic Church relied upon itself as a witness against Hus.
- Jury (the Church): -3
- Grand Jury (the Church): -1

THE FOUR CORNERS OF JUSTICE—GALILEO GALILEI

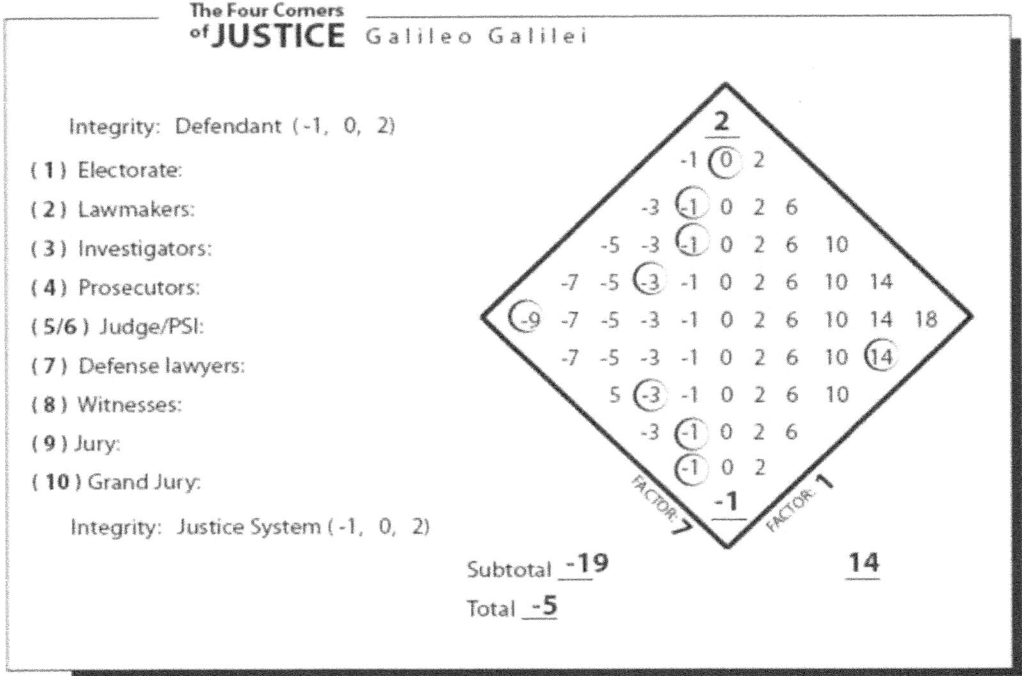

ANALYSIS OF GALILEO GALILEI

As with Hus, Galileo confronted the raw power of the Catholic Church. Over two hundred years later the culture of the church had not changed. Does the nature of man ever change? Galileo was guilty of nothing other than the pursuit of an innate and inquisitive genius that was independent of any other body of beliefs. The church, however, would not reconcile Galileo's belief that science could be separate from the sanctity of scripture and the church's monopoly of biblical interpretation.

Interestingly, Galileo tempered his pursuit of scientific advancement in deference to the church. Notwithstanding his fear of the autonomous and rigid posture of the Vatican, Galileo's perspectives progressed. We sense the respect officials afforded Galileo, a man of distinction. Though, in the end, church authority and its interpretation of scripture reigned supreme. Any absolute ruling power will not allow celebrity or maverick to advance a truth which counters the lie—a lie that must not be denied.

The Galileo case, as with most judicial injustices, reflects the adage that power corrupts, and absolute power corrupts absolutely. The church exercised mammoth influence over society. This is not unlike today as governments expect and demand control. As a result of the overbearing influence of church authority, Galileo conceded. This was his only practical choice. His intellectual curiosity and honorable scientific conclusions ended with his imprisonment at a ripe age.

Galileo had to be silenced. So, the church reverted to subterfuge. When Pope Urban VIII granted Galileo permission to compare two separate bodies of thought, Galileo was accused of failing to disclose a former order issued by the previous Pope not to engage in such activity. Galileo claimed the order never existed; rather, he said a warning was issued, a warning he honored. Only with Urban's permission did he move forward. It is plausible that Urban spoke prematurely and had to, consequently, cover his mistake.

The Catholic Church acted as the judge, prosecutor, investigator, lawmaker, witness, jury, and grand jury. The church had all the power. The only witness for Galileo was Cardinal Bellarmine. However, since Bellarmine was deceased, he could not testify. It was obvious Bellarmine's affidavit had no impact and did not counter the church's agenda.

FOUR CORNERS OF JUSTICE SCORE—GALILEO GALILEI

- Lawmakers: -1
- Investigator: -1
- Prosecutor: -3
- Judge: -9
- Defense Lawyer: 14 Galileo represented himself.
- Witness: -3 If only because the church ignored Bellarmine's testimony.
- Jury: -1
- Grand Jury: -1

Note: In 1979, Pope John Paul II reopened the case against Galileo. He determined the renowned astronomer may have been mistakenly condemned. A church commission concluded that Galileo was innocent and disclosed all documents relating to the trial.

The Four Corners of Justice—Giles Corey

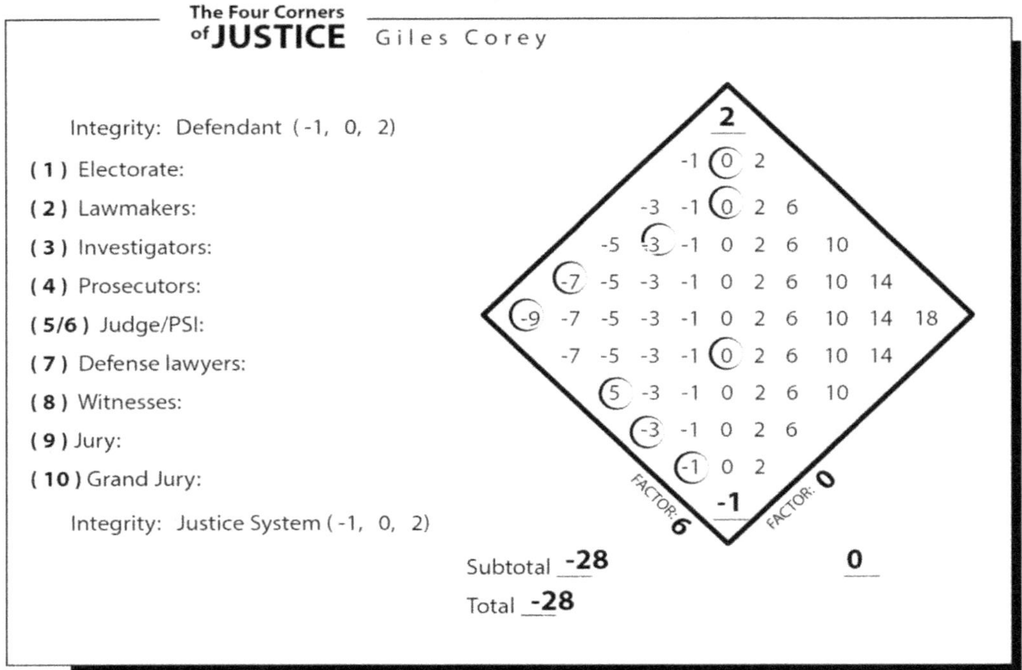

The Four Corners of JUSTICE
Giles Corey
Integrity: Defendant (-1, 0, 2)
(1) Electorate:
(2) Lawmakers:
(3) Investigators:
(4) Prosecutors:
(5/6) Judge/PSI:
(7) Defense lawyers:
(8) Witnesses:
(9) Jury:
(10) Grand Jury:
Integrity: Justice System (-1, 0, 2)
2
-1 0 2
-3 -1 0 2 6
-5 -3 -1 0 2 6 10
-7 -5 -3 -1 0 2 6 10 14
-9 -7 -5 -3 -1 0 2 6 10 14 18
-7 -5 -3 -1 0 2 6 10 14
-5 -3 -1 0 2 6 10
-3 -1 0 2 6
-1 0 2
-1
FACTOR: 6
FACTOR: 0
Subtotal -28
0
Total -28

Analysis of Giles Corey

This period of history is not unlike others; the nature of man contends with unique issues, perhaps only peculiar to its day. We cannot discount that the power of emotions of man are some of the most formidable forces known. The raw hysteria which ensues from emotions can be alarming. This is one of the reasons our founding fathers derided "democracy" and deferred to a republican form of government. Democracy is mob rule, often laden with passion that may overrule truth and justice.

The Salem Witch Trials reflect mob rule and the influence of emotions. The life of Giles Corey was taken as upheaval and fear ensued. The people feared reprisal of a public sentiment gone awry and lacked the courage to stand for truth and justice. They were fearful of being accused of witchcraft and did not defend those wrongly accused.

We can easily discern the injustice. Regrettably, separation from such injustice by time alone causes man to see more clearly.

Four Corners of Justice Score—Giles Corey

- Investigators: -3 Officials collected evidence, affidavits, and witnesses without objectivity. They were complicit with the arrests of innocent people.
- Prosecutor: -7 Without a plea, there was no trial. The *system* served as the prosecutor for his plea of innocence or guilt. Since Corey did not subscribe to the wave of pandemonium and the emotions of the time, he refused to participate.
- Judge: -9 The judge admitted to errors as extrajudicial and we will rate his conduct severely. The judge participated in and added to the hysteria.
- Witnesses: -5
- Jury -3 The jurors allowed Corey to be physically pressed to get a plea.
- Grand Jury: -1 Formed and executed against the wisdom of the more discerning.

THE FOUR CORNERS OF JUSTICE—SCOTTSBORO BOYS

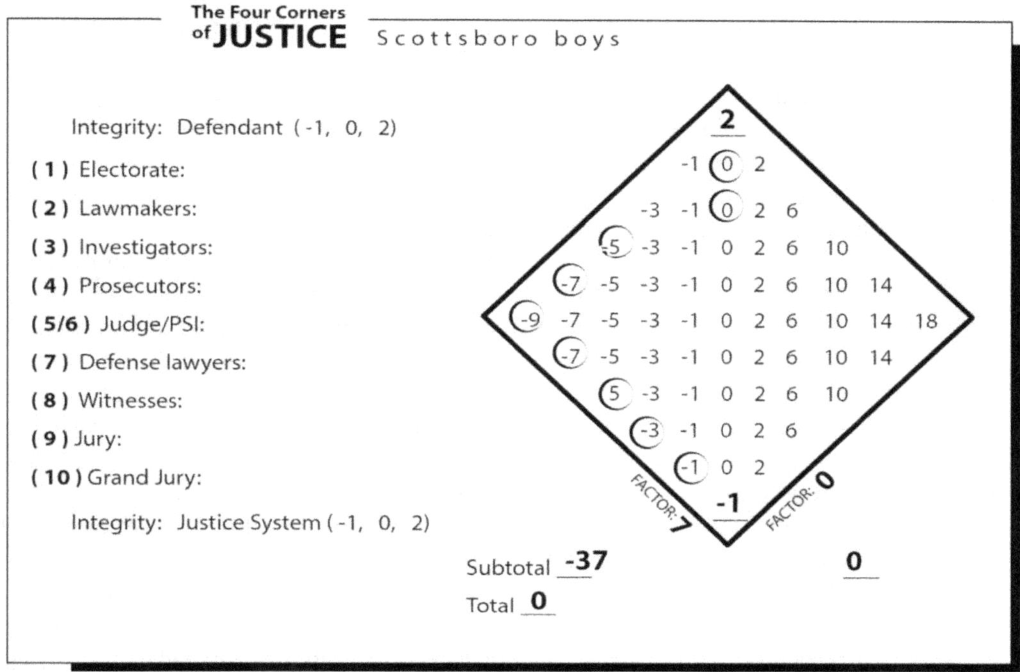

ANALYSIS OF THE SCOTTSBORO BOYS

Whether through the context of time or location, the motives of man are suspect. We need only consider the plights of Hus and Galileo. They lived during periods and in venues which wrought injustice. Since the heart of man remains constant, history tends to repeat itself. The Scottsboro Boys were victims of both time and location. The southern United States was fraught with racial strife. These boys, it cannot be denied, were guilty only of being black. It proved disastrous that they lived in Alabama in the 1930s. It proved disastrous that they were on the wrong train car that fateful day.

After an altercation, two white girls alleged they were raped by the nine boys. An exhaustive manhunt ensued, and the alleged criminals were apprehended, charged, and indicted. Their futures were in jeopardy and the factors of time and location would always be against them. The polarization between whites and blacks assured that truth and justice would not be attained.

FOUR CORNERS OF JUSTICE SCORE—SCOTTSBORO BOYS

- Electorate: 0 It would be easy to characterize this component negatively; but restraint is in order. Rape is a crime, a legitimate law accounts for this wrongful act. The electorate supported the exaction of justice for rape. The distinction that should be made is that public interests from the north fought against a racial prejudice which unduly swayed the *electorate* of the location of the crime.
- Investigators: -5 Investigators were witting or unwitting pawns for the prosecution as they collected evidence. These investigators had at least eleven witnesses. Yet, in the racially charged atmosphere, the pressure to confirm that the boys were guilty was undeniable. This was proved when two doctors concluded that no rape occurred. The investigators did not use this information to acknowledge the truth and end the case.

- Prosecution: -7 Bigots in office were uncompromising with their agenda and this included the prosecutor. The highly questionable allegation of rape did not sway the presentment of indictments and charges. Officials who were beholden to honestly discharge their authority acted on a lie. Although the prosecutor knew of the contradicting conclusion of the doctors, he represented the lie to a grand jury. The relentless and blind chase of these charges through three trials demonstrated racial antagonism and prejudice against the defendants.
- Judge: -9 Contempt for blacks was no doubt an influence even with the judge. While he had an obligation to be impartial, the collective pressure in Alabama to exact *justice* was great. The fact that the boys were sentenced to death after the first trial is confirmation that the judge did not seek justice.
- Defense Lawyers: -7 Even the United States Supreme Court determined the defendants did not have effective assistance of defense counsel. Their attorneys were likely indifferent to the protections and recourse the boys needed. The pressure of serving as defense counsel was significant and certainly not easy given the outcry for guilty verdicts. However, truth and justice should have prevailed.
- Witnesses: -5 With no evidence of a rape, unbelievably, the testimony of two white girls prevailed. The conclusions of the doctors had little impact against the victims who, obviously, did not tell the truth.
- Jury: -3 We cannot escape the obvious conflict these white jurors confronted—their own bias and public pressure for convictions. Even if some jurors were inclined to acquit, they were surrounded by other white jurors who had a heavy racial prejudice. Truth and justice were sacrificed with relative ease.
- Grand Jury: -1 Had the grand jurors done what was right, this travesty would never have occurred. Injustice begins and ends with the people. While most people hear only what they want to hear and believe what they wish, the conclusions of the doctors, if presented to the grand jurors at all, could have challenged the idea that a crime had been committed. IN the end, there was no injured party. There was only a brazen and arrogant prosecutor with a sensationalized story.

The impact of the Scottsboro case was a defining chapter in the history of the United States. This miscarriage of justice was credited as a cause of the civil rights movement. A time of upheaval for nine innocent black boys accented the need for a color-blind justice in a venue where whites cornered the market on hatred.

The Four Corners of Justice—Arlon Jones

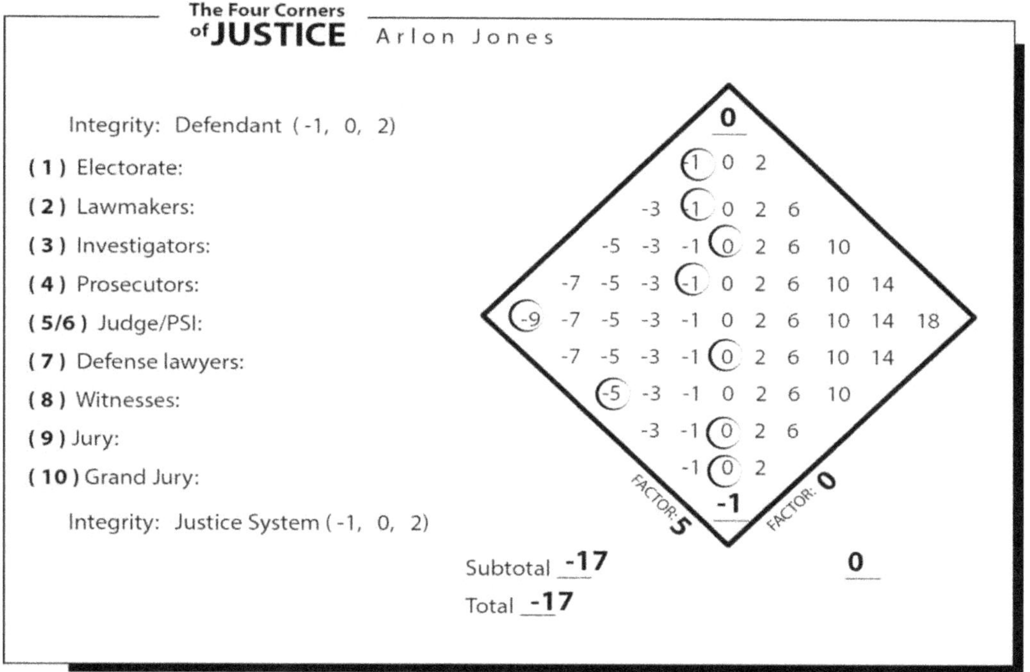

Analysis of Arlon Jones

There can be no doubt that a grave injustice occurred in the Arlon Jones case. We don't need to be legal scholars to reach this conclusion. This is the point. Legal scholars were the reason for the injustice. Actors within the legal system playing the game of court are the reason for the absence of truth and justice. The sooner we realize this, the sooner we may solve the problem. Any solution requires engagement and understanding. With the FCOJ diagram, we see the marked contrast between right and wrong. Keep in mind, with an impartial and fair judiciary, no score should cross to the left of the Zero Line. All parties should seek equity and justice.

We must ask the basic question. Did Arlon Jones commit a crime? In a legal and technical sense, we must answer affirmatively. But did he have malicious intent? We must answer negatively. His intent was to feed his family. This response is not offered to condone the theft of another man's property, but to square the crime with the intent and the eventual punishment. Note, the court did not require Jones to pay for the heifer and serve thirty days in jail. The sentence was life in prison. In a moral and compassionate society, we expect that mercy might to prevail and the people (think community or equitable standard) might aid a husband and father in need. Alas, forgiveness was lacking, and the condemnation and punishment were excessive.

Four Corners of Justice Score—Arlon Jones

- Electorate: -1
- Lawmakers: -1 We score the electorate and lawmakers negatively simply because an old statute allowed the judge to impose a harsh sentence. Both components were disengaged with the law and its current misapplication.
- Prosecutor: -1 Jones' circumstances coupled with the fact that the prosecutor tried

the case are justification for a negative score.

- Judge: -9 This score is for an obvious reason. The judge imposed a sentence that was reprehensible. Moreover, he allowed his office to be influenced by a friend.
- Witnesses: -5 The rancher's influence upon the judge was inexcusable.
- Grand Jury: 0 While many may readily conclude that the jury and grand jury executed their responsibilities appropriately, we must hold them suspect. Yet, we will score them as reflected.

THE FOUR CORNERS OF JUSTICE—ELIZABETH RAMIREZ

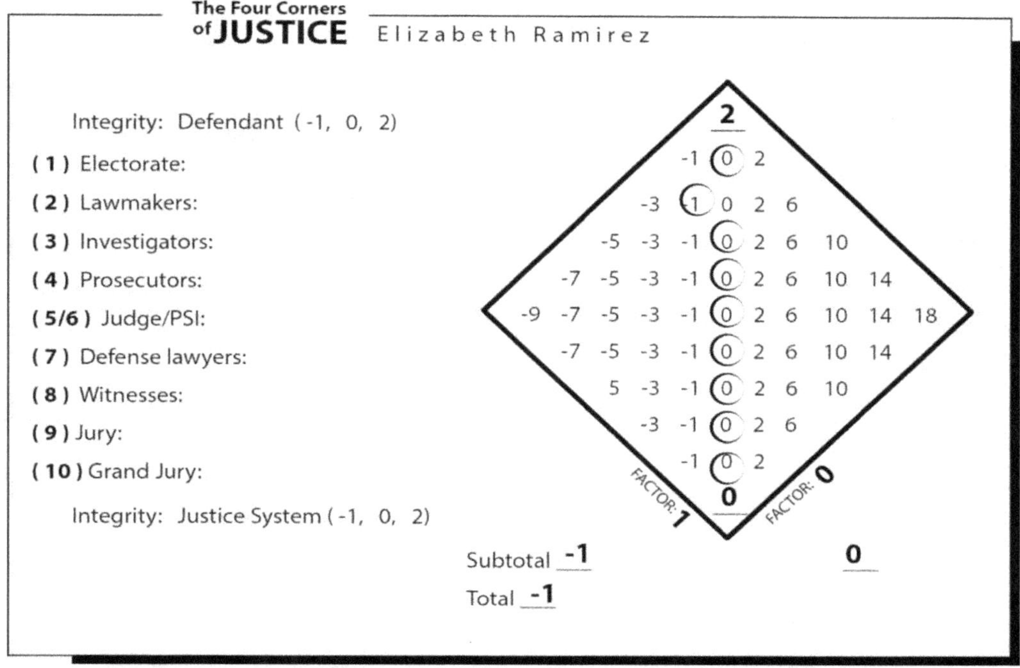

ANALYSIS OF ELIZABETH RAMIREZ

With the Elizabeth Ramirez case, we may easily conclude that the legal system failed to ensure justice. Even without an in-depth analysis, since we know little of the particulars of the case, the FCOJ diagram still reflects a disparity.

FOUR CORNERS OF JUSTICE SCORE—ELIZABETH RAMIREZ

- Lawmakers: -1 We must reach the conclusion that, although the collection and analysis of forensic evidence was handled at the time with an *objective standard*, the actual evidence was not sound. The emphasis on the given "standard," upon which the judicial process relied for the forensic evidence, must be held to account. Since the actors throughout the legal process were accustomed to this forensic protocol, we will give them the benefit of the doubt, even though we may be inclined to hold their motives suspect. If only because the lawmakers are the appropriate "authority" with the objective oversight to establish the standard for proper forensic evidence, we will rate this component negatively.
- With the foregoing, we will give deference to all other components and score as each as 0.

THE FOUR CORNERS OF JUSTICE—KEN WAHLER

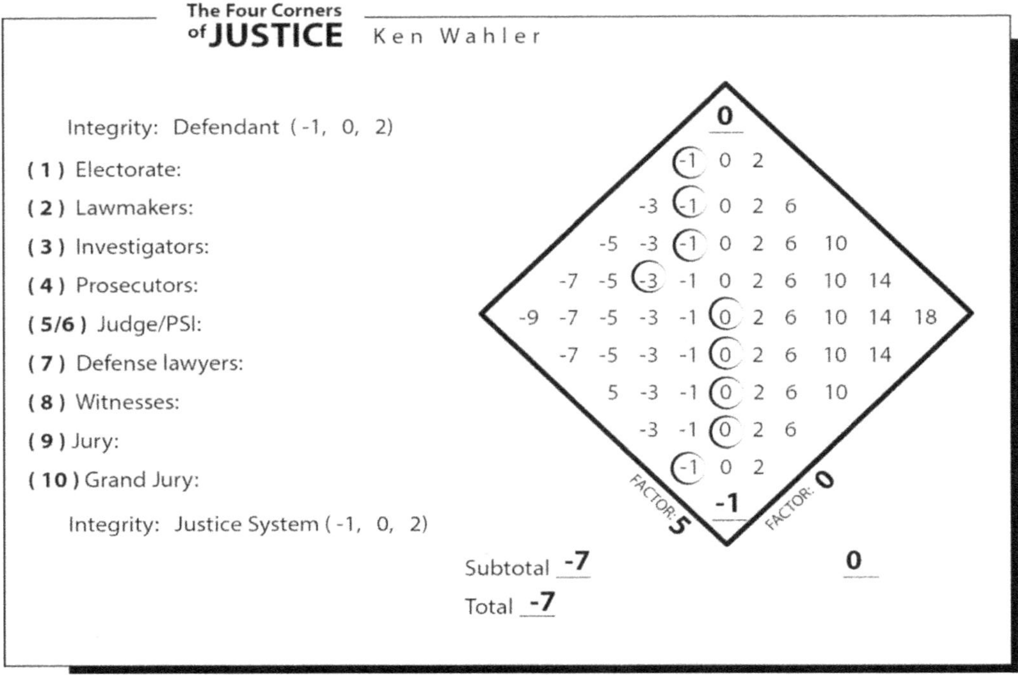

ANALYSIS OF KEN WAHLER

The case against Ken Wahler proves that sometimes wealth cannot buy justice in American courts. Ken had the means to stage a strong legal defense, but he accepted a one-way ticket to a federal prison instead. He could not afford or tolerate a severe sentence if he lost in a jury trial. The price he and his family suffered was already too costly. Ken freely admits he made a mistake. He entered a private server after he gave up ownership. Was he a criminal with willful intent? You decide. For, that is what the U. S. Attorney did. He determined that Ken deserved to spend three years away from his wife and children. The prosecutor saw no other solution, and this demonstrates that the legal system cares little for equity and balance.

FOUR CORNERS OF JUSTICE SCORE—KEN WAHLER

- Electorate: -1
- Lawmakers: -1
- Investigators: -1
- Prosecutor: -3
- Grand Jury: -1

THE FOUR CORNERS OF JUSTICE—BUTCH RICHARDSON

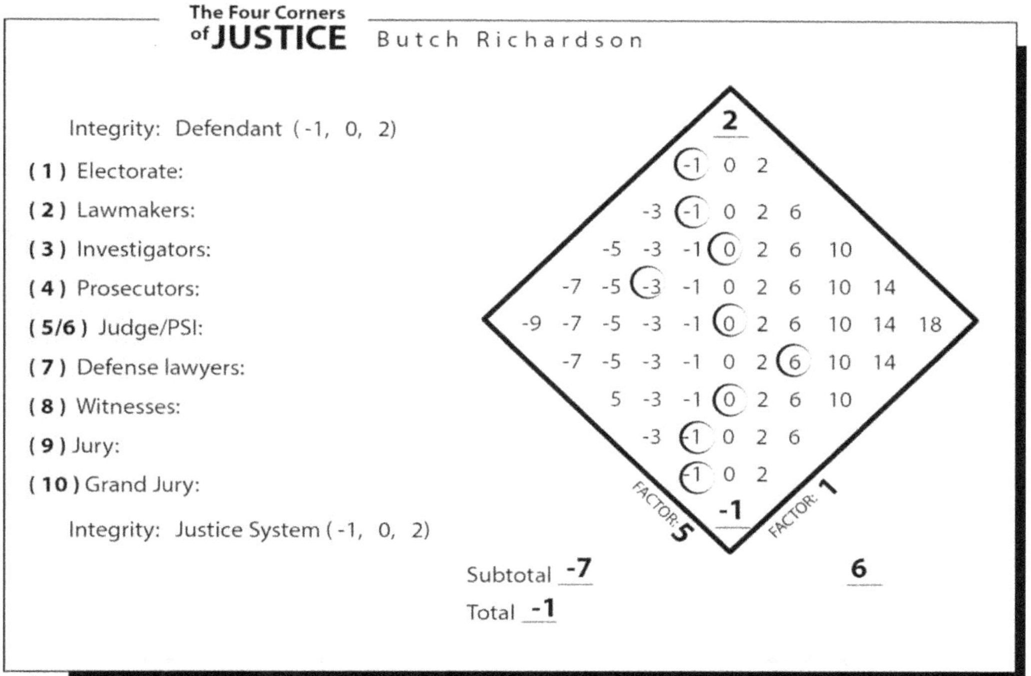

ANALYSIS OF BUTCH RICHARDSON

Did Butch commit a crime? Did he have malicious intent? Was there a victim who suffered loss of life, liberty, or property? As a husband, father, grandfather, and educator, he never imagined there would be a cloud over his reputation. His life and retirement were destroyed for a *crime* which did not match the punishment. We have a case whereby a public figure, believed to be contemptible by some of those he served (simply because of policy decisions), was subjected needlessly to a criminal investigation and conviction.

We may reasonably conclude that the prosecutor was either obligated to prosecute because of public pressure, or he wanted to pursue questionable charges which could have been remedied with a solution that scaled to the offense. Was the U. S. Attorney amenable to alternatives? No. He saw no benefit. He was confident of a conviction.

This case exemplifies that justice results in unjust penalties for mere infractions of policy. To characterize Butch's decision and actions as *criminal* reflects a rather ominous culture within the judicial system. Those who passively observe such cases, as they unfold or after the fact, are complicit with their creation and prosecution. For they condone the use of laws that demand conformance to unreasonable standards.

FOUR CORNERS OF JUSTICE SCORE—BUTCH RICHARDSON

- Electorate: -1
- Lawmakers: -1
- Prosecutors: -3 The prosecutor could have accepted Butch's offer. He could have secured a conviction while dignifying the mistakes for what they were.
- Defense Lawyers: 6
- Jury: -1
- Grand jury: -1 Prosecutors manipulate; grand jurors blindly follow.

The Four Corners of Justice—David Ingalls

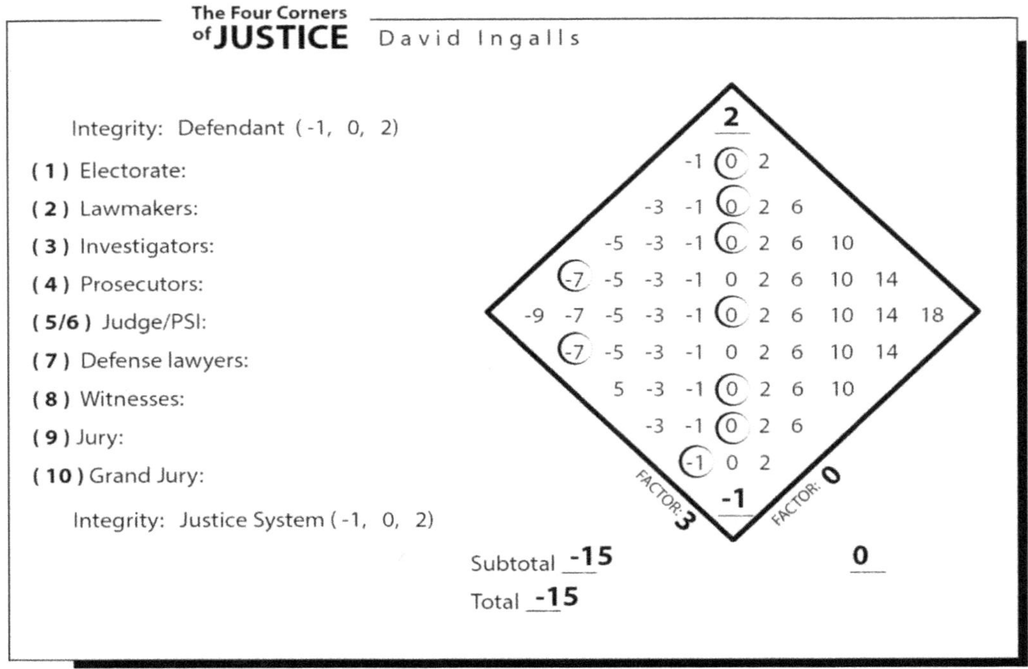

Analysis of David Ingalls

If ignorance is bliss, then innocence is unaware. David Ingalls is one such person. He plods along daily in a consistently slow speed, often oblivious to the full import of his decisions. He is not dumb. He is just—well—unaware. His receipt of SSI disability for his inability to make sound decisions reflects his innocence.

The Ingalls case offers a clear contrast of two worlds, the calculating and the meek. Jesse and Amanda were deviously calculating. David was the meek and unsuspecting pawn in their scam. The U. S. Attorney was equally calculating. He harshly condemned a man who could have used an understanding mind or a listening ear.

Picture an alternative ending to this ordeal. Suppose David was outside Wal-Mart reflecting upon his tendency to make unwise decisions and he did what was a rarity. He asked a stranger for advice. Once David explained the situation, this random bystander, who listened with a genuine sense of humanity, gave his answer. This stranger, who happened to be a federal prosecutor, told David not to cash the checks. He said it was a scam.

What is the difference between this story and the actual events? In the story, the federal prosecutor was human and real. In the legal system, he was simply an actor doing his job. He was responsible for convicting *criminals*. Let's recall, David asked the cashier three times if the checks were good. Consider this next point. David may as well have spoken with the U. S. Attorney on the street. For whether he spoke to him or the cashier, David's question reflected his intent.

Did David make a mistake? Yes. Was he a criminal? No. If anyone had criminal intent, it was the defense lawyer—the man who failed to defend his client, the man who hid behind his title, the system, and the rules of the game of court. At a minimum, he could have helped David correct a mistake.

There are several reasons why David's defense lawyer could have prevailed, even if the case had gone to trial. First, his client was on SSI disability, a factor which could have heavily swayed a jury. Second, David's story squares with the facts alleged by the government. He cashed three checks at one time for the amount stated which proved his one and only occasion to help Jesse. Most of the others involved in the scheme cashed multiple checks at different times. Third, the Wal-Mart cashier would have been an appropriate witness. She would have confirmed David's queries and cautious posture. Certainly, the defense could have established reasonable doubt.

David's *defense* lawyer was just as calculating as Jesse and the federal prosecutor. He did not even listen to David. I personally read the indictment and the plea agreement. David's lawyer wanted to get rid of the case from his personal docket as expeditiously as possible. David was inconsequential to him. David was an inconvenience, for, the lawyer was paid but a modest flat fee by the court. The only way to make the case profitable was to dispense with David with a brief meeting at the jail. He convinced David to accept a plea.

The defense lawyer's failure to provide for his client's best interests reflects the worst possible neglect of a legal advocate, the incarceration of an innocent man. Not only are lawyers limited by the rules of court as to what they may and should accomplish, they impose personal judgments and preconceived notions upon their clients. In the case of Ingalls, we see an attorney use the standard ploy that a trial would net a harsher sentence and ignored the evidence and witnesses which may have secured an acquittal.

Four Corners of Justice Score—David Ingalls

- Prosecutor: -7
- Defense Lawyer: -7
- Grand Jury: -1

THE FOUR CORNERS OF JUSTICE—KRISTER EVERSTON

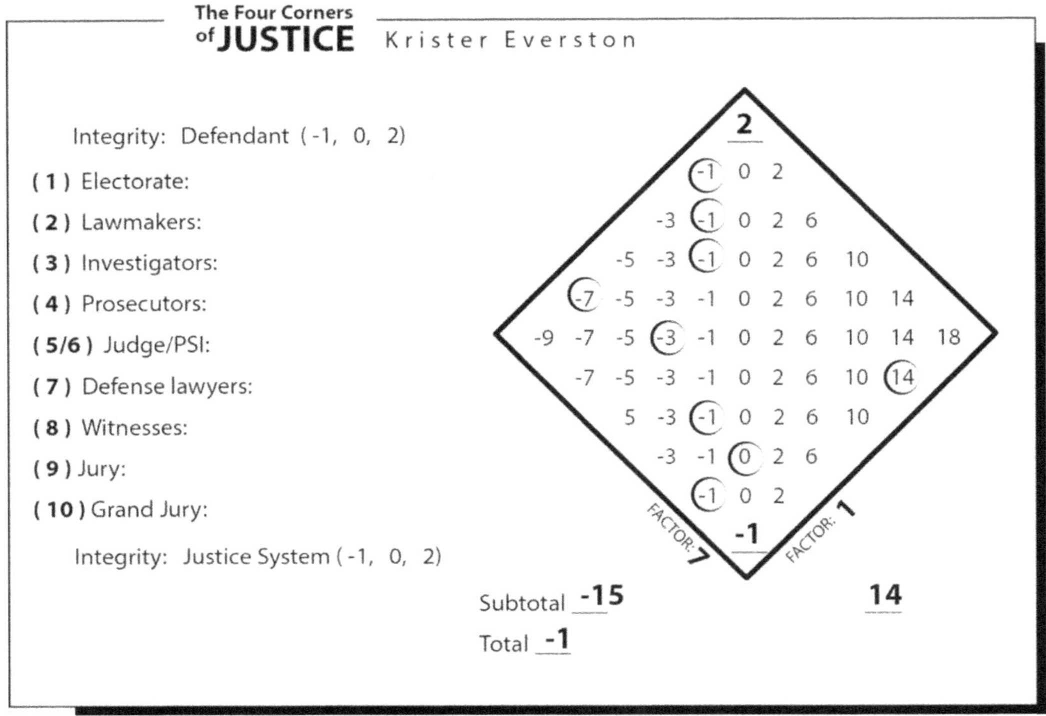

The Four Corners of JUSTICE
Krister Everston
Integrity: Defendant (-1, 0, 2)
(1) Electorate:
(2) Lawmakers:
(3) Investigators:
(4) Prosecutors:
(5/6) Judge/PSI:
(7) Defense lawyers:
(8) Witnesses:
(9) Jury:
(10) Grand Jury:
Integrity: Justice System (-1, 0, 2)
2
-1 0 2
-3 -1 0 2 6
-5 -3 -1 0 2 6 10
-7 -5 -3 -1 0 2 6 10 14
-9 -7 -5 -3 -1 0 2 6 10 14 18
-7 -5 -3 -1 0 2 6 10 14
5 -3 -1 0 2 6 10
-3 -1 0 2 6
-1 0 2
-1
FACTOR: 7
FACTOR: 1
Subtotal -15
14
Total -1

ANALYSIS OF KRISTER EVERSTON

The case of Krister Everston is an example of what is often hidden in plain sight. Why did the government aggressively pursue this man? Was it for the technology he was creating? Such a question would appear preposterous if not for the filing of additional charges after Krister's acquittal. A man charged criminally for not having a label on a package is lunacy. After an acquittal, the filing of additional charges against Krister was even more suspect. Since the authorities could find nothing, they alleged that he "abandoned"[37] batteries. Did the government want to sabotage Krister's time and work? What better way to prevent the creation of something new than to reduce a man's mind and energy to the preservation of his freedom? Was this a *conspiracy* by the government to exact injustice regardless since the costs involved government or private interests?

FOUR CORNERS OF JUSTICE SCORE—KRISTER EVERSTON

- Electorate: -1 We must prevent enforcement of crimes that are policy infractions.
- Lawmakers: -1 They must limit laws to the violations of life, liberty, and property.
- Investigators: -1
- Prosecutor: -7 He could have treated this case as an administrative violation.
- Judge: -3 The judge could have intervened, especially handling the second case.
- Defense Lawyer: 14 As his own attorney, Krister fought for his liberty and truth.
- Jury: -1
- Grand Jury: -1 Did they know of the first trial and how batteries were abandoned?

[37] http://dailysignal.com/2013/06/11/clean-energy-fuel-cell-gets-inventor-a-jail-cell/

THE FOUR CORNERS OF JUSTICE—JOHN WILLIAMS

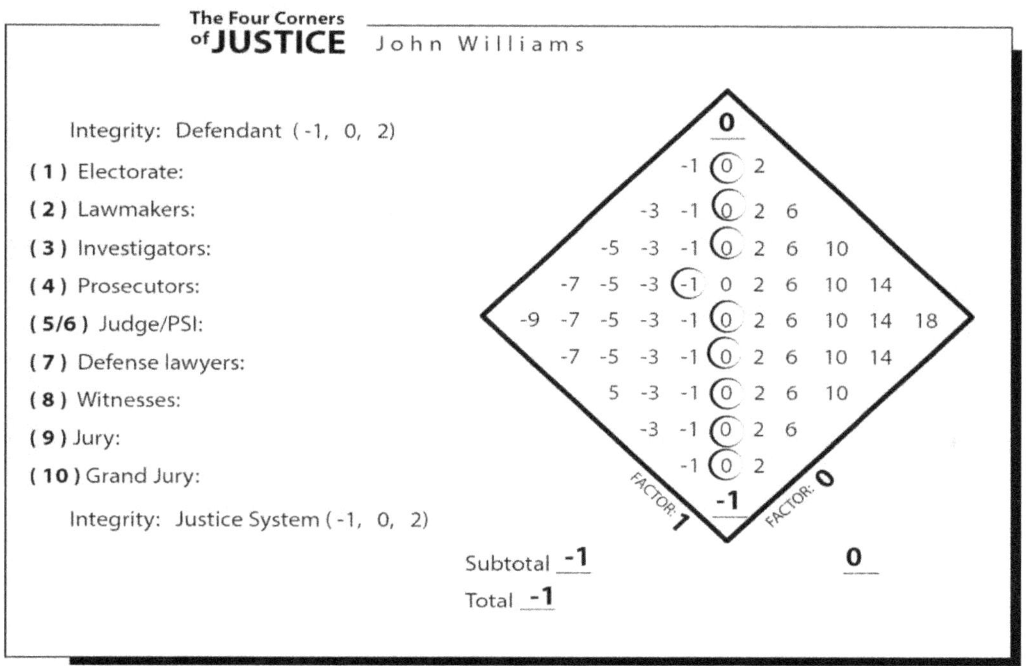

ANALYSIS OF JOHN WILLIAMS

John may represent the best example of *criminal activity* which required no willing engagement. His crime reflects the opposite—no mental or physical effort. This was a crime of omission, not commission. His absence of mind and failure to physically retrieve the pistol from his luggage after the last trip were the greatest contributors to his illegal act. Perhaps this reflects our national dilemma of unnecessarily making criminals of those who are not. When do criminals become criminals? Is it when they injure another or when they knowing or unknowingly violate a law that brings no harm? If the latter, we have sacrificed a degree of our freedom and relegated our existence to the adherence of laws simply for the sake of having laws.

FOUR CORNERS OF JUSTICE SCORE—JOHN WILLIAMS

- Prosecutor: -1 We are left with one question as a result of this analysis: How could we have secured complete neutrality along the Zero Line? We could have given credence to the conscience and intent of the man charged. John had no willful intent. If the prosecutor had willingly recognized this fact, he would never have pursued the charge and conviction.

THE FOUR CORNERS OF JUSTICE—GEORGE NORRIS

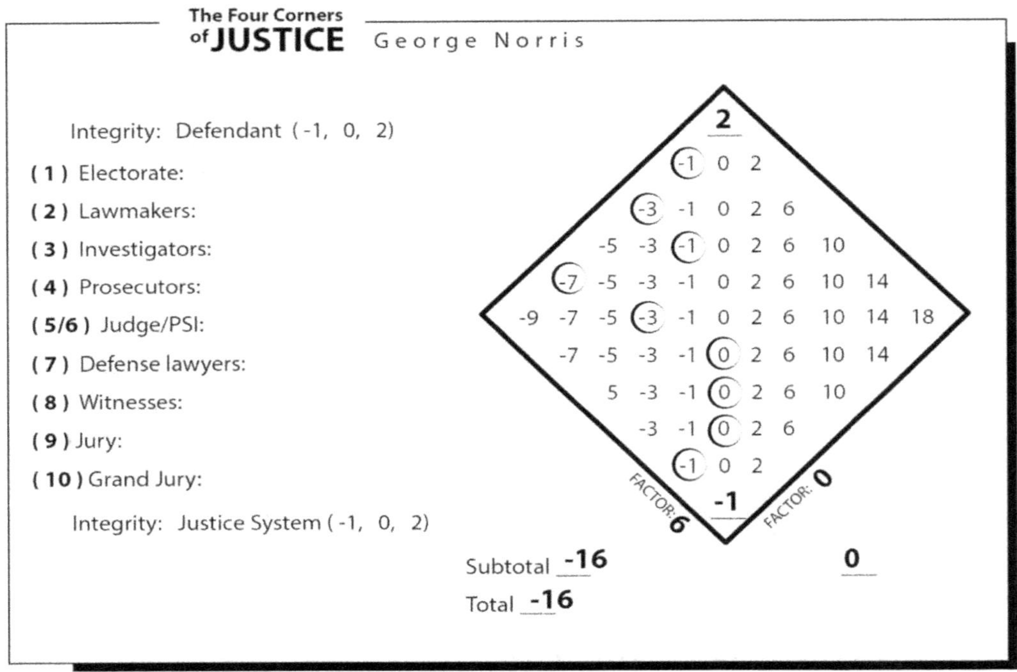

ANALYSIS OF GEORGE NORRIS

Many support the underdog whenever the odds are tilted toward a heavily favored opposition. George Norris faced the most formidable of foes, the Federal Government. The government was not a foe because of its size or strength, but for its unreasonableness. A man with an unreasonable intent is not a man who is easily influenced. Such was the case with the U. S. Attorney who asserted that George was a criminal for selling alleged illegal orchids. This official was not unlike a pit bull that bites into the neck of its victim and shakes it until it is dead. No reason and no action would convince the dog to release its hold.

The U. S. Attorney had his proverbial hands around Norris' neck and was determined to acquire a conviction. No amount of logic, reason, or passion would dissuade him from relinquishing his unjustifiable intent. Many would characterize the prosecutor's conduct and decisions as criminal. George was an innocent man who was charged and prosecuted by a legally sanctioned hitman with the powers of a federal office.

FOUR CORNERS OF JUSTICE SCORE—GEORGE NORRIS

- Electorate: -1 An uninformed and disengaged electorate merits a negative score.
- Lawmakers: -3 If lawmakers do not see and correct prosecutorial abuse and unwarranted enforcement of laws, we will continue to be over criminalized.
- Investigators: -1
- Prosecutors: -7 The prosecutor should be fired and charged criminally.
- Judge: -3 He allowed a trial without merit to continue. Moreover, his indifference to Norris' plight shows that officials are far removed from reality.
- Grand Jury: -1 The grand jury should have served as a defense for Norris.

THE FOUR CORNERS OF JUSTICE—DAN MCGINNIS

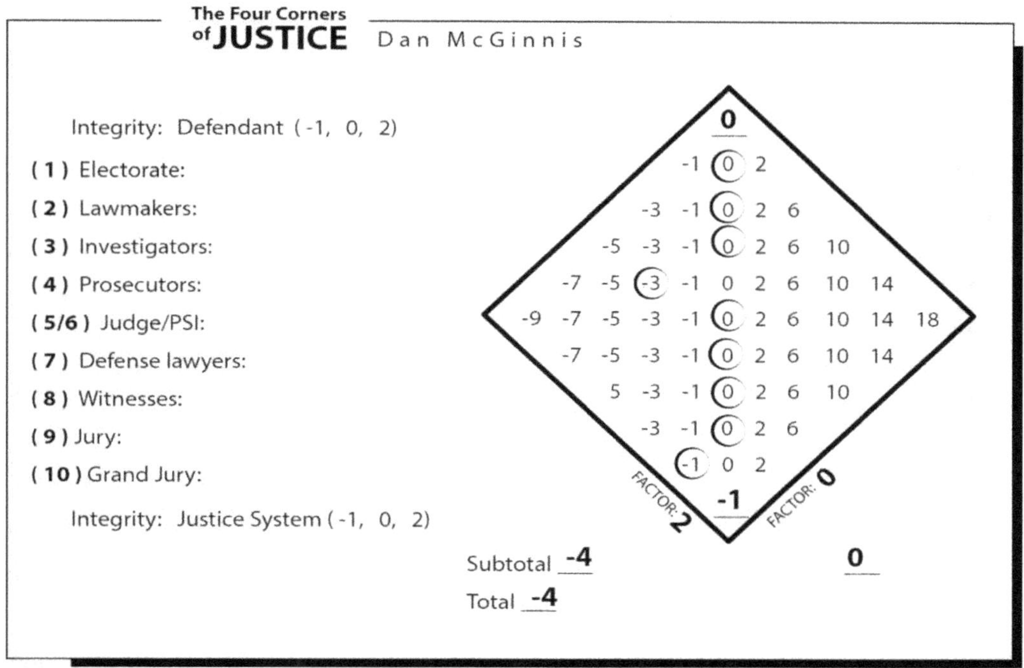

ANALYSIS OF DAN MCGINNIS

Much can be said of free will. Many believe we choose what occurs in our lives. But do we? If we learn anything from Dan's case it is that life is influenced by others and by circumstances beyond our control. Dan's life was waylaid by his roommate's mistake. Try as he might, Dan could not convince the business owners, who were equally affected by circumstances, to accept his payment. Cause and effect dynamics stifled Dan's free will and those of others. The prosecutor, who also had free will, could have ended a string of events not of Dan's creation. The prosecutor had a responsibility to convict criminals. Did he consider that Dan wanted to correct a mistake and that he was not a criminal?

FOUR CORNERS OF JUSTICE SCORE—DAN MCGINNIS

- Prosecutors: -3
- Grand Jury: -1

THE FOUR CORNERS OF JUSTICE—RON WEBB

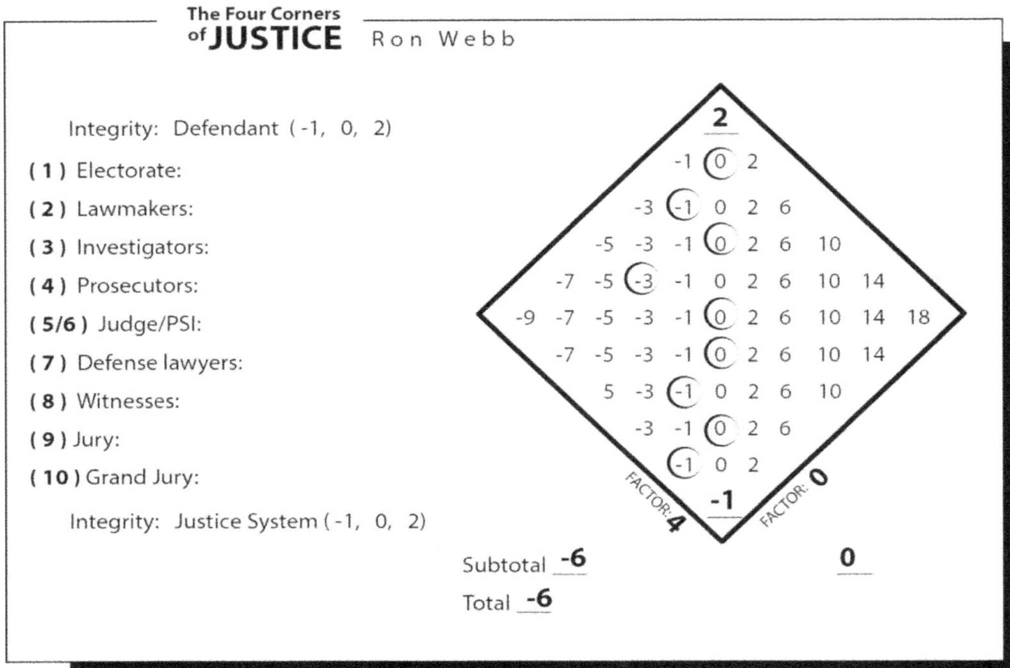

ANALYSIS OF RON WEBB

If simplicity has any correlation to honesty, Ron Webb is an honest man. With a simple life, he values what many neglect. He was imprisoned for a short sentence if only for his fear of receiving ten years if he lost at trial. To return to his life, he accepted two years in jail to avoid the unthinkable. Such is the regrettable refrain in most criminal cases. Ron was guilty of one thing, association. His wife was the reason for his demise. Otherwise, he was innocent. His case should encourage us to ask: To what extent is one responsible for someone else's behaviors and decisions? Also, what relevance should ownership of property or marriage have over one who is innocent?

FOUR CORNERS OF JUSTICE SCORE—RON WEBB

- Lawmakers: -1
- Prosecutor: -3
- Witnesses: -1
- Grand Jury: -1

Can the liberties of a nation be thought secure when we have removed their only firm basis, a conviction in the minds of the people that these liberties are the gift of God? That they are not to be violated but with His wrath. **Thomas Jefferson: Notes on Virginia**

One on One

While I was incarcerated within county jails, waiting for a forced entry into the federal penal system, I spoke with many a man who professed his guilt. Men admitted to violating someone's life, liberty, or property. Invariably, they conceded to being common criminals. I also met with those who truly believed they were innocent yet incarcerated because of the judicial process itself. As I learned of cases that were suspect, I intuitively discerned the questionable *enforcement* of laws and the *process* to mete out *justice*. The administration of justice became even more questionable when I spoke with men within the federal system.

The eight supposed criminals highlighted in the foregoing cases were oppressed by the most severe force just short of physical torture. I do not use the term *torture* to heighten the drama of their plight, but to plainly state that *absent physical punishment*, their situations could not have been any worse. The Federal Government need not resort to physical abuse even if it were allowed. The government simply employs the psychological, emotional, physical, and spiritual pressure needed by virtue of its protocol and objectives.

Men shared that they capitulated to a plea agreement to avoid more years in prison. The thought of two to three times the sentence, given their innocence, was irreconcilable. Some of them were *forced* to accept a plea within minutes of its offer. The harshness of systemic procedures obviated the government's need for any illegal method of coercion.

Except for Norris and Everston, I personally met with the other six men. Other than John Williams, I was confined with each in the same cell or compound. I watched these men. I listened. I observed their body language, tone, inflection, and word choice. I acquired a sense of their true being as they interacted with others. At planned times, I asked questions about their cases to gauge their honesty. I sought to establish whether their answers were consistent with former responses. They and others who professed their innocence were congruent with each past conversation. Those who equivocated lost credibility simply because they lacked integrity.

The obvious should be apparent. Whenever people share the most trying of times and circumstances, their character is revealed. Such is the case with those who coexist within the unfortunate dynamics of prison. The toll of the regimen and the dispiriting existence of incarceration can do nothing but reveal a man's nature. This observation is made quite easily when a mass of inmates coalesce and gravitate to a common denominator that is pedestrian, while others prove to be above the fray. Those who were resolute as to their innocence were often far removed from the influence of the *community* at large. Their thoughts, conversations, and behavior were in keeping with their personal representations.

My relationships with these men underscore the concepts of perspective and context discussed earlier. I could do nothing but confront the reality of a process that exacted what it demanded, and that was submission. As one of its victims, I never submitted. My awareness extended beyond the ordinary, beyond what was or became *comfortable* for most others. This resulted in my assessment of the integrity of these six men and their critical and honest portrayal of their own adversity.

There are two other cases of innocent men, and I met them while in isolation. I was housed with each in the Special Housing Unit, the SHU. For fourteen days, on two separate occasions and locations, I lived in close quarters with these *common criminals* who professed their innocence. Under such harsh conditions, they were even more vulnerable and expressive than they might have been. I listened as they recounted in detail the misery surrounding their arrests and subsequent destruction of their lives. As they grappled with the long days in an eight by twelve-foot cell, with the continuing unknowns in their lives, contending with the reasons for placement in the SHU, each was susceptible to a range of emotions men would typically suppress. Yes, they were vulnerable. They laughed, cried, despaired, and hoped. They were brutally honest and revealed perspectives of their cases which could not have been more genuine.

Is it possible, however, that these two and the former six distorted the truth at all? Sure, but it is unlikely. More important, their stories were consistent with the overall theme of the overbearing nature of the government. I observed. I questioned. I then reassessed until I was certain that I could dignify their representations. Based upon my life experience, I came to a relatively confident conclusion: Ryan Gosin and Tony Figueroa were authentic.

I empathized and sympathized with Ryan, for he was incarcerated over real estate transaction. I was familiar with buying and selling properties. Yet, I did not know of the law that he supposedly violated. Considering his business model, I would never have thought that he committed a crime. I came to understand see how Ryan's business attorney was unaware of the applicable federal statute and wince at the thought of spending seven years in prison for a crime both he and his legal adviser did not know even existed.

I equally empathize and sympathize with Tony Figueroa. With experience in business and bureaucracies and relationships with superiors and subordinates, I appreciate how Tony could not have known of developments that were outside his influence. I challenged myself to consider how I would have reacted to his situation. In my humble estimation, Tony could have done no differently than he did.

In both cases, especially given my own ordeal, I could see how the raw force of government crushed both men. Ryan accepted a plea to escape the unthinkable and Tony weathered a five-week trial. I concluded that both cases reflected men with integrity. As we weigh their experiences, consider that, like the eight previous cases and the men and women who suffered injustice throughout history, we are not far removed from their situation. Perhaps you will agree that these two cases represent an objective portrayal of injustice in America currently.

Ryan Gosin

Year: 2008
Occupation: Entrepreneur/Business Owner
Marital Status: Married
Children: 3
Criminal History: None
Spiritual Beliefs: Jewish
Age: 40
Education: College
Summary: Ryan is a self-starter. He makes things happen. This is why he was successful. With a family he adored, he worked to provide for them.

The Particulars

Original Charges: Mortgage Fraud/Banking Fraud
Actual Charges: Conspiracy to Commit Money Laundering
Trial: No
Verdict: Guilty
Plea: Yes
Sentence: 70 months
Appeal: No
Summary: Ryan Gosin, accused of mortgage and banking fraud, agreed to a plea agreement for one count of money laundering and conspiracy. With over thirty cooperating witnesses, who were fearful of possible prison sentences, Ryan decided to avoid the unthinkable, a guilty plea and a prison sentence.

The Case of Ryan Gosin

Ryan's family had been in the real estate business for generations. His father, grandfather, and uncles invested and did well. Ryan Gosin was no different. At the age of twenty-six, he started several businesses within the real estate industry. He became a licensed mortgage broker, a licensed contractor, and a licensed seller of renovated homes. He began his business in 2000. By 2011, he was in prison. He was found guilty of a crime he and his business lawyer did not know even existed.

At the height of Ryan's success, he was buying five or six properties at a time and selling them upon renovation. With a partner and eight employees, he owned seventeen houses, and two commercial buildings. In 2006, he sold his business, He sold each division and the real estate. He then entered a partnership as a wholesaler of exotic cars.

The only incident Ryan ever encountered in the six years he had his real estate business concerned an investor with whom he had an agreement in 2004. A woman with $450,000.00 wanted to invest. Although he did not need her money, he agreed to the joint purchase of a multi-family building. This decision turned out to be his worst. Eventually, the investor was told that Ryan was disreputable. Rather than speak to Ryan and request an immediate refund, she filed a complaint with the Nassau County District Attorney and the federal authorities.

The district attorney called Ryan's lawyer and requested that Ryan surrender. Ryan complied. Yet, the one and only time in court and only time he appeared in court, the judge stated the obvious, that this was a civil and not criminal matter. The judge then asked if Ryan planned to refund the investor's money within a year. Ryan responded that he would do so immediately. Ryan gave the investor a check for the full amount. As far as he was concerned, the issue was resolved. He believed he had done nothing wrong.

In March 2008, Ryan received a call from a friend who worked at a local bank. He learned that federal authorities were investigating his former real estate business, and particularly his banking transactions. Ryan was shocked. He called his lawyer who told him not to worry. The lawyer said the government was likely conducting a routine bank examination. The answer satisfied Ryan.

Yet, in November 2008, twenty-six federal agents cordoned off his street. At 5:00 in the morning, they barreled into his home, yelling—with weapons drawn. Clothed only in his underwear, Ryan was promptly handcuffed. Once his wife was permitted to get him clothes, Ryan was dressed and driven to JFK airport.

The agents arrived at a hangar that was used as an operations center and placed Ryan in a circle with thirty-three other people. Each was handcuffed and facing outward. Those present were Ryan's partner, employees, and business associates. They were now co-defendants in what became known in the press as a $14 to $30 million mortgage scam. Later that day, Ryan was arraigned in court and released on a $600,000.00 bond.

When Ryan left the courthouse, he was greeted by a throng of reporters. They asked him about his business. Previously, the U. S. Attorney had released a press statement touting the arrest of a major mortgage fraud ring. He stressed the diligence of the Federal Government to protect the banking industry and an unsuspecting public.

Ryan read the indictment which alleged he engineered a multi-million-dollar bank fraud scam. He hired an attorney, the first of ten, who advised Ryan to settle quickly, make a proffer and help the government indict someone bigger, like a bank. The lawyer told him this is how the system operated. According to Ryan, his lawyer seemed intent on scaring him into securing a "5K1" letter (which states one is a snitch who helps the government). This is how business was done in the game of court. However, Ryan was not willing to snitch on anyone or any bank when neither he nor the banks violated any law. Ryan believed nobody was guilty of a crime.

Ryan sold his business years earlier and resolved the one civil complaint which may have been the source of any accusation. He believed that he had conducted his business with transparency. Now he and a multitude of co-defendants faced charges for bank fraud and conspiracy. Ryan faced a minimum of fifteen years in prison if he did not cooperate.

Ryan soon learned that he had supposedly committed fraud by inducing banks to loan money based on information that was not true. He rejected this and referred to the government's premise as preposterous. He knew the banks did not suffer a loss. There was no victim. The banks even sent letters to the judge stating there was no loss, that they had no expectation of money due and payable and no desire to be involved in the proceedings against Ryan. Ryan never missed a payment and never defaulted on a loan. With the sale of his business, the mortgages for all properties were satisfied in full. Yet, Ryan would soon be sentenced for what was known as the "intended loss," a loss that could have been.

Not only was Ryan in a grave legal predicament, but it also appeared to him that the U. S. Attorney deliberately maligned him before he was convicted. How the prosecutor portrayed him to the press was significant. This affected Ryan profoundly. The news covered both him and the case frequently in New York City which further frustrated him. He did not see investigative journalists seeking the truth. Rather, he saw the press accept the representations of the U. S. Attorney. More importantly, Ryan was concerned that those who knew him would accept the coverage without question. From his perspective, the government used the press to promote and sensationalize a lie.

Ryan claimed that the truth was important. As he explained his past, before he began his real estate venture, he operated a successful cleaning business which he sold for a $2 million profit. He used the funds to start his real estate enterprise. Part of his business model was to contractually agree with associates and then purchase properties in need of renovation. His use of investors was not a necessity. Ryan was liquid. His had excellent credit. Yet, he partnered with others which afforded him the ability to expand. The use of "OPM"—other people's money—is a common business practice. Ryan's entire operation was overseen by a lawyer who approved the legal aspects and handled the actual real estate closings. To appreciate how Ryan allegedly violated the law, we must understand his model.

Whenever Ryan found a property to purchase, he had a standing offer for family and friends who wanted to invest. If they secured a loan or provided funds to acquire the property, he paid them $10,000.00. This business associate became a silent partner who made a profit. This was accomplished when Ryan created an LLC (Limited Liability Company) for each acquisition. The LLC had an agreement with each investor with very clear terms. The LLC made the mortgage payments and paid for all improvements, insurance, and taxes. The LLC leased the property, collected rent, and handled all landlord particulars. The LLC was added as an owner to the deed at the courthouse. When the property was sold, both the associate and LLC signed at closing. Any proceeds were paid to the LLC. At this point, the LLC was terminated. The entire process was transparent and conducted under the complete purview of his business attorney. The banks benefitted as did all parties concerned.

What law did Ryan supposedly violate which warranted an investigation and subsequent criminal charges? There is a federal statute which makes it a crime to use a "Straw man" to purchase real estate with a bank loan. As the government asserted, the financing of any loan was made by the LLC and not the associate. The government's interpretation of Ryan's business practice was that the associate was the "straw man" and not the true purchaser. Ryan believed he and his associates were not and could not possibly be guilty. He believed he operated his business in good faith and with full disclosure. This understanding was important. So, he began to ask questions.

How could another attorney arrive at a different understanding of his operation than his own attorney? How could Ryan be charged when there were no victims or losses? How could he be guilty when he had no intent to do wrong? He even considered that his business attorney may not have known of this law. If so, Ryan asked if he was a criminal simply because he received bad legal advice.

In the early morning hours on a cold November day, the Federal Government raided some thirty-four homes in and around New York City. Families and individuals were shocked and humbled by the force used. Ryan concluded there had to be merit to the charges or the government would not have proceeded. He also concluded that he had to fight these unexpected claims. The only other option was to acquiesce to an overwhelming and seemingly insurmountable situation.

Ryan finally hired an aggressive and practical attorney, David Burns. Even though Ryan did not want to cooperate with the federal authorities, Burns wanted Ryan to accept a plea and minimize the damage. Burns knew the thirty co-defendants would accept pleas and testify against his client. He knew Ryan would lose at trial. While Burns believed the government lacked a strong case, he understood the practical reality of Ryan's predicament. He wanted Ryan to plead to one count of conspiracy to commit money laundering. He wanted the prosecution to back off and would allow him to fight the actual losses listed on the Pre-Sentence Investigation Report (PSI). Burns sought to reduce the sentencing points to as close to "0" as possible. So, Ryan complied and accepted a plea of conspiracy to money laundering, a lesser charge than those on the original indictment.

While they waited for the PSI report, Burns argued in court that the intended loss, the loss which could have been, would have been negligible, if any at all. A Fatigo Hearing, held to offer evidence of a proper sentence, would help determine the amount of the loss. Ryan wanted to prove there was none, while the U. S. Attorney equated the loss as the total of all mortgages, over $14 million. Ryan hired an accountant and appraisers who determined that the most any intended loss could have been, $496,000.00. It was at this point that Ryan fired Burns.

Marty Gatultig was his next legal advisor. Ryan considered Gatultig to be the most honest lawyer he met thus far. Gatultig told Ryan that he was going to prison. He encouraged Ryan to secure letters from family and friends. The intent was to convince the judge that a "downward departure," a reduction of sentence based upon extenuating circumstances, was reasonable. Gatultig knew there was little chance the PSI points would be close to zero. He believed the supporting letters would have a favorable impact.

When Ryan finally received the government's sentencing recommendation, he was floored by the characterizations. The U. S. Attorney portrayed him as a "diabolical fiend" and a "menace to society." Ryan was scared. Admittedly, out of desperation, Ryan fired Gatultig and hired Joe Conway. Conway did his best with a scenario that was already near its conclusion. He submitted a sentencing memorandum to the court and assured Ryan that he had a good rapport with the judge. Conway also believed Ryan would not serve any time in prison. He believed the case did not merit such a sentence or punishment.

The day Ryan walked into court for the sentencing hearing, he perceived that the judge had an attitude. It was then that Ryan realized how wrong Conway had assessed the situation. The judge listened as the U. S. Attorney portrayed Ryan as the biggest sociopath he had ever seen. He even stated that Ryan fleeced the elderly. Ryan struggled to understand just who the prosecutor was describing. It could not be him as far as Ryan was concerned. He had never conducted himself or his business with such duplicity or baseness. Ryan challenged himself inwardly. He questioned his decision to accept a plea. He asked if the plea agreement made him the fictitious character the prosecutor portrayed.

Conway addressed the judge after the government concluded its recommendation. Conway underscored the mitigating circumstances and reasons to minimize any sentence. He referred to the letters submitted by the banks. He stressed that no bank suffered a loss, and none wanted remuneration. He referenced that bank officials had no intent to impugn Ryan or his associates.

Ryan believed the judge had made her decision before the hearing began. Once Conway finished, the judge stated unequivocally that the banks were the victims. She looked at Ryan and declared with no ambiguity that he was the reason for the country's financial mess. Without hesitation and with a point total nowhere near "0," facing 51-63 months in prison, the judge sentenced Ryan to 70 months. Since the original charges carried a sentence of fifteen years, 70 months was not considered an *upward departure* and required no justification by the court. Ryan was devastated. He was a convicted felon and headed to prison. As with any plea, he had no right to appeal.

There is one important point of Ryan's case that is important to note at this time: Ryan's wife had a passive role in his business. Her name was on two pieces of real estate. The U. S. Attorney approached Ryan's lawyer and stated that his intent was to indict his wife if Ryan did not accept the plea. Heavily influenced by the threat, Ryan was left with no choice. He would not allow his wife to suffer, regardless of his innocence.

Analysis of Ryan Gosin

Ryan was a father and husband who lived in peace and freedom until the unexpected occurred. He lived in the same community for thirty-two years. His children attended the same schools he attended as a child. He was a practicing member of his synagogue. He was established. He was not a flight risk, especially since he did not know anything about an investigation and his imminent arrest. His employees and associates were as settled within their communities. Yet, the treatment of these men and women, husbands and wives, mothers and fathers, sisters and brothers, aunts and uncles, and friends was without merit.

Ryan considered himself to be an honorable man. He wanted to fight the charges. He was incensed and insulted at the accusations. As the defendant, he wanted the truth to be known, but he was forced to consider alternatives. Most defendants are at the mercy of institutional arrogance and the fear of those helplessly and hopelessly ensnared. Ryan knew his family friends and employees, out of trepidation, became witnesses against him. They sought refuge from certain prison sentences. This is the essence of human nature often revealed within the grinding of the judicial process. Self-preservation is instinctive. Power is oppressive. Even Ryan's fervor to fight was swayed by his succession of defense lawyers who recommended that he settle and accept a plea offer.

Ryan grasped at a greased rope with each hiring and firing of legal counsel. All, save one, told him the same message. "You can't win. Cooperate." Was he to cooperate when he was not guilty and did not know of anyone who committed a crime? Ryan's state of mind was troubled. While he suffered the pangs of knowing that no attorney could extract him from the unavoidable, he wanted to fight for what was the truth. In the end, he compromised his own principles. Once he accepted a plea agreement, he knew that he lacked integrity. He knew that he no longer stood for the truth. He knew that he had surrendered what mattered most. One could argue, if his family were his priority, he would have remained foursquare behind his beliefs and demanded a trial. However, one can't discount a man who seeks to outrun a tsunami, a force which destroys all in its wake.

The full brunt of Ryan's case began with the unseen undertow of the investigation. The momentum grew with the U. S. Attorney's zeal as thirty-two witnesses pleaded guilty to felonies with no prison sentence. Each had the intent to testify against Ryan. The forward progression surged with the PSI report as the onslaught raged within the entire process and crested with the government's characterizations and sentencing recommendation. The judge was the force which slammed into and crushed Ryan and the hopes he had for himself and his wife and their children.

The timing of Ryan's predicament could not have been worse. From the government's perspective, it was the perfect array of forces marshaled against another unsuspecting American. The Federal Government benefited from scapegoats, which allowed these officials to portray to the public that their actions protected banks.

Ironically, considering the national consciousness towards the banking industry, Ryan could have saved himself a great deal of heartache. He could have contrived a story and turned on the banks which loaned the funds, monies repaid without as much as a late payment. However, Ryan did not stoop to the indignant. Nonetheless, the national news at the time of Ryan's sentencing was filled with reports of bank crashes and closings as the government and financial industry grappled with lending practices which defied reason. Banks across the country had loaned money to unqualified borrowers. The market was struggling with high unemployment and overextended credit. Families were barely maintaining, much less surviving, under the burden of their financial struggles. Many walked away from homes they could no longer afford. Foreclosures were ubiquitous. The government's attempt to help banks with TARP funds—the distribution of which was suspect—and the use of highly irregular terms did not pacify public scrutiny.

Based upon his court experience, Ryan had a new perspective, that the full force of the Federal Government defeats any notion America is a free and just country. The irony is that many do not know they are not free. Many gladly embrace the idea they are free without recognition of a perception to the contrary.

On July 24, 2013, Ryan Gosin sat in a federal prison. He had already served four years. His punishment should cause those who are sober minded to pause and reflect. His wife was struggling. She considered divorce as her only option. Their children lost touch with him. We should ask if this is what we want for our country.

We may conclude that Ryan did not commit a crime. He did not have a malicious intent. There was no victim or loss. Once the investigators had the evidence to convict Ryan, they prepared for his arrest. With no loss of life, liberty, or property—he was only accused of violating words recorded in black ink on white paper—Ryan's world as he knew it would come to an end. For a crime that supposedly took place at least two years prior, the Federal Government was going to nab those who were not an imminent threat to others.

What are the psychological and emotional motives which justified the manner and number of arrests? Someone was in charge. Someone planned and approved the raids. The raids occurred in November. The agencies may have had unspent funds. The agencies may have intended to justify an enhanced budget for the coming year. Perhaps such raids substantiated future personnel and logistical demands, a part of the "spend it or lose it" doctrine within the Federal Government, whereby excess funds not used meant a reduction of future budgets. Regardless, some thirty homes were invaded. If only ten agents were available for each location (twenty-six were used for Ryan's arrest), over 300 agents were potentially employed. With the use of such force and resources, this exercise may have been how agencies validated training and justified overtime pay.

Given the subdued nature of the crime, other options were available to apprehend the suspects. Noteworthy, the suspects did not know of the investigation; and if they had known, they may not have expected to be charged. It would have been perfectly reasonable to send three agents at dinner time to make the arrests. The obvious is true. Rather than exercise restraint and moderation, these agents and their feverish invasion of quiet homes reflects a regrettable dynamic within our culture and that of various government agencies. While it could be argued that Americans are somewhat docile and naïve, whereby they allow and excuse such militant action, this furthers the claim that the government and its agents are brazenly arrogant.

The agents played the game of "cops and robbers." The arrest of over thirty paper criminals and the elaborate display of force, replete with a rally at an airport hangar, satisfied base instincts and the exertion of power. The fact that such decisions and actions were accomplished with titles, badges, and the legitimacy of authority does not dismiss the base nature of this aggressive and hostile behavior. One cannot deny that force further subdues an already sedate populace. When we as a people accept such arrests as second nature, we no longer see them as excessive and unwarranted. Consequently, the arrogance of the arresting agencies reigns supreme and unchallenged.

We may conclude that the U. S. Attorney was equally zealous in the exercise of his powers. He wanted to win victories in court at an unfortunate cost. His conclusion that Ryan deliberately committed a crime was unreasonable. Ryan supposedly convinced over thirty people to willfully violate a federal law. Or did the prosecutor, by happenstance, discover Ryan unwittingly did what he did not know was incorrect?

The following is the likely development of the government's eventual suspicions. The federal authorities in Nassau County received the complaint from the woman who invested $450,000.00. A cursory review was conducted. At that time the authorities discovered that Ryan used loans which were not actually in the name of the LLCs. It is plausible the U. S. Attorney prosecuted a crime he knew was not as he represented to the public. Ryan was not a mastermind of a $14 to $30 million mortgage fraud operation, but a businessman innocently negotiating commerce with the help of an uninformed attorney. The prosecutor's posture overshadowed the truth. After a two-year investigation, the U. S. Attorney had to justify his salary and future career prospects.

The U. S. Attorney did not give Ryan the benefit of the doubt. He did not allow for his potential innocence. Rather, he concluded that Ryan and his employees and associates, each of whom helped to finance one property, intended to commit mortgage and banking fraud. The prosecutor wanted himself and all to believe these suspects willfully participated in a known conspiracy. To make his theory plausible, the U. S. Attorney spoke the story into existence with the powers of his office, the use of his title, and the prestige of the government.

Consider the possibility that the prosecutor may have been in a precarious position, that he had to prevail with his representations. Unless he had a crisis of conscience, he had to *prove* a case many would consider to be overbearing. This is the point. He may have never reasoned that Ryan was innocent. The U. S. Attorney had clear objectives and was not likely to deviate from them. He had little cause to conclude much less consider that he was abusing the discretionary powers of his office. Pointedly, no other party was going to hold him accountable for any alternative to his perception of the crime. Consequently, his victory was assured. The proverbial deck was stacked against Ryan Gosin and the prosecutor would reap the benefits.

Ryan was doomed. The U. S. Attorney was driven by an indifference and arrogance which would result in over thirty guilty verdicts. It was apparent to Ryan that the government created a simple but strong story line for the press and the public. The people believed the story if only because the press reported what the public needed to understand. The government had a contingent of snitches who would attest to the crime. It did not matter that these witnesses were attesting to a lie to guard against a prison sentence. With such a game plan, the prosecutor had cause to seek maximum sentences.

The naïve public and Ryan have a hope that any defense lawyer, and Ryan rifled through several of them, will defend a man's innocence. The very nature of a defense is to *defend* after all. We want a virtuous attempt made by lawyers to do what is right. Yet, Ryan's lawyers may not have asked or considered that he did not commit a crime, much less demonstrate malicious intent. They did not dignify the lack of a victim and no loss. Such concerns were inconsequential to those who considered Ryan's recourse as bleak.

According to Ryan, his lawyers intended to scare him into a plea. As far as they were concerned, the system had already won. These scare tactics surprised Ryan. They would alarm most anyone with no understanding of federal prosecutions. Ryan wondered where the warriors were who sought to defend the innocence of their clients. Ryan expressed that, as far as he was concerned, his lawyers fulfilled their roles and responsibilities with their own lies and means of intimidation and portrayed themselves as heroes.

One must conclude that Ryan's lawyers had to be knowledgeable and capable. However, they were evidently not dutiful to the truth or justice, and certainly not passionate to do the right thing. Ryan and the truth were expendable. Their performance was reflected by the results of the case. Ironically, Ryan realized his situation was ominous by simply observing the posture of his legal advisers. He was guilty not because he did wrong; he was guilty because it was impossible for his lawyers to beat the system. The construct of the legal system, its very nature, compelled his defenders to react as they did. They were more adept at managing a crisis through the legal apparatus than they were at engineering a credible defense. Why? We know the answer by now. A credible defense was not viable.

Based upon David Burns' legal experience, his plan made perfect sense. Burns knew Ryan could not and would not win. Ryan would lose because the game of court and its rules ensure defeat. Burns may have been a capable advocate, but he believed it was not practical to wage war. He may have had the passion and skill to fight, but he offered the same result as a trial, an admission of guilt, and a prison sentence. Burns' tepid response contradicted Ryan's intuition. Yet—and this is quite a statement—we should not fault Burns for his legal counsel. His representation confirms what we learned from prior cases—competent defense attorneys do not prevail on behalf of the innocent in the American justice system. Defense lawyers concede defeat because of a merciless process. There is no need to fight.

In the Ryan Gosin case, one truth marched silently and powerfully unopposed to its conclusion. The truth is that *might makes right*. The government's might, as expressed by Burns' decision, compelled Ryan to decide against his better judgment. He accepted guilt to a lesser charge to avoid what was untenable, a much longer prison term. Whether his lawyers were ignorant of how to fight a just battle, indifferent to core principles, or simply a part of an institution which defied justice, it did not matter in the end. While his attorneys intended to achieve objectives, Ryan capitulated. Truth and justice were not among his lawyers' considerations.

The same could be said of the judge. She had, like any powerful jurist, her own brand of judicial discernment. Ryan knew her to be liberally minded. As with any shrewd defendant, he was concerned about the judge's bent on politics, business, social justice, etc. As the banking crisis swirled across the political, economic, and even the judicial landscape, Ryan was toppled in its aftermath. The judge's direct reference to the country's financial demise as Ryan's own making was hyperbole which she believed.

People fail to understand how and why the innocent are incarcerated when they ignore the indifference and imperious nature of judges. We fail to comprehend the disparity of their decisions which cannot be reconciled with the conscience of the community and the disproportional sentences imposed. For example, if it is reasonable to conclude there were no victims and no losses, why didn't the judge prevent Ryan's conviction if he unknowingly violated a law at a technical or administrative level? Why allow a conviction when there was no loss of life, liberty, or property? One would expect that judges would serve as regulators of errant prosecutorial power and obvious indiscretion. This judge was indifferent and validated the government's assertions of feigned fallout from a successful business operated by a private citizen.

It would be natural to discern if the judge decided the sentence fairly. We should question why Ryan faced certain imprisonment. We should challenge a process which compels a defendant to accept a plea and question why defense lawyers forecast certain sentences by judges. But for their arrogance, judges should embrace these same queries.

There are motives which influence judges. They believe they are superior to others, elevated above the rest of humanity. Ego, alone, is enough to influence their determinations. Judges are a major force, and they know that they are a key player in the game of court which functions toward its unfortunate end. The rigidity of the judiciary and judges reflects rigidity of an institutional arrogance that denies justice.

Four Corners of Justice—Ryan Gosin

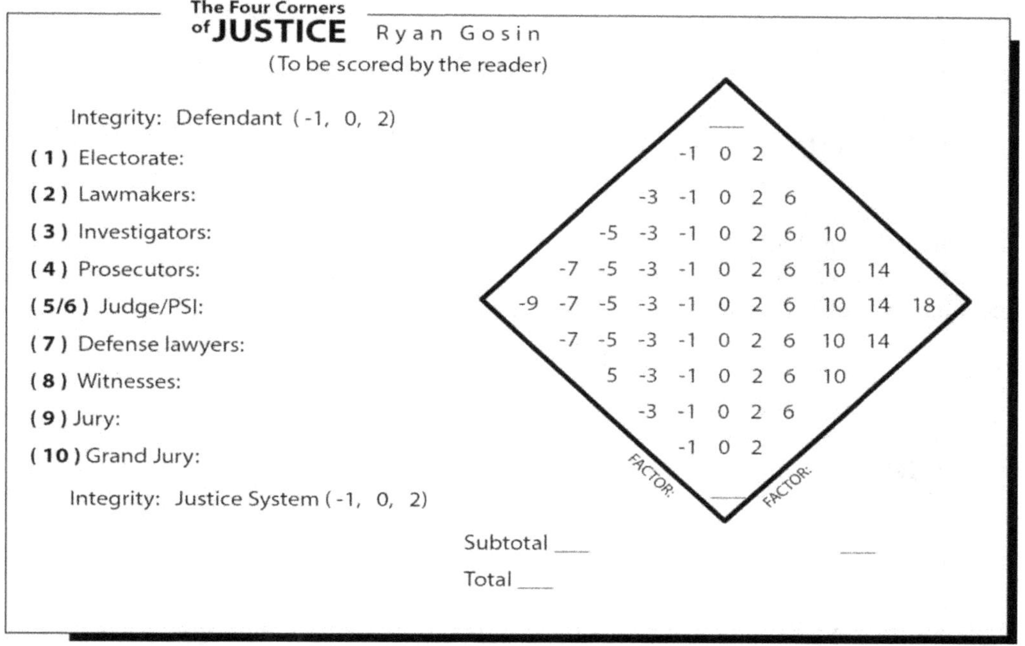

The Four Corners of JUSTICE
Ryan Gosin
(To be scored by the reader)
Integrity: Defendant (-1, 0, 2)
(1) Electorate:
(2) Lawmakers:
(3) Investigators:
(4) Prosecutors:
(5/6) Judge/PSI:
(7) Defense lawyers:
(8) Witnesses:
(9) Jury:
(10) Grand Jury:
Integrity: Justice System (-1, 0, 2)
-1 0 2
-3 -1 0 2 6
-5 -3 -1 0 2 6 10
-7 -5 -3 -1 0 2 6 10 14
-9 -7 -5 -3 -1 0 2 6 10 14 18
-7 -5 -3 -1 0 2 6 10 14
5 -3 -1 0 2 6 10
-3 -1 0 2 6
-1 0 2
FACTOR:
FACTOR:
Subtotal
Total

Author's Verdicts

Ryan Gosin: Innocent
Crime: None
Malicious Intent: None
Victim: None
Loss: None

Judicial System: Guilty
Crime: Institutional Arrogance
Malicious Intent: Yes
Victims: Ryan Gosin, his wife and children, thirty-three co-defendants, and the American people
Loss: Dignity, Honor, Truth, Justice, Integrity, time, resources, and possibility

Alternative Outcome

After an investigation, the Department of Justice determined that Ryan Gosin, a husband, father, and businessman, unwittingly violated federal banking statutes. Gosin used a "straw man" to secure bank loans for real estate. After a meeting between U. S. Attorney, John I. Dogood, Gosin, and his attorney, Gosin said he unknowingly made a mistake. He accepted responsibility and agreed to pay a fine of $10,000.00 per loan. His decision to cooperate precludes the need for an unnecessary trial that would have destroyed his life and family. Mr. Dogood's temperance and sense of dignity ensured accountability to the law and allowed federal authorities to educate the public. Mr. Dogood is a credit to his profession.

Author's FCOJ Scores: Electorate: -1, Lawmakers: -1, Investigators: -3, Prosecutor: -3, Judge/PSI: -3, Defense Lawyers: -3, Witnesses: 0, Jury: -1, Grand Jury: -1, Integrity Defendant: 0, Integrity Justice System: -1

Tony Figueroa

Year: 2012
Occupation: Mechanical Engineer
Marital Status: Married
Children: 4
Criminal History: None
Spiritual Beliefs: Unknown
Age: 45
Education: High School
Summary: Tony is everyone's friend. An affable man, his positive attitude reflects his love of people and life. This is a major reason he excelled at his work.

The Particulars

Original Charges: Bid Rigging/Conspiracy to Bid Rigging
Actual Charges: Wire Fraud/Mail Fraud/Conspiracy
Trial: Yes
Verdict: Guilty
Plea: No
Sentence: 36 months
Appeal: Yes
Summary: Tony Figueroa was originally accused of bid rigging; but he was convicted of wire fraud, mail fraud, and conspiracy. He refused to become a government witness or accept a plea. He went to trial and was found guilty.

The Case of Tony Figueroa

In 2006, the Federal Government began an investigation into the allegations of a bid rigging scam at a private New York hospital. The government eventually asserted that $300 million in funds and contracts were rigged and bids were fraudulently awarded to contractors. Since his boss was under investigation, Tony Figueroa was implicated. Yet, the prosecution never secured a conviction for bid rigging. This charge was never pursued. After a jury trial, the jurors rendered a guilty verdict for lesser charges of wire fraud and wire fraud conspiracy.

The Federal Government acquired jurisdiction through the function of banking. Since money was sent across state lines, *interstate commerce* occurred. The government applied pressure upon those who may or may not have been involved. Tony stated that he was not involved in bid rigging. Now he found himself as a defendant in a wire fraud conspiracy, a crime he did not commit. His only option was to snitch on his boss and any complicit contractor. However, Tony would not become a rat. First, he had no knowledge of any crime. Second, he would not compromise his loyalty for unfounded suspicions. He knew of his innocence and believed he would not be indicted. When he was charged with wire fraud, even though he had no responsibility for any of the finances at the hospital, he was shocked.

Tony disclosed that while he did not commit any federal crime, he did violate hospital rules. He accepted gifts from senior managers at the hospital and contractors, and from more than those accused of a crime. Tony was no different from any other hospital employee. Accepting gifts was part of the culture. Whether for holidays, birthdays or special occasions, gifts were given by contractors. This practice was no different from other companies. Contractors showed appreciation for employees.

Tony admits attending social functions or receiving tickets to professional basketball games courtesy of contractors. He received gift cards and cash bonuses at Christmas. He invited contractors to his wedding and received gifts from them like any other guest. Whoever received gifts as employees at the hospital, be it Tony, the secretary, or accounts payable personnel, this was the practice. There was nothing nefarious about these gift-giving gestures. It was not a hidden practice, but an open custom. The giving or receiving of gifts was not a federal crime. Tony was neither reprimanded nor disciplined by his superiors; but the federal authorities charged him for accepting gifts equaling more than $30,000.00 over a six-year period under mail fraud and conspiracy.

Having violated no federal law, the catch-all charge of conspiracy was available. The U. S. Attorney decided this crime occurred since the contracts and payments between the hospital and contractors were mailed through the United States (federal) Postal Service. By virtue of accepting gifts (*which were not sent by mail*), mail fraud was used.

Since Tony was charged with both wire fraud and mail fraud, the U. S. Attorney attempted to combine them into one case. Tony believed the government had no real case against him and the U. S. Attorney wanted to bolster the first charge with a second offense. The judge, however, decided these were separate issues which required separate trials. This is an important point. Tony weighed the prosecutor's heavy-handed motives. He was innocent and he knew the U. S. Attorney would not accept this fact.

According to Tony, he was a valued employee at the hospital. He was promoted based upon his performance and eventually entered management. The president of the hospital once stated Tony would be the first vice-president at the facility without a college degree; and the hospital would pay his tuition to Cornell University. Tony took his responsibilities seriously. He realized he had a tremendous opportunity.

At his level of management, he had little to do with the bidding process and had no role with the approval of contracts. He only had the ability to consent to bids under $50,000.00 which he then sent to his boss. His boss forwarded the bids to those who had the power of approval. Furthermore, Tony had no responsibility for payments or transfers of funds. With so little opportunity to commit a crime for the charges alleged, Tony wondered why the government investigated him for over six years. They could find no evidence of wrongdoing.

The U. S. Attorney did not seek an indictment until the statute of limitations was about to expire. As he pursued each crime, he enticed Tony to admit to his guilt. Tony was encouraged to snitch on his boss. The FBI agents called Tony on his cell phone early in the investigation and asked him questions and learned when he would leave work. When Tony arrived at this home that evening, the same agents approached him. They asked him about his work, finances, and his associations. They postured with the intent to agitate and instill fear. Tony remained strong.

When the agents queried how he received the funds for the down payment for his truck, Tony asked why that mattered. He had a great job and was paid well. When the agents produced a copy of the check Tony used to pay the lease, he looked at the agents and said, "This conversation is over." Scare tactics. The agents sought to intimidate and force cooperation. Tony wasn't interested.

The government had no evidence against him, but officials needed Tony's assistance. He was essential to their case. He was the pivotal person who could confirm his superior's complicity. Tony, however, secured the services of a skilled attorney, who candidly said he did not represent "rats." Tony assured him that he had no intention of turning in a case which did not involve him. His attorney received calls from the U. S. Attorney who asked if his client was ready to cooperate. He wanted Tony as a witness.

Tony soon learned that a former contractor for the hospital, who was once a policeman, copped a plea to the original big rigging charge which was never pursued in court. This witness waited over five years for the case to conclude before he could move on with his life as a felon who served no prison time. While Tony did not know what evidence this witness was shown, he knew the charge of bid rigging was not a factor. Tony believed the government wanted this witness to justify a bid rigging case. The squealing and capitulation of one witness was used by the prosecutor to pressure other suspects. Tony remained undeterred. He believed the government was on a fishing expedition.

Eventually a second witness agreed to a plea. David Porath, another contractor, once an employee for the hospital, caved to the U. S. Attorney's threats. This development was significant; for it was Porath who influenced the jury's determination of guilt for all defendants. The FBI and prosecutor used Porath to their advantage. Porath wore a wire to entrap Tony. With the wire, Porath met Tony twice at the hospital and steered the conversation to the alleged bid rigging scam. The FBI wanted Tony to offer incriminating testimony. Nothing of the sort materialized.

The recorded conversations between Porath and Tony revealed that it was Porath who offered testimony. As both men bantered about the supposed scam, Tony made a comment. He said such an endeavor (the scam), if it existed, would be one where a hospital employee "would be writing reqs (requisitions), so they (contractors) can issue checks." Porath responded by stating, "Don't want to issue checks." Tony replied, "No checks here." Tony put his feet up and onto his desk, leaned back in his chair, and, while gesturing with his arms stretched out wide, said, "No worries here." When Tony gestured, he referred to himself and his office. The U. S. Attorney used the statement, "writing reqs so they can issue checks," as the refrain which would set the tone of the trial.

Tony was not like defendants who are often forced to use public defenders, lawyers provided by the government, often private attorneys who lacked experience. Tony had an established and experienced lawyer and Tony duly compensated him. The fact that his lawyer despised snitches appealed to Tony. He was encouraged that his lawyer wanted to win. So, his attorney instructed him as to what he was to do and not to do and where to be and what to say. His legal representative took command of a client subject to a process which was often arbitrary and conflicted with what was just.

Tony's capable defense team was made stronger as each of his co-defendants had equally qualified counsel. With all four lawyers and staffs collaborating, Tony was confident the truth would prevail. Yet, when Tony was convicted, his lawyer was shocked. He told Tony that he had never seen a man convicted with so little evidence.

Before the trial began on January 9th, a court hearing on the 4th addressed the admissibility of the Porath tapes. For, in November, Porath had fled to Israel and was unavailable for questioning and cross-examination at trial. In response to this development, Tony's lawyer wrote a legal brief against the admission of the tapes and cited precedent under the Sixth Amendment to the Constitution. This amendment forbids the testimony of witnesses who are not able to be cross-examined.

> *In all criminal prosecutions, the accused shall... be informed of the nature and cause of the accusation, to be confronted with the witnesses against him...*[38]

Porath was unavailable for the prosecution and the defense could not clarify the content of the tapes. Thus, the admissibility of the tapes was crucial. In Tony's mind, the government would not be harmed if the tapes were allowed, but he would be injured.

Surprisingly, the judge denied the defense motion to exclude the tapes which were admitted without restriction. Tony's lawyer was shocked and certain the judge committed

[38] Amendment VI, The Constitution of the United States

a reversible error. He noted his objection into the record and his intent to appeal. The court knew Porath was a fugitive and unavailable for questioning. The defense requested an "in camera" hearing (a private conversation in the judge's chambers) to request access to the 302s from the FBI. The 302s are documents which summarize the content of tapes and would confirm comments made by Tony to Porath. When the U. S. Attorney assured the judge that the 302s validated what was recorded, the judge denied this request as well.

The next day the prosecutor *learned* Porath had waived his extradition hearing in Israel. When he fled the United States in November, he was apprehended by Israeli authorities shortly after. Noteworthy, Porath was not fighting his return. Tony and his lawyer did not know of this fact until after the trial ended six weeks later. Not only did the government know Porath was under arrest in Israel in November, but the day after the tapes were also admitted as evidence, Porath could have been flown to New York to testify.

Days after the trial ended, Tony's lawyer received a phone call from the U. S. Attorney. He said the call was strange. He noted that the federal prosecutor almost sounded remorseful. Yet, there was no justification for the call. The U. S. Attorney informed him of Porath's status without reason to do so. The verdicts had been issued. Nonetheless, Tony's lawyer, considering Porath's heretofore unknown availability, especially with the government's foreknowledge, filed motions under rules 29 and 33, judgment of acquittal and a new trial, respectively. The judge denied both.

At trial, when the prosecution and defense finished the presentation of their arguments, the jury prepared to deliberate. They had endured testimony and evidence that was technical and tedious. They then withstood over an hour-long monologue of jury instructions. Their deliberations would be governed by these terms, definitions, and the conditions of these guidelines. The jurors were informed that they would determine the facts; the judge would tell them the law. From Tony's perspective, the *facts,* which included the five minutes of taped conversation, admitted without the opportunity to cross-examine Porath, confirmed his guilt.

Unexpectedly, the jury asked for the tapes and transcripts during their closed-door deliberations. However, the court denied their requests and only allowed them to have the five minutes previously admitted. The jurors gave the appearance that they considered Tony's innocence only to decide he was part of the conspiracy.

When the jury foreman read the verdict, Tony stood motionless. He was stunned to hear the guilty verdict. He was in disbelief. His wife was in tears. She grieved when she realized her husband was going to prison for a crime he did not commit. He would serve time because he did not roll in a case in which he had no knowledge of a crime. Tony's wife could only hope the defense lawyer would prevail on appeal or the judge would sentence Tony appropriately with no prison sentence.

Tony had no criminal history. His record was clean. Yet, his record would have little impact on the PSI points used to determine the range of months he would serve. The only other factor that would affect the total, other than the standard number of points for the actual crime of wire fraud, was the loss to the injured party. But there was no injured party. The hospital did not suffer a loss. The hospital did not overpay for any of the work. The contractors accused of providing money to a hospital employee were not the highest bidders for the approved proposals. The hospital officials testified that all work was compliant with code and completed in a quality standard. However, while the hospital did not suffer a loss, the law allowed the judge to substitute the gain received by the beneficiary of the wired funds. The gain was $2.35 million that was transferred from the contractor to Tony's boss over a six-year period.

Tony did not have a gain. Any gifts he received would have been given to and accepted by Tony if there was no alleged crime or investigation. So the relevance of the PSI Report and the recommended points were significant. The PSI allowed for the points to be calculated at 16. After adding the points for the actual crime, the total was greater than 25. Tony, with no gain realized from the bids, received the same point value as those culpable for the crime. Everyone received the same points regardless that some were not involved and did not profit in any way. Tony was stuck to the tar baby and could not free himself. He faced a sentence of up to five years.

On the day of sentencing, Tony observed that the judge appeared as inflexible as he was during the trial. He not only denied Tony the possibility of remaining free pending appeal, but he also imposed a prison term of three years to begin almost immediately.

Tony's problems were not over though. He still faced charges for mail fraud and mail fraud conspiracy. The U. S. Attorney, after he prevailed with the first conviction, expeditiously offered Tony a deal he could not refuse. The government would not request additional prison time to his sentence if he pleaded guilty. Tony was certain he would be found guilty if he went to trial. The federal authorities secured another victory and a man, who only violated hospital rules, accepted guilt to avoid the inevitable. Though he never received gifts in the mail—with no malicious intent and no injured party—Tony was not willing to fight the second federal case. As far as he was concerned, since the prosecutor's premise was that gifts were tied to contracts and payments sent through the mail, a guilty plea was a lie. From Tony's perspective, the truth was never a concern from the beginning.

Analysis of Tony Figueroa

With a degree of objectivity, we may discern how Tony Figueroa was found guilty. The government simply presumed so. This presumption was easy and necessary. The government could not prove the bid rigging charge; so it defaulted to its secondary attack of wire fraud and wire fraud conspiracy. Trials based upon conspiracies are easy to win.

The case involved a private New York corporation and private contractors performing services for the hospital. But for the wire fraud charge and mail fraud, the federal authorities would not have prosecuted the case. Even under the guise of banking, why claim jurisdiction? Why not encourage the New York Attorney General to prosecute?

Tony asserted that he had no authority to approve bids or handle finances at the hospital. If we accept his word that he did not collude with those responsible for a crime, we will naturally question why he was charged with conspiracy. The U. S. Attorney had no evidence which indicated Tony's complicity. Give this thought the attention it deserves—there was no evidence. We may conclude that arrogance served as the impetus for a wrongful prosecution. Not only did the prosecutor want a conviction at all costs, but he would also not even consider dropping the Figueroa case after six years of investigation.

So, what did the prosecutor do along the way? He encouraged suspects to become witnesses. If he could convince Tony to cooperate, his case would gain credibility. Yet, Tony had no firsthand knowledge of a crime. He would have had no justification to assist the government. He also genuinely believed the government had no case against him. Consider one of the two witnesses convinced to cooperate. Whether or not Porath was guilty, we know he was fearful of the unknown. He fled the country. He assured his own safety and security largely because of his own ignorance. He became apathetic to whatever principles and integrity he once might have had. His comfort was a priority to the inconvenience that would ensue if he did not cooperate. Does not Porath's behavior and decisions prove that the government prevails when men acquiesce under threats and force?

The jury's guilty verdict reflects this force. With and through Porath's *testimony*, the government assured that questionable circumstances surrounding Porath's absence served its objective. The judge's willingness to pave the path for Porath's taped conversations into the proceeding facilitated the use of force. Clearly, the prosecutor knew Porath was affected by ignorance, apathy, and fear, and driven by the same psychological and emotional motives as any other witness. It was easy for the prosecutor to direct Porath's capitulation (by force) to the intended audience, the jury. The court was the conduit which ensured that the message was heard.

Thankfully for the U. S. Attorney, Porath *produced* what was necessary to win. Yet, it would be reasonable to question why the prosecutor took seven words from the tapes and crafted a limited context of their meaning. The words "writing reqs so they can issue checks" represented three seconds of five minutes of testimony, taken from five hours of taped conversation. These words and the government's interpretation did not represent the truth. The prosecutor fabricated what contained no evidence against Tony. The prosecutor knew he would be able to frame Tony into the crime.

Once the FBI finished its investigation, the U. S. Attorney had to make some decisions. Since he was not able to convince Tony to snitch or plead to a lesser charge, he had to convince the grand jury to indict him.

There are moments of truth for those public officials beholden to properly execute their authority and maintain the public trust. Is this difficult for prosecutors who must determine which *criminals* to prosecute for *crimes* against humanity? While U. S. Attorneys are motivated by each conviction, the extent to which they wrestle over any baseless charge is not known. However, we may conclude that men such as Tony are presumed guilty because they do not cooperate. Men like Tony become dispensable.

Ask the obvious. What did the prosecutor presume? Tony was direct in line to his boss. According to the presumption, Tony had to know of any illegal activity. Such a conclusion was no different than the presumption of a bid rigging scam that only ended in a wire fraud charge. As such, the *facts* portrayed to the grand jury were not as represented to the jury. Additionally, Tony was guilty by association. The grand jurors never saw this possibility; they were never shown this possibility. A mid-level manager with no knowledge of or involvement with a crime was associated with his boss by virtue of employment. He, therefore, faced the same charges as those who were truly guilty.

Had the grand jury asked if Tony committed a crime or had malicious intent, they may have had enough doubt to prevent his indictment. It is difficult for a grand jury to separate one man from a conspiracy when the government intends to implicate him. Once again, the force of government is unquestionable.

With the force Tony faced, the fact that he did not become a government snitch is noteworthy. The impact of the investigation and trial were overwhelming. He faced legal fees into the hundreds of thousands of dollars. He humbly confronted the possibility of an undeserved prison sentence. Did he make the right decision?

Since Tony did not know about the scam and was not involved, accepting a plea would have been easy. Yet, Tony could decide no differently. Had he become an informant, his decision would have been predicated upon a lie. Alas, Tony's lawyer was confident he would not be found guilty. As such, Tony felt his attorney's surprise; for he stated that he had never seen anyone convicted with so little evidence. It is not difficult to see how this verdict materialized. The prosecution relied upon the contrived. Thus, a challenge of the tapes and direct questioning of Porath were essential for Tony's defense.

The judge's decision about the Porath tapes is irreconcilable. He did not deny the admission of the tapes. He did not grant access to the 302s. He did not postpone the trial. He did not allow for a new trial once all knew Porath could have testified. The nature of the Porath developments is highly suspect. The government knew Porath waived extradition. Did the prosecutor know this fact as of the 5th of January? Did the prosecutor know Porath was arrested as of November? Did the prosecutor foreclose the fairness the defense deserved by finagling and withholding his knowledge of Porath's status? Did the prosecutor take advantage of the judge with actions and decisions that were scandalous and based upon facts he alone understood?

The idea that the prosecutor bothered to call Tony's defense lawyer after the trial is noteworthy. Perhaps he suffered from professional guilt. If he had no obligation to inform the defense of Porath's arrest in November, he certainly was not beholden to reveal Porath's current disposition. We must challenge the circumstances concerning Porath and the prosecutor's foreknowledge of his potential availability. The U. S. Attorney's conduct had to be prosecutorial misconduct. If the *system* does not consider his conduct as questionable, it should give us pause and reason to dispute the system's legitimacy.

A fundamental tenet of the judicial process is that defendants must be able to confront their accusers. Is there any doubt of the possibility that the prosecutor knowingly circumvented Tony's ability to defend himself? Is there any doubt the court sanctioned this egregious abuse? It could be determined that this was an injustice and criminal.

If we consider the arrogance which influences a prosecutor to force facts which are inconsistent with the truth, we understand such negligence as represented by the Porath situation. We know why the prosecutor did not want to secure this witness for trial. We know why he neglected to tell the defense of Porath's status before the trial began. We understand why he argued for the admission of the tapes. With Porath conveniently absent, the tapes became virtually invincible and indisputable. The U. S. Attorney opened and closed the trial with arguments which were weighed by the jury, the trier of the facts, stating the mantra "writing reqs so they could issue checks." With Porath absent, the U. S. Attorney assured himself of his objective, almost certain guilty verdicts.

Tony did not make statements or testimonials to Porath. This is a critical point. Efforts to gather evidence by wiretap are predicated upon the perpetrator making testimonials which implicate his participation in a crime. A witness who wears the wire, asks questions, and makes idle banter is not condemning. A witness who makes statements is not helpful when attempting to entrap another. It was Porath, according to Tony, who made statements to have Tony do the same. Since Tony was not involved in any criminal activity, he would have had no reason to incriminate himself.

Porath was the central figure in this trial. He caused the judge to reveal his predisposition against the defense. The judge showed his prejudice at least three different times and each centered on Porath. Tony's lawyer believed the judge was so inflexible he risked reversal on appeal. The use of the term *prejudice* is deliberate. The judge made decisions contrary to the defendant's interests and justice. His bias cannot be reconciled.

Consider the following. If the prosecutor knew of Porath's status in the least, as early as November and throughout the trial, his ploys were purposeful and cleverly orchestrated. He used the court, as he did the grand jury, to press his agenda. The judge, who was to serve as the impartial arbiter of the proceedings, was yet another tool used to secure verdicts of guilt. We would be remiss if we discounted the U. S. Attorney's intention to manipulate not only the court, but also an innocent man's rights to secure an acquittal. The prosecutor's efforts to even remotely disparage the wholesome benefits of the Sixth Amendment smacks of the arrogance required to achieve this dubious end.

The judge's deliberate or unintentional foreclosure of Tony's right to confront a witness in hopes of rebutting any innuendo or *factual* assertions was inconsistent with his authority. We must consider the arrogance of the judge and his motives. Perhaps he was not as learned about the Sixth amendment, or he cared little for such rights. Perhaps he was compelled to decide as he did because of his political or social leanings. To punish those involved with big business may have been his judicial tendency and the reason for his lack of impartiality. A judge's arrogance would serve as a *law* exercised as a personal prerogative wholly indifferent to the rights of the defendant.

The judge's decisions had grave significance and were foreshadowed at an earlier hearing well before the trial. The judge reacted to a documented comment made by one of the other defendants. The defendant purportedly stated the cliché, "Don't bite the hand that feeds you." The judge, without knowing the context of this statement, looked at the prosecutor and defense and exclaimed, "We all know what that means." The judge clearly telegraphed his sentiment. He overtly editorialized from the bench about a comment which had yet weathered exposure in a trial. Thus, Tony's lawyer should not have been surprised that this judge was so unfavorable to his filings. We should not be surprised with how he handled the Porath situation.

The judge in Tony's case happened to be liberal-minded. His brand of politics likely influenced his disdain for greed and big business. Consequently, he may have judged Tony as guilty before the trial began. In fact, the judge's decisions made post trial underscored his leanings throughout.

Tony suffered from inherent inadequacies of the judicial establishment. The actors who played the role of prosecutor and judge could have performed their parts differently. This thought should compel us to reconsider how we view the judicial system. As far as Tony was concerned, the judge lacked integrity. The prosecutor was no different. He espoused characterizations which were incomplete and portrayed them as true. The jury received these falsehoods as well as the judge's decisions and directives. Tony was at the mercy of twelve jurors who were afflicted and conflicted with what they observed.

Here is the truth. Only after the investigation began did Tony have suspicions that his boss and a particular contractor were involved with remuneration for bids which were eventually approved. The investigation prompted his suspicions, and this was the extent of his *knowledge*. Tony was an honest and loyal employee. Even the senior management at the hospital testified that Tony's promotions were based upon merit and not association.

Tony's knowledge of what was truth was diametrically opposed to the government's position. The prosecutor began and ended the trial with his "reqs for checks" refrain. It was a jingle which served as a marketing ploy. While we do not know whether a cross-examination of Porath would have reduced the effect of this refrain, we do know Tony was found guilty without challenging Porath. Tony hoped the jury would see through the lie; he hoped for what would not be.

Tony and his family were devastated. Did the jurors give up? Did they believe the prosecutor's story since the defense could not effectively rebut assertions from the tapes? We don't know what influenced their decision. But we do know they endured a long five-week trial. We can surmise they were psychologically and emotionally fatigued.

Tony could not reconcile a justice system which operated with such depraved and questionable intent. He wondered how Americans could settle for a process which encouraged what was incongruent with the truth. The answer is simple. When principles and integrity are lacking, the innocent suffer. Families suffer. America suffers. Undoubtedly, Tony and his family suffered.

The Four Corners of Justice—Tony Figueroa

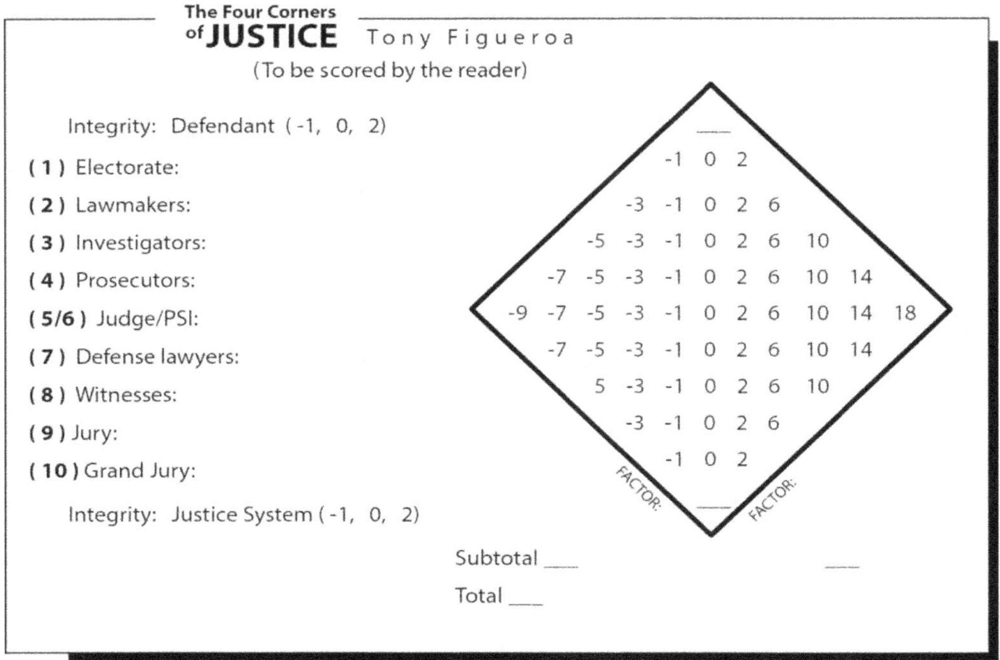

The Four Corners
of JUSTICE Tony Figueroa
(To be scored by the reader)
Integrity: Defendant (-1, 0, 2)
(1) Electorate:
(2) Lawmakers:
(3) Investigators:
(4) Prosecutors:
(5/6) Judge/PSI:
(7) Defense lawyers:
(8) Witnesses:
(9) Jury:
(10) Grand Jury:
Integrity: Justice System (-1, 0, 2)
-1 0 2
-3 -1 0 2 6
-5 -3 -1 0 2 6 10
-7 -5 -3 -1 0 2 6 10 14
-9 -7 -5 -3 -1 0 2 6 10 14 18
-7 -5 -3 -1 0 2 6 10 14
5 -3 -1 0 2 6 10
-3 -1 0 2 6
-1 0 2
FACTOR:
FACTOR:
Subtotal
Total

Author's Verdicts

Tony Figueroa: Innocent
Crime: None
Malicious Intent: None
Victim: None
Loss: None
Judicial System: Guilty
Crime: Institutional Arrogance
Malicious Intent: Yes
Victim: Tony Figueroa, his wife and children, friends, and family
Loss: Dignity, Honor, Truth, Justice, Integrity, and loss of time and money
American People: Guilty
Crime: Ignorance, Apathy and Fear
Malicious Intent: Yes
Victim: The Figueroa family and their neighbors
Loss: Freedom, Present, and future possibility

Alternative Outcome

Federal authorities investigated a "kickback" scam at a New York hospital where an official received remuneration from a private contractor for each secured bid. The U. S. Attorney met with a subordinate, Tony Figueroa, and decided Figueroa was not aware of the scam. The prosecutor did not charge Figueroa. Such fairness ensured justice.

Author's FCOJ Scores: Electorate: 0, Lawmakers: 0, Investigators: -3, Prosecutor: -5, Judge: -3, Defense Lawyers: 6, Witnesses: -3, Jury: 0, Grand Jury: -1. Integrity Defendant: 2, Integrity Justice System: -1

On December 17, 2013, I read a caption on a national news show which addressed the Eric Snowden and National Security Agency spy scandal. The headline stated that the agency justified its mining of personal data of ***U. S. persons****. I remarked how the public was, once again, the target of disinformation. Most Americans would accept and few would challenge the assertion that they were U. S. persons. They would not even question the use or definition of this legal term. How regrettable, I thought, we willingly accept the "truth" fed to us by the United States Government.* **The Author**

The Word and the Law

Words are the essence of language. Without words, most expressions would be vastly nullified. Words edify and clarify. They describe, inspire, or defeat. As equally as words are used for good, they are employed for nefarious ends. Language that is not clear leads to confusion, a condition which culminates in ignorance, apathy, and fear.

Consider the word *person.* Everyone has an idea what this word means. Yet, in the legal arena, the common man's definition is inconsistent with the meaning in law. Title 1 of the United States Code (USC), section 1 states,

> *In determining the meaning of any Act of Congress, unless the context indicates otherwise—*
> *the words "person" and "whoever" include corporations, companies, associations, firms, partnerships, societies, and joint stock companies as well as individuals;*

Person is defined as *entities* as well as individuals. This definition is unexpected.

If we look at other statutes, we learn that *person* may only be natural persons as defined under *28 USC 1915* and not an artificial entity as defined above. (Be mindful of the special treatment of the word *person* as it relates to *aliens*.)

> *Despite Dictionary Act's General rule (1 USC 1), artificial entity such as association is not "person" for purposes of 28 USC 1915; only natural persons may qualify for treatment in forma pauperis, since the sole reason for amendments changing "citizen" to person was to extend benefits to aliens... Case Notations, Section 8, 1 USC 1*

This reflects how one word is changed to accommodate the inclusion of a separate *class* of people and the exclusion of entities that are not *persons or individuals* within other sections of law.

We are confronted with a rather obvious dynamic. In the legal realm, words and definitions are changed or manipulated to fit the intent of the lawmakers. Regrettably, even after multiple readings, we may still not understand the meaning of a word much less the code. The point should be clear. While we are expected to *know* the law, with countless code sections, reading the law and comprehending the law are two separate issues. The following will be an important exercise. Since most of us have never read anything from the statutes, referred to as the United States Code, these citations will be revealing.

We may discover that common words used with little consideration are applied quite differently in law. As we survey specific terms, consider some temporary working presumptions. Let's presume *Americans* are defined as the term "*United States citizens.*" We will presume the term "*United States*" refers to the 50 states of the Union. Whenever *state* is used, we shall presume it refers to the 50 states. With the terms *person* and *individual*, we will presume both apply to "*United States Citizens.*"

Why should we accept the foregoing as our frame of reference? There are several reasons. Since the law is critical to the final case, it is essential that we apply the codes as written and challenge our conventional understanding of words. We must qualify the use of words and determine if the code agrees with our preconceptions as generally accepted definitions, or if we must accept new representations. This will lead to a critical conclusion. We may see that some sections of the code and legal terms do not and cannot apply to most of us. The law, as written, allows for a totally divergent meaning.

Consider the following observations. We will confront a meaning for *United States* which defies our comprehension. We will confront a definition of *state* and *person* and *individual* which are not in agreement with our current understanding. This will force us to reconcile that the code is relevant to an intended subject and no other. Ultimately, we will appreciate two things. First, laws are, at times, written to be incomprehensible or to deceive. Second, the enforcement of law is misapplied to *persons, individuals, citizens,* or whoever is not otherwise subject, whether in one *United States* or another.

This exercise may be tedious, but it is critical. Read the following code sections. Weigh the words and earnestly attempt to understand the meaning. Be patient. Be open-minded. Be teachable. This practical exercise should alter your willingness to accept as fact any gratuitous conclusion offered by agents, officers, representatives, senators, or bureaucrats who are (now pay attention) *employees* of the *employer*, the *United States.*

There is an important concept which is essential to understand when reading anything legal. This concept concerns classifications, groupings, or listings. For example, apples, bananas, cherries, pineapples, and grapes are a listing of a class of food—fruit. The items within the list belong. Anything which belongs and is not listed, like oranges, would be within the class. Oranges are not excluded simply because they were not included in the list, unless specifically excluded. However, carrots, a food which does not belong, would be excluded. Consider another example. All pieces contained within a board game would be part of its contents. Nothing outside of the game box would be included. We would conclude that all else is excluded.

The legal realm is governed by rules which limit what are "included" and "excluded." These rules govern how a law is understood or the rules stipulate what is included by defining the terms "includes" and "including." Since we know the law is what it is and cannot be what is not, this is a critical legal construct to comprehend. Consider the following definitions:

> ***Rule of Rank****—A doctrine of statutory construction holding that a statute dealing with things or persons of an inferior rank cannot by any general words be extended to things or persons of a superior rank.*
> Blackstone gives the example of a statute dealing with deans, prebendaries, parsons, vicars and others having spiritual promotion. According to Blackstone, this statute is held not to extend to bishops, even though they have spiritual promotion, because deans are the highest persons named, and bishops are of a higher order. —Black's Law Dictionary, 9th edition.
>
> ***Ejusdem generis*** [Latin—***of the same class***] *1. A canon of construction holding that when a general word or phrase follows a list of specifics, the general word or phrase will be interpreted to include only items of the same class as those listed.*
> For example, in the phrase "horses, cattle, sheep, pigs, goats or any other farm animals," the general language *any other farm animals*, despite its seeming breadth, would be held to include only four-legged, hoofed mammals typically found on farms, and this would exclude chickens. Black's Law Dictionary, 9th Edition.

Noscitur a sociis [Latin—***it is known by its association***] *A canon of construction holding that the meaning of an unclear word or phrase should be determined by the words immediately surrounding it.* —Black's Law Dictionary, 9th Edition.

The Supreme Court addressed the concept of *ejusdem generis* in Norfolk and Western R. Co., v Train Dispatchers, 499 US 117 (1991),

Under the principle of ***ejusdem generis****, when a general term follows a specific one, the general term should be understood as a reference to subjects akin to the one with specific enumeration.*

The court addressed ***noscitur a sociis*** in Jarecki v G.D Searle & CO., 367 US 303 (1961).

...a word is known by the company it keeps (the doctrine of ***noscitur a sociis****).* This rule we rely upon to avoid subscribing to one word a meaning so broad that it is inconsistent with its accompanying words, thus giving it unintended breadth to the Acts of Congress.

The same term was referenced by Roger Foster in his work, A Treatise on the Federal Income Tax under the Act of 1913.

Sec. 30. ***Judicial Definitions of income****. By the rule of construction, noscitur a sociis, however, the words in this statute must be construed in connection with those to which it is joined, namely 'gains and profits;' and it is evidently the intention, as a general rule, to tax only the profit...not his whole revenue.*

Consider the following definitions.

Expressio unius personae uel rei est exclusion alteruis*—The express mention of one person or thing in a written instrument is equivalent to the express exclusion of all other persons or things.*
Inclusio unuis est exclusion alteruis*—The inclusion of one is the exclusion of another. The certain designation of one person is an absolute exclusion of all others...*
This doctrine decrees that where law expressly describes a particular situation to which it shall apply, an irrefutable inference must be drawn that what is omitted was intended to be omitted or excluded. —Black's Law Dictionary, 6th Edition

We can see that legal terms follow a particular protocol of construction which is quite limiting in nature. This is consistent with the understanding that a code is applicable to a class or designation within a jurisdiction and cannot be all encompassing. The law is applicable to whom or to what it applies. Some codes even define *includes* and *including.*

The terms "includes" and "including" do not exclude things not enumerated which are in the same general class. 26 CFR 403.50. Meaning of terms

(c) ***Includes*** and ***including***. *The term "includes" and "including" when used in a definition contained in this title shall not be deemed to exclude other things otherwise within the meaning of the word defined.* 26 USC 7701 Definitions.

The Supreme Court noted this definition in Montello Salt Co., v Utah, 221 US 452 (1911):

The court [Utah Supreme Court] also considered that the word "including" was used as a word of enlargement, the learned court being of the opinion that such was its ordinary sense. With this we cannot concur.

In another decision, the court stated,

> *It is axiomatic that the statutory definition of the term excludes unstated meanings of that term.* Meese v Keene, 481 US 465 (1987)

Then, in Russello v United States, 464 US 16, (1983), the court decided:

> *[w]here Congress includes particular language in one section of a statute but omits it in another... it is generally presumed that Congress acts intentionally and purposely in the disparate inclusion or exclusion.*

The importance of the context of any given legal term, as expressed specifically within the law, cannot be dismissed. Moreover, we cannot ascribe our own ill-informed presumption of a definition. We must read the law for what it is; for any preconceived notions will likely make the meaning of a term and the law something it is not.

The people of this State do not yield their sovereignty to the agencies which serve them. The people, in delegating authority, do not give their servants right to decide what is good for the people to know and what is not good for them to know. The people insist on remaining informed so that they may retain control over the instruments they have created. **California Government Code Sec. 54950**

The Impact of Words

If the stories of John Hus and Tony Figueroa, both of whom were self-avowed innocent men, were expressed with the intent to deceive or to simply embellish the inadequacies of the injustices within the legal system, with the added intent to malign the government, we would have read a lie. However, if the intentions were honest and we received accurate portrayals of how officials operated in both cases, then the stories are credible. Even if these men were truly guilty, their experiences and the actual judicial process are no less a reality. And, if the men were innocent, they suffered needlessly. While each case may be viewed from differing perspectives, understanding the questionable conduct of government officials or the purposeful manipulation of the legal apparatus are critical. Ultimately, such conduct is manifested by the official *interpretation* and *application* of *words, facts, and law.*

This book is expressed by and through words, as is the law. The deliberate use of terms and meanings is essential. The law must be what it is and may not be what it is not. Terms and meanings are tools which lawyers manipulate and apply with one-sided and even dishonorable intent. This is how lawyers and public officials ply their trade; they parse and splice terms and definitions. Consider impeached President Clinton and his memorable statement, "It depends upon what the meaning of the word 'is' is." Such tactics are employed to obscure, deflect, or accomplish questionable and ignoble ends.

Though states and federal lawmakers create laws which are clear and knowable, some laws are less so. Laws which are not clear may be considered as void for vagueness. An American of average intelligence should be able to read and understand any law. Since we are expected to know the law, understanding law is no small concern. Reason would dictate that if laws are so vague that they are not understood, they must be void in effect.

The nature of language is neglected by happenstance and by design. Whether we recognize this misuse or abuse, the results are deleterious. Ignorance, apathy, fear, and arrogance are strengthened in an environment where language is less than transparent or incomplete. In either case, there is a lack of integrity.

If one does not know how to communicate, a skill which entails reading, writing, listening, speaking, and observing, then ignorance and apathy are inevitable. Furthermore, a lack of understanding leads to greater trepidation. If we consider those who are *educated* within the legal system, lawyers, judges, agents, and investigators, those who are adept at manipulating terms and definitions, we see a contrast. We see their presumptuousness, both written and verbal, as language, as used with specific and dubious designs. Herein rests the problem. The questionable results of the legal system may only prevail because of the force used through the language employed. Force, whether subtle or obvious, is communication. Often the mere expression of—or exercise of—force overshadows any primary message, which is often *the* message.

We need only consider the Ryan Gosin case. The raid upon his home was a display of raw force, force which trumped the message that he was under arrest for a financial crime. There was no need for a raid. A phone call and a knock on the door would have achieved the intended outcome—an arrest for an alleged *paper* crime. While the arrest of

Tony Figueroa was subdued, with his self-surrender to the FBI, the exertion of government power was implied through standard protocol. The government has the guns and resources to do as it wills. The conduct of the U. S. Attorney or judge is no different. With their positions, resources, and corresponding intent, they wield power to sensationalize and subdue an otherwise defeated party.

The presence of force is no less obvious when defendants are offered pleas. The only difference is that the force may be considered *transferred* to the defendant through another officer of the court (the defense attorney), as the defendant considers his own fate. In a formal manner, as if handing him a gun, the defendant is presented the choice to convict himself rather than be convicted by a jury of his peers. If he rejects a self-inflicted eight-year sentence, he risks a fifteen-year sentence for something he did not do. Such force, the use and abuse of power, reflects the essence of the word *arrogance*.

Understanding terms and definitions in the face of force is crucial. Understanding law is paramount. If effectively countering any use of force is unlikely, knowing the truth of what is written is still possible. Yes, in the face of unbearable force, one may still prevail. Consider an illustration which may help explain the impact of words and meanings and how one may prevail with the use of force.

Christians believe in a sovereign God. Their God is believed to be a triune God—a God of three persons. These three persons are referred to as the Trinity—three in one. (Note: Not all Christians believe in the Trinity and not all who believe in the Trinity do so in the same way.) The persons are God the Father, God the Son, and God the Holy Spirit. Surprisingly, the term *trinity* is not in scripture. Thus, we see the importance of words.

Absent definitions and explanations, the concept of this Christian God would be difficult to understand. First of all, the notion that God is actually three persons would be a challenge to accept even with a clear explanation. If scripture did not explain the nature of God, many would excuse His existence or His three-person manifestation. If God's depiction were incomplete, He would be vague and perceived possibly as being without merit. Even if the language were vague, the church, if it had the guns, resources, intent, and power, could force non-believers to *accept* this truth as credible. The force to achieve a religious end is not uncommon throughout history, as evident with the Catholic Church in and within certain sects of the Islamic faith and other religions and cults today.

Those who are not Christians may be unable or unwilling to understand or accept the *truth*—for any number of reasons—that God is comprised of three persons. One such reason is simply disbelief, even if the explanation of the Trinity were crystal clear. If words and definitions that express this God are confusing, disbelief would invariably remain. Men can't or won't be persuaded to believe what they know can't be true. A man who believes that no God exists will not likely change his belief in the advent of a full-frontal assault by church authorities.

We may reasonably conclude that if the correct meaning of a law is not understood, there are a select few who will *not* accept an improper, incorrect, or unclear interpretation and application of law. They will search and fight for the reasonable understanding of law. While most people may succumb to force out of ignorance, apathy, and fear (which would render the truth that much more elusive), the daring can and will dead-reckon toward the truth regardless of the repercussions.

Since the nature of man seeks comfort—since man tends to shrink from controversy—he seeks to preserve rather than suffer loss. If threatened to accept what is not understood or suffer the consequences, many will *believe* even if the words and meanings are unclear. Under the influence of perceived force, which engenders fear, man complies. Such submission is often rooted in ignorance, and it is crippling.

Each of the eight court cases we reviewed may be considered from the perspective of the abuse or misuse of words and the distortion of their meanings. Each man who accepted a plea surrendered as a prison sentence was presented with force. While each man was armed with the truth, their fate was sealed by their own choices. Those like Norris and Gosin, who fought the government's message, were left with no alternative but to submit. They could not win and did not win in a practical sense—although they never relinquished what they knew to be true.

Norris and Gosin were defeated by and through the manipulation of terms and meanings. Any attempt to clarify the interpretation of such terms was vanquished by force. Their efforts were futile. When language lacks clarity, there is a lack of integrity. The law which lacks *full expression* is counter to the purpose of law. There can be no justice when laws are written the avoid full expression of the truth. The result is tyranny, an environment of compelled lies and raw submission. If unable to know the specific intent of law, if the law is enforced with the smallest degree of confusion, we are at the mercy of unbridled and unchecked power alone. There will be no justice and truth is no longer a noble aim of society. Save a revolution of the mind and heart, there is no remedy.

As we explore the final case, which in some way affects all Americans, the use of terms and meanings will become acutely relevant. If we accept that the government—the justice system—acts with impunity, and terms and meanings are used as weapons, we may further appreciate that engagement, enlightenment, and sacrifice are our only solutions. This final case will raise a lot of questions. This is healthy. We need to probe. We need to examine and grapple with language. We must, when the time arises, reject the notion that the government's interpretation and application of the law is always correct.

Consider a simple example. Most believe the term "United States" means one thing alone. If we don't allow for the possibility that our understanding and interpretation of this term is incorrect or incomplete, the varied and credible legal definitions of "United States" will not be known. Appreciating or at least considering other meanings of a term is essential if we are to understand the law, any law, and the proper enforcement of the law.

The term "United States" has many different definitions in the United States Code. It certainly does not have one definition and often one which most of us would not ascribe. Besides the term "United States," we will scrutinize other words as well. For example, the term "person" has sundry definitions which serve the purpose of any given statute. If we refuse to accept these exact meanings, if we refuse to reject what we believe to be true, we reinforce our ignorance.

The law must be rightly divided by public officials and the people. An adage states, "To be forewarned is to be forearmed." If we are forearmed, we may stand firm against an insurmountable and unjust authority exercised by those with titles who act without accountability to the proper and limited meaning of the law.

Consider the following example. I was in a federal district court for an alleged violation of bond. In this hearing, I represented myself. I readily perceived that the judge was very *comfortable* in his venue—excessively so. It was his court, after all. As was evident by his attitude, conduct, and words that he was annoyed. He had already formed his opinion of the *facts* before the hearing began. His belligerent tone confirmed his posture.

I watched as he gave the U. S. Attorney respect and consideration. Yet, when he addressed me, he was condescending and divisive. His was intolerant. At one point I stopped the proceeding. I looked at the judge and directed him to the judicial canons of ethics that govern his conduct. I then specifically asked if he would grant me the same courtesy and consideration that he afforded the prosecutor.

The judge was floored. The tone of the proceeding changed dramatically. He sat in absolute silence, and, by design, he did not speak. Rather, he nodded his head in quiet acknowledgment. Why? He knew I was right, and he did not want to verbally articulate into the record an affirmation of his questionable conduct, conduct which could easily be held suspect considering his final ruling, *a ruling subject to appeal*. This federal judge was held to account for his conduct when moments before he disparaged a man's rights and recourse for justice.

If we fail to educate ourselves, we allow the system to act with impunity. We fail to assert not only rights we should covet, but we fail to restrain officials to the confines of their office and the law. Any official who exceeds his authority negates the proper application of the law. We may conclude that if we fail to assert our rights with a proper understanding and application of the law then we have no rights. We reduce our existence to one of self-imposed ignorance, a sentence which is a prelude to greater injustices.

It is worthy to note, there is a process by which laws are created. Lawmakers in Congress consider proposed legislation. With majority agreement, legislation is passed by the House of Representatives and the Senate. The bill is then forwarded to the President. He either signs or vetoes the bill. The laws are referred to as the "Statutes-At-Large." The Statutes-At-Large are then codified as the United States Code (USC) and posted in the Federal Register. The Federal Register serves as a notice to the people that the law exists. If the statute or any portion is not posted, it is not enforceable within the 50 states of the Union. The Codes are then received by the agencies responsible for the enforcement of the law. These agencies create regulations which govern enforcement by its officers and agents. These are known as the Code of Federal Regulations (CFR). The CFRs are also posted in the Federal Register. If not posted, they are not enforceable within the 50 states.

The USC is the evidence of the law for which the people are held accountable. Each section of any given code typically corresponds to a section within the CFR, the "implementing regulations." Without implementing regulations, the code is not enforceable within the 50 states of the Union.

The regulations are important. They govern not only the enforcement of the law, but they also govern the scope of authority of the agency and its officers. However, the CFR and USC are not necessarily in complete agreement. The CFRs tend to be more expansive than the language in the code. When the meaning of the CFR is not in agreement with the meaning of the USC, the constraints of the code prevail.

How the USC is written is significant. For example, the actual title to a given code section is not law and has no bearing upon the law. Consider 26 USC 1, which is contained within the tax code. The title is "Married individuals filing joint returns and surviving spouses." This title is not law and has no relevance whatsoever upon the text of the law. Section 4 of 3 USC, which concerns the President, is another example. The title, "Vacancies in Electoral College," is not law. The title may not influence the actual understanding of the law. In both instances, the titles, if not understood to be inconsequential, may skew how the codes are interpreted. This should underscore that the construction of the law is equal in importance to its words and definitions. The law is what it is and may not be what it is not.

The jurisdiction of a law is also crucial. A law may not be enforced where it does not apply. It should be transparent that the laws of the United States may not be enforced in China. China is a separate jurisdiction with its own laws. However, an alien from China who is within the United States is subject to all applicable laws according to his status.

There are codes which do not apply to the 50 states or Americans. If we are oblivious to this fact, we fail to comprehend the full extent of our freedom and the constraints of governing authorities. Conversely, when we limit our understanding of the law, we naturally impose a false application and limit our lives—physically, mentally, emotionally, or spiritually. Suffice it to say, much of the USC applies only to the "United States," the "United States Government," and the "territory" and "persons" within its jurisdiction.

We will explore the issue of jurisdiction of both the law and the agency enforcing its own power as authorized by the law. Suppose a policeman came to your house and knocked on your door. If he asked questions, what would you do? Most would freely answer without hesitation and without knowing the true motivation for the *investigation*. Few would challenge the officer's authority or the law under which he purports to operate. Yet, we have every right to refuse to respond and close the door. We have no reason to divulge information which would compromise ourselves. The policeman does not have jurisdiction simply because he has a title, authority and wears a badge. The agency for which the officer works does not have jurisdiction either, unless and until it has cause. The import of this truth cannot be overstated.

I have been approached by policemen and questioned. Since I was not in the wrong in any respect, I refused to engage them or answer their queries. To the contrary, I asked if I was being detained. When they responded in the negative, I simply walked away. Weigh the implications of being forewarned to this extent, forewarned as to the law and jurisdiction.

If the policemen had breached their proper authority and violated my rights, rights I was willing to assert, they could have been held personally liable for their trespasses against me. Any immunity they possessed would be lost with the exercise of misplaced authority. The result is that accountability is brought to public officials who may not be accustomed to such assertiveness.

As will become evident, a firm knowledge of the law must include an appreciation for jurisdiction. Before governing authorities may impose a law, it must have jurisdiction over person, place, property, or subject matter. Otherwise, the application of the law is without force and effect. While this may appear obvious, we must not take for granted that government may, nonetheless, do what it wants. Consider an illustration.

Years ago, the city council for the principality in which I lived decided to create and enforce a rental inspection ordinance. The intent was to ensure rentals were compliant with the code. The properties had to be sufficiently livable. As such, the council created a *district* which encompassed a majority of the city, a larger portion than the state law permitted.

I formed a group and challenged the ordinance. We asserted that city council exceeded its authority and jurisdiction. Our position was based upon the language of Virginia law. The terms and definitions provided that the city could not do what was done. The officials exceeded the constraints of the law. Ultimately, the council had to reduce the one large district into five smaller districts and conform to the intent of the law. Had the city council not been held accountable to its proper and limited jurisdiction, an abuse of power would have prevailed. Only by knowing the law and a governing authority's jurisdiction or purview and by challenging the wrongful conduct was accountability achieved.

The government of the United States is no different. In many respects, jurisdiction is everything or nothing. Without it, the government has no power. The Constitution identifies specific powers, property, and territory delegated to the government. By virtue of these powers, jurisdiction is established. The Federal Government has authority over these particulars alone. The Federal Government has power in relation to the 50 states in accord with Article 1, Section 8 of the Constitution. This Article lists the powers *delegated* by the 50 states to the Federal Government.

> Article 1—Legislative Department
> Section 8
> Clause 1—Power of Congress—Taxation
> Clause 2—Power of Congress to borrow money
> Clause 3—Power of Congress to regulate commerce
> Clause 4—Naturalization—Bankruptcy
> Clause 5—Coinage, weights, and measures
> Clause 6—Counterfeiting
> Clause 7—Post offices and post roads
> Clause 8—Patents and copyrights
> Clause 9—Inferior tribunals
> Clause 10—Offenses
> Clause 11—Declare war
> Clause 12—Raise and support armies
> Clause 13—Navy
> Clause 14—Government and regulation of land and naval forces
> Clause 15—Calling forth militia
> Clause 16—Organizing militia
> Clause 17—Authority over places purchased or ceded
> Clause 18—All necessary and proper laws

The government is not able to exercise powers beyond those granted. If the government were to exceed its authority, and we know it has and does, such trespasses would be extra-constitutional and outside of its jurisdiction. The same may be said for territory, property, people, and subject matter. The United States may control what it possesses or creates. The government has control over federal forests, but not those of the states. Officers and employees who work for the United States are citizens within its domain, as are resident aliens. The territories of Puerto Rico, Guam, and the Virgin Islands, as well as army posts and naval bases, are within the domain of the United States.

Specific issues or subject matter fall within the purview of the United States federal courts and are equally limited. The Constitution provides for the existence of Article I and Article IV courts, administrative and territorial courts. The Constitution also provides for courts established by Article III, Section 2, which have limited application within the 50 states of the Union.

> *The judicial power shall extend to all Cases in Law and Equity, arising under the Constitution, the Laws of United States and Treaties made, or which shall be made under their authority; to all cases affecting Ambassadors, other Public Ministers and Consuls; to all Cases of admiralty and maritime Jurisdiction; to controversies to which the United States shall be a party; to controversies between two or more states; between state and citizens of the same state claiming Lands under Grants of different states, and between a state, or the citizens thereof, and foreign states, citizens, or subjects.*[39]

The authority of the government is not all encompassing. It can't be. There are those who believe the authority of the government may exceed what others consider to be limited.

Curiously enough, when I researched this topic, seasoned lawyers were not only in

[39] Article III, Section 2, The Constitution of the United States

disagreement as to the scope of authority of the Federal Government, but they were also unaware of some basic concepts of limited constitutional power. While they had opinions and postured as if what they expressed was credible, they were no nearer to the truth than uninformed and aggrandizing politicians or the blindly compliant common man. Of course, what I explain, or present is not necessarily true either. However, I actively seek the truth. My humble attempt to gain an objective understanding, however incorrect or incomplete, is a far cry better than many lawyers, officials, or courts imposing an untruth for an unjust end. As such, let's consider a possible understanding as to how the government gains pervasive jurisdiction under *the law*.

The scope of governmental power and jurisdiction is vital to understand. We will endeavor to piece together a reasonable representation. A balanced explanation will allow us to move forward with proper context as to what the government is authorized to do since what is accomplished by government is done with and through words and definitions.

We know the states of the Union delegated powers to the United States Government under Article 1, Section 8. These powers are included in the Statutes-At-Large and distilled into the United States Code. The codes which correlate to these eighteen powers are known as *positive law*.

Before we define positive law, consider a few thoughts. First, many believe Americans have unalienable rights, rights which cannot be taken away. Second, many believe government may not encroach upon these rights without cause—the Constitution prevents such infringement. Third, fundamental rights are secured by the 50 states, as free and independent states, with the added protection of the Tenth Amendment. Powers not granted to the United States are reserved to the states and the people. With fundamental rights secured, the people recognized that the Constitution acknowledged such rights as "privileges and immunities." Consider the following from the United States Supreme Court in Saenz v Roe, 526 U. S. 489 (1999):

> *Nevertheless, their repeated references to the Corfield decision, combined with what appears to be the historical understanding of the Clauses' operative terms, supports the inference that, at the time the Fourteenth Amendment was adopted, people understood that "privileges and immunities of the citizens" were fundamental rights,* ***rather than every public benefit established by positive law.***

Not only does positive law correlate to the enumerated powers granted to Congress, but they also reflect "public benefits" as well.

Select congressional acts or codes, which have legitimate influence over the 50 states, are positive law. Acts which affect only what is under the jurisdiction of the United States Government and its territories, possessions, forts, etc., are not enacted into positive law. The Acts which are positive law and not enumerated powers under Article 1 may become "public benefits" enjoyed by the 50 states. The states or state citizens may choose to participate in public benefits or privileges created by Congress; however, both would be accountable, consequently, to the federal authority.

The implications of positive law are significant. What does positive law mean?

> ***Positive law****—A system of law promulgated and implemented within a particular political community by political superiors, as distinct from moral law or law existing in an ideal community or in some nonpolitical community. Positive law typically consists of enacted law - the codes, statutes, and regulations that are applied and enforced in the courts. The term derives from the medieval use positum (Latin "established"), so that the phrase positive law literally means*

established by human authority. Also termed jus positivum; made law. —Black's Law Dictionary, Tenth Edition

Law actually and specifically enacted or adopted by proper authority for the government of an organized jural society. —Black's Law Dictionary, Sixth Edition

Jural—*Pertaining to natural or positive right, or to the doctrines of rights and obligations; as "jural relations." Of or pertaining to jurisprudence; juristic; juridical.*
Recognized or sanctioned by positive law; embraced within, or covered by the rules and enactments of positive law. Founded in law; organized upon the basis of a fundamental law, and existing for the recognition and protection of rights.
The "jural sphere" is to be distinguished from the "moral sphere," the latter denoting the whole scope or range of ethics or the science of conduct, the former embracing only such portions of the same as have been made the subject of legal sanction or recognition.
The term "jural society" is used as the synonym of "State" or "organized political community." —Black's Law Dictionary, Sixth Edition

Enact—*To establish by law; to perform or affect; to decree.* —Black's Law Dictionary, Sixth Edition

Based upon these definitions, consider whether you agree with the following assessment: If an Act is enacted into positive law, Congress has the authority sourced in *fundamental law* (the Constitution) for the benefit of the jural society (the Union of the states) for the granting, recognition, and protection of civil rights. Positive law also reflects the powers granted to Congress to accomplish the limited intent of Article 1, Section 8, for and on behalf of the 50 states. Codes which are not enacted into positive law affect the territory, property, and people of the *United States* only. The jurisdiction of the federal authority is not reflective of a jural society. As such, the federal authority does not have the obligation to defer to the recognition and protection of rights; rather, it may control with complete autonomy all that is within its domain—not the 50 states.

The titles listed as positive law, as provided by Title 1 of the United States Code, Chapter 3, Code of Laws, section 204, History; Ancillary Laws and Directives, are:

Title 1—General Provisions
Title 3—The President
Title 4—Flag and Seal, Seat of Government and the States
Title 5—Government Organization and Employees
Title 6—Surety Bonds, Domestic Security
Title 9—Arbitration
Title 10—Armed Forces
Title 11—Bankruptcy
Title 13—Census
Title 14—Coast Guard
Title 17—Copyrights
Title 18—Crimes and Criminal Procedure
Title 23—Highways
Title 28—Judiciary and Judicial Procedure
Title 31—Money and Finance
Title 32—National Guard
Title 34—Navy
Title 35—Patents

Title 36—Patriotic and National Observances, Ceremonies and Organizations
Title 37—Pay and Allowances of Uniformed Services
Title 38—Veteran's benefits
Title 39—Postal Service
Title 40—Public buildings, Property and Works
Title 44—Public Printing and Documents
Title 46—Shipping
Title 49—Transportation
Title 26—Internal Revenue Code (Note: This will receive further discussion.)

The following Acts have not been enacted into positive law:

Title 2—The Congress
Title 7—Agriculture
Title 8—Aliens and Nationality
Title 12—Banks and Banking
Title 15—Commerce and Trade
Title 16—Conservation
Title 19—Custom Duties
Title 20—Education
Title 21—Food and Drugs
Title 22—Foreign Relations and Intercourse
Title 24—Hospitals and Asylums
Title 25—Indians
Title 27—Intoxicating Liquors
Title 29—Labor
Title 30—Mineral Lands and Mining
Title 33—Navigation and Navigable Waters
Title 41—Public Contracts
Title 42—The Public Health and Welfare
Title 43—Public Lands
Title 45—Railroads
Title 47—Telegraphs, Telephones and Radiotelegraphs
Title 48—Territories and Insular Possessions
Title 50—War and National Defense
Title 51—National and Commercial Space Programs

If we review the delegated powers granted to the government under Article 1, Section 8, and compare the Acts enacted into positive law, we clearly see those laws which are not positive law and not in agreement with the delegated powers. To illustrate, the United States Government is responsible for bankruptcy, census, copyrights, patents, armed forces, navy, post office, roads, money, and more. Enacted positive law reflects the exercise of these powers on behalf of the 50 states. The issues of Indians, Aliens and Nationality, War and Defense, Railroads, Territories, and Insular Possessions are unique to the United States Government. The government exercises these powers as a matter plenary power over what is exclusive to its jurisdiction.

Consider these examples. The matter of Indians is handled exclusively by the federal authority. The 50 states have no direct influence with either Indians or the territories and possessions within the inherent authority of the United States. Furthermore, the 50 states do not influence foreign policy. Title 20—Education and the Department of Education did not exist until 1976. The Federal Government did not have power to influence *education* within the 50 states before or after its creation. It cannot be positive law. It is only when the States agreed to participate and received financial remuneration via block grants that this Act applied. It could be said the 50 states voluntarily fell within a *district* of federal control with upon election to participate. Otherwise, Title 20 legislation applied only to federal territories, possessions, and those within its jurisdiction.

As a final example, consider Title 42—The Public Health and Welfare. This is a law created in the1930s. It is not positive law and cannot be made so. This law applies to the federal territories and possessions and *persons* within them. Over these the United States has absolute control. The Social Security Insurance scheme is a federal program designed to provide for those within its domain, which included Alaska and Hawaii at the time. At the time, these two states were territories and not part of the other 48 states. The other states became beholden to this law when each subscribed to it. As with Title 20, the states fell within a district for the purposes of federal control and administration of this law. We should note that although a state may have subscribed to the program, the citizens were not required to participate or receive a social security number. This may, undoubtedly, conflict with what you believe to be true. Yet, it is this conflict which merits a discussion of law, words, definitions, and jurisdiction.

We have covered a healthy amount of information which plainly supports the importance of *jurisdiction.* A government authority may not exercise control over anything or anyone when it lacks jurisdiction. It should be apparent that words and definitions are essential for stating the law and establishing jurisdiction. For example, we will define the term "United States." You may be surprised to learn this term is not what you have believed to be for years. *United States* is not the 50 states necessarily. Throughout the code and regulations this term is defined differently depending upon its usage.

The following definition of ***United States*** within 28 USC, the Judiciary and Judicial Procedure, is an example of what we do not understand.

> 3002 Definitions.
> (15) ***United States*** means
> (A) a federal corporation
> (B) an agency, department, commission, board, or other entity of the United States; or
> (C) an instrumentality of the United States

Most have never read anything within the code, much less a reference to the *United States* as a corporation. We are not taught this in school. What we were taught and what we believe are contrary to this definition. Let's examine meanings for the term "United States" as used throughout the code.

> 2 USC—**The Congress**
> 1966 (F) Definition of ***United States***.
> As used in this section, the term ***United States*** means each of the several States of the United States, the District of Columbia, and territories and possessions of the United States.

> 5 USC—**Government Organization and Employees**
> 5721 Definitions
> (6) "United States" means the several States, the District of Columbia, the Commonwealth of Puerto Rico, the Commonwealth of the Northern Mariana Islands, the territories and possessions of the United States, the areas and installations in the Republic of Panama that are made pursuant to the Panama Canal Treaty of 1977.

7 USC—**Agriculture**
1561 (d)
"***United States"*** means the several States, the Territories of Hawaii and Alaska, the District of Columbia and the Commonwealth of Puerto Rico.

8 USC—**Aliens and Nationality**
1185 Travel Control of Citizens and aliens
(C) Definitions. The term ***United States*** as used in this section includes the Canal Zone, and all territorial waters, continental or insular, subject to the jurisdiction of the United States.

12 USC—**Banks and Banking**
95a
(3) As we used in this subdivision, the term ***United States*** means the United States and any place subject to the jurisdiction thereof [including the Philippines Islands and the several courts of first instance of the Commonwealth of the Philippine Islands shall have jurisdiction in all cases, civil or criminal, arising under this subdivision in the Philippine Islands and concurrent jurisdiction with the district courts of the United States of all cases, civil or criminal, arising upon the high seas.]

12 USC–**Banks and Banking**
4001 Definitions
United States. The term ***United States*** means the several States, the District of Columbia, the Commonwealth of Puerto Rico and the Virgin Islands.

15 USC—**Commerce and Trade**
3301
United States: The term ***United States*** means the several States, the District of Columbia, the Commonwealth of Puerto Rico and the Virgin Islands.

18 USC—**Crimes and Criminal Procedure**
5 ***United States*** defined:
The term ***United States***, as used in this title in a territorial sense, includes all places and waters continental or insular, subject to the jurisdiction of the United States, except the Canal Zone.

19 USC—**Customs Duties**
1308
(8) **United States:** The term ***United States*** means the customs territory of the United States as defined in general note 2 of the Harmonized Tariff Schedule of the United States.

21 USC—**Food and Drugs**
(22) United States. The term ***United States*** means the 50 states of the United States of America and the District of Columbia, the Commonwealth of Puerto Rico, Guam, the Virgin Islands, American Samoa, Wake Island, Midway Islands, Kingman Reef, Johnston Atoll, the Northern Mariana Islands and any other trust territory or possession of the United States.

29 USC—**Labor**
706
(3) The term ***United States*** means (but only for the purposes of this subsection) the 50 States and the District of Columbia.

30 USC—**Mineral Lands and Mining**
(33) ***United States*** means the United States government and any department, agency, or instrumentality thereof, the several States, District of Columbia and the territories of the United States.

33 USC—**Navigation and Navigable Waters**
(8) ***United States***: The term ***United States*** means all areas included within the territorial boundaries of the United States, including the several States, the District of Columbia, the Commonwealth of Puerto Rico, the Virgin Islands, Guam, American Samoa, the Trust Territory of the Philippine Islands, the Northern Mariana Islands, and any other territory or possession over which the United States exercises jurisdiction.

48 USC—**Territories and Insular Possessions**
40102
United States means the States of the United States, the District of Columbia, and the territories and possessions of the United States, including the territorial sea and overlying airspace.

The following examples are definitions found in the CFRs. Since the regulations are often more expansive in content than the code, the meanings for "United States" may be different. The CFRs are relevant since they govern the agencies and officers charged with enforcing the laws of the United States.

5 CFR—**Administrative Personnel**
2641.201
For purposes of this paragraph, the ***United States*** means
(i) The executive branch
(ii) The legislative branch
(iii) The judicial branch

7 CFR—**Agriculture**
6.41 Definitions
(h) The ***United States*** means the Customs Territory of the United States, which is limited to the United States, District of Columbia and Puerto Rico.

7 CFR—**Agriculture**
15a.2
(5) ***United States*** means the States of the United States, the District of Columbia, Puerto Rico, the Virgin Islands, American Samoa, Guam, Wake Island, the Canal Zone, and the territories and possessions of the United States, and the term State means any of the foregoing.

7 CFR—**Agriculture**
1205.23
The term ***United States*** means the 50 states of the United States of America.

10 CFR—**Energy**
765.3
United States means the Federal Government, its departments and agencies and individuals acting on behalf of the Federal Government.

12 CFR—**Banks and Banking**
212.2 Definitions

(p) ***United States*** means the United States of America, any State or territory of the United States of America, the District of Columbia, Puerto Rico, American Samoa and the Virgin Islands.

14 CFR—**Aeronautics and Space**
440.3 Definitions
United States means the United States Government, including each of its territories.

15 CFR—**Commerce and Foreign Trade**
(m) ***United States*** means the Federal Government, its departments and agencies and individuals acting on behalf of the Federal Government.

17 CFR—**Commodity and Securities Exchanges**
7.1-1(c)
(vi) ***United States*** means the United States, its States, territories or possessions or an enclave of the United States government, its agencies or instrumentalities.

21 CFR—**Food and Drugs**
1.276
(15) ***United States*** means the Customs territory of the United States (i.e., the 50 States, the District of Columbia and the Commonwealth of Puerto Rico) but not the territories.

22 CFR—**Foreign Relations**
201.01 Definitions
(bb) ***United States*** means the United States of America, any State(s) of the United States, the District of Columbia and areas of the U. S. associated sovereignty, including commonwealths, territories and possessions.

29 CFR—**Labor**
9.2 Definitions
United States means the United States and all executive departments, independent establishments, administrative agencies, and instrumentalities of the United States, including corporations of which all or substantially all of the stock is owned by the United States, by the foregoing departments, establishments and including non-appropriated fund instrumentalities.

31 CFR—**Money and Finance: Treasury**
212.3 Definitions
United States means
(1) A federal corporation
(2) An agency, department, commission, board, or other entity of the United States, or
(3) an instrumentality of the United States as set forth in 28 USC 3002 (15)

31 CFR—**Money and Finance: Treasury**
510.309 ***United States***
The term ***United States*** means the United States, its territories and possessions, and all areas under the jurisdiction or authority thereof.

31 CFR—**Money and Finance: Treasury**
536.315 ***United States***
The term ***United States*** means the United States, its territories and possessions,

and all areas under the jurisdiction thereof.

34 CFR—**Education**
8.2
United States means the Federal Government of the United States and any of its agencies or instrumentalities.

37 CFR—Patents, Trademarks and Copyrights
11.1 **Definitions**
United States means the United States of America, and the territories and possessions of the United States of America.

37 CFR—**Patents, Trademarks and Copyrights**
104.1
United States means the Federal Government, its departments and agencies, individuals acting on behalf of the Federal Government, and parties to the extent they are represented by the United States.

46 CFR—**Shipping**
221.3 Definitions
(5) ***United States,*** when used in a geographical sense, means the States of the United States, Guam, Puerto Rico, the Virgin Islands, American Samoa, the District of Columbia, the Commonwealth of the Northern Mariana Islands, any other territory or possession of the United States; when used in other than the geographic sense, it means the United States Government.

The meanings of the term ***United States*** in the codes and regulations are as varied as they are numerous. Consistently though, ***United States*** is defined as the government and its possessions and territories. Obviously, the ***United States*** is not simply the 50 states, and rarely is it defined as such. Significantly, note that the term "several States" is often used throughout the different definitions of **United States**. If the definition of "several States" is not provided, one cannot simply accept that it refers to the 50 states of the Union when the balance of the items listed in the definitions of **United States** are possessions and territories. The use of "several States" may be limited to "States" uniquely within the jurisdiction of Washington D.C. and not the 50 states at all. The Federal Government has unique "States" within in its dominion, such as Guam, that are not the "50 states of the Union."

Then there are some definitions, such as, 28 USC 3002 and 5 CFR 2641.201 which do not include the several States. Yet, 7 USC 2116 clearly depicts the *United States* as the United States of America, the 50 states. These differences in meanings reveal that the government may craft definitions for the same term that vary from code to code. A declared meaning serves the intended purpose for a given power or scope of a specific law. The implication is that we typically do not know how a term is properly defined unless we read the law. With a lack of understanding, we instinctively conclude how a term is defined regardless of what the law decrees. This is quite unfortunate.

It should be transparent that *United States*, or any term for that matter, must be viewed within the context of the code for which it is defined. We should not blur the proper understanding of a term or its meaning or we misunderstand the law. If we gratuitously conclude *United States* is the 50 states, we fail to understand that the law applies to places most Americans do not realize even exist, much less are a part of the *United States*. The definition in 29 CFR limits what can be the *United States,* and none are what we would have expected. The definitions in 30 USC and 14 CFR leave no doubt the

United States is the Federal Government. Section 221.3 of 46 CFR even distinguishes the *United States* in a geographical sense and in an "other than geographical sense." The definition separates the Federal Government from its territories and possessions. Without such exactness we will not know the true meaning of any given law.

The government—the ***United States***—may define any word in any way. Legislators may and do write laws with the specific intent to limit a term to a particular meaning. They must do so to comply with the limited scope of their powers. The various definitions of the term *United States* underscore this practice. The *50 states* could not be viewed as applicable for most of the definitions of *United States.* Yet, legislators may write laws with the intent to devilishly expand their power to *include* the 50 states; and we are none the wiser. We will discuss this later.

Consider that within the code and regulations the *United States* is:

- a federal corporation
- an agency of the government
- an instrumentality of the government
- the 50 states
- the United States Government
- the Customs Territory of the U. S.
- the several States, District of Columbia, Commonwealth of Puerto Rico, and the Virgin Islands
- the executive branch
- the legislative branch
- the judicial branch
- individuals acting on behalf of the Federal Government

The United States of America, as noted in the Declaration of Independence and the Constitution, is not the *United States*. The term *several States* is often how the codes and regulations refer to the 50 states, the United States of America, "the Free and Independent States."[40] However, *United States* also refers to "several States" that are the *States* within the exclusive jurisdiction of the Federal Government, States which are not the 50 states.

There are definitions which include the several States as part of the United States. The 50 states are identified within the definition of the United States for two main reasons. First, the government is exercising a delegated power granted by the several States, a power which affects the several States. Second, a power exercised by the government, which is not granted by the States, and does not directly affect them, may be a power with which the several States agree to comply on a voluntary basis. The result is that the government creates a *district* and, thereby, acquires jurisdiction. Consider an example.

The federal Social Security Insurance scheme is an act which was written for the ***United States***, not the 50 states. The Federal Government sought to provide old age insurance to its employees within its jurisdiction and, as a result, offered the program to the 50 states. This is a power the federal authority may exercise. The federal ***United States*** may do as it deems appropriate within its domain. However, the Federal Government could not impose this federal scheme upon the Union without agreement. Each state had to accept participation in the program. Does it make sense that only when the states agreed to participate the government acquired jurisdiction for the purpose of providing social security? A template or district was created. Isn't it appropriate that the states be included in the definition of the *United States* under section of 42 USC—The Public Health and Welfare, but only for those states which agree to participate?

---

[40] The Declaration of Independence

As we study law, we will gain an appreciation for when these templates or districts are applied. Otherwise, the States are autonomous and not subject to the *United States*, the Federal Government. Since jurisdiction is essential for the proper enforcement of the law, we must know when an authority is granted by a specific act when that power begins and ends. We should avoid being cavalier with our innocent and uninformed understanding of authority and enforcement of law.

We will now define the term *United States citizen*. Since we know the term *United States* does not mean what we expected, does not include all that is within the United States of America, and involves more than we realized, we should anticipate that the definition of *United States citizen* will be no different. We may find that the varied definitions are not as we believe or understand. Additionally, the meanings may not be clear or easily reconciled. This exercise may require patience and mental effort. Consider the following:

> 42 USC—**The Public Health and Welfare**
> 9102 Definitions
> (18) ***United States citizen*** means
> (A) *any individual who is a citizen of the United States by law, birth or naturalization*;(B) *any Federal, State, or local government in the United States, or any entity of such government*; (C) *any corporation, partnership, association, or other entity organized or existing under the laws of the United States or of any State, which has as its president or other executive officer and as its chairmen of the board of directors, or holder of similar office, an individual who is a United States citizen and which has no more of its directors who are not United States citizens than constitute a minority of the number required for a quorum necessary to conduct the business of the board.*

As we learned earlier, Title 42 is not positive law. This code was written for the federal United States and its territories and possessions. The 50 states became willing participants under this law by choice. As we consider the definition of *United States citizen* within section 9102, we must ask some basic questions:

- Does *individual* mean anything other than what we generally accept?
- Is a *citizen* one who is born within the federal *United States*?
- Are those who become citizens by *law, birth,* and *naturalization* exclusively *federal*?
- Is the word *birth*, which is between the terms *law* and *naturalization,* subject to the concept *ejusdem generis,* which would limit *birth* to a federal application?
- Does the term *law* include participation in the federal Social Security Insurance scheme, a statute within Title 42?
- If so, are citizens within the 50 states citizens of the United States (Government) by virtue of having a social security number? If the answer is positive, to what extent are they *U. S. citizens* before they are Citizens of the 50 states?
- Does the status of *U. S. citizen* diminish the relevance of state citizenship?
- If we look under section 9102 (B), we see that any federal, state, or local government in the United States is a U. S. citizen. How is "in the United States" defined? Is it only in the federal territories and possessions—the United States?
- How is *state* defined? Are *States* inclusive of the several States, the 50 states of the Union? Or are the several States only federal possessions?
- What else could be a *state*? How and why?
- Are the several States *U. S. citizens* simply because they agreed to participate in

the federal Social Security Insurance scheme?

These questions regarding the proper meaning of *State* are warranted. We must know with certainty the extent of the law, which requires that we know the definition of terms. Consider the Supreme Court language in Downes v Bidwell, 182 US 244, (1901):

> *...the following propositions may be considered as established:*
>
> *3. That the District of Columbia and the territories are* ***states*** *as that word is used in treaties with foreign powers, with respect to ownership, disposition, and inheritance of property;*

Another reference of *State* within the code reflects the following:

> *The word "State" when used in this Title shall be construed to include the Territories and the District of Columbia.* Revised Statutes XXXV - Internal Revenue, section 3140 (see 26 USC 7701(a)(1) and (10) and 26 USC 7651.)

The relevance of the above is significant. The understanding of *State* within the tax code is consistent with federal law. This is confirmed using *State* in Title 42 at the start of our query. Consider 42 USC 303. This section concerns old-age assistance grants paid to *states*.

> (a) *Computation of amounts*
> *From the sums appropriated therefore, the Secretary of the Treasury shall pay to each State which has a plan approved under this subchapter, for each quarter, beginning with the quarter commencing October 1, 1960...*
> (2) *in the case of Puerto Rico, the Virgin Islands, and Guam, an amount equal to one-half of the total of the sums expended during such quarter as old-age assistance under the* ***State*** *plan...*

The District of Columbia and the federal territories and possessions are States. This fact underscores the merit of our investigation and queries.

If we consider 9102(c), we see the words "organized or existing under the laws of the United States or of any State." Again, the questions should be obvious. Do the "laws of the United States" refer exclusively to laws created by Congress for the Federal Government? May we conclude that the "laws of the United States" include the laws of 50 States? Even more to the point, does "or of any State" include the 50 States only if they are participating in social security? Or is *State* an entirely separate entity within the direct domain of the federal United States? Finally, is it possible that "several States" refers only to federal States of the *United States* and its federal territories and possessions?

Consider this discussion from a purely philosophical perspective and momentarily dismiss the legal significance of terms. We could and should surmise that we are "United States Citizens," members of a greater whole than the States in which we live, one of the States of the Union, the free and independent States of the United States of America. In the everyday vernacular, we are Citizens of the United States of America. We are Americans. This is beyond refutation.

Our challenge arises when the legality of a term is applied in the context of a crime. Who we are is a paramount concern. Who we are not is of equal importance. We can no sooner be "Jewish," "Buddhists," or "Christians" than "United States citizens" based upon the application of a term in law. If we consent to being what we are not we become what we never were. Moreover, we will become what was never intended and we may not even be aware of the change. If we allow the presumption to remain uncontested, we, by tacit acquiescence, are what we never would have allowed otherwise. In the legal realm, this silent acceptance is all that matters. We may readily conclude that the legal system feeds upon ignorance and unresponsiveness.

We want to know how a law is properly applied and, conversely, how a law is misapplied. We want to avoid confusion with the meaning of terms. We want to discern any interpretation, application, or manipulation of a law which cannot be. By doing so, we may effectively appreciate how a law does or does not apply to Americans. As we proceed, we should do several things.

1. Look at the title of a code and determine if it is positive law.
2. Ask if a State of the Union subscribed to a federal program which binds it to the United States.
3. Ask if the law applies to Americans—citizens of the 50 states.
4. Assess whether a term is adequately defined. Does the definition create confusion? Is the term used to define itself? If so, would this not create ambiguity?
5. Are the terms within the definition in need of clarification or explanation?

Now weigh the full extent of the term *United States citizen* as expressed in the codes and regulations.

The Definition of *United States citizen* or *citizen of the United States*

16 USC—**Conservation**
2402 Definitions
History; ancillary Laws and Directives
(16) The term ***United States citizen*** means
(A) any individual who is a **citizen or national** of the United States;
(B) any corporation, partnership, trust, association, or other legal entity existing or organized under the laws of the United States; and
(C) any department, agency, or other instrumentality of the Federal government or of any State, and any officer or employee or agent of any such instrumentality.

19 USC—**Customs Duties**
2601 Definitions
(10) The term ***United States citizen*** means
(A) any individual who is a citizen or national of the United States;
(B) any corporation, partnership, association or other legal entity organized or existing under the laws of the United States or any State; or,
(C) any department, agency or entity of the Federal Government or of any government of any State.

30 USC—**Mineral Lands and Mining**
1403 Definitions
(14) ***United States citizen*** means
(A) any individual who is a citizen of the United States
(B) any corporation, partnership, joint venture, association, or other entity organized or existing under the laws of any of the United States; and
(C) any corporation, partnership, joint venture, association, or other entity (whether organized or existing under the laws of any of the United States or a foreign nation) if the controlling interest in such entity is held by an individual or entity described in subparagraph (A) or (B)

33 USC—**Navigation and Navigable Water**
(4) ***citizen of the United States*** means any person who is a United States citizen by law, birth or naturalization, any State, any agency of a State or a group of

States, or any corporation, partnership, or association organized under the laws of any State which has as its president or other executive officer and as its chairman of the board of directors or holder of a similar office, a person who is a United States citizen by law, birth or naturalization and which has no more of its directors who are not United States citizens by law, birth or naturalization than constitute a minority of the number required for a quorum necessary to conduct the business of the board.

46 USC—**Shipping**
2102 General Definitions
History; Ancillary Laws and Directives
(3a) ***citizen of the United States*** means a national of the United States as defined in section 1101 (a)(22) of the Immigration and Nationality Act (8 USC 1101 (a)(22)) or an individual citizen of the Trust Territory of the Pacific Islands who is exclusively domiciled in the Northern Mariana Islands within the meaning of section 1005 (e) of the Covenant to establish a Commonwealth of the Northern Mariana Islands in Political Union with the United States of America (48 USC 1681 note).

Compare the foregoing definition with the following from the corresponding regulation which deals with Shipping—46 CFR.

46 CFR—**Shipping**
104 ***Citizen of the United States***
In this title, the term ***citizen of the United States***, when used in reference to a natural person, means an individual who is a national of the United States as defined in section 1101 (a)(22) of the Immigration and Nationality Act.

46 CFR—**Shipping**
221.3 Definitions
(c) ***Citizens of the United States*** means a Person (including receivers, trustees and successors or assigns of such Persons as provided in 46 USC 50502), including any Person who has a Controlling Interest in such Person or is a Person whose stock is being relied upon to establish the requisite United States citizen ownership and includes any Controlling Interest stockholder, any Person whose stock is being relied upon to establish the requisite United States citizen ownership who, in both form and substance at each tier of ownership satisfies the following requirements - (1) An individual who is a citizen of the United States by birth, naturalization or as otherwise authorized by law (2) A corporation organized under the laws of the United States or of a State… (3) A partnership organized under the laws of the United States or of a State (4) An association organized under the laws of the United States or of a State (5) A joint venture, if it is not in effect an association or partnership, which is organized under the laws of the United States or of a State. (6) A trust described in paragraph (t)(1) of this section.

46 CFR—**Shipping**
295.2 Definitions
(g) ***Citizen of the United States*** means an individual or a corporation, partnership, or association as determined under Section 2 of the Shipping Act of 1916, as amended (46 App USC 802)

46 CFR—**Shipping**
298.2 Definitions

Citizen of the United States means a person who, if an individual, is a Citizen of the United States by birth, naturalization or as otherwise allowed by the law or, if other than an individual, meets the requirements of Section 2 of the Shipping Act, 1916, as amended (46 App 802) as further described in 46 CFR 221.3(c)

8 CFR—**Aliens and Nationality**
212 ***United States citizen*** means a U. S. citizen or a United States non-citizen national.

14 CFR—**Aeronautics and Space**
47.2 Definitions
U. S. citizen means one of the following:
(1) an individual who is a citizen of the United States or one of its possessions.
(2) a partnership each of whose partners is an individual who is a citizen of the United States
(3) A corporation or association organized under the laws of the United States or a State, the District of Columbia, or a territory or possession of the United States which the president and at least two-thirds of the board of directors are citizens of the United States, and in which at least 75 percent of the voting interest is owned or controlled by persons that are citizens of the United States.

14 CFR—**Aeronautics and Space**
243.3 Definitions
United States citizen means United States nationals as defined in 8 USC 1101 (a)(22)

22 CFR—**Foreign Relations**
41
United States citizen means a United States citizen or a United States non-citizen national

United States citizen means a person who acquired United States citizenship at birth or upon naturalization as provided by law and who has not subsequently lost such citizenship.

45 CFR—**Public Welfare**
671.3 Definitions
United States citizen means any individual who is a citizen or national of the United States; any corporation, partnership, trust, association or other legal entity existing or organized under the laws of any of the United States; and any department, agency or other instrumentality of the Federal Government or of any State, and any officer, employee or agent of such instrumentality.

50 CFR—**Wildlife and Fisheries**
680.2
United States citizen means:
(1) Any individual who is a citizen of the United States, or
(2) Any corporation, partnership, association, or other entity that is organized under Federal, State or Local rules of the United States or that may operate legally in the United States.

29 CFR—**Labor**
1986.101 Definitions
(d) ***Citizen of the United States*** means:

(1) an individual who is a national of the United States as defined in section 1101(a)(22) of the Immigration and Nationality Act (8 USC 1101(a)(22)) or a corporation, partnership, association, or other business entity, if the controlling interest is owned by citizens of the United States. The controlling interest in a corporation is owned by citizens of the United States if:
(i) Title to the majority of the stock in the corporation is vested in citizens of the United States free from any trust or fiduciary obligation in favor of a person not a citizen of the United States.
(ii) The majority of the voting power in the corporation is vested in citizens of the United States;
(iii) no more of its directors are non-citizens than a minority of the number necessary to constitute a quorum.

38 CFR—**Pensions, Bonuses and Veteran's Relief**
17.601
(g) ***Citizen of the United States*** means any person born, or lawfully naturalized in the United States, but subject to its jurisdiction and protection and owing allegiance thereto.

45 CFR—**Public Welfare**
506.2 Other Definitions
Citizen of the United States means a person who under applicable law acquired citizenship of the United States by birth, by naturalization, or by derivation.

As with the term *United States, United States citizen* has various definitions. The actual meaning encompasses more than most of us would have imagined. We have been told, even if we told ourselves, that everyone in the United States is a *citizen of the United States*. Yet, most Americans are not *citizens* of the *United States* as defined in some of these examples. Rather, we are citizens of the 50 states of the United States of America, often referred to in the vernacular as the *United States*.

A citizen of one of the 50 states is deemed a citizen of any of the 50 states. This status does not make such a citizen a Citizen of the Federal Government—the *United States*. We must recall that the USC and CFR apply to the federal authorities. They only affect the states and citizens when the government is exercising a delegated power. The United States Government may only regulate and control what is within its jurisdiction.

This should be a rather simple concept to comprehend. The United States Supreme Court has established that one may be a citizen of the 50 states and not a citizen of the United States. One may also be a citizen of both. For example, a man born in Washington, D.C., who lives in Virginia, would be a *United States* citizen subject to the government and still be a citizen of Virginia. The fact that the government presumes that Americans are its citizens, or we conclude such rather erroneously does not make it so.

The United States Government is a separate and distinct entity. Americans are not a part of this entity. We should challenge the presumption that *United States citizen* includes every man, woman, and child in the 50 states. We may rebut this presumption by knowing who or what by law is within the United States—the Federal Government and its territories and possessions. The following illustration may prove the point.

Countless Americans have lived their entire lives without ever stepping into or onto United States territory or property. Unless they visited a national forest, a federal courthouse, an Army post, the nation's capital, or any other federally controlled land, they were exclusively on American soil. They lived their lives within the United States of America. They were never *U. S. citizens*. They never came under the purview of the U. S.

Government. Did they casually refer themselves as *U. S. Citizens* of the union of states? Yes. This is their common identity and heritage. But, as Americans, they were not legally or otherwise within the jurisdiction of the United States. Now, if these same Americans or future generations of Americans subscribed to the federal benefit of social security or secured a bank account that was federally insured, to what extent do they become *U. S. citizens* within a limited scope? This is the rub.

We know agencies, departments, and instrumentalities of the federal United States are *citizens*; as is any state, officer, and employee or agent of such instrumentalities. *State, officer,* and *employee* must have a limited meaning and scope. These terms cannot mean all 50 states or officers and employees within the 50 states. If a Chinese military officer is in the United States attending a class under an exchange program, is he a U. S. citizen? Both the application and scope of legal terms are important. How is *State* defined and applied? Does it mean anything other than the 50 states? How is *several States* defined? The scope of the law is relevant to have a proper understanding of the meaning of different words.

We know *any corporation, partnership, trust, association, or other legal entity* is a citizen of the United States, but to what extent? Are all corporations, partnerships, trusts, associations, and other legal entities actual citizens or just those that are federal in nature? Are these same entities, which exist only within the 50 states, citizens within such states? It would be reasonable to conclude that those *organized under the laws of the United States* are U. S. citizens.

We should have no doubt as to the deliberate use of terms and the context of their meanings. Consider 46 CFR, section 221.3. The consistent use of the term *Person* as a capitalized word is noteworthy. This definition is replete with qualifiers which should raise questions. Who is this *Person*? Who may, even remotely, be the *receivers, trustees,* and *successors* or *assignees*?

We must reconcile various definitions of United States *citizen* or any other term either clarify a true meaning or are incomplete and confusing. A lack of clarity reflects a lack of integrity. A lack of integrity leads to misuse and abuse of terms and the law, as well as the use of force. Rather than accept confusion, we would be better served challenging, probing, and questioning. Who am I? Where am I? To whom or what do I have an obligation? These are reasonable questions. Equally effective are queries which would hold the government accountable to its limits of jurisdiction and power. When interacting with government officials we should challenge them. Who are you? What are you? What is your proper authority? How was your authority established? Am I required to respond to your questions?

We cannot rely upon an agency or officer for transparency when the codes and regulations do not provide the same. We cannot expect or accept that the agent or official has read the code or regulations, much less sought the proper understanding of terms and definitions. Many agents are taught what to do without clear rhyme and reason for their actions when exercising their authority. They may be unable to answer basic questions. Consider the following from the Supreme Court in Federal Crop Ins Corp v Merrill, 332 US 380, 384 (1947):

> *...anyone entering into an arrangement with the Government takes the risk of having accurately ascertained that he who purports to act for the Government stays within the bounds of his authority. The scope of this authority may be explicitly defined by Congress or be limited by delegated legislation, properly exercised through the rule-making power. And this is so... even though the agent himself may be unaware of the limitations upon his authority.*

The significance of knowing the proper context of terms and the law becomes more relevant as the language becomes more complex and obscure. Just imagine weighing definitions with the following terms: *person within the United States, person subject to the jurisdiction of the United States, United States national, resident alien, nonresident, nonresident alien individual, United States resident, United States person, alien, person*, and *individual*. This is only a partial listing of any number of terms which impact the meaning of the law and the people.

If we apply our generally accepted meanings of these terms, we fail to comprehend from the outset. We must challenge our uninformed presumptions. Even with a deliberate understanding of the terms, it is still difficult to grasp the full intent and extent of any given law. Consider an example. Title 30, Mineral Lands and Mining, is not positive law. We must conclude that this code applies to the United States Government and its territories and possessions. We may then conclude that reference to *individual* as a United States citizen excludes citizens of the 50 states. Most of us are not and will not be involved with mining and, if we were, the activity would be within the State and outside the jurisdiction of the Federal Government. This is not an unreasonable conclusion based upon what we have learned thus far. Moreover, if the Federal Government has jurisdiction over mining operations within the 50 states, how is this oversight established?

The Definition of *State*

If we allow for the possibility that our common understanding of the term *State* is incorrect, which would mean the *50 states* is not the definition of *States* within some of these definitions, we prove the Federal Government may not control what is not within its jurisdiction. Usually, the 50 states are autonomous. They are not within federal control unless there is legitimate power, or an agreement exists for a power to be exerted for a public benefit. For example, if any of the 50 states do not accept funds from the Federal Government, would these states be obligated to the controlling statutes under Title 30, Mineral Lands and Mining?

The jurisdiction of the Federal Government and the autonomy of the 50 states are evident with 29 CFR, Labor, Section 1986.101. This section does not even use the term *state* within part (1) of (d) *Citizen of the United States*. One would think this would be appropriate since this statute is not positive law. Second, this definition qualifies a *citizen* as an *individual* who is a *national* as defined by 8 USC, Aliens and Nationality. Title 8 is not positive law. The federal authority alone controls immigration. These *individuals*, these *citizens*, are *nationals* who enter the *United States* and not the 50 states. They become *United States citizens* before or as they become citizens of the states.

Part (1) of this definition discloses that *individuals* are *corporations, partnerships, associations,* or *other business entities* controlled by these Title 8 citizens of the United States. Can these citizens be citizens of the 50 states? Is the intent of this definition limited to a *national or federal* status? There is no suggestion that these citizens could be anyone else. We would misapply the meaning and scope of this term and law by gratuitously concluding that it applies to all Americans.

Note the term *state* is used in part (2) of this definition and qualifies how a corporation, the *individual*, becomes a citizen of the United States.

> *...a corporation is only a citizen of the United States if: (1) It is incorporated under the laws of the United States or a State;*

This *State* cannot mean the 50 states. The 50 states have not been a part of this definition from the beginning. The *State* must be in reference to those within the direct authority of the United States Government. Let's recall that the issue is *citizenship* of a corporation *incorporated under the laws of the United States*.

The limited scope of the term *State* is confirmed by reference to the "chief executive officer" and chairman of its board of directors as being "citizens of the United States." These very citizens are individuals who are nationals as defined in Title 8, section 1101(a)(22) of the Immigration and Nationality Act. Is it possible that others may be this citizen? A corporate citizen may be those within *States* which are within the jurisdiction of the Federal Government. The government controls what it creates, after all.

Consider that the foregoing analysis is wrong. Herein is the greater concern. A reasonable parsing of terms of definitions, if incorrect, begs the question: What is the proper understanding and application of the law? If analysis offered is not correct, we are no less informed and we proceed with an incorrect interpretation. Confusion must be eradicated to negate the possibility of the law being misapplied. Such is the value of this brief but tedious study of terms and meanings. We must have a proper context of the law.

With the sundry definitions of the term *State*, can you imagine both observing and asking questions about several codes and regulations? As will be evident, it is difficult to know the proper meaning of certain terms and laws. Note the title of the code or regulation. What falls within its jurisdiction? Does it apply to the 50 states? Does it apply to the States exclusively within control of the United States, a separate "several States?" What other terms are used within the code which merit explanation? Is there certainty as to what the law means and what the law requires? As with any term, it would be easy to assume *State* includes the 50 states. Yet can this be true since there is a need to define the term in the first place.

2 USC—The Congress
Chapter 4 Officers and Employees of Senate and House of Representatives 60c-3
Withholding and remittance of State income tax by Secretary of Senate
(f) ***State*** defined. For purposes of this section "State" means any of the United States and the District of Columbia.

Author's Note: Chapter 4 deals with officers and employees of the Senate and House. Must we conclude that the 50 states are the *United States* which these representatives serve? Secondly, the District of Columbia is defined as a *State*. Any "State income tax" is withheld appropriately by the Secretary of the Senate.

60 e-lb State income tax withholding; definitions
For purposes of this resolution—
(1) The term ***State*** means any of the several States, the District of Columbia, the Commonwealth of Puerto Rico, or any territory or possession of the United States.

Author's Note*:* The territories and possessions of the United States are *States*.

Chapter 12 Contested Elections
381 Definitions
(8) The term ***State*** means a State of the United States and any territory or possession of the United States.

4 USC—Flag and Seal, Seat of Government, and the States
Chapter 4 The States
105 State, and so forth, taxation affecting federal areas; sales and use tax History; Ancillary Laws and Directives
(4) the term ***State*** means a State of the United States, the District of Columbia, or a territory or possession of the United States.

5 USC—Government Organization and Employees
Part 1. The Agencies Generally

Chapter 5 Administrative Procedure
500. Administrative practice; general provisions
(A) for the purpose of this section -
(2) ***State*** means a State, a territory or possession of the United States including a Commonwealth, or the District of Columbia.

Author's Note: This section deals with the United States Government and its employees and agencies. Does *State* refer to the 50 states? Why would it? "For purposes of this section," are the *States* only the United States territories, possessions, and the District of Columbia? The agents and employees work for the *United States*, after all.

Part III Employees
Subpart B. Employment and Retention
Chapter 33. Examination, Selection, and Placement
Subchapter IV. Assignments to and from States
3371. Definitions
(1) ***State*** means
(A) a State of the United States, the District of Columbia, the Commonwealth of Puerto Rico, the Trust Territory of the Pacific Islands, and a territory or possession of the United States; and
(B) an instrumentality or authority of a State or States as defined in subparagraph (A) of this paragraph (1) and a Federal—State authority or instrumentality.

Author's Note: Once again, this section deals with *employees*. Are the employees anyone other than those employed by the employer, the United States? Are the *States* those which are within the control of the Government? Does the term *State* possibly include the 50 states? How? Note that the instrumentalities and authorities of a State are *States*.

Subchapter 1. Travel and Subsistence Expenses; Mileage Allowances
(f) For purposes of this section:
(3) the term ***State*** means any State, the District of Columbia, the Commonwealth of Puerto Rico, the Commonwealth of the Northern Mariana Islands, the Trust Territory of the Pacific Islands, the Virgin Islands, Guam, American Samoa, or any other territory or possession of the United States.

Author's Note: Are the 50 states included? This section deals with mileage and expenses in 5 USC, Government Organization and Employees. Consider the *class* of States.

Subpart G Insurance and Annuities
Chapter 85 Unemployment Compensation
Subchapter 1 Employees Generally
8501
(6) ***State*** means the several States, the District of Columbia, the Commonwealth of Puerto Rico, and the Virgin Islands.
(7) ***United States*****,** when used in a geographical sense means the **States**;

Author's Note: We have an interesting development. The title to Part III is *Employees* and *Unemployment Compensation* which is under 42 USC, "The Public Health and Welfare" and 20 CFR, "Employee Benefits." Notice that the definition of *State* is different than the previous two under the same Part III, "Employees." The definition includes *the several States*, along with the District of Columbia, Puerto Rico, and the Virgin Islands, ostensibly to the exclusion of the other territories and possessions. As mentioned earlier, when the 50 states subscribe to a federal benefit or privilege are they within the jurisdiction of the United States Government? We must conclude that those enjoying the privilege or benefit of "Social Security" and what is known as "unemployment compensation" are "citizens of the United States" Government and, thus, "employees" of the Federal Government. How does one agree to this privilege and the jurisdiction of the United States? Is this done by subscribing to the federal Social Security Insurance scheme and, under 26 USC 6013(g), electing oneself to be treated as a *resident alien* of the *United States* for the Federal income tax with the voluntary submission of a 1040 tax form?

> 6 USC—Domestic Security
> Chapter 4 Transportation Security
> 1111. Definitions
> (4) State. The term ***"State"*** means any one of the 50 States, the District of Columbia, Puerto Rico, the Northern Mariana Islands, the Virgin Islands, Guam, American Samoa, and any other territory or possession of the United States.
>
> 7 USC—Agriculture
> Chapter 3 Grain Standards
> 75 Definitions
> (e) the term ***"State"*** means anyone of the States (including Puerto Rico) or territories or possessions of the United States (including the District of Columbia).
>
> **Author's Note**: Does this definition apply to the 50 states?
>
> Chapter 6 Insecticides and Environmental Pesticide Control
> 136 Definitions
> (aa) **State**. The term ***State*** means a State, the District of Columbia, the Commonwealth of Puerto Rico, the Virgin Islands, Guam, the Trust Territory of the Pacific Islands, and American Samoa.
>
> **Author's Note**: Does "State" include the 50 states?
>
> Chapter 8a Rubber and other Critical Agricultural Materials
> 178 a. Definitions
> (a) The term ***State*** means each of the fifty States, the District of Columbia, and the Commonwealth of Puerto Rico.
>
> 10 USC—Armed Forces
> Subtitle A General Military Law
> Part II. Personnel
> Chapter 53 Miscellaneous Rights and Benefits
> 1045. Voluntary Withholding of State Income Tax from retired or retainer pay (e) In this section
> (1) the term ***"State"*** means any State, the District of Columbia, the Commonwealth of Puerto Rico, and any territory or possession of the United States.
>
> Part IV Service, Supply and Procurement
> Chapter 160. Environmental Restoration
> 2710 Inventory of unexploded ordinance, discarded military munitions, and munitions constituents at defense sites
> (6) the term ***State*** means the several States, the District of Columbia, the Commonwealth of Puerto Rico, the Commonwealth of the Northern Mariana Islands, and the territories and possessions.
> (7) the term **"United States,"** in a geographical sense, **means the States**,

territories, and possessions and associated navigable waters, contiguous zones, and ocean waters of which the natural resources are under the exclusive management authority of the United States.

12 USC—Banks and Banking
Chapter 13 National Housing
Mortgage Insurance
1710 Payment of Insurance
(6) **State**. The term ***"State"*** means any State of the United States, the District of Columbia, the Commonwealth of Puerto Rico, Guam, American Samoa, the Virgin Islands, the Northern Mariana Islands, or any agency or instrumentality thereof that is established pursuant to legislation and designated by the chief executive officer to act on behalf of the State with regard to provisions of this subsection.

Author's Note: Any agency or instrumentality is a state "…established pursuant to legislation." What does this mean? Notice we already have some understanding of the "chief executive officer" as reviewed in other code sections. The use of this term, in the manner presented here, appears to indicate that those "corporations" must be "State" corporations owned and controlled by the "State." How is "State" defined? Is it limited to the "class" listed, those in federal areas?

15 USC—Commerce and Trade
Chapter 1 Monopolies and Combinations in Restraint of Trade
15g. Definitions
(2) The term ***"State"*** means a State, the District of Columbia, the Commonwealth of Puerto Rico, and any other territory or possession of the United States.

Chapter 2D Investment Companies and Advisors
80a-3a Protection of Philanthropy under State Law
(3) the term ***"State"*** means each of the several States of the United States, the District of Columbia, the Commonwealth of Puerto Rico, the Virgin Islands, Guam, American Samoa, and the Commonwealth of the Northern Mariana Islands,

Chapter 15b Natural Gas
717a. Definitions
(4) ***"State"*** means a state admitted to the Union, the District of Columbia, and any organized Territory of the United States.

Chapter 15D Alaska Natural Gas Pipeline
720. Definitions
(8) **State**. The term ***"State"*** means the State of Alaska.

Chapter 50 Consumer Product Warranties
2301 Definitions
(15) The term ***"State"*** means a State, the District of Columbia, the Commonwealth of Puerto Rico, the Virgin Islands, Guam, the Canal Zone, or American Samoa. The term "S*tate law*" **includes a law of the United States applicable only to the District of Columbia or only to a territory or possession of the United States, and the term "federal law" excludes any State law.**

Author's Note: The reference to "State law" is significant and is applicable to the territories or possessions of the *United States*.

16 USC—Conservation
Chapter 1 National Parks, Military Parks, Monuments and Seashores

Petrified Forest National Park
119. Establishment; publication in Federal Register; administration exchange and acquisition of lands; remaining funds
History; Ancillary laws and Directives
(4) **State**. The term "State" means the State of Arizona.

Chapter 1B. Archaeological Resources Protection
470bb. Definitions
(7) The term ***State*** means any of the fifty States, the District of Columbia, Puerto Rico, Guam, and the Virgin Islands.

18 USC—Crimes and Criminal Procedure
Part 1 Crimes
Chapter 2 Aircraft and Motor Vehicles
31 Definitions
(9) State. The term ***"State"*** means a State of the United States, the District of Columbia, and any commonwealth, territory, or possession of the United States.

Author's Note: This code deals with aircraft and motor vehicles. Do these assets belong to any entity other than the United States Government? May it include aircraft and vehicles which belong to the 50 states? Does the term *State* include the 50 states?

27 USC—Intoxicating Liquors
Chapter 6. Transportation in Interstate Commerce
122a Injunctive Relief in federal district court
(4) the term ***"State"*** means any State of the United States, the District of Columbia, the Commonwealth of Puerto Rico, or any possession of the United States.

42 USC—The Public Health and Welfare
Chapter 6a. The Public Health Service
General Powers and Duties
Primary Health Care
Scholarship Program and Loan Repayment Program
254r. Grants to States for operation of offices of rural health
(i) ***State*** defined. For purposes of this section, the term "State" means each of the several States.

Finally, simply for illustration, consider the definition of "State" from the Oklahoma statutes. Note, the "United States of America" is considered a "State."

Article II(a) Oklahoma Statutes
Section 134711 (a), Title 22
"State" shall mean... the United States of America, a territory or possession of the United States; the District of Columbia, the Commonwealth of Puerto Rico.

We will define the term "territory" to demonstrate that it means the same as some of the definitions of ***State***. It would be natural to question why there is a need to define territories as *States*. The obvious answer is to fulfill a legal purpose. When ***State*** is used in a manner that is not clear, when there is doubt as to what it is, we have reason to question what the law seeks to accomplish.

The Definition of *Territory*

15 USC—Commerce and Trade
77b Definitions Promotion of efficiency, competition and capital formation

(6) the term ***"Territory"*** means Puerto Rico [the Philippine Islands], the Virgin Islands, and the insular possessions of the United States.

Chapter 30 Hazard Substances
1261 Definitions
(A) The term ***"Territory"*** means any Territory or possession of the United States, including the District of Columbia and the Commonwealth of Puerto Rico but excluding the Canal Zone.

21 USC—Food and Drugs
Chapter 9 Food, Drug and Cosmetic Act
321 Definitions; generally
(2) The term ***"Territory"*** means any Territory or possession of the United States, including the District of Columbia, and excluding the Commonwealth of Puerto Rico and the Canal Zone.

27 USC—Intoxicating Liquors
Chapter 8 Federal Alcohol Administration Act
211 Miscellaneous Provisions
(a) Definitions. As used in this title
(2) The term "United States" means the several States and Territories and the District of Columbia; the term "State" includes a Territory and the District of Columbia; and the term ***"Territory"*** means Alaska, Hawaii, and Puerto Rico.

Author's Note: Pay attention to the foregoing definition; for, they accomplish something rather sneaky. Reference is made to "several States" and "territories;" yet, the definition then qualifies "State" as a "Territory" and "the District of Columbia." The definition defines "Territory" as "Alaska, Hawaii, and Puerto Rico." Are the "several States" only those territories and the District of Columbia? This definition is critical since enforcement of the tax code falls under the Bureau of Alcohol, Tobacco, and Firearms (BATF) and 27 USC.

42 USC—The Public Health and Welfare
Chapter 129. National and Community Service
12511. Definitions
(47) **Territory**. The term "territory" means the United States Virgin Islands, Guam, American Samoa, and the Commonwealth of the Northern Mariana Islands.

49 USC—Transportation
Subtitle III. General and Intermodal Programs
Chapter 53. Public Transportation
5339 Bus and bus facilities formula grants
(2) The term ***"territory"*** means the District of Columbia, Puerto Rico, the Northern Mariana Islands, Guam, American Samoa, and the United States Virgin Islands.

16 CFR—Commercial Practices
1500.3 Definitions
(1) ***Territory*** means any territory or possession of the United States, including the District of Columbia and the Commonwealth of Puerto Rico, but excluding the Canal Zone.

24 CFR—Housing and Urban Development
576.2
Territory means the following: the Virgin Islands, Guam, American Samoa and the

Northern Mariana Islands.

27 CFR—Alcohol, Tobacco Products and Firearms
5.11 Meaning of terms.
United States. The several States and Territories and the District of Columbia; the term *state* includes a territory and the District of Columbia; and the term ***"Territory"*** means the Commonwealth of Puerto Rico.

Author's Note: Refer to the previous Author's Note above for 27 USC and review that definition.

42 CFR—Public Health
70.1 General Definitions
U. S. Territory means any territory (also known as possessions) of the United States, including American Samoa, Guam, the Northern Mariana Islands, the Commonwealth of Puerto Rico, and the United States Virgin Islands.

The Definition of *United States person*

The discussion of the term "United States person" is important. Let's first ask why we must define, much less use the term, *United States person.* Is this person any different than *United States citizen*? If not, why use it? Why not continue to use "citizen?" How and why are these two terms different? Should we conclude, as stipulated in 1 USC 1, that "person" is used to accommodate for aliens entering the *United States*?

10 USC—Armed Forces
424
(2) The term ***"United States person"*** means any citizen, national, or permanent resident alien of the United States.

15 USC—Commerce and Trade
78dd-1 Prohibited foreign exchange practices by issuers
(2) As used in this subsection, the term ***"United States person"*** means a national of the United States (as defined in section 1101 of the Immigration and Nationality Act (8 USC 1101)) or any corporation, partnership, association, joint stock company, business trust, unincorporated organization, or sole proprietorship organized under the laws of the United States or any political subdivision thereof.

Author's Note: Notice that a *United States person* is a "national," identified under Title 8, Immigration and Nationality Act, or any of the entities identified as "organized under the laws of the United States." Does "State" mean the 50 states?

4725 United States and Foreign Commercial Service Pacific Rim Initiative
(c) ***"United States person"*** defined.
As used in this section, the term "United States person" means
(1) a United States citizen; or
(2) a corporation, partnership, or other association created under laws of the United States or any State (including the District of Columbia or any commonwealth, territory or possession of the United States).

Author's Note: How is "United States citizen" defined? Does "State" include the 50 states? The parenthetical refers to a distinct class and uses the term *including.*

Chapter 107 Protection of Intellectual Property Rights
8101 Definitions
In this Act, the term ***"United States person"*** means -
(1) any United States resident or national

(2) any domestic concern (including any permanent domestic establishment of any foreign concern) and

(3) any foreign subsidiary or affiliate (including any permanent foreign establishment) of any domestic concern that is controlled in fact by such domestic concern, except that such term does not include an individual who resides outside the United States and is employed by an individual or entity other than an individual or entity described in paragraph (1), (2), or (3).

Author's Note: What does *resident* mean? Why is "citizen" not used? The domestic complement of a foreign concern is a United States person. Do you understand the language in paragraph (3)? Is the law clear?

18 USC—Crimes and Criminal Procedure
Chapter 113B Terrorism
2332d Financial Transactions
(b) Definitions. As used in this section -
(2) The term ***"United States person"*** means any—
(A) United States citizen or national;
(B) permanent resident alien;
(C) juridical person organized under the laws of the United States; or
(D) any person in the United States

Author's Note: Who or what is a United States citizen? What does *juridical* mean? Does the United States consist of the District of Columbia, territories, and possessions? Under paragraph (D), what or who is any "person?" Why use the term "person" to define the term "person?" If this statute applies to every living soul and all entities, why not state so? If the statute does not, we must conclude the scope of the law is limited. Thus, is the code clear?

22 USC—Foreign Relations and Intercourse
Chapter 38 Department of State
2712 Authority to control certain terrorism-related services
(4) ***United States person***. As used in this section, the term "United States person" means any United States national, any permanent resident alien, and any sole proprietorship, partnership, company, association or corporation organized under the laws of or having its principal place of business within the United States.

Author's Note: Note the absence of "United States citizen" and the reference to "national" and "resident aliens" and the other entities listed. Do these entities include all of those created within the 50 states? Does this definition include citizens of the 50 states?

2708 Department of State Rewards Program
(8) ***United States person***. The term *"United States person"* means
(a) a citizen or national of the United States; and
(b) an alien lawfully present in the United States.

Chapter 79. Trade Sanctions Reform and Export Enhancement
7207 Prohibition on United States assistance and financing
(c) The term *"United States person"* means the Federal Government, any state or local government, or any private person or entity of the United States.

Author's Note: The U. S. Government is a U. S. person. Does reference to *State* include or exclude the 50 States? What is a private person or entity of the United States? Are they limited to the United States, the government, and its territories and possessions?

Chapter 92 Comprehensive Iran Sanctions, Accountability, and Divestment 8513 A Imposition of Sanctions with respect to financial sector of Iran

(4) **United States person**. The term *"United States person"* means

(A) a natural person who is a citizen or resident of the United States or a national of the United States (As defined in section 1101(a) of the Immigration and Nationality Act (8 USC 1101(a)); and

(B) an entity that is organized under the laws of the United States or a jurisdiction of the United States.

28 USC—Judiciary and Judicial Procedure
Chapter 181 Foreign Judgments
4101 Definitions

(6) **United States person**. The term *"United States person"* means

(A) a United States citizen;

(B) an alien lawfully admitted for permanent residence to the United States;

(C) an alien lawfully residing in the United States at the time that the speech that is the subject of the foreign defamation action was researched, prepared, or disseminated; or

(D) a business entity incorporated in, or with its primary location or place of operation in the United States.

42 USC—The Public Health and Welfare
Chapter 152 Energy Independence and Security International Energy Programs 17373 Convention on Supplementary Compensation for Nuclear Damage Contingent Cost Allocation

(11) **United States person**. The term *"United States person"* means (A) any individual who is a resident, national or a citizen of the United States (other than an individual residing outside of the United States and employed by a person who is not a United States person); and

(B) any corporation, partnership, association, joint stock company, business trust, unincorporated organization, or sole proprietorship that is organized under the laws of the United States.

50 USC—War and National Defense
Chapter 35. International Emergency Economic Powers
1701 Unusual or extraordinary threat; declaration of national emergency; exercise of presidential authorities
History; Ancillary Laws and Directives

(21) **United States person**. The term *"United States person"* means

(A) A natural person who is a citizen of the United States or who owes allegiance to the United States; and

(B) a corporation or legal entity which is organized under the laws of the United States, any State or territory thereof, or the District of Columbia, if natural persons described in subparagraph (A) own, directly or indirectly, more than 50% of the outstanding capital stock or other beneficial interest in such legal entity.

15 CFR—Commerce and Foreign Trade
760.1 Definitions
(b) Definition of "United States person"

(1) This part applies to United States persons. For purposes of this part, the term United States person means any person who is a United States resident or national, including individuals, domestic concerns, and "controlled in fact" foreign

subsidiaries, affiliates or other permanent foreign establishments of domestic concerns. The definitions of United States person include both the singular and plural and, in addition, includes

(i) The government of the United States or any department, agency or commission thereof;

(ii) The government of any State of the United States, the District of Columbia, the Commonwealth of Puerto Rico, any territory or possession of the United States, or any subdivision, department or commission of any such government.

(iii) any partnership, corporation, company, association or other entity organized under the laws of paragraph (b) (1) (i) or (ii) of this section;

(iv) any foreign concern's subsidiary partnership, affiliate, branch, office or other permanent establishment in any State of the United States, the District of Columbia, the Commonwealth of Puerto Rico, or any territory or possession of the United States; and,

(v) any domestic concern's foreign subsidiary, partnership, affiliate, branch, office...

Author's Note*:* Consider the following definition under (4) of the same section. What do you make of its application considering all we have learned?

(4) The term "United States person" does not include an individual United States national who is resident outside the United States and who is either employed permanently or temporarily by a non-United States person or assigned to work as an employee for, and under the direction and control of, a non-United States person.

17 CFR—Commodity and Securities Exchanges
275.203(m)-1
(8) ***United States person*** means any person that is a United States person as defined in 230.902 (k) of this chapter, except that any discretionary account or similar account that is held for the benefit of a United States person by a dealer or other professional fiduciary is a related person of the investment advisor relying on this section and is not organized, incorporated, or (if an individual) resident in the United States.

31 CFR—Money and Finance: Treasury
129.2 Definitions
(d) United States person means any person resident in the United States or subject to the jurisdiction of the United States.

596.313 **United States person**
The term United States person means any United States citizen or national, permanent resident alien, juridical person organized under the laws of the United States, or any person in the United States.
1010.350 Reports of foreign financial accounts
(b) **United States person.** For purposes of this section, the term "United States person" means—
(1) A citizen of the United States;
(2) A resident of the United States. A resident of the United States is an individual who is a resident alien under 26 USC 7701(b) and the regulations thereunder, but using the definition of "United States" provided in 31 CFR 1010.100 (hhh) rather than the definition of "United States" in 26 CFR 301.7701(b)-1(c)(2)(ii); and
(3) An entity, including, but not limited to, a corporation, partnership, trust, or

limited liability company created, organized, or formed under the laws of the United States, any State, and District of Columbia, the Territories and Insular Possessions of the United States, or the Indians Tribes.

Author's Note*:* Under Paragraph (2), with reference to 26 USC (the tax code), at least for this code section, we have an idea who is a *resident*. Note, there is a particular definition of *United States* that must be used; this section makes a deliberate citation to the *United States* which must apply. For, the definition of *United States* under the regulations that deal with taxes is not the correct one. While the tax code provides for the correct definition of "resident alien," who is a "United States person?"

31 CFR—Money and Finance: Treasury
1010.100
(iii) **United States person.** (1) A United States citizen; or (2) A person other than an individual (such as a corporation, partnership or trust) that is established or organized under the laws of a State or the United States.

Author's Note*:* Who is a United States citizen? *Individual* is something other than the entities listed. *Individual* is an artificial creation or designation of government.

The Definition of *Person*

2 USC—The Congress
431
(h) ***"Person"*** means an individual, partnership, committee, association, corporation, labor organization, and any other organization or group of persons."

Author's Note*:* What is an *individual*? This is critical. We have learned too much to accept a word at face value considering our preconceived notions. We saw in the section defining *United States person* that *individual* was grouped with creations of governments, which underscores concepts like *ejusdem generis*. Is individual and person in this definition a fiction, creation, or label of government? Finally, note that 2 USC deals with "The Congress," which is the "United States."

5 USC—Government Organization and Employees
7103
(A)(1) *"person"* means an individual, labor organization or agency

7 USC—Agriculture
241
(7) **Person.** The term *"person"* means—
(A) a person (as defined in section 1 of Title 1)
(B) a State; and
(C) a political subdivision of a State.
1308
(4) **Person.** The term *"person"* means a natural person, and does not include a legal entity.

Author's Note*:* For the first time we have a definition which distinguishes between a natural person to the exclusion of a legal entity.

4612(a) Definition of **Person.** In this section, the term *"person"* means a producer, importer or handler.

Author's Note*:* The term *person* is used specifically.

8401(1)(5) The term ***"person"*** includes Federal, State and local government entities.

Author's Note*:* Does *State* include the 50 states? Note that this title is 5 USC—Government Organization and Employees.

8 USC—Aliens and Nationality
1322(d) As used in this section, the term "person" means the owner, master, agent, commanding officer, charterer or consignee of any vessel or aircraft.

12 USC—Banks and Banking
95a
As used in this section, the term ***"person"*** means an individual, partnership, association, or corporation.

635F(iii)
The term ***"person"*** means natural person as well as a corporation, business, association, partnership, society, trust, any other non governmental entity operating as a business enterprise, and any successor of any such entity.

15 USC—Commerce and Trade
77b (2) The term ***"person"*** means an individual, a corporation, a partnership, an association, a joint stock company, a trust, any unincorporated organization, or a government or political subdivision thereof. As used in this paragraph, the term "Trust" shall include only a trust where the interest or interests of the beneficiary are evidenced by a security.

Author's Note*:* This is a curious definition. A "government or political subdivision thereof" follows the entire list of entities. This is no small observation. Does it suggest that the list of entities is only governmental in nature?

78c (9) The term ***"person"*** means a natural person, company, government, or political subdivision, agency, or instrumentality of a government.

Author's Note*:* *Person* is used comprehensively in this section, or at least it appears so. Is the list limited to persons related to or associated with only the government? Does *person* mean anything and everything?

18 USC—Crimes and Criminal Procedure
2510 (6) ***"person"*** means any employee, or agent of the United States or any State or political subdivision thereof, and any individual, partnership, association, joint stock company, trust or corporation.

Author's Note*:* May we conclude that "State or political subdivision thereof" is limited to the federal *United States* since "any employee or agent of the United States" precedes the text? If this conclusion is incorrect, is the law clear?

19 USC—Customs Duties
3902(8) **Person.** The term *"person"* means an individual or entity.

Author's Note*:* What is an individual?

29 USC—Labor
652(4) The term ***person*** means one or more individuals, partnerships, associations, corporations, business trusts, legal representatives, or any organized group of persons.

30 USC—Mineral Lands and Mining
1403(10) ***"person"*** means any United States citizen, any individual, and any corporation, partnership, joint venture, association, or other entity organized or existing under the laws of any nation.

Author's Note*:* We have *United States citizen* and *individual* in the same definition of *person*. What is an *individual*? Is it an alien which is a label or designation of the government? Who is a United States citizen?

31 CFR—Money and Finance: Treasury

351.3 ***Person*** means an entity including an individual, trust, estate, corporation, government entity, association, partnership, and any other similar organization. Person does not mean a Federal Reserve Bank.

Author's Note*:* It appears that *person* includes many things, but not a natural person or United States citizen. *Person* means "an entity" after all. Why is the Federal Reserve Bank, which is a privately owned corporation, and not part of the "Federal Government," not included in this definition of *person*?

354.1 (1) ***Person*** means and includes an individual, corporation, company, governmental agency, association, firm, partnership, trust, estate, representative, and any other similar organization, but does not mean or include the United States, Sallie Mae, or a Federal Reserve Bank.

360.2 (h) ***Person*** means a legal entity including an individual or fiduciary estate.

Author's Note*:* This section defines person as a "legal entity" "including" an individual, which must make the term a legal label or fiction of government and perhaps the designation of "alien" or "nonresident alien."

42 USC—The Public Health and Welfare
300f. Definitions
(12) The term ***"person"*** means an individual, corporation, company, association, partnership, State, municipality, or Federal agency (and includes officers, employees, and agents of any corporation, company, association, State municipality, or Federal agency.)

Author's Note*:* Does *State* include the 50 states? We must note the parenthetical emphasis on "officers, employees and agents."

8302 Definitions
(a)(2) the term *"person"* means any
(a) individual, corporation, company, partnership, association, firm, institution, society, trust, joint venture, or joint stock company,
(b) any State, the District of Columbia, Puerto Rico, and any territory or possession of the United States, or
(c) any agency or instrumentality (including any municipality) thereof.

2 CFR—Grants and Agreements
180.985 **Person**
Person means any individual, corporation, partnership, association, unit of government, or legal entity, however organized.

4 CFR—Accounts
28.3 ***Person*** means an employee, an applicant for employment, a former employee, a labor organization or the GAO.

Author's Note: A *person* is an employee.

5 CFR—Administrative Personnel
185.102 Person means an individual, partnership, corporation, association, or other legal entity; an unincorporated organization; and any federal, state, tribal, county, district, territorial or local government or agency.

Author's Note*:* What is an individual? There is no other reference to a classification that would indicate a human being. This list includes fictions of government, including an *individual*. Title 5 CFR covers Administrative Personnel.

13 CFR—Business Credit and Assistance
107.50 ***Person*** means a natural person or legal entity.

126.103 ***Person*** means a natural person.

134.101 ***Person*** means an individual or any form of business entity.

Author's Note*:* Is an individual a creation or designation of government? The two previous definitions state that a *person* is "natural."

15 CFR—Commerce and Foreign Trade
4.22(6) ***Person*** means any human being and also shall include, but is not limited to, corporations, associations, partnerships, trustees, receivers, personal representatives and public or private organizations.

Author's Note*:* We have a definition which identifies *person* as a "human being." Does this include all human beings worldwide, those in the 50 states, or only those in the United States, to include the District of Columbia, the territories, and possessions, and all who enter the jurisdiction of the *United States* by accepting a federal benefit or status?

8.3(d) ***person*** means an individual in the United States who is or is eligible to be a participant in or an ultimate beneficiary of any program which receives Federal financial assistance, and includes an individual who is an owner or member of a firm, corporation, or other business or organization which is or is eligible to be a participant in or an ultimate beneficiary of such a program. Where a primary objective of the Federal financial assistance to a program is to provide employment, ***person*** includes employees or applicants for employment or a recipient or other party subject to this part under such program.

29 CFR—Labor
8.2 ***Person*** means an individual, partnership, corporation, joint business enterprise, estate, or other legal entity capable of owning property.

42 CFR—Public Health
2.11 ***Person*** means any individual, partnership, corporation, Federal, State, or local government agency or any other legal agency.
423.100 ***Person*** means a natural person, corporation, mutual company, unincorporated association, partnership, joint venture, limited liability company, trust, estate, foundation, not-for-profit corporation, unincorporated organization, government or governmental subdivision or agency.

45 CFR—Public Welfare
60.103 ***Person*** means a natural person, trust or estate, partnership, corporation, professional association or corporation, or other entity, public or private.

46 CFR—Shipping
287.1(10) ***Person*** means any person not an individual, a corporation, a partnership, an association, an estate, a trust, or a company.

Author's Note*:* What should we make of a definition which uses the actual word to define it? Person means any *person*. Note, person means any person that is *not* any of the class listed.

503.60(E) ***Person*** means any person not an individual and shall include, but not limited to, corporations, associations, partnerships, trustees, receivers, personal representatives, and public or private organizations.

Author's Note*:* What should we make of this definition? Person is any person not from the list provided? This list includes creations and fictions of or by the government. Can one reasonably conclude that an *individual* is a government creation and any person who is not an individual must be a natural person or human being? Is this definition comprehensive in scope? Does it cover everyone and everything as persons?

The following definitions were purposely left for the end.

15 USC—Commerce and Trade
1127 The term ***"person"*** and any other word or term used to designate the applicant or other entitled to a benefit or privilege or rendered liable under the provisions of the Act includes a juristic person as well as a natural person. The term juristic person includes a firm, corporation, union, association or other organization capable of suing or being sued in a court of law.

The term *"person"* also includes the United States, any agency or instrumentality thereof, and any individual, firm, or corporation acting for the United States and with the authorization and consent of the United States, shall be subject to the provisions of this Act in the same manner and to the same extent as any nongovernmental agency.

The term *"person"* also includes any State, any instrumentality of a State and any officer or employee of a State or instrumentality of a State acting in his or her official capacity. Any State and any such instrumentality, officer or employee shall be subject to the provisions of this Act in the same manner and to the same extent as any nongovernmental agency.

Author's Note*:* This definition is revealing. The *person* is the applicant to a "benefit or privilege"—a grant from the Federal Government. We know the government has jurisdiction and expects something in return, a tax perhaps. Note the extensiveness of the definition as it relates to government. Does State include the 50 states? If so, have the states subscribed to a federal program and, thus, fall within a *district* of the United States?

Definition of *Person subject to the jurisdiction of the United States*

31 CFR—Money and Finance: Treasury
515.329 **Person subject to the jurisdiction of the United States**
The term *person subject to the jurisdiction of the United States* includes:
(a) any individual, wherever located, who is a citizen or resident of the United States;
(b) any person within the United States as defined in 515.330;
(c) any corporation, partnership, association, or other organization organized under the laws of the United States or of any state, territory, or possession, or district of the United States; and
(d) any corporation, partnership, association, or other organization wherever organized or doing business, that is owned or controlled by persons specified in paragraphs (a) or (c) of this section.

515.330 **Person within the United States**
(a) the term *person within the United States* includes;
(1) any person, wheresoever located, who is a resident of the United States;
(2) any person actually within the United States;

(3) any corporation, partnership, association, or other organization organized under the laws of the United States or of any state, territory, possession, or district of the United States; and,

(4) any corporation, partnership, association or other organization, wherever organized or doing business, which is owned or controlled by any person or persons specified in paragraphs (a) (1) or (a) (3) of this section.

Author's Note*:* We see the use of the term "district" as applied to the *United States*. Notice the comprehensiveness of this definition. What are the definitions of each?

The Definition of *United States National*

5 USC—Government Organization and Employees
Chapter III Employees
5561 Definitions

(5) The term ***United States national*** means any individual who is a citizen of the United States or who, though not a citizen of the United States, owes permanent allegiance to the United States.

Author's Note*:* This section deals with employees who owe permanent allegiance to the United States. Who is the employer? How is U. S. defined?

8 USC—Aliens and Nationality
1101 Definitions

(21) The term ***"national"*** means a person owing allegiance to a State.

(22) The term ***"national of the United States"*** means (A) a citizen of the United States, or (B) a person who, though not a citizen of the United States, owes permanent allegiance to the United States.

Author's Note*:* 8 USC deals with immigration and nationality. Is there any doubt this definition concerns those who are aliens or from a territory or possession or foreign country? Given the status of *national*, should we conclude that the previous definitions (5 USC) concern the same?

22 USC—Foreign Relations and Intercourse
6023 Definitions

(15) **United States national.** The term *"United States national"* means—

(A) any United States citizen; or

(B) any other legal entity which is organized under the laws of the United States, or of any State, the District of Columbia, or any commonwealth, territory or possession of the United States, and which has its principal place of business in the United States.

Author's Note*:* Considering all definitions that use *national* in relation to immigration, this definition poses a challenge. Title 22 deals with Foreign Relations. Are all United States citizens United States nationals? Is a *national* a label or creation of the Federal Government? Who is a U. S. citizen?

22 CFR—Foreign Relations
193.2 Definitions

(c) the term ***United States national*** means any individual who is a citizen of the United States or who, though not a citizen of the United States, owes permanent allegiance to the United States.

Author's Note*:* Who or what is an *individual?* Unlike the prior definition, this allows for those who are not citizens and owe allegiance to the United States. Are we dealing with aliens again?

31 CFR—Money and Finance
515.334 ***United States National***
As used in 515.208, the term **United States national** means;
(a) Any United States citizen; or
(b) Any other legal entity which is organized under the laws of the United States, or of any state, the District of Columbia, or any commonwealth, territory, or possession of the United States, and has its principal place of business in the United States.

Author's Note*:* How is *State* defined? How is *United States* defined?

22 CFR—Foreign Relations
51.1 Definitions
(1) ***U. S. national*** means a U. S. citizen or a U. S. non-citizen national.

Author's Note*:* We are dealing with *Foreign Relations*. Who is a *U. S. citizen* for purposes of this definition? Who or what is a non-citizen national?

31 CFR—Money and Finance: Treasury
800.227 ***U. S. National***
The term ***U. S. national*** means a citizen of the United States or an individual who although not a citizen of the United States, owes permanent allegiance to the United States.

50 CFR—Wildlife and Fisheries
300.2 Definitions
National of the United States or ***U. S. national*** means any person subject to the jurisdiction of the United States, including, but not limited to, a citizen or resident of the United States, or a person employed on a vessel of the United States. In the case of a corporation, partnership or other non-natural person, this includes, but is not limited to, any entity that is the owner of a vessel of the United States.

Author's Note*:* How is *United States* defined? Also, a person employed on a vessel of the U. S. is a national. What is a vessel of the U. S.?

The Definition of *Individual*

5 USC—Government Organization and Employees
552a Records maintained on individuals
(a) Definitions
(2) the term ***"individual"*** means a citizen of the United States or an alien lawfully admitted for permanent residence.

Author's Note*:* This definition states an *individual* is a citizen of the United States. The title is *Records maintained on individuals.* Upon whom would the government maintain records? Prior definitions show *individual* is a national (alien) or any entity.

25 USC—Indians
2201 Definitions
(8) ***"person"*** or ***"individual"*** means a natural person.

Author's Note*:* An *individual* is a *natural person.* 25 USC deals with Indians, a concern of the Federal Government. Are *person* and *individual* designations of government? Why not use "Native American" or "indigenous people?" Legal terms tend to generalize, as if by design. The government wants the broadest application possible.

29 USC—Labor
1301 Definitions
(v) ***"individual"*** means a living human being.

Author's Note*:* An individual is not only a human being, but a living one. A dead human being would not fit this definition. Who are the living humans to whom this code applies? Those within the *United States*? Title 29 is not positive law.

38 USC—Veterans' Benefits
3687
(3) In this section, the term ***"individual"*** means
(A) an eligible veteran who is entitled to monthly educational assistance allowance payable under 30159(e) of this title, or
(B) an eligible person who is entitled to monthly educational assistance allowances payable under section 3532 (a) of this title, as the code may be.

43 USC—Public Lands
390bb. Definitions
(4) The term ***"individual"*** means any natural person, including his or her spouse, and including other dependents thereof within the meaning of the Internal Revenue Code of 1954.

Author's Note*:* We have another sweeping application where *individual* is any "natural person." This definition refers to the meaning of the IRC. Why?

1 CFR—General Provisions
455.2 Definitions - For the purposes of these procedures:
(a) The term ***individual*** means a citizen of the United States or an alien lawfully admitted for permanent residence.

2 CFR—Grants and Agreements
182.655 **Individual**
Individual means a natural person.

6 CFR—Homeland Security
13.2 Definitions
(1) ***Individual*** means a natural person.

10 CFR—Energy
20.1003
Individual means any human being.

727.2
"Individual" means an employee of DOE or a DOE contractor, or any other person who has been granted access to a DOE computer.

12 CFR—Banks and Banking
2619.2 Definitions
(c) ***Individual*** means a natural person who is either a citizen of the United States or an alien lawfully admitted for permanent residence.

13 CFR—Business Credit and Assistance
102.20
(3) ***Individual*** means a citizen of the United States or an alien lawfully admitted for permanent residence. The term shall not encompass entrepreneurial enterprises (e.g., sole proprietors, partnerships, corporations, or other forms of business entities).

14 CFR - Aeronautics and Space
1212.101 Definitions
(a) The term ***individual*** means a living person who is either a citizen of the United States or an alien lawfully admitted for permanent residence.

1260.38
Individual means a Proposer/Recipient that has no more than one employee including the Proposer/Recipient.

15 CFR—Commerce and Foreign Trade
760.3
(2) For purposes of this section, a United States ***individual*** means a person who is a resident or national of the United States…

Author's Note*:* The term *United States individual* is limited to "resident" or "national." Both terms were limited to aliens in prior definitions.

20 CFR—Employees' Benefits
401.25 Terms defined.
When used in connection with the rules governing program information, individual means a living natural person; this does not include corporations, partnerships, and unincorporated business or professional groups of two or more persons.

Author's Note*:* This title deals with *Employees' Benefits,* the regulation which covers social security and employment benefits. This definition is limited to those persons who are natural and alive. No other entities may benefit. Who are these "employees?" Are those who are *employees* the ones who subscribe for the "benefit" of social security, a federal privilege? Are these *persons* considered employees of the *United States*? Should we conclude that if an *individual*, one who accepts a benefit, subscribes to the government program of social security, the *United States* may tax by excise *income* for this privilege? Are citizens of the 50 states who accept the federal benefit of social security "persons" of the "United States" within the "several States" of the "United States," which would classify them as "resident aliens" and, consequently, "individuals?"

The Definition of *Resident*

42 USC—The Public Health and Welfare
2304 Definitions
(k) The term ***"resident"*** means any person who, on the date on which the property in question is first offered for sale is either (1) an occupant in a residential unit designated for sale at the community or (2) a project-connected person who is entitled, in accordance with a lease or similar agreement, to residential occupancy of privately owned rental housing in the community.

3058F. Definitions
(6) **Resident.** The term ***"resident"*** means an older individual who resides in a long term care facility.

402 Old-age and survivor's insurance benefit payments
History; Ancillary Laws and Directives
… for purpose of this subsection, the term resident means an **individual** whose address of record for check payment purposes is located within the United States.

Author's Note*:* There are few definitions within the codes or regulations for *resident.* Given its frequent in our society, one would think *resident* would be equal in importance in the statutes. This definition qualifies one as a resident for "check payment purposes." If one does not receive checks, is he a *resident*? Since the 50 states subscribe to the social security insurance scheme, does this place them within a district of the *United States*? Does the receipt of a check from the government for social security benefits (a privilege) make a State citizen a federal citizen and a *resident alien*?

> 19 CFR—Customs Duties
> 141.31 General requirements and definitions
> (d) for the purposes of this subpart, ***"resident"*** means an individual who resides within, or a partnership one or more of whose partners reside within, the Customs territory of the United States or the Virgin Islands of the United States. A ***"nonresident"*** means an individual, partnership, or corporation not meeting the definition of "resident."

Author's Note*:* This definition falls under Title 19, *Customs Duties.* How many Americans are involved with customs? What comprises a Customs territory? How is it defined? Is it defined by Executive Order 10289? Are these territories limited or comprehensive? Are all State citizens *residents* "within" a Customs territory?

> 24 CFR—Housing and Urban Development
> 3286.3 Definitions
> ***Resident*** means any person residing in the manufactured home.

> 25 CFR—Indians
> 161.1 ***Resident*** means a person who lives on the Navajo Partitioned Lands.

> 8 CFR—Judicial Administration
> 115.5 General Definitions
> **Resident** means an individual who has been legally domiciled in a State.

Author's Note*:* What is the definition of *State*? Does it include the 50 states? What is an individual? What does it mean to be legally domiciled?

This ends our exposition of terms and definitions. A complete examination of legal terms was never the intent of this book. However, given the severity of America's incarceration epidemic, it was necessary to explore how much we do not appreciate, much less comprehend, the meaning of legal terms and the law. Most Americans will not consider our prison problem much less that it is caused by a perversion of language and misapplication of law. The notion that a law is enforced without grounds is often too easily dismissed. Discerning the use of legal terms is essential if we are to bridge ignorance of the law with truth. Accordingly, in preparation for the final case, we will cover the definitions of these same terms as defined in the Internal Revenue Code. Be mindful of the parameters these legal definitions represent. The law cannot be what it is not.

The words "people of the United States" and "citizens" are synonymous terms, and mean the same thing. They both describe the political body who, according to our republican institutions, form the sovereignty, and who hold the power and conduct the government through their representatives. They are what we familiarly call the "sovereign people," and every citizen is one of this people, and a constituent member of this sovereignty...
Boyd v State of Nebraska 142 US 135 (1892)

Legal Terms—The Internal Revenue Code

Earlier we considered that the enumerated powers under Article 1, Section 8 of the Constitution were enacted into positive law just as every public benefit is implemented by "political superiors." Natural and fundamental rights are not and cannot be created by "positive law." As defined, positive law is "distinct from moral law or law existing in an ideal community or in some nonpolitical community." No "political superior" or "human authority" grants or conveys a natural or fundamental right. We know a "jural society" is synonymous for "State," an "organized political community." With respect to positive law, the point should be transparent. Positive law applies to a jural or organized community—a State. Absent this State, man has what naturally belongs to him. Within a State, this is equally true; he still has what naturally belongs to him along with other benefits. Positive law does not diminish these rights.

The significance of positive law is important as it relates to the federal income tax. The list of codes enacted into positive law *supposedly* includes Title 26, the Internal Revenue Code. But curiously, this code is listed out of chronological order. Title 26 appears after Title 49 in the list we reviewed earlier. Moreover, the font is in bold. Obviously, reference to Title 26 was highlighted by design. Note the language used to explain the enactment. So, let's ask the question: Was Title 26 enacted as a positive law?

> **Title 26, Internal Revenue Code. The Internal Revenue Code of 1954 was enacted in the form of a separate code by Act August 16, 1954, Ch 736, 68 A Stat 1. Act Oct 22,1986, P.L. 99-514 Sec 2 (a) 100 Stat 2095, provides that the Internal Revenue Code enacted Aug 16, 1954, as heretofore, hereby, or hereafter amended may be cited as "Internal Revenue Code of 1986." The sections of Title 26, USCS, are identical to the sections of the Internal Revenue Code.** 1 USC

Is the Internal Revenue Code positive law? The listing of codes that were enacted into positive law reflects Title 26 as last. Why? Is it because it was not enacted into positive law and the explanation given above is mere subterfuge? Consider the following:

> *The Office of the Law Revision Counsel of the U. S. House of Representatives prepares and publishes the United States Code pursuant to section 285b of title 2 of the Code. The Code is a consolidation and codification by subject matter of the general and permanent laws of the United States.*
> *Certain titles of the Code have been enacted into positive law, and pursuant to section 204 of title 1 of the Code, the text of those titles is legal evidence of the law contained in those titles. The following titles of the Code have been enacted into positive law: 1, 3, 4, 5, 9, 10, 11, 13, 14, 17, 18, 23, 28, 31, 32, 35, 36, 37, 38, 39, 40, 44, 46, and 49.*[41]

[41] http://uscode.house.gov/about/info.shtml

The foregoing statement establishes that Title 26 is not positive law. Since positive law applies to a jural society, are those within the "States" liable for any excise tax they engage voluntarily and not liable for those they do not?

What becomes of natural rights in relation to a political community? We must conclude nothing happens to natural rights if those who are in the community remain and they never forfeit those rights. Men who covet and do not forsake their natural rights do so while being "without" (outside of) the jurisdiction of the "State." However, once men dispense with such rights for "public benefits" or a federal status, do the dictates of positive law prevail? At a minimum, the government has a presumption that the right was relinquished for a benefit and that it was done voluntarily. The *State* has every expectation that the excise tax will be paid. There should be little dispute that those who enter the *State* for the purpose of a benefit subordinate themselves to "political superiors." But is the tax code applicable to the 50 states as positive law or are Americans, when they subscribe to a federal benefit, suddenly within the jurisdiction of the *State*, the *United States* (Washington D.C.), which would negate the need for the tax code being positive law?

We will conclude that "human authority" with control over only the "State" cannot advance against natural rights. The State cannot impose a benefit which subverts the rights of people who are fundamentally outside of its influence. Those *without* the State may choose to enter the State with the intent to receive the public benefit and have a corresponding tax obligation to satisfy. Since the excise tax is by nature voluntary, those who are subservient to the State for that benefit must pay the tax. Those who never entered the State, because they never claimed the benefit, remain free to exercise their natural rights. What are the implications when Americans accept a benefit over natural rights whether done knowingly or unknowingly?

By now we know legal terms serve an intended purpose. They are written in such a manner to achieve a particular objective. At times, legal terms are not communicated simply and clearly. If laws were written with clarity, they would defeat any unspoken purpose. If we are willing to suspend disbelief, we must conclude that any difficulty understanding legal terms is done deliberately. If one conforms to laws simply because he is confused, he may easily accept that all laws apply to him. If there is any doubt, we need only ask why laws are written so. Otherwise, we must conclude that lawmakers know statutes must be written in such a manner as to be understood by the common man.

One observation worth noting is that the reference to "income taxes" under Subtitle A deals with just that—income taxes. An income tax is an excise tax. So why not title this section, "Excise taxes, including, but not limited to, those related to or measured by income?" The use of the term "income" without a definition is misleading. Income, as defined by the Supreme Court, is "profit" and "gain."[42] Profit is subject to excise. For example, when one invests in stocks, he pays a tax on the profit. The investor voluntarily chooses to enter the activity of investing or buying the investment and the Federal Government, the *State*, has an expectation of excising the gain. As may be clearly seen, defining "income" within the tax code would give the law proper context. Furthermore, making the distinction that one may be taxed on his "earnings," as in "income," for the federal benefit of social security would adequately define the term.

We will research the same legal terms defined in the previous chapters but do so for the Internal Revenue Code and regulations. Consider the language used and ask what the intent could be. Determine whether the text is understandable or not. Notice that the terms may be clear at times and then ambiguous. Keep in mind, the Internal Revenue Code

[42] Unites States Supreme Court, Flint v Stone Tracy Co., 220 US 107 (1911)

concerns the collection of excise taxes. Excises are voluntary and paid by those who choose to engage in a particular activity. The code does not deal with direct taxes, which by their very nature must be apportioned among the 50 states. Consequently, any excise tax imposed is legitimate. The question is to whom and when does any excise tax apply.

Title 26 USC—Internal Revenue Code
The Definition of *United States*

> Subtitle A Income Taxes
> Chapter 1 Normal Taxes and Surtaxes
> Subchapter F Exempt Organizations
> Part 1 General Rule
> 501 Exemption from tax on certain corporations, certain trusts, etc.,
> History: Ancillary Laws and Directives
> Certain Puerto Rican pension etc., plans to be exempt from tax under section 501 (A)2(d)… For purposes of this subparagraph the ***United States*** means the United States as defined in section 7701(a) (9) of the Internal Revenue Code of 1954 [1986]

Author's Note: Under Subtitle A, which deals with the income (excise) tax, section 501 provides for an exemption. Noteworthy is that "certain Puerto Rican pensions are exempt". The code references the definition of *United States* as defined in 7701 (a)(9), which provides a clear indication that the term *States* includes Puerto Rico. We have confirmation that this commonwealth is part of the United States. Curiously, the definition of *United States* is not clear under 7701(a)(9) and *States* is not qualified as in prior definitions. We may reasonably conclude that the District of Columbia, Puerto Rico, the Virgin Islands, Guam, and American Samoa are *States* which comprise the *United States*.

> Subtitle D Miscellaneous Excise Taxes
> History: Ancillary Laws and Directives
> (2) **United States**. The term ***"United States"*** means the several States, the District of Columbia, the Commonwealth of Puerto Rico and the possessions of the United States.

Author's Note: This section deals with legitimate excise taxes that are uniform across the United States. Is the definition clear? The *United States* means only what is stated. Are the several States the 50 states of the union or *States* which belong to the Federal Government? Why isn't the definition under 26 USC 7701(a)(9) as clear?

> 26 USC 7701(a)
> (9) **United States**. The term ***"United States"*** when used in a geographical sense includes only the States and the District of Columbia.

Author's Note: Let's acknowledge the use of the term *includes*. This definition is important. The *United States* falls under the *Procedure and Administration* section of the income tax code. Consider this thought as we weigh that the Bureau of Alcohol, Tobacco, and Firearms has a critical role with enforcing violations of the code. The language used in this definition is not specific. First, this definition limits the application of *United States* to a geographical sense. Why? What does this mean? Second, the term *States* is not qualified. It would be reasonable to conclude that the *States* are the District of Columbia, the Virgin Islands, Puerto Rico, Guam, and American Samoa. Then again, if the 50 states subscribe to the federal benefit of social security would they not be included? Are those "persons" or "individuals" included those who live in the 50 states yet subscribe to the benefit within the "district" of the United States, the State of the District of Columbia?

Subtitle D Miscellaneous Excise Taxes
Subchapter A Tax on Petroleum
(A) In general. The term ***"United States"*** means the 50 States, the District of Columbia, the Commonwealth of Puerto Rico, any possession of the United States, the Commonwealth of the Northern Mariana Islands, and the Trust Territory of the Pacific Islands.

Author's Note: This definition is clear. Yet, the *United States* is defined quite differently than above. Why? The tax on gasoline is a legitimate excise in the 50 States.

26 CFR—Internal Revenue
Part 1 Income Taxes
Itemized Deductions for Individuals and Corporations
1.165-12 Denial of deduction for losses on registration – required obligations not in registered form.
(a) … for purposes of this section, the term ***United States*** means the United States and its possessions within the meaning of 1.63-5(c)(2)(iv)

Author's Note: United States is used to define itself; *United States* means the United States. What does *United States mean*? The title involves *individuals* and *corporations*.

1.181-3 Qualified film or television production
(3) ***United States***. The term United States means the 50 States, the District of Columbia, the territorial waters of the Continental United States, the airspace or space over the continental United States and its territorial waters, and the seabed and subsoil of those submarine areas that are adjacent to the territorial waters of the continental United States and over which the United States has exclusive rights, in accordance with international law, for the exploration and exploitation of natural resources. The term "United States" does not include possessions and territories of the United States (or the airspace over those areas).

Author's Note: This is a clear definition of the term *United States*. We know what it is, and we know what it is not. Interestingly, for purposes of this subsection, the United States does not include possessions usually defined as part of the *United States*.

Chapter 1 Internal Revenue Service, Department of the Treasury
Subchapter G—Regulations under Tax Conventions
Part 521—Denmark
Subpart General Income Tax
Taxation of Nonresident Aliens who are Residents of Denmark and of Danish Corporations
521.101 Introductory
(1)(a) The term ***"United States"*** means the United States of America, and when used in a geographical sense, includes only the States, the Territories of Alaska and Hawaii, and the District of Columbia.

Author's Note: This code section deals with Denmark. The United States Government is responsible for treaties with foreign countries. This definition uses the term "United States of America." Even though not qualified, we may conclude it means the 50 states, or does it? However, we must acknowledge that the use of this term has been infrequent up to this point. As a possibility, since this definition refers to the territories of Alaska and Hawaii, and the treaty may have been consummated before these became one of the 50 states, we may conclude that the term "States" is limited to the territories and possessions—States of the United States. Finally, note the use of "nonresident alien" in the title, which is a term which will receive considerable emphasis.

> Subchapter C Employment taxes and collection of income tax at source Part 31—Employment taxes and collection of income tax at source
> Subpart B—Federal Insurance Contributions Act (Chapter 21 Internal Revenue Code of 1954)
> General Provisions
> 31.3121 (e)-1 State, United States, and citizen
> (b) When used in the regulations in this subpart, the term ***"United States"***, when used in geographical sense, means the several States (including the territories of Alaska and Hawaii, before their admission as States), the District of Columbia, the Commonwealth of Puerto Rico, and the Virgin Islands. When used in the regulations in this subpart with respect to services performed after 1960, the term "United States" also includes Guam and American Samoa when the term is used in a geographical sense.

Author's Note: This definition is important not so much for its content, but for its association and correlation with the definition of *State* under the same section. Be mindful, this section deals with "employment taxes." If the 48 States never subscribed to the federal social security insurance scheme, the territories of Alaska and Hawaii would have been required to participate. They were under the exclusive jurisdiction of the *United States* before their admission as *States*. We have an understanding that the 48 States may be included based upon their choice and the several States are those *States* which belong to the federal *United States*. We may conclude that Alaska and Hawaii are *States* that belong to the federal United States.

The Definition of *State*

> 26 USC—Internal Revenue Code
> Subtitle A—Income Taxes
> Chapter 1—Normal Taxes and Surtaxes
> Subchapter E—Accounting Periods and Methods of Accounting
> Part II: Methods of Accounting
> Subpart B—Taxable year for which items of gross income are included
> 457. Deferred compensation plans of state and local governments and tax exempt organizations
> (1) ***State***. The term ***"State"*** means a State, a political subdivision of a State, and an agency or instrumentality of a State or political subdivision of a State.

Author's Note: Once again, we have a term used to define a term—*State* means a *State*. This is not helpful. Is this technique designed to limit understanding? We also have an indication that a *State* is not what we might expect. A State is a subdivision of a State, or an agency or instrumentality of a State however the term *instrumentality* is defined.

> Subtitle C—Employment Taxes and Collection of Income Tax
> Chapter 23—Federal Unemployment Tax Act
> 3304. Approval of State laws
> (2) ***"State"*** means the States of the United States, the District of Columbia, Puerto Rico, the Virgin Islands.

Author's Note: The term *State* is used to define State. Are we to presume, wherever State is used that it means the 50 states? The title to this section is "Approval of State laws" for "employment taxes and collection of income tax." If the 50 states submit laws, this makes each a State for this code section. Are any of the 50 states which do not subscribe to this federal program *States*? Consider that if none of the 50 states subscribed to or submitted State laws or withdrew their State laws, the remaining States would be States within the purview of the *United States* as defined in 3121(e), the District of Columbia, Puerto Rico, the Virgin Islands, Guam, and American Samoa.

Subtitle D—Miscellaneous Taxes
Chapter 36—Certain other excise taxes
Subchapter D—Tax on use of certain vehicles
4482 Definitions
(1) ***"State."*** The term ***"State"*** means a State and the District of Columbia.

Author's Note: *State* means a *State*. Contrast this definition with Subtitle F.

Subtitle F—Procedure and Administration
Chapter 61—Information and Returns
Subchapter B—Miscellaneous Provisions
6103. Confidentiality and disclosure of returns and return information.
(5)(a) In general. The term ***"State"*** means
(i) any of the 50 States, the District of Columbia, the Commonwealth of Puerto Rico, the Virgin Islands, the Canal Zone, Guam, American Samoa, and the Commonwealth of the Northern Mariana Islands…

Author's Note: We have another example of a clear definition of *State*. Why aren't all definitions expressed in such a complete manner?

26 USC 7701 (a)
(10) State. The term ***State*** shall be construed to include the District of Columbia, where construction is necessary to carry out provisions of this title.

Author's Note: There can be no dispute that Washington D.C. is a *State* under the tax code. When we suspend our disbelief, we learn that recipients (*persons* and *individuals*) of the federal benefit of social security fall within the jurisdiction of the Federal Government that is the *State* of the District of Columbia.

26 CFR—Internal Revenue
31.3121(e)-1
(A) when used in regulations in this subpart, the term ***"State"*** includes the District of Columbia, the Commonwealth of Puerto Rico, the Virgin Islands, the territories of Alaska and Hawaii before their admission as States, and (when used with respect to services performed after 1960) Guam and American Samoa.

Author's Note: This definition correlates with the term *United States* under 31.3121(e). The term *State* is identified as being within the class listed. The class includes Alaska and Hawaii as territories before they were states of the United States. We must recall the definition of *United States* under 31.3121(e) appears to identify Alaska and Hawaii as *States*. For the above definition, are the 50 states included? Consider a different perspective. We know the District of Columbia, Puerto Rico, etc., are not and cannot be one of the 50 states. The title to this code section is "*Employment taxes and collection of income at source*." If the 48 States never subscribed to this federal program, Alaska, and Hawaii, before their admission into the Union, by virtue of being *territories*, would be *States* within the jurisdiction of the United States for this regulation. The same would be true today. If none of the 50 states participated in this program, only the *States* within the exclusive or general jurisdiction of the *United States* would remain—the District of Columbia, Puerto Rico, the Virgin Islands, Guam, and American Samoa.

Subchapter A—Income Tax
Part 1—Taxes, pension, profit-sharing, stock bonuses, etc.,
1.403(b)-2 Definitions
(20) ***State*** means a State, a political subdivision of a State, or any agency or instrumentality of a State. For this purpose, the District of Columbia is treated as a State.

Author's Note: *State* means a *State*. Since the law has an intended purpose, the District of Columbia is treated as a *State*. What is a "subdivision" or "instrumentality?" The title conveys that this tax is concerned with investments. Would this not be an excise on *profit*?

Part 6a—Temporary Regulations under Title II of the Omnibus Reconciliation Act of 1980
6a.103A-2 Qualified Mortgage Bond
(ii) For purposes of making a designation under this subparagraph, withdrawing a resignation, or making any other submission, ***"State"*** means the governor of a State, or a State official commissioned by the governor or by State statute for such purposes.

Author's Note: This definition is useful; it shows a *State* is an abstraction and, as such, only manifested when an official represents or becomes the *State*.

Part 1—Income Taxes
Taxable year for which items of gross income included
1.457-2 Definitions
(1) **State**. *State* means a State (treating the District of Columbia as a State as provided under section 7701(A)(10)), a political subdivision of a State, and any agency or instrumentality of a State.

Author's Note: Are the 50 states included within this definition? Note, the District of Columbia is a State.

The Definition of *United States citizen*

As surprising as this may seem, the term *United States citizen* and *citizen of the United States* are not defined in the income tax code. So we will refer to 26 CFR.

26 CFR—Internal Revenue
Chapter 1—Internal Revenue Service, Department of the Treasury
Subchapter A—Internal Revenue
Part 1—Internal Revenue
Possession of the United States
1.935-1 Coordination of individual income taxes with Guam and the Northern Mariana Islands.
(v) The term ***citizen of the United States*** means any individual who is a citizen within the meaning of 1.1-1(c), except that the term does not include an individual who is a citizen of a section 935 possession but not otherwise a citizen of the United States. The term *citizen of a section 935 possession but not otherwise a citizen of the United States* means any individual who has become a citizen of the United States by birth or naturalization in the section 935 possession.

Author's Note: First, this section concerns *Possession of the United States* and *individual income taxes*. The relevance of the term *individual* has been discussed and will be discussed later. Notice that an *individual* within a 935 possession is not a "citizen of the

United States" as defined under 1.1-1(c), unless he has become a citizen "by birth or naturalization" in the 935 possession.

> 31.3121(e)-1 State, United States, and citizen
> ... The term ***"citizen of the United States"*** includes a citizen of the Commonwealth of Puerto Rico or the Virgin Islands, and, effective January 1, 1961, a citizen of Guam or American Samoa.

Author's Note: We have a clear definition of *United States citizen*, which includes the class listed. Once again, if none of the 50 states agrees with the law, the term would still be applicable to the list of States in which U. S. citizens would reside. Moreover, if Americans enter the jurisdiction of the *State* of Washington D.C. by accepting or electing to accept a federal benefit or status, would they be within the *United States* while still remaining citizens within 50 states of the Union?

> Subchapter A—Income Taxes
> Part 1—Income Taxes
> Tax on Individuals
> 1.1-1(c) Income Tax on Individuals
> Who is a **citizen**? Every person born or naturalized in the United States and subject to its jurisdiction. For other rules governing the acquisition of citizenship, see Chapter 1 and 2 of Title III of the Immigration and Nationality Act (8 U.S.C. 1401-1459). For rules governing loss of citizenship, see sections 349-357, inclusive, of such Act (8 U.S.C. 1481-1489) for rules pertaining to persons who are nationals but not citizens at birth, e.g., a person born in American Samoa, see section 308 of such Act (8 USC 1408). For special rules applicable to certain expatriates who have lost citizenship with a special purpose of avoiding certain taxes, see section 877. A foreigner who has filed his declaration of intention of becoming a citizen but has not yet admitted to citizenship by a final order of naturalization is an alien.

Author's Note: This explanation is insightful. It is also potentially limiting. This definition must be understood based upon the meaning of the term *United States*. What is the term *United States?* We know the question of jurisdiction is essential to what is within the purview of the Federal Government. If the United States means the District of Columbia, territories, and possessions, then the inhabitants therein would receive citizenship by birth or naturalization. Does the immediate reference to 8 USC and 26 USC for "nationals" substantiate the limits of citizenship to places other than the 50 states?

This definition even refers to *expatriates* under Title 26. Are Americans only able to expatriate by and through the tax code? Does reference to *expatriates* mean something else? Perhaps it means those who are Citizens of the 50 states, those who knowingly or unknowingly become citizens of the United States or the State of the District of Columbia when they accepted federal benefits or made a knowing or unknowing election to pay the federal income tax, those who decide to expatriate out of the United States (the Federal Government) back to the 50 states, by revoking any election of any federal benefits. Since the tax code is concerned with collecting excise taxes that are voluntary, why is there a need to expatriate, unless the expatriation is to avoid the voluntary act which precipitated the excise in the first place? Those from the 50 states who become U. S. citizens must be able to cease any obligation which ties them to the jurisdiction of the *United States*.

Of critical importance is the purposeful use of the term *individual*. This term, as reflected in the title, is unique to the subject of "income taxes." Why not use the term "person," "U. S. person," or "U. S. citizen?" Are Americans subject to the United States generally or only when the United States Government is exercising a granted and limited power which affects the 50 states? Recall that an excise is voluntary. Finally, it is evident that this definition deals with foreigners and nationals. It ends as it begins with reference to foreigners. It is essential to know that section 877 is titled "Expatriation to avoid tax." Notice the language:

(A) Treatment of expatriates
(1) In general. Every nonresident alien individual to whom this section applies…

Author's Note: Here we have the term *individual* associated with the alien who is nonresident, as in *not* a resident.

<u>The Definition of *United States person*</u>

26 USC—Internal Revenue Code
7701 Definitions
(30) **United States person**. The term ***"United States person"*** means—
(A) a citizen or resident of the United States
(B) a domestic partnership
(C) a domestic corporation
(D) any estate (other than a foreign estate within the meaning of paragraph (31)), and
(E) any trust if—
(i) a court within the United States is able to exercise primary supervision over the administration of the trust, and
(ii) one or more United States persons have the authority to control all substantial decisions of the trust.

Author's Note: How is *citizen* defined? How is *resident* defined? What is the meaning of *United States*? Each definition has a bearing upon the application of *U. S. person*. Consider the class of entities that are U. S. persons. Is the scope of U. S. person, which is a government designation, limited? Is it possible that only those citizens and government creations become U. S persons within this definition? Since excises are voluntary, a U. S. person would be one of those engaged in the excisable activity.

26 CFR—Internal Revenue
Part 1—Income Taxes
Export Trade Corporations
1.988-4 Source of gain or loss realized on a section 988 transaction
(2) **United States person**. For purposes of this paragraph (e), the term ***"United States person"*** means a person described in section 7701(A)(30).

Author's Note: This section deals with "export trade." *U. S. person* means the definition under 7701(A)(30). A 988 transaction is a ***foreign*** currency transaction.

Part 1—Income Taxes
Information reporting by foreign financial institutions
1.1471-1 Scope of Chapter 4 and definitions
(132) **U. S. person**—the term ***U. S. person*** **or** ***United States person*** means a person described in 7701(a)(30), the United States government (including an agency or instrumentality thereof), a State (including an agency or instrumentality thereof), or the District of Columbia, (including an agency or instrumentality thereof).

Author's Note: *U. S. person*, based upon 7701(a)(30), means the U. S.

Government or agency or instrumentality. Are we *instrumentalities of the United States* (as in part of the government) by virtue of any decisions we knowingly or unknowingly made which placed us within its jurisdiction? How is *instrumentality* defined?

The Definition of *Withholding*

26 CFR—Internal Revenue
Part 1—Income Taxes
Nonresident aliens and foreign corporations
1.1441-1 Requirement for the deduction and withholding of tax payments to foreign persons
(c) Definitions (1) **Withholding**. The term ***withholding*** means the deduction and withholding of tax at the applicable rate from the payment.

The Definition of *Foreign* and *U. S. person*

26 CFR—Internal Revenue
Part 1—Income Taxes
1.1441-1
(c) Definitions
(2) **Foreign and U. S. person**—The term ***foreign person*** means a nonresident alien individual, a foreign corporation, a foreign partnership, a foreign trust, a foreign estate, and any other person that is not a U. S. person described in the next sentence. Solely for purposes of the regulations under Chapter 3 of the Internal Revenue Code, the term foreign person also means, with respect to a payment by a withholding agent, a foreign branch of a U. S. person that furnishes an intermediary withholding certificate. Such a branch continues to be U. S. payor for the purposes of Chapter 61 of the Internal Revenue Code. See 1.6049-5(c)(4). A ***U. S. person*** is a person described in section 7701(a)(30), the U. S. government (including an agency or instrumentality thereof) or the District of Columbia (including an agency or instrumentality thereof).

Author's Note: The last two sections deal with a nonresident alien and withholding agent liable for the collection and payment of the income tax, the tax assessed against nonresident alien individuals and foreign corporations. Are nonresident alien *individuals* foreign to the *United States*? The withholding agent may withhold for a foreign branch of a U. S. person. Are those who are citizens within the 50 states *foreign*, as in not a resident or a nonresident, to the United States, the Federal Government? What is a foreign branch? Note the foreign branch is liable for Chapter 61 "*Information and Returns*" under subtitle F. If we consider the definition of *U. S. person*, it rests upon the language of 7701(a)(30) and includes the United States Government.

Ask yourself this question: Is there anything Americans do which make them on par with the status of nonresident alien individuals? Do Americans, who become U. S. persons by election, have "foreign" branches, foreign to the "United States?" Does the U. S. Government treat citizens of the 50 states any differently when they choose to receive a government benefit such as social security or unemployment insurance, or elect to be treated as a "resident alien" under 26 USC 6013(g) for purposes of the federal income tax? What is the definition of *instrumentality*? If Americans accept the federal benefit of social security and elect to be treated as nonresident aliens and, therefore, as residents of the United States for income tax purposes, do they become *individuals*?

26 USC—Internal Revenue Code
Subtitle A—Income Taxes

Chapter 1—Normal Taxes and Surtaxes
Subchapter N—Tax Based on Income from sources within or without the United States
Part II—Nonresident Aliens and Foreign Corporations

Subpart B—Foreign Corporations 881. Tax on income of foreign corporations not connected with U. S. businesses
(3) Definitions
(A) ***Foreign Person***. For purposes of paragraph (1), the term ***"foreign person"*** means any person other than—
(i) a United States person, or
(ii) a person who would be a United States person if references to the United States in section 7701 included references to a possession of the United States.

Author's Note: This section is under Part II, "*Nonresident Aliens and Foreign Corporations,*" within Subchapter N as described above. This clever definition makes anyone who is not a U. S. person a foreign person; yet it offers a twist. Those who find themselves or reside in possessions of the U. S. and not within the definition of United States under 7701(a)(9) are, for this section, *U. S. persons*. Those who are *not* U. S. persons *would be* if the term *United States* included those possessions. What about citizens of the 50 states who do not become U. S. persons? Would they be foreign to the United States? Is this not a reasonable conclusion? We must remember, an excise tax is voluntary. Please note, "Foreign person" is not defined in Title 26 CFR.

26 CFR—Internal Revenue
Part 1—Income Taxes
Effects on Corporations
1.367(A) - 1 Transfers to foreign corporation's subject to 367(A)
In general:
(d)(1) **United States person**. The term ***"United States person"*** includes those persons described in section 7701(a)(30) [26 USCS 7701 (a) (30)]. The term includes a citizen or resident of the United States, a domestic partnership, a domestic corporation, and any estate or trust other than a foreign estate or trust (for definitions of these terms, see section 7701[26 USCS 7701] and regulations thereunder). For purposes of this section, an individual with respect to whom an election has been made under section 6013(g) or (b) [26 USCS 6013 (g) or (h)] is considered to be a resident of the United States while such election is in effect. A nonresident alien or a foreign corporation will not be considered a United States person because of its actual or deemed conduct of a trade or business within the United States during the taxable year. (emphasis added)

Author's Note: This section deals with foreign corporations. *U. S. person* is limited to the class under 7701(a)(30). This section explains that an individual who makes an election under section 6013 is a *resident of the United States*. Is this the limited application of *resident* in the tax code? What is the last sentence attempting to convey? The term "trade or business," just like all legal terms, must mean something specific. What is the definition? Consider the following carefully. Section 6013(g) is titled "*Election to treat nonresident alien individual as resident of the United States.*" Section 6013(h) concerns "Joint Return, etc. for the year in which Nonresident Alien becomes Resident of the United States." Is it possible that citizens of the 50 states are not residents within, as in nonresidents of the State of Washington D.C. and, as such, alien or foreign to the United States? Is it reasonable to conclude that corporations (at least those corporations which are federal) are "residents" and "citizens" of the United States, along with those who accept federal privileges, and are "individuals" and "employees" of the government?

26 CFR—Internal Revenue
Part 1—Income Taxes
Grantors and others treated as substantial owners
1.679-1 U. S. transferor treated as owner of foreign trust
(2) **U. S. person**. The term ***U. S. person*** means a United States person as defined in section 7701(a)(30), **a nonresident alien individual who elects under 6013(g) to be treated as a resident of the United States**, and an individual who is a dual resident taxpayer within the meaning of 301.7701 (b)-7(a) of this chapter. (emphasis added)

Author's Note*:* The title to this section deals with foreign trusts. What is a U. S. transferor? In this definition, a nonresident alien becomes a United States person by making an election under 26 USC 6013. In the previous definition, an individual becomes a *resident*. Is a resident a *U. S. person*? We also see the reference to *individual* in relation to nonresident aliens. Consider the significance of the term *elects* in relation to an activity subject to excise based upon a voluntary choice to engage that activity. May a citizen of the 50 states elect to pay the federal income tax and, consequently, be treated as a *U. S. person, U. S. resident, taxpayer,* and *individual*?

The Definition of *Person*

26 USC—Internal Revenue Code
Subtitle F—Procedure and Administration
Chapter 79—Definitions
(a)
(1) **Person**. The term ***person*** shall be construed to mean and include an **individual**, a trust, estate, partnership, association, company or corporation.

Author's Note: First, we must underscore that, in this definition, the term *person* shall be **construed**. What does this mean? Why can't the term be defined? Notice *person* is not defined as we would expect in the common use of the word. We should ask the obvious. Why is there a reason to define person at all? Yet, we are dealing with legal language. But this does not preclude us from asking why there is a need to define *person* separately from *U. S. person*. As for the definition, we see that the entities or titles in the listing are creations of the government and within the jurisdiction of the federal authority. **This includes the term *individual*.** What is unique about an individual? Is an individual one who elected to be a particular status or employment? As has been ascertained, a foreigner is regarded as a resident alien **individual**. Those who are nonresident aliens may become **individuals** who are treated as U. S. residents upon election under 26 USC 6013(g). Who is an individual? The term cannot mean all within the 50 states. The class is one which represents fictions or constructs of the United States Government by designation because of an act (election). Even if citizens within the 50 states are deemed to be nonresident and alien to the *United States*, they must still become *individuals* within this class of persons.

Chapter 61—Information and returns
Subchapter A—Returns and records
Part III—Information returns
Subpart B—Information concerning transactions with other person
6050B Returns relating to unemployment compensation

(c)(2) **Person**. The term ***"person"*** means the officer or employee having control of the payment of the unemployment compensation, or the person appropriately designated for purposes of this section.

Author's Note: As with section 1.1441-1, "... *withholding of tax payments to foreign persons*", this section concerns Chapter 61. *Person* under 6050B means the same as the withholding agent who has control of the payment. An *officer* or *employee* has a similar function relating to *unemployment compensation* of other *persons*.

Chapter 68—Additions to the tax, additional amounts and assessable penalties
Subchapter A—Additions to the tax and additional amounts
Part 1 General provisions
6652 Failure to file certain information returns, registration statements, etc.(5)(c) **Person**. For purposes of this subsection, the term ***"person"*** means any officer, director, trustee, employee, or other individual who is under a duty to perform the act in respect of which a violation occurs.

Author's Note: This definition clearly defines *person*. Notice the use of *employee* and *individual*. Are Americans deemed *employees* by the U. S. Government if they voluntarily accept the federal benefit of social security insurance or elect to pay the federal income tax? When do the citizens of the 50 States become *persons* or *employees*? Consider the title of this section— "*Failure to file certain information returns*". *Persons* or *employees* would have an obligation to file a return.

26 CFR—Internal Revenue
Subchapter A—Income Taxes
Possessions of the United States
1.936-10 Qualified Investments
(9) ...term ***"person"*** means a person described in section 7701(a)(1) or a government (within the meaning of 1.892-2T(a)(a)) of a qualified Caribbean Basin country.

Author's Note: This section deals with possessions of the U. S. as defined in 7701(a)(30) or a government under 1.892-2T(a)(1), the title of which is "*Foreign government defined.*" Section (A) is "*Foreign Government,*" with section (1) titled as "*Definition.*" The term *foreign government* means only the integral parts or controlled entities of a foreign government. The subject of this regulation is within exclusive federal jurisdiction—federal possessions and matters foreign in nature.

26 CFR—Internal Revenue
Subchapter D—Miscellaneous Excise Taxes
Part 50—Regulations relating to tax imposed with respect to hydraulic mining
50.3 General definitions and use of terms
(b) The term ***"person"*** means an individual, a trust, estate, partnership, company or corporation.

Author's Note: *Person* applies to the activity of hydraulic mining, an activity subject to excise.

Subchapter F—Miscellaneous Provisions
301.6111-3 Disclosure of reportable transactions
(4) **person**—The term ***"person"*** means any person described in section 7701(a)(1), including an affiliated group of corporations that join in the filing of a consolidated return under section 1501.

Author's Note: This definition makes direct reference to *person* under section 7701, but with an addition. It is important to recognize the addition includes only one concern, corporations, a subject already within the class.

Part 301—Procedure and Administration
Additions to Tax and Additional Amounts
301.6652-2 Failure by exempt organizations and certain nonexempt organizations to file certain returns or to comply with section 6104(d) for taxable years beginning after December 31, 1969
(d)
(1) **person**—The term ***"person"*** means any officer, director, trustee, employee, member, or other individual whose duty it is to perform the act in respect of which the violation occurs.

Author's Note: This definition is almost consistent with section 6652. Who are these officers, directors, etc.? Who has a duty to act?

301.9001-2 Definitions
(c) ***"Person"*** means an individual, firm, corporation, association, partnership, consortium, joint venture, or governmental agency.

Author's Note: Why is this definition so different than 26 USC 7701 (a)(1)? Does the language include citizens of the 50 states? Notice the nature of the class listed, government creations or designations and agencies of the government.

The Definitions of *nonresident alien* and *resident alien*

26 USC Internal Revenue Code
Subtitle F Procedure and Administration
Chapter 79 Definitions
7701 Definitions
(b) Definition of resident alien and nonresident alien
(1) In general. For purposes of this title (other than subtitle B) [26 USC 2001 et seq.]—
(A) ***Resident Alien.*** An alien individual shall be treated as a resident of the United States with respect to any calendar year if (and only if) such individual meets the requirement of clause (i), (ii), or (iii).
(i) Lawfully admitted for permanent residence...
(ii) Substantial presence test...
(iii) First year election...
(B) *Nonresident alien.* An individual is a nonresident alien if such individual is neither a citizen of the United States nor a resident of the United States (within the meaning of subparagraph (A)).

Author's Note: We saw in prior definitions the consistent reference to *individuals*; yet, we did not have a definition. It appears that resident and nonresident aliens define *individual*. These two designations appear to be *individuals*. First, we must recognize that resident aliens are *residents*, which is a term not used often. Why are resident and nonresident aliens referred to as *individuals* and not simply as *resident and nonresident aliens*? Or are they possibly *aliens* or *individuals* depending upon the circumstances? The answer is likely that resident aliens and nonresident aliens are classified as *individuals* for purposes of *employment* under the federal income tax code.
Consider that *individual*, as used within the definition of "person" under 26 USC 7701(a)(1), is the only possibility to define or include a human being and obscures the fact

that *individuals* are only resident and nonresident aliens. However, is one able to be a resident and nonresident without being an individual? What does the term individual imply? Does it mean a government position, title, or employment? Is such legal language ambiguously written in a manner to accomplish a specific objective? What is the intent of using the term *individual* within the definition of *person*?

Failure to define *individual* as *resident and nonresident aliens* creates the impression that, by presumption, more than those affected are individuals, as in all Americans. We must consider whether citizens of the 50 states are residents of the *United States*. It would appear they cannot be. Are they nonresident then? Citizens of the 50 states do not go about their business saying, "*I am a nonresident alien.*" They do not consider themselves residents of the *State of the District of Columbia*, the United States Government. They don't know of this distinction. But does the United States Government consider citizens of the 50 states as *nonresident aliens* and *nonresident alien individuals*? Why would it do so?

To apply the tax code, the government would need to dignify who is not within the jurisdiction of the federal income tax. For those who are not beholden to the federal income tax, certainly not all are beholden to this excise, the government would describe them with a legal title. Would that title be *resident* or *nonresident?* Americans are nonresident to the federal United States. Yet, the government, through the tax code, states when those who are not liable for the federal income tax become liable. Is this when a *nonresident alien* elects to be so under 26 USC 6013(g). Is it at this point that the government treats those nonresidents as *individuals* and *U. S. residents*, who become *U. S. persons*, *U. S. citizens,* and *taxpayers*?

> 26 CFR Internal Revenue
> Subchapter A—Income Taxes
> Part I—Income Taxes
> Pension, Profit-sharing, stock bonus plans
> 1.409A-1 Definitions and covered plans.
> (j) ***Nonresident alien***—(1) Except as provided in paragraph (j)(2) of this section, the term **nonresident alien** means an individual who is (i) A nonresident alien within the meaning of section 7701(b)(1) [26 USCS 7701(b)(B)] or (ii) A dual resident taxpayer within the meaning of 301.7701 9 (b)-7(A)(1) of this chapter with respect to any taxable year in which such individual is treated as a nonresident alien for purposes of computing the ***individual's*** **U. S. income tax liability**. (emphasis added)

Author's Note: This definition is consistent with the foregoing. But note, *individual* is a nonresident alien within the meaning of 26 USC 7701(b)(1). A *nonresident alien* would become an *individual* and subject to the tax code only by doing a specific act or making an election under 26 USC 6013(g). Otherwise, the nonresident alien would remain a nonresident alien and not a *nonresident alien individual*. If we have learned anything, we should discern that the *United States* has a jurisdiction which *includes* certain classes subject to the federal income tax. The definition of *person* as defined in 26 USC 7701 would be that class. Those not within the class would be without and not obligated to file a federal U. S. *Individual* Income Tax Return. Recall, the above definition deals with profit (income) from investments.

> Part I—Income Taxes
> **Nonresident alien individuals**
> 1.871-2 Determining residence of alien individuals

(a) General. The term ***"nonresident alien individual"*** means an individual of the United States. The term includes a nonresident alien fiduciary. For such purpose, the term fiduciary shall have the meaning assigned to it by section 7701(a)(6) [26 USCS 7701(a) 6)] and the regulations in part 301 of this chapter (Regulation on Procedure and Administration).

Author's Note: To define *resident alien* and *nonresident alien,* the regulations have a section which appears to define *individual.* Paragraph (3) below is titled simply enough, *Individual.* Consider the government's motivation as you read the definition. Please note, the above definition clearly states the nonresident alien individual is an ***individual*** of the **United States**.

26 CFR—Internal Revenue
Part 1—Income Taxes
Nonresident aliens and foreign corporations
1.1441-1 Requirement for the deduction and withholding of tax on payments to foreign persons
(3) **Individual**—
(i) ***Alien Individual***. The term alien individual means an individual who is not a citizen or national of the United States. See 1.1-1(c)
(ii) ***Nonresident alien individual***. The term nonresident alien individual means a person described in 7701(b)(1)(B) [26 USCS 7701(b)(1)(B)], an alien individual who is a resident of a foreign country under the residence article of a foreign country of an income tax treaty and 301.7701(b)-7(A)(1) of this chapter, or an alien individual who is a resident of Puerto Rico, Guam, the Commonwealth of Northern Mariana Islands, the U. S. Virgin Islands, or American Samoa as determined under 301.7701(b)-1(d) of this chapter. **An alien who has made an election under 6013(g) or (h) [26 USCS 6013(g) or (h)] to be treated as a resident alien individual for purposes of withholding under Chapter 3 of the Code and regulations thereunder.**

Author's Note: Section 1.1441-1 underscores beyond doubt that an *individual* is either an alien or a nonresident alien who has made an election to be treated as a *resident alien individual.* We cannot deny or ignore the frequent, consistent, and specific use and correlation of the term *resident* or *residence* of these *persons*. Significantly, there is the *election* made under 6013 that causes the government to regard one who is *foreign* (nonresident) to the *United States* as a *resident alien individual*. This is done, undeniably, for federal income tax purposes. Do not forget, *individual* is a *person* as defined under 7701(a)(1). What is the definition of *United States*? Recall that the listing of individual is a *resident* within the *possessions* of the U. S. when the nonresident alien requests to enter the *United States* for this status.

301.7701(b) -1 Resident Alien
(b) **Lawful permanent resident**—(1) Green card test. An alien is a resident alien with respect to a calendar year if the individual is a lawful permanent resident at any time during the calendar year. A lawful permanent resident alien is **an individual** who has been lawfully granted the privilege of residing permanently in the United States as an immigrant in accordance with the immigration laws.

Author's Note: Resident aliens are individuals. We see that *lawful permanent residents* are *individuals*. The *individual* is granted the privilege of residing in the United States in accord with what? The immigration laws.

For the benefit of our well-rounded education, we will define the term *residence* as it applies to *individuals* or, we will say, *resident aliens* and *nonresident alien individuals*.

26 CFR—Internal Revenue
Part 1—Income Taxes
Nonresident alien individuals
1.871-2 Determining residence of alien individuals
(b) Residence defined. An alien actually present in the United States who is not a mere transient or sojourner is a resident of the United States for purposes of the income tax. Whether he is a transient is determined by his intentions with regard to the length and nature of his stay. A mere floating intention, indefinite as to time, to return to another country is not sufficient to constitute him a transient. If he lives in the United States and has no definite intention as to his stay, he is a resident. One who comes to the United States for a definite purpose which, in its nature may be promptly accomplished, is a transient. If his purpose is of such a nature that an extended stay may be necessary for its accomplishment, and to that end the alien makes his home temporarily in the United States, he becomes a resident. Though he may have the intention at all times to return to his domicile abroad when the purpose for which he came has been consummated or abandoned. In the absence of exceptional circumstances, an alien whose stay in the United States is limited to a definite period by the immigration laws is not a resident of the United States within the meaning of this section. (emphasis added)

Author's Note: The term *residence* is finally defined. We have the comparison between *transitory* and the definite intention to stay (permanently) in the *United States*. Those who intend to stay are classified as *residents*. Are citizens of the 50 states residents? Americans do not come to the United States of America with the intention of leaving. They are born in the 50 states. Are Americans *domiciled* within the 50 states? Are they transitory with respect to the *United States*? Does this definition, in a subtle manner, confirm that the federal income tax is *foreign* in nature? We know the United States Government may tax things or persons which enter the United States and are foreign.

If Americans, who are foreign to the *United States*, enter the *United States* by election to be treated as resident aliens or accepting a federal privilege (social security or employment), are they *residents* within the *United States* and within the jurisdiction of the Federal Government for the application of the tax code?

26 USC—Internal Revenue Code
Subchapter A—Income Taxes
Chapter 1 Normal Taxes and Surtaxes
Subchapter N—Tax based on income from sources within or without the United States Part 1—Determination of Sources of Income
865 Source Rules for personal property sales
(g)(1)(a) **United States resident**. The term ***"United States resident"*** means
(i) any individual who
(1) is **a United States citizen or a resident alien** and does not have a tax home (as defined in section 911(d)(3) [26 USCS 911(D)(3)] in a foreign country or (II) is **a nonresident alien** and has a tax home (as so defined) in the United States and (ii) any corporation, trust, or estate which is a United States person (as defined in section 7701(a)(30) [26 USCS 7701(a)(30)]
(B) **Nonresident**—The term ***"nonresident"*** means any person other than a United States resident.

Author's Note: Each definition we considered is in some manner connected to others. The tax code has limited application. Just as the Internal Revenue Code cannot be applied in foreign countries, it may not be applied in some respects within America. After weighing the definitions of *individual* and *residence*, compare *U. S. resident* and *nonresident*. The connected nature of these two terms is transparent. Would it be a surprise that a *U. S. resident* is an *individual* who is a *U. S. citizen* or a *resident alien* without a *tax home*? If so, how does the nonresident alien acquire the U. S. as a tax home and become a *U. S. resident*? The tax code is consistent with respect to *individual* as a government designation with a foreign status. For the above definition, who is a *citizen of the United States*? What is the *United States*? Are citizens of the 50 states, who make an election or accept the federal benefit of social security and employment within the *United States, individuals* and *persons* who are *residents* with *residence* in the same *United States* for purposes of the federal income tax? Are these citizens treated as if they are *U. S. resident alien individuals* when they were once nonresident and non-persons?

The following section, which concerns *Identifying Numbers*, is referenced to express a point. Note how social security numbers are recognized. These numbers belong to a *U. S. citizen* or a *resident alien individual*. We must identify who is a U. S. citizen for this section. The title does not apply to all Americans. We know that those who enter the "jurisdiction" of the federal United States Government by election for a federal status or benefit would be identified with such titles. The income tax would be due and payable to the federal authority from these appropriate *citizens, persons,* and *individuals*. Finally, it is noteworthy that the records in the IRS database may be altered to designate the status of *foreign* for one who chooses to alter his *resident alien individual* status. Is this change of status accomplished by the *revocation of election* by a nonresident, an election which made him an *individual*, which imposed the status as a *U. S. resident alien* and, consequently, one who is a *United States citizen, U. S. person, person, individual,* and *taxpayer* for purposes of the tax code?

> 26 CFR—Internal Revenue
> 301.6109-1 Identifying Numbers
> (g) Special rules for taxpayers identifying numbers issued to foreign persons
> (1) General Rule—
> (i) **Social security number**. A social security number is generally identified in the records and database of the Internal Revenue Service as a number belonging to a **U. S. citizen or resident alien individual**. A person may establish a different status for the number by providing proof of foreign status with the Internal Revenue Service under such procedures as the Internal Revenue Service may specify. Upon accepting an individual as a **nonresident alien individual**, the Internal Revenue Service will assign this status to the **individual's** social security number.
> (ii) Employer identification number. An employer identification number is generally identified in the records and database of the Internal Revenue Service as a number belonging to a **U. S. person**.

All, too, will bear in mind this sacred principle, that though the will of the majority is in all cases to prevail, that will to be rightful must be reasonable; that the minority possess their equal rights, which equal law must protect, and to violate would be oppression.
Thomas Jefferson, First Inaugural Address

The Application of Tax Law

In a previous chapter, we considered an important question: When or how do Americans become subject to the law which imposes the federal income tax? Many comply with the law simply because they are told to do so. Most believe, without justification—and perhaps out of fear—that they have a tax liability. Regardless, the ultimate question must be asked: Who is liable? Naturally, those who believe they are not liable would challenge the authority of the law and the jurisdiction of the government. They would seek proof as to whether they have a liability. In the interest of expanding what we know, the following five arguments are most often considered as reasons why one is not required to file federal income tax returns.

When fully appreciated, these five arguments provide cogent substantiation against a federal income tax liability. Unless there are credible counterarguments, unless there is a greater truth which defeats each of these five positions, one would have no reason but to accept their relevance. However, we cannot escape the ever-present problem—legal language which comprises the law itself. The law, with its use of terms, often fails to clarify whether there is a legal obligation for the federal income tax. One may conclude that, by happenstance or by design, the tax laws create confusion.

If only for this confusion, many are content with what they *know*. Most, however, are unaware that they do not know. Many, whether realized or not, refuse to understand any differently. Regardless of anyone's given perspective or unwillingness to consider an alternative, the fact that the law is difficult, far too difficult to comprehend, is problematic. If Americans truly believe these five arguments, but file annual tax returns anyway, they cannot be faulted. Equally true, those who believe these five arguments and rely on them as reasons not to file cannot be faulted. Are those who do not file a federal income tax return *common criminals* for simply seeking the truth? Are they criminals for attempting to comprehend and comply with the law?

These five arguments may prove that most Americans would not be required to file tax returns unless they somehow elected to do so. As such, it would be wise to consider what else remains unknown. What is there about the law that we do not understand? Recall the previous ten court cases. We reviewed them without weighing the laws that were supposedly violated. However, the law for the final case—a tax case—will be considered extensively. As such, these five arguments, which factor heavily against the enforcement of the federal income tax, are posed as legitimate grounds for a defense in a federal criminal prosecution. If this last case ends in a guilty verdict with the use of these arguments, we must conclude one of two things. First, these arguments are without legal merit. Second, they have merit, but were ignored or considered to be inconsequential within and by the legal and judicial systems.

We have discussed how those with titles within the judicial system are complicit with the conviction of innocent people. The mechanics and application of each component of the legal system culminated in guilty verdicts. We know this to be true. Obviously, we would expect the reverse to be true as well, that the law would have some influence and relevance in the positive outcome of cases.

If there is no law which requires Americans to file federal tax returns, we should question why the Federal Government pursues those who fail to comply. We may conclude that there are no differences between cases we reviewed without examining the laws supposedly violated and a case where the law may be found wanting or misapplied with its enforcement. If there is no law which requires most Americans to file federal income tax returns, or if the law is enforced improperly, we must conclude that any conviction is a result of the legal system itself. However—and this is an extremely important consideration—if we fail to realize why convictions are secured, especially if genuine good faith beliefs of a defendant are not considered at trial, we fail to comprehend either the full scope of the law or its improper enforcement.

If a man comes to know that no law exists, ignorance gives way to understanding. Yet, if his beliefs are false, incorrect, or based upon a lie, ignorance remains. This is quite a conflict. A man who believes he is doing right, when in fact he is not, is no nearer the truth simply because he genuinely believes his decisions or actions are just. Yet, his decisions and actions, in the face of absolute ignorance, do not make him a criminal. Why? He does not have evil intent and, therefore, he does not have criminal intent.

We will proceed with one simple objective. We will accept these five arguments as valid, as proof that there is no law which requires Americans to file federal income tax returns. If these arguments are credible, we will or should be able to refute the supposed law which imposes a tax liability. If we approach these arguments in this manner, having established their validity, we will confirm that the legal system ignores the good faith beliefs of those who are innocent and incarcerates them upon their unjust convictions. However, we shall play devil's advocate and question, with equal sincerity and intensity, each argument. If the arguments do not pass muster, we have reason to question them as legitimate challenges of a law which is, at a minimum, difficult to comprehend.

After we weigh each argument, if we determine that no law exists, we will have a new perspective. We will no longer consider the need to file a federal income tax return as a legal liability. However, apathy and fear may still influence newly and fully informed Americans. Many may continue to file simply because they don't care that there is no law or the law is misapplied. Most may fear reprisal by the Federal Government for failing to comply. Given the ominous threat of the IRS, it is easier to acquiesce than to acknowledge the truth. It is more comfortable to comply than to restore our own integrity and the integrity of our laws, institutions, and country.

THE FIRST ARGUMENT

The first argument which supports the position that an American may not be liable to file a federal income tax return is: a vague law, a law which cannot be understood, is a law which cannot be enforced. A law which cannot be understood is likely confusing, perhaps purposely so. Confusion is a form of force. When people comply with a confusing statute for fear of reprisal there is little practical enforcement required by the authorities.

Americans comply with tax laws out of confusion and fear. The following example is a statute which lacks clarity and one which could be misunderstood. Title 26 USC, Internal Revenue Code, Section 6001 states, "Everyone person liable" as the language which creates a presumption that all Americans must file an income tax return. "Every person" means every person, right? No. Every person does not mean *all*. The terms which make up a statute may not be anything other than what is stated. If we don't know what is stated, if we do not understand, the law is vague. Generalized language, such as *every person*, is not specific. The statute does not state with particularity who is liable, even if those liable know they are.

Consider this illustration. Suppose you had a party at your house and invited ten guests. Only two within the group are responsible for cooking, you and your son. When you announce that "every person liable" for cooking must report for duty, who must comply? You and your son. Who already knows the law? You and your son. Do the other guests have an obligation to comply? No. Would the guests misunderstand the *law* as applicable to them? Well, the likely answer is no. Consider the following carefully. Is it possible for the guests to help on a *voluntary* basis? Yes. Even though the guests are outside the scope of the law, they may assist those within the class of "every person liable." This truth should be apparent.

The United States Supreme Court, in Foley Brothers v Filardo, 336 U. S. 281 (1949) succinctly addressed this matter by stating,

> *Nothing in the legislative history supports the conclusion of respondent and the court below that "Every contract" must of necessity, by virtue of the broadness of the language, include contracts from work to be done in foreign countries.*

The term *every* is not all inclusive. The court went further and explained,

> *...words having universal scope, such as "Every contract in restraint of trade," "Every person who shall monopolize", etc. will be taken as a matter of course to such legislation, not all that the legislator may be able to catch. (quoting American Banana Co., v United Fruit Co.)*

Given that Supreme Court decisions are considered settled law, the previous two quotes are insightful. We cannot presume a term is all encompassing.

We have a dynamic whereby codes, which are only evidence of law (Statutes-At-Large are law) are written with a lack of clarity. This confuses people and agents alike and allows for the assumption and presumption of a legal liability. We must have clear, concise, and knowable laws. Anything less renders laws as vague and, one would think, void. The void for vagueness doctrine is a serious matter. The Supreme Court in Grayned v City of Rockford, 408 US 104 (1972) stressed this obvious concern with language that cuts to the heart of the void for vagueness doctrine.

> *The critical question in all cases is whether the law affords a reasonable individual of ordinary intelligence fair notice and sufficient definition and guidance to enable him to conform his conduct to the law; those laws that do not are void for vagueness.*

As with any law, Americans must be able to understand the scope and application of tax laws. Courts must construe them with the intent to preclude ambiguity. In Billings v United States, 232 US 261 (1914) the high court stated:

> *Tax statutes should be strictly construed, and, if any ambiguity be found to exist, it must be resolved in favor of the citizen.*

The court explained in Tandy Leather Company v United States, 347 F. 2d 693 (5th Cir. 1965) that the collection of a tax could only be made if the liability was clearly laid. Note, the judges referred to this understanding as a "fundamental rule."

> *That the burden in such a case is always on the collector to show, in justification of his levy and collection of an excise tax, that the statute plainly and clearly lays the tax; that in short, the fundamental rule is that taxes to be collectible must be clearly laid.*

With Winters v. New York, 333 US 507 (1948), the essence of this fundamental concept is expressed. A clear application of law is vital. Uncertainty is unacceptable. Consider what the Supreme Court stated: "The vagueness may be from uncertainty in regard to persons within the scope of the act." There can be no doubt, in the wake of unclear and poorly constructed statutes, that the rights of the citizenry are jeopardized. The Supreme Court stated so in Ashton v Kentucky, 384 US 195 (1966) "[V]ague laws in any area suffer a constitutional infirmity."

Clarity of terms is a necessity. Yet, the meaning and purpose of a law may be defeated by other influences. Mere presumptions may obscure the meaning of a term and law. The Supreme Court stated in United States v Cleveland Baseball, 532 US 200 (2001)

> *Nierotko thus does not compel symmetrical construction of the "wages paid" language in the discrete taxation and benefits eligibility contexts. Although we generally presume that "identical words used in different parts of the same meaning," Atlantic Cleaners and Dryers, Inc. v United States, the presumption "is not rigid", and "the meaning [of the same words] may vary to meet the purposes of the law." Ibid. Cf. Cook, "Substance" and "Procedure" in the Conflict of Laws, 42 Yale L.J. 333, 337 (1933) (The tendency to assume that a word which appears in two or more legal rules, and so in connection with more than one purpose, has and should have precisely the same scope in all of them... has all the tenacity of original sin and must be constantly guarded against".)*

The court stresses the "purposes of the laws." The definition of legal terms is dependent upon the intent of the legislature. The justices went further into its explanation of the construction of statutes.

> *It is, of course, true that statutory construction "is a holistic endeavor" and that the meaning of a provision is "clarified by the meaning of the statutory scheme... [when] only one of the permissible meanings produces a substantive effect that is compatible with the rest of the law." United Sav. Assn. Of Tex v Timbers of Inwood Forest Associates, Ltd. The company's examples leave little doubt that the Government's rule generates a degree of arbitrariness in the operation of the tax statutes.*

How many of us outside of the legal realm would characterize the construction of a statute as a "holistic endeavor?" We expect the law to be whole and complete—with integrity. This endeavor is paramount. Why? The "meaning" of any provision may be affected by or affect the rest of the law.

Not surprisingly, the Supreme Court, with Justice Jackson's concurring opinion in United States v Spelar, 338 US 217 (1949), addresses the dilemma of statutory construction. He underscored that the intent of Congress and the purpose of a law may not be understood by the courts. He emphasized that different terms may describe the same thing. The way a statute is written and interpreted may be inconsistent.

> *To those uninitiated in modern methods of statutory construction it may seem a somewhat esoteric doctrine that the same place at the same time may legally be both a possession of the United States and a foreign country. This disparity results from holding that Congress, when it refers to our leased airbases, at one time calls them "possessions" and at another "foreign countries." While Congressional incoherence of thought or speech is not unconstitutional and Congress can use a contrariety of terms to describe the same thing, we should pay Congress the respect of not assuming lightly that it indulges in inconsistencies of speech which make the English language almost meaningless. There is some reason to think the inconsistency lies in the Court's rendering of the Statutes rather than in the way Congress has written them.*

As with any law, tax laws should be clear. Weigh the clarity of the following hypothetical tax laws:

> *Every American above the age of eighteen, who earns Federal Reserve Notes (dollars) from any and all sources, is liable to file tax returns on an annual basis.*
>
> *Each and every born or naturalized American, between the ages of 27 and 64, with brown hair and blue eyes, a red bicycle and a broken harmonica, who earns at least $600.00 a year, shall file an annual federal income tax return.*

Laws written with such specificity would preclude confusion, assumptions, or presumptions. We would know exactly what the law requires and to whom it applies. Such laws would not be void because they would not be vague.

Vague laws and their enforcement have dire consequences. The wisdom of the Supreme Court appropriately addresses the destructive influence of presumption, fraud, and force as an assault on the rights protected by the Constitution. Consider the following from United States v Butler, 297 U. S. 1 (1935):

> *If so, constitutional guaranties, so carefully safeguarded against direct assault, are open to destruction by the indirect but no less effective process of requiring a surrender, which, though, in form voluntary, in fact lacks none of the elements of compulsion.*

Surrendering of a right through the appearance of compulsion is juxtaposed with the Supreme Court's declaration in United States v LaSalle, NB.

> *The IRS at all times must use the enforcement authority in good faith pursuit of the authorized purposes of the code.*

Appropriately, the court reverts to the purpose of the code as essential to the authority of IRS enforcement.

The Constitution was written with the express intent that it be understood. It had to be. It was and is fundamental law. The law must be knowable if it is to be known. The Supreme Court acknowledged that this fundamental law, which governs the conduct of the Federal Government, was clear. Consider the court's decision in United States v Sprague, 282 U. S. 716 (1931).

> *The Constitution was written to be understood by the voters; its words and phrases were used in their normal and ordinary [meaning] as distinguished from [their] technical meaning; where the intention is clear there is no room for construction and no excuse for interpolation or addition.*

Naturally we would expect the codes and regulations to be equally clear. Often, we have the reverse. We have a government which, by happenstance or design, has created a body of law that is beyond comprehension. Former IRS Commissioner Shirley Peterson stated in "Tax Policy Lecture" at Southern Methodist University, April 14, 1993:

> *Eight decades of amendments... to [the] code have produced a virtually impenetrable maze... the rules are mysterious to many government employees charged with administering and enforcing the law.*

The concept that a law is void for vagueness is important. Whether or not courts decide to enforce a vague law is a separate matter. However, lawmakers should not write laws or allow the creation of subsequent regulations which are either unclear or create confusion. Enforcement agencies should not execute ambiguous laws. Courts should not adjudicate cases which involve vague laws.

Title 26 USC Internal Revenue Code, Section 1, states: "There is hereby imposed upon the taxable income of..." This language appears to be clear. Yet, without knowledge and discernment, we fail to notice the tax is upon "taxable income" and not upon any person, much less "every person." This code does not create a legal liability that requires Americans to file tax returns. The language was crafted by design to create the presumption of a legal liability. Confusion is inherent when laws, like this one, are not clear.

In United States v Butler, 297 U. S. 1 (1935), the Supreme Court affirmed that presumptions were to conform to the mandates of Congress and fundamental law—the Constitution. The conclusion reached by the court is definitive. A statute which violates the Constitution must be acknowledged for doing so.

> *Every presumption is to be in the oldest in favor of faithful compliance by Congress with mandates of the fundamental law. Courts are reluctant to adjudge any statute in contravention of them. But, under our frame of government, no other place is provided where the citizen may be heard to urge that the law fails to conform to the limits set upon the use of a granted power. When such a contention comes here we naturally require a showing that no reasonable possibility can the challenged legislation fall within the wide range of discretion permitted to the Congress. How great is the extent that range, when the subject is the promotion of the general welfare of the United States, we hardly need remark. But, despite the breadth of the legislative discretion, our duty to hear and to render judgment remains. If the statute plainly violates the stated principle of the Constitution, we must so declare.*

When taxing statutes presume, contrary to the virtues and principles of the Constitution, indiscretions occur. In 51 American Jurisprudence, the solution is apparent; doubtful laws, laws of confusion, must be considered in favor of the citizen.

> *Although it is sometimes broadly stated either that the tax laws are to be strictly construed or, on the other hand, that such enactments are to be liberally construed, this apparent conflict of opinion can be reconciled if it is borne in mind that the correct rule appears to be that where the intent of the meaning of the tax statutes, or statutes levying taxes is doubtful, they are, unless a contrary legislative intention appears, to be construed most strongly against the government and in favor of the taxpayers or citizen. Any doubts as to their meaning are to be resolved against the taxing authority and in favor of the taxpayer.* Sec. 316 "Strict or Liberal Construction"

The Seventh Circuit rendered an opinion which addressed the role of courts with respect to statutory construction, as well as stressing that the Secretary of the Treasury could not change language used by Congress.

> *It is a basic principle of statutory construction that courts have no right first to determine the legislative intent of a statute and then, under the guise of its interpretation, proceed to either add words from the statute's language. Desoto Securities Co., v Commissioner, 235 F. 2d 409, 411 (7th Cir. 1956); see also 2A Sutherland Statutory Construction 47.38 (4th Ed. 1984). Similarly, the Secretary has no power to change the language of the revenue statutes because he thinks Congress may have overlooked something.* Water Quality Assn. v United States. 795 F.2d 1303 (7th Cir. 1986)

There are laws which specifically identify a legal tax liability. The following examples indicate those liable and the amount of the tax. With such specificity, we must ask why 26 USC 1 and 26 USC 6001, among others, are not clear and exact.

26 USC Internal Revenue Code
Subtitle D Miscellaneous Excise Taxes
Chapter 32 Manufacturers Excise Taxes
Subchapter A - Automotive and Related Items
4071
(a) Imposition and rate of tax. There is hereby imposed on taxable tires sold by the **manufacturer, producer, or importer** thereof a tax at the rate of **9.45 cents** (4.725 cents in the case of a bias ply tire of super single tire) for each 10 pounds so much of the maximum rate load capacity thereof as exceeds 3,500 pounds.

Chapter 31 Retail Excise Taxes
Subchapter A Luxury Passenger Automobiles
4001 Imposition of Tax
(a) Imposition of tax
(1) In general. There is hereby imposed on the **1st retail sale of any passenger vehicle** a **tax equal to 10 percent of the price** for which so sold to the extent such price exceeds the applicable amount.

Chapter 36 Certain Other Excise Taxes
Subchapter B Transportation by water
4471. Imposition of Tax
(a) In general. There is hereby imposed a tax of **$3 per passenger** on a covered voyage.
(b) By whom paid. The tax imposed by this section shall be **paid by the person providing the covered voyage**.
(c) Time of Imposition. The tax imposed by this section shall be imposed only once for each passenger on a covered voyage, either at the time of the first embarkation or disembarkation in the United States.

Subtitle E Alcohol, Tobacco and Certain Other Excise taxes
Chapter 52 Tobacco Products and Cigarette Papers and Tubes
Subchapter D Occupational Tax
5731 Imposition and rate of tax
(a) General Rule. **Every person engaged in business as -**
(1) A manufacturer of tobacco products
(2) A manufacturer of cigarette papers and tubes, or
(3) An export warehouse proprietor **shall pay a tax of $1,000 per year** in respect of each premises at which such business is carried on.

These codes state exactly what is intended. The law is knowable. Those who are liable know of their tax burden. There is absolute clarity. They alone have an obligation, a legal excise liability. These examples underscore the importance of terms and definitions and the clear purpose of the law. The literal interpretation of tax statutes is critical. The Supreme Court stated in Gould v Gould, 254 US 151 (1917) that:

> *In the interpretation of statutes levying taxes it is the established rule not to extend their provisions beyond the clear import of the language used, or to enlarge their operation so as to embrace matters not specifically pointed out.*

The court went further and explained that courts had a right to stop the arbitrary exercise of power. This sentiment was expressed in United States v Lasalle NB. The IRS must use its "enforcement authority" in accord with authorized purposes of the code:

> *The court is free to act in a judicial capacity, free to disagree with the*

administrative enforcement actions if a substantial question is raised or the minimum standard is not met. The District Court reserves the right to prevent the "arbitrary" exercise of administrative power, by nipping it in the bud. United States v Morton Salt Company, 338 US 632 (1950)

We cannot escape that the purpose of the code is paramount. Terms are the bedrock of the "import of the language used." The court, once again, determined that any doubt of the meaning must be "resolved against the Government." Consider the Supreme Court's words in United States v Merriam, 263 US 179 (1923):

On behalf of the Government it is urged that taxation is a practical matter and concerns itself with the substance of the thing upon which the tax is imposed rather than with the legal forms or expressions. But in statutes levying taxes on literal meaning of the words employed is most important, for such statutes are not to be extended beyond the clear import of the language used. If the words are doubtful, the doubt must be resolved against the Government and in favor of the taxpayer.

Internal Revenue Service publications use the term "voluntary" in reference to the filing of a federal income tax return. The IRS cites "voluntary compliance" as how it receives returns. This behooves us to define the term "voluntary." Voluntary means a volitional act. It does not mean a volitional act until one fails to volunteer, at which points at IRS will force compliance. Consider the definition of "voluntary" in Merriam Webster's Dictionary and Thesaurus, 2007:

***Vol-un-tary** – 1) Done, made or given freely and without compulsion. 2) done on purpose, 3) of, relating to, or regulated by will, 4) having power of free choice. 5) provided or supported by voluntary action.*

Why use the term "voluntary" if the filing of an income tax return is not? Other terms would be more appropriate. For example, "required compliance" or "mandatory performance" are fitting if the obligation is not volitional. If "voluntary" is used because the filing of an income tax return is *voluntary*, there must be no law which requires this act. We may conclude that the use of force is the objective—compelled compliance. How ironic to have no law *and* note the voluntary nature of filing while using legal terms within the tax code that implies a liability. The use of government power to perpetuate a presumption is the answer to questions or confusion concerning a supposed liability.

THE SECOND ARGUMENT

The second argument which substantiates that Americans may not be liable to file federal income tax returns is: a man's labor is his property, a natural right, granted by Nature's God and outside the control and influence of the Federal Government. Man's labor and his earnings cannot be taxed. His property is an inalienable right which cannot be taken away. The Supreme Court captured the essence of life, liberty, and property (the pursuit of happiness), underscoring that labor (property) serves as the foundation of individual and national prosperity.

Life is the gift of God and the right to preserve it is the most sacred of the rights of man. Liberty is freedom from all restraints but those justly imposed by law. Beyond that line is the domain of usurpation and tyranny. Property is everything which has exchangeable value, and the right of property includes the power to depose of it according to the will of the owner. Labor is property and as such merits protection. The right to make it available is next in importance to the rights of life and liberty. It lies to a large extent at the foundation of most other forms of

> *property and of all solid individual and national prosperity.* Slaughter House Cases, 83 U. S. 36 (1873)

The court noted the importance of one's right to work as "the most precious liberty." To work "means to eat" and "means to live". The essence of labor can be no more aptly described.

> *The right to work, I had assumed, was the most precious liberty that man possesses. Man has indeed as much right to work as he has to live, to be free, to own property. The American ideal was stated by Emerson in his essay on Politics, "A man has a right to be employed, to be trusted, to be loved, to be revered." It does many men little good to stay alive and free and propertied if they cannot work. To work means to eat. It also means to live.* Barsky v Bd of Regents of N.Y., 347 U. S. 442 (1954 (1954)

The Justices in this case were compelled to highlight the limitations of government.

> *[The Bill of Rights] is not an instrument of dispensation but one of deterrents. Certainly a man has no affirmative right to any particular job or skill or occupation. The Bill of Rights does not say who should be doctors or lawyers or policemen. But it does say that certain rights are protected, that certain things shall not be done. And so the question here is not what government must give, but rather what it may not take away.* Ibid.

Consider the wisdom of Justices Bradley, Harlan, and Woods in their consenting opinion. They asserted that the "pursuit of happiness" encapsulated the fundamental notion that a man's right to work is inalienable.

> *These inherent rights have never been more happily expressed than in the Declaration of Independence, that new evangel of liberty to the people: "We hold these truths to be self-evident"—that is so plain that their truth is recognized upon their mere statement—"that all men are endowed"—not by edicts of Emperors, or decrees of Parliament, or acts of Congress—but "by their creator with certain inalienable rights"—that is, rights which cannot be bartered away, or given away except in punishment of crime—"and that among these are life, liberty and the pursuit of happiness, and to secure these"—not grant them but secure them—"governments are instituted among men, deriving their just powers from the consent of the governed".*
>
> *Among these inalienable rights, as proclaimed in that great document, is the right of men to pursue their happiness, by which is meant the right to pursue any lawful business or vocation...*
>
> *It has been well said that, "The property which every man has in his own labor, as it is in the original foundation of all other property, so it is the most sacred and inviolable..." Adam Smith's Wealth of Nations, BK I. Chap. 10.* Butcher's Union Co., v. Crescent City Co.

The Supreme Court continued by stating:

> *The right to follow any of the common occupations of life is an inalienable right; it was formulated as such under the phrase "pursuit of happiness" in the Declaration of Independence, which commenced with the fundamental proposition that "All men are created equal, that they are endowed by their Creator with certain inalienable rights that among these are life, liberty and the pursuit of happiness." This right is a large ingredient in the civil liberty of the citizen.*

The Supreme Court accurately described the significance of the right to labor.

> *Whether "fundamental" or not, "the right of the individual to engage in any of the common occupations of life" has been repeatedly recognized by this court... the Court recognized that "all men are entitled to the equal protection of the law in their right to work for the support of themselves and their family."*
>
> *In so far as man is deprived of the right to labor, his liberty is restricted, his capacity to earn wages and acquire property is lessened, and he is denied the protection which the law affords those who are permitted to work. Liberty means more than freedom from servitude, and the constitutional guarantee is an assurance that the citizen shall be protected in the right to use his powers of mind and body in any lawful calling.* Massachusetts Bd of Retirement v Murgia, 427 U. S. 307 (1976)

Finally, when it appeared as though nothing else could be said, the court removed any doubt as to the quintessence of labor:

> *There is no more sacred right of citizenship than the right to pursue unmolested a lawful employment in a lawful manner. It is nothing more or less than the sacred right to labor. Butcher's Benev. Asso. v. C.C. Livestock Co.*

America was founded upon time-honored principles that man is free. The Federal Government was created with delegated and limited powers. The government is to protect against the encroachment of freedom and inalienable rights. The government may not violate them. The Declaration of Independence acknowledges the source of our freedoms as the laws of Nature and Nature's God. Short of violating another man's life, liberty, or property, Americans are free. This pursuit of life, liberty, and property in freedom allows for all a man is and may be. There is no need or justification for government to control the people. This is the essence of the great "American experiment"[43] of self-government. Man's property represents all he has—his ideas, talents, and energy. A man's efforts and abilities are his possessions not subject to arbitrary limitation.

No law was ever written which allowed the government to directly tax man's labor. The government did not then and does not now have the authority to take his property. The government may not exceed its delegated powers and seize something as fundamental, innate, and vital as a man's means to support himself and his family. Supreme Court Justice Marshall stated in McCulloch v Maryland, 17 U. S. 316 (1819), "the power to tax is the power to destroy." Anything the government may tax, may be destroyed.

Suppose the Federal Government legalized marijuana. This decision would bring the production and selling of this plant within its taxing control and regulation. Such a decision would necessitate an excise simply to raise revenue for the infrastructure required to govern the oversight of this industry. A government tax on marijuana means its potential destruction in the marketplace. The government may increase taxes to such a prohibitive level and make it impossible for consumers to purchase. This would effectively destroy the enterprise and create a black market.

We intuitively know a man's life cannot be destroyed by the government by either gradual or drastic diminution. Man's life and labor is not a commodity subject to reduction by means of any power save God himself.

Every man has a natural right to the fruits of his own labor, as generally admitted;

---

43 http://www.heritage.org/research/commentary/2007/07/the-american-experiment

> *and no other person can rightfully deprive him of those fruits; and appropriate them against his will.* The Antelope, 23 U. S. 66 (1825)

> *The right to labor and to its protection from lawful interference is a constitutional as well as common law right. Every man has a natural right to the fruits of his own industry.* 48 American Jurisprudence, 2d 2, pg. 80.

In Murdock v. Pennsylvania, 319 U. S. 105 (1943), the court determined that an evangelist could not be charged a license fee in order to exercise his religious freedom. We have already learned how much more sacred is his right to labor.

> *But an itinerant evangelist, however misguided or intolerant he may be, does not become a mere book agent by selling The Bible or religious tracts to help defray his expenses or to sustain him. Those who can tax the exercise of this religious practice can make its exercise so costly as to deprive it of the resources necessary for its maintenance.*

We may easily conclude that, but for the exercise of the right to labor, man would not be able to exercise his religious freedom. The sanctity of labor is not without distinction. In Holden v Hardy, 169 U. S. 366 (1898) the Supreme Court affirmed Blackstone's classification of fundamental rights.

> *The third absolute right, inherent in every Englishmen, is that property, which consists in the free use, enjoyment and disposal of all his acquisitions, without any control or diminution, save only by the laws of the lands.*

A repeated theme within court decisions is that man has life and must labor to sustain life. The government, which is limited, cannot infringe upon this right. It has no such authority.

> *Included in the right of personal liberty and the right of private property are taking of the nature of each is the right to make contracts for the acquisition of property. The chief among such contracts is that of personal employment, by which labor and other services are exchanged for money or other forms of property. If this right be struck down or arbitrarily interfered with, there is a substantial impairment of liberty in the long established constitutional sense. The right is as essential to the laborer as to the property.* Coppage v. Kansas, 236 U. S. 1 (1915)

The United States may not, therefore, tax a man's property—his labor—much less tax it to the point of destruction. Government may not tax man's property—his labor—until there is no longer a benefit for man to labor. This concept is illustrated by what is known as "Tax Freedom Day," which is now in June. Man must work from the beginning of the year until this day in June to pay for all taxes before he begins to provide for himself. He must work six months to satisfy all government pecuniary demands.

The Laws of Nature dictate that a man's property is his alone. He can't be separated from his property or its fruits just as he can't be separated from his five senses. Man's property cannot be severed from his being without his consent. Considering the implications of Tax Freedom Day, it is unjust and unnatural to take a man's time or what he exchanges for his time. If taken to the extreme, there would be a point at which it would be futile for man to work. He would become a slave. It is not a legitimate power of government to consider how much time from a man's life is appropriate to tax. Man's right to labor is within the domain of nature and outside the jurisdiction of government. Government does not have and cannot have this power. Since man's labor is his property, a mere extension of himself, such a power would defy the laws of nature.

In Meyers v Nebraska, 262 U. S. 390 (1923), the court expanded upon the import of liberty. While the concept of liberty had not been defined, the court even suggested freedoms inherent with liberty, namely, "to contract" and "to engage in any of the common occupations of life."

> *While this Court has not attempted to define with exactness the liberty thus guaranteed, the term has received much consideration and some of the included things have been definitely stated. Without doubt, it denotes not merely freedom from bodily restraint but also the right of the individual to contract, to engage in any of the common occupations of life, to acquire useful knowledge, to marry, establish a home and bring up children, to worship God according to the dictates of his own conscience, and generally to enjoy those privileges long recognized at common law as essential to the orderly pursuit of happiness by free men.*

A tax on man's labor, while not only illegal and unlawful, is counterintuitive to liberty and counterproductive. Government, which is force as stated by George Washington, and must be recognized as force, cannot have the ability to destroy what is as natural as breathing. Such power and influence over the life of man has never been within the purview of government. However, government exercises this power as if it had authorization—but under what pretext? The answer is by confusion through vague laws which are enforced for what they are not.

The vigilance of the courts to evangelize the virtues of fundamental rights is conspicuously absent today. We must question if our natural rights to labor are as credible and sacrosanct as in prior centuries. Is the need for labor or property any different today? Note the passion of the Supreme Court in Yick Wo v Hopkins, 118 U. S. 356 (1886):

> *But the fundamental rights to life, liberty and the pursuit of happiness, considered as individual possessions, are secured by those maxims of constitutional law which are the monuments showing the victorious progress of the race in securing to men the blessings of civilization under the reign of just and equal laws, so that, in the famous language of the Massachusetts Bill of Rights, the government of the Commonwealth "may be a government of laws and not of men." For the very idea that one man may be compelled to hold his life, or the means of living, or any material right essential to the enjoyment of life at the mere will of another, seems to be intolerable in any country where freedom prevails, as being the essence of slavery itself.*

The American people are sovereign. Supreme Court cases, such as Yick Wo v. Hopkins, assert that sovereignty and sovereign power reside with the people. The States delegated powers to the Federal Government for the administration of limited authority of, by and for the people. The people never intended for their property, labor, and means of existence to be subject to exaction. They never intended that government, which serves at the behest of the people, would diminish their ability to survive or thrive. The court reinforced the importance of the sovereignty of the people when it declared:

> *With the exception of the powers surrendered by the Constitution of the United States, the people of the several States are unconditionally and absolutely sovereign within their respective territories.* Butchers' Benev. Asso. V. C.C. Livestock Co.

The court also stated:

> *There is no such thing as a power of inherent sovereignty in the government of the United States... In this country sovereignty resides in the people, and Congress can exercise no power which they have not, by their power entrusted to it. All else is*

> *withheld.* Julliard v Greenman, 110 U. S. 421 (1884)

> *In the United States, sovereignty resides in the people... the Congress cannot invoke sovereign power of the People to override their will as this declared.* Perry v United States, 294 U. S. 330 (1935)

The government, by design, only has those powers "surrendered," as in delegated or granted, to it by the people. The ability to tax the labor of the sovereign was not one of those delegated powers. Any argument contrary to this position is dispelled by the court with its elucidation about the Bill of Rights.

> *The very purpose of a Bill of Rights was to withdraw certain subjects from the vicissitudes of political controversy, to place them beyond from the reach of majorities and officials and to establish them as legal principles to be applied by the Courts. One's right to life, liberty, and property, to free speech, a free press, freedom of worship and assembly and other fundamental rights may not be submitted to vote; they depend on the outcome of no elections.* West Virginia State Board of Education v Barnette, 319 U. S. 624 (1943)

For numerous reasons, largely ignorance, apathy, and fear, we no longer appreciate that our freedoms are gifts from God and may not be transferred or taken away. They are absolute. A man may not give away his right to speech just as the authorities may not take it away. His ability to walk or breathe may not be surrendered or taken. His ability to labor is no different. The Supreme Court, in Adams v Tanner, 244 U. S. 590 (1917), stated:

> *The liberty mentioned in that amendment means not only the right of the citizen to be free from the mere physical restraint of his person, as by incarceration, but the term is deemed to embrace the right of the citizen to be free in the enjoyment of all his faculties; to be free to use them in all lawful ways; to live and work where we will; to earn his livelihood by any lawful callings; to pursue any livelihood or vocation.*

The foregoing case is complemented with the following wisdom. The court artfully expressed taxes—all taxes—as "gifts of the people." Such purposeful prose speaks to a deference, if not a reverence, for not only the power and sovereignty of the people, but their property—earnings—their source of livelihood.

> *A violation of one of the fundamental principles of that Constitution in the colonies, namely: the principle that recognizes the property of the people as their own, and which, therefore, regards all taxes for the support of government as gifts of the people through their representatives, and regards taxation without representation as subversive of free government, was the origin of our own revolution.* Butcher's Benev. Asso. V. C.C. Livestock Co.

We must consider the auspices under which government presumes to either control, take, or transfer a man's property regardless of the percentage or degree. We must consider whether a decree, which results in the taking, transfer, or control of property, places man in a state of involuntary servitude. We have a condition today whereby man is forced to *voluntarily gift* to government what is his alone. There can be little doubt that the voluntary federal income tax scheme is a direct assault upon the natural rights of a free people. Americans either have natural rights or they don't.

A brief look at the Constitution of Massachusetts, which was referenced in Yick Wo v. Hopkins, reflects the tone of the time of its creation, when natural rights were paramount. This tone parallels the sentiment of the Constitution and the Bill of Rights.

> *All me are born free and equal, and have certain natural, essential and inalienable rights; among which may be ranked the right of acquiring, possessing and protecting property.* Robertson v Baldwin, 165 U. S. 275 (1897)

Consider the opinion of the Supreme Court of the State of Tennessee:

> *Since the right to receive income or earnings is a right belonging to every person, this right cannot be taxed as a privilege.* Jack Cole Company v. Alfred T. McFarland, Commissioner, 694, 337. S.W.2d 453 (Tenn. 1960)

Referring once again to Murdock v Pennsylvania, the United States Supreme Court, which refers to the Illinois Supreme Court, validated that a man could not be compelled to purchase a right protected by the Constitution.

> *As stated by the Supreme Court of Illinois in a case involving the same sect and ordinance similar to the present one, a person cannot be compelled to purchase, through a license fee or license tax, the privilege freely granted by the Constitution.*
>
> *Freedom of press, freedom of speech, freedom of religion are in a preferred position.*

We have a recurring theme. Man is free. Man has inalienable rights. Government cannot directly tax what belongs to man.

THE THIRD ARGUMENT

The third argument which establishes that an American may not be liable to file a federal income tax return is: the Federal Government does not have jurisdiction to demand this act. Jurisdiction is tantamount to power and equates to the ability to control a person, place, property, or issue. Merriam-Webster's Dictionary & Thesaurus, 2007 defines jurisdiction as:

> ***Ju-ris-dic-tion*** (noun) *1) the power, right, or authority to interpret and apply a law, 2) the authority of a sovereign power, 3) the limits or territory within which authority may be exercised.*

Consider the following. How does the Federal Government acquire jurisdiction over free people within the 50 states? The answer is simple; it doesn't. The United States has control over specific lands, property, and people—and delegated powers granted to it by the 50 states. Over these alone the government exercises jurisdiction. Understanding what government is, to include its creation, answers the question concerning its jurisdiction. The Supreme Court distinguishes the scope of government authority.

> *The government of the United States was born of the Constitution, and all powers which it enjoys or may exercise must be either derived expressly or by implication from that instrument. Even then, when an act of any department is challenged because not warranted by the Constitution, the existence of the authority is to be ascertained by determining whether the power has been conferred by the Constitution either in express terms or by lawful implication, to be drawn from the express authority conferred, or deduced as an attribute which legitimately inheres in the nature of the powers given, and which flows from the character of the government established by the Constitution. In other words, while confined to its constitutional orbit, the government of the United States is supreme in its lawful sphere.* Downes v. Bidwell, 182 U. S. 244 (1901)

The Justices validated this authority in Reid v Covert, 354 U. S. 1 (1957). The Constitution is the beginning and ending of this "creature" that is the United States

Government. The United States is entirely a creature of the Constitution. Its power and authority have no other source. It may only act in accordance with all limitations imposed by the Constitution.

If there is any remaining doubt, we may rest on a simple idea. The Government is an abstraction. It is a concept. It is a fiction with limited power. This power, exercised by this fiction, is done so by an officer or agent. Consider the following explanation.

> *The "Government" is an abstraction, and its possession of property largely constructive. Actual possession and custody of Government property nearly always are in someone who is not himself the Government but acts in its behalf and for its purposes. He may be an officer, an agent, or a contractor. His personal advantages from the relationship by way of salary, profit, or beneficial personal use of the property may be taxed...* United States v County of Allegheny, 322 U.S. 174 (1944)

The court stated in Republican v Sweers, 1 U. S. 41 (Dall.) (1779) that the United States is not a "land mass." It is not the country referred to as America. The United States—the Government—is a corporation. The officers and agents who take "actual possession and custody of Government property" do so for this corporation.

> *United States is a corporation and that it existed before the Revolutionary War. The United States is not a land mass; it is a corporation.*

The Constitution gives shape and substance to and for this fiction. This revered document gives the Government, a fiction, the requisite force for clearly stated and limited purposes.

> *The fiction of a state within a state can have no validity to prevent the state from exercising its power over the federal area within its boundaries, so long as there is no interference with the jurisdiction asserted by the Federal Government. The sovereign rights in this dual relationship are not antagonistic. Accommodation and cooperation are their aim. It is friction, not fiction, to which we must give heed.* Howard v Commissioners of Louisville, 344 U. S. 624 (2011)

We know the fiction of the United States may exist within the 50 States by "cooperation" and each State respects the jurisdiction of the other.

An examination of the Constitution confirms the intent of the founders and the explanations by the court. Article 1, Section 8, Clause 17 grants the Federal Government the power to legislate over only certain territory:

> *To exercise exclusive legislation in all cases whatsoever, over such District (not exceeding ten miles square) as may, by cession of particular states, and the Acceptance of Congress, become the seat of Government of the United States, and to exercise like Authority over all places purchased by the Consent of the Legislature of the State in which the same shall be, for the erection of Forts, Magazines, Arsenals, dock-yards, and other needful Buildings.* Art. I, Sec. 8, Cl. 17

Article IV, Section 3 addresses power relating to "property belonging to the United States."

> *The Congress shall have power to dispose of and make all needful Rules and Regulations respecting the territory or other property belonging to the United States...* Art. IV, Sec. 3, Cl. 2, Territory or property of United States

Article 1, Section 8 lists eighteen powers granted to the United States by the states. Only these powers may the government exercise. The Tenth Amendment to the Constitution states unequivocally that powers not delegated to it belong to the states or people:

> *The powers not delegated to the United States by the Constitution, nor prohibited by it to the states, are reserved to the states respectively, or the people. .*

The import of the Tenth Amendment cannot be overstated. The Supreme Court exhaustively underscores the role and limits of the Federal Government. The following dissenting opinion in U. S. Term Limits, Inc. v Thorton, 514 U. S. 779 (1995), discusses the significance of the Tenth Amendment and the ultimate power of the people.

> *When they adopted to the Federal Constitution, of course, the people of each State surrendered some of their authority to the United States (and hence to entities accountable to the people of other States as well as to themselves). They affirmatively deprived their States of certain powers, see, e.g., Art 1, 10, and they affirmatively conferred certain power upon the Federal Government, see, e.g., Art. 1. Sec. 8. Because the people of the several States are the only true source of power, however, the Federal Government enjoys no authority beyond what the Constitution confers: The Federal Government's powers are limited and enumerated. In the words of Justice Black: "The United States is entirely a creature of the Constitution. Its power and authority have no other source." Reid v Covert. 354 U. S. 1, 5-6, 1 L Ed 2d 1148, 77 S Ct 1222 (1957)*
>
> *In each State, the remainder of the people's powers—"[t]he powers not delegated to the United States by the Constitution, nor prohibited by it to the States," Amdt 10— are either delegated to the state government or retained by the people. The Federal Constitution does not specify which of these two possibilities obtains; it is up to the various state constitutions to declare which powers the people of each State have delegated to their state government. As far as the Federal Constitution is concerned, then, the States can exercise all powers that the Constitution does not withhold from them. The Federal Government and the States thus face different default rules: Where the Constitution is silent about the exercise of a particular power—that is, where the Constitution does not speak either expressly or by necessary implication—the Federal Government lacks the power and the States enjoy it.*
>
> *These basic principles are enshrined in the Tenth Amendment, which declares that all powers neither delegated to the Federal Government nor prohibited to the States "are reserved to the States respectively, or to the people." With this careful last phrase, the Amendment avoids taking any position on the division of power between the state governments and the people of the States: It is up to the people of each State to determine which "reserved" powers their state government may exercise. But the Amendment does make clear that powers reside at the state level except where the Constitution removes them from that level. All powers that the Constitution neither delegates to the Federal Government nor prohibits to the States are controlled by the people of each State…*

As cited in United States v County of Allegheny, 322 U. S. 174 (1944) certain officers represent the government and exercise its powers. Some of these "representatives" come from the 50 states. The people elect those beholden to accomplish what is required of the United States within the confines of its powers. Congressional representatives are chosen to serve this limited role.

> *Representatives and direct taxes shall be apportioned among the several States which may be included within the Union according to their respective Numbers…*

Art. I, Sec. 2, Cl. 3

These representatives enter by election into the domain or jurisdiction of the fiction of the United States. These elected officials are the class subject to or within the realm of the government and, therefore, subject to its constraints by virtue of fundamental law and subsequent limited federal jurisdiction. This is a significant thought. Our elected representatives *are* the United States. They have an allegiance to the *United States*. Their purpose is to ensure the United States complies with the limits of the Constitution.

The office of the President of the United States is no different. He is no more than the Chief Executive Officer of the corporation. He executes the laws of the United States. He is strictly beholden to "protect and defend the Constitution of the United States." He is not elected to rule the 50 states of the Union. He is not elected to operate or manage any of the 50 states. He is responsible for the fiction—the Federal Government—and only that entity. The Oath of office states his limited role as "President of the United States."

> *Before he enters on the Execution of his office, he shall take the Following Oath or Affirmation: "I do solemnly swear (or affirm) that I will faithfully execute the Office of President of the United States, and will to the best of my ability, preserve, protect and defend the Constitution of the United States.* Art. II. Sec. 1, Cl. 8

Note, the President is to preserve, protect and defend. What is it he is to defend? The 50 states? No, he is to defend the Constitution!

The jurisdiction of the court is equally limited as expressed by the Supreme Court in State of Rhode Island v The State of Massachusetts, 37 U. S. 657 (1838)

> *But as this court is one of limited and special jurisdiction, and parties over which the Constitution and laws have authorized it to act, any proceeding without the limits is **coram non judice,** and its action a nullity. 10 Peters 474; S.P. Russ. 415 and whether the want or excess of power is objected by a party or is apparent to the court, it must surcease or proceed extra judicially.*

The United States Code reveals that "original jurisdiction" belongs to the courts for actions authorized by Acts of Congress for "offenses against the laws of the United States."

> *Except as otherwise provided by Act of Congress, the district courts shall have original jurisdiction of all civil actions, suits or proceedings commenced by the United States or by any agency or officer thereof expressly authorized to sue by Act of Congress.* 28 USC 1345

> *The district courts of the United States shall have original jurisdiction, exclusive of the courts of the states, of all offenses against the laws of the United States.* 18 USC 3231

As a side note, and to serve the purpose of foreshadowing the final case, the jurisdiction of the courts can and must be challenged where and when appropriate. For example, are the district courts referred to above Article III courts or Article IV Courts? There is a vast distinction. The former falls under the actions within the jurisdiction of the "one supreme Court" and the latter is a territorial court. There is the possibility that the district courts of the United States exercise authority only over people, territory, property, or subject matter within its domain. For one who is not subject to what is positive law, it would be unjust to try him in a territorial court, which is the proper venue to adjudicate such a case. The Supreme Court, in Hagans v Lavine, 415 U. S. 528 (1974), stated:

> *When jurisdiction is not squarely challenged, it is presumed to exist. In the courts*

there is no meaningful opportunity to challenge jurisdiction, as the court merely proceeds summarily. However, once jurisdiction has been challenged, it becomes the responsibility of the plaintiff to assert and prove jurisdiction.

The Supreme Court stated in Balzac v People of Porto Rico, 258 U. S. 298 (1922):

The United States District Court is not a true United States Court established under article 3 of the Constitution to administer the judicial power of the United States therein conveyed. It is created by virtue of the sovereign congressional faculty, granted under article 4, 3 of that instrument, of making all needful rules and regulations respecting the territory belonging to the United States. The resemblance of its jurisdiction to that of true United States courts, in offering an opportunity to nonresidents of resorting to a tribunal not subject to local influence, does not change its character as a mere territorial court.

We have a much clearer depiction of the jurisdiction of the government as represented by the Constitution and Supreme Court. The United States is something specific—a corporation, a fiction, an abstraction—through which officers possess property and exercise powers which apply to the United States exclusively. To substantiate this, refer to the Supreme Court for elucidation. But first, acknowledge one final thought. The Constitution had to be interpreted "in light of the law" at the time it was adopted.

We are bound to interpret the Constitution in the light of the Law as it existed at the time it was adopted... Mattox v United States, 156 U. S. 237

The definitive role of the United States and its limited jurisdiction, especially in light of Mattox, was expressed by the high court. Consider the following:

First. The canon of construction which teaches that legislation of Congress, unless a contrary intent appears, is meant to apply only within the territorial jurisdiction of the United States, Blackmer v. United States, is a valid approach whereby unexpressed congressional intent may be ascertained. Foley Bros. Inc. v. Filardo

The Banana Co. Case confined the Sherman Act in its "operation and effect to the territorial limits over which the lawmakers have general and legitimate power". Steele v Bulova Watch Co., 344 U. S. 280 (1952)

While a statute is presumed to speak from the time of its enactment, it embraces all such persons or things as subsequently fall within its cope, and ceases to apply to such thereafter fall without its scope. DeLima v. Bidwell, 182 U. S. 1 (1901)

The laws of Congress in respect to those matters do not extend into the territorial limits of the States, but have force only in the District of Columbia and other places that are within the exclusive jurisdiction of the national government. CAHA v United States, 152 U. S. 211(1894)

We know the government, whether the legislative, executive, and judicial branch, may not exceed its authority. As officers, agents, or representatives of the United States, an official's power is limited.

The Foley Brothers case presents an apt scenario which distinguishes the limited application of federal power. In the following quote, the *United States* is mentioned three times in reference to "work of a citizen of the United States," under a contract with the United States," and a "corporation domiciled in the United States." The court rejected the language in a statute that "every contract made to which the United States... is a party" as not applicable to the above referenced "United States" in the absence of a "clearly expressed purpose."

> *We are here confronted by a statute which in terms covers "every contract made to which the United States... is a party."* 37 Stat. 137, c 174, 40 USCA 324, 9A FCA title 40 Sec. 324. *Yet the court construes it as inapplicable even to work of a citizen of the United States under a contract between the United States and a corporation domiciled in the United States because "An intention so to regulate labor conditions which are the primary concern of a foreign country should not be attributed to Congress in the absence of a clearly expressed purpose."*

The court in United States v. Spelar, 338 U. S. 217 (1949) underscored the message in Foley. Unless a purpose is stated or a "contrary intent appears," congressional legislation is to "apply only within the territorial jurisdiction of the United States."

> *In Foley Bros. Inc. v. Filardo we had occasion to refer to the "canon of construction which teaches that legislation of Congress, unless a contrary intent appears, is meant to apply only within the territorial jurisdiction of the United States..." That presumption, far from being overcome here, is doubly fortified by the language of this statute and the legislative purpose underlying it.*

In Downes v Bidwell, the Supreme Court leaves no latitude with the interpretation that the *United States* is limited to what is within its domain. Pay particular attention to the fact that this case deals with a *territory*, Puerto Rico. The "inhabitants" of the "territories" have personal rights and the government is restrained by the Constitution with respect to these rights. However, their "political rights" are "franchises," referred to as privileges subject to the discretion of Congress. Such "privileges" exist at the mercy of congressional control. Congress does not have control with respect to the citizens of the free and independent states and without the jurisdiction of the *United States*.

> *In Murphy v. Ramsey, 144 U. S. 15 (1885), Mr. Justice Matthews said: The personal and civil rights of the inhabitants of the territories are secured to them, as to other citizens, by principles of constitutional liberty which restrain all the agencies of government, which they hold as privileges in the legislative discretion of the Congress of the United States.*

The autonomy of the States is beyond dispute. The Federal Government was neither designed nor intended to exert undue influence over sovereign countries that are separate and distinct from the United States. The court went so far as to declare,

> *No political dreamer was ever wild enough to think of breaking down the lines which separate the states and compounding them into one common mass.* McCulloch v. Maryland

The court ably described the independence of both the states and the United States.

> *It is fundamental, under our dual system of government, that the Nation and the State are supreme and independent, each within its own sphere of action and that each is exempt from the interference or control of the other in respect to its governmental powers, and the means employed in their exercise... Except as otherwise provided by the Constitution, the sovereignty of the States "can be no more invaded by the action of the general government than the action of state governments can arrest or obstruct the course of the national power."* Worcester v. Georgia 6 Pet. 515, 570 (This is from Justice Sutherland's dissenting opinion.)

The court noted in Farrington v. Tennessee, 95 U. S. 679 (1877), that the federal authority is limited with respect to the 50 states:

> *Yet every state has a sphere of actions where the authority of the national*

> *government may not intrude. Within that domain the State is as if the union were not. Such are the checks and balances in our complicated but wise system of state and national polity.*

We must challenge whether the government, be it legislative, executive, or judicial, has autonomy over man, his property, and his earnings. Since jurisdiction is a legitimate question, if not the main question, we must determine if the governing authorities have the power to directly tax the people. The scope of the federal authority to tax is no different from the exercise of any other power it possesses. This authority is limited. In the renowned case of McCulloch v. Maryland, the court expressed with exactness that the "constitutional measures" of separate governments were beyond question:

> *That the power to tax involves the power to destroy; that the power to destroy may defeat and render useless the power to create; that there is a plain repugnance in conferring on one government a power to control the constitutional measure of another; which other, with respect to those very measures, is declared to be supreme over that which exerts the control, are propositions not to be denied.*

This decision serves the purpose of further delineating that the United States may not trespass where it has no authority. Trespasses, aptly called "a plain repugnance," reinforce the inherent constraints of the Constitution. The "power to destroy" requires no less than disobedience to these constraints. In United States v. Hill, 248 US 420 (1919), the court stated that a "revenue law" must be "directly traceable" to the Constitution:

> *This clearly implies that the term "revenue law," when used in connection with the jurisdiction of the courts of the United States, means a law imposing duties on imports or tonnage, or a law providing in terms for revenue; that is to say, a law which is directly traceable to the power granted to Congress by 8, Art. I of the Constitution, to lay and collect taxes, duties and excises.*

Referring to McCulloch, the court states "the power of taxation." With Hill, we must ask an obvious question. From what source do we trace this right? The answer provided by Justice Marshall in McCulloch is superlative in its representation. "The sovereignty of a state extends to everything which exists by its own authority or is introduced by its permission." The government may control what it has or what it is given.

> *It may be objected to this definition, that the power of taxation is not confined to the people and property of a state. It may be exercised upon every object brought within its jurisdiction. This is true, but to what source do we trace this is right? It is obvious, that it is incident of sovereignty, and it is co-extensive with that to which it is an incident. All subjects over which the sovereign power of a state extends, are objects of taxation; but those over which it does not extend are, upon the soundest principles, exempt from taxation. This proposition may almost be pronounced self-evident. The sovereignty of a state extends to everything which exists by its own authority, or is introduced by its permission.*

An illustration of a taxing power which exceeded its scope was determined in Murdock v. Pennsylvania, 309 US 105 (1943). The tax of a "freedom" was cited as beyond the power of the governing authority and, therefore, denied.

> *The power to impose a license tax on the exercise of these freedoms is indeed as potent as the power of censorship which this court has repeatedly struck down.*

The court even declared that taxing interstate commerce was not the authority of a state:

> *A state may not impose a charge for the enjoyment of a right granted by the Federal Constitution. Thus, it may not exact a license tax for the privilege of carrying on interstate commerce, although it may tax the property used in, or the income derived from, that commerce, so long as those taxes are not discriminatory.*

The same holds true for the United States Government. The court stated,

> *But very different considerations apply to the internal commerce or domestic trade of the states. Over this commerce and trade Congress has no power of regulation nor any direct control. No interference by Congress with the business of citizens transacted within a state is warranted by the Constitution, except such as is strictly incidental to the exercise of powers clearly granted to the legislature.* License Tax Cases, 72 U. S. 462 (1866)

> *...that the internal trade of the State is not subject, in any respect, to legislation by Congress and can neither be licensed nor prohibited by its authority.* Ibid.

In Gibbons v. District of Columbia, 116 U. S. 404 (1886) the court rendered an opinion which conclusively depicts the "limits" of a state and Congress:

> *As the jurisdiction and sovereignty of a State legislature is confined to the limits of a State, so Congress as the legislature of the District of Columbia is confined to the exercise of its powers to that district and cannot lay a tax on the merchants of New York for the benefit of the district.*

The wisdom of the Supreme Court compels us to appreciate a macro perspective of sovereignty and control. The people are sovereign; the States are autonomous. The Federal Government may exercise it prerogatives to a limited extent. A miscarriage of these truths would have—and do have—disastrous effects. The justices expressed this potential abuse in Bailey v. Drexel Furniture Co., 259 U. S. 20 (1922), suggesting that "all Congress would need to do... would be to enact a detailed measure of the subject and enforce it..." The court paints the unjust ends of such efforts, citing that it "would break down all constitutional limitation" and "wipe out the sovereignty of the States."

> *It is the high duty and function of this court in cases regularly brought to its bar to decline to recognize or enforce seeming laws of Congress, dealing with subjects not entrusted to Congress but left or committed by the Supreme law of the land to the control of the States. We cannot avoid the duty even though it requires us to refuse to give effect to legislation designed to promote the highest good. The good sought in unconstitutional legislation is an insidious feature because it leads to citizens and legislators of good purpose to promote it without thought of the serious breach it will make in the ark of our covenant or the harm which will come from breaking down recognized standards. In the maintenance of local self-government, on the one hand, and the national power on the other, our country has been able to endure and prosper for near a century and a half.*

> *Out of respect for the acts of a coordinate branch of the Government, this court has gone far to sustain taxing acts as such, even though there has been ground for suspecting from the weight of the tax it was intended to destroy its subject. But, in the act before us, the presumption of validity cannot prevail because the proof of the contrary is found on the very face of its provisions. Grant the validity of this law, and all that Congress would need to do, hereafter, in seeking to take over to its control any one of the great number of subjects of public interest, jurisdiction of which the States have never parted with, and which are reserved to them by the*

> *Tenth Amendment, would be to enact a detailed measure of complete regulation of the subject and enforce it by a so-called tax upon departures from it. To give such magic to the word "tax" would be to break down all constitutional limitations of the powers of Congress and completely wipe out the sovereignty of the States.* Child Labor Tax Case

The absolute necessity for defined powers is inarguable. Let there be no mistake, as with all powers, the exercise of revenue laws is limited to sanctioned spheres and a legitimate scope. This scope distinguishes between taxpayers and those who are not.

> *The revenue laws are a code or system in regulation of tax assessment and collection. They relate to taxpayers, and not to non-taxpayers. The latter are without their scope. No procedure is prescribed for non-taxpayers, and no attempt is made to annul any of their rights and remedies in due course of law. With them Congress does not presume to deal, and they are neither of the subject nor the object of the revenue laws.*
>
> *The distinction between persons and things within the scope of the revenue laws and those without them is vital. ***To the former only does section ***apply*** and the well-understood exigencies of government and its revenues and their collection do not serve to extend it to the latter. It is a shield for official action, not a sword for private aggression.* Stewart v Chinese Chamber of Commerce, 168 F 2d 709 (9th Cir. 1948)

We have a clear distinction between a class of persons within the purview of the Federal Government, taxpayers, and those who are not taxpayers. This class of taxpayers within federal control is not new or unique. There is a need to identify taxpayers within federal authority.

Consider a prime example. The first internal revenue law was approved on July 1, 1862. This tax was passed by Congress for collection by the Commissioner of Internal Revenue and his assessors and collectors. The target for collection was a specific class. The enactment of the law discloses that class.

> *And be it further enacted, that on and after the first day of August, 1862 there shall be levied, collected and paid on all salaries of officers, or payments to persons in the civil, military, naval, other employments or service of the United States, including Senators and representatives and delegates in Congress...*

The Public Salary Tax Act of 1939 expanded the definition to include,

> *Employees of the United States the District of Columbia or any agency or instrumentality thereof whether elected or appointed.*

Consider the definition of "Gross Income" under Section 22a, 213:

> *Gross Income Defined. Section 213. That for the purposes of this title, (except as otherwise provided in section 233), the term "gross income"(A) includes gains, profits, and income derived from salaries, wages, and compensation for personal service (including in the case of the President of the United States, the judges of the Supreme Court and lower inferior courts of the United States, and all other officers and employees, whether elected or appointed, of the United States, Alaska, Hawaii, or any political subdivision thereof or the District of Columbia, the compensation received as such.*

Note the class of persons subject to the tax is still inclusive of those who work for the employer, the *United States*. Interestingly, Alaska and Hawaii were within the jurisdiction of the United States, for each was a territory not yet admitted as a state of the Union. The Public Salary Tax Act of 1939 qualified the definition of "Gross Income" as follows:

> *Public Salary Tax Act of 1939, Title 1 - Section 22 (a) of the Internal Revenue Code relating to the definition of "gross income" is amended after the words "compensation for personal service" the following: including personal service as an official or employee of a State or any political subdivision thereof, or any agency or instrumentality of any one or more of the foregoing.*

We can see the ever-increasing generalization of language in the last qualified definition compared to the specificity used in the 1862 enactment and subsequent definitions. The general use of *State* implies a greater reach than should be attributed. As we learned in the definition of *State*, the territories and possessions of the United States are States. If we weigh the definition of "trade or business," the relevance of the income tax assessed against the intended class of persons is congruent with the origins of the very first income tax law. According to 26 USC 7701(a)(26):

> *The term "trade or business" includes the performance of the function of a public office.*

Congress may only tax those within its jurisdiction. It stands to reason that since the Federal Government creates positions of "employment," it may tax those who make a voluntary decision to work in those positions for the employer, the United States. This premise is confirmed by Taxation Key, West 933:

> *The right to receive income or earnings is a right belonging to every person and realization of income is therefore not a privilege that can be taxed.*

Consider Taxation Key, West 53:

> *The legislature cannot name something to be a taxable privilege unless it is first a privilege.*

There can be little doubt that the government could not tax all earnings in 1862, as most earnings of the people within several States were outside its jurisdiction and powers. The government could only tax those within a definitively liable class. Confirmation that the Internal Revenue Code applies to "individuals" and "employees" within the jurisdiction of the United States is provided by the Department of the Treasury, which published the following by its Division of Tax Research:

> *For 1936, taxable income returns filed represented only 3.9% of the population...*
>
> *The largest portion of consumer incomes in the United States is not subject to income taxation. Likewise, only a small portion of the population of the United States is covered by the Income Tax.* ("Collection at Source of Individual Normal Income Tax (1941))

Not all Americans were liable to file an income tax return. The government did not have within the class subject to the tax those who were not and could have been employees of the United States. Why? The second truth explains the answer; man's labor was and is his property. His earnings were and are his property. His earnings were not the result of a *privilege* granted by the government. The government had no power to tax those clearly without its jurisdiction; Congress knew—and knows—this truth.

Anyone reading this material would naturally question how most Americans become *liable* for a tax when previously they were not. While the answer is not the specific intent of this third argument, the reasons offered are varied. Yet, one answer cannot be denied. Americans became ignorant which led to their apathy and, ultimately, to fear itself. At the same time, the Federal Government, by subterfuge, manipulated words, definitions, and language and created the presumption of a liability. This manifestation, which will be discussed later, is nothing more than fraud and force.

Let's belabor the significance that Congress may only tax the class within its domain. The Supreme Court stated in Railroad Co., v Collector, 100 U. S. 595,

> *Whether Congress, having power to enforce the law, has the authority to levy such a tax on the interest due by a citizen of the United States to one who is not domiciled within our limits, and who owes the government no allegiance, is a question which we do not think necessary to the decision of this case.*
>
> *The tax, in our opinion is essentially an excise on the business of the class of corporations mentioned in the statute.*
>
> *...The tax is laid by Congress on the net earnings, which are the results of the business of the corporation, on which Congress had clearly a right to lay it; and being lawfully assessed and paid, it cannot be recovered back by reason of any inefficiency or ethical objection to the remedy over against the bondholder.*

This decision reveals several relevant points. First, the tax could not be returned for the benefit of the foreign person who was outside the jurisdiction of Congress. Second, Congress had a lawful right to lay the tax on a railroad corporation, a "United States citizen." This citizen, a creature or fiction of the United States, was within "the class of corporations mentioned in the statutes." Third, the tax was an excise on the results of the "business of the corporation." Clearly, Congress had the jurisdiction to collect the tax.

Those persons and entities within the federal jurisdiction speak to a larger classification of citizenship, that is federal citizenship and *United States citizenship*. Over these citizens the United States Government may tax by excise. Let's explore this distinction by drawing a contrast which will distinguish state citizens from federal citizens. Consider the words of the Supreme Court as stated in the Slaughter House Cases:

> *It is clear, then, that here is a citizenship of the United States and a citizen of a State, which are distinct from each other and which depend upon characteristics or circumstances in the individual.*

Consider the following:

> *We have in our political system a Government of the United States and a government of each of the several States. Each of these governments is distinct from the others and each has citizens of its own.* United States v. Cruikshank, 92 U. S. 542 (1875)

While the next quote is not a Supreme Court case, but from the inferior courts, a United States Appellate Court, it is instructive:

> *Both before and after the Fourteenth Amendment to the Federal Constitution, it has not been necessary for a person to be a citizen of the United States in order to be a citizen of his State.* Crosse v. Bd of Supervisors of Elections, 221 A. 2d 431 (1966)

We can easily surmise that, before and after passage of the Fourteenth Amendment, a man could be a citizen of his state and not be a United States citizen. We may also conclude that he was not and could not be within the class created by the United States Government for whatever reason. Consider the Supreme Court decision reflected in the United States v. Wong Kim Ark, 169 U. S. 649 (1898):

> *The object of the Fourteenth Amendment, as is well known, was to confer upon the*

colored races the right of citizenship.

The following cases from California and Indiana echo the same sentiment:

> *No white person born within the limits of the United States... or born without those limits, and subsequently naturalized under their laws, owes the status of citizenship to the recent Amendment to the Federal Constitution.* Van Valkenburg v. Brown, Cal.43 (1872)

> *One may be a citizen of a State and not yet a citizen of the United States.* Thomas v State, Ind.

With the end of slavery, Congress had to create the purposeful distinction of a United States citizen, which, prior to the 14th Amendment, did not exist. Rightly, the Federal Government had to classify and protect those who had no citizenship since some states were hostile toward granting citizenship or bestowing rights and protections upon the newly freed people. The Federal Government conferred the privileges and immunities commensurate with national citizenship whether a now free people had state citizenship. Consider the following case from Maine, which predates the Fourteenth Amendment and the Civil War.

> *... for it is certain, that in the sense in which the word "citizen" is used in the Federal Constitution. "Citizen of each State," and "Citizen of the United States" are entitled to all the Privileges and Immunities of Citizens in the several States and "citizens of the United States" are, of course, Citizens of all the United States.* 44 Maine 518 (1859)

Citizens of one state are Citizens of all the 50 states. In Downes v. Bidwell, the Supreme Court established the main distinction between a United State citizen and a state Citizen.

> *In the Slaughter House cases, Mr. Justice Miller observed: "It has been said by eminent judges that no man was a citizen of the United States except as he was a citizen of one of the States composing the Union. Those, therefore, who had been born and resided always in the District of Columbia or in the territories, though within the United States, were not citizens. Whether this proposition was sound or not has never been judicially decided." And he said the question was put to rest by the amendment, and the distinction between citizenship of the United States and citizenship of a State was clearly recognized and established. "Not only may a man be a citizen of the United States without being a citizen of a State, but an important element is necessary to convert the former into the latter. He must reside within the State to make him a citizen of it, but it is only necessary that he should be born or naturalized in the United States to be a citizen of the Union.*

Consider the following quote as we delve into the significance of the topic of citizenship and federal income taxes:

> *The phrase, "privileges and immunities" was used in Article 4 & 2 of the Constitution, which decrees that "The Citizens of each State shall be entitled to all Privileges and Immunities of Citizens in the several States." As has been said, prior to the adoption of the Fourteenth Amendment, there had been no constitutional definition of citizenship of the United States, or the rights, privileges and secured thereby or springing therefrom.*

> *At one time it was thought that this section recognized a group which, according to the jurisprudence of the day, we classed as "natural rights;" and that the purpose of the section was to create rights of citizens of the United States by*

> *guaranteeing the citizens of every state the recognition of this group of rights by every other State.* Hague v. Committee for Industrial Organization, 307 U. S. 496 (1939)

Then there is the following:

> *Mr. Justice Bradley also said: The question is now settled by the 14th Amendment itself, that citizenship of the United States is the primary in this country and that State citizenship is secondary depending upon the citizen's place of residence. The States have not now, if they ever had, any power to restrict their citizenship to any classes of persons.* United States v. Wong Kim Ark

Given this discussion of citizenship, what is our net understanding? We know there never was a distinction of United States citizens of the Union of states until the 14th Amendment. We know this United States citizenship, whereby a citizen of one state is a citizen of all states, is of prime importance. We know this collective "fifty state citizenship" does not change the relevance of state citizenship and the attendant rights therewith. We also have a clear sense that to be a citizen of one State is to be a citizen of another State or of any State and, therefore, a citizen of the several States, the United States of America. The foregoing has nothing to do with whether one is subservient to the Federal Government, the *United States*, as defined in a restrictive sense. Citizens still enjoy the natural rights inherent with a constitutional construct governed by the limitations properly imposed upon the United States Government. The Federal Government is still limited with respect to its powers. The power to tax was still governed by the constraints of the Constitution.

Since we know Americans are not liable for the income tax simply for being citizens of the united (50) States, which makes them citizens of individual States, we must ask if they have somehow entered the jurisdiction of the United States Federal Government as a creation or fiction within its law that would classify them as U. S. citizens of the federal corporation, similar to the citizen cited in Railroad Co., v Collector. Even if the Federal Government operates with the presumption that all state citizens are U. S. citizens, in the sense they are citizens of all 50 states, this classification does not bring Americans within the purview of the government in the sense that they are within the jurisdiction of the *United States*. If Americans are presumed to be, in whatever form or fashion, and for whatever reason, *employees* of the United States, we must ask how this is accomplished. For, as demonstrated in Brady v. United States, 397 US 742 (1970):

> *Waivers of constitutional rights not only must be voluntary, they must be knowingly intelligent acts done with sufficient awareness of the relevant circumstances and consequences.*

Has the government, as it did in the days of the Civil War, created a class of citizenship to which most Americans have unwittingly subscribed? Are most Americans now considered *employees* of the *United States*? Do we now have two classifications of *United States citizen*, one of the collective 50 states and one of the corporate United States? As we learned previously, the use and crafting of terms, meaning, and codes are suspect. Furthermore, since most codes apply to the United States corporation and its officers, agents, and employees, does a new derivation of citizenship make most Americans beholden to the tax code the same as officers of the United States in August of 1862? Let's explore the extent to which the United States Government may exercise its authority to tax within its prescribed jurisdiction.

Under Articles 1, Section 8 of the Constitution, the Federal Government has the power to collect direct and indirect taxes. However, the power to directly tax the American people is a qualified power. As a practical matter, it isn't a direct tax at all. Direct taxes upon people and property must be "apportioned" among the 50 states. This is known as "The Rule of Apportionment." Apportioned means to distribute or allocate proportionately. Any federal tax which falls upon the people or property must be passed to the sates for collection in accordance with this constitutional constraint. This rule defeats any attempt by the federal authority to do the taxing. Such a power was not and is not within the federal arsenal of power granted by the people and the 50 states.

Consider how an apportioned tax would be assessed. Congress determines that it needs $100 billion dollars. This sum would have to be apportioned among the 50 states. The percentage of a state's population, proportional to the population of all states, would be the amount of the total it would collect. The individual states would determine how to collect the tax and from whom. The Federal Government would have no influence in this regard. If Virginia had 10% of the nation's population, it would be responsible for 10% of the $100 billion. Virginia would assess, however it deemed appropriate, $10 billion from its citizens.

There is an important reason why the Constitution was written to ensure the Federal Government could not directly tax the people and property of the citizens of Virginia. Governments, by their very nature, have an historical propensity to control and destroy. The drafters of the Constitution deliberately prevented the United States Government from exercising direct power over the people. The requirement that direct taxes be apportioned was a precaution. Our forefathers sought to defend the people's rights against infringement and destruction. We did have and should have absolute assurance that Americans are free from the undue and illegitimate influence of errant government power. The power of direct taxation as defined under the rule of apportionment still exists; but it is no longer used.

> *No capitation, or other direct, Tax shall be laid, unless in Proportion to the Census or Enumeration herein before directed to be taken.* Art. I, Sec 9, Cl. 4, Constitution

We should question why the government does not exercise this legitimate power. Perhaps the federal authority is able to control and destroy by means of its indirect taxing power. The "income tax" law has the appearance of legitimacy upon the American people when applied with force and fear.

The other form of taxation exercised by the Federal Government is indirect. Indirect taxes as cited in Article 1, Section 8, and includes duties, imposts, and excises:

> *The Congress shall have Power to lay and collect taxes, duties, imposts and excises, to pay the Debts... but all duties, imports and excises shall be uniform throughout the United States...* Art. I, Sec. 8, Cl. 1, Constitution

Duties and imposts typically relate to foreign trade. Excise taxes are those imposed to collect "internal revenue" from within the states. These excises are a viable means of collecting revenue for the government. Excises are quite different than direct taxes in one specific regard. Excises are voluntary. As discussed, we have a dynamic in America today whereby Americans are forced to voluntarily gift property (earnings) when they file federal income tax returns. Such forced gifting is a contradiction of natural rights.

Since excise taxes are voluntary, a man must choose to pay it by willingly engaging that activity or benefit which requires the tax. The volitional nature makes the tax indirect. A man must choose to pay the tax and the government may not force him to do so from the outset. If a man were compelled to pay the excise without deciding to participate in the activity or benefit subject to excise, this would be tantamount to a direct tax which would require the tax be apportioned. It is that simple of an explanation.

Consider some practical examples of excises or indirect taxes. If a man chooses to buy cigarettes, he voluntarily agrees to pay the required excise tax assessed with the purchase of this product. The same applies with the excise tax collected on the sale of every gallon of gasoline. This tax, which must be uniform across the country, is paid only if a man chooses to voluntarily buy gas. We can see that while excise taxes are legitimate, they are not at all obligatory unless a choice is made.

Herein rests the significance of direct and indirect taxes. The "federal income tax" is an excise tax and, therefore, voluntary. Understanding the definition of terms is critical. Since the income tax is an indirect tax, we must define "excise." In the Flint v Stone Tracy Company, 220 U. S. 107 (1911), The Supreme Court stated:

> *Excises are taxes laid upon the manufacture, sale or consumption of commodities within the country, upon licenses to pursue certain occupations, and upon corporate privileges.* Cooley, Const. Lim 7th Ed. 680

This definition supports our understanding that the manufacture, sale, or consumption of cigarettes, gasoline, or any other identified commodity is a viable source of excise. These taxes are paid by free men with their earnings from labor when they voluntarily purchase such products. Legitimate taxes are revenue for the operation of the Federal Government.

The definition of excise includes "licenses to pursue certain occupations" and upon "corporate privileges." These two are legitimate sources of excise within the federal jurisdiction. The Federal Government may tax only certain occupations and only corporate privileges within the federal domain. What are these occupations? Are these occupations created by or within the control of the Federal Government? Aren't those who work for the Federal Government doing so voluntarily? Those who work for a federal agency or contractors who work on behalf of the government are performing certain occupations subject to excise. Are military, Federal Bureau of Prisons, and Department of Energy personnel those who work at "certain occupations?" These examples are people—employees—involved in a *trade or business* on a voluntary basis. They voluntarily accept *employment* from the employer—the *United States*. Since the government has the power to create these occupations, it has the power to tax them as a source of privilege or license subject to excise.

Americans who are not connected with federal employment would not be within the jurisdiction of this taxing authority. Those who work in the private sector are not voluntarily engaged in a federal employer/employee relationship. The government did not create these "occupations" and does not employ the people who are exercising a natural right within the 50 states. Why are most Americans now liable to file a U. S. Individual Tax Return or to pay the federal income tax? The Federal Government may only tax those *individuals* within the jurisdiction of the United States who realize income of an excisable nature on a voluntary basis. Those who voluntarily enter such a relationship must comply with the requisite obligation, file returns, and pay the tax.

The United States Government may only tax those "corporate privileges" that are within the federal domain. Corporations, which are outside of the federal jurisdiction, are not entities created by virtue of its laws. We must realize the Federal Government may control only what it creates or what is granted or ceded to its jurisdiction. Moreover, federal laws apply to government's legitimate creations and delegated powers.

We know that IRS publications state that the submission of the federal income tax form is *voluntary*. We must consider if this term is used because a man entered a business activity willingly and, as a result, has an obligation to pay the excise tax. If income, as defined by the Supreme Court, is something he chooses to engage, just like buying cigarettes, the decision is voluntary. However, man does not decide to work or not to work. He must work to live. Akin to breathing, man must labor to sustain his life. A tax against the earnings of a man exercising his right to the common occupations of life would be direct in nature and subject to apportionment.

We may clearly distinguish that jurisdiction is essential to the execution of a legitimate power. The enforcement of an illegitimate power would be extra-jurisdictional, unlawful, and illegal. The government may not force anyone to become a federal employee or to work for an "American employer." It does not have this power. A man may not be compelled to create an income or conduct his affairs in such a manner that an income is derived from his labor or his coveted earnings.

The Fourth Argument

The fourth argument that Americans may not be required to file federal income tax returns is: a man's earnings from his labor are not "income" as defined by the Supreme Court. The term *income* is not what most Americans understand. The concept of income is no longer appreciated. The term is not even defined within the Internal Revenue Code or its regulations. When the code does define *income*, the IRS uses the actual term: "income is income." The term is used to define itself. This inadequacy underscores the void for vagueness doctrine and renders the code legally insufficient and unresponsive. One cannot know the meaning of a term if it is neither defined nor properly defined.

Compound terms within the tax code use *income* to define something else, "gross income" or "net income." To understand the meaning of *income*, we must rely upon the definition established by the Supreme Court. In Stratton's Independence v Howbert, 231 U. S. 399 (1913), the court defined income as "gain derived from capital from labor or from both combined."

> *...And, however the operation shall be described, the transaction is indubitably "business" within the fair meaning of the Act of 1909; and the gains derived from it are properly and strictly the income from that business; for "income" may be defined as the gains derived from capital, from labor, or from both combined.*

Furthermore, since the Supreme Court established this definition, it is settled law and binding upon all courts. As we delve into this definition, we will understand why Congress chose not to adequately define *income* within the tax code. The proper definition of income clarifies the nature of the "income tax" and defeats the vague language of the code and regulations. If people only accept that "income is income" without context of the Supreme Court's definition, their presumption of the definition precludes understanding the actual law and its limits.

As represented in Stratton's Independence, the limits of law are largely determined by definitions of the terms employed. In fact, in 1923, the Supreme Court refused to "enter into the refinements of lexicographers" concerning the definition of "income."

> *... there would seem to be no room to doubt that the word [income] must be given the same meaning in all of the Income Tax Acts of Congress that it was given to it in the Corporation Excise Tax Act, and what that meaning is now has become definitely settled by the decisions of this Court.*
>
> *In determining the definition of the word "income" thus arrived at, this court has consistently refused to enter into the refinement of lexicographers or economists and has approved, in the definitions quoted, what is believed to be the commonly understood meaning of the term ["gains and profits"] which have been in the minds of the people when they adopted the Sixteenth Amendment to the*

Constitution... Merchants Loan & Trust Co., v. Smietanka, 255 U. S. 509

A salient point reinforced by the high court is that the meaning of the term *income* is what the people intended at the time the Sixteenth Amendment was adopted.

A testament to the spirit of the court's accurate interpretation of the Constitution is evidenced by one of the Senators from that period. With the passage of the 16th Amendment, the Federal Reserve Act, and the most recent income tax act, Senator Albert Cummins stated forthrightly that income was already defined, and people did not grant Congress the latitude to tax "all property" without apportionment.

> *I assume that every lawyer will agree with me that we cannot legislatively interpret the meaning of the word "income." That is purely a judicial matter... The word income has a well defined meaning before the amendment of the Constitution was adopted. It has been defined in all of the courts of this country as gains and profits... If we could call anything that we pleased income, we could obliterate all the distinction between income and principal. The Congress cannot affect the meaning of the word "income" by any legislation whatsoever... Obviously, the people of this country did not intend to give Congress the power to levy a direct tax upon all property of this country without apportionment.* 1913 Congressional Record, pgs. 3843, 3844

Not only is the definition of income limited, but the Constitution constrains congressional ability to alter its meaning:

> *It becomes essential to distinguish between what is not "income" ...Congress may not, by any definition it may adopt, conclude the matter, since it cannot by legislation alter the Constitution, from which alone it derives its power to legislate, and within whose limitations alone, that power can be lawfully exercised... [income is] Derived-from-capital-the-gain... The words "gain" and "income" mean the same thing. They are equivalent terms.* Congressional Globe, 37th Congress, 2nd Session, pg. 1531

The point is made even stronger with the following court decision:

> *The Treasury cannot by interpretive regulation, make income of that which is not income within the meaning of revenue acts of Congress, nor can Congress, without apportionment, tax as income that which is not income within the meaning of the 16th Amendment.* Helvering v. Edison Bros. Stores, 133 F 2d 575 (8th Cir. 1943)

Of equal import to what income may be, is what income may not be:

> *...income, as used in the statute, should be given a meaning so as not to include everything that comes in. The true function of the words "gains" and "profits" is to limit the meaning of the word "income".* Southern Pacific v. Lowe, 247 U. S. 330 (1918)

In Doyle v Mitchell Brothers, 247 U. S. 179 (1918), the Supreme Court admonished the government and its position that all receipts are income.

> *Yet, it is plain, we think, that by the true intent and meaning of the Act the entire proceeds of a mere conversion of capital assets were not to be treated as income. Whatever difficulty there may be about a precise and scientific definition of "income," it imports, as used here, something entirely distinct from principal or capital either as a subject of taxation or as a measure of the tax; conveying rather the idea of gain or increase arising from corporate activities. We must reject in this case... the broad contention submitted in behalf of the government that all*

receipts – everything that comes in are income with the proper definition... of "gross income"

Gain is the inherent nature of income. Two references from Georgia and Louisiana effectively explain the essence of income as analogous to fruit:

> *So that, perhaps, the true question is this: is income property, in the sense of the Constitution, and must it be taxed at the same rate as other property? The fact is property is a tree; income the fruit, capital the tree; income the fruit. The fruit, if not consumed (severed) as fast as it ripens, will germinate from the seed... and will produce other trees and grow into more property; but as long as it is fruit merely, and plucked (severed) to eat... it is no tree and will produce itself no fruit.* Waring v City of Savannah, 60 Ga. 93, 100 (1878)

> *Fruits are things that are produced by or derived from another thing without diminution of its substance. There are two kinds of fruit; natural fruits and civil fruits. Natural fruits are products of the earth or animals. Civil fruits are revenues derived from a thing by operation of law or by reason of a juridical act, such as rentals, interest, and certain corporate distributions.* Louisiana Civil Code, Art. 551, Kinds of Fruits.

Income is narrowly defined. Consistent with a number of prior quotations, the court attributes gain "as a result of corporate activity"—the result of business. Within the United States Annotated Code, the correlation of gain to income is unquestionable.

> *Under the Internal Revenue Act of 1954 if there is no gain, there is no income.* 26 USCA '54, Sec 61(a)

Consider that:

> *There must be a gain before there is "income" within the 16th amendment.* 26 USCA, Const. Am 16

While defined as a gain or profit, the Supreme Court referred to income as an excise:

> *... taxation on income was in its nature an excise entitled to be enforced as such...* Brushaber v Union Pacific R.R. Co., 240 US 1 (1916)

> *Thus, in Springer v. United States, 102 U. S. 586, (1881) it was held that a tax on gains, profits, and income was an excise or duty, and not a direct tax within the meaning of the Constitution, and that its imposition was not, therefore, unconstitutional. Hyde v Continental Trust Co.*

The court posited that:

> *...the requirement to pay taxes involves the exercise of privileges, and the element of absolute and unavoidable demand is lacking.* Flint v. Stone Tracy Co.

As we learned before, a "privilege" is consistent with the definition of an excise:

> *Excises are taxes laid upon... licenses to pursue certain occupations, and upon corporate privileges.* Ibid.

In American Airways v. Wallace, 57 F.2d 877 (M.D. Tenn 1932), an inferior court stated:

> *The terms "excise tax" and "privilege tax" are synonymous. The two are often used interchangeably. Whether a tax is characterized in the statute imposing it as a privilege tax or an excise tax is merely a choice of synonymous words, for an excise tax is a privilege tax.* 71 Am. Jur. 2d Sec. 24, pgs. 319-320

What is a "privilege"? Three definitions from as many legal dictionaries explain this important term.

> ***PRIVILEGE*, rights**. *This word, taken its active sense, is a particular disposition of the law which grants certain special prerogatives to some persons, contrary to common right. In its passive sense, it is the same particular law*. Bouvier's Law Dictionary, 6th Ed. (1856)

> ***PRIVILEGE.*** *A particular benefit or advantage enjoyed by a person, company, or class beyond the common advantages of other citizens. An exceptional or extraordinary power of exemption. A particular right, advantage, exemption, power, franchise, or immunity held by a person or class, not generally possessed by others.* Black's Law Dictionary, 6th Ed.

> ***PRIVILEGE***. *A right peculiar to an individual or body. Ripley v. Knight, 123 Mass., 519. An advantage held by the way of license, grant or permission, not possessed by others. Special enjoyment of a good or exemption from an evil or burden. Wisener v. Burrell, 28 Okla 546, 118 p.999. An immunity existing under the law. For tax purposes, any occupation or business which the legislature may declare to be a privilege and tax as such.* Seven Springs Water Co., v. Kennedy, 156 Tenn 1, 299 SW 792, 56 ALR 496. Ballentine's Law Dictionary, 3rd Ed.

A privilege is, if anything, a distinction created and granted by government under law. This distinction is the antithesis to what is known by common man as a matter of common right. "For tax purposes," Ballentine's Law Dictionary cites a privilege as excisable. Moreover, F. Morse Hubbard, in testimony before Congress, stated:

> *The income tax is, therefore, not a tax on income as such. It is an excise tax with respect to certain activities and privileges which is measured by reference to the income which they produce.* Treasury Department of Legislative Draftsman, House Congressional Record, May 27, 1943. Pg. 2580

Hubbard explained that:

> *... the amendment made it possible to bring investment income within the scope of the general income—tax law, but did not change the character of the tax. It is still fundamentally an excise tax or duty with respect to the privilege of carrying on any activity or owning any property which produces income.*

Finally, Hubbard offered that:

> *The income tax...is an excise with respect to certain activities and privileges which is measured by reference to the income which they produce. The income is not the subject of the tax; it is the basis for determining the amount of the tax.*

Hubbard's statements underscore not only that government may tax what it creates, but since the excise is paid voluntarily, those who partake of a privilege or elect to an obligation or status must pay the tax. As such, *income*, which is income by virtue of the privilege, is used to measure the amount of the tax. The following statement validates the essence of an excise—a "voluntary action" involves an "obligation."

> *The obligation to pay an excise is usually based upon the voluntary action of the person taxed either for enjoying the privilege or engaging in the occupation which is the subject of the excise, and the element of absolute and unavoidable demand, as in the property tax is lacking.* Harvey v. United States, 234 F. Supp. 887m (4th Cir. 1964)

The government expects a return for any privilege it grants. Any employee who works for the United States Government does so as a *privilege*. The government has every intention as the employer to tax the *income* realized by the employee. In Murdock v Pennsylvania we learned that the court appropriately prevented a tax by license of a man exercising a natural right, a right protected from infringement by the Constitution.

> *It is claimed, however, that the ultimate question in determining the constitutionality of this license tax is whether the State has given something for which it can ask in return. That principle has wide applicability. State Tax Commission v. Aldrich. 316 US 174, 86 L Ed 1358, 62 S Ct 1008, 139 ALR, 1436, and the cases cited. But is it quite irrelevant here. This tax is not a charge for the enjoyment of a privilege or benefit bestowed by the State. The privilege in question exists apart from state authority. It is guaranteed the people by the Federal Constitution.*

There is no doubt a natural right may not be encroached. Yet, it is also clear that when people voluntarily accept a privilege "bestowed by the State," the privilege must be dignified and is often done so by means of excise. If people unknowingly accept a privilege they may have suffered the loss of a right. Such is the toll of ignorance. However, the message in Brady v. United States bears repeating:

> *Waivers of constitutional rights not only must be voluntary, they must be knowing, intelligent acts done with sufficient awareness of relevant circumstances and consequences.*

Given our understanding of natural rights and the limitations of jurisdiction, along with the proper definition of *income*, we know labor is property and cannot be subject to excise. Rather, direct taxes upon people and property must be apportioned. The Supreme Court effectively cited this in Bromley v. McCaughn, 280 U. S. 124 (1929)

> *Whatever may be the precise line which sets off direct taxes from others, we need not now determine. While taxes levied upon or collected from persons because of their general ownership of property may be taken to be direct, this court has consistently held, almost from the foundation of the government, that a tax imposed upon a particular use of property or the exercise of a single power over property incidental to ownership, is an excise which need not be apportioned, and it is enough for present purposes that this tax is of the latter class.*

As recently as 1992, Jack R. Lackey, Legislative Attorney stated:

> *When a court refers to an income tax as being in the nature of an excise, it is merely stating that the tax is not on property itself, but rather it is a fee for the privilege of receiving gain from the property. The tax is based upon the amount of the gain, not the value of the property.* Library of Congress, C.R.S. Report, Congress 92-303A

Obviously, Americans do not labor by permission of the government as a privilege. We do not pay a "fee" for the benefit of labor by legal grant of any authority. We do not petition the United States for the use of our bodies. The lower court in Connor v. United States astutely recognized the 16th Amendment, the Eisner v. Macomber, 252 U. S. 189 (1920) decision, and section 61(a) of the tax code of 1954 and asserted that, if there is no gain, there is no income. The court declared, "Congress has taxed income, not compensation."

> *Whatever may constitute income, therefore, must have the essential feature of gain to the recipient. This was true when the sixteenth amendment became effective, it was true at the time of the decision in Eisner v. Macomber, it was true under*

> *section 22(a) of the Internal Revenue Code of 1939, and it is likewise true under 61(a) of the Internal Revenue Code of 1954... Congress has taxed income, not compensation.* 303 F. Supp. 1187, 1191 (5th Cir. 1969)

The district court in Pennsylvania arrived at a similar conclusion. Specifically, income is:

> *received by or drawn by the recipient for his separate use, benefit and disposal—that is income derived from property.* 21 F. Supp.737, 739 (Ed PA 1937)

This message is consistent with Edwards v. Keith, a decision from the Second Circuit in 1916 shortly after the Income Tax Act of 1913 was passed.

> *...the statute and the statute alone determines what is income to be taxed. It taxes only income "derived" from many specified sources; one does not "derive income" by rendering services and charging for them.* 231F. 110 (2nd Cir. 1916)

Imagine a Governor of a State at the time of the ratification of the income tax amendment contending with the concerns of constituents and the implications of altering the Constitution. Governor Wilson assuaged the concerns of voters by stating:

> *The poor man or the man in moderate circumstances does not regard his wages or salary as income that would have to pay its proportionate tax under this new system.* Governor A.E. Wilson on the Income Tax Amendment, New York Times, part 5, Pg. 13, February 26,1911.

The overall theme since the enactment of the "new system" of income taxation did not regard a man's livelihood as income. The United States v. Ballard decision from the 8th Circuit expressed a similar sentiment:

> *Of course gross income and not gross receipts is the foundation of income tax liability, for it is only earnings, profits and gains which the statute subjects to tax... The general term "income" is not defined in the Internal Revenue Code...* 535 F. 2d 400 (1976)

By now we should have dismissed any possibility that man labors as a privilege, as a grant of government. Man labors as a matter of necessity and right. Among these privileges is "the right to hold specific employment and to follow a chosen profession." Leis v Flynt 439 US 439 (1979) (citing Greene v. McElroy 360 US 474 (1959))

The word "privileges" as used in the Constitution, as we read before, concerns rights as matter of common law, not as a franchise or benefit granted by the government. We may reasonably conclude that the taking of "property" is interference with a right. To bolster the capstone argument that labor and the receipt of a livelihood from labor is not a "privilege" or "benefit" granted by the government subject to excise, consider the Supreme Court's words in the Eisner v. Macomber decision:

> *What was said by this court upon the latter question is equally true of the former. "A stock dividend really takes nothing from the property of the corporation, and adds nothing to the interests of the shareholders. Its property is not diminished, and their interests are not increased. The proportional interest of each shareholder remains the same. The only change is in the evidence which represents the interest, the new shares and the original shares together representing the same proportional interest that the original shares represented before the issue of the new ones." Gibbons v. Mahon, 136 US 459. In short, the corporation is no poorer and the stockholder is no richer than they were before.* Logan County v. United States, 169 US 225 (1920)

This representation is telling. The court embraced three arguments we have discussed thus far and substantiated its wisdom that a stock dividend could not be taxed. The dividend was property possessed by right; the dividend was not income—as in profit or gain—but capital; and the jurisdiction of the government and its limitations would have necessitated a direct or apportioned tax upon the same.

The relevance of this decision is heightened when we substitute a man's labor for a stock dividend. Are not a man and his labor (property) and earnings (property) on par with a dividend or of greater import than a dividend? The exchange of a man's labor for another form of property is nothing more than a dividend, is it not? While the recipient of a man's labor may have to account for a "profit" or "gain"—that is an "income" from another man's labor, for which he would potentially owe an excise—the laborer himself is no richer than he was before he exchanged his labor. He merely bartered or traded his efforts to sustain himself for the possibility of yet a future exchange. Curiously, is a man richer for trading his labor for $10.00 in Federal Reserve Notes (dollars) versus a $10.00 meal so that he can have the energy to work more? Clearly, the transaction in either case does not reflect a "profit." If a man receives $10.00 instead of the meal and invests the money and eventually realizes a net return of $1.00 in "profit," would there be an excise tax on the "income?"

If a man invests $100,000.00 into a Certificate of Deposit and receives a 6% annual rate of return, the $6,000.00 "profit" is "income." The $100,000.00 is capital, otherwise known as the principal. The "profit" is derived from the capital. The income, the profit and only the profit, is taxable. The capital is not taxable and remains to be reinvested. The man made a voluntary decision to invest his capital into an excisable source and would not be subject to the Rule of Apportionment as a direct tax upon property.

The following example will illustrate how income is derived by labor. ABC Inc. is a corporation, a painting business which provides its services to the Federal Government. As a federal contractor, it hires Steve WannaSurvive to paint offices. ABC charges the government $100.00 a room and pays Mr. WannaSurvive $50.00. Any profit ABC derives from WannaSurvive's labor is income at the end of the calendar year. ABC must pay a tax on this "gain." There can be no doubt that, from labor, ABC derived profit.

Was the $50.00 that Mr. WannaSurvive realized a gain or income? Based upon an uninformed understanding, one would likely consider that Mr. WannaSurvive's earnings represent "profit." This is our *only* understanding. However, this is, as we now know, a flawed legal representation. A man's livelihood cannot be "profit." Mr. WannaSurvive's exchange was not a gain. He merely traded his time, efforts, and talent (his capital), all that belongs to him, for something else. His labor is his property and is the most vital of his sacred rights, perhaps second only to his very existence, his breath of life. But for his coveted ability to labor Mr. WannaSurvive could *not survive.* This simple exchange is necessary for him to live. What he possesses he uses for his survival and benefit.

Recall that the Federal Government was established with limited powers. This limitation was by design to prevent its direct involvement with a free people unless Americans deliberately enter federal employment or elect a particular status or accept specific federal benefits. Any tax that would be direct upon the people, like Steve WannaSurvive, had to apportioned.

Many who have not adequately considered the concept of "income" may question why Mr. WannaSurvive's "earnings" are not profit. The answer is simple. Steve exchanged property for property, capital for capital, principal for principal. Nothing was derived from the earnings; there was no "income" to be had, no fruit. We should not casually acknowledge the Supreme Court's definition of income. The nature of income is critical to appreciate its meaning and application in law. Simply stated, income is profit. The fact that "capital" or "labor" or "both combined" are referenced by the court should be obvious by now. Both are used to create income. Nothing else can. Both are one and the same. As reflected in the examples, both are "principal" used to generate a profit. Gain or profit is that which is derived from, as in harvested from, the principal.

All that is required for Mr. WannaSurvive to labor stems from his limited resources—resources which will never be used again. Once his day, energy, and efforts are expended, they are gone. It is property which cannot be reinvested. Hypothetically, if a "profit" were realized, it would have to be derived. One would have to account for an actual profit. With the examples of the Certificate of Deposit and ABC Inc., there was "income" derived from or severed from the source. If it were possible to separate income from the hard costs that accounted for Mr. WannaSurvive's efforts, which would include a cost for all involved with the production of his labor, how would it be derived? How would the principal be determined and then separated from the "income?"

Steve WannaSurvive would have to account for everything that required him to labor whether tangible or intangible. Would $50.00 cover the costs? If ten hours were required to complete the job, would $5.00 an hour equate to a "gain?" If he earned $500.00, would $50.00 an hour cover costs and net a profit? Even if a theoretical profit were realized, the issue becomes severability. Steve would have to sever any income/profit from the exchange. He must account for principal and costs; then he must contend with deriving a profit. The CD investment had $6,000.00 in profit, distinct from the capital and easily subject to excise. This is not the case with WannaSurvive and his earnings. The Supreme Court in Eisner v. Macomber addressed the inherent severability of income.

> *Brief as it is, it indicates the characteristic and distinguishing attribute of income, essential for a correct solution of the present controversy. The government, although basing its argument upon the definition as quoted, placed chief emphasis upon the word "gain" which was extended to include a variety of meanings; while the significance of the next three words was either overlooked or misconceived—"derived from capital"—"the gain derived from capital," etc. Here we have the essential matter: not a gain accruing to capital, not a growth or increment of value in the investment; but a gain, a profit, something of exchangeable value proceeding from the property, severed from the capital, however invested or employed, and coming in, "being derived," that is, received or drawn by the recipient (the taxpayer) for his separate use, benefit and disposal; that is income derived from property. Nothing else answers the description.*

Capital and labor are essential for the creation of income. Income is a fruit produced and derived from the source. As a tree produces fruit, capital and labor produce fruit—a profit—which is distinctly separate, as in severed from the source. This is not the case with Mr. WannaSurvive. Did he produce fruit? If he produced fruit, we would naturally concede that he ate the fruit to survive. The fruit did not produce income. However, a more appropriate analogy is that Mr. WannaSurvive is a repository of a limited resource used in exchange for what he needs. He uses what is a limited supply within his repository to produce the labor he exchanges. Any subsequent exchanges cannot be income derived from the source.

A critical point that must be considered is exactly what Mr. WannaSurvive does with his livelihood, his exchange. He supports himself and his family. He consumes. He sustains—which enables him to labor another day. If he invests a portion of his earnings into a CD, this would be as if he used seeds from fruit which became a tree which produces yet more fruit. The CD would produce income from which an excise would be paid. He would have generated an income "derived" from his labor. As it stands, Mr. WannaSurvive is still exchanging property for property which allows for subsequent "income" from the CD.

A man's labor is no different from a mine which contains ore deposits. The mine does not produce a fruit. It does not produce a finished product. It is a repository, an asset base which is depleted as the ore—the capital—is extracted. When the ore is gone, the mine is gone. The mine is no longer a mine. It is a hole in the ground which offers nothing because it has nothing. When the mine is in operation, the ore is sold, exchanged, traded. Income is not derived in a conventional sense. There is no fruit. This principle became an issue which the Supreme Court had to resolve when the question arose in Stanton v. Baltic Mining Co., 240 U. S. 103 (1916). The ore was not a commodity that was manufactured and upon which an excise could be laid. So, the Supreme Court settled this question by determining that mining corporations were exercising an "excisable activity." This was the only reasonable decision the court could make.

Tommy Cryer, a lawyer from Shreveport, Louisiana, ably expressed in a court memorandum the dilemma of taxing both income and capital:

> *The Supreme Court...resolved the problem by determining that the tax, insofar as Baltic was concerned, was not an income tax at all, but a tax on the exercise of corporate privileges and the privilege of conducting mining operations that was "measured in income."* [44]
>
> *The court had only two options: 1) Find that the income tax was taxing both the income and the capital and, therefore, unconstitutional, or 2) find that the income tax was taxing something else. It went with something else.*[45]

In Baltic, the court stated:

> *...independently of the effect of the operation of the Sixteenth Amendment it was settled in Stratton's Independence v. Howbert, 231 US 399, that such a tax is not a tax upon property as such because of its ownership, but a true excise levied on the results of the business of carrying on mining operations.*

Cryer continued with:

> *The clear and unmistakable message here is that the only tax that could tax more than income, gross receipts without allowance of deduction for the depletion of the ore body, was a corporate or manufacture of commodities based excise tax.*[46]

The owners of a mine do not know how much ore is available. They do not know how long the mine will be in existence. The value of the mine cannot be ascertained. There is no way of determining a profit. A mine would have to be exhausted of its ore before a gain could be calculated. Even then, how would the corporation sever the profit?

The mine is not unlike having stacks of gold bars in your basement. You must mine the bars and carry them upstairs. A buyer waits at the front door to exchange—as in "buy"—the gold for its value. This is an equal exchange. A man's life parallels the operation of a mine. A man extracts a resource contained within him, a non-renewable resource. Once the resource is used, it is gone. Man's time and energy are of a limited quantity. Furthermore, a man does not know how long he will live. He does not know how much time he has available, time which will be traded or exchanged. Whether two years or twenty, his "mine" will cease to exist or the ore will be depleted at some point before his

---

[44] http://wethepeoplefoundation.org/MISC/Cryer/CRYER--MotiontoDismiss.pdf

[45] Ibid.

[46] Ibid.

death. Once his time is gone or his ability to labor has ended, he can offer nothing. Like an abandoned mine, he is unproductive. We may conclude that it is difficult to place a value on a man's time to determine a profit. Not only is the amount of his time unknown, but the value of his time is also unknown as well.

Ironically, the Federal Government considers all of a man's earnings as "income." Most people believe their earnings are income. This is a result of ignorance. It is not possible that the amount a man earns on an annual basis is "income." Our new understanding of the definition and concept of income defies this possibility, notwithstanding the other arguments discussed.

The question of severing a profit from a man's labor is, ultimately, inconsequential. A man's earnings are not and may not be profit or gain. A man's labor is his property and, as such, any exchange he receives is a resource of a limited supply. What he receives for the exchanges becomes his property or capital and cannot be severed.

THE FIFTH ARGUMENT

The fifth argument which demonstrates that Americans may not be required to file federal income tax returns is: the Sixteenth Amendment to the Constitution did not grant Congress any new taxing powers beyond what it already possessed.

> *Congress shall have the power to lay and collection taxes on "incomes," from whatever source derived, without apportionment among the several States and without regard to census or enumeration.*[47] Sixteenth Amendment

The Constitution is a written agreement, a contract of sorts, a trust which binds the Federal Government. This document states what the United States may and may not do. The constitution and government do not grant or convey rights to the people. The reverse is true. The government receives its powers from the people. The government ensures and protects the rights of the people by staying within these distinct powers. It is limited by constitutional constraints and may only do what is permitted.

This understanding is important to the passage of the 16th Amendment. An amendment is approved by the several States and, therefore, the people approve it as well. For, the people grant the ultimate authority or clarify an existing authority as it relates to the Federal Government. The purposes of the 16th Amendment were to clarify that "income" "from whatever source derived" was not subject to apportionment.

This new amendment did not and could not, as law, create confusion. It could not and should not be vague, which would render it void. Law must be what it is and cannot be what it is not. We must conclude that Congress did not write the 16th Amendment with ambiguity. We must conclude the amendment means what is stated. Congress knows the constraints imposed by the Constitution. We must conclude the amendment stated exactly what Congress intended and the language is clear. It is, however, misunderstood by the people. More importantly—if only for the ignorance of the people—the amendment and subsequent tax laws and court decisions have been misapplied by law enforcement agencies. The reverse must be true. If the people understood the amendment and all related laws and decisions, they would know that agencies properly enforce the law.

Congress sought to validate those sources of "income" subject to excise before the 16th Amendment could be regarded as within or subject to the Rule of Apportionment (direct taxation). Legal and lawful excise taxes assessed against "income" "from whatever source derived" were clarified as within the jurisdiction of the Federal Government. The "income" was not property which would necessitate a direct tax; rather it was profit or

---

[47] Amendment XVI, The Constitution of the United States

gain from a voluntary choice to participate in whatever was subject to excise.

This discussion takes us back to the issue of direct taxes and the concept of apportionment. Any tax upon people or property must be apportioned. The government does not have the authority to tax the people directly. This amendment, therefore, substantiated that "income" was already and had always been within the government's jurisdiction to tax indirectly—that which was a source subject to excise. Otherwise, "income" would be incorrectly presumed as direct in nature.

We know conclusively that people and property may only be taxed under the Rule of Apportionment, and this remained as such after the passage of the 16th Amendment. Think about the significance of this point. The Rule of Apportionment did not go away. It still exists. Why? Man and his property, his labor, were not taxable and still may not be. Before and after the amendment was passed only "income"—profit and gain—was taxed. This is the truth of the matter. "Sources" of income, "from whatever *source* derived" were clarified. These sources of income, sources which created income, could not be the focus of the income tax, thereby dismissing the possibility that the "property" could be directly taxed. Rather, income "derived" from the source (property) was the subject of the excise.

The Sixteenth Amendment did not grant Congress any new taxing power. As stated in Supreme Court cases, such as Stanton v. Baltic Mining Co., and Taft v. Bowers, 278 U. S. 470 (1929), the taxing authority which Congress exercised before its passage was the same as it exercised afterward. Nothing changed. Consider the following:

> *Under former decisions here the settled doctrine is that the Sixteenth Amendment confers no power upon Congress to define and tax as income without apportionment something which theretofore could not have been regarded as income.* Taft v. Bowers

Consider what was explained in Stanton v. Baltic Mining Co.:

> ... *the provisions of the 16th Amendment conferred no new power of taxation, but simply prohibited the previous complete and plenary power of income taxation possessed by Congress from the beginning from being taken out of the category of indirect taxation to which it inherently belonged, and being placed in the category of direct taxation subject to apportionment by a consideration of the sources from which the income was derived, - that is, by testing the tax not by what it was, a tax on income, but by a mistaken theory deduced from the origin or source of the income taxed.*

Congress still raised taxes in accord with the taxing provisions of the Constitution. The 16th Amendment confirmed what could not be considered a direct tax. "From whatever source derived" denoted sources whereby the "income" was taxed and not the source itself. The point is that property which could not be taxed before the passage of the amendment was not taxable by excise. In fact, property which was incorrectly presumed to be subject to direct taxation was forever altered. Regardless of the source (from whatever source derived), the tax was on the income—and not the property—as an indirect tax, an excise.

The Rule of Apportionment could not be considered; it did not apply. We know the source of the income became central to the enforcement of the excise tax; the source was inconsequential. We also know, based upon the language used to craft this amendment, the intent of Congress was far more definitive and limited in application than our cavalier, uninformed, and generally accepted misunderstanding. Thus, the law is not vague and, therefore, not void. The amendment stated exactly what was intended.

Beginning with the Constitution, which is the *source* of congressional taxing power, we must conclude that the 16th Amendment passes constitutional muster. The often referred to case of Eisner v. Macomber stated the matter simply:

> *The 16th Amendment must be construed in connection with the taxing clauses of the original Constitution and the effect attributed to them before the amendment was adopted.*

As late as 1979, this fundamental limitation was reaffirmed by Howard Zaritisky, Legislative Attorney for the Library of Congress:

> *The Supreme Court, in a decision written by Chief Justice White, first noted that the 16th Amendment did not authorize any new type of tax, nor did it repeal or revoke the tax clauses of Article I of the Constitution quoted above. Direct taxes were, notwithstanding the advent of the 16th Amendment, still subject to the rule of apportionment...* 1979 Report No. 80-19A, "Some Constitutional Questions Regarding the Federal Income Tax Laws"

An uninformed view of the "income tax amendment" would and has caused undue confusion. However, the language of the amendment complies with the jurisdiction of the congressional taxing authority.

The purpose of the 16th Amendment is quite simple. Since we know the proper definition of income—profit or gain—and an income tax is an excise tax and "voluntary" in nature, the amendment validated that income was not subject to a direct tax; for, it was not a tax upon property. That's it. The source, the capital, or property which generated the income was irrelevant. The income was the central concern regardless of the source.

The Supreme Court addressed this matter in the first challenge of the amendment:

> *It is clear on the face of this text that it does not purport to confer power to levy income taxes in a generic sense - an authority already possessed and never questioned, - or to limit and distinguish between one kind of income taxes and another, but that the whole purpose of the amendment was to relieve all income taxes when imposed from apportionment for a consideration of the source whence the income was derived.* Brushaber v. Union Pacific R.R. Co.240 US 1 (1916)

Notice the court said that Congress already possessed the authority to levy an income tax. The 1915-16 issue of the Cornell Law Quarterly offers the same message:

> *The Amendment, the court said, judged by the purpose for which it was passed, does not treat income taxes as direct taxes but simply removed the ground which led to their being considered as such in the Pollock case, namely, the source of income. Therefore, they are again to be classified in the class of indirect taxes to which by nature they belong.*

Consider the 45th Congressional Record:

> *The sole purpose of the Sixteenth Amendment was to remove the apportionment requirement for whichever incomes were otherwise taxable.* 45 Congressional Record, pgs. 2245-2246 (1916)

Several citations reveal the obvious—the amendment did not grant Congress any new taxing power. To do so would have been extra-constitutional. The court even refuted erroneous contentions that were inconsistent with constitutional constraints and congressional intent. For example, in the Brushaber decision, the court stated:

> *We are of the opinion, however, that the confusion is not inherent, but rather arises from the conclusion that the 16th Amendment provides for a hitherto unknown power of taxation; that is, a power to levy an income tax which, although direct,*

> *should not be subject to the regulation of apportionment applicable to all other direct taxes. And the far-reaching effect of this erroneous assumption will be made clear by generalizing the many contentions advanced in argument to support it.*

We will consider three final cases which underscore that the federal taxing authority had not been altered and "income," regardless of its source, was of singular importance. The income tax is an excise and cannot be subject to apportionment.

> *It was not the purpose or effect of that amendment to bring any new subject within the taxing power. Congress already had power to tax all incomes.* Bowers v. Kerbaugh- Empire Co., 271 US 170 (1926)

> *As repeatedly held, this did not extend the taxing power to new subjects, but merely removed the necessity which otherwise might exist for an apportionment among the States of taxes laid on income.* Eisner v. Macomber, 252 US 189 (1920)

> *The 16th Amendment, although referred to in argument, has no real bearing and may be put out of view as pointed out in recent decisions, it does not extend the taxing power to new or excepted subjects, but merely removes all occasion, which otherwise might exist, for an apportionment among the states of taxes laid on income, whether it be derived from one source or another.* Peck & Co., v. Lowe, 247 US 165 (1918)

With the background of the first four arguments, the last one is simple to understand. Ignorance is less of a foe when knowledge and understanding are abundant. One would be hard-pressed to contend that the 16th Amendment is unlawful. With proper context of terms, definitions, and language it is transparent. Congress cannot exercise what is contrary to its authority to reach an otherwise lawful outcome. Consider the directness of the Supreme Court in South Carolina v. Baker, 485 US 505 (1988):

> *The United States cannot covert an unconstitutional tax into a constitutional one simply by making the tax conditional. Whether Congress should have imposed the condition is irrelevant; Congress cannot employ unconstitutional means to reach a constitutional end.*

The 16th Amendment is quite the opposite; it is a constitutional expression of power to satisfy a legitimate constitutional end. Although one may argue that the word "whatever" is misleading, Congress was purposeful in its usage. Income which was already taxable could not be confused with or considered to be property subject to apportionment. Since man and his property (labor) were his alone, the 16th Amendment did not apply. With a proper understanding of this law, we appreciate why this amendment was necessary in the first place. The history behind it is as fascinating as it is revealing.

Congress passed an income tax act in 1894. A challenge to this act occurred when a man by the name of Pollock filed suit when his stocks and bonds were taxed. Pollock considered his stocks and bonds as property and, thus, not taxable by the Federal Government. The case made it to the Supreme Court. Pollock argued that a tax on property required a direct tax subject to apportionment. The Supreme Court agreed. The Court's decision was written in Pollock's favor. The tax was declared to be unconstitutional.

The implications of this decision were huge. Congress had a problem to solve. They had to clarify that the source of the "income," the stocks and bonds, was not the focus. Rather, income from the stocks and the bonds was the focus. The stocks and bonds, while considered property, were the source and, therefore, could not be subject to tax.

Yet, apportionment did not and could not apply. The "income" was the result of a voluntary activity engaged by Pollock. The activity was the purchase of stocks and bonds.

The income from both was subject to excise. The 16th Amendment was the solution to a court decision which thwarted the original intent of Congress to tax the income and not the source. Congress wanted to tax the income "from whatever source derived."

We must note that the tax was not upon Pollock's earnings. Pollock did not argue that his earnings from his labor could not be taxed. The Congress and courts, as well as the people, knew man's labor or earnings were not taxable. This should be self-evident by the Pollock decision. Since the Supreme Court rejected a tax upon Pollock's stocks and bonds the court would dare not consider a tax upon man and his labor.

Now, here is the interesting twist about the Pollock decision. The Supreme Court was wrong. As discussed previously, an excise tax is a voluntary tax. A man chooses to pay the tax when he decides to buy what was taxable, the same as if he bought cigarettes and gasoline. While the stocks and bonds were "property," they were a "source" for an indirect tax upon the *income derived*. Congress knew income from stocks and bonds was not considered property and could not be subject to a direct tax. After the Pollock decision, Congress had to clarify that income derived from "whatever source" was excisable. Congress had to prevent the Supreme Court from stopping the assessment and collection of revenue because of an incorrect understanding of terms, definitions, and tax law. Congress had to express that the law taxed income and only income from sources from which income was derived.

Congress remedied the problem by crafting the artful and purposeful language of the Sixteenth Amendment and the Supreme Court agreed with this congressional intent. In Eisner v. Macomber, the court stated:

> *The same fundamental conception is clearly set forth in the 16th Amendment—"incomes from whatever source derived"—the essential thought being expressed with a conciseness and lucidity entirely in harmony with the form and style of the Constitution.*

With the passage of the 16th Amendment, the Income Tax Act of 1913 was open for a challenge that came quickly. A man by the name of Brushaber filed a lawsuit. His stocks were subject to an income tax. As with Pollock, Brushaber's case went to the Supreme Court. Justice White, an associate justice during the Pollock case, had dissented against that majority opinion. White was now the Chief Justice and wrote the Brushaber decision. White acknowledged that the court erred in Pollock. He stated that the tax then, as in Brushaber, was an excise tax and not a tax on property subject to apportionment.

White distinguished between "sources" of income subject to excise and property subject to direct taxation. He knew that not every source was encompassed within the language of the 16th Amendment. Chief Justice White stated a truth of immense import.

> *Moreover, in addition, the conclusion reached in the Pollock case did not in any degree involve holding that income taxes generically and necessarily came within this class of direct taxes on property, but on the contrary recognized the fact that taxation on income was in its nature an excise entitled to be enforced as such unless and until it was concluded that to enforce it would amount to accomplishing the result which the requirement as to apportionment of direct taxation was adopted to prevent, in which case the duty would arise to disregard form and consider substance alone and hence subject the tax to the regulation as to apportionment which otherwise as an excise would not apply to it. (emphasis added)*

We know the 16th Amendment did not grant Congress any new taxing power. This fact was confirmed since neither the Pollock nor Brushaber cases concerned earnings from labor. Congress never had this power regardless of the 16th Amendment. The amendment ensured exactly what was intended, income, would be taxed without confusion or misunderstanding as to the source. Pollock and Brushaber voluntarily acquired stocks, a source which produced an income outside the scope of direct taxation.

The relevance of the words "from whatever source derived" is noteworthy. The term "whatever" could be replaced with "regardless." The term "whatever" has a dismissive tone, as if to say, "Who cares about the source, 'whatever'" or "regardless, it doesn't matter". The tone suggests that income is the primary concern, and the source is secondary. The only reason the source would become primary is if substance took the place of form and man or property—not income—were taxed. If this occurred, as noted by Justice White in Brushaber, the Rule of Apportionment would apply.

REVIEW OF THE FIVE ARGUMENTS

These fives arguments are sound reasons as to how and why a legal liability to file an income tax return does not exist. These arguments are more than sufficient to establish that a new and proper understanding of the tax law is warranted, and our conventional and untested understanding is not. These arguments support the premise that no law exists, or an existing law is limited in scope and either misunderstood or misapplied

Each of the five arguments stands alone. Yet, each supports the others. We know the Federal Government, the United States, has no legal or lawful justification to exert or misapply its power, especially when the power does not exist. We must conclude that such power is unlawful and certainly extra-constitutional. Consider what we have learned:

- Laws that are vague are void;
- Man has natural and inalienable rights which can't be encroached by government;
- Man has natural rights to his property;
- The Federal Government has no jurisdiction over that which it did not create;
- Man is a creation of Nature's God and is free to pursue life, liberty, and property;
- The government exercises direct/indirect taxing powers within the Constitution;
- People and property may only be taxed directly by Rule of Apportionment;
- The Rule of Apportionment denies government what is without its jurisdiction;
- The term "income" means profit or gain;
- The income tax is an excise tax, an indirect tax;
- The Sixteenth Amendment clarified that the Federal Government could tax "income" from sources which are of an excisable nature and produce income;
- These sources, and only these sources, are not subject to apportionment;
- The phrase "from whatever source derived" does not mean from any and all sources, but only those sources from which profit and gain are derived;
- A man's earnings are not "income" and have never been "income" as the term is defined by the Supreme Court;
- Certain occupations created by the Federal Government are sources of excise. Americans who voluntarily engage the United States Government for such employer/employee relationships are subject to excise;
- The 16th Amendment did not grant Congress new taxing powers, it did not already possess. The government could not tax a man's labor before or after its passage.

The concepts revealed by these arguments are not easy to accept, much less comprehend. Attempting to discern that earnings are not "income" is a challenge. The language offered in the 16th Amendment does not mean Congress may tax all sources. Additionally, the term "income" is not defined based upon our common understanding;

rather, it has a specific legal definition. One must be willing to suspend disbelief. One must be teachable. Otherwise, most Americans will forever believe the government may tax from all sources, "from whatever source derived."

Consider the following pictorial and explanation of these five arguments:

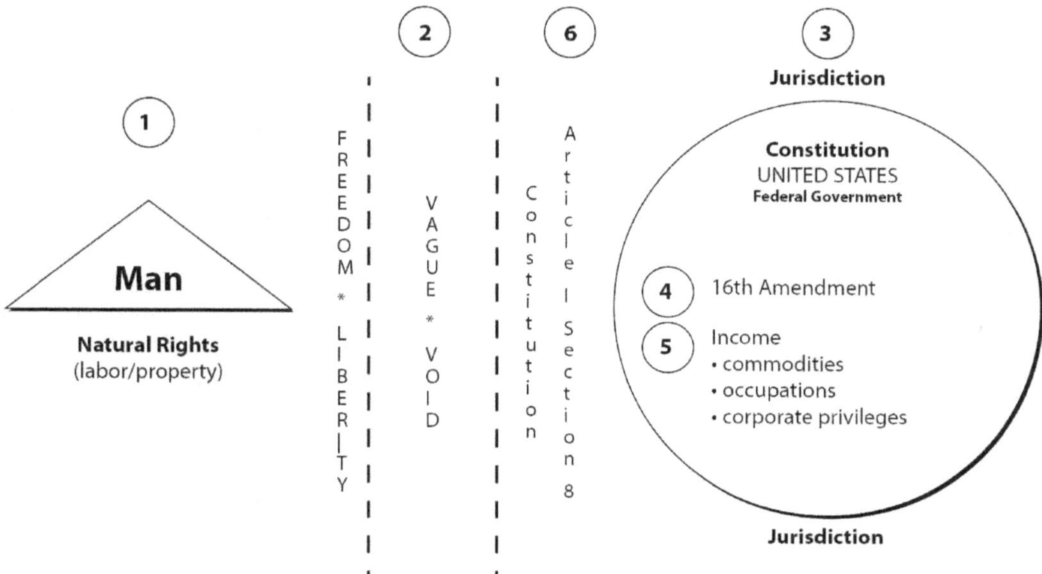

Since the founding of America, the enjoyment of life, liberty, and the pursuit of happiness (property) has been our endeavor. The Federal Government, unless operating under a granted power, has no authority to adversely affect these noble ends. The role of the United States Government was and is limited. Americans live without onerous expectations. We enjoy freedom. Short of violating another man's life, liberty, or property, we enjoy natural rights bestowed to us by Nature's God. The Constitution serves as a line of defense to protect man's rights. Americans may not be influenced by powers that the government does not have and laws which may not be understood.

- Poorly written laws (2) may not encroach upon man's natural rights (1);
- The jurisdiction of the United States is defined and limited in scope (3);
- The government (3) may not influence what is outside (1) its authority (3);
- The 16th Amendment (4) clarifies a power within federal jurisdiction (3);
- The United States (3) may tax income (5) (an indirect excise) as a matter of law;
- Sources (1) without federal power (3) are not subject to the Amendment (4);
- The 16th Amendment (4) did not grant Congress taxing powers; it clarified the sources of income (5) subject to its power (6) under the Constitution;
- The only means of taxing (6) what is outside (1) the jurisdiction (3) of the United States is by apportionment, as stipulated in Article I, Section 8 (6).

Americans are plagued with decades of conditioning which has shaped their mental and emotional perspectives. Their understanding of the role of the government and taxation has been deeply ingrained and is now largely unalterable. Fortunately, these five arguments explain with relative simplicity that most Americas are not required to file U. S. Individual Income Tax Returns (form 1040), unless they have somehow, unwittingly, become liable. Even with this simple explanation, many will require time—lots of time—to unlearn and accept this new paradigm. Keep in mind, we took the time to dignify the merits of these five arguments as a prelude to the final case. For, as certain as the sun will rise, Americans will face criminal charges for asserting reasonable good faith beliefs that the federal "income" tax law does not apply.

Hopefully these five arguments provided a credible representation that *facts* as we know them are not true. We may appreciate that we believe and live that which lacks integrity. We believe and live a lie. Once we confront this truth, we must make a choice. Do we alter our beliefs or continue to embrace the lie? Finally, as we discuss these five arguments, it will be apparent that each is intimately bound to the others. When jurisdiction is discussed the essence of natural rights will ring true. When income is covered jurisdiction must be addressed. When the 16th Amendment is the focus, the fact that codes and regulations are vague and misapplied will escalate in importance. Harmonizing these arguments will defeat the misunderstandings and ignorance we don't even know we possess. Candidly, we don't know that we don't know.

While understanding is a noble objective, how this knowledge is used is another matter. Whether we continue to live a lie or choose to stand for truth, we at least know that we have a choice. If we appreciate the truth behind the tax laws, we may finally grasp that the legal system is responsible for incarcerating those who dare to honor the law.

REJOINDERS TO THE FIVE ARGUMENTS

A man of average intelligence may accept the five arguments and rightfully question the legitimacy of the federal income tax. Taken collectively, they are a seemingly impenetrable defense against the criminal charge of willful failure to file tax returns. Students of law intent on obtaining the truth cannot be faulted for adhering to these positions. However, there is always the possibility of not knowing what a valid counterargument to these supposedly grounded fundamental principles.

Many a man has held tenaciously to these beliefs only to wind up in prison. Why? Is there something they did not know? Since these arguments rarely, if ever, prevail in court, an earnest researcher would be wise to understand how the opposition—the almighty United States Government—overcomes them. Knowing the government's response would be a remarkable feat. Convictions for willful failure to file charges are an orchestrated annual government marketing campaign designed to instill fear in the people. The intent is that fear will ensure compliance with the law. Given this regrettable show of force, knowing the federal authority's elusive rejoinders would be valuable.

We established that language is used contrary to what we might expect. We also learned that the law is specific and written to achieve results. We know the Federal Government may only exercise its powers to a limited scale and within certain venues or over certain persons and property. Thus, whatever the government's response to these five arguments, they are not readily, if ever, disclosed by officials. The rejoinders are not, therefore, received and considered by the American people. Naturally, we don't consider what could be the response because we are convinced that we already have the answers. We are certain these five positions are irrefutable. This is understandable since these positions establish a ***good faith defense*** to any federal criminal prosecution.

Here are responses to the five arguments as the government might express them.

First Argument:

A law that is vague is a law that cannot be enforced.

Response:

The law is not vague and, therefore, it is enforceable. When people lack the full context of basic concepts, they cannot understand the tax laws as written. For example, if the terms "excise," "income," and "jurisdiction" are incomplete and not properly understood, the laws are perceived as vague, when they are quite clear.

Second Argument:

A man's labor is his property, a natural right, which may not be taxed.

Response:

A man's labor may be his property and may not be taxed, but, if a man, whether knowingly or not, exchanges this right for a federal privilege or benefit, or elects to be treated under a status beholden to the Federal Government, the argument is nullified. Stated differently, if a man acquires a new "status" or "classification," he may no longer claim to be one who may not be taxed upon his labor and earnings.

Third Argument:

The government does not have the jurisdiction to impose the federal income tax.

Response:

The United States Government does have the jurisdiction to tax the "income" of all those who are within the scope of its authority. The government would not and could not tax those who are not "co-extensive" with its purview, or without its "permission." The government would be violating fundamental law if it did so. Therefore, those who pay the income tax must be within the taxing authority of the *United States*.

Fourth Argument:

A man's earnings are not income as defined by the Supreme Court.

Response:

A man's earnings are "income" for purposes of the federal income tax laws. While the Supreme Court defined "income" as "profit" and "gain," a man's livelihood, if brought within the jurisdiction of congressional taxing authority under Article I, Section 8, namely, indirect taxation, is "income" for the purposes of measuring the amount of the tax due and payable based upon a federal privilege or status.

Fifth Argument:

The 16th Amendment did not grant Congress any new taxing powers.

Response:

This amendment may not have granted Congress new taxing powers; but it clarified that, by power of excise, the government may tax what was misunderstood as not able to be taxed. Since Congress may tax all that is excisable, its power was not enhanced; rather, it was clarified to be more expansive than previously realized.

Separately or collectively, these rejoinders are credible. The responses indicate that the Federal Government presumes the five good faith arguments, which are often sincerely held beliefs by Americans facing criminal charges, are "frivolous." With our study of legal terms and the apparent soundness of the five arguments, we must reconcile that there is more to the story. What is it the government refuses to reveal to the American people? What you are about to learn completes what we do not know.

When Americans accept federal benefits or elect to be treated under a federal status, they enter the jurisdiction of the United States Government as "United States persons" and "taxpayers." This basic concept is consistent with the legal terms and the five arguments. If only because of the acceptance and election of federal benefits and status, the five arguments cannot prevail. Since the government presumes that Americans knowingly altered their taxable disposition, it expects them to voluntarily comply. If they fail to comply, the government will force them to do so. We may conclude that Americans have unknowingly entered the jurisdiction of the "United States" by election or acceptance of both a status and privileges subject to federal excise. Americans became legally obligated to a federal excise tax that the Federal Government could not otherwise collect. For further insight, we will delve into the final case.

The people of this State, as successors of its former sovereign, are entitled to all the rights which formerly belonged to the King by his prerogative. Through the medium of the Legislature they may exercise all the powers which previous to the Revolution could have been exercised either by the King alone, or by him in conjunction with his Parliament; subject only to those restrictions which have been imposed by the Constitution of this State or of the U. S. **Lansing v Smith, 21 D. 89, 4 Wendel 9 (1829) (New York)**

The Case against James Johnson

I do not like injustice; I abhor it. I despise man's inhumanity to man. My disdain for inequity comes from two main sources—my personality and experience. I have always contended with adversity. I was an underdeveloped small child and struggled to overcome difficult odds. Born into poverty and a family with six children, want was a constant. Whether for a lack of food, heat, water, or clothing, we did without tangibles that many enjoyed as commonplace. In a world fraught with suffering, doing without often defines one's heart and mind. This was my experience. From a perspective of need, I acquired an acute appreciation for inequity and equity. The disparity between the strong and weak was striking to me. Personal experiences inculcated and refined an innate sense of fair play. Fairness, deference, and equity became cornerstones of my being.

Truth and justice matter. They *must* matter. There is a distinction between right and wrong. Without this distinction life is prone to confusion. I came to understand that when might dictates the outcome, inequity reigns. My inherent affinity for equity became a calling. Furthermore, I was willing to act on my beliefs and right the wrongs inflicted in a world which deserves better. I wanted to deprive confusion of its stranglehold.

My hope is that truth, honor, and justice will serve those who deserve them. Truth and equity are essential for life. Without them life is without integrity.

Allow me to share a little about who I am. I have four beautiful children. I love and adore them. Relating with them and people brings definition and depth to my life. Time spent with my children, family, and friends is more meaningful than anything. I don't hang out with the "guys." I don't golf on the weekends. I don't play cards on a special night. Some may even consider it odd that I have not had television or cable in my home for over thirty years. I value time. Time is a precious commodity which should not be squandered. I enjoy working and learning. I find that life defining lessons from failure are more rewarding than accomplishments. Whether working with my hands or mind, I take satisfaction in the effort and seek to persevere. Challenging the conventional, I have found, is a direct path into the unknown and eventually greater understanding. Moreover, observing, listening, and conversing give shape and substance to life.

I am a college graduate and a former United States Army Officer. I have succeeded in business. Success is fine; but it is the journey I have traveled which has instilled principles and furthered my undeterred resolve. In my humble estimation, if not for the ability to know the truth, defy confusion, and aspire for what is equitable, life would be shallow and hollow.

Serving a four-year prison sentence is a testament of a search for what is equitable and just, especially after years of studying law and broadening my appreciation for the proper and limited role of government. From my perspective, freedom has a direct correlation to truth. Without truth, freedom is elusive, if not a fiction. If the law is inconclusive, it is a lie. And I am an innocent man, if not a martyr for the truth. I would never have reached these conclusions but for the journey.

In 1987, I was a Distinguished Military Graduate from the Virginia Military

Institute in Lexington, Virginia. I received a commission as a Second Lieutenant and entered the field of Military Intelligence. This experience gave me direct exposure to the reaches of the military and the United States Government. With a Top-Secret clearance, my understanding of our intelligence collection efforts, programs, reporting procedures, and technological applications were broadened. This experience altered my once limited view of the world.

When I resigned my commission from the Army, I moved to Seattle, Washington, and worked for an estate planning firm which provided legal and financial services for the retired and affluent. It was with this company that I learned about trusts and trust law. I began to study the Constitution, the role of government, and the inherent rights of the American people—which included property rights. I was struck by my level of ignorance. I realized how little I was taught in the public educational system.

In 1994, I moved back to Virginia and continued to study. By 1999, I was secure in my knowledge and was no longer fearful to act upon sound principles and beliefs. I contracted with a firm which established common law trusts for their clients. These trusts are used as a legal and lawful means of increasing privacy, reducing tax liability, and limiting litigation exposure. Our family home was conveyed into a trust. Our automobiles were transferred into trusts at the local DMV office.

A Board of Trustees was responsible for the trusts. The trustees hired a manager for the direct oversight and operation of the trusts. I knew Americans had an inviolate right to contract. Trusts are an agreement between three parties. It is an instrument which cannot be defeated unless there is impropriety or illegality. The firm which provided the trusts included a letter sent from a certified public accountant, Gregory Karl, from Saluna Beach, California, to the IRS. Karl asked if pure trust organizations were required to receive EINs for tax reporting purposes. An official from the IRS, Chief Felthaus, replied that pure trusts had no tax liability and could not receive an EIN. I had no doubt these trusts were lawful structures. Confirmation from the IRS only added credibility.

My research into the tax laws led me to conclude I was no longer a "United States person," "person," or "taxpayer" as defined in the tax code. I had a distinct appreciation for how the government used terms in a legal capacity, which was nothing like the usage of words in the normal course of life. I was an American, a Citizen of Virginia state, one of the free and independent states which comprise the United States of America. The only nexus which bound me to the federal "United States" Government was my election to a federal income tax liability and acceptance of the federal social security and employment insurance programs. I realized this status and these benefits created the obligation and classification which made my "income" subject to excise. However, I rebutted any presumption that I was within the jurisdiction of the Federal Government by categorically revoking any election and federal privilege.

In 2000, I formally revoked any election and my intention to change my status. I sent formal notification to the Secretary of the Treasury (IRS) and the Secretary of State that I was a Citizen of Virginia and was without the jurisdiction of the Federal Government, the United States. I cited Supreme Court cases such as Yick Wo v. Hopkins and asserted that sovereignty resides with the people. I clearly stated having no intention to subscribe to federal citizenship and rebutted any presumption of the same.

In 2000, I revoked and rescinded my signature and intent to the social security number and benefit. I mailed this formal notification to the Social Security Administration in Baltimore, Maryland. I also hand delivered a copy to the local Social Security Administration office and received a signed acceptance of the original. As far as I was concerned, I no longer had an obligation to or with the Federal Government.

I also believed, for all the grounded reasons discussed earlier in this book, that I was not in the "United States" as defined in the tax code, 26 USC, section 7701. I was not within the "State" for the enforcement of the tax statutes. I was also not within the District of Columbia. I was not an "employer" or "employee." I was not a "taxpayer."

THE INVESTIGATION BEGINS

In 2004, the Department of Internal Revenue began a civil investigation into me and my wife. We had not filed tax returns for the last five years. Agent Robert Biggs came to our home, unannounced, to ask some questions. We declined to answer and asked him to put any queries in writing. He left a letter informing us of a formal civil probe. He gave us a summons to appear for questioning.

I forwarded the documents to a personal representative who had an Internal Revenue Number and was able to represent people before the agency as one's Power-of-Attorney. My representative, John Kotmair, wrote Biggs several letters. Biggs, however, never responded. Rather, Biggs wrote directly to me and stated that Kotmair was not qualified. Biggs gave no other explanation. Meanwhile, I wrote a letter to Biggs and requested that he provide the law which required Americans to file U. S. Individual Income Tax Returns. Biggs never answered the question. This was the same query asked by Kotmair. He asked how I was one of "Every person liable..." under 26 USC 6001.

In 2005, the investigation became a criminal matter. An agent of the Internal Revenue Service, Criminal Investigation Division (CID), Nicholas Pompei, came to my home unannounced. He identified himself and stated that he had some questions. I directed him to put any queries in writing. He never did.

To clarify what we had done wrong, in effort to assure myself that I had a proper understanding of our tax liability, I sent Pompei the same letter I sent to Biggs. I asked Pompei for the law which required us to file federal tax returns. Pompei never responded. Rather, he referred to the pamphlet Biggs sent which addressed arguments considered to be "frivolous." This was a publication which offered nothing responsive to the question I asked. The pamphlet offered no clarification as to our tax liability under the law. It was a document that was misplaced considering the severity of the investigation and the repercussions, as if it were a pro forma response to anyone with the courage to ask the *one* interrogatory which mattered. Furthermore, Pompei went so far as to state that he would not respond to any further correspondence. Not only was Pompei negligent with respect to answering a credible question, but one could also easily conclude he was ethically, morally, and professionally bound to respond.

I was in a precarious position. To resolve any criminal prosecution, I wrote to elected and government officials. I appealed to Congressman Frank Wolf and Senators George Allen, John Warner, Jim Webb, and Mark Warner over the period of the investigation. They refused to provide a direct and substantive response to a simple query. As elected "lawmakers," I had every reason to believe they would be willing and able to provide the law which obligated me to file a federal income tax return. I was wrong. Surprisingly, each did as the others. They forwarded my letters to the IRS and requested the agency conducting the criminal investigation to answer a constituent's concern.

Not surprisingly, the IRS replied with boiler plate responses which failed to answer my one basic question. When my elected representatives received these IRS responses, they attached a perfunctory cover letter and forwarded the agency's answer to me. These elected officials considered the matter closed.

I began to realize that, while Americans are expected to know the law I had studied, lawmakers were not willing to provide answers as authors of the law. They refused to do so. Why? Since my plight involved the most ruthless, unresponsive, destructive, and feared agency in the world—the IRS—one would expect these representatives, with staffs to assist in addressing such grave concerns, to be forthcoming. They deflected the queries outright. Was I expecting too much? It did not occur to me that this was a complicated matter. I presumed the reverse was true. The issue at hand was so simple that a cogent response would have ended any criminal probe and resulted in my compliance with any credible law. Or any response would have been confirmation that no law compelled my performance. Since both the IRS agents and all elected representatives failed to disclose the law, the intensity of my situation was heightened significantly.

We have already discussed the investigative component of the judicial process and how agents are a part of the apparatus used to convict innocent men. The roles of both Biggs and Pompei and their lack of responsiveness allow us to reach several conclusions. First, they refused to provide a proper answer to a legitimate query. Second, they applied only what they knew or what they were told to offer. Third, these agents could do one of two things: offer either the truth or what was designed to deflect the truth. They did the latter. Fourth, because of their neglect, they failed to comply with the IRS mission statement.

MISSION OF SERVICE

> *The purpose of the Service is to collect the proper amount of tax revenues at the least cost to the public, and in a manner that warrants the highest degree of public confidence, integrity, efficiency and fairness. To achieve that purpose, the Service encourages the highest possible degree of voluntary compliance in accordance with the tax laws and regulations, advises the public of their rights and responsibilities, determines the extent of compliance and the causes of noncompliance, properly administrates and enforces tax laws and searches for new methods to implement the collections of taxes more efficiently.* Handbook for Special Agents, Department of Treasury, Criminal Investigation Division, Internal Revenue Service, Section 49.01

PRIMARY RESPONSIBILITIES

> *In addition to collecting tax revenues, the service is responsible for interpreting the tax laws, informing taxpayers of what is required of them, insuring that reports required by the tax laws are promptly filed, auditing tax returns and making certain that they correctly reflect tax liabilities and collecting and accounting for taxes gathered.* Ibid.

It was apparent that Pompei failed to help an alleged *taxpayer* voluntarily comply with a legal liability. No answer from him or any other official was an answer, if not *the* answer. The silence was deafening and certainly destructive.

The idea that elected lawmakers would forward correspondence to the IRS without responding on their own is untenable. I even stated in subsequent letters to these members of Congress that I wanted them to provide their own understanding of the law. I underscored that, if I was expected to know the law, they should clarify my ignorance or confusion as *authors* of the law. I emphasized that I did not want them to accept mere template replies from the IRS. Are elected officials busy? Yes. However, they are not so busy that they couldn't address this key concern. A signed letter from them with a canned response from the IRS, which excused the agency's leadership from holding itself and Pompei to the IRS mission statement is, in fact, what will happen when one asks a simple question.

These lawmakers were complicit with the intent of the agency and any underlying motives inherent with avoiding the disclosure of the law.

- Did they exert efforts to hold the agency accountable? No, there were none.
- Where was the righteous indignation? There was none.
- Where were the legislative mavericks who would either demand the executive agency reply truthfully and completely, or defy the conventional and answer the question themselves? There were none.

Should we consider the possibility that these lawmakers failed to do right because *they had to perpetuate the fraud*? Will a United States Congressman or Senator state in writing the law which requires an American to file a tax return or that there is no law? No. A representative who dared to demonstrate such moxie would be excoriated.

A truthful or credible response would be an invitation to scrutiny. Elected officials do not want scrutiny. They don't want to explain what is controversial. Their careers and re-elections depend upon operating within what is conventional. They want to deal with what is generally accepted. It is far more convenient to feign a genuine interest by forwarding any volatile issue to a third party, even if it is the party criminally investigating a constituent. Consequently, the IRS and its agents receive cover—a pass—while elected representatives create the appearance of accountability. Ultimately, the agents are encouraged—perhaps emboldened—to continue with a presumption of the legal liability of a taxpayer while summarily dismissing the taxpayer's grounded queries which were far from frivolous.

Take a step back and consider an observation. I was innocent. I believe with certainty that I was not a "taxpayer" liable to file a federal income tax return on a voluntary basis. I no longer lacked knowledge and understanding. I refused to acquiesce in the face of raw power and fear. I decided to assert the rights and beliefs I held dear.

Inadequate responses from not only two IRS agents but five elected officials were telling. Why were they unwilling to provide a rather simple answer to a simple question? Why did it appear as if they were willfully avoiding and evading the substance of my letters? The absence of a concrete answer was damning. Their unwillingness to respond validated the early implementation of the fraud and force necessary to perpetuate the federal income tax scheme. I experienced firsthand how the agency, agents, and lawmakers manifested the apathy and arrogance required to foster and advance the scheme.

I could allow for them not knowing that no law required me to do what was an alleged legal liability; however, I am not that naïve. I recognized their personal or even professional predisposition against providing an answer did not prevent them from honoring an inherent ethical responsibility—cite the legal reference that would assist an errant taxpayer. I recognized their obligation to dignify the IRS mission statement and correct an American who asked if he was making a mistake. Otherwise, one could naturally conclude these officials were indifferent and acted not only with complete disregard for one's right, but the rule of law. For, if there was no law or the laws were misapplied to me, these agents and co-conspirators would be a law unto themselves.

The arrogance of the lawmakers was notable for obvious reasons. They knew I faced an almost certain prison sentence. They knew Americans studied the law and challenged it on an annual basis. Yet, they treated such grave matters as run of the mill concerns. Do their elected positions insulate them from doing what should be done? If so, how does anyone reconcile such striking unresponsiveness? The only answer is arrogance—even if they hide behind institutional arrogance—the arrogance of Congress. Curiously, ironically, the U. S. Attorney's position during the trial was that I was the one who was unwilling to answer questions posed by the agents. How convenient.

The exertion of any fraud and force was initiated by a mere failure of anyone to respond. Had one official dignified my question, I would have gladly complied with the law which compelled my *voluntary* submission of a federal income tax return. I would have had no choice. If this had occurred, there would have been no investigation in 2005 and the Federal Government would not have wasted manpower and resources through 2013 **to convict a man who was seeking an answer, not a prison sentence.**

The impact from the IRS investigation was devastating. My family suffered needlessly. Our livelihood was destroyed. The stress was unbearable. We were under a microscope. The CID agents followed me undetected to the stores which I serviced. Once I left the store, they would enter and flash their badges. This led to a series of questions from customers and the almost certain loss of an account.

I wrote a letter to the Commissioner of Internal Revenue, Charles Rossotti, and pleaded for assistance. I asked him for the law which established a filing requirement, especially since I had revoked any election and revoked and rescinded my signature and participation to the federal benefit of social security. I clarified that I no longer had a pecuniary relationship with the United States Government. I asked Rossotti to satisfy his obligation by law and file a return on my behalf if I was liable. Rossotti never responded.

Without recourse, I drove to a local IRS office ninety miles away and requested that an IRS agent provide me a bill for any taxes owed. The agent responded that no amount would be known unless the tax returns were filed. I then handed her a letter which asked the Commissioner to file a tax return on my behalf. Weeks later, I received an unsigned computer-generated form in the mail which stated that an answer would be sent within forty-five days. The answer never came. Rossotti failed to comply again.

A telling exchange occurred at this local IRS office. I asked the agent to stamp my personal copy of the letter as "received" by the agency. She replied that they did not exercise such a practice. I was not deterred. I stressed to her that the agency did practice the confirmation of correspondence as a routine protocol. I requested that she do so. "I would like my copy stamped 'received' with today's date," I told her. Once again, she replied that this was not done. When I asked for her identification number and her supervisor, she turned around in her chair, unlocked a safe, withdrew a stamp and affixed it to my letter. Amazing. Noncompliance and subterfuge were ingrained at every level of the IRS.

In 2009, I received a letter from a Mr. Salad, from the Department of Justice. He stated that I was recommended for prosecution. I responded to him immediately and explained my numerous attempts to have any number of responsible parties give me assistance and a resolution. I even asked Salad to clarify if I had made a mistake. I said that I wanted to comply with the law and asked him to provide the statute which declared my liability. Mr. Salad never responded.

There was a recurring theme with each component of the "system" which included the Department of Justice. Based upon the lack of responses, no one was willing to help me understand my obligations under the law. No one was ready, willing, or able to do the right thing. I was nonplussed. Did all these government officials know that, given my circumstances, there was no law which required my performance? Were they part of a conspiracy to ensure the "voluntary" compliance of the greater public achieved through the fear generated from the conviction of well-intentioned Americans on an annual basis?

I knew the government had the guns, money, and power with the means and intent to conduct an eight-year investigation, and complete disregard for the truth or the constraints of its own limited powers. The sanctity of a man's freedom, natural rights, marriage, and family were of no consequence to them. All of this was collateral damage. The United States Government needed "poster children" for its annual April fear campaign achieved by force and buttressed by the arrogance needed to prevail.

Much can be said of IRS investigations into the private affairs of Americans. First and foremost is that the government invariably fails to follow its own protocol or standard operating procedure. However, what needs to be emphasized is that agents and those who can influence them had no intention of honoring the inquiry of one who was a criminal target. I could do nothing other than endure years of waiting while officials exhaustively explored every facet of my life. No stone remained unturned. Yet, I continued to be a stand for the truth. I reconciled that in the presence of silence—government silence—I had to contend with the inevitable. I could do nothing else. As I lived through the anguish, I conducted my affairs as I had before the investigation began in 2004. Regardless of the outcome, I intended to honor my principles. This included my unwillingness to have an unresponsive government adversely influence what was otherwise right and just.

Eventually I learned the Department of Justice was charging me with a felony for obstructing a federal investigation under 26 USC 7212 and three misdemeanors for willful failure to file under 26 USC 7203. Was I guilty of either charge? No. How did I arrive at this conclusion? I studied the law and relied upon my good faith belief. Moreover, the government's failure to answer my question supported the premise that I was correct in my conclusion. In good conscience, I knew I was not liable to file a federal income tax return on a voluntary basis. Additionally, I knew officials were unwilling to rebut this position. Such unwillingness gave credence that there was something to hide, or the government needed an expected result. The truth was inconsequential.

I was no longer ignorant or apathetic. I no longer feared the IRS or the Federal Government. I recognized the psychological and emotional motivations of the CID agent. He was trained or conditioned and controlled to prevail. He was a government lackey. He had no intention to ask questions of his superiors, as did former CID agent Joe Banister. Banister a CID had been an agent who learned the law. *Banister came to realize that his actions against Americans may have been the result of a simple misunderstanding and misapplication—originating with him alone—of the very laws he was expected to enforce.* So he wrote to his superiors and asked simple questions. Not only did the IRS not respond to his queries, but Banister's superiors also asked for his resignation.

Was Pompei willing to suspend disbelief and do the same? No. He was not willing to dispense with the last eight years of destroying a man's life and potential gain, whether professional recognition, personal satisfaction, and financial remuneration. He was a part of the federal machine which sought to convict and incarcerate while avoiding accountability. Winning was everything; winning was expected. The investigation was a necessary evil to reach this preordained result regardless of the cost. The imprisonment of an innocent man who held good faith beliefs of merit was of no consequence. Compliance among the public was a necessity. The loss of a man's freedom was a prerequisite to ensure such compliance.

I came to the realization that the world in which we live is not what was envisioned by the likes of Thomas Jefferson. The nature of the United States Government has changed. No longer is the scope of the federal authority limited. No longer is the "general welfare clause" properly understood or applied. In the past, the "United States" had an extremely restricted role in the lives of Americans. The philosophy that a man was autonomous if he injured no one's life, liberty, or property was a truism.

Man did not question if his labor and earnings which provided for his very existence were his and his alone. His labor was his property. His labor was an extension of himself. If man labored for gold or silver coins, the coins were exchanged for his labor. This was an equal exchange. The labor was property or substance. The coins were property or substance. The coins were his and his alone. The natural rights possessed by man that dignified this exchange was also property. Since I revoked the election of a federal status and a tax liability, as I no longer subscribed to the federal benefit of social security, this was my belief as well.

It was not lost on me that we no longer have a cultural or individual conviction that this natural right is ours to be coveted and protected. If Americans were taxed at a rate of 10% annually in the days of Jefferson—which was not so—we are now taxed at a rate of 30-60% collectively at all levels of government. We work for all levels of government for six months of every year before we provide for ourselves. This time is no longer ours. This time, which represents and is our existence, is no longer coveted property. Rather, we have relegated our existence to voluntary servitude. *We simply believe that we are free.*

These were some of the distinctions and insights I understood. As I faced ruin for a law to which I was no longer beholden, I asked myself what went wrong with Jefferson's great "American experiment."[48] Where was the jealous regard for our rights and freedom? These are questions Americans should ask themselves and each other. This would compel us to ask if I committed a crime. Did I have malicious intent? Was there an injured party? The answer to each was "No." Regrettably, this was no longer my wife's belief. If only out of convenience and fear, she now believed I was a liar.

THE GOVERNMENT INFORMANT

Most federal cases involve an informant, a snitch. We saw this with Figueroa in David Porath, or with Gosin and the thirty friends, family, members, and associates. My case also involved a snitch—my wife. She became a willing government informant.

As the criminal probe intensified, it was evident she no longer supported our past efforts and beliefs. At a minimum, she no longer supported me. My wife began to meet secretly with the IRS agents at her father's office in our hometown. She answered their questions and complied with their requests. She provided them information—my personal contacts, reading material, bills, customer lists, emails—anything that would serve the government's interests and a conviction. She asked a friend to write and type a thirty-page statement describing our marriage, my personal efforts, and the particulars of our private life. This was the length the IRS pushed her so that she could absolve herself of any culpability. The sanctity of a marriage was inconsequential to all concerned.

I understand why my wife became a government operative. She was a mother of two small children and did not want to risk what she valued most. Already with a great sense of insecurity, our children were her priority. It was convenient to seek refuge in her father's coffers and the safety and security he offered. I knew, however, that—with unbreakable loyalty—many spouses refuse to compromise their marriage vows for anything. The IRS did not deserve the credit for her dishonoring of our marriage vows.

I recall speaking with my wife in our living room one afternoon when I noticed a striking change in her words and tone. I had withheld my knowledge of her spying activities. Perhaps out of disbelief, I wanted her to reveal this fact to me. She never said a word. In a trying moment, I disclosed this revelation. I looked at her with compassion and told her that, if she continued to provide information to the government, I would not be able to provide for her and our family. We were not making it financially as it was. Her complicity had adversely affected our bottom line.

When I asked her for help with the finances, the conversation became heated. Without admitting to her spying, she declared, "You are the one responsible to provide according to the Bible!" I could not believe her response. I looked at her and shared that we were one, husband and wife, and no one could take this from us. I stressed that we

[48] http://www.heritage.org/research/commentary/2007/07/the-american-experiment

could not be forced to testify against each other, and we should support each other in times of need. Perhaps out of desperation, perhaps out of a defensive posture to protect and preserve—or to take the opportunity to distance herself psychologically and emotionally—she yelled, "You lied to me!" It was then that I knew with certainty she had no intention to help with the finances or in any way defend our decisions regarding taxes.

When we were married in 1997, I shared with her about my studies into our country's history. As years passed, I introduced articles, books, events, and insight which exposed the truth about any number of issues, such as taxation. My wife knew how firmly I believed the problems which needed redress in America. I supported the "We the People Foundation" and "givemeliberty.org." I attended classes and functions offered by the "Save a Patriot Fellowship" and became a member. I met Joe Banister, John Turner, and Sherry Jackson, former employees of the IRS who were outspoken about the truth and the abuse of this despised agency. I was involved with educational efforts to spread the truth to all Americans.

In 2004, before the IRS investigation began, Bob Schulz, the founder of www.givemeliberty.org, filed a class action lawsuit against the United States under the First Amendment clause for the "petition the government for redress of grievances."[49] I approached my wife and explained my desire to become a member of the plaintiff class. I stressed that this would bring unwanted scrutiny upon us. Nonetheless, she gave me her support. She knew I was not a fair-weather friend to my beliefs.

This lawsuit addressed several issues: America's involvement in undeclared wars, the abolishment of the Federal Reserve Bank, the use of electronic voting machines, and taxation, among others. I was encouraged to have a wife who supported my efforts to right the wrongs which ailed our country. As husband and wife, we were a testament to our beliefs. We used trusts to restructure our affairs, as do many informed and wealthy Americans. When our children were born, we decided not to get birth certificates or social security cards from the hospital. We created a "Certificate of Live Birth" as documentation of these events.

In another situation, I had successfully compelled the State of Virginia to expunge the social security number from its voting records. After researching the law, I convinced the Secretary of the Board of Elections that the law did not require this number to vote. She had initially refused my request as unlawful. After speaking with me and reading the law, she agreed and complied with my request. I was one of a handful in Virginia who voted without this number.

I share this information to demonstrate that my wife and I were a team, even if she was a mere passive participant. For years, we pursued a path of truth with genuinely held good faith beliefs. Perhaps reflective of a degree of naiveté, I never saw my wife as an undercover government informant. Never did I envision that she would gather evidence for her lawyer and government agents who were perfecting a *criminal* case against her husband. Over the years I met any number of couples within the Tax Honesty Movement with the intent to change the course of this country. They were God-fearing people who earnestly defended the truth. I marveled as wives wholeheartedly supported their husbands. Such unity was vital to prevail against injustice. I was convinced that my wife was one of the champions who supported her husband.

My intention for highlighting my wife's role in the investigation and trial is not to denigrate her, but to show how and why the Federal Government operates and relates to witnesses. The fact that my wife was a key witness is immaterial in the final analysis.

[49] Amendment I, The Constitution of the United States

While it may have shattered all prized presumptions of marriage and life-defining relationships, the practical result is all that mattered. I knew she believed, in the end, that she had to give up her husband to preserve what mattered most to her. While I witnessed couples face the IRS and government together, while I expected that we would do the same, this did not happen. It would not be unreasonable to ask why. Why was my spouse no longer supportive and, in fact, antagonistic of our or my previous efforts? Why did she help the IRS? The answer should be obvious. She was subject, exclusively, to her own fear. She submitted to the overall impact of institutional arrogance and her own ignorance, apathy, and fear.

I recognized the government must have approached my wife with pressure and threats, especially since she had direct knowledge and involvement in alleged "criminal activity." The fear in her mind and heart must have been overwhelming. Regardless of the strength of one's faith in God, relationships, truth, or a noble cause, threats have intended consequences. Fear is a prime motivation, and it is used deliberately. Fear is the prime means for IRS actions. My wife was forced to decide between her own security and the integrity of our marriage. While many would fault her for deciding as she did, I am not willing to do so. I also understand that a challenge from and with the government did not have to destroy all that we had—or would have—once this ordeal passed. But for fear.

But for fear any number of couples stands foursquare with their collective resolve. Let there be no doubt that fear overwhelms and alters how and why we decide to either exist or live powerfully. Fear is the very primal influence which drives one to indifference and away from what was previously paramount. Many would chastise me for allowing my wife to be in such a compromising position. I understand. I also understand this situation could have been perceived as other than a completely compromising position. And, yes, hindsight provides clarity. If we allow ourselves to question the path of any man, woman, or couple throughout history—those congruent with the pursuit of the truth—we are susceptible to question anything and everything before seeing the results of their efforts.

A man may be disparaged for any belief that, by virtue of misperception of others, jeopardizes his family. Such is the latitude of opinions in the face of what is uncomfortable when the opinions come from those on the sidelines. A woman's resolve for the truth may be challenged if it unsettles her comfortable state and that of her loved ones. It is easy to question without understanding. Suffice it to say, the concerns of others for my wife and family did not minimize my own concerns for them. Furthermore, we did not know how the investigation or eventual trial would end. Our marriage and family did not have to suffer such loss. We could have resolved to stand together and possibly succeed.

How easy it is to condemn when the trek proves arduous. Any number of families has endured far worse only to persevere. This trial could have strengthened our marriage. Our suffering could have been a testimony to our children and others that principles and truth are worthy of battling. There was no need to reduce the turmoil to a "lie" told by a husband to his wife. This was not the truth. A Men have gone to prison for challenging the tax laws; many of those are the ones who know the truth.

I intended to spend time discussing the critical role of informants within the judicial system. They are essential to the number of convictions secured by the government. The fact that my wife spied on me illustrates how authorities operate with disregard for the repercussions to those on the periphery, like children. Once I knew my wife had capitulated, I knew my fate and the future of our children were all but certain. I had the unfortunate experience of losing my wife and children while waiting for a judgment of guilt and an undeserved prison term. At least I had the peace of mind knowing my "snitch" did not face any legal challenges or incarceration. This also would have been the case had we withstood the adversity together. I would have accepted any unjust punishment for our beliefs and actions.

THE ARREST

On April 6, 2012, I received a phone call from Agent Pompei. He left a voice mail message that a grand jury was convening. It appeared as though I would be afforded the opportunity to attend and participate. However, I had conflicting reports about the grand jury process. Some stated that I would be able to speak. Others said that while I could speak the grand jury was a rubber stamp for the Department of Justice and my testimony would have no impact. I decided not to appear.

At precisely 6:30 the morning after the grand jury met, a SWAT team raided my home. I was not there. I received a phone call while it was occurring. An acquaintance told me that some fifteen agents were "swarming" the place. Since I was absent, the SWAT team went to my aunt's house and then to a house where my friend lived. I was at none of these locations. I was traveling at the time. I was completing paperwork that I hoped would resolve the entire legal matter.

Approximately three weeks later, I contacted the man who originally called me about the raid. We planned to meet at a restaurant in Front Royal, Virginia. Little did I know he had already been contacted by Pompei. They had traced the "swarming" phone call back to him. It was evident he had been forced to assist in my arrest or he would face charges as an accomplice. Within an hour he appeared in the restaurant. I had just finished dinner with my sister and four-year-old niece, Maddie. The place was empty save three other customers who dined at three separate tables. The acquaintance came into the place texting on his phone. We greeted and spoke briefly. I then told him that I was going to say goodbye to my family.

In a sudden burst, some fifteen individuals barged through the doors. I had been standing in the middle of the restaurant. Initially, and this may be hard to believe, I did not know what was happening. I was as shocked as any customer. I did not realize at first who these agents were. I reacted instinctively. I turned to canvas the area for my niece. What would an uncle do if a bunch of thugs barreled into a store and brandished weapons? I failed to locate her. I turned to the right in the direction of our table. I still could not find her. By the time I reached the table, some five agents, with one obese Agent Pompei laboring heavily in the lead, were on top of me. Ten other agents had their weapons trained on my back. The red lasers danced upon me. When my eyeglasses fell, I reached to retrieve them. Pompei, who was still breathing with difficulty, took them away. I was then handcuffed and taken outside and directed to sit on the curb.

Miraculously, Maddie was never in harm's way. She was off to the left and never saw a thing. My sister, however, saw the entire scene. She is a federal administrative law judge for the Social Security Administration. She was shocked and horrified by the conduct of the United States Government. She and I both knew Pompei need only have walked in and asked me to accompany him. Had I known an indictment and warrant for my arrest had been issued, I would have complied voluntarily. The zealous show of force was a matter of course and underscores the psychological and emotional motivators which reinforce their agenda—force and control with the intent to instill fear.

Would it have been plausible for Pompei to orchestrate a simpler and safer arrest? Consider the manpower he had available. He could have directed the fifteen agents to surround the building and place their vehicles to prevent egress out of the parking lot and facility. He could have beckoned me with a bullhorn or had an agent approach me inside with directives to exit with him. If I were an escape risk, with agents stationed at all exits, I would have been contained. Why risk the potential harm and unnecessary upheaval involved with storming a private business when no force was required. The motivation of the government is revealed by their actions. We need only refer to the Gosin case.

Gosin was not even aware of the imminent raid on his home, much less an investigation. Yet agents assaulted his house and family on an early November morning. Ryan was not armed and dangerous. The overbearing posture of federal agencies is widespread and humbling. As seen with Norris, what other reasons would there be to raid their home? Were they suspected of gun running, gang violence, armed bank robbery, or a underage sex operation? No, they were charged with selling illegal orchids.

The trite cliché that the devil is in the details is often true. As I sat on the curb in handcuffs, with my arms behind my back, a federal agent spoke to me. "Sovereign Citizen, huh?" There it was. "Sovereign Citizen." This was the title the Federal Government applied to me. Where did this nameless agent get this impression and moniker? And why was he characterizing me as one? Had this label been the overarching theme to the agent's raid? Never had I declared that I was a Sovereign Citizen or one of a group which used this "title" to a divisive end. I did send a declaration to the Secretary of the Treasury and Secretary of State in 2000 with a notification that I was not a "United States citizen" as defined in the tax code. I cited Supreme Court cases which clearly stipulated that sovereign power resides with the people, cases which state the people are sovereign.

The concept of sovereignty must have significance. Power does reside with the people. If not, we must question why. Has this dynamic and fundamental truth changed? Why does the Federal Government look upon Americans as mere subjects? Why do the 50 states of the Union no longer assert power given to them by the people? Why doesn't the Federal Government respect its constitutional constraints?

Consider the scene that was unfolding. Having endured what was outrageous in a private business, having researched for years about freedom, natural rights, status, jurisdiction, and taxation I was at the mercy of a brutal system. I had just received the first indication as to how the government would malign me, "Sovereign Citizen." This was consistent with how the government operates; it labels, marginalizes, and subdues.

I spent the next two nights in two county jails until I appeared at the Initial Hearing before United States Magistrate, James Welsh, in Harrisonburg, Virginia. I presumed the Department of Justice would offer charges against me. What is noteworthy, however, is that no one had identified me, and I had no identification on me when I was arrested. I had not identified myself to anyone. I answered no questions. I remained silent. I was even denied blankets at the Rockingham County Jail for my unwillingness to answer questions with the jail's intake process. My unwillingness to comply or answer in court was no different.

The average American may perceive that my mindset was belligerent. However, most of us are conditioned to comply and comply we do. *Most do not consider that if we fail to assert our rights, we have none.* This is a well-known maxim of law. I believed the Federal Government had no jurisdiction over me. With my good faith belief, I intended to assert my rights and defeat any federal jurisdictional presumption and claim. Since I had declined to participate in any federally taxable activity to which I was once beholden and revoked any election of a federal status, I knew I was not liable for a federal income tax.

I saw my situation as I would any other unwarranted detention. Consider a ridiculous example. If your child were "arrested" by another couple and forced to live within that couple's "domain," would this be acceptable? If another businessman took you and forced you to "cooperate" for his financial interests, would this be acceptable? If a foreign power seized you on vacation and forced you to live in its territory, would you simply comply? Would you not challenge the authority of each lawless kidnapper in each situation? I saw my plight no differently. Ask yourself why the Federal Government had or has jurisdiction in a situation such as mine, especially since I had rebutted any presumption that I was liable for the federal income tax. How did the United States acquire jurisdiction? Are you able to answer this fundamental question? Would you even think to *ask* this question? I did and I wanted the government to prove jurisdiction.

THE INITIAL HEARING

The tax laws did not apply in *my* situation. These laws applied to federal employees, United States citizens, entities within the federal jurisdiction, and those who subscribed to federal benefits and elected to be treated with a certain federal status. These laws applied to those who received "income" subject to excise. I had no doubt that I was no longer within the jurisdiction of the IRS. I did not have income subject to taxation. If only Americans comprehended the simplicity of this jurisdictional concern they would agree with this grounded premise. They would ask the question: *If this man no longer enjoyed a federal status or privilege, how does the Federal Government claim jurisdiction?*

I was ushered into the courtroom with shackles around my ankles and wrists and a chain around my waist. My clothes had been taken from me and I was forced to wear a striped white and orange jumpsuit. I was led by U. S. Marshals and slowly made my way, shuffling six inches at a time, as this was the range granted by the chains. Each step caused the cuffs to dig into my ankles. When I was seated next to the Public Defender, Andrea Harris, the marshals removed the handcuffs and chains were removed, while my ankles remained bound.

When Harris introduced herself, I politely interrupted and stated that she did not represent me. When the case was announced by the clerk, the U. S. Magistrate proceeded with his customary court formalities. The first time he identified me as the Defendant, I objected. I stated that I was not the defendant and then challenged jurisdiction. This was important to assert. The government assumes jurisdiction without fail. Jurisdiction is everything, and without it the government and court cannot proceed. I knew I was not and could not be what the government asserted. I was without (outside of) the authority of the federal United States. I was not a "taxpayer," "U. S. person," or "employee" as defined in the tax code. I was a free man, a Citizen of Virginia state, one of the independent states of America. I was an American without a federal obligation.

From my perspective, if I did not impress upon the court—a supposedly impartial body—that I was who I was and not as claimed by the Department of Justice, then I would automatically cede to federal jurisdiction. So, I asserted my status and rights. When the magistrate asked me who I was, since I denied being the defendant, I asked him for his name. He glared at me and said," I am James Welsh. Who are you?" I responded, "You can call me 'Friend.'" I shared that no one identified me since the arrest. I had not identified myself. The magistrate stated that the government believed I was the correct person.

I replied that I was not this "person" and asked in open court if anyone had a claim against me. The magistrate looked around the room as I waited for a response. No one said a word. The courtroom was deathly silent. I then repeated my question. "For the second time, is there anyone who has a claim against me?" When nobody responded, I stated, "Let the record show that no one has a claim against me. I hereby move this court to dismiss this case with prejudice and set me at liberty." What did or did not happen next was revealing. Although unschooled as to matters of court, I sensed America was no longer a country concerned with natural rights and freedoms. Our public officials are no longer constrained by their oath of office and the Constitution. It did not matter how their procedures and rules excused what any common man believed should have been done. At a minimum, I expected to know the injured party and to see an affidavit of the claim. This did not occur.

Naturally, I refused to be the defendant. I had rebutted the presumption that I was liable to the jurisdiction of the income excise tax laws. I wasn't in the purview of the court as stated under Article III, Section 2, of the Constitution. I was without the jurisdiction of the Federal Government. I even asked Harris, before the hearing began, if this was an Article 3 or 4 court, to which she responded "3." Meanwhile, the court simply presumed it had jurisdiction and summarily ignored my challenge.

I had just endured two of the most horrendous days of my life. I was cold, angry, and frustrated. Being chained and transported like a murderer was abhorrent. To then ask twice in court if any party had a claim against me and to receive no response was encouraging. I concluded that the magistrate was obligated to dismiss the case.

However, I could not have been further from the truth. Without the slightest hesitation, the magistrate declared, "Denied!" He gave no explanation whatsoever. I was promptly shackled again, led out of court, and taken to a holding cell. I recall stating while exiting that this was an outrage. Those who remained burst into laughter.

Pause to consider the role of the magistrate. He fulfills a function of form and formality and substance. He has a tremendous responsibility. He is a party to whom the authorities provide testimony by affidavit or formal grievance that the accused committed a crime. He receives the formal charges or indictment as confirmation that the defendant is culpable. His acceptance of this documentation grants forward progression of a case within the court. What if he does not receive affirmation of a crime? We cannot have a system whereby men are held without substantiation. If there is no injured party, those unjustly accused would have to be released. Did the magistrate have an affidavit in this case? I did not know. I asked for the claim by the injured party. With no response, I concluded that if one asserts that he could not possibly be the defendant and was without the court's jurisdiction and established that no one had a claim, the court must dignify these facts.

How does a court reconcile moving forward otherwise? Does the magistrate ignore the lack of a response to a credible challenge? As far as I was concerned fraud and force—planted from without the court—took root within the court. A valid query and a petition for dismissal of a case were not handled in a manner one would think is just, at least from the common man's perspective. Is the magistrate so limited that he cannot act, even if it required him to do what would be unthinkable within the conventional practice of court? Is he not responsible for marrying a crime with an affidavit?

I personally witnessed a tax trial when a woman requested the "True Bill" and viewed it. Why didn't this magistrate require the government to prove there was a legitimate claim against me which would confirm that I was quite possibly the defendant? The government had the ability to hide behind its unresponsiveness to my letters and questions for the last eight years. Were these officials going to receive a pass and not be accountable to an innocent man's request for proof of a legitimate claim in court?

I presumed the magistrate was obligated to show a valid claim of an injury or injured party. I could conclude that he was unaware of his responsibilities to my question, but this would be a foolish position. I could conclude that he was arrogant, and would do as he pleased because he could, regardless of his obligation to hold the government accountable.

I may never know why this court official responded as he did. He may never have had anyone in a pro se capacity ask for anything close to a "True Bill." Perhaps the expectations that he could simply dismiss the case in the absence of a valid claim were too much. What scrutiny would he have received had he done so? These observations raise questions. First and foremost, do judges not challenge what may appear to be specious charges? Are they, consequently, complicit with the incarceration of innocent people when they fail to scrutinize the credibility of a charging instrument? Do they fail to follow protocol because they can?

To deprive the people of the assurances that no errant trespass will come upon their rights is inconsistent with the constraints of the Constitution. Fraud and force cannot take root unless cultivated by those responsible for causing disharmony. It was evident that this magistrate ignored my claims and refused to compel the government to respond.

SOLITARY CONFINEMENT

As unbelievable as the Initial Hearing had been, the events which unfolded defied reason. I was placed into an unmarked white van with several other "prisoners" and transported to Orange County Jail about an hour away. We were placed in a holding cell with twenty other men and waited to be processed. Hours later we were led down the labyrinth of hallways and, either one by one or in groups, assigned to units designated as "general population." I was the last to be placed. Two guards directed me to what was known as the SHU—Special Housing Unit. This, unbeknownst to me, was isolation—solitary confinement. The SHU was the unit which housed murderers serving life or multiple life sentences or those awaiting trial for murder.

I was placed into a cinder block and concrete cell with a solid metal door and remained alone for the next fifty-five days.

I should not have been surprised at the extent the government would go. However, this was beyond the pale. I was bewildered and angry. I questioned why. What was the motivation for such treatment? A year ago, I was a husband and father working, attending church, living a respectable life, although not filing a piece of paper and paying an excise for which I was no longer bound. Now I was on par with those who killed people. Who made this decision? What was their motivation and expectation for isolating me?

Imagine being confined to your room for a day or longer. The thought is not appealing. Why? It is not necessarily because you are confined. No. You are controlled and are made to be alone, without contact. Granted, being in your room may have benefits. You have amenities, television, computer, books, window, phone, chair, etc. It is a relatively pleasant environment. However, you are alone without the ability to leave.

I was in a cell that was seven feet wide and twelve feet long. A steel bunk was anchored to a wall with a thin mattress covered in vinyl. There was a stainless-steel sink and toilet mounted to the wall. The solid metal door had no window. It had a drop-down opening six inches tall and eighteen inches long through which meals and mail were delivered. A single window to the cell was three inches tall and forty-eight inches long and eight feet off the floor. A fluorescent light illuminated the cell from a twelve-foot ceiling and was on twenty-four hours a day. The cinder block walls, and concrete floor were made colder by a single metal vent which ushered in cold air. Finally, utter silence—interrupted only by the clanking of heavy keys and cranking tumblers within locks or the cracking sound of doors being closed—enveloped the cell with an austerity that was as ominous as it was oppressive. An occasional inmate yelling for a "CO" (Corrections Officer) jarred the mind-numbing stillness. The days slowed to a crawl. With no clock, I determined the time by the schedule of the meals. The COs made regular checks by opening a metal plate on the upper and outer portion of the steel door, which allowed them to look through a thick piece of Plexiglas three inches by four inches.

Every day I was shackled at my ankles and handcuffed with my wrists behind my back. I shuffled to a shower some twenty feet to the left. I was then unshackled once locked in a solid steel container with a thick wire mesh on the upper third of the door. Once finished, I was shackled again and taken back to the cell for the rest of the day.

This was my life. This was how I spent, not a day or a week, but two months.

I thought to myself, as a former Army officer, trained and disciplined for combat and stark conditions, of the justification for such treatment. I could arrive at only two answers—to isolate to limit a man's influence or to break his will.

The only other answer is because the government could. The government could do what was impossible or seemingly impossible, and, therefore, it did. There was no doubt in my mind that the government was using force to break my will. In part, the agenda was to label and malign. As such, time was the element used to cause a man to question his own motives, purpose, and resolve. From my vantage point, the use of force, under an obvious fraud, was used to defeat me.

As the weeks crawled past, the COs assessed me as they did any inmate. They could not reconcile my placement into isolation. One CO mentioned a note on the folder left by the marshal which read, "Use extreme caution!" Once the guards understood who I was and the charges I faced, they laughed at the antics of the federal authorities. They confirmed this was typical of their modus operandi. They validated the intent was to intimidate and to break men, whether mentally, emotionally, or spiritually. The goal was to deplete any fight within a man forced to be alone with his thoughts and emotions.

The COs' observations deserve merit. They may not be the absolute authority as to the internal operation of the penal system, but they are privy to the policies and procedures of the sister agencies and agents who frequent their facility. Just as these COs had contempt for the murderers housed in the SHU, they held the Federal Government in disdain. They categorically rejected the treatment given to men like me, Americans who supposedly violated what amounted to black ink on white paper, without harm to anyone's life, liberty, or property. They saw no justification for decent men to be isolated.

While in the SHU, the guards befriended me. They brought books, pencils, paper, and the portable library, a computer wheeled from cell to cell. One CO moved me from the second story to the first floor just so I could get frequent computer access. The COs tried to smuggle in hard cover books from the law library which were prohibited in the SHU. I mention this development and relationships simply because the COs who serve at the pleasure of the jail system had an appreciation which confirmed my intuition—the system was unjust from the very beginning and from the top downward. They knew it as well.

One must be willing to suspend disbelief if he is to acquire any understanding that the system, the legal process, is arbitrarily applied—with the clear intention to have "inmates" capitulate by the end or at some point along the way. This is why I placed so much emphasis upon each component of the judicial process in the Four Corners of Justice diagram. Each component may be uniquely applied to engineer a conviction without the absolute necessity to conform to the law.

Consider my situation. Given my extensive studies, I realized the law was not relevant at this point, just as it was not relevant when I asked Biggs and Pompei for the law which obligated my filing of a tax return. After the Initial Hearing, when concern for the law was equally lacking, I realized I was a political prisoner placed into isolation for my beliefs and attempt to bring accountability to a government and system which shunned it. What better way was there to dissuade those who would dare oppose the authority and power of the Federal Government? Placement into the SHU was a direct assault upon my body and being and an insidious means to control and intimidate.

The great unknown was how I would respond. How would the time in isolation affect me? The authorities did not care how long I remained. Time was to their advantage.

I readily acknowledged I did not know how to play their game. I did not know their rules and protocol. I had never been in such a situation. I did know what I believed and why I believed as I did. I knew the fundamental precepts upon which this country was founded. I knew the limits of federal taxing authority. I knew I was *without* federal authority for the income tax. Yet, I did not know what I did not know. I did not know how long they could confine me in this manner. I did not know if my posture was or would be effective to whatever degree. Should I continue this approach? My hope was to remain true to my principles.

Throughout the time in isolation, thanks to my sister, I had the ability to make phone calls. This was obviously positive. And I became ever more present with my anger and sadness. I missed my two little children. My now ex-wife did not answer my calls to them. Factors like these made me realize even more that my *not knowing* was the consideration which influenced my psychological and emotional states. I did not want to decide or act rashly. I did not want to falter and regret steps that I should have considered, or compromise what I intended to achieve or who I was being.

While in isolation, I submitted a Writ of Habeas Corpus. My sister had mailed me some documents which I sent to the Federal Government in 2000. It was an affidavit stating that I was one of the people of the United States of America, a status as one without the "United States Government," and that I was not one with the status of "U. S. Person." In this Habeas Corpus Writ, I cited Supreme Court cases which stated that sovereignty resides with the people. Significantly, I rebutted the presumption that I was a taxpayer as defined and applied in the tax code.

As discussed, the people are the source of power in America who gave rise to the sovereign states and the federal Constitution that established the United States Government. The legal terms we learned, and their respective definitions, are relevant to my situation and this case. With these terms and definitions, how could the government acquire jurisdiction? This is what I wrote in the writ of habeas corpus.

> *Johnson reserves his sovereign rights granted by "The Laws of Nature and Nature's God." (Jefferson) The United States has no authority over Johnson and he is without the geographic power of the same, especially since formally revoking/rescinding any benefit claim to the federal social security insurance program in 2000, thus rebutting the presumption of being a United States employee. As the United States exercises its sovereignty, just as the States exercise sovereignty, Johnson enjoys and exercises sovereignty.*

While, perhaps, I could have been more complete with my representation, I had limited resources and lacked my legal material. Yet, the intent of this message was transparent. How could anyone question the basis for my good faith belief and the subsequent and underlying claim that the Federal Government to include, but not limited to, the IRS and federal judiciary, did not have jurisdiction over me?

While the writ of habeas corpus is typically submitted after a verdict of guilt and sentencing under the provisions of 28 USC 2255, for this is the protocol of the courts, I believed then and still believe, as a man who was unjustly incarcerated, I had no alternative. I had the absolute right to appeal for my immediate release. My intent was to invoke my rights to be free from unlawful incarceration and direct the court to release me. The District Court denied my request in writing and stated that I had inappropriately submitted documents without use of defense counsel. I was unaware the public defenders were counsel of record. What happened to allow this mistake? I soon learned the answer.

Approximately a week after the Initial Hearing, I was transported back to the magistrate for "Arraignment" when one is expected to enter a plea of guilty or not guilty. I postured myself as I did during the previous hearing. I refused to be identified as the Defendant and, again, challenged jurisdiction. I underscored that no one had a claim against me. The magistrate ignored my concerns and entered a plea of "not guilty." He then cited for the record that the federal public defenders were to represent me. I immediately objected and reasserted the lack of jurisdiction. The magistrate ignored my objection.

Did he refuse to hear my objection on purpose? I will never know. However, I was taken out of court thinking I had the last word, that my refusal to accept counsel was recognized. I was unaware of the binding nature of Welch's decision. When the habeas corpus was received by Judge Moon, he stated that legal counsel was responsible for all interaction with the court. There was no doubt I had rejected legal representation. But Harris stated that my objections had not been "timely submitted." I could not have been timelier in asserting my refusal to Welch. With the rejection of the habeas corpus filing, a petition which *still* should have been reviewed by Judge Moon, I had to petition the court to remove the public defenders.

By this point, I had decided to stay in isolation for as long as the government left me there. Harris even stated I would remain until I recognized the jurisdiction of the court. However, after a series of phone calls with my sister, and given her understanding that people were willing to help, I made the decision to accept counsel. Most would say I had no choice. From a philosophical perspective, this was a bitter pill to swallow. I knew everything to which I was subjected was done under fraud and force. Each decision I was required to make was under threat, coercion, and duress. What had transpired was against my rights and status and was a dictate of the system without grounds or authority. But, I was without recourse. My only hope, short of convincing a jury of my innocence, was to gain release on bond and implement a remedy.

DEFENSE COUNSEL

During my time in isolation, I occasionally met with Andrea Harris. While I believed she was not my lawyer, she was a resource. These meetings gave me insight. From our conversations, I further appreciated that she was an officer of the court before she was an advocate of any client. This thought was underscored when she said that she was bound by the rules—which included the Canons of Ethics of the American Bar Association (ABA). Her allegiance to these canons was paramount and even further underscored when I explained my good faith belief.

When I shared how and why I could not be liable to the federal income tax and articulated the reasons, she rejected my belief as "frivolous." Her response was automatic. She was not inclined to probe. She then stated the ABA prohibited her from advancing a claim which was without legal merit. I was shocked. I was dismayed. I could not believe the ABA had the influence to prevent a lawyer the wherewithal to defend a client with a legitimate legal challenge. I found myself speaking with an attorney who was not willing to delve into the constitutional merits that Congress could not exact a tax from one without its excise authority. Yet, Harris was rigid.

When I further explained the relevance of my belief, replete with supporting arguments, Harris said she would be sanctioned by the court for raising a jurisdictional claim. She even stressed that I would be prohibited from doing so as my own representative. How could this be? With no experience and limited understanding, I felt uneasy. I sensed a grave inconsistency between Harris' position and the weighty expectation that anyone in such a situation would have a hearty and vigorous defense from the one who would do battle for him. This *warrior*, my attorney, was telling me that neither she nor Randy Cargill, the senior attorney, would take hold of the one weapon they had to defeat the charges. Why? **They would be fined for attempting to do so.** The limitations upon them made my situation surreal. I sat and shook my head in disbelief.

When I first met Cargill, he stated exactly what Harris asserted. He reflexively rejected and unequivocally stated that he could not and would not advance my good faith belief. I asked him if he wanted to think about it, to investigate, to somehow square my actions and decisions regarding my revocations of any status and federal benefits with the constitutional limitations of the Congress and its limited taxing authority. Cargill was as intractable as Harris. He responded that the ABA dictated against arguing frivolous positions. He further stated that the courts had ruled certain positions "frivolous" and without legal legitimacy.

Cargill immediately asked that I provide him any of my beliefs that were *not* in any way a jurisdictional claim. I realized then that Cargill would "defend" me without substance, without the truth, without a viable premise. I was humbled with the understanding that the federal prosecutor would not contend with an opposing party of strength. The prosecutor, if only because my "defense" counsel could not and would not investigate grounded constitutional positions, would present his case without a contest.

The interaction I had with these public defenders was disappointing. As officers of the court, as professionals who worked for the Federal Government, I viewed them, more than I did before, as an inherent part of the judicial process. They were trained and conditioned by the system. They were weathered and worn by a routine, a pattern, an expectation. This was not unlike anyone performing a job repeatedly for decades and becoming desensitized. They simply went through the motions. This was not difficult to see. Their role was to facilitate, as in help people though the process which ended in convictions more than 98% of the time. This was not a matter of fighting for the liberty of each new client. They had a rote and mindless exercise, as if placing the round peg into the round hole.

Am I being too harsh? No. Consider that I was discussing my case without the possibility of arguing my only good faith belief. These defense advocates were without the desire to defend me for fear of being fined for advancing the one position which would set me free. I was devastated. Instead of a healthy discussion as to why the IRS and the government could not have jurisdiction, or presume I was a taxpayer, instead of appreciating potentially groundbreaking constitutional arguments that Congress was without the ability to tax one who was outside its excise authority, they asked questions which more than hinted of their established protocol. Their posture and questions reflected restraint rather than possibility. To illustrate, I shared that it was not possible for me to be classified with the status of "taxpayer or a "United States person" defined in the tax code.

Cargill and Harris did not want to hear or discuss these facts. They did not want to consider that my status was outside of congressional taxing authority. They reinforced that they could not and would not introduce such positions into court. Even if they understood my concerns, they would not proffer a jurisdictional argument. These "advocates" would serve as gatekeepers, obligated to filter what was impermissible from entering court. Why? Was it to prevent the truth from being known as a matter of public record? Was it to prevent the people from hearing what had been effectively squelched for six decades? To me it seemed apparent. For the past eight years, I had asked numerous agents and agencies and elected officials to provide me the law which required one in my circumstances to file a federal income tax return. I received no response. I was at the threshold of arguing my circumstances in a federal court, where I could expose a constitutional juggernaut of immense proportions; yet my legal warriors would not touch the substance of my position. This smacked of a conspiracy.

One thought must be considered. If my legal representatives were willing to balk at a founded claim anchored in Supreme Court settled law in several respects, then any claim, remotely jurisdictional, would be considered "frivolous." Yes, any lawyer faced with the possibility of arguing any jurisdictional claim in a tax case would be foreclosed from doing so by the ABA and prior court rulings. Does this not appear particularly odd? To those who understand the limitations of Congress and the Executive Branch, which would inherently limit the Judiciary, it is odd.

It would be a rather foreboding condition if all Americans are presumed to be obligated to congressional legislation without the opportunity to contest jurisdiction whatsoever. This simply cannot be. Yet, this is exactly what Cargill and Harris were telling their defenseless client. Their refusal to investigate my genuinely held belief was an absolute denial of a credible defense. We will see how Cargill simply argued I had a "belief" that the tax code did not apply to me. He did so without offering substantiation. He did not explain why the tax did not apply. To make matters worse, he told the jury I was a "taxpayer" with an obligation to file a federal income tax return and that my belief to the contrary was "crazy."

Contrast his argument with a truth based partly upon the legal terms and definitions we labored through earlier. I had stressed to Cargill and Harris that I was not an "employer," "employee," or an officer of the United States. I stressed that I was not a "U. S. person" or a "taxpayer" beholden to a specific excise tax. I was not operating under a license or exercising a privilege subject to excise. I no longer had a status which placed me within the purview of the IRS for tax purposes. I said that I could not be, therefore, within the United States Government's jurisdiction for the alleged charges.

I asked Cargill and Harris a reasonable question. "How am I a U. S. person within the jurisdiction of the federal tax laws?" I asked them how the Federal Government, a fiction, a construct by virtue of the Constitution, an abstraction with delegated and limited powers and jurisdiction, could come to any city within the sovereign states and arrest a free and innocent man who was not even involved in interstate commerce? How could this be, especially since this one man had rebutted the presumption and prima facie evidence of any jurisdictional claim? Their response was as telling as much as it was unconvincing. "You are a U. S. person," they exclaimed. This was their only response.

So, there I sat. I did not know the court process. I did not know the rules. Yet, I knew I had not violated any criminal statute. As far as I was concerned, I did not have to know the rules. I was in the unenviable position of sitting with "professionals" who supposedly knew the rules of court and the law; but they superimposed the canons of ethics as superior. Any advantage to be had by applying Rule 12 or Rule 17(b) for example and striking at the heart of the government's case for lack of jurisdiction, was not accomplished. These lawyers had no intention to challenge jurisdiction. Rather, they presumed, just like the opposition and the court, that the government and court had jurisdiction.

Were Cargill and Harris ignorant? Yes, they did not want to know or consider another possibility. Yes, they did not understand tax law as well as they could or should have in this instance. Yes, they were willfully indifferent to my position. Their ignorance was woven directly into their state of apathy. They did not care and would not care simply because of their concerns of financial sanctions. They were concerned with self-preservation. *In the end, the system allowed for their indifference.*

Were these defense advocates arrogant? Yes. They were products of their environment. They had an air of superiority and were not teachable. Defending their client was permissible to the extent they were willing. Even if the legal system was arrogant in its overall execution, they were guilty of arrogance by association. Lawyers will zealously defend to the limits of their allegiance to the system, be it the ABA, the court, or their personal level of comfort and professionalism. Consider Ingalls' lawyer, who arrogantly dispensed with his client in one meeting with a plea agreement. This was the extent his *professionalism* would defend an unwitting and *defenseless* client.

As far as I was concerned, the legal system was rigged. The entire institution was arrogant. Those who work for or within this system take comfort in knowing they can defend to their limits or those of the system. They are conveniently stopped from doing what is right and just simply because other authorities, to include their own judgment, permit it. May we conclude that if the "common man test" is not applied, that is, if it does not make sense to a common man from a defense perspective, justice can and will be denied? What would the common man do? Notwithstanding the "rules," what would a reasonable man offer to the defenseless? He would not refuse to defend a man based upon his only good faith belief.

I enclosed significant portions of two documents which more than adequately detailed my sound legal arguments. These documents were created after the trial for the appeal process. Any person who has been convicted may claim his counsel was ineffective and seek a reversal of the judgment. This is known as the 2255 Motion or habeas corpus process. Typically, the defendant will submit a Declaration as "testimony" or "evidence" for his argument. This is the first document you will read. (Appendix A) The second document is a portion of the actual Memorandum in Support of the 2255 motion. (Appendix B) In this document you will read two of the central claims as to why my attorneys were ineffective.

RELEASED ON BOND

A hearing was scheduled to address a number of issues before Judge Moon—the Writ of Habeas Corpus, the issue of legal representation, and a bond for my release. After Moon admonished me for filing documents without the use of counsel, he addressed the matter of my status. A discussion ensued between the Assistant U. S. Attorney (AUSA) Hogeboom, Cargill, and Moon concerning the citizenship of Americans. Noteworthy, Moon stated all Americans were citizens of the United States. Cargill conveniently failed to introduce the jurisdictional argument by asserting that I was not a "U. S. person" or "citizen" *as defined in the tax code*. He did not raise the argument that I was not within the jurisdiction of the "United States" or "State" as defined for tax purposes. If allowed to speak, I would have asked the court how "United States" was defined and how I was legally obligated.

None of my good faith belief entered the discussion. Cargill ensured this unfortunate development. Everyone, to include Cargill, presumed I had a tax liability and, more importantly, everyone willingly ignored that I had rebutted the government's presumption. Cargill's presumption denied the court the ability to understand my status as one outside of its purview as well. The court would not be able to make a distinction that I could not be a taxpayer. The court was allowed to presume I was a "citizen" without distinction. With the government's knowledge of my belief and its refusal to answer my question for the last eight years and with Cargill's unwillingness to investigate or advance my position, the veil of fraud and force was perpetrated upon the court and to my ultimate detriment. This, as far as I was concerned, was no different than being told who I was and was not and directed to move forward as if by gun point.

At no point since 2004 was the government willing to answer my simple question. The question and its answer directly affected my status as to whether or not I was a "taxpayer." The government's presumption in court, that I was whatever it concluded, certainly did not answer the question. This is why, whether by gunpoint or edict of the court, the result was the same. Such a scenario has no accountability.

Having been placed in a "class" presumptuously by all parties, to include the court, I was in the unenviable position of seeking a viable solution. Because Cargill would not and did not listen or investigate, I had no expectation that I would prevail at trial. I was coerced through a judicial process which would adjudicate a case by exceeding limited powers under the Constitution. Refer to George Norris as a parallel. He never did anything wrong. Yet, he was forced to endure the unimaginable. Under threat, coercion, and duress the unsuspecting are without a credible challenge. The justice system is merciless.

Within a week after the hearing, I was moved to a local jail in the city of Lynchburg two blocks from the federal building. Placed into general population with some seventy other men, I waited for the pending bond hearing and my release. At the bond hearing Hogeboom and Agent Pompei became more aggressive. Like Hogeboom's performance at the habeas corpus hearing, he protested, ranted, and waxed hyperbolic for sensational effect. He did not want me released at all. If bond were granted, he wanted the most stringent conditions possible. He was simply following the typical prosecutorial game plan. Hogeboom wanted me sent away for psychological evaluations for two months. He proclaimed that I was no different than Timothy McVeigh and Terry Nichols, the infamous Oklahoma City, Federal Murrah Building, bombers. He called me a domestic and financial terrorist. Pompei testified under oath that I had resisted arrest, a complete falsehood. They created the impression I was a flight risk.

Once again, we must discern the psychological and emotional motivations which guide these officials and the process. There should be no doubt, because of the system, they had no intention of dignifying an opponent's claim of innocence. They defied what I already referred to as "The Common Man Test." The common man, the reasonable and average man on the street, will generally listen to someone else, almost regardless of the topic or circumstances. He will deal with good faith, genuine empathy, flexibility, understanding, and even love. This is not so in a court of law. The legal process is adversarial, governed by rigid rules and form, absent the sense of humanity demonstrated by common men. Frankly, as we have seen, officials who work within the system, those who are not common men did not care that innocent men are sacrificed by them and them alone.

At the end of two weeks and one bond hearing, I was released. My mother pledged the equity in her house as collateral. I was in her custody and accountable to certain conditions. I had to report to her house no later than 10 every night. I could not travel outside the western district of Virginia without permission from the probation officer. I had to call him by a certain time every week. I could not apply for credit. I could not file any frivolous documents in court; and anything I offered into court needed defense lawyer approval. I was released in early July and the trial was scheduled for mid-September.

Without a Defense

Let's pause and ask a serious question. Given that all quarters of the legal system avoided and evaded answering my one question, do we, the people, expect justice to prevail when the legislative, executive, and judicial branches exceed their limitations? Consider another question. At what point will the government, with the aid of the courts, cease encroaching upon the people, their property, and rights? We have already seen efforts in all facets of our lives when the government gains greater control. Incrementally, the government expands its reach to the point that its jurisdiction is broadened to encompass what was previously without its orbit.

This is what my defense lawyers did. They ceded control to an opposing authority by failing to establish a legal claim. The government advanced and the people relinquished. In a practical sense, the limits placed upon defense lawyers, even if self-imposed, juxtaposed those of the prosecution. The prosecutors, while governed by the same rules, were free to disparage a defendant to the extreme; yet the defense was prevented from stating what was considered extreme, extreme as far as they, the ABA, and the court were concerned.

Consider the following pictorial:

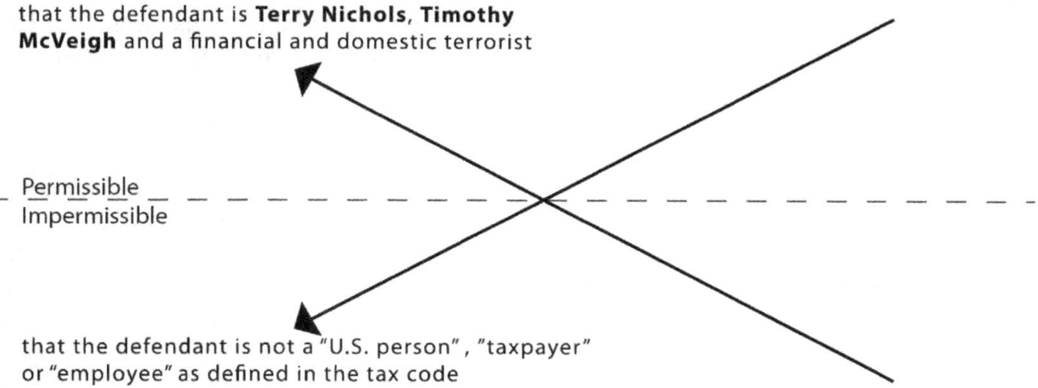
that the defendant is **Terry Nichols, Timothy McVeigh** and a financial and domestic terrorist
Permissible
Impermissible
that the defendant is not a "U.S. person", "taxpayer" or "employee" as defined in the tax code

We see language above the line that the court permitted and language below the line the court did not permit. The former is the truth; the latter is not. The truth is denied and lies are fostered in a justice system most Americans believe is honorable and just.

We are confronted with important questions. Are Americans able to challenge the jurisdiction of the Federal Government regardless of the law? How and when are the people able to challenge jurisdiction? When or how is the government able to presume jurisdiction over those without its purview, those within the free and independent states? What are circumstances under which the government does not have jurisdiction, whether of United Stated citizens or citizens of the 50 states? Are there any?

Even through the perceived autonomy of the Federal Government, we gauge the ignorance, apathy, and arrogance of prosecutors. Are they afflicted with these conditions as severely as public defenders? Probably more so. Prosecutors bring charges against private citizens, and they do this with absolute immunity. They cannot be sued for wrongful prosecution. This immunity is like a mighty cape or superpowers which make them invincible psychologically, emotionally, and otherwise. They cannot be harmed and so they exert all the influence they can, whether warranted or not. However, they, ironically enough, are also officers of the court and beholden to the public trust as well as their client, the United *States*. Yet, they are subject to the same rules and procedures within an adversarial system as defense lawyers.

From the defendant's perspective, there is little civility or few attempts at resolution in a manner equal to how the common man settles disputes. Prosecutors have the power and resources and apply the evidence and *skill* to gain a conviction. They exhibit little concern that their tactics and words in court are not the equivalent of their conduct in their private lives. Would a U. S. Attorney accuse a neighbor or handle a disagreement with him as in court, according to court rules? Would he treat him with such disdain by referring to him as a terrorist or Timothy McVeigh?

Prosecutors cloak themselves with superiority. They are actors perfecting a role and a process. Their power advances what is not easily defended in a civilized setting. This means their objective is to denigrate, frustrate, and overwhelm. Only the indignantly arrogant would mount their pedestals and besmirch decent men as being none other than mass murderers. The polarization achieved by prosecutors in numbing. The fact is that an innocent man cannot be who he is, innocent, and must be as the prosecutor proclaims. I cannot be one who rebutted the presumption that I was a taxpayer and, therefore, not liable to the excise in question. I must be the vile terrorist Hogeboom claimed.

It occurred to me that Hogeboom forced what could not be, while the defense lawyers would not accept and argue what was truth. While the prosecutor painted the most unbelievable characterizations, Cargill and Harris continued to reject what was real. My conversations with them about issues other than my status revealed their reluctance to reach the truth. Two examples stand out and involve the issues of property and plea agreements. Their questions about each topic and refusal to accept my answers showed how grafted they were with the prosecutor, not unlike the other cases we discussed.

Cargill and Harris asked if I owned any property. I responded in the negative. They did not believe me. They asked me again, a sure sign that they thought I was lying. My response was the same. For a third time they challenged my response. They asked, "What about this property?" It was then I shot back with my own question. "Why do you not accept the answer I offer?" After all, I sensed they were doing some of the heavy lifting the IRS or the prosecution might have done.

Their posture was troubling. Their response concerning the nature and validity of trusts was equal to their treatment of my good faith belief and their insistence that I was obligated to file a tax return. If they refused to accept that any property was not owned by me, property presently in a trust, which was property that could not be reached by the IRS, how were they going to defend me when these issues surfaced during the trial? Did they not understand or accept that when someone conveys an asset into a trust ten years earlier, they don't own it ten years later? What was the motivation of these public defenders? Do they refute that the Kennedys no longer own Hyannis Port, their famous seaside home? Or do they give the wealthy a pass because they are rich and trusts are, therefore, legitimate?

When I pressed these court appointed attorneys as to their agenda, their response was sobering. "We need to know how much is available to negotiate a settlement with the government." It was then I realized why they rejected my answers with subdued hostility. Why didn't they disclose this fact beforehand? Even though they told me that anything I shared was protected by attorney-client privilege, their approach was less than forthright. It was transparent that they did not confide in me as I was expected to do with them.

The issue of the plea agreement reflected the same sentiment. In most court cases the government will offer a plea. The acceptance of a plea assures the prosecutor of a victory while reducing his effort and costs. Defense lawyers are duty bound to present plea offers. When Cargill and Harris attempted to share Hogeboom's offer, I rejected it without consideration. Harris was surprised. "Why?" she asked. I told her I was innocent. I stressed that in good conscience I could not and would not consent to what would be a self-imposed verdict of guilt. I had done nothing wrong. She then asked, "Don't you want to know what is being offered?" I responded that it did not even matter. Yet, she said that they were obligated to disclose the particulars of the plea agreement.

The government offered to drop two misdemeanor charges while enforcing the other misdemeanor and the felony. Cargill and Harris projected that I would spend some twenty-six months in prison. When they asked if I was inclined to accept the offer, I reiterated that I would not accept a plea, especially one which included a felony. "So make a counteroffer," Harris replied. "No." I replied. "I am not guilty of a crime."

I'll never forget the reaction from Harris. She looked at me and rather bluntly asked, "Are you trying to be a martyr?" Her disdain for my stand and the arrogance she exuded, which prevented her from any earnest drive to advocate on my behalf, was striking. My attempt, once again, to explain my good faith belief was an exercise in futility. I was convinced that had the judicial process demonstrated any compunction to achieve truth and justice my lawyers would have at least tried. They did not because the system did not allow it. My beliefs were secondary to the protocol which drove my legal representatives. Their suggestion that I sought to be martyr defied the possibility that I was able to prevail.

While I agreed with my attorneys that the odds were against a victory in court—few prevail—I was certainly not willing to concede defeat. Wherever I stood after a verdict, the truth would be as it always was and as it would always be. This was the heart of the matter. Everything else was circumstantial. The ignorance, apathy, and fear of both Cargill and Harris, impediments to understanding my innocence, did not make me in any way guilty. They were jaded by the process; but I would be victorious regardless of the outcome. They would move on to the next case. I would remain congruent with my core belief. They were unable and unwilling to move beyond the confines of their own profession. *I was free—free because I knew the truth even if convicted and imprisoned.*

Any man worth his salt would agree that a worthy battle must be fought regardless of the aftermath. Those who have the mettle to wage war may discern it is far nobler to have ventured where the trepid will not. President Theodore Roosevelt's "Man in the Arena" aptly speaks to this point:

> *It is not the critic who counts; not the man who points out how the strong man stumbles, or where the doer of deeds could have done them better. The credit belongs to the man who is actually in the arena, whose face is marred by dust and sweat and blood; who strives valiantly; who errs, who comes short again and again, because there is no effort without error and shortcoming; but who does actually strive to do the deeds; who knows great enthusiasms, the great devotions; who spends himself in a worthy cause; who at the best knows in the end the triumph of high achievement, and who at the worst, if he fails, at least fails while daring greatly, so that his place shall never be with those cold and timid souls who neither know victory nor defeat.*[50]

Much can be said about the integrity of one who withstands the pressures which test his resolve. When a man *battles* within the scripted parameters of court, he contends with the world of the contrived. For example, any defense lawyer believes he is with integrity in court. Little does he realize this battlefield (court) and the war (trial) are fictions—a microcosm of the government's creation. This creation represents a supposed *truth* or pursuit of truth shaped by terms and meanings used exclusively in court. The integrity by which courts operate is wholly dependent upon its rules, rules which substantiate and govern its existence. When the rules are compromised, the system and those who violated them are without integrity—within the fiction of court.

Those accused of crimes and forced to enter this battlefield are still with integrity and have not sacrificed their honor or wholeness. However, they are compelled to comply with what may easily be viewed as fraud and force. In essence, there are dual realities, two realms of truth. These two truths cannot exist together. To illustrate, my defense lawyers are with integrity within the court and their canons of ethics while I am with integrity outside this realm. When I am coerced to go where I do not belong, this does not make me a man who is out of integrity. This is the rub. The public defenders are not permitted to

---

[50] www.theodore-roosevelt.com/trsorbonnespeach.html

argue what has always been true since the founding of America, that, unless warranted, a man is outside the scope of the Federal Government. There must be grounds for courts to adjudicate a case.

The Federal Government has limited jurisdiction and may not control those outside its purview. The distortion and misapplication of law does not nullify this inherent truth. The misuse of tax laws cannot alter what is a reality. The unseen and unknown collision of two separate truths, two concepts of integrity, must have a victor. They cannot co-exist. There is only one truth, and the truth must prevail.

The circumstances in my case reflect this dynamic. The government, defense lawyers, and court presumed the *truth* that I was within the jurisdiction of the Federal Government for in the income tax. This was achieved by the assertion that, by law, I was either A, B, C, or D. Cargill believed that, because of the fiction he was in, he could not argue I was outside the scope of the law, the IRS and, therefore, the court. All parties involved ignored the assertion of my natural rights. The prosecutor's (and defense lawyers') *integrity and truth* collided with a universal integrity and truth. This is the point at which fraud and force prevailed, at least for a time. There is a point certain when fraud takes hold and progressively metastasizes into a greater injustice.

Consider the following pictorial:

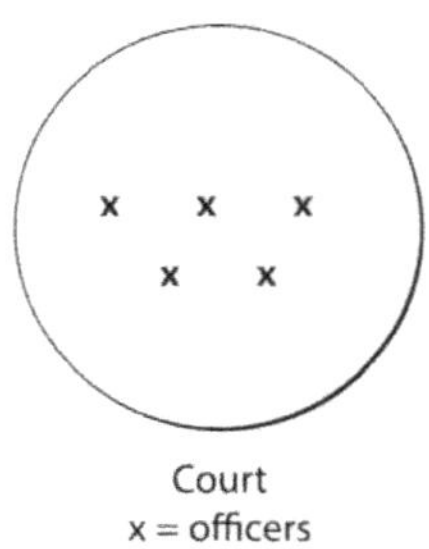

Court
x = officers

The officers of court are congruent and have integrity within the court only. Each believes and practices what is consistent with this "integrity"—the reality of court.

Compare the *truth* of court with truth of the American experience, whereby men are free with inalienable rights. Freedom is not some construct borne of the machinations of man. It's not contrived. Natural rights exist by virtue of our being, of life, and its manifestation of all that is possible in freedom. Natural rights represent what is congruent with nature and nature's God, as the people, who are outside the legitimate and limited powers of government, yearn for freedom into an unrestrained and lawful state of being.

Consider this pictorial.

Freedom
of
Man

0 ⟵ Court

Natural
Rights

Man is free and remains free. He is outside the venue of court. If he violates the life, liberty, and property of another, commits a crime or is a party to a civil action, the court acquires jurisdiction. Only then would he be brought within the venue of court.

The court serves a purpose, to exercise powers granted for the adjudication of proper matters within its domain. Exercise of a power beyond these parameters is an aberration. When rules, procedures, and the form and function of court trump natural rights of man, we have a perversion, a lie that obscures. The *integrity* of court, when it operates on a false premise, subverts the constitutional integrity that allows for its existence.

If only Americans appreciated the magnitude of the foregoing. We have an inversion of reality accomplished by fraud and force. This fraud and force originate within the world of the fictitious, as it seeks to control the integrity of universal truth, which we know is impossible. The attempt to control this truth necessitates vanquishing its presence within the fiction of court. All court actors must prevent this truth from entering in the first instance.

Consider the following pictorials:

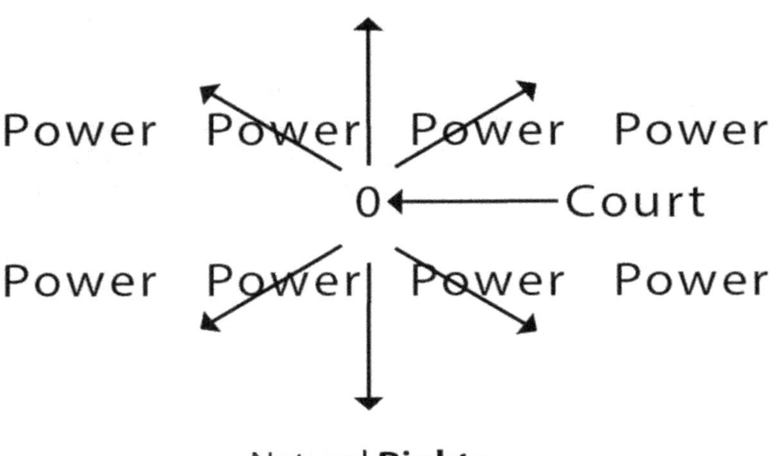

The court and culmination of its power, with the full force of government and its money, guns, laws, agencies, agents, etc., exert an unlawful enforcement of its "integrity" over what is indisputable truth. The court is all-powerful and extra-judicial in scope.

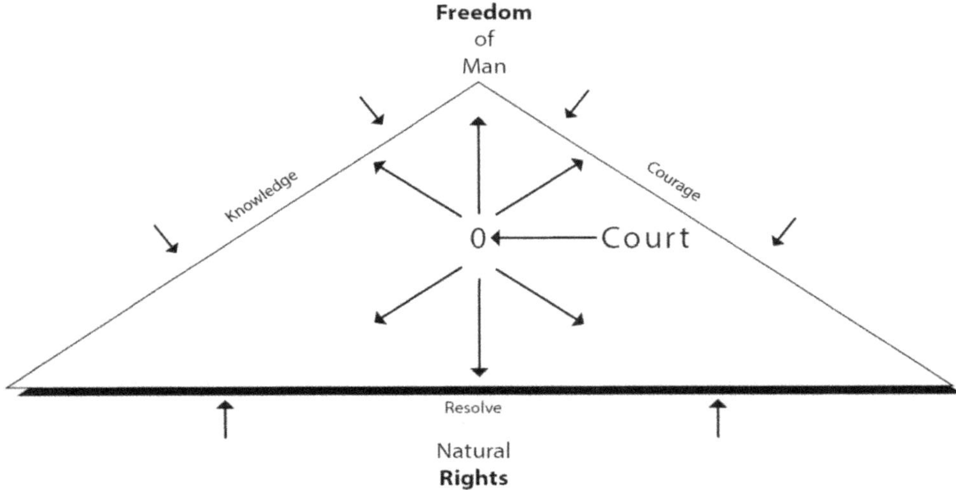

If we, the people, had the knowledge and intrepidness to withstand government force, we would not have the abuse and fraud which will continue into tomorrow. Our knowledge, resolve, and courage would bind the United States and its courts to constraints which would ensure our freedom and natural rights. The courts, as with the other branches of government, would be contained within their proper constitutional constraints.

It should be evident that my public defenders were subject to an alternate reality. It should be evident as to why there is an all-out assault upon our natural rights. If there is any doubt, consider the question I asked in 2004: "What law required me to file a U. S. Individual Income Tax Return?" To this day nobody has answered or is willing to answer this query. My lawyers were not willing to answer much less investigate something they did not fully appreciate. They were not willing to entertain that I had reason to believe there was no law applicable in my circumstances. They moved forward with the presumption I was a taxpayer liable to file a tax return. This was their *truth.* Consequently, they imposed their *integrity* upon what was otherwise beyond dispute—a universal truth.

If only for the purposes of court, this presumption was the primary means of enforcing the fraud that such a law existed without citing its existence. This was the force needed to further the fraud, an accomplishment realized by arrogance. The government, with the backing of the court, would not and will not dignify an answer to a credible question. Such is our legal system which ostensibly serves the ends of justice. If my lawyers did not stand for or represent my good faith belief to the court, they, it may be argued, did not have the knowledge, resolve, or courage to do other than what was allowed in their realm of court. They were part of a system driven by arrogance.

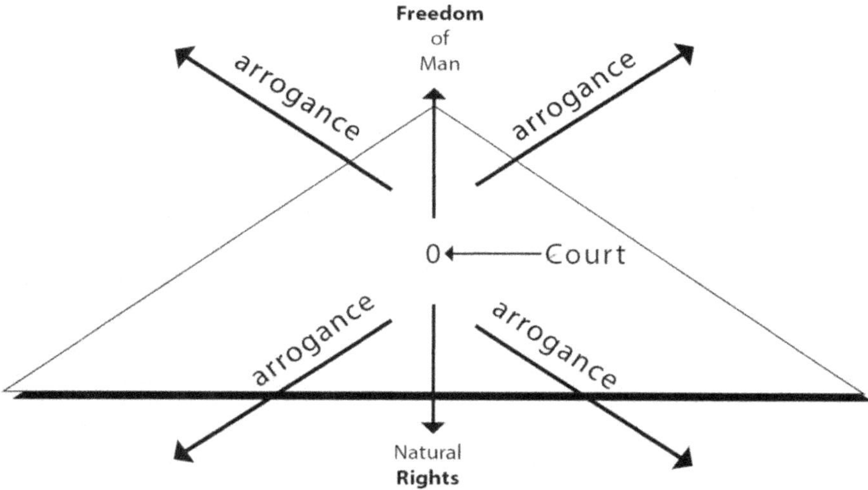

Regardless of my efforts to hold all parties accountable, the arrogance of all prevailed. Each party within the realm of court vanquished me, my freedom, and natural rights.

Knowledge, resolve, and courage are some of the qualities my attorneys lacked. Because of these deficiencies, I was not provided effective assistance of counsel. My sworn declaration (Appendix A) supports this claim. (Appendix B) With the content discussed between me and my lawyers, you should have a clearer sense as to why I believed Cargill and Harris failed to investigate my good faith belief.

A Possible Remedy

With my imminent release from jail, I had to acquire a solution. I was contending with the Federal Government and lawyers who would not argue my reasonable belief, which was a one-way ticket to a conviction and a prison term. What was one to do in such circumstances? The irony is that I relied upon the Constitution of the United States for the last eight years. Only after I was notified by the DOJ of my pending prosecution did I seek alternative solutions. Whoever was available to assist me had to offer a credible approach. I was not willing to waste my time and efforts on theories.

Thankfully, when I called those my sister said were available, they shared that I would be applying trust law with the use of government forms which would privately resolve the charges. Since I already had a grasp of trust law, the prospect of using government forms was appealing. Once I received an overview and understood the goal, I agreed to move forward. My instructors set up weekly conference calls with a deliberate curriculum. They stressed that I had to understand the totality of the process in order to appreciate how it worked and to correctly apply the solution.

Given the complexity of the process, I will attempt to give an overview. To begin, we must look at trusts and trust law. There are three parties to a trust, the Grantor, Trustee, and the Beneficiary. Typically trusts operate with a trust indenture, which contains the agreement or directives and responsibilities of the parties. The Grantor often conveys an asset into the trust to be held in "trust." This asset is referred to as the "corpus" or "res." The trustee agrees to manage the trust and preserve any assets until received by the beneficiary. There can be more than one Grantor, Trustee, and Beneficiary. A Grantor can be a Beneficiary. A Trustee can be the Grantor. But a single person cannot be all three. The spirit of a trust is that something is in trust, in the care of another party.

Ultimately, the trustee receives the corpus and res on behalf of the grantor for the eventual benefit of the beneficiary. If one person served in all three roles, there would no "trust;" there would be no reason to trust. Consider an example. Suppose you left your bicycle at the local food market. You called the owner and asked him to keep the bicycle until your sister came to get it the next day. As the Grantor, you placed the asset into the hands of the owner, the Trustee, to care for the bicycle, in trust, until the Beneficiary was given the asset. I used a rather innocuous example to demonstrate that our lives are made up of trusts or trust dynamics. We trust people. We place our trust in people. We leave items with people and trust they will care for them. Officials are beholden to the public trust. We have trusts which are memorialized on paper to serve business and legal needs. We have trusts which occur in the commercial and legal realms by happenstance because of circumstances of a transaction. As with the bicycle, once the item is given to the beneficiary, the trust ceases to exist.

Henry Gibson, in A Treatise on Suits in Chancery, explains trusts in a legal sense.

> *A trust, in the most enlarged sense in which that the term is used in our jurisprudence, is a beneficial interest in property, real or personal, distinct from the legal possession and ownership thereof. In trusts, the legal title and possession of the property are in one person, called a trustee; the equitable title and beneficial use of the property are in another person, called a c'estui que trust, or beneficiary. The trustee holds the direct and absolute dominion over the trust property, in view of the courts at law; while in the view of courts of equity, the trustee is a mere steward to hold, manage and account for the proceeds of trust property for the exclusive benefit of the beneficiary. In the sight of the court of Law, the beneficiary has no interest in the trust property; while in the sight of the Court of Equity, the beneficiary has all the enjoyable interest. In short, the trustee holds the legal title and the possession of the trust property, but all the benefits arising from the property, its income or profits, belong wholly, or in part, to the beneficiary.*
>
> *As a general rule, property of every kind and form, real and personal, may be made the subject of a trust. Any person, who has the capacity to hold and dispose or property, can impress a trust upon it; and generally, any person capable of holding property may be made a trustee, or a beneficiary. Courts of Chancery have exclusive jurisdiction of all kinds, express, resulting and constructive.*[51]

Note that:

1. Legal title and possession are different than equitable title;
2. In Courts at Law the trustee is in control;
3. In Courts of Equity the beneficiary is of paramount importance;
4. Property of every kind and form may be subject to a trust;
5. Courts of Equity have exclusive jurisdiction of trusts, highlighting express, resulting, and constructive trusts.

As an example of a constructive trust, Judge Cardozo stated:

> *A constructive trust is the formula through which the conscience of equity finds expression. When property has been acquired in such circumstances that the holder of the legal title may not in good conscience retain the beneficial interest, equity converts him a trustee.* 122 N.E. 378,380 (N.Y. 1919)

Consider the definition of "constructive trust" in Black's Law Dictionary, 10th Edition.

> *An equitable remedy by which a court recognizes that a claimant has a better right*

---

[51] Henry Gibson, A Treatise on Suits in Chancery, (Gaut-Ogden Co., Printers and Binders 1907)

> *to certain property than the person who has legal title. This remedy is commonly used when the person holding the property has acquired it by fraud.*

Recall the situation I faced in court. I was being forced into a proceeding to answer criminal charges for which I could not be liable. I had lawyers who were unwilling to argue that the government could not possibly have jurisdiction to bring the charges. To be clear, the government, through agents Biggs and Pompei, did not answer my one question for eight years. So, the government presumed jurisdiction without any accountability. I asserted that the government acted upon and pursued a fraud. The government no sooner had a claim to my property—that is me and my body—than they had a rightful claim to a man in Germany or China. Without the proper authority, without the proper constitutional basis in this case, without the taxing authority to demand an excise for a status which no longer applied and benefits which had long been revoked, the government could not act. This was no different than a government demand that I pay an excise for the manufacture and sale of tires, a legitimate excise, when I did not manufacture and sell tires. The government could not arrest, charge, and prosecute me for failure to file a return or pay a tax for tires. This point cannot be any more transparent.

With respect to constructive trusts, with my illegal and unlawful arrest, the government was the HOLDER of me. The government was in POSSESSION of me. The government claimed LEGAL TITLE, of whatever sort, to me. The government acted presumptuously when it "in good conscience" could not "retain the beneficial interest" to me. Note, Gibson states that if the holder is not able to retain the beneficial interest, EQUITY "converts [it] to a TRUSTEE". (Emphasis and brackets added) In the definition offered in Black's Law Dictionary, the court "recognizes that a claimant has a better right to certain property than the person who has legal title"—which is constructive. Of great significance is that this "remedy" is used when the person holding the property "has acquired it by fraud."

This is exactly what I had claimed from the beginning. Fraud was used to pursue charges that were extra-constitutional; fraud was used to arrest and secure my body without a legal or lawful right or claim. Who would not agree that my objective—especially since my lawyers would not raise the issue of subject matter or in personam jurisdiction before Judge Moon (which was the only way he would be able to know of the fraud and any ultra vires ((beyond one's power)) actions of the government)—was to raise the equitable claim to my own property, property which rightfully belonged to me?

My only recourse was to establish an Express Trust. Black's Law Dictionary, 10 Edition, defines an Express Trust as

> *A trust created with the settlor's express intent, usually declared in writing, an ordinary trust, as opposed to a resulting or constructive trust.*

From my vantage point, as I understood trust law and the dynamics of a court case, a clear intent had to be established in writing which redefined the relationships of the parties to the action. To remedy the fraud, a presumptive claim to my property had to be employed. Since trusts were recognized by Courts of Law and Courts of Equity, I knew equity was essential.

Allow me to belabor a critical element before I develop the element of equity. Trust relationships govern the affairs of man. When we relate with others, we do so with trust. A wife trusts her husband (grantor) to keep his marriage vows (corpus/res) for her alone (beneficiary). The mayor of a city (trustee) vows to protect and preserve the public trust for the people (beneficiaries). My effort to solicit information from Agent Biggs was a trust relationship. With his oath of office, he had a trustee obligation to answer my query.

With respect to the Court of Law, there was a trust relationship with respect to the charges and the parties involved. This is what Gibson explained.

I realized quickly that the court presumed I was the trustee with the expectation to perform. We know the trustee has the responsibility and liability. We know it is better to be the beneficiary and to receive the benefit of the trust. The owner of the store keeps the bike safe. The husband honors his vows. Agent Biggs must answer a question. Undoubtedly, each of the above parties has an obligation to perform or the beneficiaries suffer. If the trustees do not perform and they pursue subsequent wrong action—directly or indirectly—the ill-advised occurs. The germination of fraud is manifested. Since Biggs did not answer my question, under a fraud, he moved against the beneficiary of the trust.

If you appreciate these trust relationships, you may also recognize that all parties viewed me as trustee of a trust dynamic and I was beholden to perform. The court and government expected me to satisfy my responsibilities. Thus, we reach a defining understanding. Since I could not be the defendant, as I was not subject to the excise in question, I should never have been a trustee. This point is even more poignant when we consider that I rebutted the government's presumption back in 2000 and relied upon the Constitution (a trust) for my just "remedy." I was now in the unfortunate situation, as I fought for my freedom, of rebutting a presumption that I was a trustee. I had to demonstrate that I was other than the one with the obligation to perform. Rather, I had to show I was representing the beneficial interest and that other parties were the trustees.

This brings us to a critical juncture. The government brought charges against me into a Court of Law. I was not in a Court of Equity. The Constitution allows for both venues. Article III, Section 2, Clause 1, "Subjects of Jurisdiction," states, "The judicial power shall extend to all cases, law and equity, arising under the Constitution, the law of the United States…" I had to invoke the Court of Equity. It was at this point that I learned about equity. I learned equity was superior to "at law" venues. The reason is quite significant, and we need only refer to Gibson's Treatise.

History is replete with the revelation that Courts of Equity were preferred to Courts at Law. They were two separate courts. Equity and at law courts have since merged; however, they remain distinct law forms. This means one court may be invoked over another, depending upon the matter and the circumstances. According to Gibson, there were advantages to the Court of Equity. Courts at Law were rigid with definitive forms and procedures which demanded conformity. Courts of Equity sought the conscience of the court and man as well. Gibson makes the distinction that equity was concerned more with substance than formality. He states:

> *The common law was then utterly incapable of doing complete justice… It had certain rigid molds or formulas… and if the cause could not be run into any of these molds, there was no redress…*[52]

This is exactly the situation in which I found myself. Gibson further said:

> *The fictions, formalisms and arbitrary technicalities of the common law, and its dialectical refinements, were inexplicable and incomprehensible jargon to the public, and often a costly mockery of justice to the litigants. Those who asked for bread were often given a stone, and those who applied for a fish sometimes received a serpent.*[53]

Gibson states:

---

[52] Ibid.

[53] Ibid.

> *Equity, on the other hand, disregarded forms, ignored fictions, subordinated technicalities to the requirements of justice, and indulged in no dialectical refinements. Its pleading was simple and natural and its doctrines were founded upon the eternal principles of right as interpreted by a lofty Christian morality. Its great underlying principles, the constant sources, the never failing roots of its particular rules, were the principles of equity, justice, morality and honesty, enforced, according to conscience and good faith, and so adapted to the requirements of each case and the complications of business affairs, that the rights and duties of all parties were fully determined.*[54]

Gibson's words were music to my ears, enlightenment to my mind, and a salve to my heavily burdened heart. My experience in a Court at Law was nothing like the picture he painted of equity. I wanted the "rights and duties of all parties" to be "fully determined." Since Judge Moon refused to dignify my jurisdictional claim, even if he was unaware, for defense counsel did not argue it, I had to petition the Court of Equity. I sought justice, honesty, and a moral outcome in accord with conscience and good faith in the business affairs of men.

The historical context of equity is rooted in Roman and English law. The King of England was regarded as the *"fountain of justice"*[55] and deferred all suits for redress to his Chancellor. The Chancellor had full authority to "give relief in matters of 'Grace.'"[56]

> *The principles on which the Chancellor based his decisions were those of honesty, equity and conscience. By "Conscience" was meant those obligations one person is under to another to exercise that good faith the other has a right to expect.* [57]

In good faith, did I not ask Biggs to answer how or under what law I was liable to file a federal income tax return? Did not honesty, equity, and conscience mandate that Biggs and Pompei satisfy their obligations in accord with the IRS Mission Statement?

The colonies of America, like so many customs and traditions, acquired the philosophy of equity from England. The people sought equity in their affairs among others. The people back then had a greater appreciation for the difference between equity and law. Gibson compares both at great length:

> Section 8. The Divine Law of Justice the Rule of Decision
> *The statement, often made, that the Court of Chancery [Equity] was established to mitigate the rigor of the common law, and to supply its defects, is not wholly true. The court was established to do justice, regardless of any and all law. The King deemed it a duty imposed upon his conscience, both by his oath and by religion, to "decree justice" and in decreeing justice he deemed himself bound rather by Divine Law than by human law; and when the Chancellor acted in his stead, he based his decisions, not upon the law of the land, but upon honesty, equity and conscience, for he was so commanded to do in exercising the King's prerogative of Grace. In short, the Chancery Court was established rather as a court based on the precepts of Religion than as a court based on the rules of law.*
>
> *It is unquestionably true that the harshness of the common law, its unfitness to cope with fraud, its incapacity to do justice in many cases, the defects in its remedies, the opportunities it gave the strong to oppress the weak, and its general*

[54] Ibid.
[55] Ibid.
[56] Ibid.
[57] Ibid.

> *inadequacy to meet the requirements of equity, greatly contributed to perpetuate the existence of the Chancery Court, and to enlarge and justify its jurisdiction. Nevertheless, the vital principle from which the court sprung was the prerogative doctrine that the king was the "fountain of justice," and that, when a citizen could not get justice in ordinary courts, he might come to the fountain. The king in administering justice in such cases deemed himself above all the laws and customs of his conscience and will. As it was a matter of right in a citizen to draw on this reserve of justice, when remedy was given, it was deemed granted as Grace.*[58]

Gibson clearly stresses the rights of citizens. He condemned the inability of the Court at Law to effectuate justice. He cited a lack of "remedy." Do we not see a striking parallel in my case and the former cases we reviewed? Since a lack of remedy, given the element of "fraud," meant that citizens were not able to "get justice in ordinary courts", the venue of equity was at their disposal. We see Courts at Law, with its cumbersome rules and procedures, severely limit the weak in the face of the strong. Rights and justice are relegated as inconsequential.

Not only did I face the almighty IRS (Federal Government), which is as foreboding as any agency in the world, I was entangled within a federal court and its rules which prevented an honest and open airing of my defensive position. Additionally, the defensive stalwarts who were to come to my side with an arsenal of wisdom and power cowered behind the "rules" that prevented them from defeating the government's specious claims. Yes, the Canons of Ethics of the ABA thwarted justice as much as the maligned agenda of the prosecutor. With my accumulated knowledge, I was beginning to appreciate that the Court of Equity was the remedy to claim my freedom and property—my being.

Gibson spoke to the sanctity of rights and specifically addressed property rights. He was mindful that labor, acquisition of property, and the ability to engage in any lawful business were part of "individual ownership."[59] This sentiment reflects the period of time in which he wrote his treatise in 1907, the period just before the Income Tax Act, the 16th amendment, and the Federal Reserve Act, after the Pollock case was decided—when the Supreme Court sided for the sanctity of property. Moreover, the people were more educated than we are today, more sensitive toward such issues. They were cognizant that property ownership was inviolate. Equity and the Courts of Equity were a vital part of the cultural mindset.

Gibson proclaimed the pinnacle premise. When property is subject to loss, even in a criminal case, the Court of Equity must take precedence. To appreciate his teaching, consider his definition for "property," which is nothing less than transcending.

> Section 56. To Protect and Enforce Rights to Property the object of Suits in Chancery
>
> *The term "property" as used in this section, includes everything that is in the subject of exclusive individual ownership: or to be more specific, includes not only lands, houses, goods and chattels, rights and credits. But also, a man's person and his wife and minor children, and his right to work and to sell and acquire property, and engage in any lawful business, and his and their reputation, health and capacity to labor, and his and their right to enjoy the senses of sight, smell, hearing and taste and his and their right to speech and locomotion, and his and their right to enjoy their sense of moral propriety when normal. As men live by their labor and property, no man is presumed to part with either without receiving*

58 Ibid.

59 Ibid.

> *or expecting an equivalent in value. Hence, whenever one person has obtained either the labor or property of another he should pay or account thereof, unless he can prove it was a gift; and so, whatever injury one person does to another's property or capacity to labor should be made good.*
>
> *To declare and define the rights of property and regulate its tenure, possession, enjoyment and transfer, is the business of the legislature; and to protect and enforce those rights, compel atonement for their violation and conform to law and equity, so that each person may have what is another's, is the business of the courts.*
>
> *Questions involving partisan politics, denominational religion, ecclesiastical controversies, scientific theories, mere breaches of moral rectitude and violations of criminal law, are not within the domain of Equity Jurisprudence, and the Chancery Court has no jurisdiction of them, unless they violate rights of property and then only to such rights.* (emphasis added)

Read this definition again. Read it thoroughly. Acquire a true appreciation of its depth and reach. Property means everything to man. Property *is* everything to man. Property defines a man's existence, his very being. Without property, he may, it could be said, cease to exist. Gibson's definition addresses a man's reputation, his senses, and that "labor" is his alone. Not only had I asserted my right to my labor and its byproduct, I rejected the notion I would part with my labor and its bounty for a federal status or privilege subject to excise. A federal agent's knowledge of this fact and his failure to answer my query as to any legal obligation to file a tax return was a direct assault upon my property. To make the argument unassailable, we must recognize that the government's criminal charges were but the forcing of the fraud of the agent's violation of my property. The Court of Equity could note the deprivation of my right to property, the taking of my being—taking all that I represented from my control, from my own possession.

If we astutely examine Gibson's words, we easily identify with the government's inconsistency in this case. The government seized "property" without cause. I exercised my natural right to labor and property outside of federal authority. Yet, the government charged me with a crime, a crime deemed to be "commercial" and a violation of the revenue laws. Presuming authority and jurisdiction over my body, the government seized me, all that I was and had. As such, my intention was to invoke the Court of Equity and assert the loss of this property. I wanted my life back and to be set free. While I had already challenged jurisdiction and failed, by moving the court to acknowledge equity I would be defeating the "at law" venue as inferior and appointing the Court of Equity as superior.

Gibson expounds that, "in the Federal Courts, the principles, pleading and practice of Equity remain wholly unimpaired."[60] Given that the Constitution refers directly to the Court of Equity, my concern was how to effectively invoke it. I also wanted to know how to respond if the request was denied. My situation was precarious. I had before me a judge who—perhaps with good reason—had no understanding as to why I challenged the jurisdiction of the court. Without a lawyer advocating such a position, even worse, with a lawyer stating that the court had subject matter and in personam jurisdiction and indicating that my position was "frivolous"—was the judge at fault for ensuring the adjudication of the case? I had to get Judge Moon's attention. I had to convince him there was a

[60] Ibid.

compelling reason to weigh the fact that, under the auspices of the Court of Equity, there was an equitable claim, and if this claim could be established, the argument of jurisdiction would be realized. With the right understanding of my equitable claim, the judge would be able to exercise his judicial latitude and dignify an adversarial testing of the Federal Government's authority.

We need only refer to Gibson to appreciate that equity is "to do justice, regardless of any and all law."[61] Equity is predicated upon fundamental precepts which speak to "underlying principles" that demand justice. These principles are referred to as "maxims". Equity is such a vital concern that I will take the time to share some of these maxims. We will begin with the definition of the term maxim:

> *Maxim ita dicta quia maxima est ejus dignitas et certissima auctoritas atque quod maxime omnibus probetur. (A maxim is so called because its dignity is maximum and its authority the most certain, and because approved at maximum by all.)*[62]

Gibson further explains that:

> *There are certain underlying principles, often called Maxims, which are the fruitful sources of a vast number of particular rules concerning both rights and remedies. The principles are a component part of Equity Jurisprudence. They lie at the foundation of universal justice; are the sources of municipal law; and have been worthily and aptly called legume leges - the laws of the laws. These maxims are, in the strictest sense, the principia, the beginnings, out of which has been developed the entire system of Equity jurisprudence by a process of natural evolution.*[63]

The third footnote states:

> *So fundamental are these maxims that he who disputes their authority is regarded as beyond the reach of reason. Contra negantem principia non est disputandum. Coke says, "Maxims of law are holden for law." Bacon says, "They are the fountains of justice from which flow all civil laws." In Box vs. Lanier, 4 cates, 409 Beard, Ch. J., says, "Maxims have their foundation in universal law; they are embodied in the common law, and are an essential part of its warp and woof."*[64]

Finally, footnote four states:

> *Principia probant, non probantur. (Maxims are proof and need no proving.)*[65]

The full import of equity may not be easily apprehended by a lay person; but, its universal scope cannot be denied. Based upon language used by Gibson, maxims, which are the essence of equity, are the wellspring for all law. Maxims are the source of municipal law and the common law. Maxims (equity) are universal; they are undeniable in their application to life itself. Judge Moon, I was convinced, would have to recognize equity once I invoked it. Furthermore, since equity applied in criminal cases to the extent of the violation of the property in question, it was evident that Judge Moon would have to reconcile the taking of a man for criminal charges when there was no crime. Moon would have to reconcile the taking of a man when the taking of such property was done ultra vires and without the power of even Congress. The constitutional question of

---

[61] Ibid.
[62] Ibid.
[63] Ibid.
[64] Ibid.
[65] Ibid.

congressional reach had to be resolved if only to the extent of the seized property. If Moon did not dignify equity, I would regard him as "beyond the reach of reason."

I relied upon these time honored, moral, and lawful principles—laws of laws, maxims which clearly had relevance to this case and the court. Consider the list of some maxims. Weigh the strength of these truths and their universal application.

- Equity will not suffer a wrong without a remedy;
- Equity delights to do complete justice and not by halves;
- He who seeks Equity must do Equity;
- Equity acts upon the person (forcing him to do what conscience requires);
- Equity acts specifically and not by way of compensation;
- Equity imputes an intention to fulfill an obligation;
- Equity regards that as done which ought to be done;
- Equity regards the beneficiary as the real owner;
- Equity looks to the intent rather than to the form;
- Equity delights in equality;
- Equity requires diligence, clean hands, and good faith;
- Equity will undo what fraud has done;
- Equity aids the vigilant, not those who sleep on their rights;
- No one can take advantage of his own wrong;
- Equity follows the law;
- Where there are equal equities, the first in order of time shall prevail;
- Equity enforces what good reason and good conscience require;
- No one shall be condemned without a chance to be heard.[66]

The significance of maxims is as apparent as the denial of equity from the agents who investigated me since 2004. Any one of the maxims listed had an application in this case. A reasonable and discerning man need only make a cursory review to ascertain how equity should be a universal presence in the affairs of men. Noteworthy is the maxim which states, "No one shall be condemned without a chance to be heard." This is complemented with the maxim, "Equity looks to intent rather than to form." Within these two, I could easily argue the Court at Law should grant the role of equity as just.

What I faced was rather simple. The agents did not do what "conscience requires;" they did not answer a question which would have compelled me to comply with a liability. The agents did not "hear" either me or my concern. The agents did not aid the "vigilant" who did not "sleep" on his rights. The agent's failure to respond was a "wrong" which could not be suffered "without a remedy." It cannot be denied that I acted with "clean hands and good faith." I was simply asking the government to "follow the law" by disclosing the law. In total, with the government agents' failure to dignify my "intent" and their application of "form" alone, the fraud prevailed from the outset. It was, therefore, equity which would hopefully "undo what fraud has done."

The unjust formula written by the government rested with the court. Based upon the strength and broad application of the maxims, I could see the judge using the maxims with added emphasis that a man will have the chance to be heard. If no party was willing to grant my intent to touch the conscience of those who received it, there would be no opportunity to reverse the fraud. Yet, if the judge granted the possibility by applying equity and overlooking the form of court he could ensure "complete justice and not by halves." This would be particularly true as equity relates to trusts and the parties involved. As "the

---

[66] Ibid.

beneficiary, as the real owner," the judge was in the position to dignify the ownership of property to the rightful owner. This is all I wanted, to cease any and all unjust claims against me and my body. I was the rightful owner.

Since I was solely concerned with the question of jurisdiction, I was sensitive to the role equity played to this end. Consider the following maxims:

- Equity will not suffer a wrong without a remedy;
- When Chancery has jurisdiction for one purpose, it will take jurisdiction for all purposes;
- The Chancery Court never loses its jurisdiction by implication.[67]

Hypothetically, if the court sees a wrong, we must conclude, beyond argument, the judge could not and would not allow the wrong to remain. He would have to apply a remedy.

We must acknowledge the true role of judges. With respect to any and all parties, even in a Court at Law, if there is an injury suffered, the judge must remedy the wrong. The form and rigidity of law must be shunned. For example, if someone, anyone, were hauled into court, be it for a civil or criminal claim, and he had nothing to do with the alleged wrong, wouldn't the court have a requirement to seek clarity and truth?

Consider an illustration. I personally know a man in prison who was charged criminally for bank fraud. The fraud concerned a $4 million loan. However, the loan never existed. He told the court, his attorneys, and the government of this fact. No one listened. Form and the rigidity of the process prevailed. He was sentenced to 15 years in prison. He has served six years already. Had this man invoked equity from the outset, one would think the judge would have had to discern the charges with respect to the consciences of all parties. The judge would have had an obligation to prevent a wrong from prevailing against a man who injured no one.

Since the man never had a loan with the bank, the judge, had equity been invoked, would have had a moral obligation to reconcile that this man's life (his property) was unjustly harmed. The judge would have had jurisdiction for one purpose, and it would have had "jurisdiction for all purposes." There is peace of mind behind this principle. A man facing fifteen years for a crime he never committed, a man accused of securing a loan that was imaginary, a man who was never given the chance to be heard, could rest in the strength that equity would prevail when and where the Court at Law would fail. Furthermore, had this man invoked equity as the appropriate venue, he could rest knowing the Court of Equity could not lose its hold. This equitable maxim is the saving grace for cases borne of fraud and encouraged by authorities with the intent (conscience) for conviction at all costs. Whether by the government—or by those who maliciously foster false claims—there must be recourse for those who suffer wrongs by the system. Equity was that remedy, I thought.

There are key questions which may be asked concerning the charges I faced. If I invoked the Court of Equity, could the judge apply equity and its subsequent jurisdiction? Could the court lose this jurisdiction by implication? If the court saw that I had not committed a crime by virtue of my claim of lack of subject matter and in personam jurisdiction, would he correct the wrong with the appropriate equitable remedy?

Consider some maxims that apply directly to courts:

- An act of court injures no one;
- A judicial act outside of the Judge's authority is null and void;
- Consent makes law;

---

[67] Ibid.

- What ought to be done is valid when done;
- What does not appear in the record, and what does not exist in fact, are one and the same in law;
- In a judicial proceeding, nothing is believed unless proved by oath;
- The situation of the defendant is preferable to that of the complainant;
- He who does anything to another, does it to himself;
- Anyone can waive a law made for his benefit;
- He who enjoys the benefit ought also to bear the burden;
- Where the law requires anyone to show cause, the cause must be just and legal;
- Written instruments should be liberally construed so that they may stand rather than fall;
- Suits involving dower, life, liberty, and revenue are favored in law;
- That is deemed certain which can be made certain;
- No suit can be brought to enforce a fraud;
- The law arises out of the transaction;
- The law does not require anyone to do what cannot be done;
- What is improbable or dishonest is never to be presumed; on the contrary, the law presumes in favor of truth, honesty, and probability;
- When the foundation is removed the superstructure falls;
- The suppression of truth is equivalent to the suggestion of a falsehood.[68]

I established that equity was largely civil in its reach—that is, in a civil society, in the civil affairs of men, equity is accorded to all, in the sense that all are deserving of what is honest and truthful. It made sense that those charged as criminals were those who had subverted the planks of equity. They were those who took from the greater equitable nature of life, liberty, and revenue. With this appreciation, I further understood why equity could apply in criminal cases only if the charges violated rights to property and only to that extent. If the man charged with bank fraud never had an obligation for a $4 million loan, his property, his being, which was subject to incarceration, was a just claim to assert. In essence, the man wrongly convicted for this "crime" would not prevail under the fraud argued in court unless he had the chance to distinguish the fraud. This would require the court to embrace an equitable claim which would trump what the court should never have been required to adjudicate—a charge for a crime that never existed. This made sense. By invoking the Court of Equity, I would be accomplishing the same. I would be asserting a claim to my property that the court could honor as just. Why? Equity afforded the oversight of a "criminal" charge that was either fraudulent or nonexistent.

The maxims which govern the Court of Equity are as telling of the strength of equity as the overall maxims we viewed earlier. To highlight a few, recall that I never consented to the charges. This may sound like a laughable position; however, given my rebuttal of a federal status and privilege, I no longer consented to pay an excise. Naturally, my "consent" could not be realized by the force of the government's manipulation of the force of the court. Second, I was willing to assert by oath that I had rebutted the government's presumption that I was a "taxpayer." I hoped the court, once it honored my invocation of equity, would test the veracity of the charges, and require the opposition to attest under oath that I had not rebutted their jurisdictional claims.

This maxim is consistent with the fact that where the "law requires anyone to show cause, the cause must be just and legal." The government could not commit the

---

[68] Ibid.

illegal and unjust to achieve an equally abhorrent aim, an unjust conviction. I could rely upon the maxim that written statements should be liberally construed so they will stand. My habeas corpus pleading submitted before trial was testimony as to why I had grounds to overcome these specious criminal charges. By invoking equity, Judge Moon would have the wherewithal to deem "certain which can be made certain." His simple acts would further strengthen my jurisdictional claim that failed in the Court at Law. Moon would be aided in his assessment of an innocent man's hope for an equitable solution simply because he would realize the government's suit could not be "brought to enforce a fraud."

The discussion about equity establishes the contention that I could not be required to do "what cannot be done." I could not file an income tax return. It was not a possibility to the point of being "improbable or dishonest" and, therefore, beyond presumption. Yes, this truth had to be presumed. For, the probability is that I was not liable for the charges; the government never had jurisdiction. Without the "foundation" of the presumption of a legal liability, the "superstructure" of the government's charges must fall. The claim that I was liable to file a tax return was the "suppression of truth," the "suggestion of a falsehood."

As far as I was concerned, I asserted the truth, however inadequately. I was outside the jurisdiction of the government. I could not be the defendant. My body, my property, as defined by Gibson, was held against my will. I saw no reason why the invocation of the Court of Equity with its maxims would not prevail. This remedy was supported with the fact that the enforcement of trust law and trust relationships within the case had an equitable basis. If there was yet another presumption that I was the trustee with the obligation for criminal charges, I would, out of an equitable position of strength, ask the court to respect that the beneficiary could not be denied what was just, simply by the working of fraud.

The history of this case reflects that I asserted a natural right; yet the Federal Government pressed forward with its form and procedure. I treaded water and was expected to sink in an ocean of unresponsiveness.

Timeline

2000	I revoked federal benefits	Government did not respond
2000	I revoked any federal status with Department of Treasury	Government did not respond
2004	I did not file federal income tax returns since 99	Government began a civil investigation
2004	I asked Biggs for the law that made me liable to file a tax return	Biggs never answered and he presumed jurisdiction
2004	I asked Pompei for the law that made me liable to file a tax return	Pompei never answered and he presumed jurisdiction
2005	I asked elected representatives for the law	They never answered the question
2007	I asked Commissioner of Internal Revenue for the law that made me liable	He never responded
2009	I was informed by Mr. Salad (DOJ) of	Department of Justice presumed

	impending criminal prosecution	jurisdiction
2009	I asked Salad for the law	Salad never responded
2102	I was arrested – my body was seized	Federal Government and Court presumed jurisdiction
2012	I challenged jurisdiction in court	Court presumed jurisdiction
2012	I conveyed good faith belief to attorneys	Attorneys rejected my belief as frivolous, presumed the government had jurisdiction

Given my earnestness for an answer to one question and the arrogant unresponsiveness and unreserved presumption of authority by the government, I relied upon a natural and inalienable right and was not obligated to a specific excise. With the emphasis on the nature of equity and its universal application, at least from an historical context, I was confident a solution would come with the invocation of equity and the private remedy I intended to submit this to the IRS with the court receiving a courtesy copy. Consider the substance of what equity afforded based upon the content covered:

Solutions

Equity – justice, truth, conscience	At Law – form, procedure, rigidity
Trusts exist	Trusts exist
Beneficiary considered to be the owner	Trustee has the obligation to perform
I would invoke the Court of Equity	Moon would or would not apply Equity (Maxims) as superior
I would challenge jurisdiction	The court would or would not compel the government to prove jurisdiction
I would make a rightful claim to property	The court would or would not consider that the government seized property by fraud
I would represent the beneficial interest	The court would or would not project me as the trustee with the obligation to perform

Two questions remained. How to apply the remedy? What would the solution entail? With the guidance of my instructors, I created an Express Trust. We defined the trust earlier as one created with the Settlor's express intent. This trust was a *c'estui que trust* (beneficiary trust), where the "equitable title and beneficial use of property are in another person," as stated by Gibson, with legal title in yet another. With the advice I received, I filed the appropriate paperwork with the IRS to establish what we will refer to as the "IRS Trust." This trust, much to my surprise, and in accordance with IRS regulations, received an EIN without the use of another EIN/SSN. Then, by affidavit and agreement, I became the "Authorized Representative" of the Grantor and Beneficiary. I then filed tax returns with the IRS for the last 25 years, which the IRS accepted. The Trust was a legally established structure in accordance with the law and with a lengthy history of tax filings. This represented a significant development and gave me reassurance I was on the right path.

A Security Agreement was created between me and the trust. This document gave the trust a secured priority interest to anything and everything that belonged to me. This meant the trust had complete "beneficial interest" inherent with a *c'estui que* trust. The trust had a "first in line" and "first in time" claim to my body and included the interest in any court case. The Security Agreement had a comprehensive listing of all the assets and property rightfully claimed by the trust. The court case was one of those items.

Since this may be a foreign concept, allow me to share a corollary. Suppose you own a car in your name. You don't have a loan with a bank, which means you have a first in line and first in time claim to that property. If you convey the car into a trust, the trust will assume the first position. As a *c'estui que* trust, the beneficial interest would be held by the beneficiary, with the legal title held by the trustee. It is that simple.

Consider the following illustrations:

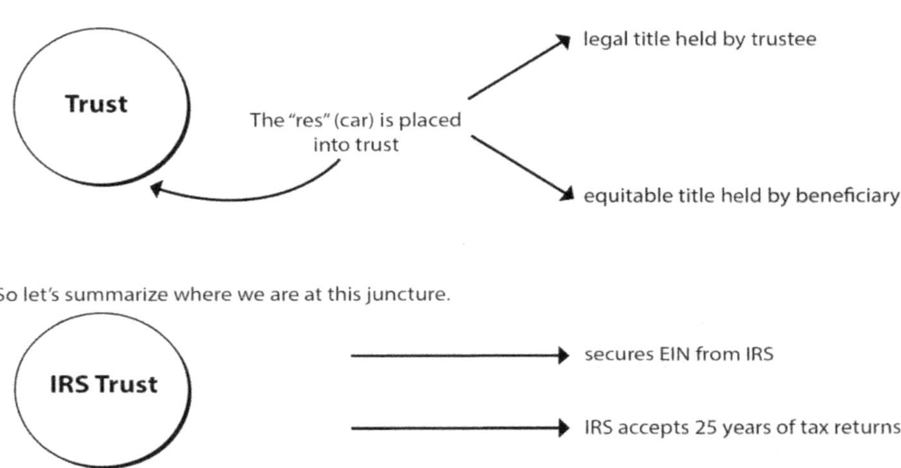

The next step was to record the trust's rightful claim. In effect, this amounted to giving notice of the claim as one would record a document at court. This was done by filing a UCC-1 Financing Statement in Washington, D.C. The UCC is the Uniform Commercial Code and is defined as:

> *A general and inclusive group of laws adopted, at least partially, by all the states to further uniformity and fair dealing in business and commercial transactions.*[69]

The UCC, adopted in some form by every State and the District of Columbia, is a generally accepted and uniform means of acknowledging rightful claims in commerce. The UCC filing, which was done electronically, included a Security Agreement. With this filing complete, the IRS Trust had a perfected claim in commerce.

[69] http://legal-dictionary.thefreedictionary.com/Uniform+Commercial+Code

Consider the following:

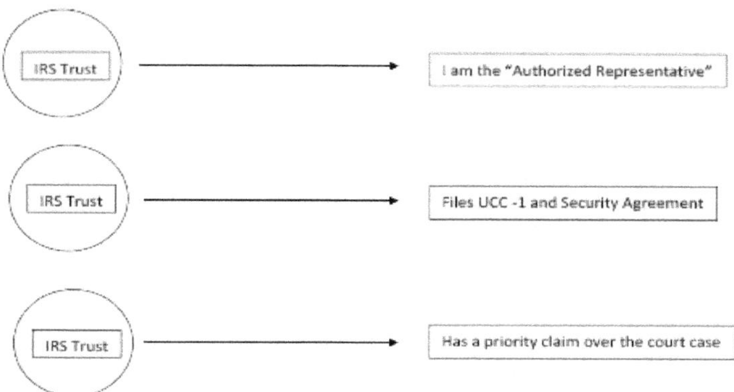
IRS Trust
I am the "Authorized Representative"
IRS Trust
Files UCC -1 and Security Agreement
IRS Trust
Has a priority claim over the court case

- ***I was the "Authorized Representative" of the Grantor and Beneficiary.***
- ***A Security Agreement and a UCC 1 were filed.***
- ***The "IRS Trust" had a priority claim over the court case.***

Confronted with all but certain defeat against the government that included a certain prison sentence, it would be appropriate to assess my progress. The situation could not have been any worse. Yet, with the instruction I had received, the information was consistent with what I knew about trusts and tax law. More importantly, every phase of the process was executed with the agencies exactly as my teachers expected. They resolved all of my reservations. They were as knowledgeable as they were confident. This dynamic put me at ease.

With these fundamentals in place, the IRS Trust created an Express Trust for the criminal case before Judge Moon. The case, 6:12-cr-00015, was named "6:12-cr-00015 Express Trust." In effect, the IRS Trust expressed its superior claim in writing with an expectation to receive the property in question or a disposition, as in an even exchange. The IRS Trust, a distinct legal entity, sought to bring accountability to the parties who presumed jurisdiction over me.

If I was expected to perform as the trustee, for example, the Express Trust would change that presumption. The trust did so by appointing Hogeboom, Pompei, and Moon as trustees for the Express Trust for the criminal case. These appointments were not only in the written Express Trust, but they were also cemented by the submission of IRS Form 56. This form served the purpose of appointing those who have a fiduciary obligation to perform. The language on the back of the form allows for the fiduciary to accept his fiduciary relationship. The language of 26 USC 6903, listed at the top of the form, states:

> Notice of fiduciary relationship
> (a) Rights and obligations of fiduciary.
> *Upon notice to the Secretary that any person is acting for another person in a fiduciary capacity, such fiduciary shall assume the powers, rights, duties, and privileges of such other person in respect of a tax imposed by this title (except as otherwise specifically provided and except that the tax shall be collected from the estate of such other person), until notice is given that the fiduciary capacity has terminated.*

I was told that these new trustees, who had a fiduciary relationship with the obligation to perform, would sign the forms and enforce the private remedy I would submit to the IRS.

Form **56**
(Rev. December 2011)
Department of the Treasury
Internal Revenue Service

Notice Concerning Fiduciary Relationship

(Internal Revenue Code sections 6036 and 6903)

OMB No. 1545-0013

Part I Identification

Name of person for whom you are acting (as shown on the tax return)	Identifying number	**Decedent's social security no.**

Address of person for whom you are acting (number, street, and room or suite no.)

City or town, state, and ZIP code (If a foreign address, see instructions.)

Fiduciary's name

Address of fiduciary (number, street, and room or suite no.)

City or town, state, and ZIP code	Telephone number (optional)
	( )

Section A. Authority

1 Authority for fiduciary relationship. Check applicable box:
- a ☐ Court appointment of testate estate (valid will exists)
- b ☐ Court appointment of intestate estate (no valid will exists)
- c ☐ Court appointment as guardian or conservator
- d ☐ Valid trust instrument and amendments
- e ☐ Bankruptcy or assignment for the benefit or creditors
- f ☐ Other. Describe ▶ ______________

2a If box 1a or 1b is checked, enter the date of death ▶ ______________

2b If box 1c—1f is checked, enter the date of appointment, taking office, or assignment or transfer of assets ▶ ______________

Section B. Nature of Liability and Tax Notices

3 Type of taxes (check all that apply): ☐ Income ☐ Gift ☐ Estate ☐ Generation-skipping transfer ☐ Employment ☐ Excise ☐ Other (describe) ▶ ______________

4 Federal tax form number (check all that apply): a☐ 706 series b☐ 709 c☐ 940 d☐ 941, 943, 944 e☐ 1040, 1040-A, or 1040-EZ f☐ 1041 g☐ 1120 h☐ Other (list) ▶ ______________

5 If your authority as a fiduciary does not cover all years or tax periods, check here . . . . ▶ ☐ and list the specific years or periods ▶ ______________

6 If the fiduciary listed wants a copy of notices or other written communications (see the instructions) check this box . . . . . ▶ ☐ and enter the year(s) or period(s) for the corresponding line 4 item checked. If more than 1 form entered on line 4h, enter the form number.

Complete only if the line 6 box is checked.

If this item is checked:	Enter year(s) or period(s)	If this item is checked:	Enter year(s) or period(s)
4a		4b	
4c		4d	
4e		4f	
4g		4h:	
4h:		4h:	

For Paperwork Reduction Act and Privacy Act Notice, see the separate instructions. Cat. No. 16375I Form **56** (Rev. 12-2011)

Form 56 (Rev. 12-2011) Page **2**

Part II Court and Administrative Proceedings

Name of court (if other than a court proceeding, identify the type of proceeding and name of agency)			Date proceeding initiated
Address of court			Docket number of proceeding
City or town, state, and ZIP code	Date	Time ☐ a.m. ☐ p.m.	Place of other proceedings

Part III Signature

We have the following:

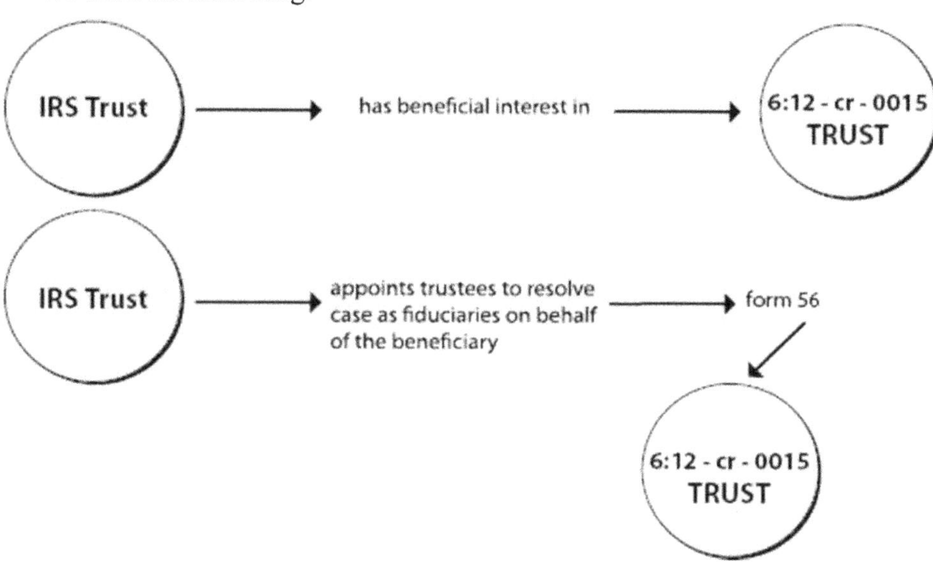
IRS Trust
has beneficial interest in
6:12 - cr - 0015
TRUST
IRS Trust
appoints trustees to resolve case as fiduciaries on behalf of the beneficiary
form 56
6:12 - cr - 0015
TRUST

The IRS Trust is the Beneficiary with a priority claim over the court case with a financial value. With form 56, the IRS Trust appoints Trustees to act for the Beneficiary.

The intent of the IRS Trust was specific and deliberate. The trust was asking for the return of the property secured by the court case. With a superior claim, the IRS Trust and the Express Trust sought the release of my body.

My one concern was what to do if the court did not recognize the equitable claim. What was I to do if Moon did not dignify the invocation of the Court of Equity? Although the equitable claim in the court case was established by the Express Trust and the UCC-1 filing, I did not understand how the IRS Trust could compel the government to perform. It was one thing to appoint Hogeboom and Pompei as trustees, it was quite another to have them satisfy all obligations. To me, the problem was self-evident. The Federal Government presumed jurisdiction since 2004 when I wrote to numerous officials and asked for the law which required me to file a federal income tax form. No one answered the question. No party addressed the issue of jurisdiction. Why would it be any different now? As far as I was concerned, the government could still assert jurisdiction and remain unresponsive to any of my current claims or questions.

It was at this phase of my education that my instructors asked me to pay particular attention. They introduced specific government forms to use. Had it not been for fundamental knowledge of trusts and equity and government forms that tied in with trusts and equity, the balance of the process would have been difficult to accept. Let me explain.

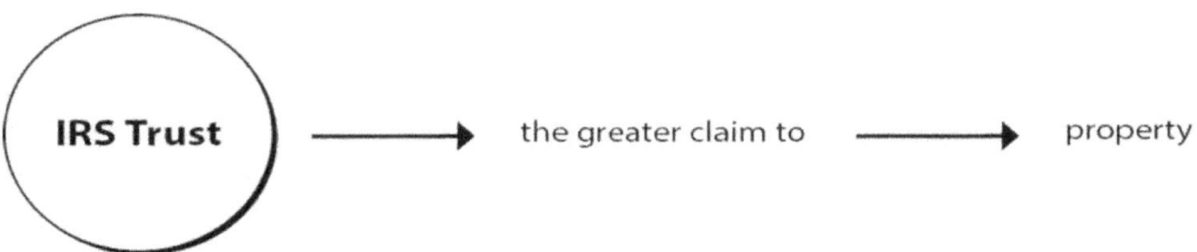
IRS Trust
the greater claim to
property

We know the IRS Trust had a superior claim to the court case because the IRS Trust had a superior claim to me.

I learned that the court case represented a value to the United States Government. My instructors stated that the court case was backed by traded securities. Like mortgage-backed securities, court cases—as underscored to me—were securitized and sold. While the explanation is simple, it is beyond belief of those unfamiliar with this concept. As a matter of course, the government already had an "asset" collateralizing the security; the asset was the prisoner warehoused in the court/penal system. The asset was me.

While I allowed my mind to process this possibility, my instructors asked me to provide the court case number to a man they knew who had direct access to a securities broker. I paid a nominal fee, and a broker produced a report which itemized the following:

CUSIP (Committee on Uniform Securities Identification Procedures)
Symbol: FASMX
CUSIP: 316069103
Fund Number: 314
Fund Inception Date: 12/28/1988
Annualized Turnover Rate: 14.00% as of 9/2011
Net Assets: $6,775,187,157.58 as of 4/30/2012
Portfolio Assets: $6,893,889,829.67 as of 4/30/2012

With this information, according to my instructors, I had proof the court case was traded as a security. They advised me to apply this CUSIP on all of documents with the court and government. With this insight, I applied the rest of the remedy.

My instructors then gave me a fax number to an IRS office to request specific forms: 1099-A, 1099-B, 1099-OID, and 1099-C. These forms, I was told, were given only to financial institutions. The IRS Trust qualified as a financial institution. Within two weeks, I received a stack of each of these forms directly from the IRS.

- Form 1099-A - stands for "Acquisition" or "Abandonment"
- Form 1099-B - stands for "Barter"
- Form 1099-OID - stands for "Original Issue Discount"
- Form 1099-C - stands for "Cancel"

Each form serves a purpose. While they are similar in format and requirements, each is unique. Noteworthy, the forms asked for the names of the parties involved in the transaction and the fiduciaries appointed with form 56. I entered each of the names and addresses of the trustees: Hogeboom, Pompei, and Moon.

- The 1099-A form is used to indicate that the IRS Trust was "Acquiring" the value of securities involved in the court case. My goal was to receive the "disposition." The disposition is the exchange, the even trade (barter), for the securities. The "barter" for the securities would allow the government to keep the realized value of the securities from the court case. The "disposition" for the IRS Trust was the dismissal of the court case with prejudice, an even exchange.
- The 1099-B form is the "Barter" for the securities. With the value of the securities worth $X and the value of the dismissal of the case the same ($X amount), the terms of the barter were established. The exchange of $X for $X is an equal barter.
- The 1099-OID determines the "Difference" between what remained after the barter. In the above example, $X - $X = 0. So, the OID would be "0."
- The 1099-C form is used to "Cancel" the transaction, if necessary. If the trustees failed to provide the disposition, the transaction would be canceled. The trustees would then be obligated for the difference of the value of the securities ($X) and the value of the barter (0). So the OID would be $X - 0, which equals $X.

8080 ☐ VOID ☐ CORRECTED

LENDER'S name, street address, city or town, state or province, country, ZIP or foreign postal code, and telephone no.

OMB No. 1545-0877

2016

Form **1099-A**

Acquisition or Abandonment of Secured Property

LENDER'S federal identification number | BORROWER'S identification number

1 Date of lender's acquisition or knowledge of abandonment

2 Balance of principal outstanding $

Copy A For Internal Revenue Service Center

File with Form 1096.

BORROWER'S name

3

4 Fair market value of property $

Street address (including apt. no.)

5 If checked, the borrower was personally liable for repayment of the debt ▶ ☐

City or town, state or province, country, and ZIP or foreign postal code

6 Description of property

Account number (see instructions)

For Privacy Act and Paperwork Reduction Act Notice, see the **2016 General Instructions for Certain Information Returns.**

Form **1099-A** Cat. No. 14412G www.irs.gov/form1099a Department of the Treasury - Internal Revenue Service

Do Not Cut or Separate Forms on This Page — Do Not Cut or Separate Forms on This Page

7979 ☐ VOID ☐ CORRECTED

PAYER'S name, street address, city or town, state or province, country, ZIP or foreign postal code, and telephone no.

Applicable check box on Form 8949

OMB No. 1545-0715

2015

Form **1099-B**

Proceeds From Broker and Barter Exchange Transactions

1a Description of property (Example 100 sh. XYZ Co.)

1b Date acquired

1c Date sold or disposed

PAYER'S federal identification number | RECIPIENT'S identification number

1d Proceeds $

1e Cost or other basis $

Copy A

1f Code, if any

1g Adjustments $

For Internal Revenue Service Center

File with Form 1096.

RECIPIENT'S name

2 Type of gain or loss: Short-term ☐ Long-term ☐

3 Check if basis reported to IRS ☐

Street address (including apt. no.)

4 Federal income tax withheld $

5 Check if noncovered security ☐

City or town, state or province, country, and ZIP or foreign postal code

6 Reported to IRS: Gross proceeds ☐ Net proceeds ☐

7 Check if loss is not allowed based on amount in 1d ☐

Account number (see instructions) | 2nd TIN not. ☐

8 Profit or (loss) realized in 2015 on closed contracts $

9 Unrealized profit or (loss) on open contracts—12/31/2014 $

CUSIP number

10 Unrealized profit or (loss) on open contracts—12/31/2015 $

11 Aggregate profit or (loss) on contracts $

14 State name | 15 State identification no | 16 State tax withheld $ $

12

13 Bartering $

For Privacy Act and Paperwork Reduction Act Notice, see the **2015 General Instructions for Certain Information Returns.**

Form **1099-B** Cat. No. 14411V www.irs.gov/form1099b Department of the Treasury-- Internal Revenue Service

Do Not Cut or Separate Forms on This Page — Do Not Cut or Separate Forms on This Page

9696 VOID CORRECTED

PAYER'S name, street address, city or town, state or province, country, ZIP or foreign postal code, and telephone no.		1 Original issue discount for 2016 $	OMB No. 1545-0117	Original Issue Discount
		2 Other periodic interest $	2016 Form 1099-OID	
PAYER'S federal identification number	RECIPIENT'S identification number	3 Early withdrawal penalty $	4 Federal income tax withheld $	Copy A
RECIPIENT'S name		5 Market discount $	6 Acquisition premium $	For Internal Revenue Service Center
Street address (including apt. no.)		7 Description		File with Form 1096.
City or town, state or province, country, and ZIP or foreign postal code		8 Original issue discount on U.S. Treasury obligations $		For Privacy Act and Paperwork Reduction Act Notice, see the 2016 General Instructions for Certain Information Returns.
	FATCA filing requirement	9 Investment expenses $	10 Bond premium $	
Account number (see instructions)	2nd TIN not.	11 State / 12 State identification no.	13 State tax withheld $ $	

Form 1099-OID Cat. No. 14421R www.irs.gov/form1099oid Department of the Treasury - Internal Revenue Service

Do Not Cut or Separate Forms on This Page — Do Not Cut or Separate Forms on This Page

8585 VOID CORRECTED

CREDITOR'S name, street address, city or town, state or province, country, ZIP or foreign postal code, and telephone no.		1 Date of identifiable event	OMB No. 1545-1424	Cancellation of Debt
		2 Amount of debt discharged $	2016	
		3 Interest if included in box 2 $	Form 1099-C	
CREDITOR'S federal identification number	DEBTOR'S identification number	4 Debt description		Copy A For Internal Revenue Service Center
DEBTOR'S name				File with Form 1096.
Street address (including apt. no.)		5 Check here if the debtor was personally liable for repayment of the debt ▸ ☐		For Privacy Act and Paperwork Reduction Act Notice, see the 2016 General Instructions for Certain Information Returns.
City or town, state or province, country, and ZIP or foreign postal code				
Account number (see instructions)		6 Identifiable event code	7 Fair market value of property $	

Form 1099-C Cat. No. 26280W www.irs.gov/form1099c Department of the Treasury - Internal Revenue Service

Do Not Cut or Separate Forms on This Page — Do Not Cut or Separate Forms on This Page

After careful study, I understood the forms and the purposes for each. There was one question which remained unresolved. I did not know the value of the securities in the court case. I soon learned there was no way to know. As the CUSIP report from the broker indicated, the trading fund in which the securities were registered was valued in the billions of dollars. The securities in the case represented only a fraction of the fund. The key was to factor a value for each criminal charge so that the estimated value was not under the amount of the value of the securities associated with the court case. My instructors explained, if the projected value was greater than the actual value, the IRS would enter the lower value and calculate the final amount.

As a rule of thumb, they said a felony was valued at no more than $300 million and misdemeanors at no more than $100 million. With these figures, I reached a value of $600 million, one felony and three misdemeanors. Whatever the actual value of the securities, the IRS Trust sought an equivalent disposition, a dismissal of the charges. The government could keep the value realized from the securities.

The result would mean that, if the trustees/fiduciaries (the government) provided the disposition (the dismissal), the IRS Trust would release all rights and interests to the securities to the government regardless of their value. The "Acquired" assets would be "Bartered" with a difference of "0" with no need to cancel the transaction and no tax owed from a cancellation or an equal exchange (Barter).

If the trustees refused to provide the disposition, the trustees/fiduciaries would be fired and this would result in a "merger of equities."[70] Recall, one person may not be all three parties to a trust. If the trustees were fired, the IRS Trust would automatically become the trustee and demand that the original securities be returned. The trust would collapse and cease to exist. The government would realize the sale of securities, something that would have already occurred even before trial. Securities are apparently sold well in advance of a court conviction. Consequently, any tax burden from this sale would be owed by the trustees, as they would have the obligation to perform.

Given the extent of information relating to the government 1099 forms, consider:

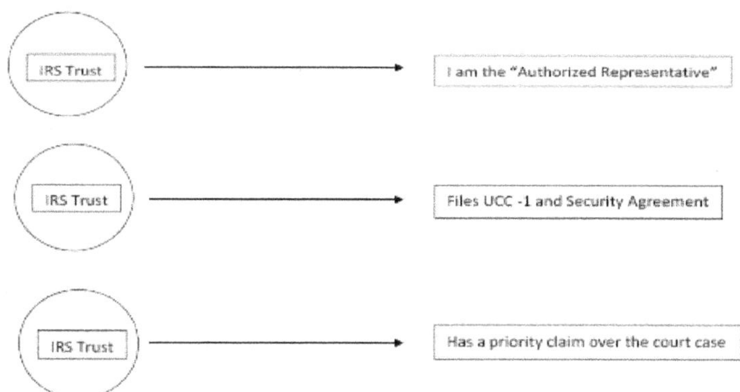
IRS Trust
I am the "Authorized Representative"
IRS Trust
Files UCC -1 and Security Agreement
IRS Trust
Has a priority claim over the court case

If the court case involved securities, by and through the Express Trust, the IRS Trust had an equitable claim and would seek a resolution to the criminal charges against me by seeking a "disposition" or a trade with the submission of the 1099 forms.

These forms are sent to the trustees in the following sequential order:

1. 1099-A
2. 1099-B/1099-OID
3. If necessary, 1099-C, and a request for the original securities

Before proceeding to the next component of this private remedy, consider an important fact. The 1099s asked for the CUSIP. This piece of information could do nothing but confirm the authenticity of this entire process. While I had never heard of this remedy before, the process and information were reassuring. I gained confidence that if Judge Moon did not honor the invocation of the Court of Equity, the government was beholden to complete the paperwork, nonetheless. This was a private process, after all.

I prepared a package for each trustee and those who would receive a courtesy copy of the private remedy. The most important person involved, other than the trustees, was

70 Henry Gibson, A Treatise on Suits in Chancery, (Gaut-Ogden Co., Printers and Binders 1907)

Renee Mitchell. She was the Director of the IRS Service Center in Covington, Kentucky. This was the location that handled such matters for criminal cases. In a letter to Mitchell, I asked that she direct her personnel to set off, settle, and discharge, as in, do a ledger to ledger set off, of the obligations associated with the case.

There were two looming factors. One was whether the court would view this private remedy as a "filing" or a "frivolous" submission. The second factor concerned how the judge and I would handle my request. Some elements of the execution of this remedy were simply out of my control. Based upon this uncertainty and the arbitrary nature of any court decision, I had to consider one final action. If the court deemed this remedy a "filing," it would mean that I violated bond conditions and would be arrested. I would be without any access to computers and unable to mail legal work. I would be without the ability to access the UCC system. If the government did not respond to the private remedy in time, I would not be able to file a UCC-3 Amendment, which would preclude me from recording any taxable liability of Hogeboom and Pompei.

The information from my instructors was that government officials would be accountable for their failure to enforce this private remedy. They stressed that, in good faith, based upon their oaths of office, agents had a responsibility to process a civil remedy, akin to a request under the Administrative Procedures Act or the handling of an administrative remedy under federal law. The consequences of any failure would result in a recording of any liability within the UCC system with a UCC-3 lien.

When I asked my instructors of the implications to officials and any repercussions to me. They stressed a UCC recording of any liability only affected the agents in a professional capacity. Moreover, they stressed this was the only recourse, ultimately, to compel them to perform. They explained that a man in my circumstances could not rightly expect to face certain imprisonment without recourse to compel an agent who would not otherwise honor his responsibilities. They stressed that I was knowingly executing a legal and lawful process with the just aim of satisfying the best interests of all parties and that I had given these officials ample notice and time.

My instructors finally underscored that, if the worst of all scenarios unfolded, and I was sent to prison, the officials could request the removal of any UCC-3 recording through a formal process. With the understanding that any recording on a UCC-3 was limited to their official capacity, I believed there was no way one could determine that I knowingly or maliciously harmed any agent who either did not perform their jobs, or at a minimum, failed to respond, which is what they did for the last eight years. With this particular and final remedy, I asked Hogeboom and Pompei to immediately notify me of any defect or deficiency. Not surprisingly, they never responded.

With the likelihood I would be arrested and the probability that the officials would not respond to my request for a private remedy, the UCC-3 lien would be recorded. The instructors were correct; this was my only recourse. If the judge honored the equitable claim, or if the officials processed the remedy, any recording could and would be prevented, and if filed, it could be rescinded with a UCC-3 Amendment. As far as I was concerned, given the destruction to my family and life, I was enforcing a valid process.

Consider one final thought. The discharge of debts is not uncommon to the IRS. If there was a tax owed because of a commercial offense against the revenue laws, if there were securities traded, the IRS, a bookkeeping and collection agency for the International Monetary Fund (IMF), would want to balance its books. Notice what is written in 22 CFR, Foreign Relations, under section 213.14,

> *"Contracting for Collection Services," "(h) Report written off/discharged debts to IRS on the appropriate form 1099."*

Who would not see that I was attempting to satisfy the obligation for all concerned with the IRS and with the same forms?

Given the amount we have covered, it would be wise to review the critical elements which support the submission of the private remedy. They are:

- Trusts
- Equity
- Government/IRS 1099 forms and
- UCC

Consider the following points:

- Trusts are inherent and prevalent in Courts of Law and Courts of Equity;
- Equity is superior to the Court of Law and preferred venue for universal justice and honesty;
- A trust, the IRS Trust, was created and secured a priority claim to my property as recorded within the UCC;
- The IRS trust had a claim to the court case and any securities;
- Hogeboom and Pompei were appointed as trustees of the Express Trust;
- The IRS trust was asking for the disposition, the exchange of any securities tied to the case for a dismissal of the charges;
- With the 1099 forms, the request for the discharge of all liabilities was given to Hogeboom and Pompei and sent to the IRS for processing;
- If Hogeboom and Pompei did not satisfy their obligations, they would be fired as trustees which would collapse the trust;
- With the filing of a UCC-3 form (lien), Hogeboom and Pompei would be accountable for any obligation for their failure to perform; $X – 0 = $X, the resulting tax liability;
- As Authorized Representative of the Grantor and Beneficiary, I would invoke the Court of Equity and ask Moon to dignify the equitable claim and private remedy.

It would be appropriate to provide some context as to my mental and emotional states. I was overwhelmed. I was concerned about creating the appearance of wrongdoing by my actions. Why? I had done no wrong to warrant the first charges. Seeking an answer to an earnest question did nothing but ensure harm by the government. I was convinced that I should not have faced the first charges at all. If I've said it once, I will say it again, I was outside the jurisdiction of the federal authorities for the excise in question. The fact that no agency, agent, or official answered my question over an eight-year span was telling. Given my certain fate, I decided to overcome the fear of the unknown and fight for the truth. The only potential shortfall was the continued failure of the government to respond. Would the officials not respond to this new request as well?

The unresponsiveness of government agents was such a concern during the criminal investigation that—after the trial and the appeal some two years later—I filed a suit into the federal court and asked the Department of Justice a "Federal Question." The sentiment of this question is so relevant, I am inserting it for your review. (Appendix C) Pay particular attention to the language in the Supreme Court case, <u>Federal Insurance Crop Corp, v Merrill</u>, and the role of "fraud." Imagine the Federal Government not responding a second time, in a situation such as mine, with the submission of the private remedy.

If I thought employing the private remedy was legally insufficient, I would not have done so. Just as I knew that I no longer had a legal obligation to file a federal income tax return and did not commit a crime, I acted knowing my intent was sound. Perhaps this is the point I should make. To commit a crime, one must have a *guilty mind* coupled with *the act.* In the legal realm, these two elements are known as *mens rea* and *actus reus*.

> *Mens rea is the second of two essential elements of every crime at common law, the other being actus reus... expressed by the adverbs purposely, knowingly, recklessly, and negligently...* Black's Law Dictionary, 10th Edition
>
> *Actus reus...* 1. *The wrongful deed that comprises the physical components of a crime and that generally must be coupled with mens rea to establish criminal liability; a forbidden act... Also termed deed of crime; over act.* Ibid.

Since I sought a private and civil and legal remedy to criminal charges which should never have been filed, I knew my intentions were true. I did not commit a wrongful act, much less have a guilty motive.

This thought is even more poignant when one considers that the government has a tendency not to respond. If the agents failed to answer this second query, I could only conclude that, as with the first query, the government wanted me to *commit* a *crime* so they could score a conviction. If I did not receive a response from Hogeboom and Pompei with the private remedy, I would ask the same question. Would they not answer and then assert that I had the intent (*mens rea*) and committed the crime (*actus reus*)?

VIOLATION OF BOND

One of the bond conditions to which I was subject was that I could not "file" any documents into court. Also, I could not file any "frivolous" documents with any agency. Anything I submitted had to be through my attorneys. One could easily ask why these conditions were necessary. First, who determines whether any document is frivolous? Second, why not allow a defendant to "make lemonade" (George Norris case) out of a very difficult situation, especially if he is not filing something into court, but merely giving the court a courtesy copy of private correspondence to the agency leveling the charges. Finally, if the filings are truly frivolous, why not allow the defendant to injure himself further. The court's conditions serve one purpose—intimidate the defendant to the point of absolute control. This should cause those who are discerning to note how the government benefits from these constraints.

As I neared the date to the private remedy, I submitted a motion to remove legal counsel and move forward *pro se*. I could not have sent these documents to anyone with Cargill and Harris as my legal representatives, which clearly would have been a violation of bond conditions. This hearing took place in November. By then, Cargill had already secured a continuance. The trial was rescheduled for January 15, 2013. When the judge approved my request to proceed without attorneys, I spent my time finalizing the private remedy.

Let me to underscore a thought. I believed that I was still operating under fraud and force. But for my concession to acknowledge the court's jurisdiction, I would still be in solitary confinement as stated by my public defenders. Conversations with defense lawyers and my efforts with the court were ineffective. Only the ABA Canons of Ethics and court rules and procedures had any influence. This made me wonder if the private remedy was going to work. I did not know; but I had no other option. With a 98% probability that I would be convicted, I was not optimistic with airing a defense before a jury, a defense which did not include my good faith belief.

My hope was the IRS would process the private remedy. My intent was to ask the court, if necessary, to stay the trial until the agency acted on the paperwork. Since the government had a responsibility to process the remedy, I believed such a request was reasonable. Additionally, since I asked all concerned to notify me if the remedy was defective or legally deficient in any way, no response would only support a grant of leave from Judge Moon for the IRS to process the remedy.

By the end of November, I mailed the private remedy to the IRS and trustees. I specifically stated that in no way should the documents be considered a filing. These papers were not a matter of record for the trial proceedings in any manner. I also sent courtesy copies to the Clerk of the Court, the Chief Judge, and the U. S. Attorney. Less than a week later, on December 7, 2102, while I was at the local court to notarize a document, I was arrested by the local sheriff. The government had issued a warrant for my arrest.

I had spent the morning and early afternoon with my son and daughter at their home school. ***It was the last time I was to see them for almost four years.***

I was placed into solitary confinement in the local jail for the weekend. On Monday morning, I was transported and jailed in the Orange County facility for two weeks. I was then moved to the jail in Lynchburg. Although I had a strong suspicion, I wanted to know why I had been arrested. In my view, I had not violated any bond conditions. I did not file anything into court. Moreover, these were not frivolous documents. I was a man in a precarious position attempting to solve a problem with a civil or private administrative remedy with the opposing party before any court action began. If the IRS accepted and processed my remedy, there would be no reason for the trial. The matter would be settled.

I eventually learned that I was arrested for violating bond conditions. I was accused of filing documents into court. I believed this conclusion continued the fraud and force. By virtue of its stringent rules and procedures, the court denied justice once again. I did not "file" anything. In the cover letter to the court, I stated that at no time should these papers be considered a filing. These documents were not frivolous in nature. And if considered frivolous, who made this determination and by what standard?

The other consideration is that I would not have violated bond conditions knowingly and placed my mother's house at risk. (Not that the government could have seized her house for the mere mailing of documents, for the bond was to ensure I did not flee.) I also would not have risked the loss of time to prepare for the trial and the invocation of the Court of Equity. Moreover, I needed time to coordinate efforts with the IRS to process the private remedy. Then there was the issue of my children. I coveted my time with them. The upcoming Christmas holiday was important since I faced seven years of prison.

Early one morning, I was taken to a probable cause hearing and, as a pro se litigant, I handled my own defense. Harris was there as standby counsel. The purpose of the hearing was to establish if there was probable cause for violating bond conditions. Hogeboom made the argument that I had done so. I underscored in my opening statement that I made no filing. Rather, the court received a courtesy notice of a private remedy sent to the IRS. Aside from the heightened hyperbole from Hogeboom that I was a "domestic" and "financial terrorist," here are two thoughts.

It was apparent that the presiding judge, Judge Crigler, had an agenda. He came to the hearing with an aggressive posture. He was caustic and treated me with disdain. Primarily because of him, this appeared to be a kangaroo court with a predetermined outcome. This is the same judge and scene to which I referred earlier in this book. I cited his behavior and treatment of me as a violation of the Judicial Canons of Ethics. The second observation is that Hogeboom used the Probation Officer (PO) to validate that I violated bond conditions. I was accountable to the PO. He discussed the conditions for bond with me and had me sign an acknowledgment of receipt. Did I violate the conditions? No. But the government disagreed, and Hogeboom needed a witness to corroborate this conclusion. The man who enforced the conditions, the PO, was in the position to make a legal determination that conditions were violated.

When the PO was called to the stand, the prosecutor asked him to confirm the signature on the private remedy. "Is this the defendant's signature?" he asked. "Yes," said the PO. What occurred with this simple exchange? The government offered evidence into court that the documents were a violation of the bond conditions. Hogeboom did not ask the PO if I had "filed" anything into court. Why? Hogeboom knew I had specifically stated these documents could in no way be considered a filing. Hogeboom established a "filing" based upon a "signature." More importantly, he was furthering another lie into the court system. Hogeboom had no integrity, except for the *integrity* permitted by a corrupt judicial process.

When I cross-examined the PO, I asked him if he was an "expert" with signatures and handwriting. He said, "No." I asked him if he had firsthand knowledge of the documents or their significance. Again, he said "No." Finally, I asked him if he knew the "intent" for the signature, underscoring that intent was the reason for the signature. For the third time, the PO said "No." When I challenged the PO, he agreed that he could not conclude that the papers were filed or frivolous.

The court process and the court's decisions are often quite arbitrary. There was no doubt that, based upon the capricious nature of this hearing, I would be found guilty. When Hogeboom gave his summation to the court and stressed that I was a rogue citizen determined to defy specific orders. He recommended that there was probable cause for a violation of bond. In my summation, I argued that the PO was not an expert witness for signatures or handwriting. I cited the fact that he did not know of the intent for the signature which, as I understood the definition in the law, is the essence of a *signature*. I then stated the obvious; these documents were not frivolous and not filed into court.

My argument was unsuccessful. Crigler concluded there were probable grounds that I had violated bond and remanded me until a subsequent hearing at which time Judge Moon would decide whether to revoke bond outright. Moon did just that. Without hesitation he revoked bond as a mere formality. I would remain in jail until trial. The significance of Moon's decision is telling. The application of court rules and procedures were conveniently employed to steer the defendant to a determination of guilt, when guilt had little to do with the law, as has been suggested throughout this work. Guilt had a direct correlation to the operation of the system and the repercussions were huge.

I was unable to adequately prepare for trial or move the private remedy forward. It was critical that I coordinate the remedy with an IRS agent familiar with the process and government forms. With this thought, let me be clear. The IRS received an honorable and legal remedy from an established trust. The IRS, the victim of the alleged *crime*, was in receipt of a potential resolution tendered with the express intent to resolve the matter in the best interests of all parties. Ironically, the court dismissed this good faith effort as a violation of bond. The judge did not consider the remedy to be a genuine solution. Meanwhile, the IRS could still process the remedy at any time.

Consider the significance of the "signature" on the remedy. The court and government gratuitously considered that the signature at the bottom of the documents was mine, even though the "office" under which it was signed was different than my personal capacity. Without belaboring the point, an example may be helpful. When the CEO of a corporation signs a letter, he does so in the capacity of his "office." He does not sign (think of intent) in his personal capacity. His intention is to sign as the CEO—and nobody can declare his intent to be otherwise. Moreover, he can't be liable personally for his legal and lawful acts as CEO on behalf of the corporation. My situation was no different.

This remedy was offered in the capacity or office other than me since the IRS Trust was the remedy. Consider what may or may not have happened if another private party had signed as the "Authorized Representative." Anyone could have agreed to be the "Authorized Representative." Would the government or court have had recourse to revoke bond and jail me had someone else signed? In the end, we know the court refused to accept that I was not personally the one who submitted the papers. We know the government willfully rejected a solution to the case and, thus, dismissed my intent to avoid a trial, while others were only concerned with having a trial. Was there continued fraud and force applied to this case? I believed so.

Within the court and the legal system generally, there is a subtle and sometimes not so subtle manipulation of the process and the defendant. This is often achieved through a deliberate interpretation or representation that something is true when it is not. This dynamic may be defined by the legal term *colorable*. Colorable is defined as:

> ***Colorable***—*(of a claim or action) appearing to be true, valid, or right... 2) intended to deceive; counterfeit...* Black's Law Dictionary, 10th Edition

Consider the term *color of law.*

> ***Color of law***—*The appearance or semblance, without the substance, of a legal right. The term usually implies a misuse of power made possible because the wrongdoer is clothed with the authority of the state.* Ibid.

One last definition will help explain this concept:

> ***Color of process***—*The appearance of validity and sufficiency surrounding a legal proceeding that is later found to be invalid.* Ibid.

To *color* is the malleable application of law or process to a given situation. From a layperson's uninformed perspective, *colorable* is not a black and white application of law. For example, the PO's perception that the bond was violated with a *signature* was a *colorable* conclusion. Such a position allows the prosecution to advance a colorable interpretation of the law and advance the fraud and force through court. The proper application of otherwise non colorable law is avoided.

As of mid-December, I was in the same jail as before I was released on bond. Sadly, I was without options. All I could do was wait. The best that could be done under these circumstances was to apply pencil to paper and prepare for what I would state to advance the Court of Equity argument. In the meantime, with the use of mail or phone, I had someone confirm whether the trustees responded in writing to the private remedy. Without a response, I asked someone in advance of my arrest to mail the sequential packages with the appropriate 1099 forms and papers that would facilitate the filing of the UCC-3 liens. I hoped, at a minimum, to dignify this solution by offering the entire private remedy to the IRS. I would wait for any response.

Invoking the Court of Equity

On January 2, 2013, I was transported to court for a hearing on the government's motion that I be committed for psychiatric evaluations. This is a standard ploy. Prosecutors use this tactic as a tool to further frustrate the defendant in tax cases. I intended to use this opportunity to invoke the Court of Equity. I had submitted a motion for the same reason. In accord with Gibson's work, I was seeking honesty and justice and couldn't be faulted for making a claim to my property under equity.

Unfortunately, Moon had no intention to honor the motion. He denied it. To the extent I was able, I responded to his decision. Rather than explain the event, I am including a copy of the entire transcript. Please note that being in court is an overwhelming situation for anyone. Imagine being in a federal criminal trial proceeding, faced with the threat of mental evaluations for months, and attempting to request that the court accept an alternative to the "Court at Law" jurisdiction. I was in an uncomfortable position. (Appendix D)

I failed. The judge decided against my equitable claim. However, after hearing what he said—and certainly after reading the transcript—I could not escape the idea that Judge Moon held a tight line to the role of law, the absolute jurisdiction of criminal law. It appeared that he did not so much rule against an equitable right as Gibson defines it in a criminal venue, but ruled for the prosecution of a criminal violation, as if Moon ignored the role of equity completely. It occurred to me that Moon would not even dignify the appropriate application of equity. Based upon my education to date, the trustees (Moon, Hogeboom, and Pompei) were now *trustees de son tort*.

> ***Trustee de son tort****—Someone who, without legal authority, administers a living person's property to the detriment of the property owner.* Ibid.

I also concluded that the court's refusal to acknowledge my decisions and request for the Court of Equity did not alter the trust dynamics inherent with the Express Trust for the court case and the relationships of the parties. Pointedly, the private remedy was an administrative and civil remedy that was still in play. The court's refusal to honor the role of equity did not grant the government or IRS a pass with the acceptance of a legitimate solution. The court had simply refused to give the role of equity the universal consideration due. However, this issue was not closed.

JAILED

Before I discuss the next component of the legal process, the trial, I want to share about the experience of incarceration, specifically the five weeks leading to this foreboding event. Imprisonment before a trial serves a purpose—a purpose that is taken for granted by the government and one which is largely unspoken. It forces a man to endure further loss. Confinement brings defeat before the real battle begins. Other than separation from loved ones there were two elements I came to detest. One is the abhorrent tendency of becoming incrementally more comfortable in a situation and an environment that was as unnatural as it was reprehensible. Secondly, as with solitary confinement, the other was defaulting to the only known events which defined the day—three meals and "counts" by the Cos. This was apparent in general population as well.

The days were scheduled by three meals. The only other notable time-appointed activity was the count held in the morning, afternoon, and evening. Counts are a religious daily event for prisons. The remainder of the day was filled with my own initiatives of limited scope. I read, wrote, and exercised within the confines of the unit. When I was tired, I would nap. I tried to keep a continuously refreshed mind. Every element of prison was surreal with a constant grinding upon my psychological, physical, emotional, and spiritual being.

One of my main contentions had to do with the men housed with me. I generally avoided others. I was selective with whom I interacted. My priorities were more important than developing relationships. I had to focus on my case. Several inmates were from gangs. Many were there for actual crimes against people and property, assault and battery, grand larceny, etc. The level of education and emotional wisdom of these men were varied, but largely deficient. Many lacked the maturity, discipline, and temperance to cope with a modicum of civility, as well as self-respect and respect for others.

There were five physical fights during the time I was there. Theft was rampant. The atmosphere was loud, as men communicated by shouting. The noise lasted into the early hours of the morning as men gambled. With the constant drone expected in such a venue and from such a large group, sleeping was difficult. The television was on from morning until night and the volume was high. It was an ordeal to focus in this constant cacophony of noise. While most of the men were disruptive, there were some who stayed to themselves. They were civil and respectful. They simply wanted to serve their time and go home. Their lives were uneventful. They, too, were at the mercy of those who operated without much structure in their lives. Most of the men appeared to be *comfortable* and as if they had been programmed within this environment. They were inmates who accepted their lot in life.

The food was poor in quality and minimal in quantity. Hunger was a constant and nagging presence. It was not uncommon to find hair and rocks in the food. The lack of nutrients had a direct impact on my health. Within a twenty-four-hour enclosure, never seeing the sun or breathing fresh air, it was easy to become dispirited. The dark and condemning atmosphere, both literally and figuratively, was made even starker by the hardness of life in prison: cinderblock walls, concrete floors, steel bunks in a row, like stacked coffins waiting for the burial ground, and metal tables and seats were as cold and uninviting as their color, dark forest green, and the temperature of the unit. With a chronic arthritis condition, I struggled with the thinly soled shoes and lack of clothing. I received neither socks nor T-shirts. These luxuries were obtained through the commissary system. If a man did not have funds to supplement his diet and attire, he did without.

There was no privacy. We were constantly watched by COs and each other. One could never escape. The bathroom stalls were in the open. We were without the decency once taken for granted. Even conversations were subjected to constant interruptions. Few exercised the deference and restraint to wait until people finished talking.

The cumulative experience was one of self-preservation. One had to cope with what was once thinkable, as the "system" managed bodies in as efficacious a manner as possible. I quickly learned that—though not unexpected—bureaucrats were indifferent towards those imprisoned. Inmates were no longer human beings, but assets to be warehoused until relocated or discharged.

The other element of incarceration I detested was the phenomenon of not knowing. Never had not knowing become pronounced. Man may contend with most anything; yet, not knowing may be the most difficult. Why? The mind is our nemesis, endlessly and tirelessly wrestling with possibilities which never come to pass. The mind ruminates over outcomes and their sundry permutations. The mind never stops. It is a reservoir of thoughts, mostly negative, which disaffect the soul.

A second reason not knowing is powerful is because man hopes—like an eternal beacon, even in the face of inevitable despair. I did not know my fate, though I believed it was ominous. However, I hoped. There was always that prospect—the element of the fight which wills a man forward. A man's heart equals the influence of the mind. Such is the irony of the unknown. For, as the mind tends to berate and despair the heart longs for growth and change. Good or bad, the mind considers and settles upon the undesired, while the spirit of man angles for what is possible.

To illustrate the prominence of not knowing, consider this comparison. Appropriately, the expectation or hope of a gift for a birthday parallels times of struggle. One does not know what is inside the box; but one hopes. Not knowing is what spurs the mind. One cycles through ideas. Questions surface: What if the gift is not what is wanted? What if it is the wrong color? What if? Yet, one hopes—still.

I was in the battle of my life. Not knowing was heightened. What would happen? How could I affect the outcome favorably? Would I? If found guilty, where would I be sent? How would my children be impacted? Would they have access to me? How long would I be gone? The rabbit trails of thoughts were seemingly limitless. The future and its particulars were not known, and this challenged my conscious and subconscious states of being incessantly. Yet, it was only a matter of time before the unknown became a reality.

Yes, jails are a necessary evil; but they are a tool for the establishment. A man who is jailed is limited and defeated. As demonstrated in my case, what better way to aggravate a man's efforts to gain an acquittal than to accuse him of a frivolous claim that he violated bond conditions? I was separated from my research material. I could not prepare for trial. I was limited to survival. Whatever hope I had to prevail was constantly suppressed. Those who were able to manipulate the rules and laws (think of the terms *color* and *colorable*) created the most restrictive conditions possible.

As it stood, the IRS took over eight years to conduct its exhaustive investigation. The government had over 20,000 pages of discovery—all fluff and no substance. These pages were more for show. All prosecutors do this, as they wheel large boxes into court to suggest the ironclad case against the villain they intend to convict. Like the Norris case, the federal corporation, the United States, did not care that a man's life was destroyed. The authorities ensured complete destruction by any means. This was a known fact to me which I detested as much as not knowing.

<u>THE TRIAL</u>

By January 15, 2013, the first day of the trial, the apex of pressure was reached, especially since I suffered from a lack of sleep. Inmates gambled behind my bunk until two in the morning. The CO had little control. He did not care either. Sleep deprived and weary, I could do nothing but face the impending doom as best as able. The jail staff went through its protocol and took me to a holding cell at 5:30 AM. I waited until the U. S. Marshals arrived. At 8:00 AM sharp, they drove me two blocks to the courthouse where I was placed into another holding cell until the trial began. At the appointed time, the shackles and handcuffs were temporarily removed. I changed into a suit my mother brought from home. The three-act play was about to resume with its second act.

My mind was numb. The Court was a machine which could not and would not be stopped. Rarely did anyone escape its path. The government would exact *justice* no matter the cost. If a trial were necessary, so be it. If a "not guilty" verdict was somehow obtained, fine; but the damage was already done. A family and finances had already been destroyed. Even with an acquittal, the government would pursue civil charges and a certain judgment. With this understanding, we will examine the next phase and all it presents—the trial.

It's a play upon a stage, perhaps life's biggest stage. Actors perform their roles and follow a loose script which only needs but a little improvisation. Nonetheless, the plot was as predictable as any of the prior performances at any federal court across the United States. There is the judge, clerk, bailiffs, stenographer, prosecutors, defense lawyers, jurors, and defendants. Some are protagonists; others are antagonists. Each was expected to perform. They had a specific role to play. From my vantage point, they had performed as expected thus far. This was their business. They were professionals.

I was not, however. I was not an actor. My life was not a business, or a play and I was not going to perform the role of the defendant. Obviously, my approach was an anomaly. Most did not view the court as I did. Most would not, even if they had the gumption, defy the force used to compel cooperation. The majority would not even perceive the fraud.

I am not advocating lawlessness. I am, however, seeking two noble aims, if not three. I hope to distinguish between true crimes and the questionable *crimes* for which so many Americans are imprisoned—mere infractions of black ink on white paper. I hope for a restoration of treasured fundamentals of freedom once coveted by our ancestors. Finally, I hope, because of a love of liberty, to relegate the Federal Government to its proper subservient role mandated in and by the Federal Constitution. As I shared with my wife, this was not about taxes; this struggle was about truth.

Consider for a moment the cases we viewed earlier. How did each man become the defendant? George Norris? By force. Kristen Everston? By force. Did Webb and Ingalls commit a crime? What of Gosin and Figueroa? Was it their intent to harm, which resulted in their compelled performance to act as defendants? Or did each man arrive on this stage to perform this assigned role by the sheer weight of the Federal Government and the judicial system? How did I arrive at this point at this time? To me the answer was rather simple. The agents and agencies failed to answer my question as to the law which required me to file a federal income tax return. They presumed I was what I had rebutted. Also, my defense lawyers refused to investigate the basics of my good faith belief—the tenets of which were sound and beyond dispute. They only had to dignify their roles and *perform* as advocates for the accused.

This point is important. Had the agencies or agents answered my question, I could and would have complied years ago. The fact is the government and prosecutor ignored my belief and arrogantly presumed jurisdiction. This is the main contention I had with my lawyers. If I had to be on this stage, largely engineered by a subplot of fraud and force, I would have had peace of mind if my legal team attacked a constitutional question which would have likely resulted in an acquittal.

Cargill and Harris, had they not reflexively regarded my belief as "frivolous," would have set a precedent-setting benchmark in the legal community. Sadly, they did what the government did. My lawyers presumed I was what I had refuted. This left me effectively defenseless as I faced Goliath on the very stage upon which I should never have been.

To prove this fact, I am going to pause at this point and introduce a second Federal Question (Appendix E) which I filed into the federal court two years after the conviction. This question is the same as the one posed to agents Biggs and Pompei. What law made me liable? Failure of the federal court to mandate that the Department of Justice answer this question would be telling; for it would be the third branch of our government to evade this issue. As with Cargill and Harris, there is no accountability when there is the direct and unequivocal rejection of accountability.

Just imagine a seasoned veteran like Cargill digging into the laws, regulations, and Supreme Court cases to construct a defense like the argument I provided in this Federal Question. Imagine the horror of the prosecutor as he faced the strength and soundness of a man's principles and belief, a belief the government ignored over an eight-year investigation. Imagine the amazement of jurors who suddenly realized their last twenty to fifty years of living was based upon a false premise—with the revelation that one could not be liable for the federal income tax, one could be outside the jurisdiction of the Federal Government for this excise. This argument, my belief, would have provided the adversarial testing the government's case deserved.

The weight of these considerations, the import of my belief, is staggering. By contrast, we should ask what my attorneys did. Other than *not* investigate my belief, how were their efforts ineffective and, quite frankly, destructive? This revelation will be provided shortly as the trial unfolds. However, before we continue, based upon my federal question, consider a defining point. If Cargill and Harris had argued my belief early in the proceeding, would the trial have ever occurred? Or would the judge have decided that his court did not have jurisdiction, that an American had a superior claim to his property, his life, and the Federal Government had none? Would he have confirmed what was undeniable and wholly neglected, that the federal United States Government was limited in scope after all, and I was outside of congressional taxing authority?

When Judge Moon began the formalities which set the trial in motion, he asked if each side was ready. I stood and addressed the court. I emphasized the private remedy I sent to the IRS. I stated,

> *I have another filing that I would like to tender as the grantor and beneficiary appearing by special appearance, which is the entire document sent to the Department of Treasury, Department of Internal Revenue, Renee Mitchell, which seeks the disposition and the ledger-to-ledger set-off for the liability in this case. And I do so now.*

Judge Moon responded, "All right. You can proffer it to the court. We will proceed." Moon did not care at all about my filing. He was there to conduct a trial. So I stated,

> *Judge Moon, I would like the record to reflect that I do not concede and I waive all benefits. I'm here by special appearance as the beneficiary in this case. And I demand, as I did on the 2nd of January, the disposition in this case. The trustees were fired for failure for specific performance, which is required under a Court of Equity. And the responsibility lies, I believe, at this court, as far as Judge Moon being the executor of this court, with the taxable termination and the liability for the securities in this case.*

Again, Judge Moon simply ignored my comments. He was moving toward the trial. When Judge Mood asked if I wanted to make an opening statement, I said,

> *I stand by my comments on the record earlier. I appear here specially as the beneficiary of [the IRS Trust] that has an equitable claim over the James... Johnson estate...*

I willingly concede that I was out of my element. Other than observing a tax trial years earlier, I had never experienced federal court. My experience and knowledge came from lower state courts or by reading or listening to others. However, I moved forward with the courage to engage the process. While most would default to the trite saying, "a man who represents himself has a fool for an attorney," I would suggest they are ill-informed and fearful reactionaries. Whether scarred in defeat or battle-tested in victory, until we experience, we will not appreciate redemption gained through perseverance.

The judge began with jury selection. The prosecution and the defense were to question a pool of people and determine a jury of twelve with two alternates. I was expected to participate. When the first group was escorted in, Moon explained the procedure to them. Then the prosecutor asked questions and silently noted his observations. When the judge deferred to me, I declined to engage the process. As unbelievable as this may sound, since I had rebutted the presumption and prima facie evidence of liability over a decade ago, I objected to being the defendant. In front of the potential jurors, I stated for the record that I was not the defendant, and the court had a remedy to discharge this matter through the IRS. The judge simply acknowledged my statement. I repeated this for the second set or jurors, as well as the third group. In the end, I did not select any of the jurors who decided my fate.

Noteworthy is that before the second group of potential jurors were brought in, I stood and asked a question of the court and prosecutor. I asked if either the court or the government filed a "Bid Bond" or "Performance Bond" into the case. What occurred was remarkable. Without a lengthy explanation as to what these bonds are, allow this to suffice. If there is credence to the idea the government trades court cases as securities, to guarantee the value of the securities from loss (which would result if the trial ended in an acquittal), the government secures a bid and performance bond, as if providing insurance. In theory, the rationale is perfectly plausible.

Judge Moon looked directly at me and stated he did not enter either of these bonds. I then turned my attention to the U. S. Attorney. Rather than answer the question, he stood and magnanimously explained to the court that I was asking for something based upon some "patriot mythology," some "mumbo jumbo" theory. I interrupted his answer and asked the court to direct him to respond to my query. The judge looked at Hogeboom with every expectation that he would and should. Once again, and very telling, Hogeboom rambled unresponsively. Meanwhile, the next group of jurors was at the door. Time was short. For a second time, I asked the court to direct the prosecutor to respond. Amazingly, this master wordsmith, with his ability to obfuscate, chose his words very carefully. "I did not personally enter such bonds into the case." I knew, as before, the integrity of the judicial process was relevant and whole only within its confines. While he answered the question, he also failed to disclose the truth. It was apparent; however, someone filed these bonds into the case; it just wasn't Hogeboom.

Did Hogeboom direct his subordinates to file these bonds once he completed them? Did his superior file these bonds as a matter of practice? He did answer with a limited scope, leaving no doubt that the bonds were viable. I looked at the judge and stated, "Let the record show the U. S. Attorney was unresponsive to my question." The answer given by Judge Moon was simple and direct while the prosecutor gave the court an explanation as his response. The judge knew of these bonds. He did not need a lecture from a federal prosecutor. Moreover, who was Hogeboom to suggest that Judge Moon did not know the nature of the question when Moon had replied directly? Instead of answering the first time, Hogeboom showed his understanding of the truth by evading an answer on the second attempt. He did not want to address the matter! Hogeboom finally offered a qualified *truth* which failed to address the concern. In hindsight, I wish I had pressed the issue. I wanted the truth. Consider the definition of "truth-seeker."

> ***Truth-seeker****—Someone who strives to reveal the truth (the trial lawyer should be a truth-seeker).* Black's Law Dictionary, 10th Edition

The following is the definition for "truth, the whole truth and nothing but the truth."

> ***truth, the whole truth, and nothing but the truth****—The words used in the common oath administered to a witness who is about to testify (do you swear or affirm that you shall tell the truth, the whole truth and nothing but the truth?) The purpose of the second part of the oath is to preclude the possibility of* ***suppressio veri,*** *the purpose of the third party is to preclude the possibility of* ***suggesto falsi****.* Ibid
>
> ***suppressio veri****—Suppression of the truth; an indirect lie; whether by words, conduct or artifice; a type of fraud.* Ibid.
>
> ***suggesto falsi****–A false representation or misleading suggestion.* Ibid

Granted, Hogeboom was not "under oath," but he was an officer of the court. We must acknowledge that the rules of the game of court permit him to be less than forthright, less than complete, less than truthful, and less than honorable. There is no doubt that had he answered the same question under oath—while he would have selected his words carefully, while he would have placed these words in an order and with such limitations as to offer a controlled complete truth—his response would have been different.

Before the third group of jurors entered, I addressed the court again. I had arranged for two pre-1933 silver dollars to be in court the day the trial began. I intended to employ whatever options were available to avoid this predicament. I attempted to pay the debt of any tax owed with lawful currency. There is a belief that House Joint Resolution 192 of June 5, 1933, made it impossible to pay debts. The Federal Reserve Note (U. S. dollar) was no longer backed by gold or silver (lawful currency). Any debt to be paid had to be done so with another *debt* instrument. Herein rests the problem. A debt cannot be paid with another debt instrument. Debt is merely exchanged when another debt instrument is used. Debt always exists unless paid with real money or discharged. My private remedy was an attempt to discharge a debt. With the two silver dollars present in court, I wanted to pay any liability with a hard asset currency for any pecuniary liability. Judge Moon denied this remedy. With his oath of office, was it unreasonable to have him uphold the Constitution and accept constitutional money? Or did the Constitution not apply because this was possibly an Article IV court and I was presumed to fall within the *State* of Washington, D. C. and the *United States* as a federal employee?

As is evident, I had been and remained determined to seek a solution for the charges I faced. I was resolved that a solution was available. Was I foolish? Was I reckless? Many would say so.

The jury of twelve was selected without my participation. I did not ask questions. I did not select or reject jurors. The jury was seated with input from the U. S. Attorney alone. Whatever advantage gained from my involvement was lost. To make matters worse, the jurors heard my claims that I was not the defendant. Their perception of me was already prejudiced. Who would deny that my words and actions adversely affected the proceedings thus far? Had I harmed what little chance existed for the jury deciding in my favor?

However, since I was not offering a defense, did the perceptions of the juror's matter? As far as I was concerned, the jury would not hear my good faith belief anyway; so, it did not matter what they believed. They would not hear the truth, the real facts. Furthermore, Hogeboom had already asked leading questions. For example, he asked if they could decide fairly in a case in which a "fellow citizen" had not filed taxes, especially when they knew of this obligation. The jurors now had to reconcile my denial that the court had jurisdiction over me. They would not learn the reason why I was no longer obligated to a federal income tax return that they, in fact, were legally required to honor.

The judge adjourned the trial for lunch. Opening statements would be made upon our return. Once the jurors received the instructions which governed their actions while away from court and were escorted out, I was handcuffed and taken to the elevator. Descending one floor, I was locked in a large cell with a brown bag lunch. I sat in solitude and waited. The random questions which weigh upon men in such situations were present in my mind. Am I doing the right thing? Is it possible to prevail? Should I pursue the truth at all costs? Will my efforts have any favorable impact? If justice is not equitable, why pay the price?

When the court reconvened, Judge Moon addressed some issues before the jury returned. When he acknowledged me, I held to my position; I was not the defendant—both the government and court did not have jurisdiction. The questions I had asked myself during the lunch changed nothing.

When the court asked the government to make an opening statement, Hogeboom's assistant spoke to the jury. What she offered was not unexpected. She stated that I had *knowingly* violated the tax laws with nefarious intent and circumvented my known legal duty. She stated that I refused to pay my bills, which included taxes, and deliberately obstructed the Federal Government and its investigation. She told the jury that I *intended* to dishonor what was in years past an annual ritual, the filing of a federal income tax return.

I viewed the opening statement as a sad indictment upon the legal profession, the judiciary, and America. Officials, who had never bothered to speak with me, maligned my reputation and motives, not to mention the truth. They didn't seek a just conclusion. The government wanted a conviction which would keep the populace in compliance.

From my position, I made repeated overtures to the opposition over the span of a decade for an answer to a simple question. Since my own attorneys were unwilling to answer or research this question, the conclusion I reached was unimpeachable. The question would never be answered, and men like me would be convicted to discourage others from asking it. The actors, those who recite their lines in an opening monologue before unwitting and ignorant jurors, who are a product of the entire system, jurors who would not discern for themselves, were doing exactly what was expected. The actors upon the stage of court were following an agenda scripted for a specific ending, the continued ignorance, apathy, and fear of the people. Since form, function, and rules dictate the operation of court, the government's representations were contrived and incomplete, and certainly not the "truth, the whole truth and nothing but the truth." Why? Officers of the court were not "truth-seekers."

Once the government finished its opening, the atmosphere was surreal. I sat in a state of disbelief. Her diatribe was pointed. A discriminating observer would not have failed to note her use of language. But where were these discriminating observers?

Even if I had waged a vigorous defense, it would have been nearly impossible to influence jurors who had lived with concrete beliefs for up to fifty years. They were products of their own limited history and education, a history and education they would project upon me, the supposed defendant. They were conditioned. The court was the conduit through which they would be guided to make a rather clinical decision in a classic tax case. Who would not argue the jury already believed I was guilty?

When the judge asked for my opening statement, I reiterated what I stated earlier. Moon nodded and proceeded to allow the prosecution to call its first witness. Sure, my posture was suicidal; I would not disagree. But I was not going to win anyway. As you learned in my Declaration (Appendix A), Cargill and Harris already stated I was a "U. S. person" and a "taxpayer" as defined in the tax code. They already stated I had a tax liability. Without a competent defense team behind me, I had no chance. With a 98% conviction rate, what I did made little to no difference. The system is designed for plea agreements. While the following analogy may seem extreme, my situation was no different than being shot in the head or forced to jump off a 1,000-foot cliff. My fate was sealed. As it stood, I refused to accept a plea and I would not go through a trial willingly, if only because legal counsel would not argue the element of jurisdiction.

Ironically, as happens in life, the totally unexpected occurs. Timing, the random dynamics of life and the evolving flux of human nature tend to influence a man's soul. The convergence of timing, life, and human nature were about to impact me in an unexpected way. My mother and some friends were in the gallery, obviously in disbelief. They knew nothing of tax law or what I believed. They did not take the time to research the law, much less question the idea of jurisdiction. The fact that they were as incredulous as the twelve jurors was not unexpected.

This battle was never fair or just. It was never meant to be so. My mother may as well have watched me in an arena with ten hungry lions and no exit. I may as well have faced ten Goliaths. No sling or stones would prevail against the formidable marshaled against me. What I realized years ago, and what my mother did not see, was the omnipotent Federal Government was not the primary foe. Beyond the force of government was the pervasive fear of the American people. The ominous presence of institutional arrogance thrived if only for the fear of an ignorant, apathetic, and submissive populace. If only my mother knew that I stood in truth and with integrity and without the need to battle Goliath. I did not have to fend against the beasts. I believed those who could not be stopped—which included complicit and ignorant defense lawyers—were without the authority to compel a man to be where he should not have been. No, those in the gallery and jury box did not see. They only saw what their worst nightmares could conjure. Those inside and outside court would never consider my beliefs. I was at the mercy of the merciless and observed by those without understanding.

During the recess, my mother and friends spoke. Based upon their conversation, she wrote a letter and encouraged me to offer a defense. Defend yourself was her cry to a son against the odds. As if I was not under an egregious amount of pressure already, the receipt of her plea was as unsettling as much as it was unexpected. This letter, handed to me by Cargill, caused me to question. While Hogeboom continued to ask questions of the first witness, I writhed in agony. I looked at the letter, my mother, and friends. I looked at the judge and back down at the table. Cargill, who sat to my right, knew I was struggling. In my mind and heart, I had a clear path to follow. Would I surrender?

General Thomas "Stonewall" Jackson once said, "You may be whatever you may resolve to be." As a former VMI cadet, I championed this sentiment. But, I was conflicted. Cargill pleaded with me to allow him to assert a *defense* on my behalf. I felt as if I were in a movie, with the protagonist caught in an unexpected dilemma so overpowering his world collapses under the weight of the decision he must make. With grave implications, which way would I go? What would I decide? Would I break under the pressure?

If there is any difference in the portrayal of this case and the others we viewed, one is the consideration of those who observed the trial. While they are part of the electorate, family and friends have a relationship with the man being prosecuted. Naturally, their influence is not inconsequential. My mother's letter reflects the import of this thought. I knew that I was doomed if I did not mount a defense and doomed if I did. I likened my situation as one who was kidnapped and threatened by the perpetrator. With the kidnappers having no credible claim to my life, any conditions for release would be a fraud. If I complied with his demands, the kidnapper would be granted legitimacy. Even the government does not overtly negotiate with terrorists. I was humbled that my mother asked me to do something, anything. I was about to make an irreversible decision. I collected my thoughts and wrote a brief statement. I was about to address those who had possession of my property, my body.

When the judge asked me if I had any questions for this witness, I rose to speak. What I was about to do would quiet the unsettled hearts and minds of those watching. With great reservation I stated,

> *I would like to correct a mistake. Reserving all rights and waiving none, I would like the Public Defender to make an opening statement and provide a defense.*

Did I capitulate? Was I out of integrity? Was I no longer congruent with my principles? Had I conceded defeat that was all but certain? I sat in a cloud of bewilderment, believing the enemy had not only won the case, but had vanquished me. Everything I believed to be true was dishonored. Was I a coward in retreat or did a grasp at the last straw?

Other defendants had secured victories in criminal tax cases. Vernie Kreuglin was acquitted of criminal tax charges. Her attorneys put on a vigorous defense. Tommy Cryer, a lawyer from Shreveport, Louisiana, defeated the IRS. I, on the other hand, had not "prepared." Cargill and Harris had assured that my good faith belief would not be aired. Anyone without context for my belief would have difficulty appreciating my struggle. This is why I have taken the effort to convey my thoughts. Ask the obvious question. When would you decide and stick to a course regardless of the outcome? If your child were abducted, would you endure until the bitter or better end? Would you pursue her until you found her smiling face, or, God forbid, her lifeless body? Would you do the same for a friend? For a stranger? How far would you fight for a noble cause without looking back?

George Norris was in his sixties when a rogue U. S. agency and U. S. Attorney stole his liberty, his very life. He was ruined financially. Should Norris have acquiesced as he eventually did? At what point do we, as a people, no longer prostrate our beings and no longer concede our souls to an authority originally designed to be our servant? When? I ask this question knowing I clothed myself with shame as I shunned my core beliefs; for I surrendered to the fraud and force. Is this not the very intent of force? Submission to the inevitable is sobering especially when one knows he has been defeated. The idea that I had no recourse was a tragedy, an utter travesty.

Cargill found himself in a situation he had never experienced. He was delivering an opening statement after the second government witness was excused. If the situation was not already untenable, the jury's perspective ensured as much. They must have viewed these events as pure absurdity. So, with the judge's approval, Cargill backtracked and gave his opening statement. He tried to create order out of chaos, but only within the integrity of court rules and his ABA Canons of Ethics. In short, he told the jurors that believed I did not have a liability to file. Yet, he offered nothing to support why I held this belief. He never told the jury the income tax is an excise tax predicated upon the election of a status and acceptance of federal benefits. He never told them that, since I had revoked and rescinded this taxable status and benefits and rejected the privilege that subjected one's "income" to taxation, I could not be liable. Cargill never equated the "voluntary" nature of subscribing to social security as the catalyst for this federal filing requirement which made it mandatory. He never argued the law! No. This is what Cargill told the jury.

> *He thinks that when the IRS and the Federal Government tell people that our tax system is a voluntary tax system—this is for example—that they cannot come to you then and say, "You must file taxes and you must pay taxes," because if it is voluntary, then you can't force someone to do it. He thinks that one's labor should not be subject to taxation.*

Do you see the conflict with Cargill's "representations" compared to what I shared earlier? Cargill was lying to the jury. He did not offer the truth, the whole truth, and nothing but the truth. He was not a truth-seeker. Cargill never articulated that if I no longer had a taxable status or subscribed to a federal privilege, my labor and earnings were no longer subject to the federal income tax. A tax upon someone like me would be a direct tax and would be unconstitutional unless handled in accordance with Apportionment.

Why did Cargill argue this line of reasoning instead of the truth? Clearly, he did not want to state that his client was outside of the jurisdiction of the Federal Government for the federal income tax. Was it really because he knew he would be sanctioned and fined? Or was he part of the collective effort to prevent a cogent argument which revealed the true nature of the federal income tax? Was Cargill part of a conspiracy? It was evident to me, had Cargill argued what I believed and explained my decisions and actions, which proved I was without the jurisdiction of the federal and legislative authority for this indirect excise, the jury would have had a reasonable basis to grant an acquittal.

Rather than do the right thing, rather than defend his client, Cargill told the jury,

Now, he stands here charged, as the court advised you, with four criminal charges; three counts of failing to file tax returns and one count of obstructing the IRS. And, quite honestly, if the question was whether he should have filed returns and whether he owes taxes to the Federal Government, the case would be over, done. Of course he does.

Cargill continued to poison the jurors with a twisted premise by stating:

And so that's what it comes down to: good faith. Did he act in good faith? Did he act willfully? Or in his obsession with the tax code—to put it bluntly—and I know he's not comfortable with me saying this, but is he misguided? Has he just made a mistake? And, that's, in the end, what you are going to have to decide.

Alas, have we reached the limits of the wisdom of a veteran defense lawyer who throws out that his client had a mere good faith, but cited no reason for that good faith, and who suggested rather directly that his client's good faith was an obsession and a mistake? Ironically, Cargill concluded his opening statement to the jury with,

He's - he's scared. Anyone in his position would be scared. Not because he's guilty—not because he feels guilty, but because he's afraid that you might make a mistake and find him guilty.

Unbelievable. Absolutely unbelievable. Perhaps you understand why I never wanted these kangaroo attorneys to represent me. I was not scared. As I stated in my 2255 Motion and Federal Questions, I had a sound argument and Cargill flatly refused to run with it. I was angry—not scared—angry that I was in this most unfortunate situation, to have a fear-laden legal representative who was more afraid of being fined for raising a credible jurisdictional claim than zealously defending me with the truth. I was angry because I was going to prison because of ineffective legal counsel.

AGENT BIGGS

The first witness that Cargill cross-examined was Internal Revenue Agent Robert Biggs, the government's main witness. Hogeboom had just accomplished two objectives when he questioned Biggs directly. He had Biggs assert at least five times that an agent must be able to speak with the taxpayer to acquire a sense of his tax liability, that if a taxpayer is not willing to speak, any agent's task is much more difficult. With this message, the jurors were automatically made to consider that Agent Biggs had to investigate at length and piece together a puzzle without assistance from me. This was an effective strategy. Hogeboom was able to convey the impression that I was uncooperative and unwilling to speak with Biggs, consequently, cost the government time and money. The second accomplishment Hogeboom achieved was to have Biggs admit that John Kotmair, my power of attorney, was not authorized to represent me before the IRS and the questions and assertions Kotmair posed were "frivolous." This reference allowed Hogeboom to assert that my belief was less than credible—whatever that belief happened to be.

These two accomplishments are extremely relevant since Cargill had an opportunity to refute the government's tactics and overall objectives. Cargill could have aggressively held Biggs to a completely juxtaposed perspective. Regrettably, Cargill did nothing of the sort. He never addressed these issues. Was Cargill to blame? He had from May until January to read Kotmair's letters. He was only standby counsel for two months. The discovery material was available for his review. He knew we were going to trial.

As a defense lawyer, Cargill was—at least I thought—expected to attack the government's theories. For example, since Cargill knew both Kotmair and I wrote to Biggs at least six times with simple questions which he refused to answer. Cargill could have rebutted the idea that I refused to speak with Biggs. I had communicated with Biggs directly. Cargill could have proved that Biggs refused to respond by asking:

> *How can you expect the "taxpayer" to respond, Mr. Biggs, when you refused to respond to his request for the law that required the filing of an income tax return?*
>
> *Didn't you refuse to answer the defendant's questions? Didn't you refuse to show him the legal authority under which you presumed to ask him for information regarding taxes that he believed he no longer owed? Didn't you refuse to offer the exact authority that would have informed the defendant to simply answer your queries and that you presumed you had the authority to do so? Didn't you presume that the defendant was obligated to respond?*
>
> *Mr. Biggs, is it possible that there are people in this country who are not liable to file a federal income tax return? Could it be, to whatever degree of probability, the defendant no longer had a responsibility to file a tax return and that you had an unfounded and untested belief to the contrary? Mr. Biggs, didn't the defendant send you and the Government a reason why he was no longer liable for filing a federal income tax return? Mr. Biggs, what was that reason? He certainly did not simply believe that he was no longer liable, did he?*

Yes, Mr. Cargill could have asked several questions. Consider the following:

> *Mr. Biggs, the Supreme Court, in* Federal Crop Insurance Corp, v. Merrill *stated that a citizen must guard against a federal agent exceeding his authority, if only because the agent may not know of his own limitations. Is it possible that you exceeded your authority? Was it not reasonable for the defendant to question your actions and decisions and that you may have acted "**ultra vires**?"*

Such queries would have placed Biggs on the defensive and given the jury every reason to believe I did not refuse to communicate with Biggs. Cargill could have established the foundation that, however unbelievable, I did not have a tax liability and I rebutted the presumption I was a "taxpayer" as defined in the tax code. These questions could have been asked without Cargill making a direct reference to a jurisdictional argument, a supposed violation of the Canons of Ethics of the ABA.

The significance of Kotmair's letters could have been more insightful with minimal effort. Cargill could have established the critical fact that Kotmair, with an Internal Revenue Number, was authorized to represent me. Had Cargill investigated the matter, which would have included reading Kotmair's letters, he would have learned Kotmair's ability to serve as power of attorney was not terminated until at least December 2004. Even Biggs testified he would have been required to speak with him.

> *If he had've—if he was qualified to do that, then I was required to then respond Mr. Kotmair and deal with Mr. Kotmair, and to not deal with Mr. Johnson directly.*

Cargill, armed with the basic fact that Kotmair was qualified after all, could have discredited Biggs and the government's case. He could have asked Biggs, "Why was Kotmair not qualified?" Biggs had already testified that:

> *The information came back from the manager and counsel that Mr. Kotmair did not qualify to represent Mr. Johnson as power of attorney.*

Cargill could have hammered Biggs with "Why? Why was Mr. Kotmair not qualified?" Biggs did not know. He was only told by his manager and counselor what he needed in order to proceed with his investigation and without bothering with a force such as Kotmair. Cargill was in the enviable position to ask Agent Biggs a powerful question.

> *Mr. Biggs, you already stated that you have handled some 600 investigations. Is it typical for you to run to your manager every time you receive a letter from a party with power of attorney for another? Or is there a standard protocol by which you can confirm that the representative's number is current and that he is qualified? For example, does the agency have a database that shows the numbers that have been issued and their status? Wouldn't it be cumbersome for all agents to ask the "manager" to verify each number? Mr. Biggs, why would you consult your manager and counsel for such a routine matter?*

We don't know how Biggs would have answered; but we know these queries could have been asked. This line of questioning would have been a perfect set up for the following:

> *Mr. Biggs, at what point was Mr. Kotmair not qualified to represent the defendant? Are you aware of the date that Mr. Kotmair was no longer qualified? Would you have been required to communicate with Kotmair if the number had been active through December of 2004? Mr. Biggs were you aware that Mr. Kotmair was qualified until December 2004, which meant that you were required to communicate with him and not Mr. Johnson? After hundreds of investigations since 1993, isn't it true that you sought cover from your manager and counsel because you did not want to answer Kotmair's questions? Isn't it true that you never saw such questions in the past, questions that challenged your authority? Isn't it true that you were confronted with a simple question as to Mr. Johnson's presumed liability and you just did not want to respond? Mr. Biggs, since Kotmair was qualified to represent Mr. Johnson up to December 2004, what law would you have cited as your authority to investigate the defendant? What would you have offered as the law that required Mr. Johnson to file a federal income tax return?*

Questions such as these would have served an extremely important purpose. These questions and Biggs' subsequent answers would have conveyed to the jury that Biggs, the investigating agent, was not forthcoming in his testimony. Consider the obvious. Biggs stated to Hogeboom, "the information I got back from the manager and counsel." This seemingly generalized representation paints the picture that Biggs hid behind "information" and his superiors. The "information" excused him from offering any substantive official response to legitimate queries which were worthy of answers. Biggs avoided what was required of him (refer to the Merrill case) so he could proceed with the presumption that he had authority without further investigation. He presumed I was liable to comply with his requests and the law. This occurred because Cargill never once challenged the government's assertion that Kotmair was not qualified.

Cargill's failure was equally transparent concerning Biggs' "frivolous arguments" testimony. Since the legal defense team has a responsibility to defend, naturally, one would expect any defense lawyer would attempt to destroy the opposition's arguments whenever possible. Cargill should have attacked Biggs' continued investigative ploys, ploys that allowed him to avoid communicating with Kotmair. Cargill should have challenged whether Kotmair's letters were in anyway frivolous. Let me explain.

Cargill had the perfect opportunity to argue that Kotmair was qualified as of July 2004 and Biggs simply did not want to respond. Why? Because the agency did not want Biggs to respond. Kotmair's letters were obviously not something Biggs or the IRS frequently saw; but the letters were professional and reasonable. Thus, Biggs should have simply confirmed Kotmair's status and replied.

We shall take the essence of Biggs' avoidance scheme and apply it to the "frivolous argument" directly. After Biggs testified that Kotmair "did not qualify to represent Mr. Johnson as power of attorney…" Biggs stated:

> *And they also advised me that the IRS has published a response to frivolous arguments and I should attach that, because Mr. Kotmair's, you know, letter did raise some issues, and that would have been the official IRS response to it.*

Cargill, lawyer for the defendant, who had access to Kotmair's letters, letters discussed briefly with his client in the summer of 2012, heard Biggs' testimony. Cargill then heard Hogeboom ask Biggs the following question.

> *And what was the (if you recall), what part of it was considered to be frivolous by the arguments being made?*

Biggs responded, "The part of the IRS response or the part…"

This is when Hogeboom interrupted and said, "Yes, the IRS considered to be frivolous."

Now watch carefully; the next exchange is important. Biggs replied, "The - I'm sorry. You mean Mr. Kotmair's frivolous -"

Then Hogeboom, to get their rehearsed testimony straight, said, "Yes, Mr. Kotmair's."

Biggs stated, "I would have to read back. It was advice I got from counsel."

The questions and answers continued until Hogeboom asked, "Okay. And then, in particular, this section there, did you find that to be somewhat unique, beginning 'Finally?'"

Biggs said, "It was unusual to me, yes."

Hogeboom came back with, "Had you ever received that type of response before?"

Biggs, "No, I had not."

Hogeboom, "When you talked to counsel, was there anything that you were doing outside of what you had determined to be your authority?"

Biggs, "Oh, absolutely not, no."

Agents Biggs had received questions from Kotmair which challenged his authority. Biggs had received questions from Kotmair which asked for the law that required me to file a tax return. Yes, Biggs received what? Questions. That's right. Two questions. These questions were in no way "frivolous."

Yet, Cargill was silent.

Had Cargill been effective, he would have attacked Biggs on this grave matter.

> *Mr. Biggs, since you avoided answering Kotmair's letters, because he was supposedly not qualified, isn't it true that you avoided legitimate questions that were not frivolous? Did Kotmair or Johnson pose a frivolous position or did they ask legitimate questions?*
>
> *Were the questions frivolous? Why were the questions frivolous? Mr. Biggs, can questions regarding your authority or a citizen's tax filing obligations be deemed frivolous? Are questions asked in good faith frivolous?*

Cargill could have continued with the following.

- *Mr. Biggs, if Mr. Kotmair was not qualified to represent Mr. Johnson, why did you bother to address the "frivolous" nature of Kotmair's questions?*
- *Did you respond in this manner <u>because you did not want to answer the questions, questions</u> which challenged your authority?*

- *Is it because you did not want to respond as to the law that made Mr. Johnson liable to file a return?*
- *Mr. Biggs, isn't it true that you never asked your manager or counsel as to how or why Kotmair's questions were frivolous?*
- *Wasn't it your manager and counsel who proffered the unsolicited advice that you send the IRS publication about the "frivolous arguments?"*

Obviously, Biggs would have been in a more difficult position had he been required to answer these questions. Accountability to the truth before the jury would have been apparent if Cargill had asked Biggs the following:

- *Mr. Biggs, were the questions that Kotmair asked frivolous? Or were the questions so fundamentally sound, you did not want to answer them?*
- *Didn't you simply ignore the questions by presuming Mr. Johnson was a taxpayer and you had the power to investigate and request information?*
- *Mr. Biggs, you stated, "that would have been the official response to it." Does the word "it" refer to the "issues" Kotmair raised?*
- *Isn't it true that, when one asks a valid question, based upon the "advice" you received from counsel, the IRS will consider it "frivolous" and send the official IRS publication?*
- *Doesn't this practice allow the IRS and agents, such as you, to avoid accountability? To avoid providing answers to reasonable questions?*
- *Mr. Biggs, isn't it true that if you or the agency are not required to answer such basic questions then no answer would ever be given?*
- *Isn't it true that if you or the agency were not required to answer such basic queries, a citizen will effectively have no recourse, that under the threat of force, they would have to respond or face imprisonment?*
- *Isn't this tantamount to ignoring Kotmair's and the defendant's letters?*
- *If neither you nor the agency responds, no one gets answers, correct?*
- *They can expect nothing but the brunt of an unwarranted investigation?*

Cargill could have fully vetted Kotmair's letters with Agent Biggs.

- *Mr. Biggs, let's take a look at Kotmair's letter, Government exhibit 5-2. Mr. Kotmair asks, "Mr. Biggs, what issues are you referring to?"*
- *Kotmair never posed any issues, did he? In his letter dated August 24, 2004, Kotmair asked you to provide the requirement and your authority to make that determination and your delegation of authority authorizing you to act. Based upon this content, is there anything frivolous?*
- *Do you not see that if no one is able to make these requests, your authority and the authority of the agency can never be challenged?*
- *Then, with respect to the word "finally," highlighted by Mr. Hogeboom, Kotmair states, in part, "The problems we are trying to resolve are based upon the IRS failure and/or refusal to obey and apply those laws as Congress intended." As you confirm in your letter, the Congress enacts the tax laws, and in Subtitle A, Congress imposed an income tax and made a class of persons liable for the payment of that tax." Mr. Kotmair then concluded that Mr. Johnson was not within that class. Mr. Biggs, is this a frivolous conclusion or is it a legal position of merit which requires an equally worthy response?*

Yes, Cargill could have underscored the failure of Biggs and the agency to deal constructively with all questions and requests.

Consider the potential questions Cargill could have asked Biggs.

- *Didn't Mr. Hogeboom ask if you did anything outside of what you had determined to be your authority?*
- *Isn't the issue that you were the one who was outside of the parameters of the lawful authority established by the agency and Congress?*
- *You were the investigating agent, correct? Do you know whether you were outside any authority as it relates to the defendant's circumstances?*
- *Is it possible that you, in any way, exceeded your authority and both Kotmair and Johnson asked you to, therefore, cite that authority?*
- *Isn't it true that by offering a publication about frivolous arguments, you effectively avoided responding to this primary question?*
- *Mr. Biggs, your testimony is, regarding what was frivolous in Kotmair's letters, "I would have to read back. It was the advice I got from counsel."*
- *Did you ask your manager and counsel in writing or verbally?*
- *Is your reference to counsel your legal counsel?*
- *Were you speaking with a lawyer who represented the agency?*

We will conclude Cargill's hypothetical questioning.

- *Now, Mr. Biggs, whether you must think back or read back, isn't it true counsel never cited anything specific in Kotmair's letters as frivolous?*
- *Isn't it true counsel simply gave advice to send the publication of frivolous arguments to avoid the substance of Kotmair's words?*
- *Isn't it true that, by sending the publication, neither you nor the agency had to respond to legitimate concerns, if only because both the agency and you answered unresponsively with a publication that was unresponsive and wholly frivolous?*
- *Isn't it true you presumed that both your authority and Mr. Johnson's liability existed while exceeding your authority and ignoring Mr. Johnson's lack of a liability?*
- *Doesn't your failure to answer such questions equal the failure of the IRS Commissioner, the Department of Justice, Congressman Wolf, and Mr. Johnson's elected representatives in the Senate to answer these questions?*
- *Finally, Mr. Biggs, does Mr. Johnson have a right to ask these questions? Does he have a right to receive a non-frivolous response from you?*
- *Does he have the right for answers to his non- frivolous questions and concerns before he communicates with you?*

What would the jury have concluded with such direct queries from a defense lawyer fighting for his client? Cargill would not have argued a jurisdictional claim that would have resulted in sanctions. He would have simply held the witness and government to account for its representations in a court of law. Cargill would have provided the adversarial testing the government's case deserved.

Tragically, Cargill's one crucial decision—to avoid sanctions that would never have occurred in the first place—left him unprepared for this trial in every respect. As such, he was incapable of making strategic decisions or weighing tactical options that would have defeated the government's case. The jury, as witnessed with Biggs, did not see a disparity between the opposing parties. As evident with Cargill's opening statement, they saw agreement. This will become even more pronounced as the trial unfolds. As

Hogeboom proceeded to develop his argument with a string of witnesses, Cargill was—and remained—inconsequential.

Since Cargill did not depose any of the government's witnesses, he was unprepared for cross-examination. I watched as Hogeboom selectively queried each of his witnesses for a very limited objective. As with the other ten cases, the prosecution had a narrow focus. Hogeboom wanted to offer the jury only what would result in a conviction. The truth had no relevance.

Consider the Norris case. The government did not care that Norris did not sell illegal orchids. The prosecutor knew Norris did not sell illegal orchids. The prosecutor's objective was predetermined. He wanted to present the unfounded argument with ample evidence which could be squared with the *letter* of the law. If done satisfactorily, the jury could do nothing less than place the proverbial round peg into the round hole. In an extra-legal sense, this is how federal prosecutors define "truth-seeker." With a finite understanding, the jurors determined the "facts" which proved Norris was guilty, if only in a strict legal sense. He became a criminal with the clinical application of the codes by a compliant jury. When the judge tells the jurors of the law, it is the final information they receive besides the jury instructions. The jury is left with little doubt that the *facts* correlate with the law.

The impact from the witnesses in the Norris case or my case are significant, with the understanding that the smallest advantage, the smallest of incomplete truths which secure that advantage, leads to the injustice necessary to attain, so called, *justice*.

Even if Cargill had prepared for each witness, it would not necessarily have negated the perceived legitimacy of any given response from a witness. For example, one witness stated that I took a cruise to an "offshore" venue to attend a seminar which promoted and sold tax avoidance products. I never did so. I never traveled farther than just across the border of the U. S. into Canada and Mexico back in the 1980s. Yet, the witness was certain we met in Cancun. What is the jury to believe—my testimony that I had never made the trip?

Another witness claimed I owned rental property, and I collected rent, but never gave a receipt. The truth is I managed the building, and the witness was a tenant that was indigent. The owner allowed the witness and her desperate boyfriend to live there while they worked through their financial problems. She did not disclose that she lived rent free for eighteen months of her "lease" and would not have received a receipt. The prosecutor and Cargill did not ask her why she no longer lived at the property. They did not have her testify that she was evicted in December, the month prior to trial. No. Hogeboom targeted information which served his agenda, the truth be damned.

Another witness, Mark Dreyer, a man I knew from church, a recent acquaintance from a mutual friend who suggested Dreyer would be a worthy tenant, testified that I was his landlord. He said that I used this title to describe myself. He lied. He knew I was not the owner of the property. He knew I was under a criminal investigation. Why would a seemingly reasonable man misrepresent the truth? Dreyer, who would, in jest, remark that I was his landlord, knew why I deliberately corrected him and asked that he not refer me in this way. This was important to me—because it was the truth—and I knew such characterizations could prove injurious. Why would I promote myself as something or somebody I was not while under a criminal probe?

The truth is that, months before trial, Dreyer leased the property from the owner directly. When on the stand and testifying against me, he was the landlord. He was the one whose name was on court documents which secured the eviction of the woman who testified that I never gave a receipt. Yes, Hogeboom did not care for such incidentals, the complete truth; and Cargill, the legal advocate who rejected my one belief, never availed himself to such inconsistencies.

After I was convicted and sentenced, months after I was in prison, Dreyer sent me a letter in which he said, "I know you hate me." Why would he offer such a remark? Why would I hate him? If he told the truth, there would be no reason to hate. Was Dreyer offering an apology? Was he admitting he lied? He knew he did wrong, and this was his way of expressing this admission. Such is the nature of our revered justice system. Two separate factions, prosecution, and defense, elicit the incomplete and parlay it into the *truth*. Both camps seek to convey *facts* to an audience that will determine the real *facts, facts* as they perceive them. This requires the prosecutor to dismiss veracity while coloring the real facts. Only a tainted truth scales with and conforms to his perception of the crime.

Granted, many a defense lawyer has the same objective—to shape strains of truth which "serve the end of justice." What is a jury to do? Jurors may not realize this subtle gamesmanship. They may not perceive the nuanced. It occurred to me that there was a gradual drawing of jurors' collective conscience into the fraudulent, as one would pull a kite through the various and shifting winds. And there I sat. I had no lawyer "shaping" any truth; no, Cargill was advocating a lie; he had no need to counter Hogeboom's agenda.

Hogeboom built an argument piece by piece. He crafted the idea that I criminally failed to pay taxes and obstructed an investigation. It did not matter to him that I had done neither. Of prime importance was his assertion that I had done so. He then cultivated these thoughts with half-truths and untruths from testimony. Hogeboom used the technique of repetition mastered by most lawyers. He repeated these facts after he already told the jury what he wanted them to hear. He then summarized what he told them. As I observed the jurors, I imagined how easy it would be for them to determine my guilt, even if Cargill had prepared a strong defense.

Why would it be easy to convict? Simply because the prosecution told them I committed the crimes. This is where it begins. The authority and influence of the Federal Government has an impact on people. Also, the jurors paid their "income" taxes. Both the prosecutor and defense lawyer had already stated the absurdity of not filing tax returns. Cargill already conceded that we all owe taxes, and I believed in good faith I had no liability. With the prosecution's argument and with witnesses insinuating a corrupt intent and questionable actions, it was easy to render a verdict of guilt.

How does a jury reconcile beliefs contrary to their own? How do they overcome their cognitive dissonance? How do they overcome such profound personal prejudice supported by strong prosecutorial arguments and slanted testimony with no counter by the defense? The jury would not believe a man who did not do exactly what was expected of all Americans. The jury would not believe otherwise unless a strong defense team overcame the prejudice of their own making and defeated maligned testimony.

My Testimony

When Hogeboom concluded direct examination of his witnesses, when he entered his *evidence*, the defense presented its case. Did Cargill have a case? Did Cargill have an argument? No. But he did have one witness. Cargill had one witness because he had no others. He was not prepared to offer other witnesses. His one witness was me.

Cargill told me that my objective was to answer each question simply and honestly. So, with no preparation, we were left with what amounted to a tap dance. Cargill said they would ask about my background, family, schooling, and work history. He said the goal was to make me likable to the jurors. I needed to appear credible, someone they could believe. "Ah, yes," I remarked to myself. "What are they to believe when they are not able to hear exactly what I believe?" Meanwhile, without Cargill's knowledge, I intended to inject answers which hinted if not spoke directly to the question of jurisdiction. I would attempt to explain to an ignorant jury that the government never had authority to require me to file a federal tax return in the first place.

After establishing some historical context of my past, Harris asked questions directly related to my understanding of tax law. I asserted firmly that the tax code was constitutional but misapplied in my circumstances. When asked how and why I formed this belief, I cited the Constitution of the United States. I wanted to explain how this critical document and its taxing provisions granted the Federal Government limited taxing powers. It was at this point that Judge Moon abruptly interrupted my testimony and asked why this was relevant and what this had to do with the 16th Amendment. I was shocked. Without making a direct reference that I was without congressional taxing authority, questions about the taxing powers of the Constitution were crucial. Why did Moon intervene and introduce the income tax amendment? The 16th amendment had little to no significance in my circumstances. I looked at Harris and saw she had no intention to object to the Moon's decision other than to state that she would have me focus.

The judge was accelerating my testimony to where he believed it should go—to the 16th Amendment—which he believed granted Congress the authority to tax all incomes "from whatever source derived." He wanted me to address why I was not liable under this law. Harris took me to that law. It was clear that Moon and Harris were ignorant or deliberately indifferent as to the historical context of the 16th Amendment. They willingly allowed for the presumption that I was liable under this amendment. Harris resigned herself to the tone that Moon established. She went directly to the 16th Amendment.

I answered that the 16th Amendment did not grant Congress any new taxing powers. When Harris asked me to explain, I referred to a Supreme Court case, Stanton v. Baltic Mining Company. This court case confirmed that Congress did not receive additional taxing powers. To emphasize this point, I wanted to explain that "income" had a specific definition. Income had to be derived from, severed from capital, labor, or both combined. I wanted to establish a jurisdictional distinction. If one accepted a federal status or benefits, it was only then that his earnings were subject to excise. Other than the acceptance of a federal status or privilege, his earnings were not *income* under the 16th Amendment.

Supreme Court cases are considered settled law unless and until a future court or Congress alters a decision. The Stanton case, among others, was essential to my explanation. I had to explain the limited powers of Congress and that *income* was not as we understood and could not include a man's earnings, that is, until he willingly became liable. Unfortunately, just as with my response with the Constitution, Judge Moon interrupted again. He looked down from his bench and asked firmly, "Were you running a mine?" I was in disbelief. I wondered if he sought to prevent any reference to a jurisdictional claim.

What was happening? There was no need for an aggressive U. S. Attorney given how Moon effectively prosecuted the case. Moon's posture confirmed the court's complicity with the legal system. Even if Moon were completely oblivious to the truth of the 16th Amendment, he was a part of the problem. Even if he believed he was being fair and impartial, he, even if unwittingly, was the antithesis. If defeat and submission were his goals, his contributed to this end. I was effectively denied the opportunity to discuss cases which would have confirmed and explained my good faith belief. Meanwhile, Harris stood at the podium like a deer in the headlights. **She never said a word**.

To say I was bewildered was an understatement. I could not believe what was developing. In the context of a fair trial, these actions and decisions defied what I expected. Why did Moon decide so? What were his responsibilities? How did he determine what he did or did not do? To say or not say? To allow or not allow? Was he an impartial arbiter, an indifferent referee between two opposing parties? We lay people may easily conclude the obvious, at least what is obvious to us. We would expect Moon to be fair. This was his role within this adversarial process. Yet, he was objecting in a manner I would have expected of Hogeboom.

I was under no illusions about the unjust nature of American justice; but Moon's interference was unexpected. When he interrupted for the second time, I said in a near-whispered tone, "I see how this is going to be." It occurred to me that a federal judge would prevent any oblique reference to my jurisdictional claim—my good faith belief.

Did Moon have an agenda? What were his psychological and emotional motivations? Since he had an oath to support and defend the Constitution, why deny a question and an answer which addressed the constitutional limits of Congress to tax or not tax? Or did Moon want to prevent the possibility of the jurors knowing Congress could only tax in accord with the direct and indirect taxing clauses, which would include the acceptance of a federally excisable status or privilege? These taxing clauses, which are as valid today as they were one hundred years ago, confirm the limited purpose of the 16th Amendment. Is this why Moon stopped me from explaining the relevance of Stanton? He knew this case validated the constraints of Congress and the settled definition of the term *income*. If he didn't know, I was a victim of judicial ignorance, apathy, and arrogance.

Allow me to beat this issue to death. Did Judge Moon intend to thwart the jury from understanding that the 16th Amendment concerned only *income* "from whatever source derived?" Or did he believe all *income* and "all sources" were subject to the 16th Amendment? Such a position would contradict the fact that congressional taxing power was not enhanced with its passage. This is what Stanton represented—the truth. With a reasonable explanation, the jury would have known *income* was something specific and legally within reach of congressional authority by and through the indirect taxing clause of the Constitution and only this clause. They would have realized that my revocation of a federal status and benefits prevented my earnings from being considered *income* subject to excise and no longer from a source within congressional authority.

Why did Moon ask if I was running a mine? Of all questions, why this one? He already knew the answer. Moreover, does Stanton apply only to mines, miners, and mining operations? Of course not. This is why his question is fallacious or even frivolous. Supreme Court cases have universal application. Court cases apply across professions, to life, and humanity, with the import of judicial decisions resting upon the lucidity of universal wisdom as it relates to the operation of law. Moon had to know of the inherent worth of Stanton and its credence for issues relating to taxes, specifically as to what and who may be taxed and why.

Moon's interference was a grave injustice. He prevented me from explaining further that the Stanton decision supported the idea that mines could not be taxed as a traditional business. They jury did not hear that a mine had a limited repository of ore, like a man having a finite number of days to labor. They did not hear the argument that if a man did not want to pay an excise by election of a federal status or acceptance of federal benefits, his entire repository of time, labor, and resulting limited earnings were his alone. This meant, and this brings the Constitution and congressional authority into the discussion again, the jury did not hear that one who did not have the requisite federal status or did not subscribe to federal benefits could not be taxed. Such a tax would be a direct tax and would, therefore, be unconstitutional.

If the mining operation could not be taxed, why would a man, not beholden to the

Federal Government for an excise, be taxed? Without ore, a mine ceases to exist. Without time, a man's life ends. Moon prevented me from explaining that man uses his time for his survival and his earnings are not subject to excise unless by election.

Just as with a mine, whereby the taxation of ore would be a direct tax on property—and unconstitutional—the same applies to a man's life and earnings. How would the jury understand this unless I explained Stanton and the application of the taxing clauses of the Constitution? The operation of law is not so much specific as it is universal. Be it the definition of *income*, the taxing powers of Congress, or the concept of property, the scope of Supreme Court cases is broadly applied. Would it be unreasonable to conclude that Moon's interruption was for dubious intent or sourced in his raw ignorance of the law? Do we not see that, but for his interruption and Harris' failure to object, the jury did not hear any semblance of the explanation you just read?

Moon's behavior plainly represents judicial arrogance, if not judicial *ignorance*. He condemned a man's explanation and belief before each could be developed and fully expressed to the jury. Just as the judge encouraged Norris to make lemonade, Moon was equal, if not greater, in his disregard. Moon prevented answers designed to not only make lemonade, but lemon meringue pie. Moon's disruptions ensured only rotten lemons would remain. If Moon's decisions may be perceived as fair, we are in a far more difficult state than previously considered. The concept of fairness, as we learned earlier, should be guided by what is favorable to the *taxpayer* or the defendant when there is confusion. My confusion stemmed from a less than impartial judge who stymied an attempt to express a coherent and valid argument with one of the most difficult of subjects, taxes.

Moon's decisions reinforced why I did not want to "fight" within their legal system. I was already there under threat, coercion, and duress. Nothing I stated, questioned, or submitted was effective. Moon denied me the chance to explain the truth of the tax laws as I *believed* they applied in my circumstances. The arrogance of the judge was unquestionable. These federal jurists have a lifetime appointment. Are they so enamored with their office and powers that they are disassociated with the common man and truth? A judge's elevated status causes me to consider another motive for the legal system, other than truth and justice. I entertained that a financial incentive motivates the parties, including the judge. Such an incentive would further the institutional arrogance which casts an unjust influence over a trial. Would it be unfair to ask what the judge stood to gain financially from my conviction?

Unless my public defenders were disingenuous, they could not believe the judge prevented me from testifying. Yet, when I asked why they did not object, they summarily dismissed my concerns. "Why not object and preserve any possibility of appeal?" I asked. They were not interested in answering and flatly ignored the query. They were more concerned that I had not responded to their questions effectively. Cargill and Harris deflected my concerns by citing my "mistake." I replied that I had told the truth in the best manner I could under the circumstances.

CROSS-EXAMINATION

Harris questioned me on the stand for no more than forty-five minutes. I was then cross-examined by Hogeboom. He asked queries tied to doubt. He wanted to eliminate the appearance of truth which, in anyway, rebutted his *truth*. Hogeboom was his typical contentious self. He was condescending. He treated me in a hostile manner. He obviously wanted to unsettle me, to agitate and frustrate. He steered me to answers with which I did not agree. This would create the appearance that I was confrontational and rigid. Hogeboom introduced issues with no relevance to the charges. Everything he did was with purpose. Hogeboom wanted me to be unbelievable.

Let me illustrate by sharing that Hogeboom introduced a child support issue into the case. If only for the eight-year criminal investigation and the subsequent financial impact, I had fallen behind with payments. To their credit, Cargill and Harris objected. The prosecutor wanted to discredit me as one who would not pay his obligations. He stated I would not provide for my own children much less pay taxes. He challenged my character so the jury would believe the moral turpitude he intended to imply.

The facts, never conveyed to the jury, were that I had superior credit and never had missed a payment until the IRS investigation reached critical mass. As proof, in 2007, I received a "no doc" loan for two mortgages. The bank did not require me to provide tax returns, income verification, or bank statements—nothing like a conventional loan. My reputation was enough. The jury was not told that Biggs' failure to answer my one question would have ended the investigation and the financial demise. They did not hear that the one child support issue was not reflective of my past, my character, or beliefs about taxes.

More importantly, Cargill did not argue that if one did not owe a federal income tax, there would be no tax bill to satisfy. He should have exposed Hogeboom's disingenuous representations. To the contrary, since Cargill advocated that I was required to pay a tax, he did not express the idea that my character was reflected in my inordinate challenge to stand on principle and confront the feared IRS and an all-powerful government.

Regrettably, Judge Moon agreed with the ridiculous notion that a one-time child support issue was not prejudicial. He allowed this evidence for its "probative value." Moon, who also presumed I had a tax liability, allowed the jury to know that he equated a failure to pay a tax as the same as my failure to feed my children. In a sidebar discussion with the attorneys, he opined that if the defendant is not prepared to provide for his family, he won't pay his income taxes.

Like the prosecutors in the other cases, any "good" prosecutor will stoop to the absurd to win the game of court. The absurdity continued with Hogeboom's cross-examination. Hogeboom asked about John Kotmair, my power of attorney.

"Do you know what happened to Mr. Kotmair?"

"As far as what?" I replied.

Hogeboom asked, "As far as the help he was giving other taxpayers. What was the end result of that help?"

"I wasn't aware particularly of any given case, no." This was my truthful response.

What was Hogeboom trying to accomplish? What did he want the jury to understand? Notice, he stated that Kotmair helped taxpayers. Notice, Hogeboom refers to "the end result of that help." First, Kotmair did not help taxpayers. He and the Save-a-Patriot-Fellowship helped those who were *not* taxpayers. Kotmair studied the law. He understood what Hogeboom did not know and refused to understand. Why was Hogeboom questioning me in this manner?

Hogeboom then asked, "You weren't aware of him doing time in prison for tax evasion?"

"Are you talking about him? I thought you said helping others?" I asked.

Then Hogeboom admits, "Yes, himself."

Let's analyze this exchange. Hogeboom knew Kotmair did not go to prison for helping others, "the end result." He knew Kotmair went to prison several decades ago for failing to file income tax returns. Hogeboom knew Kotmair formed the Save-A-Patriot-

Fellowship, an education and advocacy group, to help people understand the law and their rights. Hogeboom knew the Federal Government had been trying for years to shut Kotmair's operation down. This is what the government does. It destroys truth-seekers.

We have a federal prosecutor in Hogeboom who refused to represent the truth, the whole truth, and nothing but the truth to the jury. He lied. He perpetrated the fraud which began with Agent Biggs' failure to provide the truthful answers to Kotmair in 2004. Hogeboom created the impression that Kotmair spent time in prison for helping *taxpayers* and now he was helping me. Did Hogeboom's intent as a public official or officer of the court reflect the truth? Was he a *truth-seeker*?

Quite telling, Cargill just sat there. He never accounted for Hogeboom's manipulation of the truth. Why? Hogeboom and Cargill were members of a brotherhood, a fraternity, a class which protected themselves, just like the "blue line" of police officers. Cargill would not dare accuse Hogeboom of playing with the truth. Secondly, during our private conversations in the summer, Cargill asked me why I ever sought help from the likes of Kotmair. Cargill was in disbelief. "He doesn't file tax returns. He went to prison for not filing tax returns," Cargill exclaimed. I looked at Cargill and Harris and said, "Kotmair knows the law." Yet, they did not care. Cargill's intent was clear. He impugned me for associating with Kotmair.

Hogeboom's distortion of the truth was not an isolated event. He did it consistently throughout his questioning. With his untruths and subsequent character assassination, the jury formed an impression. I will share two more examples.

Hogeboom asked, "How did you travel up and down 81?"

"In a car." I replied.

"A car? Okay. Were the roads maintained there? Were they paved?"

I responded, "There's an excise tax on gasoline."

"And did they have police officers?"

"Sure, and that's—it is by revenue collected from the state or the Federal Government by means of whatever excise tax collected."

Hogeboom eventually asked, "Now, when you were renting property, did you rely on fire and police protection?"

I replied, "I don't know that relying—or renting property has anything to do with relying on them. The property taxes were paid, if that's your—if that's the point."

Hogeboom continued. "I mean, there's other things besides—the property tax doesn't cover all public services, does it?"

There are two critical points to Hogeboom's posture. First, Hogeboom, if he believed his questions were appropriate, was woefully ignorant of basic tax law. Second, if his intent was to craft the *truth* so the jurors would receive the impression that I was benefiting from several services at the local, state, and federal level without paying for them—whether any of the jurors understood fundamental tax law—Hogeboom re-created that *truth*. He was abusing and misusing his office. He lied again. He perpetrated the fraud which began with Biggs in 2004.

This is an important issue. Excise taxes are specific exactions collected at the local, state, and federal levels of government. They are collected for a particular reason or for general revenue purposes. The federal "income tax" is supposedly collected for the purpose of paying the interest on the national debt. Social security benefits are paid for by specific excise. Pointedly, a man's payment of the "income tax" or FICA tax has nothing to do with paved roads, fire protection, trash collection, and other services. Hogeboom's ploy created the appearance this was so. He preyed upon the known ignorance and prejudice of the jurors. He wanted the jurors to conclude that I was a leech sucking in the benefits of society without paying the costs. The truth was that I paid for all services. The truth was that since I did not have a federal status and was not obligated for the income tax or federal benefits subject to excise. I did not pay those particular taxes.

My intentions were truthful and congruent with the law. Hogeboom did everything to dissuade the jury from perceiving this possibility. His intent was corrupt and dishonest. His ignorance and motivation were highlighted by his legal posturing capped with this question; "Now, isn't it true not only did you deliberately revoke your social security number, you also deliberately evaded your tax liability?"

Notice how he made the implication that revoking social security is illegal. Notice how he implies a "tax liability" is *disassociated* with social security.

Permit me to conclude this section by answering Hogeboom hypothetically:

> *Mr. Hogeboom, notwithstanding your willful ignorance and illegal and unconstitutional enforcement of federal excise tax laws, notwithstanding your deliberate intent to mislead the American people by perpetrating a fraud, especially upon jurors, people who are equally uninformed about basic tax law, I would like to state that I revoked any federal status I once elected under a voluntary basis and I revoked and rescinded the use of any federal benefits which once made me liable for a federal excise tax, the "income tax." I am outside the jurisdiction of the "United States" Government for these excises. Mr. Hogeboom, an excise is voluntary. I once voluntarily, without fully informed consent and while under the age of majority, chose to participate in the federal income tax scheme. This uninformed decision made me liable. Therefore, allow me to respond that I am no longer liable for an excise on my earnings. You must see, then, I cannot evade a tax for which I am no longer obligated.*

Those who read this book and acquire a more accurate portrayal of the "legal system" and gain a fundamental education of legal terms and tax law are likely to appreciate that Hogeboom is not a practitioner of law. He is not a professional concerned with what is just and true. He is not a man of principle and character. No, most will see him as they would a circus barker at a sideshow, shouting the fantastical of his own making. They may see him as the unscrupulous purveyor of half-truths and untruths, the snake oil salesman proclaiming the far-fetched. They may see him as the slick-haired, smooth-talking con who spouts the sensational. Yes, we can begin to see the judicial system cannot be and should not be perceived as for *justice*, simply because it *works*. We cannot view a verdict as *just* simply because a man is in prison. Hogeboom's tactics and antics speak to this concern.

Consider the second and final example which epitomizes how and why both Hogeboom and the system should be held suspect.

During Hogeboom's questioning he asked, "Now, you stated that you do not live in the United States during direct examination, do you recall that?"

"Yes sir." I replied.

Hogeboom shot back, "Okay. Now, since you don't live in the United States, do you allow your—when you had renters, do they pay you in foreign currency? Give pesos or anything for rent?"

For the benefit of understanding Hogeboom's purpose for emphasizing this point, we must look at my testimony on direct. Harris asked, "And you renounced your social security number?" I answered by stating,

> *I researched the issue. I asked myself—I said what binds me as far as the nexus to the United States that compels me to file a tax return? And I looked at the issues I was trying to explain about the role of the government. I didn't live in the jurisdiction of DC or a territory of the United States. I was no longer a military officer, an officer of the United States. What bound me?*

We can plainly see that Hogeboom misrepresented the term "United States" when he asked his question. Why? The answer is simple. He knew the jury understood only one definition for the term "United States." He knew he was playing to an audience which knew nothing of the law or the use of legal terms. Did Hogeboom know the definition United States is often isolated to a statute and a section to which the definition would apply? Yes. Did he know I specifically used the term United States as it applied to the tax code? Yes. And, if he did not know, it only speaks to his lack of knowledge, akin to "willful blindness, deliberate ignorance." He closed his eyes to avoid learning and/or disclosing the truth.

Consider Hogeboom's comments to the jury during his closing statement.

> *Now, the element of knowledge in willfulness can be satisfied by inference drawn from proof that Mr. Johnson deliberately closed his eyes to avoid learning that he was not in compliance; he was violating the law. That's the deliberate ignorance. It is sometimes referred to as the ostrich instruction, in that ostriches allegedly stick their head in the sand and just ignore everything that is going on. And I submit to you the proof of his willful blindness and deliberate ignorance is quite simple.*

The fact that Hogeboom knew of the varied and limited definitions of legal terms underscores how disingenuous he was as an officer of the court. There was no doubt in my mind Hogeboom knew I had a valid jurisdictional claim. He knew defense counsel would not argue this good faith belief. And Hogeboom was still without a governor to temper his approach. He was without discrimination. Consequently, he stooped to the ridiculous. He belittled not only a man who had a firm grasp of tax law and the issue of jurisdiction, Hogeboom belittled the law itself. Moreover, he abused the court.

By now you have an appreciation for the use of legal terms. You have a sense that legal definitions of a term are numerous and not at all what was expected. You may appreciate that Hogeboom, one of thousands of prosecutors, was pandering to the jury's base prejudice by introducing the acceptance of foreign currency and pesos, which had absolutely no relevance. Whether or not I am in "U. S. territory," which is not the 50 states, has nothing to do with what is received as payment in the course of business. Any American may accept pesos or the yuan when transacting business. Hogeboom's antics should be as transparent as much as they are reprehensible. He, like all *good* prosecutors, shapes the *truth* by gratuitously linking one disassociated *fact* with another.

The fact was that I was outside the jurisdiction of the *United States* for the federal income tax. My status had nothing to do with the acceptance of or payment of anything with Federal Reserve Notes or French francs. In Hogeboom's distorted argument, he wanted to assert the *fact* that I was not in the *United States,* which somehow related to the receipt of foreign currency. His approach was an absurdity. I may accept any currency I choose in whatever *United States* I happen to be in at the time.

How can a man articulate a good faith belief based upon the legal terms and definitions within the tax code if both the prosecution and defense do not provide for the complete disclosure of these facts? The answer is simple. He cannot. Since Cargill agreed with Hogeboom's position, he never argued the jurisdictional belief that I was not within the authority of the *United States* for the income tax. Since Cargill believed as Hogeboom, Cargill allowed Hogeboom to perform and argue without objection. The jury listened to Cargill's and Hogeboom's *facts* to arrive at the *truth*.

Hogeboom left nothing to chance though. His prospects and promotions were on the line. His reputation and tally of convictions had to be assured. He peppered his argument with doubt whenever possible. He even referred to the Internal Revenue Code as the Internal Revenue *Service* Code. Was this by design? I looked directly at Hogeboom and stated its proper name. How far is too far? How far should a prosecutor advance an argument before it is beyond the bounds of reason?

This is an issue for the public at large. How far should officials operate before an institution compromises the greater public interests? While there are groups which monitor the conduct of courts, these efforts are quite small with limited impact. When officers of the court and judges become a law unto themselves, we suffer the consequences as a community. When we blindly accept the conduct and decisions of authorities, justice suffers. Without exception, blind acceptance encourages institutional arrogance.

Is it possible to prevent a prosecutor's extremes? Perhaps. We may take solace that the opposing sides exchange evidence through the "discovery process." We may take comfort that each knows the opposition's strategy to whatever extent. Yet, it is impossible to govern how a lawyer parses words, splices definitions, and manipulates information. As was the case with Hogeboom, knowing an untruth was introduced into the record is not readily perceptible. Lawyers use tactics which deviate from what is true. These tactics divide and destroy the truth. With subtle agendas, the unreal is manifested, doubt takes root and questionable goals are veiled with *legitimacy*. Inescapably, when a prosecutor fires untruths at a semi-automatic rate, neither the opposition nor the jury can recall the particulars. In the end, lies and half-truths mix and mingle into a seemingly comprehensive representation and draw the mind to a conclusion anchored in the incredible. The jury is subconsciously told the prosecution is right and the defendant is wrong. When the jury hears 72 times by a United States Attorney that a man has a $4 million loan guaranty that never existed, the jury believes the imaginary. When the jury is told repeatedly that a defendant has a tax liability, why should the jurors believe otherwise?

Once Hogeboom finished his cross-examination, after Harris conducted a brief redirect, both parties rested. The case was effectively complete.

GOVERNMENT'S FINAL WITNESS

Inexplicably, before Hogeboom rested, he had a final witness. Since the witness saw the government's case before testifying, her presence is even more suspect. Her sole purpose was to testify that a tax liability was owed, and I had a tax liability. Cargill immediately objected. The judge overruled him.

Hogeboom asked this witness to answer questions which concerned the content of the trial thus far. She was to respond as the *expert* with the opinion that I should have filed tax returns. I could not believe what I saw and heard.

First, the witness was not needed for the government's benefit. I had done an excellent job of destroying any chances for an acquittal. Without a strong defense attorney arguing my good faith belief, evidence presented by the prosecution stood as conclusive because it was not rebutted. If our goal was to create *reasonable doubt* that I did not have a tax liability and did not willfully fail to file tax returns, we failed already. Admittedly, the case was never approached with the intent to be victorious against the charges. So, as the grand finale to the government's case, an expert witness was on the stand to testify under oath to the conclusiveness of my guilt *before I testified.*

The outrage I felt from this unexpected development was palpable. Not only was she untimely placed before the defense presented its failed case, but the jurors would also be less inclined to rely on their own discernment as to the facts and truth even with the defense representation of the facts. The jurors heard an expert's assessment which, based upon the government's evidence, was legally unassailable. Since the expert authenticated *facts*, the jury would have less need to weigh them independently in the end.

Why did the court allow the government the opportunity to offer this witness? The jury did not have all the facts or the whole truth at this point. How could the expert know the truth? How was she able to conclude as she did? I had not discussed the Constitution or specific Supreme Court cases. How could she have reached a thorough opinion? How could she have squared my good faith beliefs with her expert conclusions? She could not state that I had taxable *income* unless I explained why my *income* was not subject to excise. The definition of *income* was incomplete for her expert testimony. There was no direct evidence of any income in my name. Was this expert a stooge with the singular aim of summarizing exactly what the prosecution wanted the jury to distinguish and determine?

If this expert was concerned about the truth, she would not have been able to, morally, ethically, or professionally, testify until *all the evidence* was presented. As an expert, how could she testify that I had a tax liability since there were no W-2s reflecting "wages" or 1099s showing receipt of payments? How could she in good conscience speak to the profit or loss of the LLC or trusts when no balance sheets or confirmation of my involvement were offered as evidence? On what basis could she extrapolate any profits or losses from the LLC or trusts as mine? I had no ownership or management role in either. These questions are telling and speak to the government's fraudulent agenda.

How could this expert reconcile that I was obligated to the federal income tax if I had rescinded and revoked my signature and intent to any taxable federal status or benefits which tied me to the federal jurisdiction? How could she justify a tax liability as if I was not a federal employee or federal citizen? How could she justify my liability to file tax returns when she did not hear any testimony or weigh any evidence from the defense as to why the law that governed this federal excise did not apply? Did she presume I was a "United States person" as defined in the tax code? Did she consider that I was not a "U. S. citizen," "employee," "person," "individual," or "taxpayer" as defined in the tax code? Did she consider that I was not engaged in interstate commerce and was not within federal jurisdiction? Of course not. She was testifying with a rehearsed script. Here is the point. Why did the government need someone to determine the facts when the jurors were responsible for determining the facts?

I did not know when or why courts began to allow such experts to testify in tax trials. Obviously, the witness served as a fail-safe measure against any possible loss by the government. She was to validate the prosecution's position. Could such testimony be perceived as balanced and credible? Absolutely

The defense was not afforded the same latitude. An expert witness for the defense could not summarize that, according to the evidence, there was no liability to file a tax return. No expert could confirm that I was not and could not be within the jurisdiction of the federal authorities or court, or one of the legal classes within the tax code with this federal obligation. The defense could not have had a witness testify as to the proper definition of *income* or reveal that I did not have an income subject to excise. He could not confirm such a conclusion based upon my rejection of a federal status and benefits, or that my labor was property, a mere extension of me, for which I could seek an equal exchange.

An expert for the defense could neither validate that Congress could not tax other than stipulated by the direct or indirect taxing clauses of the Constitution. He could not proffer that the 16th Amendment had no relevance. The expert could not stipulate that I had rebutted the government's presumption and prima facie evidence of a tax status or liability. Such a witness could not have substantiated that Congress did not have and never had the ability to tax the natural rights of Americans who never made a federal election or revoked the election which originally created the liability.

An expert witness for the defense could not posit that the private remedy I tendered to the IRS was a viable solution to the charges and all parties concerned. He could not conclude that, under equity, the judge and prosecutor failed to satisfy their obligations to an equitable claim. The court would not allow an expert witness to underscore facts according to the defense. Court rules prevent these questions and representations from being considered by the jury. We may conclude the government's expert witness reflects the arrogance of the system. The prosecutor's legal positions were given credibility by the affirmation of an expert who observed the trial. I recognized this development as a sham.

If we willingly accept the testimony of this expert, we are far removed from the viable solutions desperately needed to change America's dire course. Innocent people will continue to be found guilty—not for violating the laws, but for the operation of the legal system. This system alone guides defendants to plea offers or guilty verdicts and prison.

Once this expert witness told the jury that the evidence required the filing of tax returns, Cargill agreed; for he told the jurors I was required to do so. Why did he object to the prosecutor's expert witness in the first place? What can be more conclusive to jurors beholden to determine a verdict than a defense which agrees with the government?

CLOSING ARGUMENTS AND JURY INSTRUCTIONS

The jurors had spent the last four days observing and judging facts of a federal tax trial. They did not want to be there. Yet, they were duty bound to a civic responsibility. The final formality before their responsibility to reach a verdict was to hear closing arguments and jury instructions. For the closing arguments, the prosecutor spoke first. The defense followed and then Hogeboom offered a final rebuttal.

As expected, Hogeboom's conclusion could not have been more caustic. It was equal to the distortions within his cross-examination. Yet rather than catalogue his distortions, I will emphasize one of the objectives for highlighting this case.

Throughout this book, I sought to examine the "legal system" within the context of the law. The other cases were discussed without the law and revealed that individual and collective components of the legal system contributed to the eventual injustice achieved. This tax case, *with an understanding of tax law*, reveals that the components of the legal system failed to result in justice. If the law is ignored, if the government or system presumes the law applies even though it doesn't, injustice is achieved without accountability to the law.

Before reviewing the closing arguments, consider the jury instructions as to the law the judge provided. (Appendix F) Pay particular attention to page 583. Moon references 26 USC 7203, willful failure to file tax returns. On page 585, the judge states, "A person is required to file a tax return if his gross income…exceeded $14,600…" If this information is overwhelming or if it is difficult to understand the statute, consider the following summary:

- The Constitution, the supreme law of the land, allows for direct and indirect taxes;
- The tax code concerns excise (indirect) taxes;

- Excise taxes are paid when one engages (voluntarily) in a status, activity, or benefit subject to excise;
- The tax code is constitutional;
- When one voluntarily elects to be a particular federally taxable status and accepts federal benefits, he is subject to the excise on his income or wages. He becomes one of "any person required." (See Charles Steward Machine v. Davis (1937));
- If one does not elect or revokes/rejects an election of a status or benefit, he is not one of "any person required to make a return...";
- Those who do not elect or accept a federal status or privilege are not within the excise authority of Congress;
- I revoked and rescinded any election and acceptance of any federally excisable status and benefit in 2000;
- I sent letters to 12 federal agents, agencies and officials since 2004 and asked for the law which required me to "make a return;"
- Not one agent, agency, or official answered the question;
- I had a good faith belief that I was without the indirect taxing authority of Congress for the federal income tax;
- I could not be subject as one of "Any person required," as stated in 26 USC 7203;
- The government prosecuted me with the *presumption* that I was a "taxpayer;"
- Cargill and Harris *presumed* I was a taxpayer and refused to investigate much less argue my good faith belief. They called it "frivolous;"
- The court refused my challenge of jurisdiction and *presumed* I was a taxpayer, one of "any person required;"
- The court did not mandate that the government prove jurisdiction. The court denied my rebuttal of the government's presumption.

With the foregoing summation, one may readily appreciate that my good faith belief was not only credible, but consistent with the law. Much later after the trial, the Federal Government's response (Appendix G) to my 2255 Motion (habeas corpus) simply stated that I was a "taxpayer" and Cargill was not ineffective for not arguing my good faith belief. In response to the government's assertions that both it and the IRS had jurisdiction and that Cargill was not ineffective, I submitted a Reply (Appendix H) which struck at the heart of the issue.

If you fully appreciate the content of my reply, realize that Cargill foreclosed on the opportunity to argue a constitutional question. He avoided the challenge that Congress does not have the authority to tax those who are without its excise authority. Why did Cargill avoid this constitutional question? Was his decision deliberate or one sourced in his own ignorance of both tax and constitutional law? With this comprehensive and not at all exhaustive review of the law (a more detailed look at the question of congressional jurisdiction and tax law will be developed as we progress), we will weigh the closing arguments from Hogeboom and Cargill.

Hogeboom had a very clear objective. He wanted to preach the message that I was a "taxpayer." He wanted to promote the presumption that I was liable for the excise. He made this presumption knowing full well that no one had answered my one question since 2004: What law required me to file a federal income tax return? Hogeboom wanted the jury to presume I was a taxpayer. How did he do this? He stressed the *law*—the law as he saw it. Hogeboom began by stating:

> *...you heard in the testimony - listen to the testimony here, evaluating the evidence admitted, that in the years charged, Mr. Johnson was required to file a tax return.*

> *That, in these types of cases, normally is not the issue of whether someone has a requirement to file or not. Those are number crunching as set up by statute. The real issue is the willfulness, violation of a known legal duty. The law imposed a duty upon the defendant, as it does upon everyone.*

Look at Hogeboom's sweeping generalization and conclusion—*everyone*. Note that he explains what the law is, something the court prohibited the defense from doing. One should ask whether Hogeboom even knows what an excise tax actually is. If he did, and if he were honest with the term's application, he would admit that not everyone could be liable. Hogeboom continued:

> *Mr. Johnson deliberately closed his eyes to avoid learning that he was not in compliance; he was violating the law. That's the deliberate ignorance.*

Was I ignorant of the law? Or was the jury unaware of the law and its limited application because of Hogeboom's efforts and strategy? Hogeboom then suggests that I "...sought out people, got the advice of people who shared the views [I] had...." He continued by stating:

> *... he avoided asking those people who might give him an answer he didn't want to hear, so he could stand before you and say, I believed this in good faith. I wasn't required to pay taxes. That is intent. And I submit to you, based on that alone, you can convict him.*

Hogeboom's theme of the *law* was so important to his case, he stressed that I read the law.

> *And, surprisingly, he admitted reading the Internal Revenue Service Code and reading the very statutes that he's charged with. He admitted that he read 7212a, that he read 7203. He knew what the law was, by his own admission. He chose to disregard the law.*

Hogeboom's words are important for one reason. How did Hogeboom know of my understanding of the law? The answer is he didn't. He merely presumed I understood the law as he did. He wanted the jurors to believe as he understood that I simply said, "I believe it doesn't apply to me." This is what Hogeboom wanted the jurors to embrace.

Conveniently, he emphasized the jury instruction which served his purpose. He said, "And as the jury instructions pointed out, you know, a disagreement with the law is not enough." Hogeboom offered a very thoughtless premise: I avoided the law because I disagreed with the law. Hogeboom even encouraged the jury to consider an instruction which the court did not give—an instruction to punctuate his baseless application of the law. He said, "... one of the instructions not given is to leave you[r] common sense at the courthouse steps." He continued:

> *The reason the jury system works, there are people coming from different walks of life, different economic places, different stages of life, come together for one thing: to decide the guilt or innocence of a defendant. And it is important that the—you know, the common sense that you develop throughout life is used, you apply what you know to the facts and to the law as the judge has given you. Use your common sense.*

We must surmise that Hogeboom is a proponent for jurors not to use their common sense to know or understand what the law means—to include its limited application. He did not want them to know that I no longer had a federal status that obligated me to file tax returns and no longer participated in a federal benefit program. Hogeboom wanted the jurors to ignorantly apply the law exactly as he wanted them to understand the law.

Since words and thoughts are important, we will conclude our review of Hogeboom's closing argument with a few observations. First, he said I "closed my eyes to avoid learning that [I] was not in compliance" with the law, while he ignored my letters to Biggs and Pompei and others for the law as it applied to me. Yet, unbelievably, Hogeboom told the jury I "avoided those people who might give [me] an answer [I] didn't want to hear." However, Hogeboom said I read the code. I read the law. But, during the trial, he asserted I didn't read the "frivolous arguments" publication that had no relevance to the law. Hogeboom's logic was so incongruent and inconsistent as to defy the "common sense" he wanted jurors to employ. His logic and reasoning were not consistent with the *facts and truth* he used. Why? He was not concerned with either the facts or the truth. His goal was to mislead the jury. He didn't want them to consider that, just maybe, not all Americans are liable for the federal "income tax," an excise/indirect tax.

Let's now weigh Cargill's closing argument. His succinctness was in sharp contrast to Hogeboom's long-winded and rambling monologue. It appeared as though Cargill was on a mission. What purpose would his mission serve? Since he did not argue the fundamental legal tenets of my belief, I was not sanguine that he would alter his approach. Then, true to form, Cargill busted out with two points which ill-served my cause.

> *Here is what we agree with. One, we agree that in these three tax years under consideration, you'll see the indictment has three years, 2005, 2006, 2007—we agree in those years Mr. Johnson had sufficient income attributable to him to trigger the requirement to file tax returns. The evidence is clear. The government has proven that plainly... he plainly had sufficient income so that he should have filed tax returns.*

Cargill had spoken. Cargill embraced *the law* without countering any flawed premise or analysis offered by the prosecution.

Let me be clear. During the entire trial, the government referred to LLCs, corporations, and trusts which may or may not have received gross income. I did not own these entities. The checks, bank accounts, and papers belonged to these structures, not me, just as I did not own a major national chain or the local gas station. More importantly, the government had no W-2s, W-4s, 1099s, or any documents which reflected my personal income for any given year. What did this mean? My attorneys agreed with the prosecutor's claim that any gross income associated with these entities, which may have filed their own tax returns, was mine. Cargill did not contest this conclusion. He handed the government a conviction because he never argued that the government could not convict a man on a charge if the prosecution could not prove I had personal income. Cargill assured that the jury could and would conclude I had income because other "persons" may have had gross income.

Cargill continued by granting concessions to the government's position when he said, "Second, we agree with the obvious. He didn't file returns in those three years." It is noteworthy that Cargill said, "we agree." It is undeniable that he was supposed to *represent* his client, which implies that he should have represented his client's belief. Obviously, I did not agree to either the first or the second concession. How is an attorney able to defend a client when he agrees with the opposition, which is contrary to his client's belief? Cargill stated:

> *He felt like the system didn't apply to him, he had no obligation to file tax returns, so he didn't. To be sure...Mr. Johnson still believes that the tax code doesn't apply*

to him and he still had no obligation to file a return. But, as a matter of law, as a matter of who is correct, we all know that he should have filed returns, I mean, come on, he should have...

As I looked at and listened to Cargill address a rather somber jury, I felt the proverbial noose tighten around my neck. My defense lawyer was not refuting the government's contention of liability. Twice Cargill agreed with the prosecution without rebutting Hogeboom's claims. Cargill may as well have said, "My client is guilty of the first two elements cited by the government." Cargill then secured his agreement by stating:

And so if this case were about whether he should have filed the returns and whether he owes tax money, it would have been over Tuesday morning.

Cargill cited points which were technical in nature and dealt with the law, He shared a rather simple equation. If a man has income of $X, he must file a tax return.

Critical to this equation is whether Congress has the authority or jurisdiction to subject a man to an excise. Does he manufacture cigars? Does he sell tires? Does he subscribe to the federal benefit of social security? Does he have a status recognized by the Federal Government as taxable? All of these are excisable in nature. This is the point. There is a constitutional question of jurisdiction and power to tax in the first instance. If Congress lacks jurisdiction, a man may be outside of congressional authority. A man's belief should not be the object of scrutiny when Congress is already without authority. The man's belief is secondary when, in fact, a congressional lack of power is primary.

Weigh the following thought. A man could believe he is within the jurisdiction of a governing authority even though his belief is wrong. If the governing authority knew it had no jurisdiction over him, what is the significance of the man's belief to the contrary? My belief that I was without the authority of Congress for the tax in question was subordinate to the fact that Congress and its legislation were without autonomy over me. The scrutiny should have been on Congress from the outset. This is why courts exist, to challenge errant and unlawful application of statutes and regulations.

Cargill had the ripe opportunity during pretrial and trial to declare my belief as relevant because it warranted an overarching constitutional question. As a matter of constitutional and settled law, Congress may not assess an "income tax" upon anyone outside of its excise authority. Cargill could easily have argued to the court or jury that Congress may not tax what the Constitution prohibits. With this argument, Cargill could have dispensed with any claim that I committed a felony by obstructing a federal investigation. Frankly, since I knew Congress could not tax my earnings, what I did during an investigation was no different then what I did before the investigation. I did no differently!

My relationship with any structures was not illegal. I had a contract for my services—a private agreement. Even the IRS agents stated during the trial that there was nothing wrong with trusts. Even Hogeboom agreed trusts were lawful and served a purpose. My actions were consistent with my belief and the law. This is the argument Cargill failed to articulate. Why? He was preoccupied with establishing my liability as a taxpayer in accordance with the law while avoiding sanctions for arguing a *frivolous* argument.

Cargill then addressed the element of willfulness. Was I willful in my failure to comply with the law? Cargill gave the jurors his answer. He looked at them and said his client "sincerely believes the tax code does not apply to him, that he has no obligation to file." He shared that I sent letters to the IRS stating, "I don't believe I'm subject to the tax code. Tell me why I am wrong." However, this was not my posture with the IRS. Cargill exceeded my greatest concerns when he told the jury that I told the Federal Government, "I don't believe I'm supposed to file."

Cargill then proclaimed, "Now, is he right? No. It is crazy."

Cargill attempted to convince a jury that I could not have been willful of failing to file tax returns with a meritless argument by stating. He said, "because my client believed that the law did not apply." That's it! Nothing more. Cargill did not shore up his argument with anything of substance. He simply threw these words at the jury without even a hope that they would leave a favorable impression. He did this immediately after conceding that I had a tax liability which I had failed to satisfy. This was no defense.

Hogeboom referred to "common sense" in his closing. Perhaps Cargill should have heeded this advice and tapped into any common sense as he *defended* his client. I am not purposely disparaging Cargill just to denigrate him. I merely acknowledge that the lack of a defense is not a good defense, and a bad defense is even worse. This is common sense.

Recall that Cargill refused to argue a frivolous argument for fear he would be sanctioned. This was not common sense either. This was instinct anchored in fear for self-preservation. He wanted to protect (defend) himself from injury. He did not want to be fined. His wallet was more important than me or my children. Cargill had boxed himself into a position which was perfunctory at its best and hackneyed at its worst. Cargill's performance only degraded into the unimaginable when he told the jurors:

> *It is sad, really, that a man of his talent, who started out life in the way that he did—it is really sad. He went to VMI. He honorably served his country. And then he veered off on this path.*

Cargill reduced his argument to ridicule and defaulted to his outrageous refrain; "He sincerely believes... but he does sincerely believe..." Permit me to restate the obvious once again. Cargill never explained why I believed as I did. He never once offered rhyme and reason as to why I was not then and am not now liable to the federal income tax. Cargill was about to end his remarks.

> *And as the judge instructed you, a person who acts on a belief or an opinion honestly held is not punishable under the tax law merely because that belief turns out to be wrong. And that's his case.*

Cargill restated the point he made at the beginning of his closing. "Don't focus on whether he's right or wrong as a legal matter. That's the easy question." Yes, Cargill already agreed that I failed to comply with the law. He asked the jurors to "Focus on the relevant question: whether he's guilty of the serious charges." In Cargill's wisdom, he asked the jury to reconcile guilt on the legal matters and not to do so on the nature of the charges.

Upon what did Cargill base his argument? His client had a belief. Other than that, it was a sincere belief. There was no litmus test to gauge the merits of this belief. Cargill expected the jury to wrap its collective mind around this absurd position. "The defendant had a belief. He simply and knowingly believed. Yes, he believed the tax code did not apply to him." Cargill's words were empty and not very convincing in the least.

I could as easily have claimed that my neighbor's car, dog, and golf clubs belonged to me. Why? I believed it. I sincerely believed it. Does acting upon a belief that I "honestly held" protect me from the crime of theft for stealing a car, dog, and golf clubs? No. If, however, I produced a bill of sale as the basis for my sincere belief, are my actions credible? Certainly. My belief would no longer be without merit. I believe the car, dog and golf clubs are mine because I bought them. I have the agreement. I have the proof which supports my good faith belief!

Cargill's efforts to explain how I was not guilty according to the law were, at most, a rote formality to justify his presence (performance) and salary; otherwise, he made a sophomoric attempt to excuse the alleged crime. He never contended with the premise that honestly held beliefs, which served as a predicate for my decisions and actions, must pass the laugh test. Without grounds to support my sincere belief, Cargill's argument was simply laughable and unbelievable to the jury. Had Cargill proffered that my belief was consistent with the Federal Constitution, that Congress had no indirect taxing authority over my earnings—upon the basis that I no longer had a status or accepted federal privileges—he would have told the whole truth with supported facts. This would have netted no derision or sanctions from the court at all. And if it did, to hell with the court.

To establish a benchmark for the argument which Cargill should have offered, consider this hypothetical closing for the jury:

> *Ladies and gentlemen of the jury, earlier I explained to you that legal terms and legal definitions have significance. Legal language serves a purpose. You learned that Mr. Johnson no longer enjoys a federal status or federal benefit. This means he is no longer within federal jurisdiction and, therefore, not liable for the federal income tax. As such, he cannot be a "taxpayer" within congressional indirect excise authority.*
>
> *Since Congress may not tax what is beyond the limits of the Constitution, my client, the man I am to zealously defend to my utmost in knowledge and ability, cannot be within the purview of the IRS and its investigatory powers. My client cannot be subject to the alleged charges.*
>
> *Logically, you must conclude, if Congress does not have the requisite authority to impose a tax which does not apply, the executive branch, represented by the Department of Internal Revenue and the Department of Justice, is without the authority to compel my client to comply. In fact, I entreat you to consider that the very reason no agent, agency, or elected official ever answered my client's singular question is for the simple fact that they can't or won't.*
>
> *For eight years my client stood in truth and weathered an unconscionable criminal investigation based upon an unfounded presumption by the Federal Government that he had a legal tax liability. For eight years Agents Biggs and Pompei avoided and evaded their responsibility to show my client the law which applied to his circumstances. Why? Mr. Johnson was right. No law exists and the presumed law does not apply.*
>
> *The Federal Government cannot allow for a man to have a well-founded good faith belief which is validated by the supreme law of the land—the Constitution. The Federal Government cannot allow for an America to gain a victory in a criminal tax case, a victory which would invite unwanted scrutiny; the truth would be exposed to an ignorant, apathetic, and fearful people. The people would incrementally appreciate that they are not required to subject their earnings to an income tax.*
>
> *Yes, Mr. Johnson's belief, which is more than a belief, is not crazy. His belief is both sound and lawful. His belief is constitutional. His belief is the truth. Mr. Johnson, my valiant client, educated himself and courageously risks a prison sentence to uphold the sanctity of the Constitution. I ask you, members of the jury, to reject the frivolous presumptions offered by the government. I ask you to reject the prosecution's ill-conceived conclusions which defy common sense; I ask you to silently acknowledge the noble calling of my client with a resounding proclamation for his acquittal and a declaration of his innocence.*

Since this was not the message the jury heard, since Cargill offered nothing more than that I had a belief that was "crazy," since he told them I was obligated to file, as reflected in his, "I mean, come on, he should have" capitulation, there was nothing left but to await the jury's decision and verdict of guilt. For, it appeared as though the jurors would receive Cargill's information unquestionably. Who could blame them? Both the prosecution and defense claimed I was guilty. The judge stipulated the law which pointed to the same conclusion. The jurors had no reason to challenge that I was outside of congressional taxing authority. Consequently, I knew my fate was sealed.

JURY DELIBERATION AND THE VERDICT

If we consider the depth of our problem—the highest incarceration rate in the world—why would we expect jurors to have the capacity to think beyond what they are spoon fed by the "legal system." Our entire lives have been one of conditioning. From an early age we are taught to comply. Could it be said these jurors were my "peers?" They did not know the law as I did. They did not know me and my character. They had different values and priorities. Statistically, they were likely plugged into the television six hours a day—the average for an American. This is likely how they identified with life. This is how they learned what they *knew*. They were told what to believe. By relative comparison, I did not allow the system to tell me what or how to think.

We as a people no longer epitomize being. To *be* implies a volitional intent to be into an understanding which precipitates action. To the contrary, *existing* implies an unchallenged receptivity, indifference even, with the intent to conform. We may easily surmise that when a white-haired senior judge, robed in black, sitting atop a mahogany bench, unerringly declares that the "law" requires one to file a tax return, the jury willingly accepts this edict. Why wouldn't they? The jury's responsibility is to determine the facts. The judge states the law.

The jury does not contend with anything else. Once the facts are determined, the jury squares the facts with the law. Did the defendant file tax returns? Yes or no. If the facts show that he did not, the jury need only ask if the defendant violated the law. Did the defendant obstruct the IRS investigation? Yes or no. If the facts show that he did, the jury need only ask if the law was violated. The jury's task is rather facile.

Ironically, the role of the juror is touted as the quintessence of the judicial process. I did not share this perspective. I was disheartened. I was humbled that my life and liberty were relegated to a simplistic formula which would net a decision from such an uninformed and uninitiated people. Whether realized or not, my situation reflected the lot of all Americans. In most cases, it would take confronting the system for others to appreciate that the problems are real and dire.

What occurs within the confines of the jury room is central to what Americans do to themselves. Consider the following. Who sits as jurors? Americans. Who determines the guilt or innocence of Americans? Americans. Who squares the facts with the law? Americans. There is a reason for these largely rhetorical questions. Not much is involved to determine the facts of a case. Jurors are not deliberating the reasonableness of the law. Their aim is not to discuss attorney bias or challenge questionable practices of the investigators. They are not to weigh the conduct of the judge or discriminate how the defendant was maligned by the process. Why would jurors ever question such nuances? They wouldn't. Rather, jurors wrangle over the interpretation of the facts or they are collectively predisposed to a foregone conclusion. This is how the system operates.

We can have a rather simplistic formula. The task of the jury is very elementary. Juries accomplish the following:

1. Determine the facts;
2. Determine if the law was violated;
3. Comply with the jury instructions.

The role of the jury is quite limited, if not crippling. We must question what Americans do to other Americans as jurors. We, quite unthinkingly, are led through the motions and reflexively apply the formulaic which invariably ends in guilty verdicts. *This is what Americans do to other Americans.*

If you are inclined to believe the jury process is virtuous and credible, there is but one question to ask: *Are Americans more corrupt, immoral, and criminally predisposed than the rest of the world?* If not, with only five percent of the global population, why do we have nearly twenty-five percent of those incarcerated? As jurors, Americans serve on an assembly line of sorts, working for the system, as if by design, a system which churns out guilty verdicts. Americans exercise their "civic" responsibility and offer their seal of approval. Such is the role of the unenlightened.

The jurors in this case in my case experienced just how overbearing an influence the court has upon the jury and its deliberations. At one point during their discussions, the jurors made a written request for the entire law for the felony (26 USC 7212). The request, once received by the judge, was presented to the prosecution and defense. Judge Moon read the request, considered input from both sides, and decided that the jury *should not receive the full text*. Moon decided that the limited portion of the law the jury possessed was sufficient for their efforts.

What happened? Why did the jury want the complete language of the law? Did the jurors want to understand the context of the entire statute for a specific reason? Were they attempting to reconcile the *facts* within the complete and proper legal context of the *law*? Why did Moon deny what was reasonable? Why did he deny the jury's search for edification and clarification? Did granting the request injure my position or help? Obviously, the jury must have been willing to discern, as if there was some reasonable doubt to resolve.

This exchange between the jury and the court was a major revelation. Plainly stated, the jurors' efforts were extracurricular to what was rote and expected. Their inquiry defied the parameters designed to limit the engagement and initiative of the jury. Yet, the court refused what was outside *the scope* of their discussions. I firmly believed there was a specific reason the jury wanted the full text of the law. What follows is that reason.

When I was cross-examined by Hogeboom, he asked me questions which concerned banking and finances. His intent was to establish that, even if only circumstantially, I obstructed the IRS investigation into my private financial affairs. Since I did nothing different during the investigation than before, I disagreed with his premise. I never prevented IRS agents from investigating what I would have done or did as a matter of course. I lived my life as normally as possible given the circumstances. What I did or did not do during the IRS probe unquestionably, unjustifiably, and adversely affected me at trial. Why? Because I never deviated from my normal way of being! My normal way of being before the investigation began was presumed to be obstructive behavior. In my mind, had I any intent to obstruct the investigation, I would have done the reverse; I would have changed all my decisions and actions to thwart the IRS investigation.

When the prosecutor asked if I impeded the IRS agents, I stated,

> *I never sent threatening letters or used physical force with the intent to kill anyone or their family members.*

Hogeboom was blindsided. He never expected my response. Why would he? Hogeboom concluded that everything I did during the IRS probe amounted to obstruction. I, on the other hand, without realizing Hogeboom's mindset, thought he referred to the "felonious"—the truly criminal nature of the obstruction charge. So, I introduced a partial text of the law to the jury; the portion the judge refused to grant.

Hogeboom recoiled from this unexpected disclosure to the jury. I had just interfered with his agenda. I just offered something to the jurors which would cause them to think. I had just introduced an aspect of the law he would have to rebut. He did not want them to hear what I revealed. Why? And why did the judge deny this portion of the law? We may hazard a reliable conclusion, but we will never know the answer. The court determined that some words of that portion of the statute were not relevant. However, we may appreciate that denying a jury's reasonable request confirms the system is complicit with the imprisonment of the innocent.

We must consider the actual language of the law to understand the insight which would have been gleaned by the jury. Otherwise, we must conclude the limited text offered was used to substantiate that I committed a felony. A felony is a life-altering label which drastically affects the futures of those labeled as felons. Felons can't vote, possess guns, and their vocational opportunities are severely limited. My unexpected challenge to a federal prosecutor's felony charge was significant and one Hogeboom had to address.

Hogeboom had to recover from my assertion that I never threatened or used force with the intent to kill or harm. He had to dismiss this idea as something he never suggested. He had to isolate the felony to a selective section of the code, the section just before the part which addresses the use of force. The jury, as best I could discern, wanted to understand why I testified in such a manner. Ostensibly, they wanted to determine the facts considering not only what was suggested as truth by Hogeboom based upon circumstantial evidence, but to appreciate my understanding of the law and the true scope of all facts and the entire law.

Moon's decision not to provide the whole law stood in sharp contrast to the search for substance cited by Gibson in his treatise on equity and the limited scope of the jury's deliberations. The rules, form, and procedures of court limited and defeated the call for conscience. From my perspective, justice prevented is justice denied, just as the prevention of full disclosure denies understanding. The full text of the law was denied its relative association to the supposed crime. With the jury's request, Hogeboom argued against allowing the jury to see the entire text of the law. Surprisingly, my attorneys agreed with Hogeboom. The judge made his decision. This brings us back to the essence of the jury's role. They are to determine the facts. The judge provides the law, *or a small portion thereof*. Once the jurors have the law and have decided of the facts, referring to the basic formula, they can ask the question: Did the defendant commit a felony?

The prosecutor wanted certain facts portrayed. He wanted to exclude what he did not intend. He was not a truth-seeker. My reference to force through threatening letters was a prime example. Hogeboom wanted the law stated succinctly and nothing more. If he could accomplish this objective, he would minimize reasonable doubt before the jury. Such is the power of rules and procedures in court. Meanwhile, he knew that I had sent letters repeatedly to the IRS agents. I had every reason to refer to a statute which imposed a felony for *sending letters* with threats of force. I had every reason to refer to this *law* when my letters were requests that agents provide the law which required my compliance. I had every reason to refer to the law when I simply asked for their authority (force) under which they presumed to act against me.

We can easily project what may have occurred had the jury been given the full context of the law. If they read the context of threats and force, the jurors would have weighed Hogeboom's incomplete representations considering the whole truth and the whole law. The judicial process is restricted by design and provides for greater control and targeted use of the jury. For ease of comparison, consider the judge's interruption of my testimony. He prevented full disclosure of my good faith belief. We know the judge denied full expression of facts as equally as he denied full expression of the law. Why not allow jurors to comprehend the relevance of the Constitution and Supreme Court cases? Why not allow them to read the entire code? Why not let jurors determine the factual basis of any letters sent by me or those sent on my behalf to the IRS, especially given the import of a felony?

Consider the full text of the statute for 26 USC 7212(a), which is a felony.

> 7212. Attempts to interfere with administration of Internal Revenue Laws
> (a) *Corrupt or forcible interference.* ***Whoever corruptly*** *or by force or threats of force (including any threatening letter or communication) endeavors to intimidate or impede any officer or employee of the United States acting in an official capacity under this title, or in any other way corruptly or by force or threats of force (including any threatening letter or communication)* ***obstructs or impedes, or endeavors to obstruct or impede the due administration of this title, shall*** *upon conviction thereof be fined not more than $5,000, or imprisoned not more than three years, or both, except that if the offense is committed by threats of force, the person convicted thereof shall be fined not more than $3,000 or imprisoned not more than one year, or both. The term "threats of force", as used in this subsection, means threats of bodily harm to the officer or employee of the United States or to a member of his family.*

Please weigh the next sentence. *The highlighted words above were the only words from the statute offered to the jury.* Out of the entire text, the jurors were directed to these words alone. This is how narrowly and refined the jury is controlled. With this limited language, the jury was governed by the jury instructions, the rules of court, and the law, however parsed. Their thinking and deliberations were funneled to a verdict of guilt.

Given the strict adherence to the formula, the jury would ask: "Did the defendant corruptly obstruct or impede or endeavor to obstruct and impede the due administration of the tax code?" Obviously, the prosecution was aided by the limited way the charge was framed. A mere handful of words from a rather comprehensive description of the law made it convenient for the prosecutor's circumstantial *facts* to fit a rather bland representation, while the balance of the law was replete with notations of force and threats.

Instead of referring to the letters I sent to agents Biggs and Pompei, which did not have any semblance of threats or force, Hogeboom was able to implicate the changing of banks or the use of unconventional banking by other entities and the titling of assets as the acts which fit the definition of "corruptly endeavoring" to obstruct the IRS. Yes, how I lived before the investigation, which was the same as during and afterwards, and acts that did not involve me, was somehow impeding the efforts of an agency which had no jurisdiction over me. Hogeboom's unstated suggestion was that since the charge under 26 USC 7212(a) was enforced, everything done by whomever could be perceived as an effort to stifle or obstruct the agents and the investigation.

Hogeboom may as well have suggested that, once under investigation, a man should cease all decisions and actions and allow the IRS to easily determine what was needed for a conviction. As with the IRS, Hogeboom ignored letters from the defendant. If I had dubious intentions, I would have stopped everything that would have been, in any way, suspicious to any ignorant Americans and uniformed jurors.

More importantly, the reference to *force* is made in conjunction with the efforts to *corrupt*. The words *corrupt or forcible* are combined with the conjunction *or.* A conjunction, as defined in Merriam-Webster's Dictionary & Thesaurus, 2007, is "the act or instance of conjoining: the state of being combined." The word *corrupt* means "to make evil," "deprave," or "morally degenerate: characterized by improper conduct." Synonyms for *corrupt* are: "*dishonest, unethical, unprincipled, degenerate, evil, immoral, nefarious, sinful, vicious,* and *wicked.*" The word *force* means "to compel by physical, moral or intellectual means: coerce." Synonyms for force are *"browbeat, bully, intimidate, menace, terrorize*, and *threaten.*" We plainly see that one who exercises *forcible interference* would be *corrupt*—or one who is corrupt would likely consider threats of force.

With these definitions, a series of rather obvious questions become relevant. If a man knows of no IRS investigation, is he in any way corrupt or forceful? Once he learns of an investigation, if he conducts his affairs as before, is he corrupt or forceful? Finally, if he knows of an investigation but does not know how it is conducted or to what extent is he corrupt or forceful towards the agents' efforts? Wouldn't a man know how to corrupt an investigation to corrupt an investigation? To illustrate, if a man goes to the local DMV office while under investigation and changes the title to a car from his name to a trust is this legal, lawful, and public transaction corrupt or forcible?

I did not care that I was under investigation. This fact did not influence my decisions or how I lived. I knew that I was outside the jurisdiction of the government. I was innocent. I was not doing anything wrong. I was *outside* the jurisdiction of the IRS. I was consistent with my decisions and actions whether under investigation or not.

I concluded that Hogeboom hoped the jury would not expend the time or effort to ferret through the distinctions of terms. He wanted the jury to accept the suggestion that I committed a felony which he supposedly supported with circumstantial facts, *facts* which had nothing to do with obstructing the IRS or its probe. The facts had everything to do with Hogeboom crafting the appearance that circumstances indicated the obstruction of the investigation. This brings us back to the issue of the jury's query to the court. Even with the limited language of the law the jurors received, the word *corrupt* implies a heavy-handed or intent to harm.

We have the heart of the jury's request. The jury wanted to clarify my assertion that I did not threaten anyone and was not corrupt with my behavior, whether written or physical. I was not corrupt in my conduct or forceful in any form or fashion with any investigator. That the court denied the full text of the law severely limited the juror's deliberation and flexibility. They could not act on an inquisitive initiative that would have provided a broader perspective for an incomplete topic. When the judge foreclosed the opportunity to understand the whole text of the law, the jury was placed back into deliberation for purposes of deciding. This is exactly what Hogeboom wanted. This is what the court did.

Some may argue that I handled the explanation of the terms *corrupt* or *forcible* and the context of the code like a seasoned lawyer. I narrowly directed the focus of the law in a fashion not in keeping with the entire code section. My response would be "Exactly!" This is just what lawyers do. This is what Hogeboom did. This is what the court facilitated when it spurned the genuine probative inquiry of a jury responsible for determining the guilt of a man for a felony. The question which should be asked is which option would have better served the interests of truth and justice, my complete application of the law or that of the court's which was restrictive and dishonest? Was the truth manifested more with the court's decision or would truth have been discerned by giving the entire law to the jury?

This query reflects the demise of the legal system. The text of the law and the terms and definitions are a means to an end. The language was created by legislators for an intended aim. If a self-serving prosecutor can selectively apply terms within the statute, he is more likely to engineer an outcome of his own design. If he couples his efforts with loose factual representations of a defendant's *crime*, he adds the appearance of congruency or veracity with the parsed law. At this juncture, prosecutors only need willing recipients to take the combination of select words and a representation of allegedly criminal acts to reach a contrived conclusion. The jury accomplished this when it deliberated within such constraints. The search for truth and justice was dismissed; a guilty verdict was reached.

When the jury received the judge's denial for the complete text of the law, they quickly finished their deliberations. I was soon escorted to court to hear the verdict of my peers. When the actors were settled in their choreographed positions, Moon directed the Marshal to bring in the jury. Noticeably, each juror avoided eye contact with the defense table. This was the tell-tale sign the verdict was not favorable.

My sister was in the gallery. She was my one supporter who knew how firmly I believed in the proper understanding of the law. She knew I could not and would not deviate from the truth. We both waited those few moments before the judge addressed the twelve who had weighed the *facts*. Whatever the verdict, it had their seal of approval.

Moon looked across the expanse of the chamber. "Have you reached a verdict?" he asked. The jury foreman stood and acknowledged in the affirmative. After Moon reviewed the verdict, the charges were read aloud. For each, one felony and three misdemeanors, the word "guilty" sounded solemnly in the air. I was now a convicted felon. My fate was known. I turned to my sister and offered a reassuring smile. As close as we were, this was a sober moment and a sad ending to this chapter in our lives.

The path I traveled had profound implications. It would affect relationships for years to come. Why? How? I was, according to prevailing perception, a criminal—a common criminal—for violating a law which did not exist or was grossly misapplied in my circumstances. Yes, I had rebutted any presumption and prima facie evidence that I was one with a status subject to the federal income tax law, as I was not a "U. S. person" or "taxpayer" as defined in the tax code—a position my lawyers considered frivolous. Those who understand and have researched tax law know that men like me, those willing to confront the system and stand for truth, are incarcerated to keep the populace in fearful compliance.

The tax laws we discussed demonstrate that the government has limited jurisdiction. I was not within federal jurisdiction for the tax in question and the United States did not have authority over me. I did not commit a crime or violate the tax laws. However, the government needs you to believe that I did. I was found guilty because the legal system allowed the prosecutor to reach this objective. I dared to confront an agenda which, invariably, cannot be defeated.

Many will not agree with the proposition that the tax laws do not apply to Americans. Most will not accept that the tax code applies to U. S. persons and taxpayers alone. Such is the belief of those who reflect the ignorance, apathy, and fear discussed in this book. From my vantage point, I knew with certainty that I was not a U. S. person, taxpayer, or any other federal classification designated within the tax code. I did not have the obligation to voluntarily comply. This was the truth and my good faith belief—a belief I established in the year 2000.

A QUESTION OF MOTIVATION

As we reflect upon these eleven cases, is it reasonable to conclude that the legal system is responsible for jailing men and women who have not committed a crime? Those who are innocent and imprisoned suffer needlessly because of institutional arrogance, arrogance that is a crime against humanity, an injustice considering the laws of nature. Such arrogance is a crime against American ideals that are no longer revered as supreme. A timely question is: Why does the government pursue *crimes* so vigorously? Beyond the obvious answer that government simply *can*—if only for the fear of the people and arrogance of officials—is there is a financial incentive? Is there a little-known financial agenda tied to the imprisonment of inmates? Profit may be one of the psychological and emotional motivations.

There is a tremendous cost associated with the operation of prisons. While there is an expense to the government, it is a gain to the Federal Bureau of Prisons (BOP). The BOP benefits from more than prisoners. As an agency of the government, unless there is a significant drop in the number of inmates, it must maintain or plan for growth. As long as the funds are available, there is no incentive to downsize the BOP. Unless the BOP is forced to operate at a loss, prisons will continue to be a growth industry, a cash crop. There are aspects of the penal system which speak to a profit motive. First and foremost, there are publicly traded stocks on the exchange directly tied to the private prison industry. This thought alone is abhorrent. The idea that we, as a people, earn *income* from the warehousing of men and women is reprehensible. Secondly, prisons are now privatized; some facilities are owned and operated by outside firms.

Based upon these two observations, we should question who has ownership or interest in this business. Do judges, elected officials, and others have a vested financial benefit when prisons are operated at maximum capacity? Are officials somehow associated with arm's length transactions with select companies receiving contracts tied to the prison industry? Who owns the land upon which prisons are built? Is the land leased or sold? Are there laws which prohibit public officials from realizing monetary gain? If so, are there loopholes which circumvent these laws? Is there even the remotest pecuniary incentive to impose prison sentences upon unsuspecting Americans?

In *Newsday*, December 17, 2013, Rosa Brooks, in her article, "A country within a nation," cites that ten percent of America's incarcerated are in prisons operated by private companies. She notes one private company, CCA, had annual revenue in 2011 of $1.7 billion. Damon Hininger, CEO of CCA, personally earned $3.7 million that year. He encouraged investors by referencing "highly compelling corrections industry dynamics.

Who benefits from UNICOR, known as Federal Prison Industries, a "manufacturing" and "processing" operation within the BOP? If UNICOR does not have a profit motive, does it reduce the hard costs to prisons because of the windfall of any gains realized? Do private businesses contract with UNICOR for reduced capital outlay within their own operations and increase profits to their bottom line? Rosa Brooks cites the Defense Department as UNICOR's largest patron. The Defense Department "accounted for $357 million of UNICOR's annual sales." Brooks mentions the U. S. Army "awarded UNICOR a $246,699,217.00 non-multiyear, no option, firm-fixed-price contract… to procure interceptor Body Armor Outer Tactical Vests for various foreign military sales customers." Unbelievably, UNICOR's online video promotes inmate labor as "The best kept secret in outsourcing."[71] Since inmates earn $0.23/hour to $1.35/hour, it is

[71] http://www.post-gazette.com/opinion/Op-Ed/2014/01/05/Incarceration-Nation-by-Rosa-Brooks-What-the-U-S-prisoner-complex-would-look-like-if-it-were-an-independent-nation/stories/201401050077

advantageous for those *in the know*.

Who benefits from the prison commissary system used by inmates nationwide? The commissary is how prisoners supplement their diets and satisfy other wants and needs. Who benefits from the sale of lotion, powder, peanuts, and shampoo? Are providers, distributors, and manufacturers related to public officials? Is the "Keefe" brand in any way owned by present or formerly elected officials or their families? Did Bob Barker of "The Price is Right" game show acquire the contract to provide prison uniforms? Where does the money flow because of the prison system? Does it connect, reconnect, or interconnect to the streams which flow from or to the courts of America?

I raise these questions for an important reason. Besides the conventional and relatively unknown profit-driven relationships, are there other means of profit from the incarceration of Americans? Is there a larger profit motivation to secure court convictions? There are indicators that the federal corporation, the United States, benefits financially when "paper" from convictions or potential convictions is sold as securities, like securities from mortgages sold on the secondary market. There is conceivably a level of financial operations, a whole realm of fiscal transactions, of which we are unaware. Most Americans, because of our cognitive dissonance, would refuse to believe of the possibility of such a financial construct, just as those who may not have believed a stock tied to prisons is on the exchange, prisons are privatized, or that UNICOR is what it is. The selling of securities tied to court cases would be discounted readily by most people.

It is just as easy for the government to dismiss the possibility of the trading or selling of court cases as securities as it is for it to dismiss that one is outside the jurisdiction of Congress for the income tax. The government simply ignores the claim or discounts the notion as frivolous or conspiracy mumbo jumbo. Most Americans would accept either of these official responses just as easily as my defense lawyers rejected my belief.

Consider how Hogeboom responded to my question about the bid and performance bonds. He did not want to answer the question. He dismissed the premise as "patriot conspiracy." But when he finally answered, he parsed his words carefully. Why did he respond in this fashion? Those who have researched these bonds suggest they underwrite the value of a court case which has already been securitized, sold, or traded. As further substantiation of this possible profit motive let's recall the CUSIP number I received for the case against me. Meanwhile, when the government is unresponsive to questions concerning a credible constitutional question and a query which either strikes at what is unknown or smacks of a conspiracy, the official position is not to respond.

THE SENTENCING HEARING

After the jury's verdict against me, the process was simple and direct. I returned to the Lynchburg jail and remained there for three months. The sentencing hearing was scheduled for April 11, 2013, just in time for federal officials to make a press announcement that would serve not only to "educate," but to scare the public-at-large before the April 15 tax filing deadline. My sentence would coincide with the IRS annual "Fear Campaign." During this time, the Probation Office, which works for the court, compiled information for the Pre-sentence investigation report (PSI) for the judge. This report would contain a recommended prison term.

As evident with the previous cases, the length of imprisonment is predicated upon the number of points calculated. There is an amount of points for the criminal charges and the loss. Since I did not cooperate, as I rejected a plea and chose to withstand a trial, I did not benefit with a reduction of points. I would soon learn the points would be significantly increased because of the supposed loss to the victim. What was the loss to the victim? The prosecutor did not know. Why? The government did not know how much I earned. There was no reporting upon an "employer/employee relationship." However, the government concluded that the gross income attributed to any entities mentioned during the trial automatically belonged to me. This gratuitous assertion was beyond comprehension.

To the contrary, I had a private contractual relationship. I received whatever from whomever in exchange for my labor. The government had no knowledge of either the amount or the specie exchanged. My affairs were private and inviolate.

As if the arrogance of the government's presumptions about my earnings was not enough, officials willfully disregarded the losses suffered by these entities. The relevance of this deliberate disregard for the whole truth was irreconcilable in the face of the known. For example, the LLC lost approximately $400,000.00 to $600,000.00 during the tech bubble crash. The corporation lost $350,000.00 in a scam. With its 20,000 pages of discovery, the prosecutors knew of these losses. They had the account information and statements. Yet, as officers of the court, as truth-seekers, they did not include these accurate representations.

When I asked the public defenders why the government, for the purposes of the PSI, did not reconcile what it knew would offset any presumed gain, their response was telling. "They don't have to," Harris stated. Now I understood. The government could promote as *truth* that any revenue was mine without justification, while knowing it was a falsehood, an inaccurate total, which adversely affected the PSI points. This was Hogeboom's intent.

Harris said I should produce the records which proved there were losses. She said it was my responsibility to justify lowering the total points and lowering the potential of a stiff sentence. Out of disbelief, I laughed at her suggestion. My lawyers never lost sight of their own opinions that anything realized by other entities belonged to me. They were willing to support the falsehoods the government knew to be incongruent with the truth. Moreover, I did not have the records of any other *person*. I only had my own.

As we saw with the Gosin case, a man who contended with the "intended loss," the court determined the loss regardless that none existed. One may conclude the intent was to estimate the worst possible calculation. This is the point; the truth was and is inconsequential. If the truth mattered, the trial would have never taken place.

There was no reason to refute the government's claims if I had to prove another company's loss; a loss the government knew was not mine. The government should have gone after the LLC for any tax owed. The bottom line is the "loss" suffered by the "victim" was never credible. As with the Figueroa case, the number applied against him was a lie. Figueroa never gained. He never committed a crime from which he received profit. Under the umbrella charge of "conspiracy," his points were increased substantially.

This begs a question. Does the actual gain or loss have any relevance except to amass points to justify a harsher sentence? The amount of time a man serves in prison does not matter to the government. A prosecutor's goal is to seek what is not true to validate what is unwarranted. This practice leads to a more philosophical query. Why do government officials dignify relationships differently than how people generally relate to each other? Whether as friends, spouses, parents, children, or professionals in business, we typically exercise an equitable standard of relating. We instinctively operate with a sense of integrity. We recognize and react to injustices with a sense of fair play.

As parents, we judiciously apply honest and balanced reprisal to our child's infractions. We deal fairly with friends. We honor our relationships with spouses by offering the dignity they deserve. We do not impugn relationships by ignoring what is blatantly untrue or incomplete.

If we do, we compromise the truth and act without integrity. We allow for the consequences of what is false to prevail; and we do so with selfish and deliberate intent to achieve some questionable end. A husband who cheats on his wife cares little for honor or the sanctity of his marriage. A sister who allows her brother to suffer punishment for something she did cares little for what is right and just. One who swaps his own inferior movie camera for a friend's newer and better version denigrates a relationship for selfish gain. The truth does not matter; yet the truth exists, nonetheless. In each of these scenarios, someone suffers. The wife, brother, and friend need not prove they did nothing wrong. The culprits know the truth, the whole truth.

The same can be said of a U. S. Attorney who purposely ignores and inflates information related to the *loss* and charges. Just as a husband operates with a sense of arrogance and entitlement cloaked in secrecy, the government does the same. As the sister allows a brother to suffer, while she shrouds herself with an untouchable air of supremacy, the government advances an agenda with an equal lack of accountability. As the friend relegates a new reality, transposing what is real for a lie, the officers of the court exchange fiction for what is true and known.

The exclusion of evidence which would invalidate the charges and a presumed gain or loss is no different than crafting words, definitions, and representations to distort the truth. In the end, the courts may only achieve convictions of innocent men if the manipulation and absence of truth are effectively employed. A more severe prison term is gained by obfuscation of information and a complete dismissal of what is credible.

What are men such as Gosin, Figueroa, and I to do? Gosin's points were inflated for a loss which never was. Figueroa's points were inflated for a gain he never received. The points in my situation were inflated for a loss to the victim which could never have been. In each case, the system fostered an outcome with sentences for crimes that were never committed and validated by imaginary losses and gains. The system determined that each man was guilty. The system determined the years of incarceration. The law and the truth were of little to no consequence.

If we blindly accept *justice* without understanding what is behind the false front known as the legal system, the arrogance of those who operate this machine will do so without challenge. Discovering this dynamic after the fact is too late. Figueroa and Gosin will never know, and the Johnsons of the world may affect little when they are warehoused in federal facilities serving a prison sentence that is disproportionate to the true loss or gain, notwithstanding they are innocent of committing the alleged crime.

REQUEST FOR A NEW TRIAL

A few weeks after the government's trial, Cargill visited me. He had a copy of the PSI report to complete. He was accompanied by the probation officer. It was at this meeting that Cargill told me that he intended to file a motion for a new trial. He believed reference to the child support issue was extremely prejudicial. I was not just surprised at his suggestion but encouraged. He was going to defend me for what he believed was not frivolous. If a new trial were granted, I could fight the charges with my good faith belief, regardless of any attorney's reluctance. After what I experienced, if forced to contend with the charges a second time, I knew I had no option but to argue my belief and the lack of jurisdiction.

Unfortunately, Cargill never filed a motion. He originally encouraged me to use an outside law firm. When I asked him for the reason, he stated that Moon knew him and would deny the motion. Consider the significance of this statement. Cargill claimed a private attorney would have a better chance of gaining court's approval. This disclosure was significant and an admission by an officer of the court that a judge would give credence to a private lawyer over a federal defense attorney who often appeared before him. One would think the motion would stand upon its own merits, regardless of the messenger. Yet, I followed his advice.

I called a lawyer whom I recently met on a phone call. When we spoke, he advised me to have Cargill file the motion. The ease with which the outside attorney dismissed Cargill's recommendation was telling. With urgency, I tried to reach Cargill. I attempted to call him but could not get through the jail's phone system. I called the private attorney again and asked him to call or email Cargill with instructions to file the motion. I also mailed two letters directing Cargill to file before the deadline. Unbeknownst to me, Cargill never acted upon my request or his own recommendation. He chose not to defend his client with a professional belief that was *not frivolous*.

Cargill's neglect was no trivial matter. I argued to Judge Moon that Cargill had a responsibility to file the motion but failed to do so. As you read the Declaration I submitted (Appendix I), which is my testimony of events between me and both attorneys, as you weigh my argument in the 2255 (Appendix J), compare it with Cargill's failure to defend me during the trial. The point is rather obvious. If a defense attorney will not defend his client, the justice system cannot and will not achieve justice. Since the documents are self-explanatory, reach your own assessment. Pay attention to the emails from the outside attorney, Jay Nanavati, as confirmation of Cargill's timid nature. Read the Declaration and 2255 argument and the Motion to Amend (Appendix K). Consider the impact on a defendant who is at the mercy of a *professional* who balks out of self-preservation.

When Harris visited some five weeks later to retrieve the PSI forms, I asked her about the motion for a new trial. I had believed Cargill did as asked. Harris looked at me and then looked down, as if in shame. She disclosed that they never moved forward. She acknowledged they received the email from Nanavati and my letters; yet they did nothing. I was struck by her apparent indifference to my requests that they act upon their own advice.

Cargill, alone, recommended a new trial. With disgust, I asked, "Why? Why didn't you act?" I paused. "Why didn't you at least preserve the opportunity to file by notifying the court with an email?" Her response confirmed her attitude. "We did not think it was 'strategically beneficial' to file a motion for a new trial before sentencing." She intimated such a request would further frustrate the court and would adversely affect the amount of prison time I would receive. She said they wanted to prevent any appearance of hostility. "What?" I asked. This made no sense. When was a man to submit a motion if not before sentencing? Any motion had to be submitted prior to the filing deadline. Cargill's reasoning, as conveyed by Harris, was without merit. According to him, no one should file a motion for a new trial. No one should compromise the "strategic benefit" that comes because of doing nothing.

According to Cargill, not filing the motion was positive and would somehow suggest to the court that I was "cooperative" in a situation which could not get any worse. Not filing would be a sign, a code, a message of sorts that the judge should be lenient, and the allowance of any child support issue was excusable, regardless of how prejudicial it was to the defendant, regardless of the impact it had upon the jury's decision.

I believe the unspoken reason for Cargill's inaction was self-preservation. He did not want to suffer from a filing he knew would be denied. He did not want to be the messenger who, either on paper or verbally, argued that the judge made an error. This was the truth of the matter. This was the reason Cargill encouraged me to secure an outside attorney. He was more concerned with his own career than preserving my best interests.

The words "strategically beneficial" may be translated as "do not further burden" or "do not frustrate, aggravate, or agitate" since the sentence would be harsh already. These words meant "I must protect my career," "take the easy path," and "the defendant lost, so why bother." Cargill's psychological and emotional motives were evident.

When we examine this public defender's rationale, we see the arrogance of the legal system from his quarter. We plainly see what he valued. Did he hope I would understand? Perhaps. But he knew that *I knew* he was ethically bound to perform. He failed to act, and he did so deliberately. He justified his failure under a theory of protecting the strategic benefit of a man who was already doomed. Meanwhile, the only way to escape this fate was with a new trial. Cargill's belief was *frivolous*.

When I expressed my disappointment, Harris seemed all too prepared. She stated, "You can always submit a 2255 motion for ineffective assistance of counsel." I had not even heard of such a motion at the time. Her comments only corroborated my belief that their motivation sprang from professional preservation more than a calling to defend a client against what they saw as prejudices of the court and an obvious injustice.

One of the unfortunate and unintended consequences of institutional arrogance is the callous indifference toward those at the mercy of the system. Cargill was a twenty-year veteran. The altruistic fervor with which he entered public service had long since waned. No longer were his clients viewed as flesh and blood, as deserving people. They were numbers, statistics. Cargill was desensitized. Does this sound harsh? Is this thought overstated or unwarranted? Consider the progression of this dilemma. Cargill was no different than the prosecutor who used *discretion* to blur the facts of the case for his own purpose. As readily as a prosecutor may, under the color of law, trespass upon the rights of an innocent man, which is permissible with the rules of court, defense counsel may skirt obligations under color of professional judgment and dismiss remedies designed for justice and the rights of the convicted.

I was angry and in disbelief. I was one against the machine—the entire machine. Even my proponent was an opponent. I had no other option but to submit my own motion for a new trial regardless that the deadline had long since passed. Yet, as far as I was concerned, Cargill had received sufficient notice and squandered the opportunity. On principle alone this served as the impetus for my request. Whether effective or not, I was going to resurrect to last hope that might reverse a bleak future.

THE VICTIM IS REVEALED

Curiously, my motion for a new trial became even more significant. I received a revelation within the contents of the PSI document, an example of a fact that would have been lost otherwise. Initially, I could not fully comprehend its import because I could not believe this disclosure. The PSI stated that the victim of my supposed crimes was the IRS. I was under the impression the victim was and had always been the United States of America, however this term was defined. The United States of America was the party which filed suit, the plaintiff. Furthermore, the *United States* was the party frequently referenced within the text of court documents. One might say such an observation is of no consequence, that the IRS is, based upon what we learned in the chapter which dealt with definitions, the United States. However, why is the victim also the investigating agency? Is this not a conflict of immense proportions? Is this why the IRS never answered my question? The fact is that the victim investigated me with impunity.

Within a separate paragraph of the PSI report titled "Victim," the IRS, a collection and bookkeeping agency for the International Monetary Fund—a debt collector for the central banks—was the real party in interest with a claim against me. Questions surfaced. I wanted answers. Why? How? What? When? I wanted clarity. I asked the public defenders if this revelation was true. "Yes," Harris responded. "How could this be?" I replied. She rather nonchalantly shrugged and suggested the IRS was always the victim. I stared at her with a look of incredulity and uttered my response rather haltingly, "How could it be obvious when it was not revealed?" Harris ignored my question.

I reminded both Cargill and Harris that during the Initial Hearing I had asked if anyone had a claim against me. I noted that Pompei was sitting next to the prosecutor; neither of them spoke. I asked Cargill if the government did not respond to prevent disclosing that the IRS was the victim, and the United States was the Plaintiff by proxy. They continued to ignore my questions. Why? The questions mounted. As the days passed, I was no closer to any credible insight.

- Why was the United States of America on court filings instead of the IRS?
- Why did the victim conduct a 9-year investigation against the alleged criminal?
- How was the investigation objective and impartial? When or where in this legal system are victims able to conduct their own criminal probes?
- Does the IRS agent sit with the prosecution as a representative of the victim?

The lack of any information from the public defenders was troubling. The motion I had prepared became another challenge of jurisdiction. After all, jurisdiction could be challenged any time during the proceeding.

I believed fraud was an element of the trial. If only for how the investigation was handled from the start, with the added developments throughout the trial, I appreciated that the real victim was deliberately hidden from disclosure. It was with this contention that I renewed my challenge of jurisdiction with vehemence. With this frame of reference, permit me to offer an explanation as to why jurisdiction was important.

I explained earlier how a law comes into existence. To underscore an important point, all laws must be given public notice. To be enforceable in the 50 states, the law must be published in the Federal Register. A law that is not published is not valid. A law which does not have an "implementing regulation" is not enforceable within the 50 states. In practice, once a law is passed, there must be an implementing regulation published in the Federal Register. This allows the public to not only be informed, but to give people chance to comment.

I knew the misdemeanor charges did not have implementing regulations. The charges for the felony had an implementing regulation under CFR 27, Bureau of Alcohol, Tobacco, and Firearms, not 26 CFR, Internal Revenue. How could the IRS and the Federal Government enforce a law within the 50 states with no implementing regulations? The answer is the IRS is not enforcing the law within the 50 states; rather, the IRS is enforcing the law against those with a federal status and receiving federal benefits within the *State* of Washington D. C. Americans who elect to be treated as *resident aliens* (see 26 USC 6013) are within the *United States*.

There is a resource called the Parallel Table of Authorities and Rules (PTOAR) which, as I understand, is not permitted in courts as evidence. This is a government publication and its use in court is denied. This reference is a listing of statutes in chronological order. To the right of each code section is the corresponding implementing regulation. The PTOAR is a compilation of all codes and regulations published in the Federal Register. If the code is not in it, the code is not relevant to the 50 states.

When I was released on bond in July 2012, I validated that there are code sections within the PTOAR which are without implementing regulations. There are code sections which are not even in the PTOAR. There are code sections which have implementing regulations that are outside of the section for statutes. For example, 26 USC is the code which deals with taxes, yet 27 CFR is the source for the implementing regulation. This is what I found in my case. When I wrote the motion challenging jurisdiction after learning that the IRS was the victim, I tried to recall what the PTOAR revealed.

As we move forward, keep in mind that Cargill and Harris, as I conveyed my concerns to them, were not affected in the least. In my motion I stated:

> *... petitioner naturally questions how the "victim," the IRS or the plaintiff... the United States of America, has jurisdiction or standing to sue.*
>
> *The IRC limits assessment and collection to internal revenue districts established under 26 USC 7621. Yet, 7621 is not listed in the Parallel Table of Authorities and Rules... While 7621 is not within the PTOAR, Executive Order No. 10289 is, with implementing regulation Title 19, Part 101, establishing customer collection offices in each state... This order is the only authority for establishing revenue districts, confirmed by 26 CFR 301. 7621-1.*

The regulation, 26 CFR 301.7621-1 states:

> 301.7621-1 Internal revenue districts
> *For delegation to the Secretary of authority to prescribe internal revenue districts for the purpose of administering the internal revenue laws, the Executive Order No. 10289 dated September 17, 1951 (16 FR 9499) was made applicable to the Code by Executive Order No. 10574, dated November 5, 1954 (19 FR 7249)*

This regulation ends with "32 FR 15241, Nov. 3, 1967." This should serve as confirmation of the veracity of the posting of codes and regulations to the Federal Register and the relevance of the PTOAR.

Code section 26 USC 7212—the felony—had a cross reference in the PTOAR with an implementing regulation of 27 CFR, which deals with "Alcohol, Tobacco and Firearms." The regulation refers to a "manufacturer of cigarettes." There was no implementing regulation listed for code section 7203. I told my legal advisers that it was difficult to reconcile their willful failure to argue jurisdiction given the indicators that jurisdiction was lacking. They never once bore the cross of legal representation as I feverishly fought for my freedom and innocence.

With limited resources, I spent the next two months compiling information and writing the motion. By the time I finished, I submitted a handwritten document which argued that fraud and force were used to pursue a conviction under threat, coercion, and duress. Fraud and force are staples of the legal process which contradicted any conclusion that the judiciary was a virtuous and venerable institution.

I continued to endure the dynamic of "not knowing," especially while in prison. Regrettably, I found myself becoming comfortable. I detested the tendency to seek balance in an environment which defied what was natural and normal. This was the main reason I kept busy. I used every moment of the day with purpose. Meanwhile, with the sentencing hearing just weeks away, I read and studied a limited supply of law citations, court cases, and regulations.

With only days before April 11, 2013, I filed the motion challenging jurisdiction. Since I filed a motion to dispense with legal counsel the week prior, I was able to move forward. I would make my last attempt to prevail with the truth.

Weigh the import of the sentencing hearing in context of all that transpired. Two thoughts are salient. The first is philosophical, a notation of the self-discovery of man by and through experience. Man will never truly know himself until he grapples with the harsh reality of life. If he stumbles or retreats, he learns about himself. If he shrinks with trepidation, fails to act, loses perspective, and questions his resolve, he learns. If he faces the unthinkable, executes his battle plan, reacts to the unexpected with carefully planned contingencies or ad hoc solutions, recovers from mistakes, and endures the confusion and upheaval inherent with conflict, he learns about himself.

This sense of knowing, not who a man is or is not, but who he is becoming, is everything. We cannot dispute that life is more much more than merely existing. Life is knowing, being, and becoming into possibility. I believe knowledge begets understanding; understanding begets wisdom; and wisdom begets truth. When men ascend through this hierarchy and live into truth, regardless of the repercussions, he manifests a life of distinction and purpose.

I must admit that I questioned why I traveled this path. I surveyed the past nine years, especially the last four, and cringe in disbelief at the raw destruction. The magnitude of the loss is unfathomable, and for what? Was I self-righteous? Was I maniacally driven? Was I beyond the bounds of reason? Or was I moving into an understanding few appreciate? Was my penchant for truth the catalyst which moved me toward greater truth? Why would a man sacrifice so much? This final question is perhaps the most illuminating. I cannot escape what I believe to be a truism of life—understanding begets heart and heart begets understanding. Had my heart never entered the equation, had I never challenged the disparity between truth and the well-orchestrated lie, I would have lacked the will to venture farther than the threshold of fear. Absent the heart to act upon principles and genuinely held beliefs, I would not have sought what was uncomfortable.

Even in prison, I had a vision for my children and America. I envisioned less ignorance, apathy, and fear. I saw people coveting a solemn promise that freedom secured in the past would be freedom which will flourish yet again. I hoped for the defeat of arrogance, a sinister force which deceives and destroys. I yearn for my children to live into the possibility that lies anchored within institutional arrogance will no longer enslave them. Rather, my fervent desire is that we will be as Nature's God intended and claim our calling, ever cognizant of our birthright as kings and queens without subjects, exercising the sovereignty that resides in the people—the wellspring of freedom.

We were once a people who sought the noble aim of freedom and reaped the bounty of its harvest. We have every possibility to secure this bounty for ourselves and posterity. We need only jettison the chains which bind us to a certain fate. If we escape the chains of ignorance, apathy, and fear, we may defy a pervasive institutional arrogance.

This certain fate leads to the second thought worthy of consideration. The power that is the federal judicial system, the apparatus which turns the heavy and slow wheels of *justice*, the leviathan responsible for raw and depraved destruction of the lives of Americans and their families, can be stopped. The courts may be restored to their former heyday of virtuous jurisprudence and the exaction of a more congruent and equal justice.

With and through the power of one—one man, one group, one community, one state—we may create a revolution of the heart and mind. We may overcome a power which is rendering America to a history and future of inconsequence. I am convinced this revolution of the heart and mind may redeem and restore an individual and collective accounting for freedom and truth. This accounting will compel courts, which once esteemed discretion and discernment, to appraise justice and truth as sacrosanct. Such redemption may be realized from an inspired hope of those willing to shed the inhibitions that accompany ignorance, apathy, and fear. We may right the wrongs of the injustices largely borne of our own neglect.

I found myself confronting a certain fate, a prison sentence, the consequence of a wrong versus a right. I saw the context of a man contending for truth over the lie. It was through this experience that I was able to appreciate the extent of our national and cultural demise. But for my suffering and willingness to persevere, I would not have discerned the true scope of federal power, power which far exceeds the government's legitimacy.

Had I done anything differently, had I wavered in fear and filed tax returns at the first encounter with agent Biggs in 2004, I would be comfortable within the four sides of my home. I would be a compliant conformist because I no longer cared and no longer searched for enlightenment. I would never have met the likes of Figueroa, Gosin, Ingalls, or Webb. I would not have known their common stories of unwarranted suffering and injustice. I say with certainty, if we come to appreciate what fellow Americans endure, it is then, and only then, we will understand our challenge. Once we arrive at this juncture and appreciate the repercussions, we may pursue solutions. Solutions, after all, are the fruit of adversity. Because of my journey and understanding, I sought solutions.

The ominous prospects of the Sentencing Hearing reflected the culmination of all the adversity the legal system had wrought. No remedy would salvage my future. No solution would protect or preserve the present or future my children deserved. The truth would not be understood, and the remedies would remain unattainable until we avail ourselves to the idea that we do not know. May this one message resound without fail.

Innocent men and women are in prison, and we don't know of this reality. If you can reconcile this thought, there may be only one veritable conclusion—our deliberate indifference to any innocent man's plight assures the arrogance of a flawed process and an unaccountable judicial system. In this light, solutions which might eradicate these conditions will never come to pass. Knowledge, courage, and resolve are vital for change to occur. May we all consider that my experience, my defeat—analogous to death—is the very substance which will bring forth life. If we learn from those who have suffered from the unconscionable, we may eventually defeat our own ignorance.

Ironically, my journey into this death, the loss of my liberty, was the solace which gave me hope. I recognized how I had become even more enlightened. I realized how, through my stark experience, I would enlighten others. Not only had I withstood the power of a lie and subsequent loss, but the prison sentence would also serve as the fertile substance for greater insight, begotten by experience and the light of truth. Loss is not loss when we understand our lives are largely comprised of mere circumstances. If I prevailed with integrity, I would embrace the experience as a righteous cry for the unsuspecting. I would sound the clarion call and declare that we don't know what we don't know. If only people would listen.

THE END AND THE BEGINNING

On April 11, 2013, I was shackled and transported by armed marshals to the federal courthouse. As I was ushered into the mahogany chamber for the last time, I did not realize the strident contempt I harbored. Caged in a jail for the last three months, awaiting the inevitable, affected by a restless and fleeting hope, I rebelled inwardly. I likened my state of being to the pursuit of a lost child with unrelenting passion—never capitulating—only to know that steps away was the sad truth. This realization unhinged the depth and breadth of my despair which had to be expressed.

This unexpected and burgeoning array of emotions and thoughts, the almost unharnessed compunction to lash out indiscriminately, were bound and dignified out of necessity. I couched my angst for the purpose at hand. When Judge Moon commenced the hearing, I immediately moved the court to take judicial notice of the motion for a new trial and challenge of jurisdiction. Moon acknowledged my request as a formality and stated that he would get to these documents. When he continued with sentencing, I objected. I cited the motion again and stressed that jurisdiction could be challenged at any time. Moon was unaffected. He refused to address my claim.

After Hogeboom addressed the court with his sentencing recommendation, the judge asked for my response. Without hesitation, I moved the court to compel the prosecutor to prove jurisdiction. Moon denied my request. He refused to require that Hogeboom prove anything. I was disheartened; but Moon's rigidity emboldened my resolve. Angry, frustrated, and all but condemned to an unjust fate, the intransigence of the court was humbling. I pressed the issue and stated the government must prove jurisdiction. Moon remained steadfast. Citing Supreme Court cases which mandated jurisdiction be proved, Moon ignored my plea. I sensed I was reaching a tipping point.

With another desperate grasp for what would not be, Moon stated that if I pursued the matter further, he would hold me in criminal contempt. I challenged him and asked, "Who suffered an injury which warranted a criminal contempt charge?" Moon looked around the chamber and said, "I think we have all been injured today." He was not going to honor what I deemed to be fundamental judicial obligation. At a minimum, I believed he was duty bound to have Hogeboom respond. I expressed dissatisfaction. I withdrew a notarized affidavit from my files. The document memorialized that the judge had violated his oath of office and committed sedition and treason against the Constitution. I was steps away from encountering my fate and the turmoil within me was hell-bent for an exit.

Before I offered this affidavit, I asked Judge Moon to recuse himself. "I will not!" was his firm reply. I then noted for the record that he was fired. It was at this point that he found me in criminal contempt of court. At the same time, as two storm fronts collided, I tendered the notarized statement. I read into the record that Moon had compromised his oath, which resulted in seditious acts and treason against the Constitution. His rejoinder was his refusal to allow me to continue as my own representative. He reappointed Cargill and Harris as my legal advisers.

To say the tension was great would be an understatement. The judge was annoyed. I was angered and vehemently opposed their dog and pony show, a supposedly fair trial. As far as I was concerned, their scripted three act play was farcical—nothing but a judgment secured by fraud and force.

The public defenders sat in disbelief. I had not conformed to the parameters which governed their profession as equally as they did not comply with their ethical duty to present my belief or defend my best interests. Meanwhile, Hogeboom sat in amusement, no doubt relishing in the tragic demise of another *guilty* American. The U. S. Marshals were positioned behind me and prepared for the unexpected. I never noticed that, amidst the fury of emotions, they made their way from the right side and within feet of the rear of the defense table. My sister, who traveled to make an impassioned plea on my behalf—hoping to sway the court for a lenient sentence—sat in the gallery in complete dismay. Not only affected by the events, but she was also, unbeknownst to me, told by Cargill that her words of support were not needed. His rude dismissal of her testimony to the judge had a grave impact, akin to the tumult of my own emotions, dashed hopes and disgust for the system.

Judge Moon had not been amenable to any of my efforts, questions, and motions. He did not recognize my earnest attempts to reach a resolution, especially concerning the issue of jurisdiction and the private remedy. The reverse was true. He denied or ignored everything. He was poised to pass a stiff sentence. With a solemn air, Judge Moon, asked for me to stand. I responded that I would not. I reaffirmed that I was not the defendant and was without (outside of) the jurisdiction of the court. Moon looked at me and shrugged his shoulders and stated, "I don't care whether you stand or not."

As Cargill and Harris rose from their seats, I remained seated and as motionless as a ship at sea with no wind. Moon pronounced his sentence. He opined at length about his perception of the crime and the selfishness and greed at the root of the charges. I looked at my sister. I looked at the judge. I looked down in sobering contemplation. This was it. This was the finality of American *justice*. With certainty, I knew fraud and force served as the undercurrent which swept truth from what were once sacred halls of justice. Consider that:

- My motion for a new trial was not read;
- My prior motions appeared to have been given the same treatment;
- The remedy to off-set the charges was not honored;
- My query to know who had a claim against me went unanswered;
- My challenges of jurisdiction went unanswered;
- My public defenders dismissed my good faith belief as frivolous.

The entire court experience paralleled my attempts to have the IRS and government officials respond to a simple question: What law required me to file a federal income tax return? No response was given, and it remains unanswered to this day.

I viewed the court as a mere extension of a system which assured a fraud that was as apparent as the unjust sentence and the unbridled force needed to carry it out. The court and legal systems compelled men to endure its process under threat, coercion, and duress. There were no distinctions separating the court from any of the other components of the legal system. Through and because of this system, the court sentenced me to forty-eight months in prison for seeking the truth and an additional thirty days for criminal contempt—that is, for expending every effort to assure my freedom.

Sovereignty itself is, of course, not subject to law, for it is the author and source of law... While sovereign powers are delegated to... the government, sovereignty remains with the people, by whom and for whom all government exists and acts. **Yick Wo v. Hopkins, 118 US 356 (1886)**

IN A WORD—*DISCRETION*

On April 30, 2015, I was paged over the prison intercom system to report to the CO's office. There I met Lieutenant (LT) Hoover. "Do you know who I am?" he asked. "No." I responded. "I am LT Hoover from SIS (Special Investigations Services) and I solve problems." Hoover was responding to a complaint I had filed against the prison and LT Martin. Let me explain.

In early April 2014, on a cold, windy, and rainy day—a day that was miserable—the inmates were told they could not wear their jackets to the dining hall. The prison officials expected the men to stand in line, outside, and unprotected from the elements. The temperature was 61 degrees. The prison policy states that no jackets could be worn if the temperature was greater than 60. After speaking with LT Martin about this decision and its impact to my health, she coldly stated, "No coats!"

I promptly filed a "BP-8" form (Appendix L), which is the first stage of an "Administrative Remedy" within the Federal Bureau of Prisons. The Federal Government has an "Administrative Procedures Act" under Title 5. Anyone with a complaint against the Federal Government is expected to request an administrative remedy before pursuing legal action. The prison system enforces this remedy process with internal forms.

Two weeks after filing the BP-8, I was called by LT Martin to the Compound Office. She was caustic, calculating, and even hysterical. She explained the policy regarding the coats and asked if the issue had been resolved informally. I stated that it was not and indicated so on the bottom of the BP-8. In accordance with the administrative process, I submitted a "BP-9" that went directly to the warden. The warden has an opportunity to resolve any complaint. This is when LT Hoover entered the scene. Based upon my concerns, the warden ordered a change to the policy. LT Hoover was the messenger. From that point on, I wore my coat whenever I wanted.

To illustrate the administrative process, consider the next example. In yet another situation, on June 24, 2015, I was cited for an infraction by a prison official. Angela Lamb (who goes by the name of Ms. Stewart), stated that I had another man's Xerox copy card and she documented this on an "Incident Report." I was, as a result, required to appear before the Unit Disciplinary Committee (UDC). The prison policy is that inmates are not allowed to give anything to or receive anything from another inmate. The UDC determined that I was guilty of the charge and issued punishment. I was denied commissary and telephone privileges for two weeks. The punishment was suspended for six months with good behavior. (Appendix M)

I submitted two requests for an Administrative Remedy. First, I appealed the punishment. Second, I filed a grievance against Angela Lamb for harassment. Once again, I was seeking a resolution under Title 5. The BP-8 concerning Lamb's harassment was handled professionally. Ms. Callahan, Lamb's supervisor, spoke directly with me. She listened and understood why I believed Lamb targeted me for something which occurs daily in the law library *with* Lamb's awareness. She assured me that she would speak with Lamb. Callahan then asked if the BP-8 had been informally resolved. I agreed and noted the same on the form and thanked her for her time, efforts, and discernment.

Meanwhile, I filed a BP-9 concerning the punishment directly to the warden.

When the warden upheld the UDC's decision, I submitted a BP-10 to the Regional Office. The Regional Office reviewed my request and directed the UDC to review the matter again. The UDC decided to retract the punishment and expunge any and all reference to the charge.

What do the coat and copy card situations reveal about the Federal Government and the nature of man? The Federal Government is a fiction, a creation which owes its existence to written words. These words (law, policy, regulations, and procedures) are enforced by men and women who represent the *United States,* the U. S. Government. This is what we learned from the definitions *United States*. When enforcing their responsibilities on behalf of the United States, officials exercise discretion. "Discretion" is defined as:

> *Wise conduct and management exercised without constraint; the ability coupled with the tendency to act with prudence and propriety.* Black's Law Dictionary, Tenth Edition.

When LT Martin enforced the coat policy, she represented the BOP and the United States. She exercised discretion. When Angela Lamb cited me for the infraction, she represented the BOP and the United States. She exercised discretion. Had these situations not been resolved, the Federal Government faced potential legal action for injuries caused by its agents and employees. The point cannot be any clearer. The U. S. Government mandates that any perceived injury be reconciled with and through the administrative process. In a practical sense, this process is a necessity. With its millions of employees and the exercise of discretion used in countless transactions and interactions daily, the government must address grievances and avoid litigation.

Unfortunately, most Americans do not know of this process under Title 5 or how to redress a grievance with the federal authorities. This process, which is available at all levels of government, brings accountability to agents and agencies. As is evident with the coat and copy card incidents, agents abuse their discretion and exceed their authority. Such indiscretion reflects two things: a lack of understanding of the judicious use of power and the inherent disregard for one's fellow man.

Martin's actions and decisions were not sanctioned; rather, they were repudiated by the governing authority, the warden. Lamb's actions and decisions were a concern for her supervisor. Finally, the Regional Office provided oversight for the warden's discretion and support of the punishment issued by the UDC in the copy card incident.

The question of discretion has a direct correlation to the institutional arrogance which runs roughshod over humanity. The men and women who represent the U. S. Government are inherently arrogant to whatever degree. Such is the nature of power. Power is often errantly applied. With respect to criminal investigations, the abuse of power is heightened, and agents are prone to even greater abuse of discretion. As evident throughout history (consider Hus and the men we discussed), should we not expect abuse of discretion? Should we credit ignorance and apathy as reasons why agents abuse their own power? Certainly. Whether because of education, experience, or motivation, agents act contrary to sound judgment. Because of their education, experience, or motivation, Martin and Lamb did not act or decide prudently. The warden did not favorably consider my request to expunge the punishment and the charge from Lamb's indiscretion.

If we consider the countless decisions and actions made daily in all criminal investigations, we naturally expect countless mistakes and errors in judgment (discretion). America still has a 98% conviction rate at the federal level. This statistic would lead one to conclude that the Federal Government and its agents, without any diminution of the current case load, either perform nearly flawlessly or their discretion is not held to account for what it is—rampant indiscretion.

It would be reasonable to conclude that criminal charges subject to indiscretion in the initial stages of an investigation are forwarded to other agencies and authorities. These higher levels of power assert even more questionable actions and decisions without challenge. The net result cannot be anything less than a high conviction rate and the highest level of incarceration in the world. It is not unreasonable to state that officials and agents who act on behalf of the government exercise dubious judgment and are culpable for injuries to Americans and America—a result of institutional arrogance.

Indiscretion is a catalyst for institutional arrogance; and if indiscretion were defeated at the lowest level as well as all levels, institutional arrogance would be lessened. In 2004 and 2005, I wrote to Agents Biggs and Pompei with a simple question. Even if a citizen does not know of the Administrative Procedures Act (APA), my query to them should be considered one as governed by the APA. This can hardly be disputed. A request for assistance is a request for a remedy. What other reason would there be than to ask for assistance and a remedy? Consider that the "Frivolous Arguments" pamphlet Biggs sent, as noted by Kotmair, was unresponsive to my question. Neither Kotmair nor I raised a frivolous argument. Biggs, and his manager and counsel, ignored my query, a request for an administrative remedy.

Their education, experience, and motivation determined their actions. Their *discretion* was not used to hold themselves accountable to a citizen's concern. Why? The agency did not want to answer the questions. Since no official, elected or otherwise, provided a response, we may conclude there is a systemically pervasive and ulterior motive—tantamount to a hidden agenda. This agenda was the reason Biggs ignored my letter and the IRS refused to provide a legitimate administrative remedy.

This compels us to examine how Biggs' unresponsiveness was the catalyst for the institutional arrogance and subsequent power that was ultra vires. Biggs' investigation was forwarded to Pompei who exercised flawed discretion equal in significance to Biggs' flawed discretion. Pompei forwarded his investigation to the prosecution (the DOJ). The prosecution accepted and ignored the investigator's historical record of my "Administrative Remedy" and rebuttal of the government's presumption. The prosecutor concluded that I was a "taxpayer." He ignored that I refuted prima facie evidence of any liability. He ignored that I sought a resolution to the alleged charges in the early stages of the investigation. Hogeboom ignored my letter to the Secretary of the Treasury and my revocation of any federal status which obligated me to the income tax. He ignored my letter to the Social Security Administration and revocation of the federal benefit of social security. Hogeboom exerted his flawed discretion and validated the flawed discretion of both Biggs and Pompei.

Biggs' decision not to respond to Kotmair's letter or my letters directly and indirectly impacted my defense. Moreover, Cargill never reconciled my petition to redress a grievance with the Federal Government. Since Cargill considered my belief to be frivolous, he exercised flawed discretion which summarily jeopardized my defense. Although the Supreme Court decided in Cheek v United States, 498 U. S. 192 (1991) that an American may have an unreasonable belief which would defeat the element of willfulness, with Cargill's position, he strengthened the element of willfulness and the jury's determination of guilt. With Cargill's judgment (discretion), which adversely affected a client who had a reasonable belief, we may conclude that no belief, whether reasonable or unreasonable, may be defended.

I expressed this argument in a complaint against Cargill to the American Bar Association. I asserted that an attorney may hide behind the Canons of Ethics as grounds not to defend a client and ignore that these canons compel every attorney to provide a vigorous defense. (Appendix N) Not surprisingly, the ABA responded by stating that Cargill could not have violated the canons. The ABA *misunderstood* my claim and wrote an explanation which failed to address my central concerns. The Bar did not see a conflict between Cargill's potential and permissible defense of an unreasonable belief (Cheek) that would have conformed to the ABA's Canons of Ethics and his refusal to argue a reasonable belief that was considered frivolous that somehow also conformed to these same canons.

Let's examine Cargill's education, experience, and motivations to an even greater degree. In its response to my 2255 Motion, the Federal Government never asked Cargill for an affidavit or testimony by him rebutting my declaration (Appendix A). So I asked Cargill for his agreement as to what occurred outside the trial record—what was discussed between us—information the prosecutor and the court did not know. I sent Cargill a series of letters which served as a private administrative process. I specifically asked that he agree with the facts or state why he did not. (Appendix O)

We must not lose sight of my intent. I only wanted Cargill to help me overturn the conviction with information only he and I knew. His assistance would have given the court the full context of his failure to effectively defend me against the charges. Consider Cargill's response sent on August 3, 2015. Cargill ignored the substance of my letter and referred to the theories and language which Hogeboom introduced into the trial. Cargill ignored my one and only good faith belief even at this late date. As is evident with my subsequent letters, Cargill continued to avoid my request. In September he continued to speak of "theories" I never posed, while stating that my "good faith defense was fairly represented at trial." We already know he refused to argue my good faith belief. He deemed it "frivolous." So how could it have been fairly represented at trial? His only argument was that I had a mere "belief" that I was not liable to file a tax return. He even responded in this manner after receiving the two Federal Questions concerning an agent's failure to respond to a private citizen's query and whether the federal income tax could be assessed after revocation of the social security benefit. It appeared to me as though Cargill was avoiding and evading accountability. He refused to confirm my testimony.

Finally, Cargill offered to help if he could. So, I asked him for his assistance. For the third time, I asked him to send me copies of all communications between him and the federal prosecutors throughout the trial proceeding. This is something he could do. To this day, Cargill has yet to respond. Such is the calling for justice and truth by this veteran defense attorney. Such is his "discretion."

If the foregoing is not convincing that Cargill is less than genuine about the facts and his willingness to help, there is but one final point to make. I mentioned before that Biggs responded to Kotmair's letters by sending me the "Frivolous Arguments" pamphlet. As a professional lawyer, Cargill should have read this critical publication before trial. He should have tried to appreciate whether or not my good faith belief was addressed by the IRS in this publication. Take note of the 2013 version of this document, which is dated less than two months after the trial ended on January 18, 2013. (Appendix P) I have included page 20, which is the very page Hogeboom referred to in the trial as the frivolous argument that both Kotmair and I allegedly asked about or asserted. Yet, this IRS "frivolous argument" is unresponsive to my query and is easily contrasted with my nonfederal status. Noteworthy is that no frivolous argument in this pamphlet addresses the acceptance of or the revocation of the federal benefit of social security or a federally excisable status.

I vividly recall Cargill's reaction when I met him at the federal courthouse building in Harrisonburg, Virginia, when we discussed Kotmair's letters in preparation for trial. Cargill had not read them and chastised and questioned me for even speaking with Kotmair. "He doesn't file his taxes," Cargill exclaimed. "He went to prison." To Cargill, there was no reason to consider anything Kotmair communicated. As a result, Cargill failed to apply fundamental legal research and advocacy. He failed to read the government's one document that would have defeated the government's case. But for Cargill's discretion, he would have proved that my belief was not frivolous. Based upon the government's documents, Cargill would have defeated his own good faith belief that my good faith belief was frivolous. He would have zealously defended his client as expected under the Canons of Ethics. Cargill's discretion proved costly.

As we conclude the question of agent and agency abuse of discretion, consider the letter I sent to Senator Rand Paul (Appendix Q), which included a copy of the Federal Question concerning the issue of revoking or not accepting the federal benefit of social security. He never responded. Consider a letter to the ranking members of the Judiciary Committee. (Appendix Q) I asked them to conduct an inquiry into the inability of inmates to overcome wrongful convictions. Not one of these representatives responded. Why did Senator Paul and the leadership of the Judiciary Committee fail to acknowledge my correspondence with even a simple "thanks for writing?" Is it because I am a "common criminal," an "inmate?" Is it because they have motivations which conflict with an earnest interest in these problems? I don't know the answer. These two examples demonstrate that the legislative branch is complicit with the criminalization of America.

A theme runs through these examples. With LT Martin and Angela Lamb, Biggs and Pompei, Hogeboom and Cargill, and Senator Paul and the Judiciary Committee, indiscretion is rampant throughout the government and the legal system. Indiscretion takes a toll when one considers the number of moving parts (parties) in a criminal case. With the ten components we discussed, each has sub-components and sub-actions and decisions which, although self-contained, interconnect with the actions and decisions of the others. With so many variables, as a criminal case advances, the margin of error multiplies.

As reflected in the next diagram, there are at least eight components in the government's case against me. These parts have numerous sub-parts. The eight parts interact or influence other parts (as indicated by the solid lines); they indirectly influence other components (as indicated by the dashed lines). We may surmise that an unjust result will be realized when each or some parts fail to honor a fundamental act or decision in keeping with the truth, or when any indiscretion is forwarded and sanctioned from one part to another. This is how the justice system propels the indiscretion of an agency or agent. This is how institutional arrogance is validated.

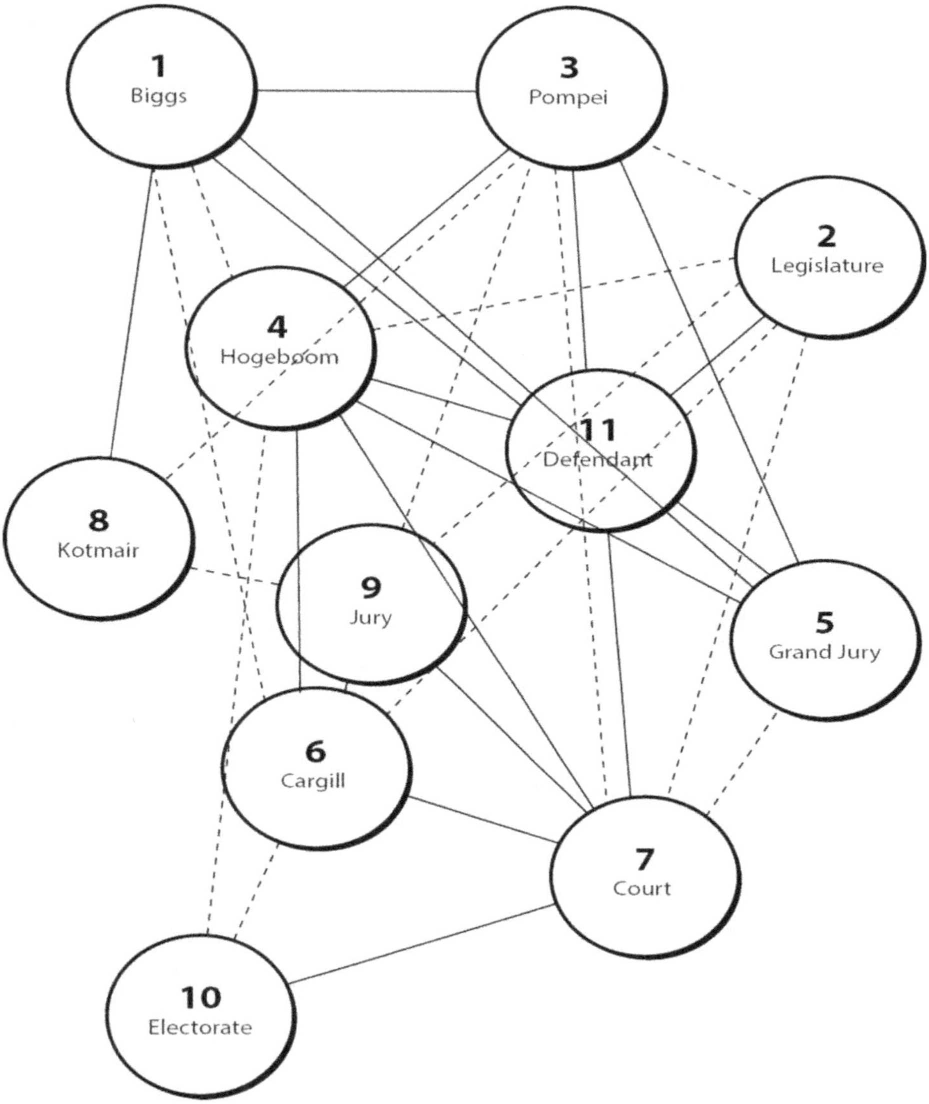

- *If Biggs had responded with the law which required my compliance to file a tax return, the issue would have ended with parts 1 or 3. An administrative remedy would have been provided and negated the need for a criminal trial.*
- *If Biggs and Pompei had dignified my circumstances as not "frivolous," as attested by their own pamphlet, the matter would have ended at 1 and 3. In either scenario, the case would not have progressed beyond 3 to 4.*
- *If 2 had responded to my requests, the case would have ended without progression. Why? I would have compiled with the law or used 2's response to defeat the investigation at 1, 3, 5, or 7.*
- *Had Hogeboom, 4, honored my rebuttal of the presumption and prima facie evidence that I was a taxpayer, he would not have gone to the grand jury, 5.*
- *Since 4 ignored the investigative record and did not square my belief, actions, or rebuttal of his presumption with the Frivolous Arguments pamphlet, he encouraged an indictment without cause.*
- *With Cargill's involvement, 6, he could have read the same pamphlet and*

realized my belief was not listed. He could have tendered a Rule 12 or 17(b) Motion and argued the element of jurisdiction before the court, 7, and moved for dismissal before the trial began. This is what I attempted to do without him.

- ***If 7 did not dismiss the case, 6 could have argued my belief before the jury, 9, and sought an acquittal with a solid defense. This would have defeated the indiscretion of 1, 2, 3, 4, 5, and 7. Since this did not occur, the electorate, 10, and 2 never heard the truth as to my belief, which made me, 11, innocent.***
- ***The people, 5 and 10, and the lawmakers, 2, did not learn that a man relied upon the Constitution, statutes, regulations, and settled law (Steward Machine v Davis), which established the nature of the excise in question.***
- ***No one learned that a man's revocation of a federal status and benefit, 11, was grounds that he was without the jurisdiction of the federal income tax.***

This simple diagram and explanation are revealing. With proper discretion and the search for the truth, the case would have ended at any of the parts. Imagine any government investigation, at any level, described in this manner. If we factor in the education, experience, and motivation, as well as the corresponding ignorance, apathy, and arrogance of any official, the margin of error increases and the legitimacy of any conclusion becomes suspect.

We need only consider the indiscretion of LT Martin, Angela Lamb, the city council with the rental inspection ordinance, the zoning administrator's handling of the business owner's table, and the police chief who provided officers for the Zoning Administrator. Now consider the indiscretion employed by all components and sub-components in the cases of Hus, Galileo, the Scottsboro Boys, Corey, Jones, Ramirez, Webb, Ingalls, Wahler, Richardson, Gosin, Figueroa, Williams, McGinnis, Norris, and Everston. Consider the thousands upon thousands of actions and decisions exercised by agents daily and weigh the multiplying effect of those actions and decisions by even higher levels of office. Every agency has its "blue line" of protection. Like the police forces across the country, agents will not compromise those who make unethical or morally questionable decisions. These dynamics portend an overwhelming and insurmountable situation. There is, seemingly, no way to defeat such arrogance and its all-consuming effect upon institutions and its agents.

This would be an appropriate point to include one, largely untouched, institution which has a direct and indirect impact upon our culture, the justice system, and the indiscretion exercised by the government. This component is the press. The press is often a tool, a weapon of the government, which is used deliberately and effectively. The press should be a means to combat the overreach of the government. Yet, there are times when the press will not express a truth which would otherwise shed light upon the reach of institutional arrogance. For example, the local and national press would not likely reveal my position or belief regarding the federal income tax. Yet, the press will and did document that the government secured a conviction against me. In another example, the press would not readily expose the unconstitutional abuse of power of select politicians for selfish interests.

Consider the letter I sent to the Editorial Board of the Inquirer, the major newspaper for Cincinnati, Ohio. (Appendix R) This letter, which included a copy of the letter sent to the Judiciary Committee mentioned earlier, was never published. The reason is simple. The newspaper was not motivated to expose local and national politicians who knowingly contributed to the imprisonment of an innocent man, husband, and father, Orlando Carter. Consequently, citizens are not informed of the truth. This is the power of arrogance, the power of institutional arrogance.

If a nation expects to be ignorant and free, in a state of civilization, it expects what never was and never will be. **Thomas Jefferson**

Cultural Decline—Decadence to Depravity

Think for a moment of the possibility that the men discussed in this book are innocent and in prison. If only *one* man were innocent, should the outcry be any less? If all were innocent should the outcry be any greater? In either consideration, what if there was no outcry at all? What would this say about our culture?

I decided to conduct a test. While in the SHU in Allenwood, Pennsylvania, I perused the news for anecdotal evidence which would support representations in our culture that the justice system is deeply flawed. I culled through a major regional news publication for confirmation that the arrogance demonstrated in the legal system is reflected in and through the affairs of government, society, and within the citizenry at large. I wanted to see if our culture is under a direct and indirect assault. Do officials or systems prey upon or add to our ignorance, apathy, and fear? Does institutional arrogance reign as a matter of course in our daily lives? Would I find that subtle and blatant decisions by those with titles and low regard for truth, justice, integrity, and principles adversely influence an unwitting people?

This foray into the news served another purpose as well. I wanted to support the premise that our collective indifference allowed the legal system to directly affect our high incarceration rate. If readers could be brought to a better understanding with examples in the news—that injustices were inflicted upon the innocent—this was my goal. Americans have a short memory and are likely to dismiss those topics which do not gain their interest. The outcry for any of the innocent discussed in this book may be negligible, if it exists at all. Referencing news accounts of ignorance, apathy, fear and arrogance with greater societal context would confirm an epidemic of immense proportions. This would validate injustice within the courts. Perhaps people would realize we have a grave problem as pervasive as it is unnoticed. What better way to underscore this prevailing dynamic within the judiciary than by surveying the same in our culture generally?

The examples I unearthed concerned the George Zimmerman trial, the glorification of heinous criminals by "fan[s]"[72] who served as jurors or potential jurors, Elliot Spitzer's campaign for Comptroller of New York City and President Obama's decision to stop enforcement of select portions of the Affordable Care Act. Any of these topics confirm cultural indifference to do right and a propensity toward subsequent moral decay. Any of the news examples are a testament of liberties (indiscretions) taken by those in positions of influence, those with *titles*. These examples are an indictment against the people for allowing such indiscretions to remain unchecked. Our failure to comprehend what is occurring on a macro scale inhibits any genuine sense of community. We create a false façade, a contrived truth. How am I able to state this proposition? It is simple. Consider that we either don't know of the potentially innocent men in this book, or we may know of them, but we give them little to no regard. Either way, a true sense of community is lacking.

The electorate is the bedrock of the great American experiment. If the electorate is comfortable with the absence of principles and integrity, the examples in the news will continue and worsen. From a micro perspective, the lawless nature of American justice will never change as long as the people are unenlightened and indifferent.

---

[72] http://www.realclearpolitics.com/articles/2013/07/12/americas_sociopath_fetish__119171.html

Thomas Sowell is an author and commentator who posed the idea that "the American justice system and of the public's faith in that system and in their country"[73] is "more important than Zimmerman's fate."[74] Zimmerman was tried and acquitted for the charge of murder of a young black man, Trayvon Martin, in Florida. Sowell reached his conclusion by asking, "Is this still America?"[75] Sowell, along with other commentators, suggested George Zimmerman should have never been brought to trial. Why? Sowell stated that the prosecution had "an absence of serious evidence."[76] So why was there a trial in the first place? The answer may be sourced in the *search* for the truth.

The Executive Branch is one of the ten components of the legal system. This component enforces the law. Whether the President of United States, governor of a state, prosecutors, or police chiefs, the executive and his agencies are expected to enforce the law. The Zimmerman case became a political football caught by the highest executive in the land—President Obama. He hoped to score political points at the expense of justice. Before the trial began, Sowell wrote that Obama stated, "If I had a son, he'd look like Trayvon."[77] The posturing of presidential power with racially parsed pandering is as telling as it is reprehensible. As the chief law enforcement authority, Obama had no greater responsibility than to seek justice objectively and impartially. Not only did he denigrate the search for truth and justice for political gain (his re-election was forthcoming), but he also sent representatives from the Department of Justice to Florida, according to Sowell, "to finance local activists who agitated for Zimmerman to be arrested."[78]

With a clinical view of Obama's agenda and comments, we can draw a parallel to any U. S. Attorney pursuing unjust charges against innocent men, or those who are subject to an agenda driven by a heavy bias. Obama wanted to make a crime and a criminal in the Zimmerman case when both were potentially unwarranted. His zeal mirrored the warped focus of prosecutors who fanatically pursued Tony Figueroa and Ryan Gosin. Is there any difference? There is reason to believe that Obama, as with any administration, had an unspoken motivation to politicize *crimes* for personal gain.

To prove the point, the Obama administration acted to stop Figueroa and a non-existent $300 million bid rigging scam. The administration protected the public when the U. S. Attorney, a political appointee, broke up a $14-$30 million bank fraud racket and its diabolical leader Ryan Gosin. Perhaps the question Sowell and every clear-thinking American should ask is: When will Americans hold unprincipled executives and their minions accountable for perverting the proper enforcement of the law? If this question were posed, we would never need to ask, "Is this still America?" However, we must know enough to recognize that the likes of Obama and his surrogates are incongruent with American justice. Their actions juxtapose what the law requires, and the people deserve.

Yet, we must reconcile that this is a *system*. Obama confirms one of the tenets of this book; psychological and emotional objectives malign decisions, thoughts, beliefs, and actions taken by law enforcement authorities which affect how the system is used. Such motives confirm a heightened level of apathy and arrogance among officials that easily masks their ignorance. This dynamic is a formula which will consistently defeat justice. This is the point as it relates to the Zimmerman case.

---

[73] http://www.nationalreview.com/article/353502/still-america-thomas-sowell

[74] Ibid.

[75] Ibid.

[76] Ibid.

[77] Ibid.

[78] Ibid.

Jacob Sullum is another commentator who espouses "ample cause for reasonable doubt about Zimmerman's guilt."[79] Sullum gives credence that "Zimmerman erroneously believed the shooting was justified, that he feared for his life, but not reasonably so, as required for a self-defense claim under Florida law."[80] This was the element the authorities overlooked in their search for the truth.

The special prosecutor did not argue this sensible and grounded perspective. According to Sullum, the authorities "implausibly portrayed Zimmerman as an angry vigilante who maliciously tracked Martin down to deliver rough justice after mistaking him for a burglar."[81] Regrettably, the prosecutor crafted her own story in hopes of sensationalizing the crime into a conviction. Thomas Sowell agrees. He states, "You don't send people to prison on the basis of what other people imagine or on the basis of media sound bites…"[82] Sullum offered, "prosecutors tell a compelling story that does not fit the facts very well."[83]

Any of the men in the court cases we explored were in similar situations. They were pursued by a prosecutor with a sensational story incongruent with the truth. The prosecutor's *facts* were inconsistent with reality. Just as Zimmerman did not act out of "ill will, hatred, or an evil intent,"[84] as asserted by Special Prosecutor Angela Corey, none of the men highlighted in this work equaled the hyperbole offered by the prosecution.

Unfortunately, the men I discussed did not have a national stage or audience. They did not have the defense counsel who would have accompanied such top billing from a nationally pronounced case. Adequate defense representation is crucial since prosecutors, such as Corey, are no different than their superiors who seek convictions for political gain at the expense of innocent lives or those who are targeted for criminal charges which exceed the circumstances. Notably, Corey was either unwilling to tell her superiors she would not pursue certain charges against Zimmerman when the evidence was lacking, or she believed her unsubstantiated claim. Either way, she served her primary objective of trying a national case—a motivation which revealed her apathy and arrogance.

Sowell was correct when he stated, "politicians… cheapen or corrupt the law."[85] This is exactly what President Obama, Attorney General Holder, and Corey accomplished. This is what ethically hampered prosecutors did in the cases we surveyed. This is what prosecutors do when they act with impunity against the interests of justice and the people. President Calvin Coolidge stated:

> *It is difficult for men in high office to avoid the malady of self-delusion. They are always surrounded by worshipers. They are constantly and, for the most part, sincerely assured of their greatness. They live in an artificial atmosphere of adulation and exaltation which sooner or later impairs their judgment. They are in grave danger of becoming careless and arrogant.*[86]

Those in authority are moved by corrupt motives, be it psychological or emotional, motives that obscure and blind.

We cannot avoid the lessons of humanity and man's feebleness in the face of hubris. The pursuit of unjust and unsubstantiated charges is often predicated upon the

---

[79] http://reason.com/archives/2013/07/10/why-george-zimmerman-should-be-acquitted
[80] Ibid.
[81] Ibid.
[82] http://www.nationalreview.com/article/353502/still-america-thomas-sowell
[83] http://reason.com/archives/2013/07/10/why-george-zimmerman-should-be-acquitted
[84] Ibid.
[85] http://www.nationalreview.com/article/353502/still-america-thomas-sowell
[86] http://www.nytimes.com/learning/general/onthisday/bday/0704.html

basest motivations. We cannot escape that man is driven by fear of loss and greed. Presidents, governors, judges, prosecutors, investigators, and more are affected by both fear of loss and greed at the same time. Ironically, though, it is the fear of loss and greed of the people, the electorate, which should serve as a damper upon executive and agency action. The people should instinctively covet, to the point of absolute avarice, the freedom they possess as they fight for fear of losing it. Without these two motivations we forsake what matters most—the desire and need to repel tyranny from within.

> *It will be of little avail to the people that the laws are made by men of their own choice, if the laws be so voluminous that they cannot be read, or so incoherent that they cannot be understood; if they be repealed or revised before they are promulgated, or undergo such incessant changes that no man, who knows what the law is today, can guess what it will be tomorrow.*[87] James Madison

Couple Madison's wisdom with the misapplication of law by the executive, legislative, or judicial branches and we have a toxic combination. Such tyranny conquers an already unknowing people.

John Adams stated, "facts are stubborn things…"[88] He is correct. The true facts of a case can never be discounted, regardless of the strong tendency to do so, just as the hysterical emotions of the people will never overthrow an inconvenient truth. This is why Adams went on to say "…whatever may be our wishes, our inclinations, or the dictates of our passions, they cannot alter that state of facts and evidence."[89]

The facts and the evidence speak to the reality that Zimmerman should never have been charged as he was. The prosecutor's claims, contrary to the truth, do not change the facts. The incessant clamoring of those who appeal for racial justice and a guilty conviction for murder, like Angela Corey and those influencing her, do not alter the fact that Zimmerman should not have been charged with a crime that was unlikely to prevail. Racial justice and a conviction would have been achieved with the correct criminal charge. Moreover, justice would have been achieved had Ron, Butch, Dan, John, George, Krister, Tony, Ryan, and Ken not been charged according to the claims made by overzealous prosecutors. Prosecutorial claims are not factual simply for being stated.

America's downfall, however, occurs when such claims are permitted merely because they are not challenged. Jean Francois Revel states:

> *A human group transforms itself into a crowd when it simply responds to a suggestion rather than to reasoning, to an image rather than to proof, to repetition of a phrase rather than to arguments, to prestige rather than to competence.*[90]

The great American experience of true self-government ends when we, the people, cede our charge to both lawmakers and law enforcers and fail to preserve our rights and responsibilities as the electorate and jury. We become a crowd, a mob, easily led to the slaughter. Few would argue that the people are not responsible for the laws which govern our culture. If not the people, who? Whether for a lack of understanding of lawmaking, electoral disengagement, or blind acceptance of cronyism—whereby politicians remain in perpetual power—we ensure our demise. Too many laws, laws designed to limit and control, are created with our approval. We get is what we put into the process. We get what we allow. We get what we deserve based upon our contribution or lack thereof.

This truth is available for the jury to nullify bad law. Yet, people cannot exercise a

---

[87] http://www.constitution.org/fed/federa62.htm
[88] http://www.quotationspage.com/quote/3235.html
[89] Ibid.
[90] http://www.freer.public.com/focus/f-news/3045999/posts

power long forgotten. Equally troubling is the quality, both emotionally and mentally, of potential or actual jurors. If a culture feeds upon the frenzy of celebrated trials, as with any excess, the jury or jurors become problematic. Author and commentator Michelle Malkin addressed this matter. Focusing on a microcosm, she effectively portrayed women with a groupie or cult-like following of criminals who committed terrible crimes. Malkin listed Boston Marathon Massacre suspect Tsarnaev, murderer Aaron Hernandez (former NFL star), fugitive cop-killer Christopher Dorner, Lyle and Eric Menendez, and others as having adoring fans who would gladly ensure their salvation.[91]

To underscore this point, Malkin referenced that Dorner, who terrorized southern California, had tens of thousands who "liked"[92] his support pages on Facebook. This is no small number. Malkin referred to the first Menendez trial and the women who served on the jury and noted that they adored the "glamorous"[93] defense lawyer and were overcome with the Menendez brothers themselves. Abramson, the defense attorney, arranged for "her jurors"[94] to meet the brothers, Malkin stated. A national television show even aired a program on "Women who would leave their husbands to marry a Menendez."[95] This is the state of our outrageous culture. Malkin's observations are shocking because they are true.

This insight should give us reason to pause and consider how jurors react to the process and players in a court case. Love-crazed and adoring fans of the vile who have taken life, liberty, and property are not isolated cases. As Malkin asserted, such jurors are aggressively sought by defense lawyers. Prosecutors select jurors with no less a calculating agenda. This practice validates the secondary importance of both truth and justice. The relevance of Malkin's observations is not for the freakish nature of these "fans,"[96] but the general concern that jurors are susceptible to the pedestrian. If just one juror were easily swayed from what should be transparent, a just verdict could and does suffer the consequences. The fate of innocent people rests within the "discerned deliberations"[97] of such ilk, not to mention the guilty could gain an acquittal.

There is a case which was not discussed in this book, in which the jury foreman asked all jurors at the start of the deliberations if the defendant was "willful" in his actions. Did the defendant act with the intent to commit the crime? All jurors agreed that he did not act with willfulness. None of the jurors believed the defendant acted maliciously. Naturally, the jury foreman asked for a vote of acquittal; but four of the twelve jurors did not want to acquit. The foreman was surprised. When the four jurors were challenged as to why they changed their decision, their responses were unsettling. Each decided, though they believed the defendant had not acted willfully, that he should have done what most Americans do anyway. These jurors deviated from an objective standard and applied a prejudicial interpretation and application of the law. What they felt influenced what they thought. According to these four, the defendant was guilty because of their own bias, which meant the defendant was no longer innocent because of the facts and the law.

Any number of influences affects the outcome of jury deliberations. Wrong influences damn the innocent more so than influences that result in acquittal of criminals. We already discussed that jurors suffer the influence of arrogance just as public officials suffer this overpowering influence. Consider Paul Johnson's observation.

---

[91] http://michellemalkin.com/2013/07/12/americas-sociopath-fetish/
[92] Ibid.
[93] Ibid.
[94] Ibid.
[95] Ibid.
[96] Ibid.
[97] Ibid.

> *The study of history is a powerful antidote to contemporary arrogance. It is humbling to discover how many of our glib assumptions, which seem to us novel and plausible, have been tested before, not once but many times and in numerable guises; and discovered to be at great human cost, wholly false.*[98]

Hubris is one constant frailty which impales those who are its eventual target. If we live in a vacuum, insulated and isolated from true awareness, we accept the effects of hubris as normal. When a U. S. Attorney speaks to the public through the press, most accept what he states as truth. We don't know any better. How could we unless there is contrast? Unless we challenge the norm, we are unaware that what is pledged as truth is not. There must be a distinction. This is like the distinction of sin by virtue of God declaring the Ten Commandments as law. This is akin to the crime of speeding by the creation of a speed limit. God's commands separate right from wrong, just from unjust. The speed limit distinguishes safe and unsafe. Man did not associate adultery as wrong, necessarily, until it was declared so. The same may be said of the speed limit. If we are unaware, we will not know officials are a law unto themselves.

Elliot Spitzer is illustrative of this unfortunate condition. As former Attorney General for New York, he created a name for himself by pursuing criminal accusations which lacked merit. Spitzer sensationalized trumped up charges. For example, an executive for AIG for two decades resigned when Spitzer used his position to impugn this man's character and threatened him with unwarranted charges. Spitzer's accusations were lies—not the truth. Hubris. Hubris comes at "great human cost," even the cost of a career, a reputation, liberty, and the life of a man. As with Spitzer, local, state, and federal prosecutors are not immune from the delusional effects of pride. We don't know that authorities operate outside the purview of not only their jurisdiction, but basic decency and goodwill. We blindly accept their decisions and subsequent behavior as normal. We accept questionable use of power as legitimate. There is no distinction.

The hubris of Spitzer escalated until he was Governor of New York. In this position, he used and abused his office and resources for trysts with high-dollar call girls. We should not be surprised. Moreover, we are aware of the distinction that his adultery was wrong, and his misuse of authority violated the law and public trust. Spitzer epitomized arrogance. If the New York electorate had been aware that this same arrogance was used to destroy men through Spitzer's unfounded claims during his tenure as Attorney General, which was a title and position which served as his ticket to the governor's mansion, he could have been stopped long before he shamed himself and embarrassed the voters. Those who mean well are not free from the haughty effects of power. Whether in the world of sports with Tiger Woods, a church leader in Jim Bakker or Jimmy Swaggart, or a local politician caught embezzling funds, the allure and fall from significance is not uncommon.

This is the heart of the issue. United States Attorneys and prosecutors are in the thick of these influences. The enticement of public acclaim and adulation is intoxicating. Their inclination to advance charges against defendants at "great human cost" is calculated for ignoble reasons. Such is the nature of man. The temptation to act with autonomy is equal to the bounty of victory itself. T.S. Elliot wrote:

> *Half the harm that is done in this world is due to people who want to feel important. They don't mean to do harm—but harm does not interest them. Or they do not see it because they are absorbed in the endless struggle to think well of*

---

[98] http://www.goodreads.com/quotes/234863-the-study-of-history-is-a-powerful-antidote-to-contemporary

themselves.[99]

The admiration we bestow upon those in office who already deceive themselves is not healthy. Our lack of understanding serves as a catalyst, an accomplice of sorts, to the destructive repercussions against humanity.

Spitzer is but one example among countless others who sacrificed the prudent for the indefensible. Whether these acts are exercised in public office or private business, in our schools or churches, by elected officials or captains of industry, federal bureaucrats or mid-level managers in the free market, the result is the same. Power is misused and abused with either minimal or significant impact. Hubris fosters this sense of entitlement.

The President of the United States is the chief law enforcement officer. We expect him to exercise his office in keeping with the law. He is the standard-bearer who serves as the epitome of law and order. Yet, how often are we confronted with chief executives who fail their commitment to their oath of office? We cannot escape that the law is what it is and cannot be what it is not. We expect the president to perform with integrity and are disappointed when failure is apparent. We shouldn't be surprised. Richard Epstein notes, "The study of human institutions is always a search for the most tolerable imperfections."[100]

We should *expect* hubris to influence Obama not to properly enforce the laws. As such, we should not have been surprised when he purposely stalled portions of his own law, The Affordable Care Act, referred to as ObamaCare.

When a president, prosecutor or any public official deliberately fails to enforce what is required, just as they enforce what does not exist, the game is over. The war has been lost. The rule of law is of little consequence. Rather, the objectives of such officials, driven by psychological and emotional factors, are of prime importance. President Obama has no standing to ignore what must be done just as prosecutors have no grounds to proclaim accusations absent merit that are eventually leveled against the innocent. This is a parallel of vast import. Neither the president nor the prosecutor has power to do what they know they ought not. Ronald D. Rotunda, a commentator, notes:

> *Obama's decision to "suspend" the employer mandate of the Affordable Care Act has no support in precedent and dramatically shifts the arc of presidential power.*[101]

He further notes that the words of the Constitution require that the president "Shall take care that the laws be faithfully executed."[102] History is replete with examples of rulers who failed to enforce laws under their jurisdiction. Such arrogance shatters any notion of credibility. In an editorial by Michael Barone, he cites:

> *King James II was ousted in the Glorious Revolution of 1688-89, in large part for claiming that he could in particular cases dispense with—that is, ignore—an Act of Parliament.*[103]

Barone posits "there is an argument that the executive has some discretion in enforcing the law."[104] He refers to the efforts of prosecutors. "Prosecutors, for example, are not obliged

[99] http://www.tsowell.com/quotes.html
[100] https://www.goodreads.com/quotes/860090-the-study-of-human-institutions-is-always-a-search-for
[101] https://www.washingtonpost.com/opinions/on-the-health-care-mandate-obama-reaches-beyond-the-law/2013/07/18/d442aefc-efb4-11e2-a1f9-ea873b7e0424_story.html
[102] https://www.washingtonpost.com/opinions/on-the-health-care-mandate-obama-reaches-beyond-the-law/2013/07/18/d442aefc-efb4-11e2-a1f9-ea873b7e0424_story.html
[103] http://www.washingtonexaminer.com/obama-forfeits-trust-by-not-enforcing-obamacare/article/2532884
[104] Ibid.

to bring criminal charges in every case where there's evidence that someone broke the law."[105] We may reasonably conclude the president is breaking the law when he fails to enforce the law. We may also conclude that prosecutors do the same when they charge innocent men when no crime was committed. Officials cannot bring into existence as a matter of convenience what should not and cannot withstand scrutiny.

If the people do not know that prosecutors exercise their powers in a capricious manner, the problem will not be distinguished, much less resolved. It is nearly impossible to determine that prosecutors fabricate their stories for prosecution. If we consider the empirical evidence, along with the tendency of officials to skirt the law, we intuitively know there is an injustice. There are some 200,000 plus prisoners in the federal prisons according to the Federal Bureau of Prisons. What would you think if an estimated 58,000 newly convicted are waiting to enter the system and an estimated 20,000 are currently under indictment and awaiting prosecution? Whatever the numbers happen to be at any given time, the system is a system in the truest sense of the word. It is a machine. A myriad of disconnected elements with various motivations ensures this machine operates without fail. The motives and role of U. S. Attorneys are critical to this operation. Just as the president chooses to enforce or not enforce a law, so does the U. S. Attorney.

Obama, as stated by Ramesh Fonnuru, "pulled back on the employer mandate… because, among other things, it threatened to depress the full-time employment before the next Congressional elections."[106] Now we know the truth. We know Obama's motives. We know why he did what he should not have been done, while what he should have been done was inconvenient. The machine, in this case, was a raw political machine.

Within the legal machine, prosecutors routinely criminalize those who should not be, even when the evidence does not support a criminal charge. Prosecutors, like the president or any official, will use or abuse the process to forward an agenda for personal gain, to "think well of themselves," regardless of the cost to humanity. Barone is correct, "Obama will not face a similar fate"[107] to James II. Neither will prosecutors who betray the truth and their conscience. Barone says Obama's reluctance and "unwillingness to faithfully execute"[108] his office and laws "is a confession of incompetence… even the incompetence of the government generally."[109] That prosecutors fail to execute their authority morally and conscientiously is a crime of immense proportions. With years lost in prison by those at the mercy of this sordid machine, the results are inexcusable.

My examination of the news was a worthy exercise. Whether with Zimmerman, questionable jurors, Elliot Spitzer, or the President's crippled gait with ObamaCare, we, the people, the electorate, cannot do anything but find ignorance, apathy, fear, and arrogance throughout our culture. When the bar is set low in comparison to the worthy end of justice and pursuit of truth, our culture does and will continue to reflect this prevailing sentiment. This sentiment mirrors the state of the American judiciary. We should not expect anything other than the result, the most incarcerated people in the world.

The appeal to understand this blight upon our society and within the legal system should not go unanswered. The time is nigh for accountability. The time is nigh for retribution, reconciliation, and remuneration for those injured so egregiously and unjustly. The time is nigh for solutions.

---

105 Ibid.

106 http://nation.foxnews.com/2013/07/10/obamacare-inconvenient-truths

107 Ibid.

108 Ibid.

109 Ibid.

I shall often go wrong through defect of judgment. When right, I shall often be thought wrong by those whose positions will not command a view of the whole ground. I ask your indulgence for my own errors, which will never be intentional, and your support against the errors of others, who may condemn what they would not if seen in all its parts. **Thomas Jefferson**

The Need for Credible and Practical Solutions

It takes more muscles to smile than it does to frown; it takes more effort to declare the truth than to state a lie.

At this point in our nation's history, the Department of Justice, the U. S. sentencing commission, and Congress are passing initiatives to alleviate the overcrowding within federal prisons. Some 40,000 prisoners will likely be released within the year.[110] However, and this reflects rather poorly, with a system which pursues the easy lie over the difficult truth, there are sobering statistics to consider. We currently have an estimated 220,000 federal prisoners. With thousands at some stage within the legal system and tens of thousands waiting to enter, the reason to ease the prison population should be transparent. The United States must make room for a free people inundated with an incarceration epidemic with no remedy in sight. Sadly, there is no reason to smile.

Our hearts should be heavy. If we do nothing constructive, our future is bleak. The "great American experiment" is finished. We have no cause to be comfortable. We have every reason to roll up our sleeves, don our work boots and, by the sweat of our brow and the ingenuity of our intellect, reconcile with the truth. For, we have but one goal—to assure our posterity of the freedom cherished by Jefferson. This alone would alter our countenance and fulfill the felicity of our hearts and the hearts of coming generations.

When in prison, I awoke every morning with anger and contempt in my mind and heart. This was a healthy reaction to what was the theft of my life and the lives of my children. I don't question this reaction. I would not want to experience anything other than this natural state, a state that is a truly human vulnerability and expression to what is an injustice. The idea of starting a day in prison with any sense of comfort would be a telling indicator. It would signify acceptance. When I went to sleep, I thought of my children absent the father they loved and needed. I wore and still wear two elastic hair bands around my wrist as a constant reminder of them.

From morning to night, I lived a regimented and purposeful day with the aim of prevailing with the truth. I never forgot that I was innocent and in the grips of a merciless system designed to defeat the truth, designed to incarcerate those who should not be imprisoned. My children deserved no less than my constant vigilance to right this wrong. They deserve no less today as I work to ensure they live in a less hostile country.

There is no doubt in my mind that America is doomed because of the ignorance, apathy, and fear of the people. There is enough anecdotal evidence to demonstrate unconscionable decisions borne of the arrogance which spring from these three contagions. I have spoken with numerous *inmates* who have suffered unjust fates. Then there are those who may weigh my words knowing beyond doubt that all who are imprisoned are *common criminals*. Such is the nature of humanity. Many will read the examples of Norris and Figueroa, but they will still follow a different path. They are disaffected by the cognitive dissonance so prevalent in our culture. It is much easier to

[110] https://www.themarshallproject.org/2015/10/09/meet-the-federal-prisoners-about-to-bereleased#.OuWDLcMzN

trust the government and its systems. It is easier to rest in the judgments of those with titles. Doing so is comfortable. This is what most people know and accept.

When we assess that only 25,000 Americans were federal prisoners in 1980, how do we justify the 200,000 plus incarcerated today with tens of thousands expected to enter? We would be hard-pressed to explain this drastic increase. At some point, the sheer ridiculousness of the numbers, the disparity of the past and present, would compel us to question how this occurred. The men in the trenches, the men who broke under pressure and accepted plea agreements which, had they not, would have netted more years to their sentences, know what is wrong. The men who fought through a jury trial controlled by the rules of the game of court can state how and why the system is rigged.

We shall revisit Zachary Liverman. He is one of the brightest and most positive people I met behind bars. He is innocent of the charges for which he was found guilty—of this he has no doubt. He served nineteen years of a twenty-year sentence. However, even after all you have read, you may exclaim, "How could this be? Surely, he was guilty!" It is at this point I would refer you to a newspaper article by Joe Jackson who disclosed the star witness in the Liverman case, a prisoner who was granted conjugal visits in the offices of the Drug Enforcement Agency as a "reward" for his testimony.

Let's suppose Liverman was guilty. Would we even allow such practices by the DEA to gain the information needed to convict him? Would we even expect such sordid deals to secure the testimony of a witness to convict a guilty man, much less one who is innocent? If we don't question the tactics and strategies of a system, we presume to be generally wholesome, we do ourselves a disservice. Why accept the word of a criminal who cooperates only if he can have sex with his wife? How is this objective or credible? Why would we give credence to an agency or prosecutor who stoops to such loathsome tactics? Liverman does not deserve the title of common criminal based upon the truthfulness of a man who demanded to copulate in a government office before being placed back in his cell as a rat that fabricated false allegations.

Consider another case. A man was a member of a photo sharing group, a website like Facebook. He entered a search for "barely legal.". As opposed to selecting the pictures he wanted, he clicked "download all" and left his house. Unbeknownst to him, he had received pictures of child pornography. Government agents, meanwhile, became "friends" with this man on this same website after the download. They were purposely tracking this illegal content. Illegal pictures were on his computer and accessible to his other "friends." Consequently, this inmate was charged with not only possession, but distribution of child pornography. He never distributed porn and deplores child pornography. Within two weeks, his home was raided, and he was arrested. He did not even know what was in the downloaded contents.

Are we to believe him? Even if we don't, weigh that he is currently serving seven years for this *crime*. The system threatened him with seventeen to twenty years if he argued his innocence and went to trial. He did what any reasonable man would have done; he accepted a plea agreement. His lawyer told him that he would lose at trial.

Most of us would object to not only pornography, but especially child pornography. While many would not willingly view such vile images in the privacy of their own home; some do. The lawmakers in this country have determined this is a crime. Does it matter that a man did not know he received what he did not want? Contrast this with another man who knowingly accessed illegal pictures of children. At the age of 62, he will spend the next twelve years in prison. He will likely die there for an act he deliberately committed. We can view both cases and determine that the system is much too severe. When men who only looked at pictures are sentenced to more time than some murderers, we have a severely flawed system.

Absent integrity, the legal system is wanting. We should expect rampant indiscretion. We should not be surprised with an eight hundred percent increase in convictions within three decades. These numbers are symptomatic of a culture in decline. The decline is a result of a complete capitulation of the American people. Consider another set of numbers as confirmation of our plight. An article in the March 2014 issue of "The Economist" states that the police in our country "have become more militarized."[111] Raids by Special Weapons and Tactics (SWAT) units were rare. According to Peter Kraska of Eastern Kentucky University, there were only 3,000 a year in the early 1980s. They are now routine, perhaps as many as 50,000 a year.[112]

There is a direct correlation between the eight hundred percent increase in federal prisons and the number of assaults into our private homes. If we apply this analysis to our courts, we can draw a parallel with the morphing of judicial thought in keeping with the "social justice' envisioned by activist judges. "The Economist" cities that

> *The courts have smiled on SWAT raids. They often rely on the "no-knock" warrants, which authorize police to force their way into a home without announcing themselves. This was once considered constitutionally dubious. But the Supreme Court has ruled that police may enter a house without knocking if they have a reasonable suspicion that announcing their presence would be dangerous or allow the suspect to destroy evidence.*

We have, and it is undeniable, a splintering, whether incremental or sweeping, of the rights of the people. With every degree of increased authority, wherever and however applied within the legal system, Americans are subjected to the intended or unintended consequences. We no longer live in Mayberry and Sheriff Taylor does not walk the streets without his firearm. As "The Economist" discloses, an estimated.

> *89% of police departments serving American cities with more than 50,000 people had SWAT teams in the 1990s—almost double the level in the mid-1980s. By 2007 more than 80% of police departments in cities with between 25,000 and 50,000 people had them, up from 20% in the mid-1980s.*

The report even drew a sobering comparison between the United States and England. There are 18,000 state and local police agencies in America and 100 in Britain.[113]

As we consume our beer, buy our lottery tickets, watch sports on our digital flat screen televisions, have three cars in the garage, and enjoy all the distractions which represent "life" in America, we are being invaded. The irony is that the enemy is we, the people. Note the following statistic as stated in "The Economist:"

> *Between 2002 and 2011 the Department of Homeland Security disbursed $35 billion in grants to state and local police. Also, the Pentagon offers surplus military kit[s] to police departments... By 2005 it had provided such gear to more than 17,000 law-enforcement agencies.*[114]

The implications are staggering. The Pentagon is a direct supplier to 94% of all police departments across the nation. Is there any doubt we have been or are being conquered by the Federal Government, which has been sanctioned by the judiciary and facilitated by the

---

[111] http://www.economist.com/news/united-states/21599349-americas-police-have-become-too-militarised-cops-or-soldiers

[112] Ibid.

[113] Ibid.

[114] Ibid.

entire legal system? As defined earlier, the "legal system" includes the electorate, the people.

Ignorance is bliss; and it is also debilitating. The militarization of our civilian police forces is reflective of a nation awash in laws that are brutally enforced. This would have been inexcusable in any other era. Citing numerous examples, "The Economist" provides details of accidents and deaths of innocent American from the escalation of high intensity police and SWAT actions.

> *Some cities use them for routine patrols in high crime areas. Baltimore and Dallas have used them to break up poker games. In 2010 New Haven, Connecticut sent a SWAT team to a bar suspected of serving under-age drinks. That same year heavily-armed police raided barber shops around Orlando, Florida; they said they were hunting for guns and drugs but ended up arresting 34 people for barbering without a license.*[115]

The End of Justice was written by design without reliance upon statistics which reveal the conquering of a nation from within. Rather, this work validated our demise by sampling a dozen court cases which prove the indiscriminate destruction of men and their families. These cases are emblematic of statistics that support a worst-case scenario, the end of justice. We may have witnessed the end of a free America. The statistics we have just considered confirms the thesis of this book.

There is an analogy which was already discussed, and it appropriately describes our situation, "How to cook a frog." The key to cooking a frog is not to place the frog directly into a pot of boiling water; the frog will leap for its life. The frog should be placed into a pot of cold water which is then heated gradually. As the water warms, the frog becomes comfortable and falls asleep. Its fate is sealed. America has become extremely comfortable. We have compromised our integrity, sacrificed our principles, and have become ignorant, apathetic, and fearful. We are cooked.

Given the range of threats from innumerable fronts, we are in no position to fight. This is why men in the court cases we surveyed are not home with their families. We no longer covet our rights and freedom as the federal establishment aggrandizes by incremental and strident degrees. The unsuspecting, like Norris and Figueroa, had their lives turned upside down with no refuge. Gosin and Figueroa had no chance. Webb and Ingalls were but two in a queue with no end in sight. Humbly, we should ask who will be next? The odds are such that any number of readers will experience the same fate.

America is over-criminalized. We have the highest incarceration rate in the world. Why? Because of the arrogance of governing institutions and officials who operate them. What is the reason this arrogance exists? The people, the supposed source of power, are ignorant, apathetic, and fearful. There is only one way to resolve our problem. We need a revolution within our hearts and minds that educates, encourages, and emboldens. As a result, those who are abusing their discretion will be held accountable. This requires solutions—solutions which restore the integrity of the American people.

Imagine a huge mountain. At the base of the mountain are millions of souls with the intent to ascend. They have no choice. Time is one of the boundaries. By virtue of this one unseen, but known influence, man must act; he must use time and do so wisely. Some will simply follow those in front, trusting that they have not failed to assess available options. The path may be perfect. It may be safe, easily traversed, and one that enlightens. The path that juts to the left may be troublesome, but negotiable. The path to the right, if riddled with obstacles, may impede to such an extent that those in front are trapped, while

---

[115] Ibid.

those behind are forced to seek an alternative route.

This mountain is life. There are many paths on which to proceed. Those who observe may discern. They will ask questions—the hallmark of initiative. They will assess their options and choose a path that satisfies a want or need. It may not be the optimum choice; but at least it's not a journey followed blindly. Yet, the decision may lead to ruin. The motivation may be so misguided that one may fall off a cliff. However, the contrary may happen, the motivation may be sound, but end with the same result. One may reach a destination that is abundant beyond measure which only clouds his judgment. He may come to know what is neither edifying nor purposeful and, consequently, squander his time—his very existence. He has no reason to venture beyond what is comfortable.

Those who are comfortable may come to symbolize the aspirations of those who are unaware. The majority, as they travel from the base of the mountain, will seek to emulate this goal. This is the travesty of group think—the herd mentality. Man is governed by two fundamental elements of human nature, fear of loss and greed. These base instincts have such a dominate influence that man fails to acquire perspective and context from and for his life. He simply exists, as if in a pre-programmed mode, intent on attaining satisfaction or mere survival. Circumstances, and he never realizes they are just that, circumstances, become conditions which should not hold sway over what is of greater import.

The antithesis to those who follow mindlessly—without clear perspective and complete context—are men who see with a clear knowing. They recognize circumstances and reject the preconceived notions that riddle the existence of many, notions which are rote at best and uninspiring. These men, even if not cognizant of the scope of their choices and actions, defy boundaries designed to limit and condition the masses. Somehow, they, as if by an innate calling, an internal voice which speaks a counterintuitive message, prevail against a rampant and cognitive dissonance that impairs. These iconoclasts know that disbelief is an unenlightened path.

To appreciate the magnitude of their choices, we need only step back and view the mountain from a distance. A few less worn paths mark the terrain. These mavericks trekked their unexpected journey elsewhere. Somehow, inexplicably, they cast aside their wants and needs for something much greater than themselves. Their purpose is clear, as if drawn by a gravitational pull, with their destiny congruent with their integrity. They live in accordance with principles that assure a reckoning with truth, a truth they know is on the distant horizon and attainable. The cost may appear irreconcilable, but the cost is circumstantial as well.

These are the extraordinary champions who are victorious in defeat. Long after their suffering or untimely and unjustifiable death, humanity will recognize their contributions. In the context of time, with a perspective which provides immense clarity, we will marvel at their seeming prescience. We will honor their intrepid nature. We will admire their selfless service to timeless truth which may, at a minimum, remind us that we are on the wrong path.

As humbling as this thought may be, we have a choice. We can change course and observe, reassess, and become more aware that we don't know that we don't even know—to include not knowing that we are being put to sleep water which is being incrementally warmed. With knowledge, we, by a volitional act, may become engaged, even if this engagement is little more than a mere acknowledgment of those who battle the imponderable. These champions are testaments of courage—change agents intent on vanquishing limitations. As we observe, we sense the enormity of their calling and would do well to simply walk in their shadows.

Lives that are fully examined, be it Hus, Galileo, Giles, or Figueroa, those who waged war against unbeatable odds and forces, or be it Norris, Everston, Webb, or Ingalls, those unwittingly trapped and, subsequently, marred in defeat, they offer lessons attained through their experience alone. These lessons may be a source of hope. By their examples, we learn of solutions. Absent remedies, we have little chance to prevail within the legal system.

The solutions we will discuss are not all inclusive and some are either short-term or long-term in nature. Our crisis took decades to create, if not longer; and with deliberate steps, it will take time to ameliorate them. Obviously, effective solutions abound, especially at the local level. While some of the solutions may appear impractical, our current legal system is impractical as well. Any perceived impracticality may be a result of our own ignorance and lack of vision or hope. As we weigh changes which must be made, keep in mind, we have no choice. Our situation is dire, and time is not our ally.

With a proper perspective and context, let's enter a world of possibility, a universe of change. We now know what was unknown. We can transform our lives with a future which dignifies the freedom and rights enjoyed by our ancestors. No different than those who suffered oppression five hundred years ago, our prospects may only improve. It matters little that the facade of the current regime masks the toll of injustice with representations that mislead. However, the truth will always be—regardless of all subterfuge.

Truth has a natural propensity to persist. Those stalwarts willing to pursue the truth are souls who invariably stitch generation to generation with a common calling. This woven thread is a constant reminder that struggles are the fabric of human existence weathered from season to season as the centuries unfold. Humanity yearns for what is proper and just. Our hearts thirst for equity. The likes of Galileo, Hus, and the blindsided Scottsboro boys are symbols which imprint our souls with a nobler calling. Norris and Ingalls are humble reminders of the weak amid the catastrophic. Let us declare to ourselves, our posterity, and even our predecessors that we will actively engage our souls for the greater benefit of humanity. Let us declare that these solutions are a modest investment for the cause of freedom and those who are innocent.

SOLUTIONS

1—The people must be informed.

The education of Americans is essential. If we remain oblivious to our plight, we will have no reason to change the path we travel. Once the crisis is understood, we may reconcile our shortcomings. There is no better place to start than at home—your home. Ask yourself the following questions:

- What do I know?
- What do I not know?
- How do I inform myself?
- How do I spend my time?
- What books do I read?
- What notions do I believe that may not be true?
- Do I take a stand for anything that is more important than me?
- Do I contribute to the well-being of my community?
- Do I exercise critical thinking or am I in a receive mode most of the time?
- Do I have a proper sense of history?
- Do I understand the Constitution and the fundamental element of jurisdiction?

- Do I know the names of the elected representatives of my district?
- Do I know my representatives at the state level?
- Do I know how my representatives vote?
- Do I visit the courts?
- Do I understand the legal process?
- Do I fear the courts and government agencies and agents?

This practical list serves an important purpose—to humble us into understanding by showing our complicity. Our failure to answer these questions affirmatively illustrates that we are not contributing to our present or future. The reverse is true—we are the cause of our current crisis. We are ill-informed. We are ignorant.

If we refer to the cooked frog, we see our comfort within the waters we find ourselves. We have no reason to care. By degrees we have become content. To be sure, if we were the same freedom-minded patriots who peopled America and we were unceremoniously dropped into our current period in history, it would be the equivalent of a frog thrown into a pot of boiling water; we would rebel and recoil, just as the frog would leap for its survival. In both situations there is contrast.

There is a clear distinction between the frog's natural climate and the pot, just as our era is dissimilar with the past. Patriots would spurn our cradle to grave dependence upon the Federal Government. The point should be transparent; we have little to no sense of contrast, much less a healthy perspective or context of our given situation. We have no reason to brace against what would otherwise be inexcusable and intolerable for a free and independent people. As America crumbles, we have become sedate and content. We are going down with the ship with a smile. Oh, how ignorance is bliss.

Without knowledge, we are not able to be powerful. With the wrong knowledge, we are as ineffective as a sleeping frog minutes from death. Americans can't save themselves while they spend six to eight hours a day watching television and playing video games. We will not improve our lot with a 6th grade education, an education that is already questionable. Our existence encourages antipathy and lethargy. These factors can do nothing but create a state of fear.

If the frog did not *know* how to jump or critically discern enough to escape either the hot or cold water, it would naturally fear or exist in blissful ignorance. It would die almost instantly in boiling water and wallow in misery as the cold water was heated. Our culture is no different. We fear because we are not powerful; we are not powerful because we don't have knowledge. Our collective and individual fear envelopes our complete sense of being. We are paralyzed. Any efforts to free ourselves would be reactionary—groundless attempts to live another day—not sentient steps to solve a crisis or thrive into a world of glorious possibility.

Regrettably, our progeny will become who we are, if not worse. Our children and their children will learn from those who lead them down paths which do not enlighten, engage or embolden. They will become more expectant, petulant, intolerant, and oblivious than us. There should be no doubt, when America's incarceration rate reaches thirty percent, few will question this statistic, for few will know or even care. The solution is obvious; the people must be informed.

Individually, we must reassess what we do, how we do it, and why. We should challenge why we are on any path and strive to change course. We have the choice to restore our integrity and abide by principles which will alter schools, churches, businesses and communities. As we acquire insight and push outwardly against resistance, the reverberations from our initiatives will be felt. We will impact the local, state, and federal level. Officials, if only for the increase in scrutiny from the subtle and deliberate exercise of the power of the electorate, will become aware of their own indiscretions. We want these government agents to question their own psychological and emotional motives and recognize that the people are no longer lemmings. We want them to know the people are an informed, resolved, and intrepid force.

2—Americans must assert their status.

If there is any one factor that will consistently appear throughout this chapter, it is the question of jurisdiction. If we know who we are in the context of a given law or situation, we will be forearmed and, consequently, more effective confronting unwarranted and unsanctioned government action. We discussed several examples earlier. Recall that I challenged the police for stopping me without cause and then I continued my way. Had I submitted to their questions, I would have been drawn unwittingly into their *jurisdiction* once they established grounds to detain me. Recall the city council created the rental inspection district which exceeded its jurisdiction as established and limited by state law. Then there is the Zoning Administrator and Police Chief who exceeded their authority when they confronted a business owner about her table.

Examples like these occur thousands of times every day in America. For our failure to assert a status or failure to challenge the jurisdiction of those who unduly affect our status, we suffer. The question of status within the legal system is equally important. The fact that jurisdiction is imposed in court implies that the system has jurisdiction beforehand. The last case is an example. I determined and documented that my status was one *without* the jurisdiction of the United States (Government) for purposes of the federal income tax. I no longer elected or subscribed to a federal status and benefit and could no longer be deemed an *employee* or any other taxable designation. I no longer had the obligation to file federal tax forms. I was not *within* the scope of this federal excise. Ironically, as if willfully avoiding and evading full disclosure of the truth, some twelve different officials and agencies refused to answer my query. What law required me to file a federal income tax return? I knew the limits of the jurisdiction of the Federal Government. The lack of a candid response to clarify my liability confirmed lack of jurisdiction.

I knew the legal system and the federal district court itself were complicit with presuming my status for what it was not and could not be. Status is everything. This is why jurisdiction is of vital importance. When the police, city council, prosecutors, courts, inspectors, investigators, legislators, the president—when officials do not have jurisdiction—they do not have authority. They have nothing. When we are cognizant of our status and the commensurate power to assert the same, we have a reason to stand forthrightly when previously we would have caved. For example, we know to close the door when the police ask questions. We know to offer those who conduct the federal census no more than the Constitution allows. There is no jurisdiction beyond the limits of constitutional power. We guard against encroachment upon our status by rejecting the enforcement of baseless authority.

The assertion of status is empowering. It is defining. When we understand the law and know the definition of *United States* and *United States person* do not apply, we realize just how many laws are irrelevant to the people. We realize how much government authority is limited by its delegated powers. This fact alone is a taproot to understanding. Once we are aware that the government is constrained, any extra jurisdictional imposition must be a result of the ignorance and arrogance of the establishment. Why? Officials *presume*. Presumption forces legal cases through the system—without jurisdiction.

Zachary Liverman, a man whose case we did not discuss in detail, is an example. His status of *free man* was changed a *felon* if only for the indiscretion of DEA agents who abused the process to gain false evidence and testimony. The DEA agents offered an already incarcerated witness an unthinkable proposition inside a DEA office in return for his testimony. Liverman was presumed guilty by investigators who acted beyond their jurisdiction—at least as to how the common man would perceive it. Although Liverman knew he was innocent, after nineteen years in prison, the legal system prevailed through extracurricular authority (indiscretion) and adversely affected his status and life.

Ron Webb and David Ingalls suffered similar fates. They were caught within the government's loose application of the conspiracy charge and unjustly punished. George Norris will die knowing he was innocent, and that the government gratuitously grafted him within the scope of its *authority* without cause. While we may not be effective asserting our status, we must, nonetheless, take a stand. Status becomes inconsequential when we allow any presumption contrary to our proper status to prevail.

It has been said that one who does not assert his rights has none. Uninformed officials who flex their power as if their power is limitless will never realize their own incapacities unless and until we intractably rebut their presumptions of authority. Such acts would correct abuses of indiscretion in the trenches of life. Our deliberate exercise of our freedom and rights would hold errant officials accountable. The assertion of status is critical and would inexorably alter the conversation within our culture. Both sides of the battle would operate within their own spheres and reconcile the truth.

Truth, which is most often ingrained and embraced by and through experience, is infectious. When citizens see victories peppered across the landscape, they would know and see accountability. When officials are held accountable, citizens secure ground lost to a creeping arrogance that should never have been. Whenever and wherever we question the ability of any official to impose his will, we intuitively rely upon our awareness and righteously assert a proper status while rejecting who we are not. In line with the first solution, we move beyond existing into being. With this heightened understanding, we have every reason to question the path we travel and the need to change course. We have every reason to challenge officials who approach us on a path they should not be traveling. We may then articulate that they have gone too far. Why? Our status.

3—If there is no violation of life, liberty, or property, there is no crime.

As absurd as this proposition may sound in our current climate, this solution is a baseline for qualifying what is criminal conduct. Let's make a comparison.

Arlon Jones stole a man's heifer, his neighbor's property. This was a crime. While Jones may have prevented his family from starving, which would compel the court or jury to consider the nature of the act and his intent, we know society cannot tolerate theft. Consider Ryan Gosin's case; he harmed no one and stole nothing. He violated one of thousands of codes without evil intent. Was there a need to classify the violation as *criminal*? Norris, even if he inadvertently bought an illegal orchid, should not have been attacked as a criminal. A penalty for unknowingly violating a regulation would have been sufficient for either Gosin or Norris.

Criminalizing codes has everything to do with status. We need only question why the government doesn't pursue these as civil infractions. What is the payoff for labeling such acts as criminal? There must be a gain. Regardless, when a man is imprisoned for what is a technicality there is a tremendous cost. The men charged and convicted acquired a new status, *common criminals*, which allowed the government to warehouse them. The public pays dearly and families suffer needlessly.

The senseless categorization of noncriminal acts as criminal must end. If the government intends to emphasize the violation of laws that do not entail the loss of life, liberty or property, the civil nature of the act should prevail. If there are egregious instances of these violations and evidence establishes a lack of evil intent—we should consider civil penalties to dignify the nature of the wrong.

Consider a hypothetical example. Suppose Norris received an orchid from a foreign provider. Suppose that the flower had noxious pollen which causes injury and possible death when touched or inhaled. Since the Federal Government has jurisdiction for international trade, it has authority to regulate what enters the country. If Norris never ordered this type of orchid, should Norris be deemed a criminal if the orchid was sent accidentally by the shipper? Now consider that the flower is not a risk to people, but it is a rare species which faces extinction and is controlled by a foreign government to prevent smuggling. Would Norris be a criminal for unknowingly receiving this flower? What if he knew of the purchase? Now consider that it was not a rare flower at all and misidentified and mislabeled on the shipping invoice. At some point, the government must reconcile that if there is no health risk or the flower is not controlled, there is no loss of life, liberty, or property. In the Norris case, it was a paperwork issue. He never should have been charged criminally for what was a minor civil infraction, an infraction evidently made by the foreign supplier.

Some of the cases we reviewed have nothing to do with the loss of life, liberty, or property. Other cases amount to nothing more than crafting a law which makes the act a crime. The receipt of Figueroa's *gifts* is an example. The government finagled the use laws governing mail to impose mail fraud and mail fraud conspiracy. Everston lacked a sticker on a package shipped through the postal system and was targeted as a criminal. Richardson mailed nine packages with his own business funds and was classified as a felon. I no longer voluntarily participated in an excisable activity within the federal income tax scheme; yet the government advanced a criminal charge on behalf of the IRS. When does the lunacy end?

We must alter how crimes are classified and pursued. If there is no *mens rea* and no loss of life, liberty, and property, the charge should be categorized as civil. If needed, levels of severity for civil infractions could be established. If the infraction is substantiated with intent of wrongdoing, a more significant fine could be imposed. Given questionable enforcement by prosecutors, innocent men have been caught in the justice system with the sole purpose of the prosecutors increasing their number of convictions. This is the real *mens rea* issue which results in real loss of life, liberty, and property.

4—We must elect discerning representatives.

Americans must elect representatives who exercise humility and restraint. These attributes are necessary to tamp the rise of pride which clouds the judgment of those with titles. An informed electorate will recognize that the Constitution binds the government and representatives are limited to the powers delegated in Article 1, Section 8. When officials misinterpret these powers and then couch their use under the "general welfare" and "commerce" clauses, the scope of government morphs into what was never intended. A shift in perspective concerning the expansion of governance comes from those in office; it is sourced within the context of the time they are living and their ignorance. They exceed the constraints of their authority established by standards established in the past.

Perhaps even Justice Cardozo, the Supreme Court Justice who wrote the opinions which established social security and employment taxes as excises (Charles C. Steward Machine v Davis, 301 U. S. 548 (1937) and Helvering v Davis, 301 U. S. 619 (1937)), would be hard-pressed to interpret the current extra-judicial experimentation as ventures into "social justice."[116] Most learned men, even those with prejudicial blinders, must reconcile that elected officials have become misguided and they manipulate the conditions

---

[113] Benjamin Cardozo, The Nature of the Judicial Process (Yale University Press, 1921)

of society into what they desire. The irony is that less seasoned officials may not know this is occurring or may not realize they are a means to facilitate this end.

Consider a basic example. If elected officials fail to appreciate that the *United States* has limited powers, yet they tout legislation which affects the 50 states, they are on a fool's errand and the errand will have the intended effects. The electorate will listen to their representatives without challenging their limited understanding and authority or the scope of the law. This is the inverse cascading of power which cripples our republic.

America's incarceration rate reflects the incongruence of the application of laws, an incongruence invariably borne of several facts. First, the culture of government breeds and feeds upon the arrogance associated with power. Second, those who enter politics, while likely altruistic, are eventually shaped by this culture. Third, their conformity to the culture of government is directly correlated to their lack of knowledge upon taking office. Otherwise, we must accept that they become unmoored from principles which once anchored their once altruistic beliefs and decisions. We could even conclude that fear of loss and greed affects their performance. They seek to remain in office, after all.

Rogue legislators and executives—and it can be argued that each is rogue to some degree—may only be checked and defeated by such drastic measures as term limits. Given the allure of elected office, which speaks to the premise that absolute power corrupts absolutely, there may be no other way to curb their exposure to power. While an ignorant electorate may never likely defeat those legislating adversely on behalf of the people, the time is ripe to elect others. When officials, whether serving on city council or in Congress, interject and impose their interpretation of life and law upon their constituents, the results are accomplished through overreach of power and outside the parameters of fundamental constitutional principles. In the end, the reverse of reasoned and sound government occurs. This is the genesis of extra-jurisdictional indiscretion. When the rights of citizens suffer in the least, we may attribute such loss to the arrogance of these representatives.

Congressman Frank Wolf was in office for half my life when I was incarcerated. As my representative in Congress, I had posed a question he would not, and in the interests of self-preservation, could not answer. He was and is governed by two universal political instincts—fear of loss and greed. An honest response to my letters for the law which required me to file a federal income tax return would have caused him problems. Wolf could not compromise his prospects with such candor. Moreover, why should he suffer rather significant inconvenience that would come with full disclosure to a constituent's concern as controversial as the federal income tax?

Imagine if I received the following response from Wolf or any of the four Senators who were in office during the nine-year investigation, namely George Allen, John Warner, Mark Warner, and Jim Webb:

Dear Mr. Johnson:

Thank you for your recent inquiry concerning the law which requires U. S. persons to file a federal income tax return.

The United States has limited jurisdiction as defined by Article 1, Section 8 of the Constitution. One of the delegated powers is the ability to tax by either direct or indirect means. Indirect taxes are "excise" taxes based upon a voluntary decision by Americans to purchase something or by their election of a particular federal status or benefit. For example, when you buy gasoline, you agree to pay the excise (indirect) tax which is ultimately paid by the retailer. The same applies to social security and the "relation of employment." The same applies when American elect to be treated with a status of a class subject to the federal income tax, as expressed under statute 26 USC 6013(g). When Americans agree to an excisable status or accept federal benefits of the social security insurance scheme, they agree to pay the requisite federal income tax upon their "income."

The United States Government presumes that, once Americans voluntarily submit the appropriate federal tax forms, they are liable for the payment commensurate with the status and benefits accepted. The initial submission of these federal forms creates the presumption of liability which becomes prima facie evidence. Consequently, the United States Government considers those who are U. S. persons within the federal United States and under its jurisdiction for income tax purposes.

It is quite fundamental that the United States Government cannot enter the domain of the 50 states. State citizens, in fact, have no reason to obligate themselves to the federal authorities, unless it is done as a knowing and deliberate act of a legitimate power.

The truth, Mr. Johnson, is that the Federal Government has no authority by law to enforce the income/excise tax until one agrees to be within the federal purview of congressional excise authority. If you have elected to be one with such a status or class or accepted federal benefits, whether done knowingly or unknowingly, you have a federal income tax liability. However, if you revoke the election for that federal status (See 26 USC 6013(g)(4)(a)) and federal benefits, you may be exempt from this obligation.

I hope this sufficiently answers your question.

Sincerely yours in the defense of liberty,

Frank Wolf

This hypothetical letter would have caused Mr. Wolf grief. It would have caused Congress grief. The disclosure of the true nature of the tax laws would create a firestorm. Why would Wolf make life uncomfortable for himself when he could pass a constituent's letter to the IRS, the agency which provides boilerplate responses? Congress is an organism with self-interests and such tactics are essential for self-preservation. This is accomplished by maintaining a status quo which is not in America's best interests.

To ensure that Congress is not preserved as an organism of self-interests, we must elect discerning, knowledgeable, and courageous representatives. The cycle of electing those who are the problem, those who represent the status quo, is insanity. We need fresh blood injected, people the resolve to abide by the constraints of the Constitution.

5—The Congress and courts must cease liberally interpreting the General Welfare Clause and the Commerce Clause. These clauses must be applied with the restraint of former days, with the intent to limit the scope of government.

In some respects, America's heyday immediately followed the Revolution. The people were joined in a common cause and a joyous spirit. With the Constitution written as the fundamental construct of a Federal Government, people were assured of their rights. Yet, successive generations have more than strayed from the then definitive understanding of limited federal authority. Curiously, our history has periods of thought which mark new sentiment, or the injection of a radical departure from the original intent of the framers. Akin to the rings within a tree trunk, which distinguish the character of the years it has lived, congressional sessions or specific terms of the Supreme Court indicate the character of our country and the character and leadership at any given time. The 1st session of Congress is different than the 50th and the 101st is dissimilar from that of the 10th. The Marshall Supreme Court varies from Story's and the Robert's Court is not like Taney's.

Why? We could ask the following rhetorical question: Don't terms and definitions remain consistent throughout each era? Pointedly, the general welfare clause or the commerce clause should have the same meaning now as in the beginning of our republic. Thomas Jefferson viewed the Constitution, and the importance of its *definition* as follows:

> *I consider the foundation of the Constitution as laid on this ground: that "all powers not delegated to the United States by the Constitution, nor prohibited by it to the States, are reserved to the States or to the people." To take a single step beyond the boundaries thus especially drawn around the powers of Congress is to take possession of a boundless field of power no longer susceptible of any definition.*[117]

Any deviations from core elements of sanctioned powers are aberrations, illegitimate initiatives of those who graft their interpretations for an agenda.

We must acknowledge the parameters the founders designed to stem the imagination of government officials from influencing the private affairs of the people. The notions of sound government were not and are not fertile ground for the vagaries of the undisciplined with the intent to experiment with esoteric ends. America sacrificed all for a coveted victory against England and guarded against the fancies of potentially wayward rulers. Distortion and abuse of the General Welfare clause are done deliberately. Note Jefferson's words against the incorporation of a national bank:

> *The incorporation of a bank, and the power assumed by this bill have not, in my opinion, been delegated to the United States by the Constitution. They are not among the powers specially enumerated... still less are these powers covered by any other of the special enumerations. Nor are they within either of the general phrases, which are the two following: 1. To lay taxes to provide for the general welfare of the United States, that is to say "to lay taxes for the purposes of providing for the general welfare." For laying taxes is the power and the general welfare for the purpose for which the power is to be exercised... They are not... to do anything they please to provide for the general welfare, but only to lay taxes for that purpose.*[118]

Jefferson did not equivocate; he left no room for the grand designs of the mischievous. The term general welfare was a preordained concept quite contrary to the current interpretation. Sequential sessions of Congress and courts are complicit with the taking of liberties that chartered a course contrary to the proper and prudent original conceptions established long ago. Jefferson foreshadowed this very misdirection.

> *But is the spirit of the people an infallible, a permanent reliance? Is it government? Is this the kind of protection we receive in return for the rights we have given up? Besides the spirit of the times may alter, will alter, our rulers will become corrupt, our people careless. A single zealot may commence persecutor, and better men be his victims.*[119]

I am suggesting, as Jefferson foreshadowed, the bastardization of formerly concrete terms and rigid definitions deconstructed an already delicate balance of proper government with the deliberate indifference of both rulers and citizens. There is a compelling need to reign in migratory intellectual forays which defeat the rights and autonomy of the people, all done in the name of general welfare or commerce. This perversion is the reason the likes of Justice Cardozo crafted the caginess of "social justice" as grounds for social engineering which ensured the social security scheme as settled law.

The solution is simple; but implementation will prove arduous. States must force a dialogue with specific goals which reassert the original intent of the Constitution. The

---

117 http://avalon.law.yale.edu/18th_century/bank-tj.asp

118 http://founders.archives.gov/documents/Jefferson/01-19-02-0051

119 http://tjrs.monticello.org/letter/1316

words of Jefferson portend the repercussions of idle and continuous misapplication of powers, "the coercion of the laws" created without foundation:

> *The error seems not sufficiently eradicated that the operators of the mind as well as the acts of the body are subject to the coercion of the laws. But our rulers have no authority over such natural rights, only as we have submitted to them. The rights of the conscience we never submitted, we could not submit. We are answerable for them to our God. The legitimate powers of government extend to such acts only as are injurious to others.*[120]

Supreme Court Justice Joseph Story, perhaps the ablest legal mind in our history, opined at length of the meaning of the scope of federal power and general welfare clause:

> 904. *Before proceeding to consider the nature and extent of the power conferred by this clause, and the reasons, on which it was founded, it seems necessary to settle the grammatical construction of the clause, and to ascertain its true reading. Do the words, "to lay and collect taxes, duties, imposts and excises," constitute a distinct, substantial power; and the words, "to pay debts and provide for the common defense, and general welfare of the United States", constitute another distinct and substantial power? Or are the latter words connected with the former, so as to constitute a qualification upon them? This has been a topic of political controversy; and has garnished abundant materials for popular declamation and alarm. If the former be the true interpretation, then it is obvious, that under color of the generality of the words to "provide for the common defense and general welfare," the Government of United States is, in reality, a government of general and unlimited powers, notwithstanding the subsequent enumeration of specific powers; if the latter be the true construction, then the power of taxation only is given by the clause, and it is limited to objects of national character, "for the common defense and the general welfare."*
>
> 905. *The former opinion has been maintained by some minds of great ingenuity, and liberality of views. The latter has been generally received sense of the nation, and seems supported by reasoning at once solid and impregnable. The reading, therefore, which will be maintained in these commentaries, is that, which makes the latter words a qualification of the former; and this will be best illustrated by supplying the words, which are necessarily to be understood in this interpretation. They will then stand thus: "The Congress shall have power to lay and collect taxes, duties, imposts and excises, in order to pay the debts, and to provide the common defense and general welfare of the United States;" that is, for the purpose of paying the public debts, and providing for the common defense and general welfare of the United States. In this sense, Congress has not an unlimited power of taxation; but it is limited to specific objects, - the payment of the public debts, and providing for the common defense and general welfare. A tax, therefore, laid by Congress for neither of the objects, would be unconstitutional, as an excess of its legislative authority. In what manner this is to be ascertained, or decided, will be considered hereafter. At present, the interpretation of the words only is before us; and the reasoning, by which that already suggested has been vindicated, will now be reviewed.* 1833 Commentaries on the Constitution.[121]

We may conclude that the whims of any given generation are not the litmus test for sound

[120] https://mirielthomasreneau.com/2016/01/20/jefferson/

[121] http://press-pubs.uchicago.edu/founders/print_documents/a1_8_1s28.html

and constitutional governance. The integrity of federal influence was established for a reason—to prevent thoughtless and emotionally-riddled meanderings void of fundamental and constitutional support.

6—The role of the judge must be scrutinized and limited. Moreover, as an impartial administrator of the court, he should be given the latitude to determine prison sentences without prescribed guidelines.

The lifetime appointment of judges is perhaps a greater detriment to our society than the residual benefits associated with their permanency of position. The arrogance of the justice system may be reviewed by a judge's sense of entitlement and superiority. They have become too comfortable in their role. This comfort comes at a cost. We need only consider the Norris case for confirmation. The judge's judicial temperament leaves a lot to be desired. Even more of a concern is not the isolated insensitivity of a single judge, but the collective impact the system has on all judges. These jurists routinely assess case after case in which they must know defendants are not guilty, where there is neither *mens rea* nor *actus reus*. The judge in Ron Webb's case expressed his reservations, which is unusual. This judge and his brethren see these examples often and, yet they do nothing. Not only is arrogance a factor, but they also become callous and indifferent. This is the regrettable aspect of the conditioning they endure over decades of service. As humanity is paraded before them, their views become jaded. They tire of the common theme of man's depravity, and it reflects in their attitude, decisions, and sentences.

I will never forget Judge Moon exclaiming "We are not going to go there." This is when I attempted to explain my good faith belief to the jury. **This was his reaction to an innocent man seeking to exonerate himself of criminal charges.** The prosecutor did not provoke Moon's response. Moon's misgivings were enough to disrupt and destroy a man's hope to defend what his attorneys would not. The factors of both time and volume of cases over which Moon presided for decades ingrained an intolerance that subverted justice. **Moon even directed Harris' questioning of me by asking how I was not liable for the income tax under the 16th Amendment. Moon introduced the amendment into the trial. Moon wanted to go there.** Yet, this amendment had no relevance to my belief. Either Moon's ignorance of tax law or his expected flow of another tax case, or both, governed his actions and decisions. Moon was intolerant of what was offered by a defendant whose views were not those reflective of a typical tax case. Moon's impact was equal to an unprincipled and unbridled prosecutor who tramples truth. A judge who suffers professional fatigue is, in all probability, ensconced within the hubris that allows him to adjudicate with increased intolerance.

Lifetime appointments ought to be heavily evaluated. The culture within the current legal system encompasses the influence of rigid minds and hardened hearts. The routine appointment or election of judges would ensure that capable jurists would temper or reverse the effects of this unfortunate dynamic. Moreover, if lawmakers dispensed with sentencing guidelines and the folly often associated with the likes of *three-strikes* initiatives, whereby legislatures determine lifetime imprisonment for three-time offenders, sentencing would become more balanced. As it stands, judges are forced to sentence criminals without the latitude consistent with unique circumstances of any given case.

7—The governor of each state and sheriff within each county must serve as the final barrier before the Federal Government may make arrests.

In a very real and practical sense, the Federal Government is foreign to the 50 states. If we appreciate this fact, we should question why or how the *United States* enters the jurisdiction of any state to apprehend her citizens. This suggestion may appear radical, at least today, but we need only consider the arrest of Norris, Everston, Wahler, Richardson, and even me. If you will permit the analogy, these arrests are no different than your neighbor walking into your home and taking your son for allegedly stealing the apple pie from his windowsill. Is the federal authority able to exercise such force simply because it has perceived power? China is not able to enter America and take anyone it accuses of committing a crime. Consider the words of Thomas Jefferson:

> *It is a fatal heresy to suppose that either our State governments are superior to the federal, or the federal to the states… each party shall prudently shrink from all approach to the line of demarcation, instead of rashly overleaping it, or throwing grapples ahead to haul hereafter. But, finally, the peculiar happiness of our blessėd system is, that in differences of opinion… the appeal is to [the sovereign citizens] ... peaceably assembled by their representatives in convention. This is no more rational than the **jus fortis**, or the canon's mouth, the **ultima et sola ratio regum**.*[122]

We may presume there is a protocol by which the federal authority operates and apprehends those accused of committing criminal acts. Presuming is a fool's game. What the protocol entails is of paramount concern. Any practice presently employed may be nothing more than the Federal Government notifying a willing, compliant, and ignorant local sheriff before an arrest is made. A reasonable neighbor would confront you with the accusation about the supposed theft of his pie. China would appeal to the corresponding authorities within the United States Government, seek a solution through Interpol (International Police), or the United Nations. There should be an established procedure whereby the governor of a state is notified. However, mere notification is not enough.

The 50 states are sovereign and their citizens even more so. The people have an expectation of safety of person, place, and property. The governor is the proper authority with no greater responsibility than to defend against federal incursions. I am not suggesting the federal and state relationship be antagonistic; rather, it should be cooperative. However, the states should confront not only the rampant indiscretion of federal power; they should assert supremacy in all jurisdictional respects. The autonomy of the state encompasses the protection of its citizenry. This would effectively subordinate federal claims of jurisdiction. Governors should demand and validate claims of federal interests before authorizing arrests.

This practical precaution would serve to humble the aggressive posture of any federal prosecutor. Norris is a perfect example. Had the Governor of Texas been thoroughly engaged, federal agencies and officials would have been prevented from injuring a fellow Texan. Secondly, the Governor would have been able to confirm the alleged crime of a constituent. Once assured that Norris did not commit the crime, once the Governor confirmed the error of a U. S. Attorney's decisions and actions, he would have preserved Norris' life, liberty, and property. For those who believe such a solution is impractical, we must recall that America is the most incarcerated country in the world. If no one checks the power of the Federal Government, who will? We would benefit by Jefferson's counsel that government is to protect against injury to others, which would include federal actions.

Obviously, there are counterarguments against this solution which are easily deflected. Some arguments against the supremacy of State superiority are the loss of the element of surprise, reduction of federal power, and the avoidance of punishment. Let's consider each. Any element of surprise would not be lost if the federal authorities planned

---

[122] http://rotunda.upress.virginia.edu/founders/default.xqy?keys=FOEA-print-04-02-02-2141

for involving governors in the first place. Moreover, since investigations take years, and are often done in secret, the argument of surprise is negated. The argument that the authority of the *United States* would be diminished is true. The intent of the solution is, both in appearance and as a practical matter, to alter the role of federal power. Federal control is not and should not be an end goal. The third argument that citizens may escape punishment for committing a wrong is a matter of parsing words and perception when there is no injury. We should exact just penalties, however, should we not prevent abuse of power that would result in unjust discipline.

There are routine examples of citizens who are unable to dodge the artful and crafty interpretation of the *truth* presented by federal prosecutors. This is the problem. If governors checked this abuse, the people would be more secure and free. The men we learned about should have avoided their unfortunate experiences. The power of the governor and careful coordination with local sheriffs would effectively secure a potential criminal without the extreme heavy-handed tactics of the "Fed." The governor, with a protocol designed to prevent injury to his constituents, would hold the United States Government to its limited jurisdiction and validate true crimes. I am not suggesting the governor adjudicate the facts but scrutinize the particulars as worthy for federal control. This would place responsibility upon the states to prosecute what are state charges and prevent handing such cases for federal action. It is not a stretch to conclude that Norris and Everston and others would have preferred their governors intercede in the interests of justice and life, liberty, and property.

8—There is a need for a federal office that would respond definitively to queries about federal laws.

There is a compelling need for a federal office that would respond directly to the queries of the governors concerning federal statutes. This office would be an agency that would be distinct from any other involved within the *legal system*. Any query sent by citizens to their states would be answered with the understanding that each citizen is within a state's jurisdiction. The governor would receive notification of any federal response from this office.

If we learned anything, we know with certainty that the Federal Government is limited in scope with its delegated constitutional powers. Notwithstanding the annihilation of the General Welfare and Commerce clauses, which are used to facilitate any view necessary to justify federal control, we may stand foursquare behind the inherent strength of the Tenth Amendment. The intent of the 50 states should be to extinguish any compunction of federal initiative that is unsubstantiated and unwanted. An office that would, with absolute transparency, explain the meaning of terms and scope of the law would assure both state and federal accountability.

Highlighting my case would be appropriate. We should have little doubt as to why one congressman, four senators, the Commissioner of Internal Revenue, the Department of Justice, the Internal Revenue Service, one Internal Revenue agent, and one CID IRS agent refused to reply to my simple question. They, individually and collectively, did not want to account for the truth. Each of these *public servants* was willing to allow an earnest interrogatory to go unanswered. The lack of a response precipitated the imprisonment of an innocent man. They failed to recognize that their abject failure to respond was like broadcasting the truth—accomplished by what was not said. Yet, their admission of the truth by their silence was and still is a means of enabling the legal system to cause injury.

The confusion caused by codes and regulations must be addressed. The inability or, more appropriately, the unwillingness of officials to explain the law must be acknowledged. Undue harm would be prevented by clarifying honest inquiries of the well-intentioned. Moreover, the extent of federal jurisdiction must be confirmed and contained. An agency responsible for satisfying queries would serve these ends.

In my case, having rebutted the presumption that I was a *taxpayer*, I was confident that I was no longer within the power of the *United States* for the excise in question. As far as I was concerned, the government was obligated to either confirm or refute my reasonable understanding. Each public official who received my letter, whether because of fear of loss, greed, or arrogance, neglected a fundamental premise of public office. They did not disclose the law to an inquiring citizen. A federal agency tasked to answer questions would ensure against those who would otherwise shirk their duty.

This federal office and the corresponding state agency would answer questions about law and regulations. It is time we default to the 50 states as a line of defense in the battle of confusing legislation and aggrandizing federal agencies. The benefit of this solution is that specious charges would immediately receive the close examination they deserved. Designed in part to challenge the actions and decisions of federal prosecutors, this office would assist the likes of Norris and provide the exact representation of the law. Appropriately, this service would potentially correct misapplications by reckless agencies and agents.

9—The grand jury and trial jury must enforce its full power.

The grand jury and trial jury must exercise its comprehensive authority to nullify bad law. Essential to this end is that those who sit on these august and powerful panels must understand the history of the power they wield, which this book has explained. When grand juries and juries defeat federal and state authorities by repudiating the laws used to convict people, we will exercise our ultimate authority as the electorate.

10—Investigations must be objective.

The objectivity of investigations must be dignified. Probes must not be tainted. Investigations which lack integrity should not lead to prosecution. Moreover, investigations which are unreasonably long are unconscionable. Four-, five-, six-, and eight-year probes are unjustified. They are cruel and unusual. In my case, the investigation began in 2004 and ended in a trial in 2013. By the time *justice* was reached, I had already lost everything. The only act left to accomplish was to lock me up. Such carnage, as if by design, is malicious and even retaliatory. Norris was no different. Everston experienced unnecessary suffering before trial.

Admittedly, much must be accomplished by investigators. When and if this heavy lifting is compromised, the integrity of criminal charges is jeopardized as well. When I was a Company Commander in the Army, we conducted urinalysis tests. The chain of custody of the samples was paramount. If a sample was compromised by a broken seal or left unattended, the test (investigation) was void. The soldier and staff had a limited time to complete the test. The same should be dignified with evidence and witnesses in criminal probes. When witnesses in jail are influenced with sexual visits for their cooperation, as happened in the Liverman case, the integrity of the investigation is compromised. When Porath was knowingly absent and then kept from the probe and trial, the entire process was tainted and delayed for an unjust end. Anything that can and does adversely influence a defendant's position is unwarranted.

Since the investigators are an integral component of the process, their independence and ethical standing should be beyond reproach. When their sworn affidavits are handed to magistrates or grand juries attesting to the crime, there should be no foul play and no doubt as to the facts involved. They should be factfinders and truth-seekers. Their search for the truth should involve sound judgment and they should investigate within a reasonable amount of time. A credible investigator would have questioned the charge against Norris and Webb—especially since Webb's wife admitted to the crime. The investigators play a pivotal role. When they forward the evidence and testimony to the prosecutor, they should do so with all due alacrity and honesty.

11—Defense lawyers must vigorously defend their clients.

We expect two opposing sides to battle in any court contest. Whether in baseball, soccer, cards, or all-out war, there is the victor and the vanquished. Each side aligns its forces, develops strategies, and executes an attack. Defending against a prosecution in court should be no different. When the accused faces damning evidence and reconciles his guilt, there is wisdom in surrendering. There is no reason to fight.

Those who are innocent and facing the challenge of refuting overwhelming and often misconstrued and circumstantial evidence should be able to rely upon a defense attorney. This is the essence of a defense—to fight and counter the opposition's argument. The defense lawyer and the system should not allow for the possibility of compromising an innocent man's only hope for exoneration. There should be no reason to consider a plea agreement. The plea is the defense advocate's ultimate crutch. It is the invitation to concede before the battle begins.

Consider this point in another way. Why is the truth inconsequential or a man's declaration of innocence immaterial? When is justice no longer the noble aim of our judicial process? The opposition has an unhealthy advantage with the plea at its disposal. The plea reflects the one-sided nature of the contest. The reflexive reaction by the defense to play the plea option is the evisceration of the fight of the accused. This is perhaps the greatest injustice outside the manufactured lies of the prosecutors. Because of the plea, considered only because the government has an unjust advantage, the defense resigns in defeat. Psychologically and emotionally, and as a practical matter, the defendant is outnumbered and overpowered by his foe. His defense is never optimum.

In the cases we reviewed, Figueroa is the best example of a defendant with an able defense. Yet even his lawyer contended with insurmountable forces. The contest was engineered for a plea since the conditions were ripe for a verdict of guilt. Had Figueroa been unable to pay for his defense, had he not secured an advocate who had an indomitable desire to win, he would have had to seriously consider a plea.

With the above primer, we arrive at the pith of this solution. When a defense lawyer is focused on the plea as a strategy, the defense of a client is *not* his intent. Even the argument that a defense is possible once the plea is refused misses the point. A vigorous defense, only after a plea is rejected, renders the defense as secondary from the beginning and secondary during battle. The plea is accepted because defeat is expected.

Even if the plea did not relegate a vigorous defense as inferior, the odds faced by the defense lawyer are invariably insurmountable. This is the crux of the matter. If we assure that, in any court battle, the defendant has an equal expectation and opportunity to defend his innocence, there is no reason for a plea and every reason for an able lawyer to do the expected, battle with a truthful and vigorous defense. We expect a strong defense of the truth and the rightful claim of the innocent until proven guilty.

The essence of American justice is a lie. The lie is that a defense against the charge is possible. This is the greatest con in the legal system, perhaps a greater con than the prosecutor's version of the facts which provides the impetus for the plea in the first place. The American people believe Webb, Ingalls, Wahler, and Richardson had a worthy defense. Americans believe their lawyers arrived at the scene of battle ready, willing, and able to defend these men. This belief is a fiction—the naïve hopes of an ignorant populace. Absent a defense for those in need, we have a crime of immense magnitude, specifically, not having a strong advocate. Why aren't defendants assured that their lawyers will prevail with as much ease as prosecutors? Otherwise, there is no contest. Rather, it is a field-slaughter with innocence laid to waste.

Consider the contrasting pictorials:

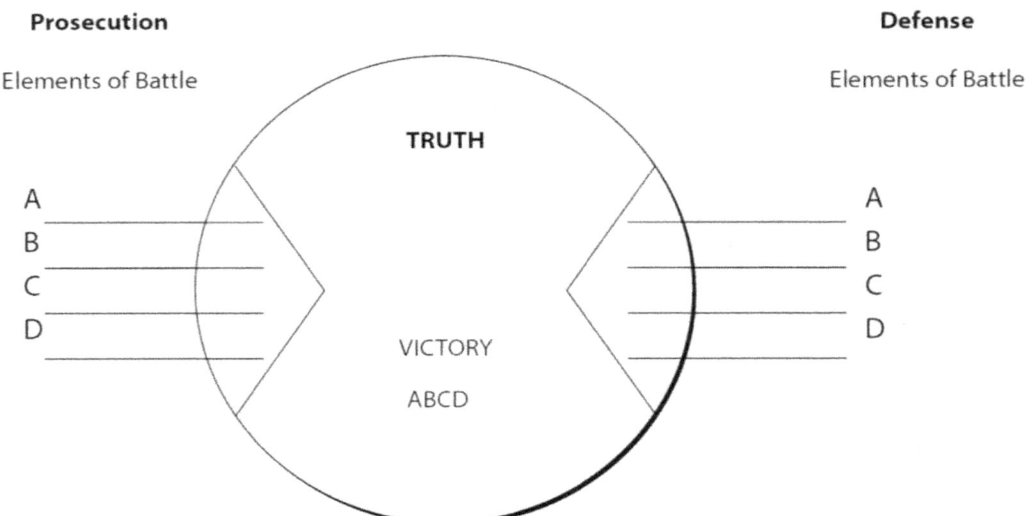

Those who wage war in court would fight for truth and justice and stake claims with their elements of battle (A, B, C, and D). When a victor emerges, we may conclude that a just conclusion was reached, and truth was attained. **We** ***know the battlefield is not cluttered with indefensible obstacles. Neither opponent is unjustly hampered. A true defense and prosecution of facts are achievable. A path to truth is accessible.***

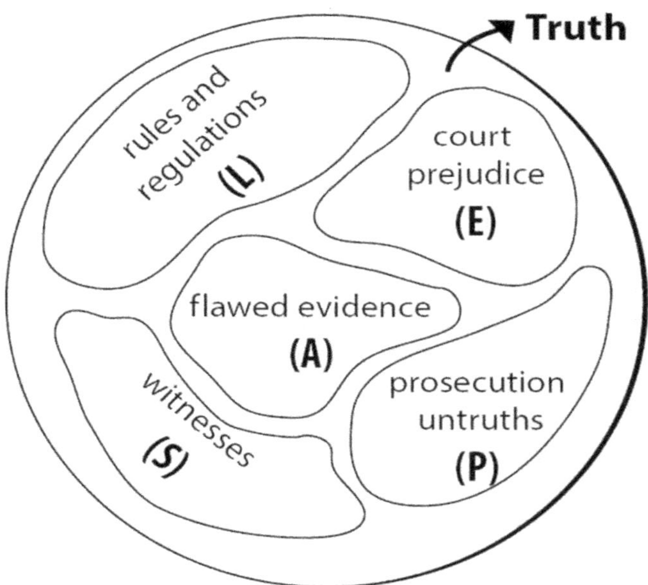

If the defense is confronted with conditions, the truth is sacrificed. If the accused must negotiate P, L, E, A, S, there is no fight for truth. There is, instead, a struggle for survival, to salvage whatever possible. A grounded defense based upon truth is lost to overcome what amounts to interference that forces the truth off the battlefield.

In the cases we viewed, the integrity of the fight was lost and the defense of both the truth and defendant were defeated. Justice was not served. When the elements of truth, ABCD, were forced out of the equation, the result is often PLEAS, a term which defines an atmosphere which discourages the possibility of any defense and defeats truth.

12—The accused may only be charged for the actual crime.

Prosecutors must charge the accused for the actual crime and nothing else. They should not have the latitude to inflate or reduce the charge to a lesser offense. Prosecutors should not have the ability to assert what is false. They should be prevented from employing catch-all phrases designed to implicate those who have no culpability with the crime. Finally, the prosecutor should not be the party that proffers a plea.

This solution, with separate elements, relies upon one significant premise: Prosecutors operate from raw force to achieve their objectives. This is tantamount to a schoolyard bully dictating the terms of a fight from the beginning until the end. The teacher may be present, the *rules* may be *applied*, but the subtle or unspoken conditions of actual conflict prevail. The weak and meek endure the unjust. They agree to conditions not reflective of a fair fight. Considering the inability of defense lawyers to provide a complete defense and their tendency to default to a plea agreement, a remedy is needed.

We will tackle the subject of the plea one more time, but from a different angle. We will then weigh the other elements. The essence of a plea is that the party with the weaker position is the party who should tender it. Here is the definition of "plea".

> ***Plea***—*Defendant's answer in law to a charge or indictment 2. Something alleged as an excuse 3. An earnest entreaty; appeal.* Black's Law Dictionary, 10th edition

There is no doubt a plea, just as the word sounds, originates from the weak, those who seek leniency. Even if a mere formality, when prosecutors offer a recommended plea, it symbolizes the power and arrogance of their position.

When we weigh the other elements, we see that the prosecutor comes from a position of strength. When he does not charge for the actual crime, he alleges criminal conduct which will not likely be proved. This is on par with sensationalizing and is a sign of hubris with the intent to use the system to leverage what should not be achieved. The prosecutor intimidates the defendant. The lesser and more accurate charge becomes palatable to the accused and, thus, the plea gains relevance. Figueroa was never involved in bid rigging and the government never charged him for this crime. Gosin was never convicted of the initial charge leveled by the prosecutor. Figueroa was not even part of any money laundering or mail fraud. Gosin was never responsible for a loss, not to mention $14 to $30 million in mortgage fraud. Meanwhile, the prosecutors in these examples were willing to reduce the charges if both accepted pleas to lesser charges.

The issue should be transparent. The government does not deal with its adversaries with integrity. The brunt of the legal system is channeled behind an escalated charge and targeted at a defendant who knows it is not true. Yet, the defendant quakes in fear of the possibility of conviction. Any plea offered by the prosecutor for a lesser charge is a reprieve and often accepted. Can it be said the government battles fairly?

The arrogance, the gall of those who manipulate the system culminates in injustice. Where else in the judicial process does any party have the means to allege what is unfounded? In civil suits, the plaintiff does not claim the loss of $1,000 when the actual sum is $100. He must prove the true loss. As such, a duel between opponents is not fought for anything less or more than what is alleged. Otherwise, people have no reason to defend their honor and they would not fight for a lie. In any fair contest, the accusations are accurately alleged. The schoolyard bully comparison is appropriate. The prosecutor is the bully. He applies a *truth* that is convenient for him. The plea, which is an enticement, becomes relevant with the force of his office. This is particularly true when the crime of conspiracy is alleged.

Justice becomes a mockery when those in power can exact a *just* charge by painting with a broad brush. The charge of conspiracy is no more credible than any inflated charges. The toil of the prosecutor is no longer like a watchmaker intent on coordinating in synchronous harmony the wheels of justice, truth, integrity, principles, evidence, witnesses, and the motive of the accused. No, the tactics are akin to hurling boulders at a weaker opponent who waves the white flag of surrender.

Who does not perceive the prosecutor as a protector of the people? He is the one who prevails against the bad guys. Yet, when he exercises power to impugn as many people as possible, he becomes the persecutor as foretold by Jefferson. The prosecutor becomes a surrogate for those in power. For example, there was nothing reasonable with the conclusion that Gosin's employees, friends, family, and investors were involved in a conspiracy. Such an approach reflects a void of prosecutorial restraint. It is an incongruous effort to achieve some benefit from a thoughtless practice involving nothing more than a blanket accusation. This practice, which is neither good nor sound, reduces the battle to one of emotions—largely fear.

In the Gosin case, thirty co-defendants were forced to defy the truth simply to avoid entrapment. The truth did not matter, and the prosecutor did not suffer retribution. He continued with the sensational by furthering a lie. The same can be said of Ron Webb. He was not involved in a conspiracy. To think the government wanted Norris to become a snitch on a supplier for what was a simple mistake would be laughable if not so contemptible. These examples are nothing more than predatory acts by government officials upon the worst fears of the people. There is certainly no mastery of the law and no distinction by the prosecutor as he plies his trade in this fashion.

Our one recourse is to require that the prosecutors be truth-seekers. If a prosecutor is limited to filing only accurate charges, the fight becomes fairer. If prosecutors are prevented from leveling charges which are not truthful, the fight is more equitable. If the government is unable to cast a wide conspiracy and forcing the innocent to concede to lies, the fight is closer to the truth. If such *power* were stripped from his arsenal, the prosecutor would have no need to proffer a plea and the defendant would be less inclined to accept a plea. When a prosecutor's case is consistent with what is true the defense might have a fighting chance to prevail.

13—The incentives and conditions provided to secure witness testimony must be disclosed to all parties.

There is no greater sense of hypocrisy than to be accused of a crime by someone who snitches. Most of us have been chastised in our youth for being tattletales. The criminal justice system relies heavily upon the self-interests of those who lack credibility. Why trust the word of someone who is merely attempting to save his skin? This makes little sense. It should be axiomatic that the eventual *testimony* of anyone who divulges the *truth* out of self-preservation is suspect. Two examples prove this point.

We learned of the witness in the Liverman case who provided testimony in exchange for sex. Why should anyone believe him? Why believe him only after he was satisfied? Is his evidence or testimony any more credible than prior to the transaction facilitated by the DEA? Or is the fact that the evidence was suddenly *available* the prime motivation? Compare this with the thirty witnesses in the Gosin case. These common folks, the average Jane and Joe, had no idea of or involvement with a conspiracy. It is just not plausible. If only from the overwhelming pressure of their potential prosecution, each, with the exception of one man who served a year in prison for the charge of conspiracy—for he alone refused to accept a plea to what was a lie—agreed to testify against Gosin. These decent law-abiding citizens agreed to a falsehood to save themselves. As with the former examples, why are these thirty witnesses somehow instantaneously credible? The answer is simple; the *evidence* was *available*, even though it was not as a matter of truth.

The use and manipulation of witnesses is a shameful practice in many respects. All too often the government depends upon *rolling* those who can *confirm* the criminal charge. The incentives for witness testimony are withheld from public awareness and is thus a dubious practice. The fact that plea agreements are not disclosed is indicative of the deceit employed. The point is, whether the testimony is true or not, the prosecutor relies upon what *becomes* viable. If he has a *messenger*, no matter how the messenger was motivated, the message alone is relevant.

Disclosure to the jury of what the witness received in exchange for the *truth* affects the context of the trial. No longer would a witness simply state what he knows; he would be required to reveal how he benefited. This disclosure may already be in place; however, as with any *rule* within the legal system or court, its enforcement is problematic.

Consider the following questions. Would the evidence from a witness alter the jurors' perspective if they knew a *friend* compromised a defendant to have sex in with his wife in a DEA office? Would the jurors rightly question his testimony? Would the jurors consider the testimony of thirty witnesses any differently if they knew the witnesses escaped unwarranted prosecution? If we weigh the sweeping charge of conspiracy, the turning of a witness who faces a criminal charge, especially if his evidence is not true, is a devastating combination to the defense and severely taints the legal system. The government applies pressure with a conspiracy charge that is a falsehood to elicit testimony from a rat which is also a falsehood.

A second concern is that the government treats ringleaders of criminal enterprises as typical witnesses. Full disclosure of any deal for a ringleader is even more important than the average snitch. Isn't the ringleader the impetus behind the crime? He is the one responsible for bringing harm to society. When he receives leniency for assisting the prosecutor, we must conclude the system is flawed if the ringleader receives less time than his subordinates. Consider two examples.

Jesse was the key criminal in the Ingalls case. He was the mastermind. He had possession of the stolen checks and solicited those who were willing to help cash them. Jesse agreed to cooperate with the government and reveal what he knew for his own self-interests. At a minimum, disclosing any reduced charge or sentence would be relevant to Ingalls.

In Ron Webb's situation, Andy was the target of interest. He operated a meth lab somewhere in the mountains of southwest Virginia. The sale of a few pain pills, which had nothing to do with Andy's meth operation, led to Ron's conviction. Disclosure of Andy's deal, and there was one, had relevance. Why? It reveals that, through force, exerted by arrogance, there was a net increase of convictions unrelated to the ringleader's racket.

Regardless of how it is interpreted (the cooperation of a kingpin who rats on his own), this prosecutorial practice is grossly disingenuous. Ultimately, it sends the wrong message: If you are instrumental in the syndication of crimes, you will benefit by tattling on your minions, even those who are innocent. The practice of rewarding key criminals, tracks with the attempted squeeze of Ryan Gosin to roll on a bank that never committed a crime. This was the goal of the prosecutor—the truth-seeker. He wanted bigger fish when there were none. Gosin would have benefited handsomely had he conceded to a lie. Alas, he suffered from the testimony of witnesses. Had Gosin become a witness seeking a plea and any leniency, he would have been no different than those testifying against him. It is ironic that Gosin's refusal to spin facts which would have enhanced the prosecutor's prospects—for he would have been able to topple a banking institution—made Gosin vulnerable to those who lied to escape prosecution.

The federal prosecutors are without integrity when they employ such tactics. The revelation of witness agreements to the jury would effectively curb the arrogance under which the system operates.

14—Every case goes to trial.

When the legal system is designed to circumvent the scrutiny of a criminal charge, truth is compromised. Within the latitude of the rules of court, the government engineers the prosecution of innumerable cases. This is equivalent to mass production of one product on an assembly line by any manufacturer. For, when *facts* are manufactured and the legal system employs a mechanism geared for volume, the truth cannot and will not be pursued.

As opposed perfecting his practice of the law and convincing a jury as to the totality of the truth, the prosecutor becomes a mere processing agent. With this understanding, we may appreciate that prosecutors do not perform as expected. If they did, they would reach the noble goal of intellectual challenge inherent with most court cases. Instead, with a cookie cutter approach, there is little intellectual effort involved. Prosecutors do not sharpen their reasoning and polish their adeptness of articulation of the law; rather, they push buttons which leverage force. The adroit use of language and wisdom are not required with such pedestrian tactics.

If we recognized the legal system for what it is not, if we realized Norris, Figueroa, Webb, and Everston were chambered into the system and rifled through a gauntlet of power which has little to do with logic and veracity, we would impede such efforts. We would compel prosecutors to do what was intended—to prosecute. We can observe the schoolyard bully and understand he does not operate by the wherewithal of his mental acuity. He relies upon power of his office, power that drives the processing of continuous convictions. The use of force is the objective. If prosecutors are not required to prosecute in the truest sense of the word, if they are free to engineer a mind-boggling number of convictions through alternative means, we have the end of justice.

Any number of analogies would be appropriate to prove the point; but we will defer to the watchmaker. If a fine watch represented truth, and each required time and effort to craft, there would be very few made relative to the inferior watches produced on a massive scale. A $5.99 watch is not comparable to a $5,000.00 handmade piece. If we value truth and the lives of the accused, as a society, as a community of truth-seekers, we would demand a system which handled each case for what it represents. If we enable a process whereby an innocent man will plead to guilt because it is not feasible to portray his innocence, we have mass produced convictions.

Consider that the solutions offered so far target the separate components of the legal system. The intent is to demand accountability and integrity and mitigate the shortcomings of any component. With these solutions, separate and collective abuses of power within the system will, to some degree, be alleviated. This leaves the defendant with somewhat of a fighting chance. Truth has the possibility of being known. There is every reason to expect that most cases would go to trial. While some may consider this approach to be naïve and impractical, we should not disbelieve what could be.

Consider the following pictorial:

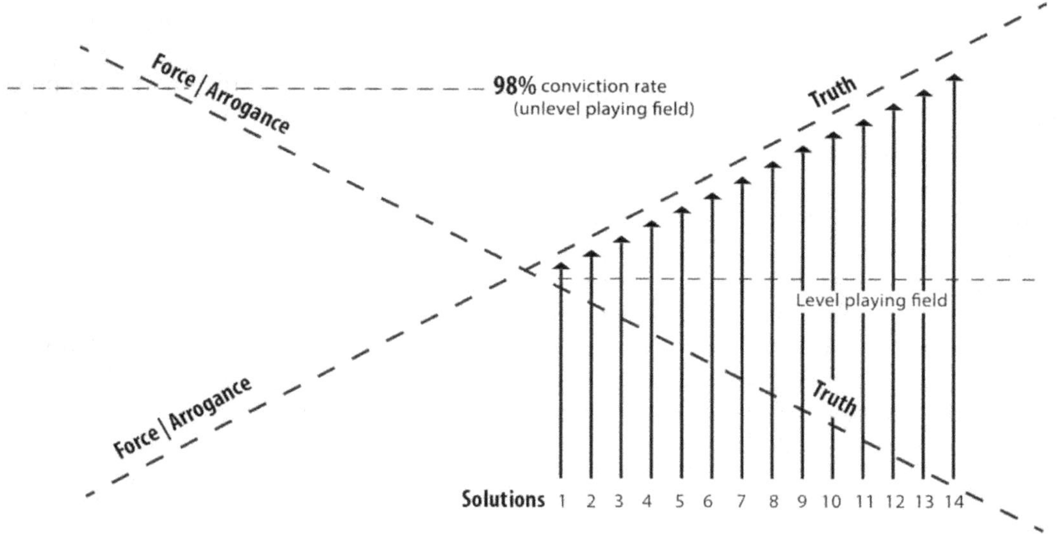

The solutions listed on the bottom right would apply pressure that would defeat the force and arrogance exerted by the judicial system. With success, "Truth" would be elevated well above the line that reflects a "level playing field." An arrogant and forceful system would be humbled as reflected on the left side of the diagram. Ideally, the conviction rate would naturally drop with increased accountability.

Credible solutions would dignify truth for its inherent value and the government would no longer exercise an unjust advantage. On a level playing field, the prosecutor would have no choice but to articulate a reasoned argument for conviction. With these solutions, we should expect an increase in the number of cases that go to trial. A just society would want more trials or, in the alternative, less charges and indictments.

I am not suggesting that conclusive evidence of guilt should not be subject to plea agreements. Rather, cases which cannot and should not be influenced by plea bargains should be tested in court. Each case deserves to be placed in the crucible of court and the elements heated by the strength of opposing arguments. The impurities of each would be burned into insignificance and yield a purer result than current practices. The consequence of *mandating* that more cases go to trial would result in fewer convictions and reveal greater truth and less fabrication. Guilty verdicts would reflect a just society with the intent to punish those who are guilty.

Behind his façade, the schoolyard bully is weak and insecure. His bravado is a mask for what he knows to be true. He huffs and he puffs; he flexes his muscles; he leans into his weaker opponent with the sole intent to intimidate. He rests upon his power and has little justification to articulate a cogent argument that would support his decisions. With the use of fear, he can achieve his desired results. He has no reason to create a delicate and informed position, one which would take time and skill, especially when he can bellow and bluster his way to another hollow victory.

Those who are aware of America's incarceration epidemic may sense that an increase in convictions over the last thirty years is not emblematic of truth and certainly a contrast from the pursuit of justice in a bygone era. To finish the watchmaker theme, the prosecutors create knockoffs of truth. They operate in a system absent integrity without an incentive to argue a healthy representation of veracity into existence before a jury. Ron

Webb's conviction is a badge of dishonor for the prosecution achieved by expediency and greed. The Norris verdict reflects poorly upon a once noble profession. The Figueroa decision is no more than a fraud. Why? The legal system authors fiction through force and arrogance.

The obvious benefit of requiring that cases go to trial is that the court apparatus, nationally and at all levels, would be clogged for decades to come. This would create the need to weed out cases which do not merit prosecution. This expected pipeline of trials would require a purging of sorts. Prosecutors would have to discern which *criminals* should not be tried. The innocent, such as Norris, Figueroa, Richardson, and Everston, would not be compelled to defend themselves. As if a great catharsis, prosecutors would be obligated to reduce the toll on both the court and society. The irony is that prosecutors (not persecutors) who secured legitimate guilty verdicts within an honest system, would be known for the truthful verdicts they attained. The concept of justice would claim its rightful stature; those responsible for seeking justice would also seek truth. The rule of law and the discernment of those who enforce the law would net credible verdicts and sentences. Integrity would be restored.

15—The Webb Doctrine may be employed at any time to challenge the illegality or unethical actions or decisions of any official. Each official or component must certify there was no compromise of either truth or justice.

The entire legal system is a mechanism prone to abuse of discretion. For those who are discerning, the amount of indiscretion is perceived to be quite vast. How is this possible? The reality is that each component is, in some manner, interwoven with the other components. This dynamic culminates in the insidious and even incestuous nature of the entire judicial process. Yet, those who operate the system view this pervasive indiscretion as normal, while most, who briefly glance from the outside, would never make this distinction. Most would not know to perceive such a distinction. Thus, the legal process deserves close examination.

Considering the cases we discussed, we know the investigators were tied to the prosecutor and the prosecutor was bound to the court, with the defense lawyer hinged to the prosecution and the jury connected to the electorate. With this realization, some Americans may cross the threshold of disbelief and into the realization that America is no longer concerned about justice. Some of us may surmise that a lack of justice would not exist but for the ignorance, apathy, and fear of the people and the arrogance of institutions and officials.

If we learned one lesson, it is that contrast is needed if we are to appreciate the full context of anything we do not understand. We do not know the full context of hot until we know what it means by cold. This explanation fits perfectly with the frog in the pot analogy. The frog never knows boiling water until the moment it is thrown in. By virtue of contrast, the frog instinctively knows something is wrong; and it instantaneously seeks a remedy—escape. It fights for survival. We are no different, except for one vital point. If we are oblivious to the threat, we can't apply a remedy. If we do apply a remedy, it is often too late. Our lack of understanding is the reason we perish. We lack the knowledge to be powerful. This point brings us to the beginning of this work. We don't know what we don't know. Ultimately, if we have no inkling of the perversion of justice and the subsequent high rate of incarceration, we don't and won't act.

With our examination of the justice system, we may appreciate the impact of indiscretion. We must act. America is no stranger to action. Note Jefferson's reason why war was inevitable in our earliest years:

> *We have counted the cost of this contest, and find nothing so dreadful as involuntary slavery. Honor, justice and humanity forbid us tamely to surrender that freedom which we received from our gallant ancestors, and which our innocent posterity have a right to receive from us. We cannot endure the infamy and guilt of resigning succeeding generations to that wretchedness which inevitably awaits them if we barely entail hereditary bondage upon them.*[123]

History is being relived into a future that is our present. We face an enemy with the intent of imprisoning we, the people, behind physical bars and within the prisons of our own minds and hearts. Meanwhile, we sit passively, immobilized by fear, unwilling to move beyond our own comfort to help the innocent. As a practical matter, we need a solution which combats this form of voluntary slavery and hereditary bondage.

Reference was made earlier to a Native American, Chief Joseph of Seattle, who said that what we do to the web of life we do to ourselves. I suggested that what we fail to do adversely affect us as well. The Webb Doctrine, in recognition of the interconnectedness of our past, present, and future, which encompasses our current incarceration problem, is a strategy designed to arrest the harm done at any stage of the legal process. This doctrine, named appropriately for Ron Webb, who was caught in the web of life and deprived of his freedom, has a basic premise. If, at any point, there is a credible ethical breach of a man's quest for exoneration or a questionable act which jeopardizes truth and justice, any party may invoke this doctrine as a means to hold the system accountable.

The Webb Doctrine is as simple and powerful as it sounds. At the completion of each phase of the legal system, the responsible official would tender a certified affidavit affirming, under penalty of perjury, that the actions and decisions of his office are consistent with the truth and the interest of justice. These documents would follow the case until it reached the court. There would be an affidavit from the grand jury foreperson, investigator, prosecutor, defense lawyer, jury, and judge. These parties would personally account for their own involvement.

If at any point the defense lawyer, defendant, or any other party believed truth or justice had been compromised, he may contact the Inspector General. The Inspector General's responsibility would be in to investigate the claim. In the event a violation unduly prejudiced the case against the defendant, the violation would be cured, or the charges would be dismissed.

Consider the role of the Inspector General (IG). The IG is an objective official, not uncommon in government, who investigates claims of a wrong. The IG has the power to halt a proceeding pending resolution of the complaint. If the claims are deemed credible, the IG would forward his findings to the appropriate party. The intent would be to correct the abuse and punish the offender.

While the DOJ has an IG, his scope would not currently encompass the intent of the Webb Doctrine. This must change. Given our current dilemma, we must employ this solution. The IG is the party responsible to investigate internal corruption within an agency and within the courts. We must ask the obvious question: How often does the court or judicial process undergo objective scrutiny? With an eight hundred percent increase in federal convictions alone, there cannot be a great deal of oversight. The cases we reviewed validate this concern.

The following examples demonstrate the soundness of the Webb Doctrine. Under this approach, the prosecutor would have been obligated to affirm his decisions and

[123] https://en.wikipedia.org/wiki/The_Testament_of_Freedom

actions as a truth-seeker. He would have certified under penalty of perjury that he had no doubts as to the veracity of the charges and the defendant's culpability. He would have affirmed by his own discretion that Ingalls willfully committed a criminal act with the requisite mens rea. The prosecutor would be required to stipulate that the *evidence* provides complete understanding of the circumstances, actions, and decisions of the accused which warrant an indictment. With the Webb Doctrine, we can plainly see that an ethical and discerning prosecutor would be judicious when attesting to such simple and expected fundamentals.

The facts in the Ingalls case would have prevented any conscientious prosecutor from moving forward with an indictment. The prosecutor would have known from the investigators, who would have complied with the Webb Doctrine, that Ingalls:

1. Did not know the checks were stolen;
2. Asked Jesse and Amanda if the checks were legal;
3. Asked the Wal-Mart cashier if the checks were legitimate;
4. Agreed to refund the full amount for his mistake;
5. Received SSI disability payments for his inability to exercise sound judgment.

Even an inexperienced prosecutor would have realized that, if truth and justice were his primary concerns, Ingalls would have received a just jury trial (if needed at all) and likely would have been found not guilty. More importantly, with the Webb Doctrine, the prosecutor would not have indicted Ingalls in the first place.

The Webb Doctrine would reduce the exercise of unethical practices. If this were not the case, the defense lawyer could invoke the Webb Doctrine before the case proceeded any further. No longer would the defense lawyer view the prosecutor as a colleague, a fellow member of a private society and granted a pass for conducting business as usual. The defense would have the intent to ensure, restore, and preserve truth and justice for those like Ingalls. This is the high calling of legal advocacy. This should also be the objective of the prosecutor.

The Webb Doctrine would give officials within the system reason to challenge their own motives before others made the challenge. Weigh the defense in the Ingalls case as confirmation. Given that the defense lawyer was so depraved and indifferent toward Ingalls, we know the lawyer should have questioned the prosecutor's agenda, decisions, and judgment. He would have resorted to the Webb Doctrine as a means of accountability to hold the prosecutor accountable. Moreover, he would not have defended Ingalls as poorly as he did. Ingalls' lawyer sold him down the river. No one held this defense lawyer accountable. The Webb Doctrine could have been employed to bring him to account for his failure to defend his client. He certainly could not have attested under affidavit that he, in clear conscience, defended Ingalls to the full extent of his ability and the law.

In the Ingalls case, we have the forward progression of an errant prosecutor's indiscretion with the complicity of an unprincipled defense advocate. Were Ingalls or a friend to invoke the Webb Doctrine and petition the oversight of the court or the Inspector General, Ingalls would have had a fighting chance. Otherwise, the system will reach its goal—another conviction of an innocent man.

Let's continue with the scenario and project its proper conclusion. With the IG involved and in possession of both the complaint and Webb Doctrine affidavits from each agency up through the defense lawyer, he may conclude that indiscretion unduly affected Ingalls' one opportunity for vindication and exoneration. The IG would appropriately cite that a one-time fifteen-minute meeting between Ingalls and his legal advisor, during which Ingalls was pressured through fear tactics to sign a thirty-two-page plea agreement, was unwarranted. Such a miscarriage of justice would be acknowledged as a professional indictment against Ingalls' attorney.

Absent the Webb Doctrine, Ingalls would be assured of injustice alone. The power of the Webb Doctrine and the role of the IG should be evident and beyond dispute. Without an independent and autonomous body policing the legal system, we will continue with our current demise.

I can personally attest to the efficiency of the IG and its competent and objective oversight. As a Company Commander in the Army, infrequently soldiers filed complaints. Major Davidson served as the Battalion IG. He was accountable to no one save the IG at the Brigade. He did not reply to or take orders in any matter concerning his role as IG from the Battalion Commander. He suffered no outside influence. His independence was complete. He investigated and accomplished his mission undeterred. His position was respected. We honored the role and the IG's capacity and intent to reach a just and prompt conclusion. The IG ensured accountability of and within the system. The Webb Doctrine could do the same within the legal system.

Any of the cases discussed are replete with junctures where the Webb Doctrine could have been used. As with the IG in other areas of the Federal Government, the intent would be clear: investigate decisions or actions which are counter to rules, regulations, and sound ethics. Without a means to hold officials accountable, there is no adequate safeguard. Even if the people were the most enlightened possible, rogue agents and agencies would still twist and mangle the truth and justify their wayward efforts within the rules of their own game.

Without oversight, the prosecution lied in the Norris case. The investigators hid facts just as they did not disclose Porath's availability in the Figueroa case. My lawyers prevented present a credible good faith belief to the jury, and they refused to require that the prosecution prove jurisdiction. The prosecutor filed charges for what was not criminal in the Everston case. The prosecution stretched the definition and application of the term conspiracy in the Gosin case. The Webb Doctrine would have deterred these officials.

Arguments from naysayers who claim the Webb Doctrine would be impractical or effectively employed are easily discounted. Unless there is a viable alternative, this is an appropriate measure. Inactivity is not an option. The status quo is not an option. Internal and external examination of the executive and judicial branches as to what defeats truth and justice is critical. The repercussions from inaction are severe. We can't "surrender freedom which we received from our gallant ancestors and which our innocent posterity has a right to receive from us," or endure a "wretchedness which [we currently endure] and awaits [our children]."

16 —The defendant may invoke the Common Man Conversation before the grand jury or the jury.

The Common Man Conversation is a dialogue any man or woman of reasonable intelligence has every day. It is a dialogue with give and take, a fluid exchange of information which serves to inform, amplify, qualify, explore, challenge and, in every respect, allows for a comprehensive understanding. Questions are posed and answers expressed. Doubts are reshaped into what is credible. What is presumed to be true is broken down until the misinformation and disinformation is exposed. What is unknown becomes known. Since our reality and truth is expressed in language, words bridge the divide from ignorance into knowledge and understanding.

When the common man has a healthy conversation, there are no questionable rules. There are no limitations. There are no controls as to what may be said. Conversations, while not always easy, are open and ripe with the possibility that the truth will be dignified. Participants extend to each other the mutual respect and courtesy they deserve and afford themselves with a malleable dynamic without impediments. While conversations are often plagued with difficulties, we cannot discount that we can fully express until the conversation is complete. When this occurs, we have integrity. We are complete and whole.

We have anything but integrity with the cases we reviewed. The *conversation* within the legal system is anything but civil. It is not a complete exchange or a common man's way of relating and dignifying others and differing perspectives. With its rules, the game of court precludes the elements of relating with the written and spoken word.

Judge Moon interrupted a man's testimony and prevented him from sharing his good faith belief. This is not normal in healthy conversations. Within the game of court, such tactics are not only employed, but they are also used to achieve a particular result. The prosecutor in the Figueroa case snipped a handful of select words from five hours of taped dialogue to craft a specific portrayal for the jury. This is neither normal nor healthy among civil conversationalists. We don't intend to reduce the discussion to a partial representation—a lie. The prosecutor force-fed the jurors the exact impression of Figueroa he desired. He had no intent to relate with others in a wholesome manner.

We cannot discount that the game of court is foreign to most of us. It is foreign because we are unfamiliar with this venue. It is foreign because it is unnatural to our manner of being. A fish that is out of water experiences what is unnatural. Outside of its environment, the fish will die. A common man's conversation, a normal way of relating and expressing, will not survive in court. The rules will not permit it. The healthy conversation dies in court. This is by design.

The game of chess has clear and established rules. The game of court is the same. The irony is that most enter court as defendants, jurors, or observers and naturally expect a somewhat normal dialogue to unfold. We naively proclaim, "I'll tell my story! I will state the truth. The system will listen and do the right thing." It is foolhardy to enter this controlled venue with the expectation that our explanations will have an impact or we will be heard at all. The rules of court, which are firmly established, dictate not only how the *conversation* will unfold, but what is or is not stated.

I marveled at the reaction of my two attorneys when I first explained my simple and clear good faith belief. They were emphatic that they could not state in court that I was not a *U. S. person* as defined in the tax code. If they attempted to do so, they would have been sanctioned. Well, there we have it. The governing guidelines of the ABA and the supposed limitations of court curtailed what Cargill and Harris, officers of the court, defenders of the innocent, could introduce into the *conversation*. They could not state the truthful position of their client. This was forbidden. Contrast this approach with my perspective. I proclaimed my innocence. I was dragged into court, akin to a fish hauled out of water. My freedom would cease if I could not communicate as a reasonable man does all the time in the outside world. I was under the false impression that I could share the truth. The following is what I would have expected my lawyers to communicate to the court and jury, or what I would have shared if permitted.

Ladies and gentlemen of the jury, the defendant has stated to this court from the very beginning that the federal income tax is not an excise which applies to him. The reasons are quite simple. The income tax law applies to whom and what are within the Federal Government's jurisdiction to tax. The government may tax by excise those persons who either have a federal status as revealed by 26 USC 6013(g) or accept federal privileges. Americans voluntarily engage both of these prerequisites.

Mr. Johnson no longer has a federal status, which is consistent with 26 USC 6013(g)(4)(A), and he no longer accepts a federal benefit subject to excise. He revoked and rescinded his participation in the federal social security insurance program. He also rebutted the presumption that he was an "U. S. person," "taxpayer," or "employee" within the jurisdiction of the federal "United States," a presumption created by his voluntary submission of his very first federal income tax form.

If Mr. Johnson had never held a federal status by electing to submit a 1040 tax form or accepted federal benefits, he would not have been obligated for this income/excise tax in the first instance. Let me be clear. Mr. Johnson cannot be within the jurisdiction of the Federal Government for the imposition of the federal income tax. Why? By virtue of his decision to disengage with or extract himself from the orbit of these federally excisable classifications and activities.

Note the tax code refers to "person" and "U. S. persons" as those liable to file. These definitions are limited in scope. Otherwise, the language would say "Americans" are liable; yet, even then, "Americans" would have to choose to engage in the very activity to incur the tax liability.

Members of the jury, consider a practical example. A child may be born without ever getting a social security number or submitting federal tax forms. The presumption would never be made that such a child was obligated for the tax, much less liable to file a return. The child, even when he becomes an adult, would not and could not be considered a "person" or "U. S. person" as defined in the tax code. Why? The tax code only applies to statuses and excises for which that "person" would be liable, within constitutional excise authority.

Mr. Johnson has altered his status by correcting the mistakes he made when he was under the age of majority and without fully informed consent. He is presently as he would have been had his parents not entered him into the social security scheme or directed him to acquire a federal status with the first submission of his first 1040 tax form.

The consequences of his past uninformed decisions are profound. Mr. Johnson, against his wishes, was hauled into federal court when the DOJ and IRS had no jurisdiction to do so. This means Mr. Johnson is here without the court having the requisite jurisdiction. The Federal Government does not and cannot have jurisdiction. Under Article III, Section 2 of the Constitution, the federal court may only adjudicate cases within the stated parameters. Both Mr. Johnson and the circumstances of this case do not fall within those parameters. He should not be prosecuted in an Article III or IV territorial court of the United States, as he is no longer within a territory of the United States or even the United States itself.

Since Mr. Johnson does not have a federal status and does not participate in a federal privilege, he cannot have a tax liability and, therefore, he can't be a "U. S. person" under the tax law, which is the law the government seeks to enforce. Since Mr. Johnson is without the scope of congressional taxing authority, he is without the scope of this court.

This is the heart of the issue. The Federal Government may not go into the 50 states and pick up, as in arrest, Mr. Johnson when he no longer has involvement with the "United States" for the excise in question. The United States may not compel him to perform and conform under a law which no longer applies to him. The fact that you are not aware of either the law or the limitations of the law should not adversely affect a man who is without any legal obligation and committed no criminal act. This tax obligation is no different than Mr. Johnson being liable to 26 USC 4071 which mandates an excise tax for the manufacture and sale of tires. If not involved in the business of tires or no longer involved with tires, he can no longer be liable for the excise tax.

Please know that a federal status and social security number are not required by law and Americans are not required to participate in or accept either. Moreover, your failure as Americans and jurors to know that the United States Government is, by fraud and force, requiring Mr. Johnson to appear in court and endure this trial, when the government lacks jurisdiction, should not bring him harm.

If the prosecutor bothered to seek understanding as to Mr. Johnson's genuine belief, just as Agent Biggs and Pompei should have answered his one simple question years ago, he would have realized the truth. The prosecutor has no grounds for an indictment much less the wherewithal to seek a conviction or imprisonment. Mr. Johnson is outside the prosecutor's authority and jurisdiction of this court.

The court was duly informed of Mr. Johnson's status from the very outset. Upon his arrest, he sought to have a conversation that would explain and then clarify his status and belief which should have required his immediate release. This is what he sought during the ungodly eight-year investigation which unduly affected his marriage, family, and life. He wanted answers which would have underscored how and why he had a legal tax liability or that his good faith belief was both legal and lawful. If he had been shown that he was liable, he would have filed tax returns and would have been no criminal charges, much less a trial. If the government had validated that his good faith belief was sound, we would not be here today, and your time would not have been wasted by the indiscretions of a political appointee aggrandizing for his own future at an innocent man's expense. No government official or agency answered Mr. Johnson's query. He was accused under false pretense.

Sadly, we are here, and the rules of court and the unspoken rules of force and fraud serve as the means for those with titles NOT to engage a man whose sole intent was to comply with the law.

As jurors, you are in the unfortunate position of determining the guilt of a man who has forgotten more about tax law than you will ever learn collectively. Regrettably, if only for the rules of court, you are not permitted to converse with either Mr. Johnson, the prosecutor, or the IRS agent. You are not allowed to question Mr. Johnson in hopes of understanding his good faith belief. You cannot question the government and challenge their weak claims and preposterous arguments. You cannot ask them why they hid from Mr. Johnson's request for full accountability, and you cannot ask why they hide behind court protocol now. You are not able to clarify any confusion you may have. You are not granted the ability to probe for greater insight. You are expected to do what is quite unnatural. You must pass judgment on a man without complete understanding. Furthermore, just as you must decide within these constraints, Mr. Johnson must await your verdict knowing you are hamstrung by these conditions.

If you were able to listen to his reasoned position, you would likely come to the revelation that Mr. Johnson cannot be a "taxpayer" or "U. S. person" as defined in the tax code. You would realize the judge never allowed Mr. Johnson to assert his proper and true status for one very important reason; this court could not have proceeded with a case which was not within its authority. The repercussions of this disclosure would have been too great a risk. You, as jurors, would come to know that if one man could effectively establish that he was not within the jurisdiction of the Federal Government for the federal income tax and not within the purview of the federal courts, others would begin to comprehend the true nature of the income tax fraud.

Perhaps this is why Judge Moon, directed Harris to address the question of the 16th Amendment, when this amendment had no relevance to Mr. Johnson's belief. The presumption that an American would be perceived as having a federal status and the federal benefit of social security program did not even exist at the time of the passage of *this amendment. It was the submission of the 1040 tax return and the social security act, along with the subsequent Supreme Court decisions in 1937 that addressed the issue of the excise and the income tax. Was Judge Moon unaware of tax law? Did he introduce the 16th amendment in order cloud and confuse? For, that is what happened. The conversation is no longer about Mr. Johnson's good faith belief; it is now, in part, about an amendment, the 16th amendment, which most people believe, erroneously, is the basis for the income tax.*

So, not only are you unable to question Mr. Johnson and the government, but you are also unable to question and converse with the judge.

Where does this leave you? Knowledge that Mr. Johnson is not liable for the income tax and outside the jurisdiction of the taxing authority would prove to be powerful.

Rest assured that the rules of court must prevail—for the rules are how the government's fraud is perpetrated. If courts can prevent the expression of a man's status and beliefs, if court protocol is maintained, you, as jurors, can do nothing but aid and abet this racket. Although your involvement in this agenda is done unwittingly, the guilty verdict that you will likely render will be the true crime.

So, I ask that you suspend your own disbelief and realize that things are not as you understand, and the tax law does not apply to Mr. Johnson. He is innocent.

As is transparent, my attorney could not have used such language with the primary aim to clearly state an innocent man's proper status. The court prohibited this approach and Cargill and Harris rejected this approach. As such, these defense lawyers did not speak with the jury in a manner that remotely resembled a common man's way of conversing. Why? They would not risk contempt of court charges.

We can imagine similar scenarios for any of the other men in the cases we reviewed. These men were denied a reasonable expression of their defense and full disclosure of their thoughts on the matter. The truth was denied. Be it Norris, Ingalls, Webb, or even Wahler, the requirements of court are prohibitive. Obviously, the jury has less to work with than if they could engage in a common man's conversation.

Imagine twelve reasonable men and women of a jury in a trial that is all but over except for one remaining act. Imagine one juror standing within the jury box and stating:

> *By the power vested in me as Juror, I hereby invoke the Common Man Conversation. I have questions and doubts that remain unresolved, even after and perhaps because of the constraints of the legal system. Therefore, I expect all parties to dignify my resolve to clarify any points of contention that I or my fellow jurors may have. As for me, I will not pass judgment upon a man who may not deserve a verdict of guilt. Since I occupy the most powerful position in this court, I expect your cooperation as I pose my queries to the defendant and, if need be, other parties to these proceedings.*

Do you see the effectiveness that would result with this solution?

From that point forward, until this conversation was concluded, the jury would satisfy their questions with a natural and unfettered conversation with the defendant and anyone else concerned. Norris would be able to express the truth that he never bought or sold an illegal flower. Moreover, the judge and prosecutors could do nothing, *absolutely nothing*, but listen to the exchange. Norris' innocence would potentially prevail because the government and court would be shackled by a *rule* used to reveal the whole story—*the truth, the whole truth, and nothing but the truth*. The jurors would be truth-seekers. Integrity would be restored. The jury would appreciate that the rules of the game of court—the legal system—were designed to compel a man to plead or to lead the jury to an all but automatic determination of guilt.

Consider another example. If only for the existence of the Common Man Conversation, suppose Ron Webb decided not to accept a plea; rather, he decided to have a trial by jury. When the trial was almost over, *Webb* invoked the power to speak plainly to the jury. He freely told the jurors his concerns. He disclosed his reservations that what they heard was not the complete or truthful representation of the facts. He stated that unless he was able to relate to them outside the unnatural and contrived constraints of court rules, they would not make an informed decision. So, Webb and the jurors defied the artificial construct of court and shared intimately as men and women with integrity.

Can you imagine Ingalls with the option to invoke the Common Man Conversation? Can you visualize the relief of the jurors with the ability to reach beyond the injustices and contrived limitations of the system and relate with a man trapped within what should never have been—a charge of conspiracy? And then there is Richardson, who would have been able to speak freely and share the dynamics of the politics within the school system which led to the original accusations of wrongdoing. Wahler would no longer have been inhibited by court mandates. He could have shared that the retrieval of a document on a server, which was his just a day earlier, should not be grounds for a verdict of guilt with the label of felon and potential prison time.

The Common Man Conversation may be the defining resolution to our current epidemic. This approach may be the best antidote to fear, where fear is most fierce—within the court of law.

If the preceding solutions were implemented, each component of the legal system would experience reform to some extent. The Common Man Conversation would ensure the occurrence of the most important event in the entire process, the relating of the defendant with the members of the electorate—the jury. No other outside influences would be permitted to interfere with this moment. Honestly, those who were truly guilty of committing a crime would likely balk at this opportunity or fail miserably if they decided to have this candid conversation with their *peers*. However, the innocent would honor and cherish the possibility to vindicate themselves.

[W]ith all these blessings, what more is necessary to make us a happy and a prosperous people? Still one thing more, fellow-citizens -- a wise and frugal Government, which shall restrain men from injuring one another, shall leave them otherwise free to regulate their own pursuits of industry and improvement, and shall not take from the mouth of labor the bread it has earned. This is the sum of good government, and this is necessary to close the circle of our felicities. **Thomas Jefferson**

The Four Corners of Justice Revisited

This book should have shocked your conscience. The content should have riled an individual and collective sense of contempt for man's inhumanity to man. We should realize that life is not as we perceive. Our perceptions are not reality. Rather, we should know America's problems are grave. Hopefully, you reached the conclusion that solutions—effective solutions—must be employed. If we fail to see the crisis and are unwilling to solve it, we validate that we, the people, are the problem.

We discussed various concepts which provided valuable insight. These concepts are integral to our understanding. The concept of contrast is essential. The absence of contrast denies us complete context. Contrast underscores the concept that *we don't know that we don't know*. Without knowing, we will never appreciate any problem, much less the solutions. The concept of not knowing is directly tied to judgment. When we judge without the context of contrast and knowing, we indict ourselves. Without these three grounded concepts, it is far too easy to impugn a man for his words and deeds.

If we fail to apply either the concepts of contrast, not knowing, and non-judgment, we place less value on life and humanity. This may appear to be a rather strong conclusion; but, given the content in this book, it must be stated. We need only consider that, as a community, we do not appreciate or respect our fellow man. Regrettably, and this cannot be argued, our indifference to other human beings reflects an indifference to our individual roles within our culture. It is worth repeating that what we do or don't do to the web of life impacts all of us.

If we refer to any of the ten men discussed as common criminals, when they are likely innocent, we demonstrate a degree of detachment. Judging others without knowledge and contrast reflects ignorance and a limited perspective. Whether or not we acknowledge cracks in the foundation of the legal system, we perceive justice, nonetheless. We prevent ourselves from seeing cracks or we are too far removed, which renders the cracks as inconsequential. We either don't acknowledge or refuse to see injustice.

The contrast contained within the Four Corners of Justice (FCOJ) diagram gives us a means to measure. This chart quantifies the extent of injustice within the legal system. No longer is the representation of a court case merely subjective, vaguely defined within our minds, or loosely expressed in a conversation with shallow words alone. The FCOJ diagram gives us something concrete. The diagram shows a disparity between positive and negative scores. Qualifying the subjective through contrast reveals what we did not know. With this knowledge, we are less inclined to judge. Our perspective is broadened, and criticism tempered.

Any new frame of reference garnered through the FCOJ diagram allows us to reassess the judicial process with purpose. This is where the use of knowledge becomes powerful. Change becomes inevitable. We realize solutions must be sought. We no longer accept the status quo. Otherwise, we will suffer the consequences of our own inaction. The sixteen solutions serve a valuable purpose—accountability. We become accountable to ourselves, and the legal system becomes accountable to itself, the electorate, and truth. With the FCOJ diagram, we visualize how solutions counter the arrogance and subsequent flaws which encourage guilty verdicts. The FCOJ strengthens the argument of a need to combat the adverse effects of the ten components of the legal system. However, before we measure how these solutions neutralize negative scores, let's establish a frame of reference.

In an ideal world, if we had justice, the scores would be congruent with the Zero Line. We would have balance. We would have two opposing parties providing reasoned arguments of the facts—truth—with each opponent exercising an equal opportunity to prevail. There would be no force, threats, denial, subterfuge, and no evil intent to deprive either party of justice.

As established by the scores from the cases we surveyed earlier, the ratings were predominantly to the left side of the Zero Line with very few to the right. Then we have total scores that were negative. Even though the point value for the positive marks was doubled, we already know the system allows real criminals to go free on technicalities. However, bad guys do not typically escape accountability. Noteworthy, the system did not err for the benefit of the innocent seeking truth and justice. We can, therefore, eliminate the right side of the FCOJ diagram. What remains is quite revealing. We have the Zero Line to the far right and points that correspond to the respective ten components on the left or UNJUST side of the diagram.

Electorate:					-1	0
Lawmakers:				-3	-1	0
Investigators:			-5	-3	-1	0
Prosecutors:		-7	-5	-3	-1	0
Judge/PSI:	-9	-7	-5	-3	-1	0
Defense lawyers:		-7	-5	-3	-1	0
Witnesses:			-5	-3	-1	0
Jury:				-3	-1	0
Grand Jury:					-1	0

Our intent should be to eliminate the ill effects of the system. With the solutions we just covered, we may defeat the influence of an act or representation which impedes or destroys any element of justice. With the solutions listed at the bottom and top of the chart and referenced by a corresponding letter, we would expect to quantify or at least visualize how each would correct the intended or unintended consequences of institutional arrogance.

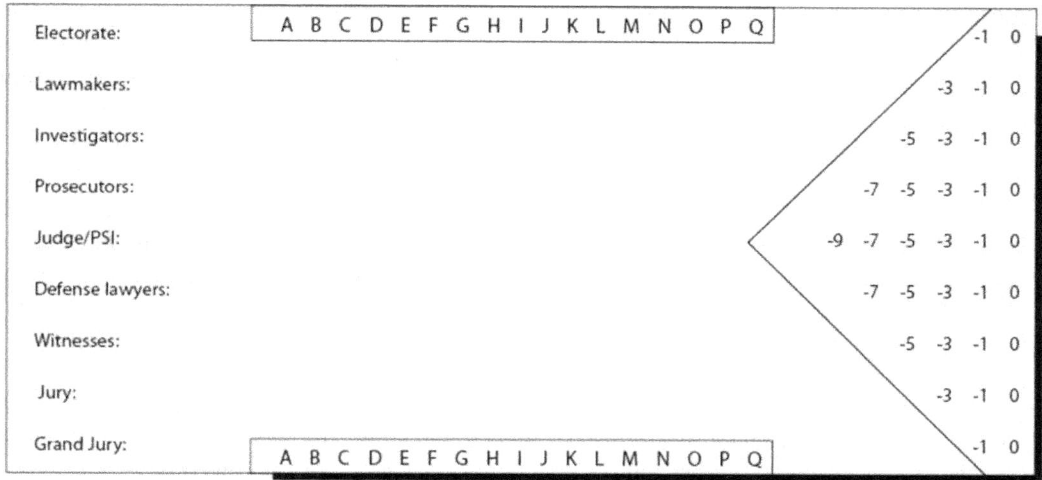

A—An informed people
B—Status
C—Must be a crime
D—Representative
E—Commerce/General Welfare Clause
F—Judge's Role
G—Governor/Sheriff
H—Federal office for queries
I—Grand jury
J—Jury
K—Objective Investigation
L—Defense provided
M—Charge for actual crime only
N—Witness Incentives
O—Trials Mandated
P—Webb Doctrine
Q—Common Man Conversation

By placing any solution with a negative score, we have the possibility to right the wrongs inflicted upon the defendant. This is no different than standing up to the schoolyard bully. If the bully attacks with his vast arsenal, the chance of the victim prevailing is negligible given his lack of knowledge, resolve, and courage. However, if solutions are available and each contributes to the battle, the bully may be defeated.

As the bully stands alone with his "might makes right" posture, if the victim relies upon the righteous persuasion of a grand jury, asserts his status as a freeman with a discerning and judicious judge (the teacher supervising the schoolyard), has a Common Man Conversation and, thus, reasons through doubt and confusion, and he uses the Webb Doctrine for accountability, the perceived dominance of the system wanes. Collectively, not that the bully system couldn't be tamed with a simple and powerful solution, all solutions chip away at the injustice.

We must recall, as with the bully, *court* is a game. Since the game of court is like any other controlled operation, it would be impractical to suggest that the rules of court could be changed easily. The court and its players thrive with and because of these rules. Our best efforts should be used to assert healthy countermeasures. Even if these solutions are not able to completely prevail over each negative score, we can make amends. We can destroy injustice with one critical remedy.

Consider examples of both possibilities. If a witness were convinced to accept a plea in exchange for his testimony and the prosecutor were required to disclose those conditions, the defendant could overcome the unfavorable impression that would result if the plea agreement was not disclosed. If the government had to limit charges to actual crimes committed, the defendant's inclination to capitulate would be lessened. The government would have to prove the more severe charge. While these two examples may not influence a particular case to the point of acquittal, they would provide clarity and accountability. Examples of complete defeat would be if the governor prevented an arrest for what was clearly not a criminal act, or a jury acquitted by nullifying a law with which they did not agree.

When the solutions prevail, justice would reign. In all other cases, our hope would be that every possible solution incrementally adds to a positive net gain to a negative score. For example, if a FCOJ score is -15, solutions would place pressure upon the negative influences and raise the score. If justice could be assured by virtue of a fail-safe solution, we mark it with a box around the letter—***G***. All other solutions would remain as a letter only. The aggregate score of all solutions, even if given half the value of each negative score, significantly increases the possibility of an acquittal. Our objective is to equal, if not exceed, any negative score. In theory, the score of "-15" would be reduced to "-7" or better. Regardless of how much the score is lessened, we seek parity.

No system will ever function perfectly. When man is involved, unsavory tendencies will unduly taint the outcome. Just as humanity chooses paths up the mountain of life, actors in the game of court and any number of government officials within the legal system make the same choices, even within their profession. Today, few will travel the just and righteous path. Most will satisfy their own agendas. Our best option is to impede their way—force them to alter course. Our solutions would permanently block their questionable and unethical means to unjust ends.

In the original FCOJ diagram, we had the reverse cascading of power, whereby the components which represent the people (the electorate, jury, grand jury, and lawmakers) were heavily influenced by the components within the court. Recall that arrogance flowed from within the legal system outward, from the judge, prosecutor, and defense lawyer as reflected by the line labeled "C"—arrogance. The new FCOJ diagram demonstrates the proper flow of power from the people who bring accountability to the legal system. With effective solutions, backed by an informed, resolved, and courageous people, the impact of institutional arrogance is marginalized.

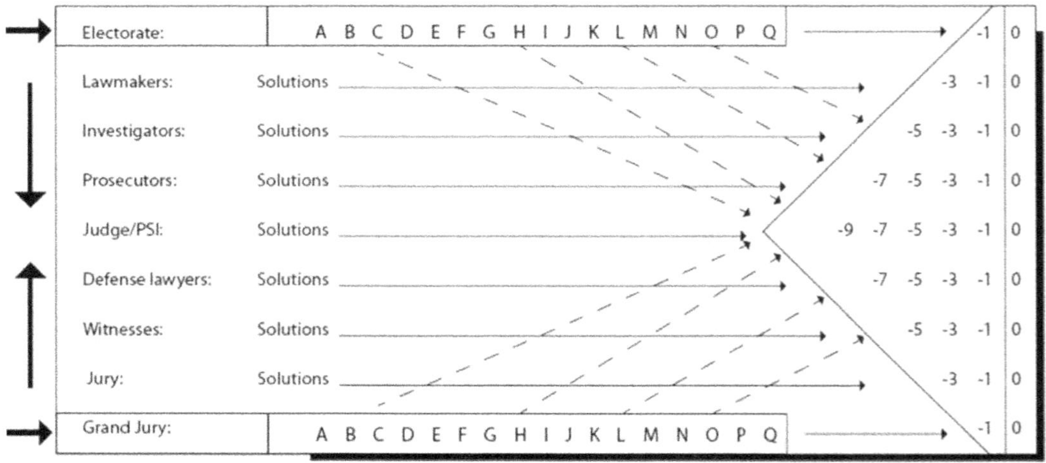

With this current FCOJ diagram, the grand jury serves as the cornerstone. In the engineering world, the cornerstone is critical to a sound structure. Every other element in the structure is square with the cornerstone. In the diagram, the electorate serves as the capstone. Unique to these two components (which represent the electorate) is that all solutions are available—which reflects the power inherent within each, even if these solutions are not used. Since the people are the source of power—the cornerstone and the capstone (the foundation and the header respectively)—the structure will be as solid as possible. Finally, notice on the left side of the diagram that the cornerstone and capstone apply equally opposing pressure to the remaining components, which serves our intent to reach the proper and just execution of all offices, powers, and laws.

We can look at the right side of the chart and note that the Zero Line is square with the cornerstone and capstone and plumb with the entire structure. With have balance within the construct that is the legal system, even if it is only a symbolic balance. With all corners anchored by the electorate, grand jury, and equitable scores of "0," we can assert that, in theory, as solutions push against all wrongs, the FCOJ is foursquare behind what is equitable and true. This sense of justice is achieved when the electorate and grand jury, which represent the people exert pressure from the top and bottom of the structure and at an oblique 45-degree angle against the negative scores. The dubious influences within the legal system are attacked from the front and sides with nowhere to retreat but back to the Zero Line. This is an optimum strategy for success.

We will review the cases discussed and consider alternative outcomes with the sixteen solutions. We will weigh the solutions which counter the more egregious prejudices in each case and recognize that all other solutions weaken the stranglehold that is injustice and institutional arrogance. As noted by the arrows coming from the electorate and the grand jury, we must recognize some solutions are always seeking corrective remedies. While a solution may not be prominent, the remedy is present, nonetheless. For example, if we elected discerning representatives, they would constantly seek parity with injustice. Or, if we were more vigilant as an informed people, we would assert our status. This alone might prevent a situation from ever escalating into an unjust prosecution. These quiet solutions provide added strength, not unlike the mortar which binds building blocks to an already firm and resolute cornerstone.

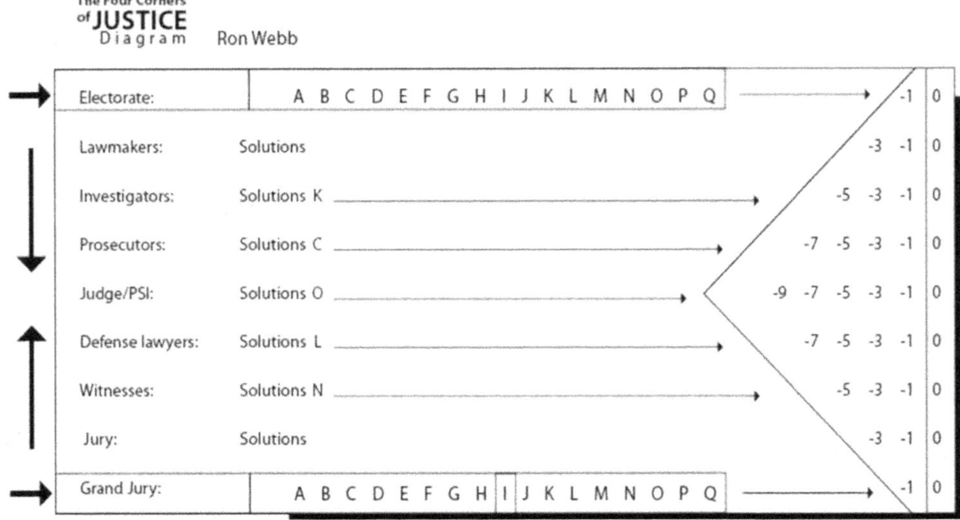

RON WEBB

Crime: Webb was charged with selling prescription pain pills and conspiracy.

Verdict: Webb entered a plea of guilty to avoid a long prison sentence.

- The investigation was not fair.
  Solution: The investigation must be objective. (K)
- The prosecutor filed charges when Webb committed no crime.
  Solution: No loss of life, liberty, or property. (C)
- The defense lawyer did not defend his client.
  Solution: Defense lawyers must vigorously defend. (L)
- There was no trial.
  Solution: Every case goes to trial (O)
- The witness, a criminal, received leniency which should have been disclosed.
  Solution: Witness incentives must be revealed. (N)
- The grand jury did not have all the facts.
  Solution: Grand jury exercises full power. (I)

The Webb case is another example in which the governor or sheriff could have easily prevented the arrest of a man who was innocent. Moreover, given the severity of the charges and punishment, the Webb Doctrine would have ensured accountability at every level. Even if the officials falsely swore of the veracity of the charges at each stage of the case, invoking the Webb Doctrine would have brought internal systemic scrutiny. Finally, invoking the Common Man Conversation would have allowed the jurors to hear from a defendant trapped within a system designed to limit his testimony. If the jurors were permitted to ask questions to resolve doubt, had Webb gone to trial, justice may have been achieved since his wife would have been found guilty of the charges.

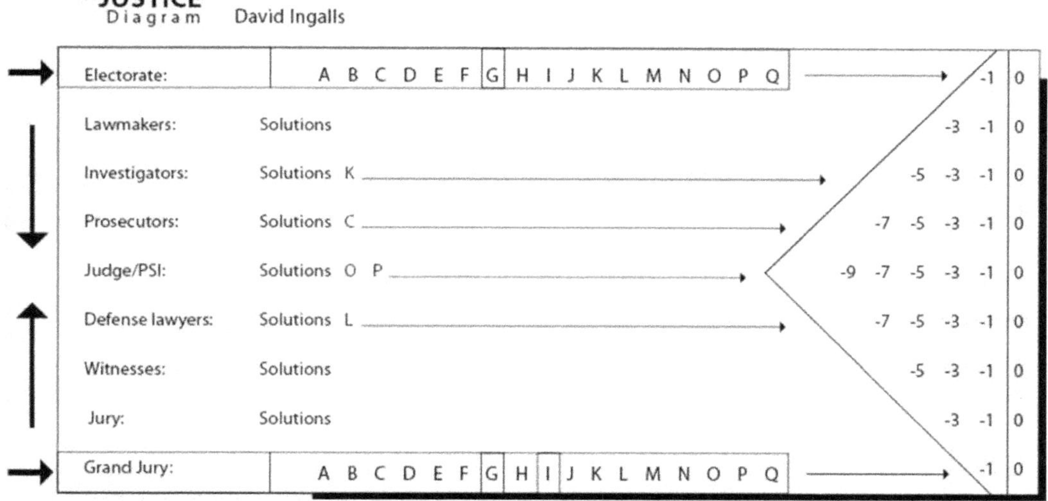

DAVID INGALLS

The Crime: Ingalls was accused of cashing stolen checks.

The Verdict: Ingalls entered a plea of guilty to avoid a long prison sentence.

- The prosecutor filed charges without criminal intent. Ingalls was a victim.
  Solution: No loss of life, liberty, or property. (C)
- The defense lawyer did not defend Ingalls.
  Solution: Defense lawyers must provide a vigorous defense. (L)
- There was no trial.
  Solution: Every case goes to trial. (O)
- The investigation was not objective or truthful.
  Solution: The investigation must be objective. (K)
- The grand jury did not have the truth.
  Solution: The grand jury exercises its power. (I)

There is no better illustration for the need of the Webb Doctrine than the Ingalls case. If each official or agency were accountable for its actions and decisions, they would have had an ethical obligation to attest to Ingalls' lack of involvement with the conspiracy. The case reflects the grave need for objective internal oversight and accountability. Three officials—the lead investigator, the prosecutor, and defense lawyer—should have been sanctioned, if not charged for criminal negligence. At a minimum, the Common Man Conversation should have been invoked at a trial that should have occurred. The jury should have been given the facts which included Ingalls' status as a recipient of disability compensation for his inability to make wise decisions.

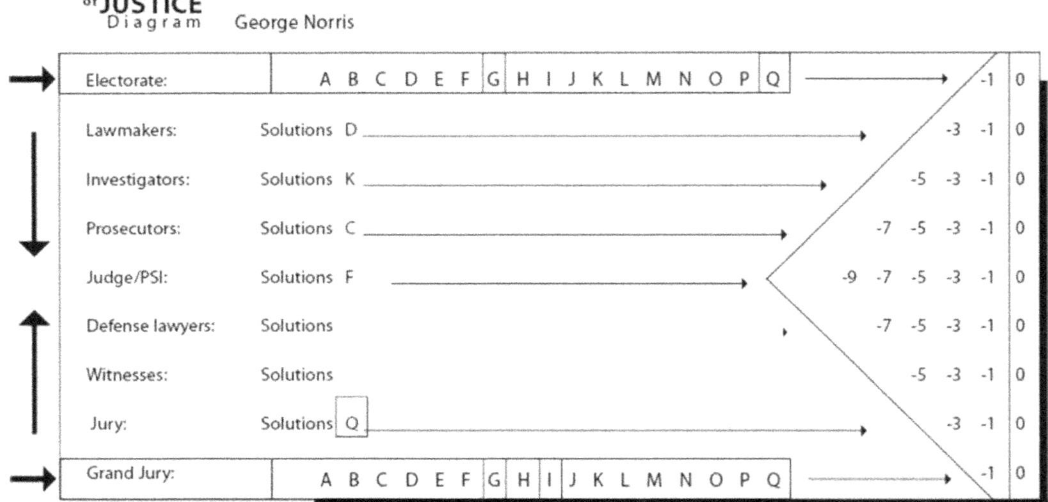

George Norris

The Crime: Norris was charged with selling illegal orchids.

The Verdict: Norris accepted a plea rather than go to trial.

- The investigation was not objective.

  Solution: The investigation must be objective. (K)
- The prosecutor pursued charges for acts that were not criminal.

  Solution: No loss of life, liberty, or property. (C)
- The grand jury did not have all the facts.

  Solution: Grand jury exercises its full power. (I)
- The judge didn't provide balanced oversight for a case that should never have gone so far.

  Solution: Judge must be impartial. (F)
- Lawmakers did not prevent the improper enforcement of the law.

  Solution: We need discerning representatives. (D)

The Norris case is another example where the governor would have prevented a tragedy and stopped the willful abuse of reckless federal authority. Norris should never have been arrested. The Common Man Conversation would have been ideal in a trial setting. It would have afforded a jury the chance to clarify the *facts*. The Web Doctrine would have caused each agency to account for its actions and decisions. Moreover, any agent and his blatant abuse of power would have been held accountable with sanctions after appropriate oversight by the Inspector General.

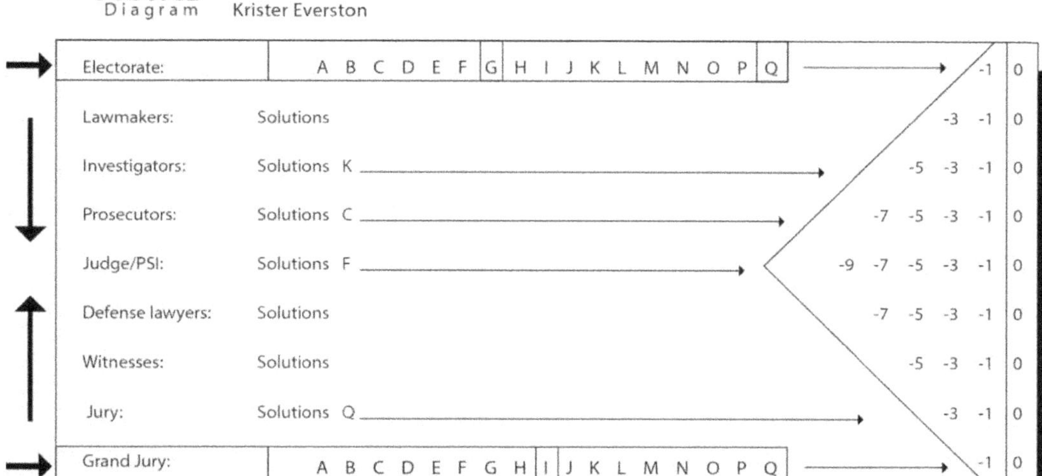

KRISTER EVERSTON

The Crime: Everston was charged with abandoning fuel cells after he prevailed against charges that he mailed an illegal package without the proper label.

The Verdict: After a jury trial, Everston was found guilty.

- The grand jury did not have all the facts.
  Solution: Grand Jury exercises full power. (I)
- The prosecutor pursued charges when there was no crime.
  Solution: No loss of life, liberty, or property. (C)
- The judge turned a blind eye to naked aggression by the government.
  Solution: Judge's role of impartiality. (F)
- The investigation was prejudicial from the outset.
  Solution: The investigation must be objective. (K)

The Everston case is another example where the governor could have intervened and prevented the arrest of a man who did not commit a criminal act. Furthermore, the Webb Doctrine would have been appropriate. Everston was subjected to an egregious abuse of prosecutorial power. Without the involvement of the Inspector General, such cases will be prosecuted without accountability. An IG would have effectively curtailed a prosecution which was nothing more than the use of raw force upon an innocent victim of government brutality.

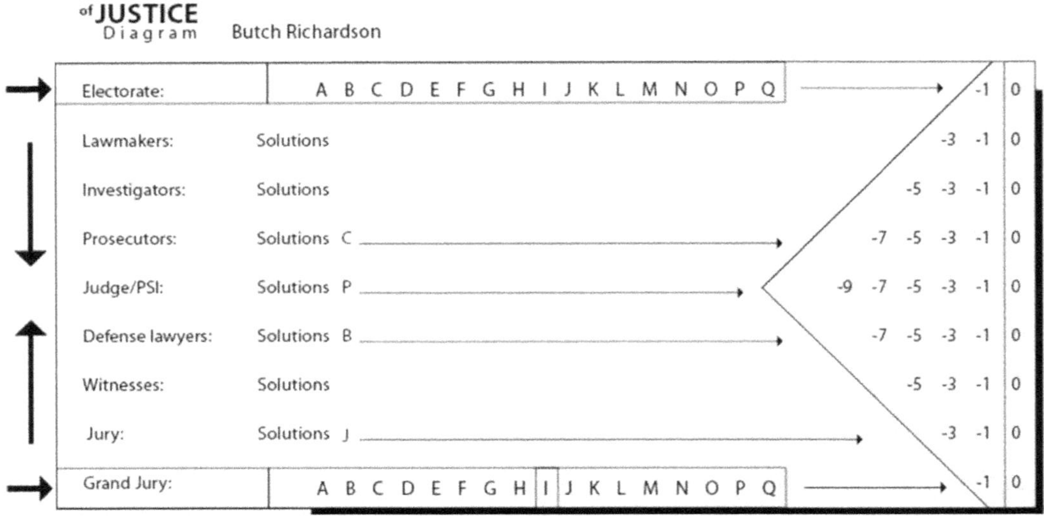

BUTCH RICHARDSON

The Crime: Richardson was accused of using of government funds illegally. He sent nine packages through the mail system and did not take leave for professional events.

The Verdict: After a jury trial, he was found guilty.

- The prosecutor pursued charges which did not involve an actus reus or mens rea.

  Solution: No loss of life, liberty, or property. (C)
- The jury did not have all the facts.

  Solution: Jury exercises its full power (jury nullification). (J)
- Richardson's status as a private business owner would have been critical to express to the jury, especially considering petty, local politics.

  Solution: Assertion of status. (B)
- The investigators should have asserted their professional discretion and attested under the Webb Doctrine that no crime occurred.

  Solution: The Webb Doctrine. (P)

The Webb Doctrine would have been appropriate in this case. Additionally, had the governor dignified the claim that there was no crime—the case stemmed from a local, political controversy—Richardson would never have gone to trial.

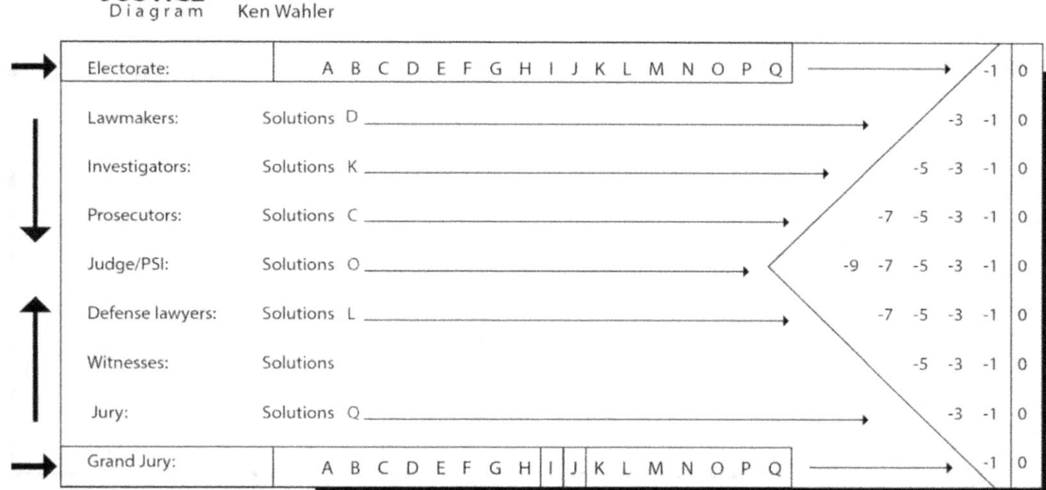

KEN WAHLER

Crime: Wahler was accused of illegally accessing a server and downloading a document, both of which belonged to him a day earlier.

Verdict: Wahler pled guilty to avoid a longer prison term.

- The prosecutor pursued charges that did not reflect a criminal act or intent.

  Solution: No loss of life, liberty, or property. (C)
- The defense lawyer did not defend his client.

  Solution: Defense lawyers must provide a vigorous defense. (L)
- The FBI agent involved in the initial complaint knew the plaintiffs.

  Solution: Investigations must be objective. (K)
- The grand jury did not have the complete truth.

  Solution: Grand jury exercises its full power. (I)

Justice may have been achieved if Wahler had not been coerced into a plea agreement. With the solution that all cases go to trial, and with the expectation of fairness and the requirement that the defense lawyer must fight for his client, an acquittal might have been the likely result. Even if the battle for his innocence proved difficult, the case would have been ideal to invoke the Common Man Conversation (Q). It is telling that the jury, with the rules of court, would have been denied knowledge of the prior civil suit between the parties, which was the plaintiff's motivation for the criminal complaint. The victim never called Wahler to ask if he accessed the server or for assistance with changing the password. They, out of spite, went for the proverbial jugular. Wahler would have benefitted if he had been able to share the truth with a jury.

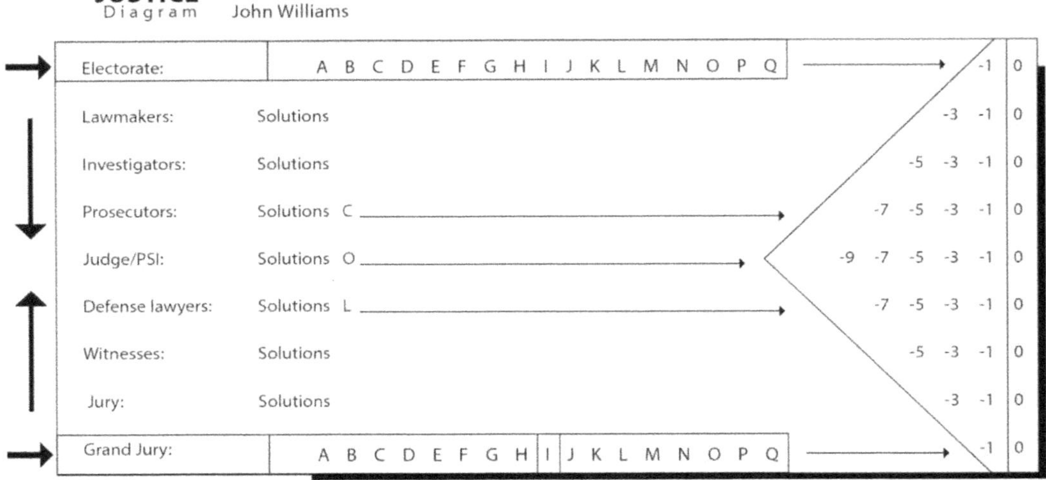

JOHN WILLIAMS

The Crime: Williams was charged for bringing a firearm to an airport.

The Verdict: Williams accepted a plea of guilty to avoid a prison sentence.

- The prosecutor pursued a charge that lacked criminal intent.
  Solution: No loss of life, liberty, or property. (C)
- The defense lawyer did not defend his client.
  Solution: Defense lawyers must provide a vigorous defense. (L)
- There was no trial.
  Solution: All cases go to trial. (O)

Williams was relatively unscathed by the legal system; but justice would have been achieved if he had challenged the charge and invoked the Common Man Conversation.

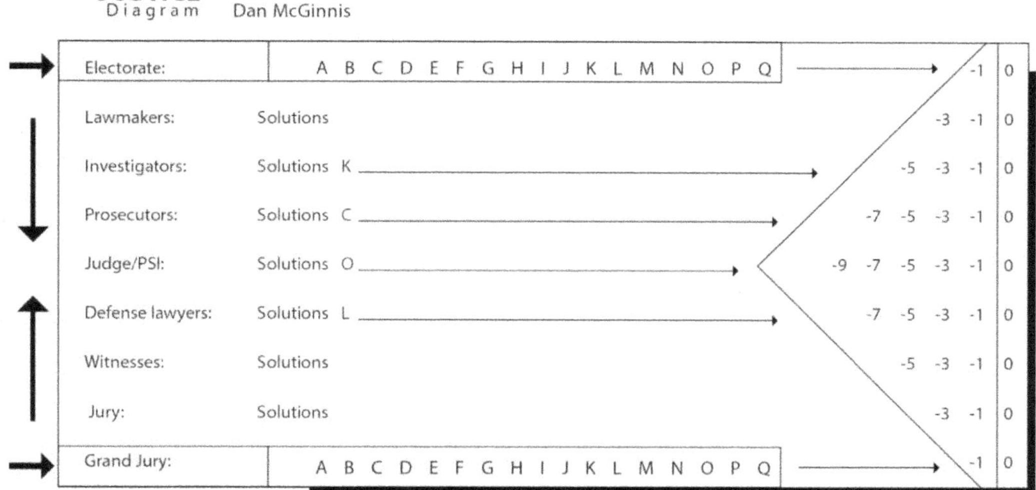

DAN McGINNIS

Crime: McGinnis was accused of writing two bad checks.

Verdict: McGinnis accepted a plea of guilty to avoid a long prison term.

- The prosecutor pursued a charge which lacked criminal intent.
  Solution: No loss of life, liberty, or property. (C)
- The defense lawyer did not defend his client.
  Solution: Defense lawyers must provide a vigorous defense. (L)
- There was no trial.
  Solution: Every case goes to trial. (O)
- The grand jury did not have all the facts.
  Solution: The grand jury exercises its full power. (I)

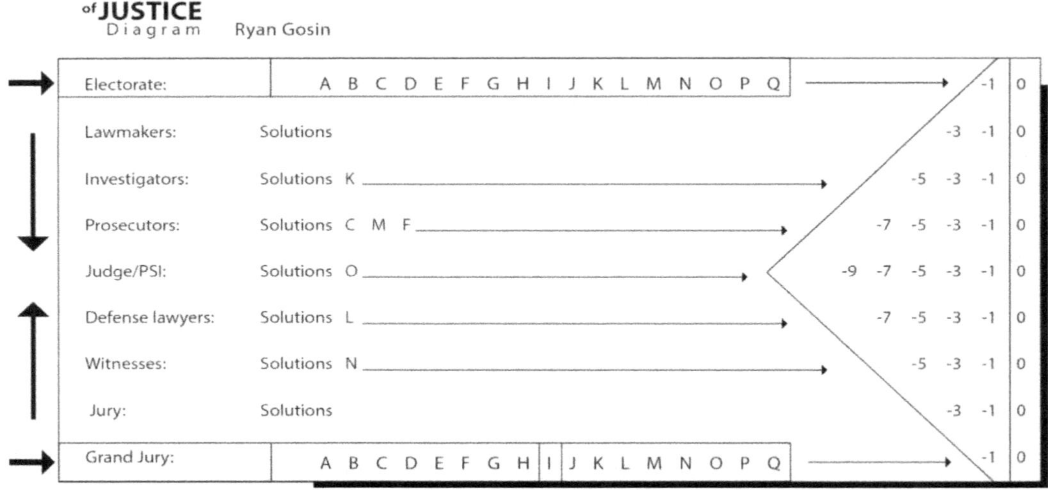

Ryan Gosin

Crime: Gosin was charged with mortgage fraud and conspiracy.

Verdict: Gosin accepted a plea of guilty to bank fraud and conspiracy.

- The prosecutor pursued a charge absent a criminal act or intent.
  Solution: No loss of life, liberty, or property. (C)
- The defense lawyer did not defend his client. They managed a plea agreement.
  Solution: Defense lawyers must provide a vigorous defense. (L)
- The investigation revealed no wrong other than a technical violation of the law.
  Solution: Investigation must be objective: (K)
- The prosecutor used secondary charges to convict.
  Solution: Charge for the actual crime only. (M)
- There was no trial.
  Solution: Every case goes to trial. (O)
- The grand jury did not have all the facts.
  Solution: Grand jury exercises its full power. (I)

Gosin would have benefitted with a balanced trial. Under the Webb Doctrine, the prosecutor would have been held accountable for the proper charges and a fair representation of the facts. Gosin could have expressed the truth with the Common Man Conversation. These solutions would have prevented the U. S. Attorney from threatening to file charges against Gosin's wife if he did not accept a plea.

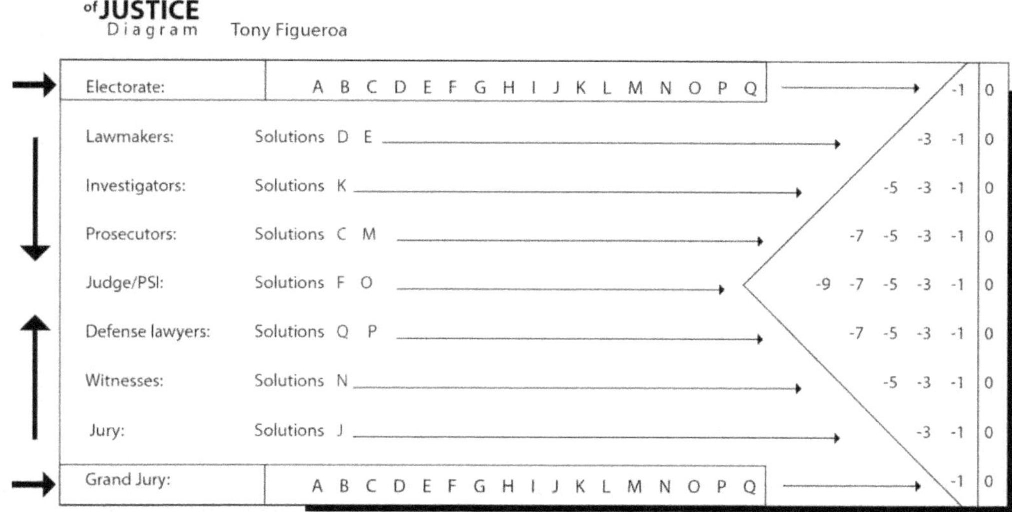

Tony Figueroa

Crime: Figueroa was eventually charged with bank and mail fraud and conspiracy.

Verdict: Figueroa was found guilty on the first charges and pled guilty to the second.

- The prosecutor pursued charges for which Figueroa had no knowledge, involvement and, therefore, no evil intent.

  Solution: No loss of life, liberty, or property. (C)
- The witness, Porath, proved instrumental. Under questionable prosecutorial practices, full disclosure of witness treatment should have been made.

  Solution: Disclosure of witness incentives. (N)
- The investigation was not objective.

  Solution: The investigation must be objective. (K)
- The judge's role concerning the tapes and the witness was prejudicial.

  Solution: Judge's role of impartiality. (F)
- The prosecutor used secondary charges and not the original charges. Figueroa was found guilty for acts he could not have committed.

  Solution: Charge for actual crime only. (M)
- The grand jury did not have all the facts.

  Solution: Grand jury exercises its power. (I)
- The jury lacked all the facts and was limited by the rules of court.

  Solution: Jury exercises its power. (J)

Several solutions would have been effective for Figueroa. Given the dubious handling of Porath, the Webb Doctrine would have had a favorable impact. The Common Man Conversation would have answered doubts and confusion.

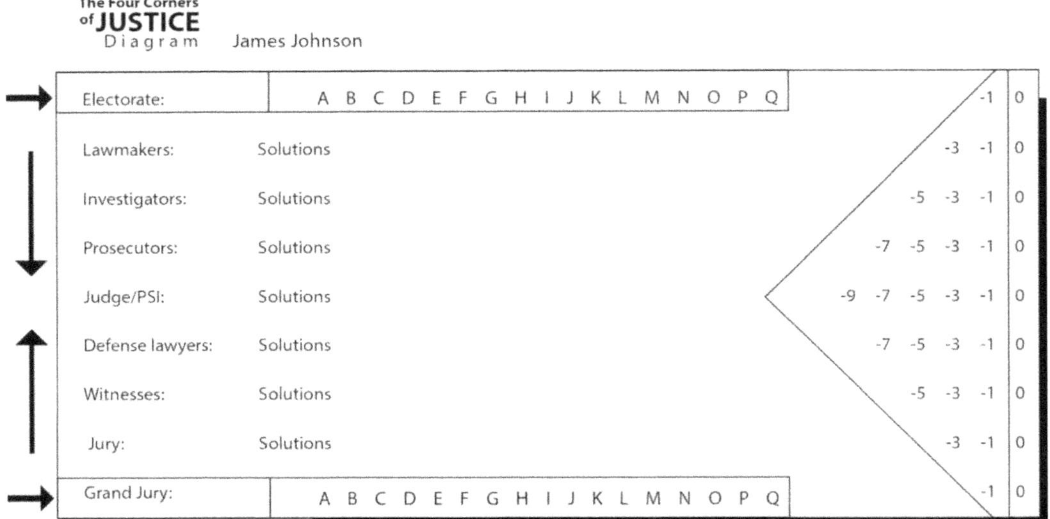

James Johnson

Crime: Johnson was charged with obstructing a federal investigation and willful failure to file federal income tax returns.

Verdict: After a jury trial, Johnson was found guilty and sentenced to four years in prison.

List the concerns you observed and note the solutions that would apply.

The revised FCOJ scoring diagram reflects not only the battle against injustice but demonstrates the pursuit of justice. With the elimination of the right side of the original FCOJ chart, we dispensed with the numbering of "factors" on the "just" and "unjust" sides of the diagram. Additionally, we no longer have the need to weigh the "integrity" of the defendant or the legal system. With an equitable process that seeks justice, the truth becomes central. We have little need to judge the integrity of any official. We expect them, with effective solutions, to be "truth-seekers." The net result of a truth-seeker, whose creed is that nothing less than the truth is acceptable, should be a process with a conclusion based upon integrity.

No longer should prosecutors compare their conviction rates and percentages with colleagues; for, this is what they do. Rather, their intent should be to convict only those who committed a crime with *mens rea* and an *actus reus*. If this were their noble aim, and no more—without personal or professional aggrandizement at the expense of humanity—the credibility of a conviction would scale with the significance it deserves. Presently, convictions are a dime a dozen, which is statistic that is not reflective of a base or immoral people, but that of an unprincipled and brazen profession and process concerned with what is contemptible. Guilty verdicts are ubiquitous and unflattering, a disgrace to those who relish and profit from them. The resulting incarceration rate is a mockery. The intended and unintended consequences of this country's crisis are grave. And the people do not even know that they must fight back. Such is the impact of their ignorance, apathy, and fear—and the arrogance of *public servants*.

The American people have no other recourse. We must act or resign ourselves to a failed American experiment of self-governance. We are a far from anything that resembles the autonomy of a free people. In the early days of America's founding there were a handful of federal criminal laws. We are presently saddled with a multitude of federal criminal statutes. This was never the intent. Thomas Jefferson presciently and aptly expressed the rather foreboding nature of man.

> *It can never be too often repeated that the time for fixing every essential right on a legal basis is while our rulers are honest, and ourselves united. From the conclusion of this war we shall be going downhill. It will not be necessary to resort every moment to the people for support. They will be forgotten, therefore, and their rights disregarded. They will forget themselves but in the sole faculty of making money, and will never think of uniting to effect a due respect for their rights. The shackles, therefore, which shall not be knocked off at the conclusion of this war will remain on us long, will be made heavier and heavier till our rights shall revive or expire in convulsion.* [124]

With a vein of thought rich in caution, Jefferson opined with a hint of optimism. He was a student of human nature. His perspective of the macro was and is congruent with life because he was sensitive to the micro. Jefferson, centuries ago, petitioned us to guard against the ignorance, apathy, and fear that riddles a troubled republic and cavalier people.

The Common Man Conversation and the other solutions may not be the best answers; but they are viable for change that is so desperately needed. We know the problem and we have perspective and context. With the verve to resurrect our individual and collective integrity, we would effectively embrace a world of possibility. Solutions abound. Otherwise, we will remain comfortable until our inevitable destruction.

Let's not allow the inevitable to unfold. As we stand afar, as we examine the mountain and its various paths, we should mark with discernment our own routes or

[124] http://www.bartleby.com/71/1208.html

follow the mavericks who paid the price into victory or defeat and contributed to humanity's progress. If we resolve to champion the truth and reverse our shameful rate of imprisonment, we will take bold steps into the untamed with a hope for enlightenment and a hope to enlighten. There is no finer distinction than to aspire beyond that which is comfortable, to be indifferent to circumstances, and to serve a purpose much larger than ourselves.

I need only reflect upon the sordid actions of the officials who operated the Federal Government and brought harm to Norris, Everston, Richardson, Figueroa, Ingalls, and Gosin. These men are my neighbors, brothers, and fellow Americans who suffered needlessly. Their wives, children, and grandchildren, who are my fellow citizens, suffered inexplicably. We have a nemesis that is as old as the ages—the nature of man and the institutions which wield power beyond the bounds of sound discretion.

History is fraught with peril, as is the present and the future. I resolve to champion truth and justice with an eternal vigilance. We must take the measures required to vanquish ignorance, apathy, and fear. Throughout this book and even now, I extend my word and solemn commitment to restore and preserve our common and hopeful future, one in which we will not be maligned as common criminals. May we stand united into unchartered territory and relish the pursuit of truth with an uncommon awareness, resolve, and courage.

Knowledge, resolve, and courage are the qualities which turn a foreboding crisis into victory. Such qualities are a direct result of experience. Experience is what gives rise to solutions. A man who withstands harsh elements is forced into cognition and action. He becomes resourceful. When he understands, he determines the appropriate remedy. Understanding and action give him the confidence to know that ingenuity will lead to success. As such, being courageous is a natural consequence to experience.

To underscore this message, refer to the letter from the Social Security Administration signed by Anna White at the beginning of this book. This letter reveals the truth: a social security number is not required for an American to live and work in the United States. Is this because the social security number (SSN) is a federal benefit which establishes a federal status? Moreover, the Federal Government has no constitutional power to influence what is an American's inherent and natural right to work and provide for himself and his family. It is reasonable to conclude that Americans within the 50 states of the Union, who are neither foreigners (aliens) nor "federal employees" (citizens within the *United States* Government), are not legally obligated to enumerate themselves or their children. They are not within, and, in fact, they are without, the jurisdiction of the Federal Government. They are state citizens exclusively and not within federal territory and not subject to limited constitutional taxing powers. Americans are, at most, *nonpersons*. This position is established in my Informal Brief to the Fourth Circuit Court of Appeals, in which I cite 26 CFR 301.6109-1, entitled "Identifying Numbers."

We must ask: Who is obligated to get a social security number? Those who are foreigners within the *United States* and *federal employees* (U. S. citizens)? Consider section C(g)(1)(i) of 26 CFR 301.6109-1.

> *Social security number. A social security number is generally identified in the records and database of the Internal Revenue Service as a number belonging to a U. S. Citizen [think federal territory and jurisdiction] or resident alien individual.*

Although NOT required to get a social security number to live and work, when Americans within the 50 states accept one, their status effectively changes. They are within federal control and designated as *U. S. citizens*, or *resident aliens*. This is easily proved when one reads the following notation on the bottom of a "Numident printout," which is a Social Security Administration response to an American's request to verify information concerning the original application (SSA-5) for an SSN. The notation states:

> *Your Social Security Card is the Official verification of your Social Security Number and* ***evidence of employment authorization****.*

Since Americans do not need an SSN to live and work, they do not need authorization for work (employment). Who would benefit with the SSN other than resident aliens and federal employees? We must conclude that those who apply for and receive an SSN, even if by uninformed Americans, are subsequently recognized by the Federal Government as resident aliens, federal employees, or U. S. persons. This fact is confirmed when we continue to review the language of 26 CFR 301.6109 which states:

> *A person may establish a different status for the number by providing proof of foreign status with the Internal Revenue Service...*

And, under section (iii), the regulation states:

> *If the Internal Revenue Service determines at the time of application or subsequently, that an individual is not a nonresident alien individual, the Internal Revenue Service may require that the individual apply for a social security number.*

Based upon the sundry definitions for *United States, State, person*, etc., an unwillingness to accept that Americans are not required to be enumerated with a social security number is a personal inhibition. Acceptance of a federal status and benefits is either a knowing or unknowing election which supersedes the status of a sovereign Citizen within the sovereign 50 states of the Union.

Ultimately, one may neither accept the truth nor change his position. If so, he will remain imprisoned behind the bars of ignorance, apathy, and fear, a cage locked by means of the arrogance of governing institutions.

Whether viewed under the disciplines of morality, ethics, philosophy, or mathematics, the premise that the justice system and its 98% conviction rate are sound must be rejected. It is simply not possible. A mathematician could prove by theorem that, given the varied permutations of variables and relationships within each component, it is not possible for a national conviction rate to be remotely close to 98%, not to mention thousands of cases would never rise to the level of indictments. Such a theorem would demonstrate nothing less than the lack of integrity of the judicial system. A sound equation would confirm that institutional arrogance is the result of the ignorance, apathy, and fear of the American people and the ignorance, apathy, and arrogance of officials.

Another way of expressing this thought is that we, as a people, are culpable for our demise. We are culpable for man's inhumanity to man. We are liable for what we do—or don't do—to and for the web of life. In other words, our actions and decisions, our lack of discretion, reflects our depraved indifference. We fail to appreciate how and why human nature is so inequitable and repugnant. This point is beautifully illustrated in Victor Hugo's Les Miserables.

In the beginning of his book, Hugo is describing Bishop Myriel, the man who forgave Jean Valjean's theft and redeemed his life. Hugo describes Myriel's response to a criminal case that was once disclosed to him.

> *In a salon one day he heard an account of a criminal case about to be tried. A miserable man—because of love for a woman and the child she had borne him—had been making counterfeit coins, his real money was gone. At that time counterfeiting was still punished by death. The woman was arrested for passing*

the piece he had made. She was held prisoner, but there was no proof against her lover. She alone could testify against him through her confession. She denied his guilt. They insisted, but she was obstinate in her denial. At that point, the king's state prosecutor devised a shrewd plan. He maintained that her lover was unfaithful and by means of fragments of letters skillfully put together succeeded in persuading the unfortunate woman that she had a rival and that the man had deceived her. Inflamed with jealousy, she denounced her lover, confessed everything and proved his guilt. He was to be tried in a few days, at Aix, with his accomplice, and his conviction was certain. The story was told and retold, and everybody was delighted by the magistrate's cleverness. Bringing jealousy into play, he had brought truth to light by means of anger, and justice had sprung from revenge. The bishop listened to all this in silence. When it was finished he asked, "Where are this man and woman to be tried?" "At the Superior Court." ***"And where is the King's prosecutor to be tried?"*** [125]

As expected, literature captures the essence of humanity. Perhaps the lesson is that history repeats itself. The prosecutor in Hugo's masterpiece is no different than the prosecutors from Hus to the Scottsboro Boys to Johnson. The fact that history repeats itself is no mere cliché; it is axiomatic of the indifference and resignation of man to the timeless and unimaginative—if not compliant—treks he makes throughout his existence. For this reason alone, we would be better served with the awareness, courage, and resolve to take a different path. If not, our plight will only worsen.

Will ignorance, apathy, fear, and institutional arrogance remain unabated? The answer may be found within yet another query.

What will you do—or not do—to the web of life?

[125] Victor Hugo, *Les Miserables*, (Signet Classic, by Penguin Group, 1997), p. 14

I think the most important bill for our whole code is that for diffusion of knowledge among the people. No other sure foundation can be devised for the preservation of freedom and happiness. Let our country men know that the tax which will be paid for this purpose is not more than one thousandth part of what will be paid to kings, priests and nobles who will rise up among us if we leave the people in ignorance. **Thomas Jefferson**

Epilogue

On August 19, 2015, I sent a FOIA (Freedom of Information Act) request to the IRS for documents which proved that the agency revoked John Kotmair's representative number. On October 6, 2015, the IRS responded that it had no documents which satisfied my request. I then submitted a Motion to Amend my 2255 Habeas Corpus petition under 28 USC 2255 (f)(4), (Appendix S), which allows for newly discovered evidence. I had no doubt the IRS purposely avoided Kotmair's questions in 2004 and into the trial in 2013. I had no doubt the IRS gratuitously labeled Kotmair's concerns as frivolous as a deliberate strategy to denigrate my good faith belief and destroy my ability to offer a complete defense. This new evidence proved these assertions. I argued that Biggs offered, and Hogeboom used perjured testimony to deceive the court and jury and to secure a conviction. *The court denied this motion.*

Based upon the submission of these documents, I sent Cargill a letter and asked, once again, that he come to my defense. I believed he had an ethical duty to acknowledge the relevance of Biggs' false testimony and how Cargill would have altered his "strategy" had he known otherwise. (Appendix T) *I never heard from him.*

I submitted an action for a Declaratory Judgment concerning the revocation of the federal social security number and benefit. (Appendix U) *The court denied this request.*

In 2015, I sent Renee Mitchell, Director of Internal Revenue Service Center in Covington, Kentucky, another letter asking for an update on the private remedy she received in November 2012 to set off, settle, and discharge any liability with the case. *She never responded.*

In 2015, I also sent a request to Mr. Jack Lew, Secretary of the Treasury, asking that he investigate the failure of the IRS to respond to my private remedy. This request was submitted under the Administrative Procedures Act. *He never responded.*

I received the decision of the Fourth Circuit Court of Appeals to my two federal questions. The court affirmed the lower court's decision that I lacked standing. The Court of Appeals did not provide any explanation whatsoever. I submitted a Motion to Reconsider (Appendix V). *The court denied this motion.*

On January 7, 2016, Judge Moon sent me an ORDER that was a full denial of my 2255 and every other request. (Appendix W)

I submitted a Motion for a Certificate of Appealability (Appendix X) to the Fourth Circuit Court of Appeals in response to Moon's denial. I included a Supplemental Brief concerning Kotmair's status as Power of Attorney. The Court of Appeals denied my motion.

The fight for truth and justice continues.

Appendices

- APPENDIX A—DECLARATION
- APPENDIX B—2255 MOTION
- APPENDIX C—FEDERAL QUESTION #1
- APPENDIX D—TRIAL TRANSCRIPTS, EQUITY
- APPENDIX E—FEDERAL QUESTION #2
- APPENDIX F—TRIAL TRANSCRIPTS, JURY INSTRUCTIONS
- APPENDIX G—GOVERNMENT RESPONSE TO 2255 MOTION
- APPENDIX H—REPLY TO GOVERNMENT RESPONSE
- APPENDIX I—DECLARATION (NEW TRIAL)
- APPENDIX J—2255 MOTION (NEW TRIAL)
- APPENDIX K—MOTION TO AMEND (NEW TRIAL)
- APPENDIX L—BP-8 (COAT INCIDENT)
- APPENDIX M—BP-8/BP-9 (COPY CARD INCIDENT)
- APPENDIX N—ABA COMPLAINT
- APPENDIX O—CORRESPONDENCE TO/FROM CARGILL
- APPENDIX P—IRS FRIVOLOUS TAX ARGUMENT
- APPENDIX Q—LETTERS TO SENATOR PAUL AND JUDICIARY COMMITTEE
- APPENDIX R—LETTER TO EDITOR OF THE ENQUIRER
- APPENDIX S—MOTION TO AMEND (NEW EVIDENCE)
- APPENDIX T—CARGILL LETTER (KOTMAIR NEW EVIDENCE)
- APPENDIX U—DECLARATORY JUDGMENT REQUEST
- APPENDIX V—MOTION TO RECONSIDER (FEDERAL QUESTION)
- APPENDIX W—MOON'S DENIAL OF 2255 MOTION
- APPENDIX X—CERTIFICATE OF APPEALABILITY/SUPPLEMENTAL BRIEF

APPENDIX A – DECLARATION

UNITED STATES DISTRICT COURT
WESTERN DISTRICT OF VIRGINIA

James Bowers Johnson, Petitioner, v. **UNITED STATES OF AMERICA,** Respondent.	))))))))	Criminal Case No. 6:12-CR-00015-NKM Declaration of James Bowers Johnson

COMES NOW, Petitioner, James Bowers Johnson, having full knowledge of the facts, who does hereby submit this Declaration in support of the Motion pursuant to 28 U.S.C. §2255 to vacate, set aside, or correct the conviction and sentence by reason of ineffective assistance of counsel.

1. In 1992, Petitioner began studying history, banking and tax law. He read books, listened to tapes, read the United States tax code and regulations, Supreme Court cases, and attended classes, joined research groups and organizations that sought to understand the law.
2. In 2004, Petitioner went so far as to join a class action lawsuit against the United States in which the Plaintiff sought to petition for redress of grievances under the First Amendment (Shulz v. United States). Petitioner also became the Virginia representative for the "We the People Congress.org," a grass roots organization with the aim of educating Americans about the law and government.
3. As expressed by defense counsel Randy Cargill in his opening statement, (Exhibit A, 107-108), Petitioner believed the tax code did not "apply to him." As disclosed in testimony by Government witness Diane Johnson, Petitioner's ex-wife, he studied and believed there "were legitimate things you could do to deal with tax liabilities." (Exhibit A 202-203). Petitioner's sister, Holly Munday, a witness called by the Government, who is an Administrative Law Judge, testified that he studied to the extent that "he is more knowledgeable about the tax

31

code than most attorneys." (Exhibit A, 458-459). Munday, who admitted she was "very close" with Petitioner, stated that he said, "he wished that he didn't believe this, that he didn't know what he knew." The witness said, "This is his personal belief, but look where it has gotten him." (Exhibit A, 468-469).

4. Petitioner continued his studies throughout an eight year federal criminal investigation, while he asked government officials for an answer to the very question at the root of the alleged crime: What law required him to file a federal income tax return? Receiving no response, even as he lost his marriage, family, home and livelihood, he believed he had effectively rebutted the Government's presumption that he was liable for the federal income (excise) tax. As such, Petitioner pursued the truth as he understood. He dignified his good belief that he was without the jurisdiction of the United States Government for the income tax.
5. Petitioner stopped filing federal income tax forms in 1999.
6. In 2000, Petitioner revoked and rescinded his signature and intent to the federal social security insurance scheme by written notification, sent by certified mail to the Social Security Administration in Baltimore, Maryland.
7. In 2000, Petitioner sent written notification by certified mail to Secretary of the Treasury, Lawrence Summers, rebutting any presumption of any nexus with the Federal Government, which encompassed the relation of employment.
8. In doing so, Petitioner effectively rebutted any presumption held by the Government that he was liable for the federal income tax.
9. Thus, in keeping with Charles C. Steward Machine Co. v Davis, 304 US 548 (1937)* and Helvering v Davis, 301 US 619 (1937), cases Petitioner

studied, he believed that he was no longer within the jurisdiction of the United States for federal income and employment tax purposes.

10. Petitioner believed conclusively that the Internal Revenue Code (IRC) dealt exclusively with excise taxes and that the code was legal, lawful and constitutional. (Exhibit A, 509)
11. Petitioner believed that upon the initial and "voluntary" submission of federal income and employment tax forms (W-2s, W-4s, 1040s, etc.), he became liable for the indirect tax, which is predicated upon social security and the "relation of employment."
12. Even though entered without fully informed consent and under the age of majority, Petitioner believed that he became a "person," "U.S. person" and "taxpayer," as defined under 26 U.S.C. 7701 and liable for the excise taxes. (Exhibit B)
13. Yet, since Petitioner rebutted the Government's presumption, he could not be defined as any of the foregoing, at least not until he engaged in an excisable activity or privilege and only to that extent.
14. Petitioner believed that a contract is null and void when entered into under the age of majority and without fully informed consent (Exhibit B).
15. Petitioner came under investigation by the Department of Internal Revenue in 2004.
16. When contacted by Internal Revenue Agent Robert Biggs, Petitioner sent a letter asking for the law that required him to file a federal income tax return. Biggs never answered the query; rather, he sent a pamphlet that explained "Responses to Frivolous Arguments." Petitioner never posed a "frivolous argument." He asked a simple and legitimate question. Yet, Biggs continued to investigate with the presumption that Petitioner was a "taxpayer."

17. Petitioner appointed John Kotmair as his Power of Attorney. Kotmair had an Internal Revenue Number, which allowed him to represent people with tax concerns before the agency. Biggs did not respond to Kotmair, who asserted that Petitioner was without the federal income tax law.

18. In 2005, the investigation became a criminal matter. Petitioner was contacted by Criminal Investigation Division (CID) Internal Revenue Service (IRS) Agent Nicholas Pompei. Petitioner sent Pompei a letter asking the same question posed to Biggs. Pompei was unresponsive. He investigated as if Petitioner were a "taxpayer."

19. Petitioner sent letters to his U.S. Representatives and asked the same simple quéstion. "What law required him to file a federal income tax return?" These elected officials never answered the query directly. They simply forwarded Petitioner's letters to the IRS, which replied with template responses that did not answer the question, which were then sent back to the representatives, who forwarded them to petitioner.

20. Petitioner sent letters to Internal Revenue Commissioners Shulman and Rossotti, detailing his rebuttal of social security and any nexus to the Federal Government and asked the same simple question. Both Commissioners never bothered to respond.

22. Petitioner feverishly sought unconventional solutions. He studied the Uniform Commercial Code, discharging debts or any remedy that would obviate a presumed tax liability. Consequently, Petitioner sought to remedy a child support obligation, asking the Virginia Department of Social Services to notify him of any legal defect. The agency did not respond. It is only when life became dire and he had no money that Petitioner attempted to "discharge" debts. He simply wanted to resolve his liabilities. Holly Munday, witness, stated, "But if my

34

brother does something, there's a reason for it. And it wouldn't be for ill-will reasons. There would be a legitimate reason, in my opinion, behind it." (Exhibit A, 63). It was not until Agent Matthew Johnson, a National Bank Examiner with the U.S. Treasury Department, Office of the Controller of the Currency, testified at trial that Petitioner learned such solutions were not viable.

23. In August 2009, Petitioner drove to the IRS office in Staunton, Virginia with a written request for a bill with the total tax liability that the IRS presumed he owed and that the Secretary of Treasury file a "substitute for return" on Petitioner's behalf. The IRS sent a letter stating that a response would be coming within 45 days. The IRS never responded.

24. Petitioner was confident of his status as one without the scope of the federal tax code. He intended to assert the truth and impress upon the Court that he was without the jurisdiction of the United States for income (excise) tax purposes. For, Petitioner had rebutted any prima facie evidence that he was a "taxpayer."

25. Petitioner was arrested in April 2012 for obstructing an investigation under 26 U.S.C. 7212(a) and willful failure to file tax returns under 26 U.S.C. 7203.

26. Two days later, Petitioner was brought before Magistrate Judge James Welsh.

27. Federal Public Defender Andrea Harris witnessed as Petitioner communicated to Judge Welsh that he could not be the defendant, challenged jurisdiction and asked if anyone had a claim against him. Both Welsh and Petitioner looked around a silent courtroom. No one responded. Harris witnessed as Petitioner asked a Second time. Again,

she saw Welsh and Petitioner canvas the room. No one said a word. Harris then witnessed as Petitioner stated for and on the record that no one had a claim against him and moved the Court to dismiss the case with prejudice and to set him at liberty. Harris witnessed as Welsh denied his request. (Exhibit D**). It was at this hearing that the Magistrate stated, "I note your objection to all proceedings in this case from the time it started." Id., 15 Petitioner believed he was without the jurisdiction of the Court.

28. Petitioner was placed into solitary confinement in the Orange County Jail. It was there he met with Harris and explained that he had rebutted the presumption that he was a taxpayer liable for the federal income (excise) and employment tax, citing his decisions and actions taken in 2000. Harris disagreed with Petitioner's good faith belief and stated that we all have to pay income taxes.

29. At Arraignment on May 3, 2012, Petitioner asked the Court to move on his "motion to quash and actually dismiss the defective claim for lack of jurisdiction." (Exhibit E, 12)

30. Petitioner asked Harris as to the extent of her knowledge of tax law. She admitted to knowing very little. Petitioner explained that the federal income tax was an excise tax and, by its very nature, voluntary. Petitioner explained that people were obligated to pay an excise tax when they enter an activity or privilege for which an excise tax is owed.

31. Petitioner explained that the Supreme Court determined that the income and employment taxes were predicated upon social security and the relation of employment. Yet, Harris was insistent that Petitioner was liable. More importantly, she stated that she could not and would not argue this defense in court.

32. Petitioner was incredulous and asked Harris why. She explained that she was bound by canons of ethics, which prohibited such a defense. She explained that she would be sanctioned by the Court if she argued either a defense that challenged jurisdiction or Petitioner's status as one without the scope of the tax code.

33. More importantly, Petitioner stated that he subscribed to the benefit of federal social security and entered the relation of employment without fully informed consent and while under the age of majority.

34. Harris refused to consider that he was not a "taxpayer" as defined in the tax code. She refused to accept Petitioner's revocation and rescission of the federal social security benefit by written notice and notification to Secretary of the Treasury, Lawrence Summers, refuting any federal nexus. Harris refused to accept that both documents served as a rebuttal of the presumption of any prima facie evidence that he was a taxpayer.

35. Given Petitioner's efforts to rebut the presumption that he was subject to the income and employment tax, he told Harris that her refusal to argue jurisdiction made no sense. Petitioner asked how a rule of the American Bar Association could prevent a lawyer from stating that her client was not within the jurisdiction of the Federal Government and the Court for an excise tax, or bind him to a privilege/benefit he had since rejected knowingly. Harris dismissed the question, stating simply that this was the rule.

36. Petitioner, therefore, underscored over several meetings with Harris the reasons why he could not be within the limited application of the income (excise) tax law, the authority of the IRS or the jurisdiction of the Court. Petitioner explained facts and law which substantiated his belief that he was without the jurisdiction of the Federal

37

Government. Petitioner discussed information and concepts that included, but was not limited to, the following:

*The Federal Government may collect direct taxes under Article 1, Section 2, Clause 3 and Article 1, Section 9, Clause 4.

*The Government may collect indirect taxes under Article 1, Section 8, Clause 1, "the Congress shall have power to lay and collect Taxes, Duties, Imports and Excises."

*Title 26 U.S.C., Internal Revenue Code, concerns the enforcement and collection of excise taxes.

*The Supreme Court determined in Charles C. Steward Machine Co. v Davis 301 US 548 (1937) and Helvering v Davis 301 US 619 (1937) that the "income" and "employment" taxes were excises.

*The Court defined excise taxes in Flint v Stone Tracy Co., 220 US 107 (1911)

*The receipt of benefits is a "privilege" subject to excise.

*Petitioner, having rejected the benefits associated with social security and employment, was not liable for them. His mother, without complete understanding signed on behalf of directed Petitioner, who was under the age of majority and without fully informed consent to request a social security number and to enroll into the federal social security insurance scheme, as well as the relation of employment, with and through sundry federal employment tax forms. Petitioner filed income tax forms for the first time on a "voluntary" basis, which established the Government's presumption that he was partaking in those privileges. Such documents became prima facie evidence that Petitioner was expected to comply with the income tax law.

*In 2000, when he sent notification to the Social Security Administration and Department of Treasury, Petitioner rebutted any and all presumptions and prima facie evidence that he was a taxpayer.

*Charles Mullen, with the Social Security Administration, stated in a letter in 1948 that a social security number was not required to live or work in the United States. (Exhibit F)

*The collection of a tax must be based upon some statute which had to be traceable to a power granted in the Constitution under Article 1 and that the statute was no longer binding on Petitioner.

*A statute may not reach those without its scope; as such, not EVERY person may be subject.

*The Federal Government may not assert a power that is a prohibition under the Constitution and that the inalienable rights of the people are secure. Moreover, Petitioner cited

38

Hale v Henkel, 201 US 44 (1906), that a man could not unknowingly concede any of his rights which were long established before the Government.

*Petitioner explained that his labor was property, exchanged for earnings, which was also property, and no longer a privilege subject to excise.

*Petitioner cited a report by the Department of Treasury in 1940, stating that only 3.9% of the population filed income tax returns, noting that the majority had no liability, indicating that the privileges of social security and employment were excisable in nature. For the Government could not indirectly tax people until they subscribed to federal social security and employment benefits.

*The legislative body may not tax something unless it is first a privilege.

*Petitioner referenced the Supreme Court decision in Brushaber v Union Pacific R.R. Co., 240 US 1 (1916), in which Justice White stated that when a tax accomplished what a direct tax was designed to prevent, the Government must look from form to substance.

*Petitioner conceded that he was once within the constitutional scope of these indirect (excise) taxes; but, he had since rebutted this presumption.

*Petitioner referenced McCulloch v Maryland, 4 Wheat 316 (1819), noting that he was no longer within the jurisdiction of the tax code, if only because he refused the Government's "permission" to be so. As such, he was "exempt," if only because Congress' indirect taxation power did not extend to him.

*Petitioner cited Butcher's Union v Crescent City Co., 83 US 36 (1873), which stated that a man's labor was his property and Coppage v Kansas, 236 US 1 (1915), which stressed personal liberty and private property.

*Petitioner noted that he believed he was without the taxing power of Congress and, therefore, without the jurisdiction of the Court under Article 3, Section 2 of the Constitution.

37. Petitioner told Harris that the submission of any and all tax and employment forms (W-2s, W-4s, 1040s, etc.) became prima facie evidence which were now rebutted.

38. Petitioner underscored to Harris that Internal Revenue Agent Biggs and CID IRS Agent Pompei were unresponsive to Petitioner's letters and his one simple question and ignored his rebuttal.

39

39. Petitioner explained that Biggs sent a document which cited frivolous taxpayer arguments which applied to "every person" liable for the income tax; and Petitioner explained that he was not one of "every person." Biggs and Pompei ignored that they were without authority or jurisdiction over the Petitioner.

40. Petitioner shared that he sent a similar request to his U.S. Representatives and that none of them were willing to directly answer his question about tax liability. Rather, they avoided the issue by forwarding his letters to the IRS, which responded with template answers.

41. Petitioner shared that he mailed the same request to Internal Revenue Commissioners Shulman and Rossotti and the Department of Justice and received no response.

42. When Petitioner asked Harris what law required him to file an income tax return, she dismissed the query, stating that we are all required to file. Petitioner stated that such an answer was consistent with the Government's unresponsiveness. Petitioner stressed that she failed to account for a status outside the scope of the tax code and the very issue of jurisdiction.

43. Petitioner eventually met senior defense counsel Randy Cargill. When Petitioner told Cargill of his good faith belief and the reasons for it, Cargill stated that he could not and would not argue that Petitioner was without the jurisdiction of the federal income tax and, therefore, the Court. Cargill said that he would be sanctioned if he violated the canons of ethics. He even stated that Petitioner would be prohibited from making such an argument as a pro se litigant.

44. Petitioner could not believe counsel's comment. He was in disbelif that counsel could not and would not zealously defend him and his

40

grounded belief, especially since his belief was predicated upon the deliberate act of a rebuttal of a presumption. Even after discussing some of the elements shared with Harris, Cargill was unaffected. His reaction was inflexible, equal to that of Harris.

45. When Petitioner explained that he could not be a "U.S. person" as defined in and liable for income tax, Cargill's response was sobering. "You are a 'U.S. person,'" he declared.

46. While in solitary confinement, Petitioner submitted a Writ of Habeas Corpus and, once again, challenged jurisdiction. As a result, counsel discussed in a hearing before Judge Moon whether Petitioner could not be a "United States citizen."

47. Petitioner did not state that he was not a "United States citizen," as in an American, one within the several States, but that he was not a "United States citizen" as defined in and subject to the tax code - a "taxpayer."

48. Defense counsel did not mention Petitioner's rebuttal of all presumptions or that Petitioner believed he was not and could not be a "U.S. person" for federal income tax purposes. They did not argue jurisdiction.

49. Cargill and Harris had but one intention; they would argue Petitioner's "beliefs" which they believed were "relevant." They would not argue Petitioner's good faith belief of jurisdiction. Counsel did not and would not present Petitioner's deliberate decisions and actions.

50. Counsel refused to consider that the United States Government was limited in its exercise of power over the several States, while it exercised plenary power over its own territories. Cargill and Harris refused to consider, by virtue of his rebuttals, that Petitioner was outside the limited indirect taxing power of the Federal Government.

51. Consequently, defense counsel rejected Petitioner's belief that, under Article 3, Section 2 of the Constitution, the courts could not exercise jurisdiction over Petitioner. Counsel refused to consider that he was not subject to the conditions under Clause 1 for which the federal courts exercised authority.

52. Petitioner explained to counsel that their refusal to understand that he rebutted the Government's presumption enabled the continuance of a fraud into the court.

53. Petitioner referred to the fact that he had challenged jurisdiction at the Initial Hearing and no one made a claim against him. He referred to the Habeas Corpus in which he challenged jurisdiction. Petitioner stated that these challenges reflected his earnest belief, which would defeat the Government's otherwise baseless charges. Petitioner stressed that absent jurisdiction, the Government and Court could not move forward.

54. Cargill and Harris were not swayed. They stated that, as officers of the Court, they had an allegiance to certain standards. They could not adequately defend their client with his fundamental good faith belief.

55. When Petitioner was released on bond, he met with counsel to prepare a "defense." Counsel asked him to provide information that did not deal with the issue of jurisdiction. Petitioner sent counsel emails that covered various topics concerning "excises," "income," natural rights and the void for vagueness doctrine. Nothing about Petitioner's rebuttal and jurisdiction was offered.

56. Eventually, unable to convince counsel to argue his only good faith belief, Petitioner, out of desperation, sought solutions that might remedy the charges. He submitted a private remedy directly to

42

Department of Internal Revenue to set off, settle or discharge any debt. He filed suit in the Court of Claims. He invoked the Court of Equity. Since he believed he was not within the scope of congressional indirect taxing authority, he continued to refuse to be the defendant. As a lay person unskilled in legal matters, Petitioner sought to do what defense counsel refused - argue his good faith defense, however possible.

57. Some of Petitioner's efforts to assert his beliefs concerning jurisdiction and, therefore, to seek a remedy, are noted in the transcripts, including, but not limited to:

* Bill in Equity (Exhibit A, 69)
* Express trust (Id., 73)
* Stating he was not the defendant (Id., 113)
* Invoking the Court of Equity (Id., 116)
* Challenge jurisdiction (Id., 118)
* Challenge jurisdiction by motion and verbally at sentencing (Id., 1805)

58. Petitioner submitted a motion to proceed as his own counsel, with the intent to argue that he was without congressional tax authority. He would stand upon his status as one who was not liable for the income tax.

59. At the start of the trial, Petitioner noted the issue of jurisdiction and denied being the defendant.

60. Petitioner did not participate in voir dire, stating in front of potential jurors that he was not the defendant (transcripts not available). He did not make an opening statement or question the first witness. Defense counsel witnessed Petitioner's assertion that he was not within the jurisdiction of the Government or Court.

43

61. After a lunch recess, counsel handed Petitioner a letter written by his mother, who was in attendance, in which she beseeched Petitioner to mount a defense. Petitioner had originally decided not to participate in a matter he had already rebutted in 2000. Petitioner decided not to participate when the Court or Government had not proved jurisdiction and counsel would not defend him.

62. Petitioner believed he was still under threat, coercion and duress since his arrest and placement into isolation. He had resigned himself to the fact that he was going to prison for a presumption he rebutted and an indirect (excise) tax that no longer applied to him. Petitioner realized he was going to prison because counsel would not argue his belief. Meanwhile, Cargill, who was seated next to Petitioner, pleaded with him that they be allowed to offer up a "defense." (Exhibit A, 621). Akin to grasping a greased rope, Petitioner asked the Court to allow defense counsel to proceed.

63. Cargill offered an opening statement with comments that did not reflect Petitioner's belief. He stated that Petitioner believed the tax system was "voluntary," in a sense that one may choose not to participate. This was not Petitioner's belief. Petitioner explained to counsel months prior that it is one's decision to voluntarily accept the federal benefits of social security and employment, at which point the tax is required henceforth. Petitioner believes one becomes a taxpayer by a knowing or unknowing act, which makes one liable for the excise tax. (Exhibit A, 108)

64. The above point was underscored by the testimony from witness Holly Munday. She offered her perspective of Petitioner's understanding of the nature of the federal social security benefit, that we "are contracted into the system against our will, so to speak." (Exhibit A

465)

65. Cargill offered statements to the jury that contradicted Petitioner's good faith defense that he was not a taxpayer.

66. Specifically, Cargill stated, "if the question in this case were whether he should have filed returns and whether he owes taxes to the Federal Government, the case would be over, done. Of course he does." (Exhibit A, 109). This supposition further undermined Petitioner's good faith belief and the fact that he was not willful. Petitioner believes that had counsel investigated the merits of his belief, they would have offered an accurate representation and, therefore, demonstrated a lack of willfulness. Cargill's comments came after the prosecution stated to the jury that Petitioner "knew he was supposed to file returns, and he just frankly did not." The Government stated, "He willfully chose not to file tax returns." (Exhibit A, 99)

67. Defense counsel did not focus on the fact that at least 12 different elected or appointed government officials and at least 7 different agencies and offices failed to respond to Petitioner's one simple question asked over a period of 8 years. Cargill didn't rely on Petitioner's good faith belief that no answer, which is tantamount to tacit acquiescence, was an answer that confirmed he had rebutted the Government's presumption.

68. Agent Biggs testified that "if you want to know what normally happens; you sit down and talk to the taxpayer one-on-one." (Exhibit A, 147). He further stated, "But, of course, the real help there would have been able - If I were to talk to him and find out why he didn't think he was over the threshold. But without a conversation, you can only go with what you get." (Exhibit A, 159).

69. Defense counsel did not challenge Agent Biggs' inability to have a "conversation" with Petitioner based upon Biggs' failure to respond substantively to Petitioner's correspondence and rebuttal. Counsel did not establish that Biggs and, therefore, the Government, had a responsibility to provide a response with the law that made Petitioner a taxpayer liable for the income tax. Counsel did not question Biggs in this regard because they did not dignify Petitioner's good faith belief that he rebutted the Government's presumption and prima facie evidence. Cargill did not, therefore, place the burden on Biggs to justify the legal grounds and statutory authority by which he presumed a "conversation" with Petitioner was necessary. Counsel did not establish that, by tacit acquiescence, Biggs conceded to Petitioner's claim that he was not and could not be a taxpayer laible for the income tax.

70. Moreover, when the Government witness Jennifer Maroulis, Internal Revenue Agent, was asked by the prosecution, "but what is the first place to go to obtain records?" she replied, "you would ask the individual taxpayer first." (Exhibit A, 479)

71. Cargill did not ask her how or why Petitioner was presumed to be a taxpayer for an excise tax based upon a privilege/benefit. Cargill did not do so because he rejected Petitioner's belief as frivolous. Cargill presumed Petitioner was a taxpayer as well.

72. Defense counsel did not investigate the merits of John Kotmair's letters (Exhibit C). They did not challenge Agent Biggs or question him as to why Kotmair, with an Internal Revenue Number, "did not qualify to represent Mr. Johnson as power of attorney." (Exhibit A, 132) Furthermore, when Biggs was questioned as to "what part of [Kotmair's letter] was considered to be frivolous," he did not answer

directly; rather, he stated, "it is the advice I got from counsel." Id. Cargill did not pursue Kotmair's observation to Agent Biggs that "it must be presumed that you can not identify any lawful authority for the actions you are taking." (Exhibit C (25 AR-1-0531)) because Cargill did not question the agent's "lawful authority."

73. Defense counsel asked witness Thomas Klepper, Special Agent CID IRS, "Now, there's nothing illegal or wrong with using a trust is there?" Klepper responded, "Not at all." (Exhibit A, 230) Petitioner, in fact, received the letter signed by Charles Felthaus, Chief, Accounting Branch, IRS, given to him by Innovative Financial Consultants, which states "a pure trust has no tax requirements." (Exhibit G) Petitioner relied upon this IRS correspondence for decisions and actions, which negates the element of obstruction and willfulness.

74. Petitioner did not receive a letter from the IRS sent to IFC clients, which said, "Warning, we believe this is an abusive trust organization. This could result in fines, penalties, audits, etc." (Exhibit A, 234)

75. The witness, Thomas Klepper, in response to a question that IFC employees admitted that they lied to people, said, "Yes, I -- it is a fair characterization." (Exhibit A, 240) Petitioner was a victim of IFC's apparent illegality, not unlike thousands who fell prey to their misrepresentations.

76. Petitioner went beyond IFC's training and advice concerning the pure trusts by resigning as Managing Director. He wanted to negate any inference that the trust was an "alter ego" and eliminate the presumption that the trust was less than pure. Moreover, Petitioner stated that IFC sent him a copy of the IRS letter (Exhibit G) explaining that pure trusts did not have a tax liability and could not get an EIN. (Exhibit A, 175) Petitioner explained to the jury that

banks were closing accounts that were just opened for the pure trusts. The only viable option was to use MYICIS, an operation Petitioner believed to be legitimate and legal. (Exhibit A, 517)

77. Petitioner did not know that Wayne Hicks was operating an illegal banking business with MYICIS. Petitioner did not receive notification from the IRS (Exhibit A, 339) that Hicks was indicted and pled guilty to conspiracy to defraud the United States. Petitioner did not know Hicks went to prison in 2009.

78. As is evident by Petitioner's passport and testimony, he never travelled to an international destination to attend seminars as claimed by witness Gary Menchoffer. (Exhibit A, 365-366) Petitioner met this witness in Ohio as Menchoffer stated to field agents Labor and Brown in January 2008. (Id.)

79. When Petitioner testified, he attempted to explain his good faith belief - the absence of jurisdiction.

80. When Petitioner took the stand, he was asked questions and spoke for some 20 pages of transcripts, at which point counsel asked the first question relating to his beliefs about taxes. After only two paragraphs into his explanation, Judge Moon interrupted at precisely the point Petitioner was about to specify what could be and were excises. Petitioner sought to explain his belief that congressional authority was specific and limited by constitutional prohibition through the indirect taxation clause. With this interruption, the Court directed the discussion to the "income tax amendment," (Exhibit A, 502-503) which had little relevance to Petitioner's belief.

81. When Petitioner attempted to explain his good faith belief as it related to labor/property, he cited Stanton v Baltic Mining,

at which point the Court interrupted again. Judge Moon asked, "Were you running a mine?" (Exhibit A, 507). The Court went on to ask, "What separates you from the rest of the citizenry when it comes to paying your taxes? That's the question, I think, is why do you believe that the tax laws do not apply to you, if they apply to others?" Id. Little did the Court realized that it asked the precise question at issue for which defense counsel stated they could not and would not argue for fear of being sanctioned. Ironically, what counsel refused to argue - the fundamental good faith belief of their client - denied Petitioner the opportunity to answer what was obviously not a rhetorical question.

82. Petitioner was separated "from the rest of the citizenry when it comes to paying [his] taxes," Id. the precise question at issue, since he rebutted the Government's presumption that he was a taxpayer liable for an excise tax based upon a privilege/benefit he had since rejected. Petitioner was, therefore, without the jurisdiction of congressional authority under Article 1, Section 8. The fact that counsel considered this position "frivolous" denied him a truthful and effective defense.

83. Petitioner, during cross-examination, even stated, "And I was not able to answer along the lines of my good faith based upon what I understand the United States to be defined as in the Constitution." (Exhibit A, 547). Petitioner knew and believed that the Constitution defines and limits the United States and its powers. If only for counsel's failure to investigate Petitioner's sole defense, the Government's lack of jurisdiction and authority, he was unable to convey to the jury how and why he was not subject to the income tax law.

84. After the third interruption of his testimony, Petitioner stated the words "given my understanding of what is apparent here," (Exhibit A, 507) as Petitioner believed it was "apparent" that he was not to be afforded the chance, even with obliquity, to make any implication of jurisdiction to the jury. Moreover, counsel did not defend their client from prejudicial queries from the Court.

85. Petitioner's question asked of government officials, as it related to his tax liability, was part of his testimony. (Exhibit A, 524-525). Petitioner underscored the failure of anyone to respond. This became evident during cross-examination when Petitioner stressed that government agencies "were unresponsive to even my simple questions." (Exhibit A, 539). Petitioner even stated his intent to bring accountability so that "other agencies take recognition of the fact that" one can withdraw from the jurisdiction of the United States Government for the income tax. Petitioner's good faith belief was one that agencies and officials refused to counter and one that defense counsel considered "frivolous."

86. Assistant U.S. Attorney Hogeboom, concerning Petitioner's tax liability, asked if "current IRS agents" or "anybody from the Tax Division, Department of Justice" were at meetings attended by Petitioner, "explaining how the tax code operates." Hogeboom asked, "How did you determine who to seek advice from " Hogeboom asked, "Isn't it a fact that you only sought advice or input from the pro side? You didn't check with the con side?" When Petitioner stated he had determined, "I'm not going to file anymore," because of his research, Hogeboom said, "I understand that." Yet, Hogeboom said, "You did not look to the other side; you deliberately closed your eyes to the other side of the argument." (Exhibit A, 561-563)

87. Hogeboom stressed that Agent Biggs sent a "pamphlet" to Petitioner, a document that concerned frivolous taxpayer arguments. These arguments, first of all, were not ones upon which Petitioner depended. The pamphlet failed to answer Petitioner's query sent to all officials.

88. Harris asked Petitioner on redirect, "And so from your review of the material, you did not find an answer that responded to that question; is that correct?" Petitioner responded in the affirmative, noting that all parties "were unresponsive." (Exhibit A, 570)

89. Concerning jury instructions, Cargill stated, "...we did submit an instruction that just said - addressing that element, that Mr. Johnson was required by law, regulations, to file tax returns in the specific years '05, '06, and '07. There's uncontroverted evidence that he was." (Exhibit A, 574)

90. In his closing argument, Cargill stated, "Mr. Johnson still believes that the tax code doesn't apply to him and he still had no obligation to file a return. But, as a matter of law, as a matter of who is correct, we all know he should have filed returns, I mean, come on, he should have." (Exhibit A, 614)

91. Cargill then stated that in a criminal case, "you look at...the defendant's state of mind. Did he have criminal intent " He He questioned openly to the jury that Petitioner believed he wasn't "supposed to file. Is he right? No. It is crazy." (Exhibit A, 619)

92. Petitioner was found guilty on all counts on January 18, 2013.

93. Prior to sentencing, with the intent to argue what counsel considered "frivolous," Petitioner dispensed with representation. He submitted a motion challenging subject matter and in personam jurisdiction, which the Court denied.

94. Petitioner stated to the Court that he raised the issue of jurisdiction as he did in April before Judge Welsh. The Court responded, "And we are well aware of that and have ruled against you over and over and over." (Exhibit A, 1805)

95. Petitioner then stated that the prosecution "was not compelled to prove jurisdiction." Petitioner stated, "the fact of the matter is I cite presumption and fraud" in the motion. Id.

96. Petitioner was intent that the Government overcome Petitioner's rebuttal of its presumption. Petitioner, unfortunately, out of frustration, alienated the Court and received a criminal contempt charge for his efforts to seek an answer to a challenge that began in 2004 with Agent Biggs.

97. Petitioner ended his comments stating, "There's no jurisdiction this Court has over me." (Exhibit A, 1818) Petitioner concluded by refusing to be the defendant, just as he began in 2004.

98. When Mr. Paul Beers became counsel of record for the appeal of the sentence and verdict to the Fourth Circuit, Petitioner sent him a letter which addressed the central concern of jurisdiction (Exhibit H).

99. In yet another letter dated 7/24/13, Petitioner underscored his deliberate efforts to rebut any presumption that he was within the scope of the federal income tax. Petitioner noted trial counsel's concerns for sanctions. He challenged jurisdiction stating that he was not a taxpayer enjoying a privilege. (Exhibit I)

100. Petitioner wrote about the nature of an excise tax which may be avoided by not choosing to engage the activities that require them.

101. Petitioner received a copy of this same letter back from Beers, who wrote handwritten question marks at the end of the final thought:

52

"Since revoking the SS#, I have removed any question of any nexus to the U.S. and any privilege and jurisdiction. I hope you see this." Id. Beers did not understand the nature of the excise tax and, therefore, jurisdiction.

102. Beers responded on August 9, 2013 (Exhibit J), stating that he found two issues that were "meritorious or colorable" for appeal. Beers continued by assessing Petitioner's jurisdictional arguments as "meritless or even irrational." He cited that he was "constrained by ethical canons in writing appellate briefs to raise only those arguments which have merit." He stated, "In my judgment, your challenges to the trial court's jurisdiction and arguments concerning the enforceability or constitutionality of federal tax laws are not well grounded in law and fact. Therefore, I must decline to include arguments along those lines in our brief." (Exhibit J)

103. Petitioner believed that Beers did not thoroughly examine the trial record, as Petitioner did not question the "enforceability or constitutionality of federal tax laws." Petitioner even testified that the tax code was "100% constitutional." (Exhibit A, 509). Petitioner believes lack of understanding by trial and appellate counsel prevented Petitioner from challenging the enforcement authority of the tax code as it applied to him alone, the precise question at issue, since "income" and "excise" taxes were ones for which Petitioner was no longer engaged. As such, just as with Cargill and Harris, Beers prevented Petitioner's good faith defense from being aired in the Fourth Circuit Court of Appeals.

104. Petitioner believed, at a minimum, that if the Government and Court presumed jurisdiction, he deserved the opportunity to understand the grounds for that jurisdiction. Moreover, he believed he should have

had the opportunity to explain to the jury why and how he rebutted the presumption that he was within the jurisdiction of the federal income tax law and, therefore, the Court.

105. After his appeal was denied, Petitioner wrote Beers a letter and asked him to file a petition for a rehearing (Exhibit K). Again, Petitioner cited jurisdiction as grounds. Petitioner stated that the Government and IRS operated by presumption, which Petitioner had long since rebutted. Petitioner referenced Steward Machine and Helvering. Petitioner was emphatic that he was without the scope of the tax code for income and employment excises.

106. Appellate counsel's understanding of Petitioner's belief was equally lacking. Beers' efforts before the Court offered nothing substantive as to why his client established his good faith belief. Not surprisingly, without even a single phone conversation with Petitioner before the appellate hearing, Beers surmised his understanding from the trial record and offered nothing about jurisdiction. Consequently, Beers failed to assert a "dead-bang-winner."

107. Beers stated in the appellate brief that Petitioner's "sole defense at the trial was that he did not act within the requisite mens rea to be guilty of obstructing the IRS or willfully failing to file tax returns. (Exhibit L, 4). This was not Petitioner's sole defense. It was not his defense at all.

108. Beers continued by stating, "in both his opening statement and closing argument to the jury, defense counsel stipulated Petitioner should have filed tax returns alleged by the government," and "he also conceded that Johnson owed the taxes the government claimed." Id.

109. Beers stated Petitioner's "position was that he did not willfully or knowingly violate 26 USCS 7212(a) or 26 USCS 7203" and that his "theory of innocence centered on his steadfast belief that he was not subject to federal income taxes." Id. Yet, Beers did not explore or argue the concrete reason why Petitioner was not subject to the income tax.

110. Beers stated that Petitioner "attended courses and seminars taught by persons who espouse the view that the Internal Revenue Code is unconstitutional or nonbinding." Id. This is not a truthful or factual statement. Petitioner did not deal with those who believed the tax code was unconstitutional. Moreover, Petitioner never stated or believed that the code was unconstitutional. Petitioner believes the tax code is legal and lawful.

111. Curiously, Beers offered that Petitioner's good faith belief was based on the "Constitution and Supreme Court precedent," Id. but he cited no reference to the precedent. Had Petitioner's truthful belief been argued at trial, the Supreme Court precedent would have revealed a credible argument which trial and appellate counsel considered "frivolous." For Steward Machine and Helvering speak to the very nature of the excise tax and its limited application (jurisdiction), a non-frivolous defense in fact and settled law.

112. Incredibly, Beers' distilled essence of the trial record was that "The central, contested issue was mens rea." (Id. 17) Beers, like defense counsel, dismissed Petitioner's belief of jurisdiction because he failed to investigate and understand its significance.

113. On June 10, 2014, Petitioner mailed Cargill, Harris and Beers a letter requesting the specific canon of ethics that prevented them from arguing jurisdiction. (Exhibit M)

114. Harris replied immediately stating "Virginia Rule of Professions Guidelines 3.1 provides that a lawyer shall not raise a defense unless there is a basis for doing so that is not frivolous." (Exhibit N)

115. In her letter, Harris stated, "your claim that you were not a 'taxpayer' or 'U.S. citizen' have been deemed frivolous." She also stated, "This does not mean that you could not argue that you misunderstood the law differently (or that you had a good faith, but mistaken, belief about what the law meant), it just means that a lawyer could not argue that your interpretation of the law was correct when courts have uniformly found the arguments to be incorrect and frivolous." Id.

116. After a second request to Cargill, Petitioner received a reply on July 16, 2014. (Exhibit O). Cargill cited Rule 3.3 of the Rules of Professional Conduct. He underscored that this rule "governs a lawyer's responsibilities regarding asserting defense or taking positions at odds with settled law." Id. Cargill continued by offering, "An attorney may not assert a position he knows has no legal basis and which he cannot in good faith ask the court to adopt." (Id.) [emphasis added]

117. Beers never responded to Petitioner's two requests.

118. Cargill stated in his opening statement, referring to Petitioner, "He's scared. Anyone in his position would be scared. Not because he is guilty, but because he's afraid that you might make a mistake and find him guilty." (Exhibit A, 110). Cargill was incorrect. Petitioner was angry, angry because he was in a position that was entirely unnecessary and inappropriate, knowing full well that defense counsel was about to argue a defense that was not the truth

and not based upon the facts. Petitioner knew that the ends of justice would not be achieved. Cargill stated during his closing argument that, concerning Petitioner's words and actions during the voir dire and the start of the trial, he "was acting on his beliefs then. He was plainly wrong. He was acting on his sincere beliefs. And we begged him, 'Please let us try to do something to help you. You cannot do this.'" (Exhibit A, 621).

119. Counsel could have helped Petitioner by investigating his good faith belief and defending him based upon truth, fact and law.

120. Cargill met with Petitioner at the jail on 2/1/13, at which time Cargill stated that he believed there were grounds upon which to request a new trial. Yet, Cargill stated that he did not personally want to submit the motion. Cargill suggested that Petitioner have outside counsel file the request. Cargill stated that Judge Moon would not likely approve the motion if he submitted it, since he practiced in Moon's Court. Cargill went on to explain that filing a motion would not be prejudicial, that if the motion were denied, both the denied motion and trial could be appealed.

121. Petitioner had the name of a lawyer, Jay Nanavati, given to Petitioner by his sister some weeks earlier. After Petitioner explained Cargill's idea, Nanavati advised Petitioner to have Cargill submit the motion for a new trial. Nanavati contacted Cargill by phone, Petitioner by mail.

122. On 3/7/13, Harris met with Petitioner at the jail. Harris told Petitioner, only after he asked about the new trial request, that they never submitted the motion. Harris stated that they decided against this course; she said it would not be "strategically beneficial" for sentencing.

Appendix B – 2255 Motion

PRELIMINARY STATEMENT

Petitioner, James B. Johnson, respectfully submits this Memorandum of Law with the attached Declaration ("Decl"), in support of this motion pursuant to 28 USC 2255, for an order vacating the conviction and sentence by reason of ineffective assistance of counsel.

PROCEDURAL BACKGROUND

Petitioner was convicted in January 2013 for obstruction under 26 USC 7212(a) and willful failure to file tax returns under 26 USC 7203. Petitioner was sentenced to 48 months on April 11, 2013. The conviction and sentence were affirmed on May 12, 2014. See 2014 U.S. App. LEXIS 8834. Appellate counsel withdrew representation for lack of grounds for a writ of certiorari.

RELEVANT LAW

It is well settled that there is a two-part test for evaluating claims of ineffective assistance of counsel. See Strickland v Washington, 466 US 688, 687 (1984). "First, the defendant must show that the deficient performance prejudiced the defense," such that there is a "reasonable probability that, but for counsel's unprofessional errors, the result of the proceedings would have been different." Id. As the Supreme Court made clear, "a defendant need not show that counsel's deficient conduct more likely than not altered the outcome of the case." Id, 693. Rather, the "reasonable probability" of a different result is a probability "sufficient to undermine confidence in the outcome." Id. See also United States v Dominguez-Benitez, 542 US 74 n.9 (2004).

("...the reasonable probability standard is not the same as, and should not be confused with, a requirement that a defendent prove beyond a preponderance of the evidence that but for error things would have been different.")

1

Finally, pro se pleadings must be construed and treated liberally, under whatever law or rule appropriate for proper avenue of relief, and are not subject to dismissal on mere technicality. See Haines v Kerner, 404 US 519 (1972), Boag v MacDougall, 454 US 364 (1982), and Hill v United States, 368 US 424 (1962).

ARGUMENT

As shown below, both prongs of the Strickland test are satisfied. Defense and appellate counsel failed to investigate their client's good faith belief and relevant law and failed to develop a strategy of defense to the alleged charges. In conflict with settled law, Steward Machine, infra, and Helvering, infra, counsel summarily dismissed Petitioner's good faith belief that, based upon his written rebuttal of the Government's presumption that he was a taxpayer liable for income and employment taxes, he could not be within the jurisdiction of the United States Government and, therefore, the Court. Counsel rejected letters that Petitioner sent in 2000 to the Social Security Administration and the Secretary of the Treasury, rebutting the presumption that he was within the Government's purview, (Decl. 6,7). Rather, counsel cited the American Bar Association (ABA) canons of ethics as justification for their unwillingness to argue what they believed in "good faith" (Exhibit O) was "frivolous." But for their timidity and "scant knowledge of tax laws," Bursten infra, counsel did not defend Petitioner's belief or argue that he was not and could not be willful. In a nutshell, counsel rejected sound strategy, viable evidence and any and all circumstances. They ignored an argument that they considered "frivolous" only to avoid sanctions. This amounted to a conflict of interest that was self-imposed.

Consequently, this was not a matter of counsel making questionable strategic decisions challenged in hindsight. This was not a matter of counsel merely engaging in poor judgment, advocacy or performance. This was a case whereby they put their own interests before their client's strategic benefit. When counsel repudiated Petitioner's sole belief as frivolous, they condemned his one strategy and grounds of defense predicated on fact and law. Thus, they were unprepared to ensure the meaningful adversarial testing of the Government's case. They were wholly unprepared for key points of the trial. Why? Because of a fear of sanctions and a lack of knowledge, counsel refused to accept or investigate his belief or argue "the precise question at issue." Chevron U.S.A. Inc v Natural Resources Defense Council 467 US 837, 842 (1984).

Instead, counsel offered a hackneyed "defense" for a tax case that was anything but typical. This was absolute foolishness and carelessness and advocacy laden with self-interests, wholly inconsistent with representation within the range of competency expected of criminal attorneys. The prejudice to Petitioner cannot be doubted. Petitioner was, therefore, denied his constitutional rights for effective assistance of counsel.

TRIAL AND APPELLATE COUNSEL REFUSED TO ARGUE THE ELEMENT OF JURISDICTION.

Trial and appellate counsel refused to argue the element of jurisdiction. When they failed to investigate and argue the element of jurisdiction, counsel failed to act as advocates guaranteed by the Sixth Amendment. Their failure to argue jurisdiction before the Court allowed this case to endure a prosecution that was not warranted. Candidly, counsel's failure to prevail before the Court allowed a jury to convict a man who had rebutted the presumption that he was within the Government's purview for income taxes.

Petitioner told defense counsel that he developed a good faith belief that he became liable for federal income and employment taxes when he accepted federal social security and employment benefits, both of which are subject to the jurisdiction of congressional indirect taxing power granted under Article 1, section 8, of the Constitution. (Decl. 3, 10, 11, 36) Petitioner explained

3

to counsel that, in 2000, he knowingly and deliberately rebutted the prima facie evidence which established the nexus that he had a tax liability. (Decl. 4, 6, 7, 8, 9, 35) Petitioner explained that he sent written notification to the Social Security Administration and Secretary of the Treasury, thereby rebutting the presumption that he was a "taxpayer" as defined in the Internal Revenue Code (IRC). (Decl. 6, 7, 12, 13) Yet, surprisingly, counsel reflexively and categorically rejected the idea that the Government lacked jurisdiction.

When Petitioner first met counselor Andrea Harris, he explained why he was outside the jurisdiction of the tax code. (Decl. 30-42). Harris said that Petitioner's belief was "frivolous" and one she could not argue in court, stating that the "Canons of Ethics" prevented her from doing so. (Decl. 43, 44). Cargill also rejected Petitioner's belief as "frivolous" and referred to the "Canons of Ethics" as his governing authority. (Decl. 43) Appellate counsel Paul Beers did the same. (Decl. 98-102) However, the argument of jurisdiction was anything by frivolous; especially since it was grounded in law and fact. Moreover, given the legal significance of presumptions, failure of counsel to weigh the element of jurisdiction was not only ineffective but, ultimately, highly prejudicial.

Appropriately, presumptions are addressed by the Internal Revenue Service (IRS). THE HANDBOOK FOR SPECIAL AGENTS CRIMINAL INVESTIGATION DIVISION, INTERNAL REVENUE SERVICE, Section 323.50 states,

> A presumption is a rule of law which permits the drawing of particular inference as to the existence of one fact not certainly known from the existence of other particular facts. Although it is not evidence, it may be considered as a substitute for evidence. (2) <u>Presumptions may be conclusive or rebuttable. (3) A rebuttable presumption is one which prevails until it is overcome by evidence to the contrary.</u> [emphasis added]

4

Ironically, while the IRS allows for the rebuttal of presumptions, defense counsel did not. Counsel did not investigate that absent any counter by the Government, Petitioner's rebuttal "prevails until it is overcome by evidence to the contrary," and that the Government, therefore, lacked jurisdiction in this case. The relevance of presumptions is further explained in Crimes-Presumptions-Validity, 13 L Ed 2d 1138.

> 1) There must be a rational connection between the fact proved and the ultimate fact presumed, and the inference of one fact from the proof of another should not be so unreasonable as to be a purely arbitrary mandate; 2) the statute must not effect a discrimination against certain persons; and 3) the subject matter of the statutory presumption must be within the constitutional limitations of legislative power. [emphasis added]

There is no escaping that the Government presumed that since Petitioner submitted federal tax returns (fact proved), he was a taxpayer expected to continue submitting tax returns (ultimate fact presumed). Additionally, the Government presumed with circumstantial evidence that, for the years charged, Petitioner was liable. The relevance of presumptions is inescapable. Although criminal statutes create presumptions:

> (1) The statute must not deprive the accused of a proper opportunity to rebut the presumption or to present his defense to it, or (2) that the presumption must not be made conclusive of the right of the accused, or (3) that the statute must lay down a "rule of evidence" and not a "rule of substantive law." Id. [emphasis added]

Petitioner impressed upon counsel that his rebuttal of the Government's presumption returned him to the jurisdiction, status and class as one without "the constitutional limitations of legislative congressional indirect excise power" Id. of indirect taxation under Article 1, Section 8. Furthermore,

5

Petitioner expressed to counsel that he, as stated in Hale v Henkel, 201 US 43, 74 (1906)

> May stand upon his constitutional rights as a citizen...and owes no duty to the state, since he receives nothing therefrom. [emphasis added]

Petitioner referred counsel to Flint v Stone Tracy Co., 220 US 107, 151 (1911), which defines "excise taxes" as those assessed upon activities and choices that are voluntary in nature. He referred to Brushaber v Union Pacific R.R. Co., 240 US 1, 17 (1916), in which the Court "...recognized the fact that taxation on income was in its nature an excise entitled to be enforced as such. [emphasis added]

Petitioner established for counsel a clear distinction between a "privilege" and a natural right, which are congruent, respectively, with the limited indirect and direct taxation jurisdiction granted to Congress under the Constitution.

Had counsel at least investigated, they would have accepted the relevance of jurisdiction as more than a "frivolous" argument that would have resulted in sanctions. Consequently, the role and limits of law and presumptions, which were ignored by counsel, were extremely relevant. In Bailey v Alabama, 219 US 219, 239 (1911), the Court acknowledged the limited jurisdiction of Congress and presumptions.

> ...a constitutional prohibition cannot be transgressed indirectly by the creation of a statutory presumption any more than it can be violated by direct enactment. The power to create presumptions is not a means of escape from constitutional restrictions. [emphasis added]

With minimal investigation, counsel would have learned that, at the heart of Petitioner's contention, Congress may not accomplish what the Constitution prohibits. Enforcing a statutory presumption would be tantamount to compelled performance upon those without the scope of congressional authority. Congress

6

may no sooner require one to engage in a federal privilege or excisible activity than to craft the presumption into law. And, counsel may not make Petitioner a taxpayer by failing to research or argue his belief. The significance of Bailey supra, would have been transparent if counsel understood that income and employment taxes are excises by virtue of settled law.

Since excise taxes are inherently voluntary, one may not be forced to pay an excise when one does not subscribe to an excise. The nature of both income and employment taxes as excises was expressed by the Supreme Court. In Charles C. Steward Machine Co. v Davis, 302 US 548, 574 (1937), the Court stated, "Every employer is...to pay...an 'excise tax'..." The Court explained, "First: The tax which is described in the statute as an excise tax..." Id., 578. In Helvering v Davis, 301 US 619, 635 (1937), the Court determined the excisable nature of the social security tax and the relation of employment and that the Social Security Act under Title VIII "lays two different types of tax, 'an income tax on employees' and 'an excise tax on employers.'"

The import of the "voluntary" and, therefore, the excisable nature of these taxes were validated in Morse v United States, 494 F 2d 876, 880 (9th Cir. 1974). The Court stated,

> Accordingly, when returns were filed in Mrs. Morse's name declaring income to her for 1944 and 1945, and making her potentially liable for the tax due on that income, she became a taxpayer within the meaning of the Internal Revenue Code. [emphasis added]

Morse "became a taxpayer" and entered the Government's jurisdiction when she filed returns some thirty years earlier. She created the presumption when she voluntarily subscribed to an excisable federal privilege. Her submissions became prima facie evidence. Moreover, Morse did this on a "voluntary" basis.

If there is any doubt as to the meaning of the term "voluntary" the Government in Burns v United States, cr-85-122-Ef, clarified the matter.

7

Samuel H. Pillsbury, who prosecuted the case, asked Burns,

> ...and it never occurred to you that they have a somewhat different meaning of the word "voluntary;" that perhaps they meant the actual initial payment of the money was voluntary? It never occurred to you that the word "voluntary" might go to the payment of taxes, or permission to withhold funds, did it?

Clearly, the Court in Morse, and the Government in Burns, distinguished the significance of the excisable and voluntary nature and subsequent jurisdiction of both income and employment taxes.

In the instant case, counsel knew that Petitioner rebutted any and all Government presumptions and prima facie evidence that he was within the Government's jurisdiction, (Decl. 6, 7, 8, 37). With initiative and insight, counsel would have pursued Petitioner's direct reference that "The Social Security Act does not require a person to have a social security number (SSN) to live and work in the United States." (Decl. 36) (Exhibit F) The contrast of this statement against the presumption attendant with a subscription into the privilege of social security is striking. Yet, even more striking is one's rebuttal of that very privilege and presumption. Counsel's failure to explore or accept the very act of their client's rebuttal reveals a lack of total performance in light of the entire body of evidence. But for counsel's neglect, it is reasonably probable that the outcome "would have been different." Strickland, 694.

Effective assistance of counsel would have required a level of competence that would have at least dignified their client's belief as something other than "frivolous" until proven to be so. Such deficient advocacy demonstrates that Petitioner was denied representation "within the range of competence of attorneys in criminal cases." Strickland, 687-688. Counsel did not touch, much less grapple with, either the facts of the case or the law. When counsel heard buzz

8

words which indicated what they believed in "good faith" (Decl. 116) to be frivolous, they had no inclination to investigate in the midst of what was obvious to them. Thus, there was no need to probe what was possible with the express intent to contradict what they believed was untenable. This thought is critical, since both Harris and Cargill admitted that they did not know much about tax law. (Decl. 30, 42-44) As such, how could they conclude that Petitioner's belief was "frivolous?" In United States v Bursten, 395 F 2d 976, 981 (5th Cir. 1968), the Court stated, "that most lawyers have only scant knowledge of tax laws." Even though counsel had scant knowledge, they certainly had the ability to investigate Petitioner's belief and the fundamentals of tax law for his strategic benefit. Absent investigation, his belief would remain frivolous and they would remain ignorant, with no strategy or defense. Sadly, counsel relied upon what they presumed to be frivolous to avoid sanctions. (Decl. 32, 43) Yet, as stated in DuBoise v North Carolina, 225 F. Supp 51, fn2 (4th Cir. 1964),

> The canons of ethics of the legal profession require a lawyer's "entire devotion to the interest of the client, warm zeal in the maintenance and defense of his rights and the exertion of his utmost learning and ability" to the end that nothing be taken or be withheld from him, save the rules of law, legally applied. American Bar Association, Canons of Ethics, Canon 15.

Counsel's reliance upon the canons (Decl. 32, 43, 106) as their ultimate authority, which prevented any exploration of their client's belief, was ineffective assistance that prejudiced the outcome of the trial. With respect to the ABA canons of ethics, the Supreme Court, in Rompilla v Beard, 545 US 374, 400 (2005), quoting Strickland, stated that they "'are only guides' and do not establish the constitutional baseline for effective assistance of counsel." The Court underscored that "The majority, by parsing the guidelines as if they

9

were binding statutory text, ignores this admonition." Obviously, these "guides," while reflective of a particular practice, are not the practice required by the Federal Constitution for effective assistance of counsel. Counsel's lack of investigation was, therefore, crippling.

> Counsel must ordinarily be prepared to discuss the reasonableness of a statutory presumption not only on the basis of the express terms of the statute, but on the basis of the application of the statutory presumption to the particular facts of the case, for various decisions have established that the reasonableness of a particular presumption may depend not only on the express terms of the particular statutory provision, but also on its application either under a particular statutory construction or in a particular factual situation. Crimes-Presumptions-Validity. [emphasis added]

Noteworthy, the Court in Strickland, 690-691 stated that,

> ...strategic choices made after less than complete investigation are reasonable precisely to the extent that reasonable professional judgments support the limitations on investigation.

Sound strategic choices are not made by incompetent counsel who unreasonably reject their client's belief and the particular facts of the case. The Court underscored that "counsel has a duty to make reasonable investigations or to make a reasonable decision that makes particular investigations unnecessary." Id. Counsel failed in this important regard. Rather, counsel's rote reaction to Petitioner's belief as meritless and their deference to their canons of ethics was the extent of their investigatory prowess. The result is that trial and appellate counsel dismissed the constitutional basis for Petitioner's belief and his rights under the Sixth Amendment. (Decl. 106, 108, 110, 111) Had counsel investigated to "prevailing professional norms," Kimmelman v Morrison, 477 US 365, 385 (1986), they would have learned that Petitioner no longer enjoyed the federal privilege of social security or benefits associated with the relation of employment. They would have realized that not all who argue that they are without the scope and jurisdiction of the federal tax code have unreasonable beliefs. To the contrary, the particular means of supporting such a good faith belief separates the frivolous from the non-frivolous. With counsel's reasoning, anyone proposing that he was without the jurisdiction of the tax code would preclude a legitimate explanation in court.

Counsel's advocacy was so unreasonable as to be a "purely arbitrary mandate" Crimes-Presumptions-Validity and discriminatory against a class not subject to the provision of the statutory presumption "within the constitutional limitations of legislative power." Id. Regrettably, counsel agreed with and aided and abetted a canned theme of the trial (Decl. 63, 65, 66, 89, 90, 91). Consequently, counsel never argued Petitioner's rebuttal and, therefore, jurisdiction. Since they did not argue jurisdiction before the Court, the matter unnecessarily went before the jury. As opposed to effectively defending their client, counsel served as gatekeepers who prevented meritorious arguments from entering the court.

> Counsel's ineffectiveness stands in contrast to the premise that they will use every skill, expend every energy, and tax every legitimate resource in the exercise of independent professional judgment on behalf of their client and in undertaking representation on their client's behalf. In re Asbestos case 514 F. Supp 914, 920 (4th Cir. 1981)

In the instant case, "representation" included a lack of attentiveness to the unique circumstances involved. As stated in Wong v Belmontes, 558 US _, _ (2009), quoting Strickland.

> In light of the "variety of circumstances faced by defense counsel [and] the range of legitimate decisions regarding how best to represent a criminal defendant," the performance inquiry necessarily turns on "whether counsel's assistance was reasonable considering all of the circumstances." [emphasis added]

11

In effect, counsel's failure to consider all circumstances denied the Government's case the "adversarial testing" required to rebut the presumption that Petitioner was liable for the excise taxes in question (Decl. 28, 45, 53, 54, 66, 89-91).

There can be no doubt that the Federal Government operates within a "lawful sphere" Downes v Bidwell, 182 US 244, 289 (1901). Just as it was appropriate to ask counsel before trial how or when one may contest the acceptance of a federal privilege and its accompanying excise tax, it is appropriate now. This question, which is more than rhetorical, speaks to the credibility of that lawful sphere. (Decl. 81, 82) Petitioner asserted that, unlike Mrs. Morse, in Morse supra, he could not possibly be a "taxpayer" as defined in the IRC; for Petitioner rebutted being in that sphere. Yet, without hesitation, Harris said he was a taxpayer with a tax liability. (Decl. 28, 31, 34, 42) With such rigidity, counsel was reluctant to accept that "taxpayers" as defined within the IRC, 26 USC 7701 (a)(9)(14), are those subject to the jurisdiction of the Government for any applicable EXCISE taxes, to and for which they are liable. [emphasis added] Counsel's lack of tax knowledge and, thus, jurisdiction, prevented them from considering that Petitioner's belief was reasonable. Since Petitioner rebutted the presumption that he was currently liable for excisable benefits, he was without congressional indirect taxation authority. He was as if he never "became a taxpayer, within the meaning of the Internal Revenue Code." Morse, supra.

A "heavy measure of deference to counsel's judgments," Strickland, 691, cannot be applied when counsel failed to investigate and proclaimed that what was credible, factual and lawful was not. This was not a reasonable strategy given all the circumstances. This was not a reasonable strategy at all. Counsel did not familiarize themselves with their client's argument and material. Their approach was not objectively reasonable under Strickland, especially since they did not argue the precise question at issue. Chevron, supra. Had counsel

12

investigated and argued all the facts, the Court and, if necessary, the jury would have discerned a reasonable alternative to the Government's representations. Ultimately, then, it can hardly be said that because Petitioner's belief was so contrary to the accepted norm that it was not arguable.

At a minimum, the Government had a responsibility to overcome Petitioner's good faith belief in order to establish that the alleged offenses were committed. For this to occur, Petitioner had to overcome reluctant counsel from the outset. Indisputably, defense counsel had a profound and inherent obligation to investigate and argue their client's defense, especially given that the Government, Department of the Treasury, IRS and Department of Justice refused to counter Petitioner's rebuttal throughout the investigation. (Decl. 67-69, 72, 85, 86, 99). Since Petitioner no longer sought either social security or employment benefits, the United States Government could not and may not expect to exact contributions from his property - his labor.

With respect to a criminal trial, it is reasonable to ask "What is fair?" As stated in Sallie v North Carolina, 587 F 2d 636, 640 (4th Cir. 1978),

> This standard does not require that representation be flawless only that all decisions materially affecting defendant's representation be the product of informed judgment, not neglect or ignorance. [emphasis added]

It is fair that, as stated in DuBoise, 53 supra,

> when the Petitioner has alleged no grounds for a defense even the ineffective assistance of counsel does not warrant the invalidation of the conviction.

Since Petitioner offered grounds for defense, which Counsel summarily rejected, his loss of liberty is all the more egregious and contrary to the ends of justice - the result of a lack of understanding and no investigation.

The trial record reflects that Petitioner continuously challenged jurisdiction. (Decl. 100-102). As stated in J. McIntyre Machine Ltd v Nicastro

564 US _, _ (2011),

> Personal jurisdiction of course, restricts "judicial power not as a matter of sovereignty, but as a matter of individual liberty," for due process protects the individual's right to be subject only to lawful power. [emphasis added]

Constitutional and judicial power to apply and enforce the tax statutes in the present circumstances is lacking. Petitioner is without congressional taxing authority and no longer subscribes to the privileges that once bound him to that jurisdiction. Since the Government's presumption was challenged, the dynamics changed. Limited and rebuttable authority, then, were pertinent facts for the Court and, if needed, the jury's deliberation. Counsel, naturally, should have argued their client's belief to the former or latter.

Notably, in United States v Cronic, 466 US 648 n15 (1984), the Court states, "...there can be no restrictions upon the function of counsel in defending a criminal prosecution..." [emphasis added] Significantly, however, at their first meeting with Petitioner (Decl. 32, 43, 106), Counsel argued for their "good faith" belief (Exhibit O) to the exclusion of Petitioner's "good faith belief," Which precluded counsel from arguing jurisdiction. Counsel's interests overshadowed Petitioner's strategic interests. Cronic, fn31, supra, states,

> We have presumed prejudice when counsel labors under an actual conflict of interest, despite the fact that the constraints on counsel are entirely self-imposed. [emphasis added]

Moreover, concerning appellate representation, as stated in Hawkins v Hannigan, 185 F 3d 1146 (10th Cir. 1999)

> Counsel's failure to raise a "dead bang winner" - an issue that is both obvious from the trial record and one which would have resulted in reversal on appeal - constitutes ineffective assistance.

Considering all the circumstances, deference to counsel should not be granted. Most certainly, had counsel acted within professional norms, without misguided dependence on select cannons of ethics, to the exclusion of other canons, all of which are only "guides," with reasonable probability, the outcome would have been different.

DEFENSE COUNSEL FAILED TO ARGUE THE ELEMENT OF WILLFULNESS

As discussed in the first claim, Petitioner developed a core belief that not every person is subject to federal income and employment taxes. (Decl. 3, 10, 11, 33, 36) Petitioner took deliberate steps that he believed, in accordance with the law, were sufficient to remove himself from the IRC and any excise tax liability. (Decl. 4, 6, 7, 8, 9, 35) These steps, whether considered sufficient or not, are indisputable proof that Petitioner, in fact, believed that his actions were protected under the blanket of the Constitution and in conformance with the law.

That Petitioner believed what he believed is important; for, it proves that he did not willfully commit an act in defiance of the law. Consequently, Petitioner's failure to file taxes, even if determined to be unlawful, cannot be construed as a crime. Why? Petitioner did not have the requisite mens rea. Pointedly, the crime of failure to file tax returns requires that the element of willfulness be met. It is, therefore, impossible that Petitioner believed that he was acting contrary to the law and that he willfully committed the alleged offenses.

When counsel failed to provide the advocacy guaranteed by the Sixth Amendment, they failed to effectively counter the necessary element of willfulness. This failure prevented the jury from understanding Petitioner's state of mind, which propelled them to a determination of guilt. The resultant prejudice, in this regard, is transparent. Even if defense counsel did not agree with Petitioner's belief, even if they thought Petitioner's actions were not in conformance with the law, they had a professional obligation to offer the jury their client's good faith belief. Had they done so, counsel would have effectively eliminated the element of willfulness, which would have, invariably, led to a not guilty verdict. Thus, counsel provided ineffective assistance which unduly prejudiced the outcome of the trial.

In Cheek v United States, 498 US 192, 200 (1991), the Court stated,

> ...the statutory term "willfully" as used in the federal criminal statutes...carv[ed] out an exception to the rule. [The presumption that one knows the law.] This special treatment of criminal tax offenses is largely due to the complexity of the tax law. [brackets added]

Moreover,

> The proliferation of statutes and regulations has sometimes made it difficult for the average citizen to know and comprehend the extent of the duties and obligations imposed by the tax laws. Congress has accordingly softened the impact of the common-law presumption by making specific intent to violate the law an element of certain federal tax offenses. Id., 199-200.

With such congressional sensitivity granted the complexity of the tax laws, we have the gravamen of the ineffective assistance of counsel concerning willfulness. Petitioner's belief, even if it is presumed that he violated the law, prevented him from understanding that he was actually committing a criminal act. Petitioner had, in fact, no willfulness, for, he never had the intent. The Court established that

> The standard for the statutory willfulness requirement is the voluntary, intentional violation of a known legal duty. Id. 201 [and] Willfulness, as construed by our prior decisions in criminal tax cases, requires the Government to prove that the law imposed a duty on the defendant, the

16

defendant knew of this duty, and that he voluntarily and intentionally violated that duty. Id.

Since Petitioner believed that he was without the jurisdiction of the tax code, he believed he had no known legal duty. Consequently, but for counsel's failure to contest the three elements of willfulness, as set forth in Cheek, the Government would not have been able to overcome that burden and prove Petitioner's guilt beyond a reasonable doubt. Furthermore, in an attempt to gain an untruthful advance, it is one thing for the Government to deliberately ignore Petitioner's genuine attempt to elicit from competent authorities a response to his repeated question: "What law required him to file a tax return?" (Decl. 16-21), but, for counsel to ignore their client's sincere efforts to cooperate with the IRS was neglectful. Rather unexpectedly, counsel, in fact, did the opposite. They underscored the Government's case to the jury that Petitioner had a tax liability without explaining his good faith belief. (Decl. 63, 65, 66, 90, 91)

In Snyder v United States, 897 F. Supp 241, 244 (4th Cir. 1995), quoting Cheek supra, the Court noted,

> We thus disagree with the court of appeals' requirement that a 'claimed good faith belief must be objectively reasonable' if it is to be considered as possibly negating the Government's evidence purporting to show a defendant's awareness of the legal duty at issue. 496 US at 203.

The Court offered,

> Thus, Cheek simply states that a good faith belief of legality, no matter how unreasonable, negates the statutory element of willfulness for tax evasion and failure to file a return, and that a jury must be allowed to consider evidence of such a belief. Id. [emphasis added]

In this regard, the significance of the jury instructions, for the tainted perspective they represent, is worth highlighting. Prior to deliberations, the Court instructed the jury that

17

> You may consider, however, the unreasonableness of the defendent's views in determining whether the defendant actually held those views, or, instead was in disagreement with a known legal duty. (Exhibit A, 579) [emphasis added]

By instructing the jury to consider "the unreasonableness of the defendant's views" the Court usurped the mandate in Cheek, which was accepted by this circuit in Snyder. Counsel did not object that the sentiment in Snyder of "no matter how unreasonable," was negated and the jury was allowed within the same thought to consider a "disagreement with known legal duty," which, if anything, marginalized his genuine good faith understanding, "no matter how unreasonable." But for counsel's neglect, the reasonableness of Petitioner's belief was NOT to be considered. Moreover, defense counsel, then, not only did not effectively argue the element of willfulness, their failure led to the introduction of extremely prejudicial jury instructions. The prejudice arising from this instruction was magnified when Cargill declared to the jury that Petitioner's belief was "crazy." (Decl. 91) Ironically, the Court further instructed the jury that

> In considering the defendants good faith belief misunderstanding of the law, you must make your decision on what the defendant actually believed... (Exhibit A, 596) [emphasis added]

However, how could the jury properly consider that which was not presented to them - Petitioner's "understanding" - not his "misunderstanding"? The truth remains that the jury never learned what Petitioner "actually believed" and the earnestness of that belief.

The Cheek Court underscored the importance of willfulness, stating,

> It would of course be proper to exclude evidence having no relevance or probative value with respect to willfulness, but it is not contrary to

18

common sense, let alone impossible, for a defendant to be ignorant of his duty based on an irrational belief that he had no duty, and forbidding the jury to consider evidence that might negate willfulness would raise a serious question under the Sixth Amendment's jury trial provision. Cheek, 203 [emphasis added]

Thus, had counsel argued what they considered to be Petitioner's "irrational belief," the jury, with reasonable probability, would have dismissed the conclusion that Petitioner had a "disagreement with a known legal duty." This thought is consistent with United States v Jordan, 112 F 3d 14, 17 (1st Cir. 1997), in which the Court, referring to Cheek, states "a defendant is entitled to present his subjective belief that he did not violate the law, even if his belief is objectively unreasonable." [emphasis added]

Counsel's failure to argue all the facts denied the Government's case any meaningful adversarial testing based upon what Petitioner understood to be reasonable and lawful. One may conclude, then, that the jurors never learned what was Petitioner's possible understanding (not misunderstanding), whether reasonable or not. The Court in United States v Pensyl, 387 F 2d 459 (6th Cir. 2004), referring to Cheek, stated,

> Actions taken in good faith cannot be willful. Therefore, if a person honestly, but incorrectly believes that they are not obliged to pay income taxes, they are not guilty...because the willfulness element is not present. [emphasis added]

In the instant case, Petitioner suffered a double blow. First, counsel failed to argue his reasonable belief, while offering what was not, which was portrayed and presumed as unreasonable. Second, the jury understood defense counsel's argument that Petitioner had a tax liability, which, coupled with jury instructions that were incongruent with Cheek, negated reasonable doubt and "transformed factual judgments into legal judgments." Id. In essence, the

19

presumption against Petitioner was no longer rebuttable but "conclusive," akin to a "rule of substantive law," Crimes-Presumptions-Validity supra. An irrefutable or conclusive presumption has grave implications, as stated in Sandstrom v Montana, 442 US 510, 517 (1979).

> Given the common definition of "presume" as "to suppose to be true without proof," Webster's New Collegiate Dictionary 911 (1974), and given the lack of qualifying instructions as to the legal effect of the presumption, we cannot discount the possibility that the jury may have interpreted the instruction in either of two more stringent ways.
>
> First, a reasonable jury could well have interpreted the presumption as "conclusive," that is not technically as a presumption at all, but rather as an irrebuttable direction by the Court to find intent once convinced of the facts triggering the presumption. Alternatively, the jury may have interpreted the instruction as a direction to find intent upon proof of the defendant's voluntary actions (and their "ordinary" consequences), unless the defendant proved the contrary by some quantum of proof which may well have been considerably greater than "some" evidence - thus effectively shifting the burden of persuasion on the element of intent. Numerous federal and state courts have warned that instructions of the type given here can be interpreted in just these ways.

But for counsel's ineffectiveness, the jury was precluded from not only understanding what was reasonable but they were led to believe that that which was tendered was unreasonable. Moreover, the jury was invited to connect "an unreasonable belief" to their determination "whether the defendant actually held those views." (Exhibit A, 579) Ultimately, then, the jury was permitted to disqualify a man's belief with an unqualified standard of reasonableness.

Ultimately, we are contending with presumptions.. Petitioner contends that he rebutted any presumption that he was liable for "federal income" or "federal

20

employment" taxes. Yet, federal agents presumed Petitioner was a "taxpayer" and neglected to answer his one question, presuming it to be "frivolous." The DOJ presumed it had jurisdiction to prosecute, never reconciling Petitioner's good faith letters to clarify his presumptive liability and DOJ and IRS presumptive authority. When the matter came before the Court, Petitioner challenged presumed jurisdiction. Meanwhile, defense counsel presumed Petitioner to be the same as the Government's presumption. Incredibly, when Petitioner asked counsel to argue his reasonable good faith belief, they refused, based upon the presumption that it was "frivolous." The Court presumed jurisdiction and the jury rendered a guilty verdict, presuming the Government's presumption was unrebuttable. When the jury understood defense counsel's argument that Petitioner had a tax liability, coupled with one-sided jury instructions, which served to eradicate any reasonable doubt, the presumption became irrefutable.

Since counsel did not argue their client's belief, Petitioner could not prove "the contrary by some quantum of proof." Id. This was especially true given the Court's three sequential interruptions during Petitioner's testimony, when he was asked the first substantive question by counsel concerning his belief. (Decl. 79-82) Counsel's failure to object, most notably after the third interruption, when the Court asked Petitioner "...why do you believe the tax laws do not apply to you, if they apply to others?" (Exhibit A, 507) was neglectful. Thus, given all the circumstances, there was only one conclusive inference the jury could make, akin to the influence of a "rule of substantive law." For, absent "quantum proof," the jury was convinced of what was actually rebuttable.

The Court, in Wong v Belmontes, supra, said the defendant must

> ...establish "a reasonable probability that a competent attorney, aware of [the available mitigating evidence], would have introduced it..." and "that had the jury been confronted with this mitigating evidence, there is a reasonable probability that it would have returned with a different sentence."

21

Since counsel never offered the jury the mitigating evidence, it would be advantageous to consider an alternative to their "strategy." As opposed to aligning with the Government's theme that Petitioner had a tax liability, had they exercised for their client's "strategic benefit" that, based upon his concrete rebuttal and settled law of the Supreme Court, he had no liability as defined in the statutes, the jurors would have considered that Petitioner knowingly did what he believed was reasonable, even if unreasonable to them.

The Court stated in THE MATTER OF SAMUEL WINSHIP, 397 US 358, 364 (1970) "There is always in litigation a margin of error..." and that "the reasonable doubt standard is indispensable..." Why? This standard "impresses upon the trier of the fact the necessity of reaching a subjective state of certitude on the facts at issue." Id. Since counsel failed to introduce all the evidence, they did not reduce the "margin of error" in fact finding. They sought only to have the jury entertain the unbelievable contentions that whatever their client believed was "crazy." (Decl. 91) Counsel reinforced the Government's presumption, which allowed the jury to infer that Petitioner was willful in committing the crime. As such, the path to conviction was achieved with agreement and ease between adversarial parties, which made reasonable doubt all the more weaker and Petitioner appear all the more willful. Considering all the circumstances, Petitioner had ineffective assistance of counsel who willfully failed to argue the precise question at issue. Chevron supra.

When the "defense" is viewed from the macro perspective, with counsel's initial dismissal of Petitioner's good faith belief, the entire process was effectively altered. Counsel imposed their trite defense. Their approach was flawed and certainly not the truth. Without effective assistance of counsel, which would include a purposeful attempt to defeat the element of willfulness, Petitioner contended with the insurmountable. As stated in Cronic, 657 supra,

While a criminal trial is not a game in which the participants are expected to enter the ring with a near match in skills, neither is it a sacrifice of unarmed prisoners to gladiators.

Clearly, if counsel had argued all the facts related to Petitioner's belief, the Government would not have proved that Petitioner acted with the necessary knowledge and intent to render his conduct unlawful. More importantly, if defense counsel had argued effectively, the Government would have, at least, contended with an adversarial testing based upon what Petitioner reasonably believed to be lawful. Consequently, counsel's failure to effectively advocate against willfulness improperly led the jury to convict Petitioner. Counsel's ineffectiveness cannot be reconciled with the standards of professional representation required in Strickland.

APPENDIX C – FEDERAL QUESTION #1

UNITED STATES DISTRICT COURT

WESTERN DISTRICT OF VIRGINIA

James Bowers Johnson
Petitioner,

v.

UNITED STATES OF AMERICA
DEPARTMENT OF JUSTICE
DEPARTMENT OF THE TREASURY
DEPARTMENT OF INTERNAL REVENUE
INTERNAL REVENUE SERVICE
Respondents.

CIVIL ACTION: 7:15-CV-00076
FEDERAL QUESTION

FEDERAL QUESTION

COMES NOW, petitioner, James Bowers Johnson, who, pursuant to 28 USC (1331) and Rule 5.1 of the Federal Rules of Civil Procedures, in light of equitable claims and rights, asks a federal inquiry under the Constitution, 5 USC 3331, 26 USC 7214 and 28 USC 1361, to wit:

> When a private citizen writes an Internal Revenue Agent and an Internal Revenue Service Agent with a specific question as to the law that requires that citizen's performance under the tax code or the agents' authority to make a request of that citizen, and the agents fail or refuse to respond with the legal authority which compels that citizen's performance or validates the agents' actions, how are the agents in violation of their oath of office and 26 USC 7214 and, therefore, how would the agents and agencies be obligated to perform a duty owed under 28 USC 1361?

PARTIES

The parties to this action are:

Petitioner
James Bowers Johnson, 16665-084
Federal Satellite Low, Elkton
P.O. Box 10
Lisbon, Ohio 44432

Respondents
UNITED STATES OF AMERICA
c/o U.S. ATTORNEY GENERAL
DEPARTMENT OF JUSTICE
950 Pennsylvania Ave N.W.
Washington, D.C. 20530

and

DEPARTMENT OF THE TREASURY
1500 Pennsylvania Ave N.W.
Washington, D.C. 20220

and

DEPARTMENT OF INTERNAL REVENUE
1111 Constitution Ave N.W.
Washington, D.C. 20224

and

INTERNAL REVENUE SERVICE
1111 Constitution Ave N.W.
Washington, D.C. 20224

MEMORANDUM IN SUPPORT

LIMITATION OF AUTHORITY

If an agent of the Federal Government exercises authority that is ultra vires (See Chevron U.S.A. Inc. v Natural Resources Defense Council 467 US 387 (1984), City of Arlington, Texas v FCC _ US _ (2013), Auer v Robbins 519 US 452 (1997)) and a citizen asks, under the blanket of the Constitution, the Oath of Office and applicable statutes and regulations for the source of the agent's authority and the corresponding requirement for that citizen's performance, the citizen's question serves as the essential element and the predicate act to obviate the risk of agency indiscretion. If an agent either unknowingly or deliberately fails to provide a cogent, complete and professional response to a fundamental inquiry, a citizen effectively has no recourse with any ensuing government action.

2

The Supreme Court stated that

> ...anyone entering into an arrangement with the Government takes the risk of having accurately ascertained that he who purports to act for the Government stays within the bounds of his authority. The scope of this authority may be explicitly defined by Congress or be limited by delegated legislation, properly exercised through the rule-making power. And this is so... even though the agent himself may be unaware of the limitations upon his authority. Federal Crop Ins Corp v Merrill 332 US 380, 384 (1974)

NEGLIGENCE

An agent's ultra vires act may be a result of negligence or "negligent misrepresentation." (See United States v Neustadt 366 US 696 (1961)) While "negligence" is not specifically defined by the courts (See Jamison v Encarnacion 281 US 635 (1930)) the term has sweeping implications. The court acknowledged that "liability arises when one suffers injury as a result of any breach of duty owed..." Id. 641 In Laird v Nelms 406 US 797 (1972), the court noted that a "duty involves exercising a reasonable care in one's activities or refraining from certain activities altogether." Id., 804 The court cited that one may not be at fault for an act of commission or omission and, therefore, not negligent. However, the court also said that "one who engages in it should make good any harm caused..." Id., 805

Yet, the duty to respond to a written inquiry increases the possibility of an agent being negligent. Inarguably, the mere presence of a citizen's question and the inherent immediacy for a response heightens the sensitivity to satisfy a duty owed and to do so with pointed resolution. Anything less would be negligence however artfully parsed in the legal arena. For the Supreme Court in Neustadt supra, referring to the Fourth Circuit, distinguished "negligent misrepresentation" and cited under footnote 16 The American Law Institute's "Restatement of Torts" (1938), Topic 3, "Negligent Misrepre-

3

sentation." occurs when one

> fails to exercise that care and competence in obtaining and communicating the information which its recipient is justified in expecting.

The court also cited Prosser, "Torts" (1941 ed) c 16, "Misrepresentation," § 87 "Basis of Responsibility," which states that "misrepresentation" is classified as "Negligence in obtaining information or in making the representation."

ACCOUNTABILITY

According to the Internal Revenue Manual, the agency states

> Our system is dependent on taxpayers' belief that the tax laws apply to everyone and the the IRS will respect and protect their rights under the law. These are fundamental principles of voluntary compliance. (Part 5, Collection Activity, 105.4.1.2, 7/27/98) [emphasis added]

Since the tax code deals exclusively with excises (indirect taxes) and given that a citizen's good faith belief is that he may not be liable to a specific excise, the IRS may only respect and protect his "rights under the law" with accountability. Agents are guided by principles that require a duty to the law and the public trust. Under their oath of office, agents are beholden with a fiduciary responsibility to the end that they will not willfully oppress under color of law, fail to perform any of the duties of their office or demand, either directly or indirectly, that which is not expressly authorized by law. (See 26 USC 7214) The agents must conduct themselves to the end that they do not recklessly or intentionally, or by reason of negligence, disregard any provision of the tax code. (See 26 USC 7433)

FULL DISCLOSURE

Any agent who receives a written communication from a private citizen has an inherent relation with that citizen and a responsibility in good faith to provide full disclosure, especially if that citizen is the subject of an investigation. There exists an expectation that the agents will not do some act or fail to do some act. The agents are to afford a citizen with transparency, honesty and fidelity.

> Every person who has business dealings with another has the right to expect that he will do whatever good reason and good conscience require. Indeed, each party... impliedly contracts... that, in making and performing his engagements, honesty, frankness and fidelity will characterize his conduct. Henry R. Gibson, Suits in Chancery, 2nd Ed. (1907), § 932

Footnote 1 appropriately states

> The law requires good faith in all transactions between man and man. Bad faith is treason to mankind, and if generally practiced would destroy human society. Id.

In the relations between men, it is implied that:

1) Neither party will make to the other any material representations concerning the subject matter... that are not true.

2) Neither party will conceal from the other anything, within his knowledge, material to the subject matter... that the other party ought to know, and cannot easily discern for himself.

3) Neither party has done, nor will do anything to hinder, delay or defeat a faithful compliance... on his part.

4) If one of the parties has trust or confidence specially reposed in him by the other, or has special power or influence over the person or property of the other, he will not avail himself of these advantages to the other's detriment. Id

<u>IGNORANCE</u>

The Supreme Court acknowledged that an agent may be "unaware of the limitations of his own authority." <u>Merrill</u> supra Yet, the fact that the agent receives written correspondence of a citizen's concern would, if anything, encourage the requisite care to prevent decisions and actions that are ultra vires. The agent would be further burdened with the due diligence incumbent with his office and responsibilities under the law. However, whether or not

5

the agent is "unaware of the limitations of his own authority" when equitable rights are involved, his ignorance is immaterial.

> While at law before a misrepresentation can be fraudulent, it must be made with a guilty knowledge of its falsity, in Equity such knowledge is not necessary. A person making an untrue statement, without knowing or believing it to be untrue, and without any intent to deceive, may be chargeable with actual fraud in Equity. Gibson supra 884

An agent who knowingly or unknowingly asserts or enforces a presumption or fact that is not true, especially when a citizen seeks the nature of the agent's authority or the law that compels a citizen's specific performance, the very merit of the agent's oath of office or statutes and regulations that stipulate his responsibilities and conduct are suspect.

FRAUD

Failure of an agent to ethically satisfy his professional obligations creates and is fraud.

> Fraud, in the sense of a court of equity, properly includes all acts, omissions and concealments, which involve a breach of legal or ethical duty, or of trust or confidence justly reposed, and which are injurious to another, or by which an undue advantage is taken of another. Id., 933

> Actual fraud is the intentional doing or saying of something, or the intentional concealment of something... Id

> All frauds grow out of relations, and are those violations of the duties arising from relations caused by bad faith. Id., 934

Moreover,

> Constructive frauds are acts, statements or omissions, which operate as virtual frauds on individuals or which, if generally permitted, would be prejudicial to the public welfare... Id

FEDERAL QUESTION

This Federal Question is necessary to clarify how an agent and agency are fraudulent or negligent. As with any foundation, be it for a building or the construct and execution of a legal act, the cornerstone must be laid so

6

that it is plumb and true. The legal basis of an agent's action that is askew from all accountability frustrates a citizen's attempt to ascertain the "bounds" of agency indiscretion, which, naturally, jeopardizes all associated equitable claims and rights.

CONCLUSION

Based upon the foregoing Memorandum, in light of equitable claims and rights, may this court clarify how an agent, as stated in the Federal Question, is in violation of the Constitution, Oath of Office, 26 USC 7214 and, therefore, how they would be obligated to perform a duty owed.

WHEREFORE, for the reasons stated herein, petitioner moves this court to decide accordingly.

Respectfully submitted, original signed

James B. Johnson
Petitioner, Pro per

7

APPENDIX D – TRIAL TRANSCRIPTS, EQUITY

(9:56 a.m., January 2, 2013)

P R O C E E D I N G S:

THE CLERK: United States of America v. James Bowers Johnson, Case Number 6:12-cr-15, Defendant Number 1.

THE COURT: Government ready?

MR. HOGEBOOM: We are, Your Honor.

THE COURT: Defendant ready?

Are you ready, Mr. Johnson?

MR. JOHNSON: Yes, sir.

THE COURT: All right. We're here on the government's motion. You may proceed, Mr. Hogeboom.

MR. HOGEBOOM: Thank you, Your Honor.

Just as a first task, I want the Court to be aware that we filed a motion in limine with the Court to exclude certain exhibits and limit certain testimony. That was filed electronically. I produced a hard copy to both standby counsel and the defendant.

Your Honor, as I prepared for this hearing, I went back and reviewed some of the prior transcripts of some of the jailhouse conversations that were recorded that were provided to the government, and what has struck me through this all is that the defendant does not have a clue as to what type of proceeding that he's -- it's -- he's involved with here.

In one of the earlier comments on May 3rd, 2012, after being arrested, he told Judge Welsh, basically, that all crimes are commercial in nature and that he wanted Judge Welsh to note -- "Note for the record, sir, that your obligation for a taxable termination." He was able to hold it enough together that the Court saw fit to set conditions down, place him on bond, a bond secured by his mother's home, but one of the restrictions was not to file anything else with the court and not to be sending this stuff off.

And what he did was, he took on a -- began almost like a fiscal terrorist campaign. In July he sends a hundred-billion-dollar offset bond to the United States Treasury on his behalf, and that bond number is the same one that he's been using sending 1099s to the Court and various other peoples on behalf of this trust.

The U.S. Attorney, the agent, my office, in December 8th of this year we received a notice that the defendant had sent to the Treasury a -- kind of like a notice that we were not in compliance, that somehow he had given us $600 million on an informational referral and that it was unreported income and we had failed to pay tax on it.

And then when he comes into court with Judge Crigler and with yourself, he begins this whole thing, arguing that the crime's commercial in nature and can be offset, which is the same position which he held back in April or May.

I also looked at and found a case in the Eastern Division of the Northern District of Illinois, Cherron Phillips, Docket Number 12-cr-872. An order was entered in that particular case on December 3rd, 2012, by a Judge Shadur from that court.

The case -- the facts are similar. Ms. Phillips had been charged with 18 U.S.C. 1523 [sic], attempting to cloud titles of certain law enforcement officials and others. While on bond she had similar restrictions, and she sent a UCC financing statement and other financial documents to the Court.

And what the Court argued, the Court had said, as this Court has, it orally reflected its concerns as to whether the nature of Phillips' filings and her in-court conduct have indicated that she may be suffering from a mental defect -- not a mental disease -- a mental defect that could render her mentally incompetent in the sense specified in 18 U.S.C. 4241(a), the inability to understand the nature and consequences of the proceedings in this case or to assist properly in her defense.

And I think that's what we're drilled down to, that particular concern. We have a pro se defendant here who doesn't seem to have any grasp of criminal law. He told the Court he could read and write and comprehend, yet he also informed Judge Crigler that he had not read the conditions of his release, which I would think would be very much of an important thing to read given the fact that your mother's home is the basis for the bond.

The other concern that we obviously have here is that he has standby counsel. He's used standby counsel from time to time. But the information that he's attempted to put before the Court is not evidence, as the Court has acknowledged, and I don't think he quite understands that these views he has about everything being commercial and that he can offset it with a 1099 and everything else, that is fiction.

That has nothing to do with the world of criminal law that he's about to face where he's going to have 12 people sitting there and the facts are going to be either did he file his tax returns, which he is required to do, did he willfully fail to file, or did he take actions to impede and impair the IRS.

And in our motion we put down the fact that these beliefs only go to the issue of willfulness but can be offset by such things as willful blindness. And these are not real complicated issues, but they're issues that a seasoned practitioner deals with all the time and knows how to handle these.

I talked to a colleague in Oklahoma who had a similar case last September, and they said one of the problems that they had with a pro se defendant is keeping him focused on what he could and could not do.

And I think the -- my worst fear is -- and I've had it happen in a case several years ago down in Norfolk where the defendant went pro se, had standby counsel. About halfway through trial he saw that the ship had left the dock and was sinking quite quickly and then wanted his pro se counsel to take over.

And the concern I have here is with all these filings, with these issues that have been raised about whether he understands it, if he is convicted, the jury finds him guilty, then all of a sudden his standby counsel who's now representing him should have known that he's -- he didn't understand what he was facing.

And so I think just out of a -- just on the safe side of this, that it would be -- to have him evaluated. We've listed cases where they've had people who have had similar views on the government and everything else, but they've been determined not to be incompetent. But at least the study was done to ascertain, do they really understand? Can they really comprehend and assist with their defense?

I know Mr. Cargill and I had one individual who

was found to be incompetent at the time of the offense, but after the evaluation by the Bureau of Prisons it was ascertained that he was competent to assist in his trial, which he ended up pleading guilty to the charges and getting time served. But at the time that we first dealt with him, he truly did have some concerns.

And that's the concern -- it's difficult to articulate, because if you look at Mr. Johnson, he appears to be competent. He's not as we see from time to time, but this -- he's been doing this tax avoidance, tax evasion scheme since at least 1999 with these antigovernment things.

He dealt with an organization early on, Save the Patriots, by Mr. Kotmair who spent time in prison for selling a program. That didn't dissuade him. Mr. Johnson then went to this warehouse bank in Arkansas to conceal his assets. Those individuals are now serving prison time. And there's others that he has relied upon that at some thing -- at some point I think a competent, sane person would say, "There's, if not a red light, there's at least a caution light here that maybe these views I have, they're just not based in reality. They may be something we can discuss on blogs or we can get up on Skype and talk with" --

THE COURT: Well, are you suggesting, though,

that we would send the defendant to Butner or somewhere and they would cure him of his thoughts and beliefs?

MR. HOGEBOOM: I'm not -- I don't think that, and that's not the concern, that they cure him of these thoughts and beliefs.

THE COURT: I mean, if he comes back, he'll still have --

MR. HOGEBOOM: My concern is, does he understand -- does he really and truly understand the nature of these proceedings, and that's what -- when he comes into court and sends in a 1099 for $600 million and then expects to walk in and walk out because the Court dismisses an indictment by a federal grand jury, that's a little bit, you know, beyond what I normally have seen in these types of cases.

I've done these for -- with these types of views for years, and even on the most hardened, they have at some point, maybe not changed their views totally, but have focused down in trying to prepare for trial. But I mean, it's not the typical situation that we see in these, and I just, out of, you know, an abundance of caution, felt that we needed to bring it to the Court because I'm concerned that more filings are going to occur until he hits the right -- until he believes he hits the right formula to turn everything into commercial and that he's now -- the Court recognizes he's not James Johnson, defendant, but he's James Johnson the trust, you know, using that name who has a hundred billion dollars waiting for him in treasury that he can offset his accounts with.

Thank you, Your Honor.

THE COURT: All right. Mr. Johnson.

MR. JOHNSON: Good morning, Judge Moon. I'm under the impression and understanding that this is a hearing with respect to the government's motion for consideration of a mental competency exam; is that correct?

THE COURT: Yes.

MR. JOHNSON: Okay. I'm concluding that you want my response to Mr. Hogeboom's comments at this point.

THE COURT: Well, yes. He filed a motion, and respond to the motion, why you believe the government -- I mean, if you want to agree to it, that makes it easy. If you disagree, then, you know, you should state why you disagree.

MR. JOHNSON: I came to this hearing today, obviously, very much against my will as I went through the probable cause and preliminary hearing with respect to the filings that were considered to be extraneous and obstructive, et cetera, irrelevant, and I encourage the Court and Mr. Hogeboom to seek legal and tax advice if, in fact, that was deemed appropriate for --

THE COURT: I'm sorry. I didn't --

MR. JOHNSON: I encourage Mr. Hogeboom and the Court to seek legal and tax advice if there was any question about those documents.

So I stand here today looking at a word on my paper here as I was taking notes listening to, again, the diatribe from Mr. Hogeboom as far as the hyperbole, looking at a "fiscal terrorist campaign," and I'm questioning his motivation. Is he looking after my best interest, does he want me to lay down and have Mr. Cargill be in my stead so that I don't harm myself, or is there some other motivation? I don't seem to understand.

If, in fact, 27 CFR 72.11 --

THE COURT: That's irrelevant. I don't pay any attention to that.

MR. JOHNSON: You don't pay attention to what, sir?

THE COURT: To the hyperbole. I mean --

MR. JOHNSON: Yeah. And that's my point. I don't either. And so I stand here and I say, I'm not McVeigh, I'm not Nichols, and I'm not the right-wing zealot with a cache of arms that Mr. Pompei was telling my neighbors and friends. I'm not that person.

I've been studying for some 15 to 20 years looking for the truth, and I stand here today not filing the documents that were received by this Court but understanding what they were and by whom. And so do I need to be subjected to a mental exam? Quite frankly, no. I wouldn't even dignify the suggestion. But I would consider, maybe, what is Mr. Johnson's motivation.

I have in my hand -- actually, on the desk over there -- a bill in equity that I sent to the Court. I don't know if you've received it yet, but I understand enough about the proceedings to know that the in-law, the procedure --

THE COURT: Mr. Johnson, address me. I don't -- I mean, it's not proper -- don't address Mr. Hogeboom.

MR. JOHNSON: I'm sorry. I was just making eye contact to dignify the roles in this courtroom. That's all I was trying to do, sir.

THE COURT: Okay.

MR. JOHNSON: There is a bill in equity, a petition for suit that I sent to Judge Conrad and to this Court -- and if you haven't received it yet, I have one copy that you can make copies of -- with the intention to seek a suit, a countersuit, for lack of a better word, in equity, and just hopefully put a rest to what's going on here and add some bounds to it.

Is there a need for a mental competency exam?

No, sir, there is not.

THE COURT: All right. We went through this before whether -- and I went through all these questions. I don't see anything different today than I saw the last time I ruled on this. I mean, have you discussed anything with your standby counsel?

MR. JOHNSON: No, sir. Very little. I mean, I've used them occasionally for the proceeding I was in because I flew in blind. I did not know why I was where I was and what was getting on, and so Andrea, Ms. Harris, answered a couple questions for me, and Mr. Cargill met with me a couple minutes before this hearing.

THE COURT: Okay.

MR. JOHNSON: So, I mean, I think there's some strident expectations on behalf of the government, and I can see why. I mean, he eats and lives and breathes this stuff, and this is his profession, and I give him his due. And this is not my venue, but I also know that coming into this I might look at it a bit differently.

And I realize you might have your protocol, which is simply why I filed this bill in equity, because as far as I understand, equity provides a search of the conscience of a man as opposed to the form and seeks the substance --

THE COURT: Well, but that -- I'll tell you

that that's not relevant to the case before the Court. That will not be relevant in this case. And the question before the Court is, are you going to be able to follow the rulings of the Court? I decide the law. You can put on any evidence you like, but I decide the law, and you have to obey my rulings.

And if you disagree with them, then you can appeal them to the Fourth Circuit. Should you be convicted, you can appeal my rulings to the Fourth Circuit, but you will not be permitted -- you'll be permitted to make your argument to me about the law out of the presence of the jury, but you will not be permitted to argue the law to the jury or to question what I say the law is before the jury.

And the big issue, as far as I'm concerned, are you going to be able to follow the rules of court which you are bound to? We're playing -- you know, you may disagree with the authority of the Court, but, nevertheless, that's where you are, and at this point, you know, you're playing in this ballpark, and you have to play under these rules if you're going to represent yourself.

And, you know, if you don't agree with what I rule, then there's a proper procedure to appeal it to the Fourth Circuit. And that's my question, is will you follow the rulings of the Court?

MR. JOHNSON: You said -- I'd like to answer your question by answering it this way, and that would be by asking a question. You said that the bill in equity or the countersuit is irrelevant. Is it irrelevant? Is a suit against --

THE COURT: It is irrelevant to this case. Now, if you want to bring a suit somewhere else, you know, if you've got a case, a civil case, which that would be, you can bring that, do a proper filing of a complaint against whomever you wish, but it's not going to be tried in this case.

This case is whether you -- it's what's charged in the indictment concerning whether you failed to file tax returns when you were supposed to and whether you endeavored to obstruct, impede, or impair the due administration of the Internal Revenue Code, and that's all this case is about. So come, you know, for the trial, they're the issues.

The government is going to have to prove beyond a reasonable doubt that you didn't -- you were supposed to file tax -- under the United States law, you were supposed to file tax returns and you did not, you willfully did not, and that you -- that with regard to Count I, that you willfully endeavored to impede or obstruct the enforcement of the Tax Code as set forth in Count I. And the proper defense is, you didn't do those things. I mean, that's -- that's what will be relevant at that trial.

MR. JOHNSON: Well, I do know --

THE COURT: You will not be permitted to tell the jury you disagree with the law. And that's the question I have about whether you should continue to represent yourself, is whether you will adhere to those rules. And if you don't like the rulings, that's perfectly all right, but you still -- in this court you'll have to adhere to those rules, and then you can do an appeal of right to the Fourth Circuit as to any ruling I should make.

MR. JOHNSON: Judge Moon, let the record show that I withdraw nunc pro tunc my actions and signature as defendant deposited generally, done so under threat, coercion, and duress, and I redeposit the same for an exact return upon demand.

I am here by special appearance as the grantor and beneficiary of the express trust demanding a disposition for this case, and I'm appointing you as trustee for the express trust, 6:12-cr-0015 Trust, with the obligation of specific performance to provide the disposition. Are you prepared to provide the disposition, which is the exact paperwork that I sent on behalf of CHTE Financial, which has --

THE COURT: I stand by the remarks that I've

United States of America v. James Bowers Johnson

Case No. 6:12-cr-00015

January 2, 2013

Page 17

earlier made.

MR. JOHNSON: Yes, sir.

THE COURT: I've told you what the issues in this case are. That is -- what you there raise has nothing to do with this case.

MR. JOHNSON: Let the record show that Mr. Heaphy, Mr. Hogeboom, Mr. Pompei, and Judge Moon are fired at trustees and CHTE Financial is appointed as trustee, culminating in a merger of equities collapsing the express trust.

I would like and I demand the return of the original securities. There's a CUSIP number on this case. There are securities being traded, and I'd like the Court to take judicial notice of the fact that this court case is a trust and there are securities being traded.

The IRS, the Department of Internal Revenue, Renee Mitchell has the appropriate paperwork to provide the disposition and a ledger-to-ledger setoff for CHTE Financial, which is a private trust, and even the Internal Revenue cannot trespass against that trust, sir, without written authorization.

And I ask you again, are you prepared to provide the disposition and order to discharge?

THE COURT: And I'm telling you again, you're charged with two counts. One is that you attempted to

(fax) (434) 975-5400 Cavalier Reporting & Videography (direct) 434.293.3300
www.cavalier-reporting.com production@cavalier-reporting.com

-73-

impede the revenue -- the enforcement of the Revenue Code, and the other is that on -- counts are that you failed to properly file.

The matter you raise has nothing to do with those issues, and you, sir, are the defendant. And if the government's wrong, if the government can't prove that you did the things you supposedly are charged with, then it will be the duty of the jury to acquit you. On the other hand, if they prove beyond a reasonable doubt that you did do those things, it will be the duty of the jury to find you guilty.

And the matters you raise, they are extraneous to these issue, and I will have nothing to do with those issues whatsoever.

MR. JOHNSON: I'm wondering, Judge Moon, if you would be willing to have an in camera review with me and Mr. Hogeboom.

THE COURT: In camera with regard to what?

MR. JOHNSON: With regard to these issues.

THE COURT: Well, what -- what do you mean? Why would there be an in camera review? I mean, are there secrets?

MR. JOHNSON: I would -- it would be my intention to speak privately with you and Mr. Hogeboom to discuss some facts that I would prefer not to keep in public. I know that, for example, there might be some application of 18 U.S.C. 479 that talks about the fact that securities aren't necessarily discussed. It would just give me an opportunity to discuss something in private and off the record. If that's not possible, then perhaps approaching the bench.

But my understanding is that the expressed trust in this case, which has been expressed by the grantor, is the operative law in this case. It grants -- it identifies the manifest intent of the grantor with the superior claim over the securities and over this case, which has been received by this Court with a settlement instrument number seeking for the disposition in this case.

And that's -- that is the -- that is the intention, is to settle this thing privately. It is feasible for this to be done by the Internal Revenue or by the opposition. All they have to do is to understand the full import of what was received and to look at this and say, "We can dignify the mistake."

Because my -- I -- the tax returns have been filed. Ever since '99 all of them have been filed in performance of a statement in lieu of return. So mistakes are correctable, and the paperwork does actually provide the opportunity for a remedy that makes this issue go away, and it restores the government in whole for any loss they believe they're suffering financially.

And so that's why I seek to approach you in camera and to discuss this matter with Mr. Hogeboom.

THE COURT: Well, there's no way the Court can have an off-the-record meeting with a party to the case. It's just not -- that's not possible. And it doesn't appear that the matter you raise has anything to do with the case at hand. So if the government -- you know, you can negotiate with the government but not with me.

I don't have any -- I don't have any place in settlement of these cases between the taxpayer and the government. That's not the way the rules are. The case is brought to me. I preside at the trial. And if the government can't prove its case, that's -- you know, that will be the end of it.

And there are always ways -- may be ways to settle matters, but not -- it's up to the United States Attorney regarding whether to bring criminal charges or not, and they've chosen to do so in this case. And my function is to determine whether they prove the case, put on enough evidence for a reasonable jury to find you guilty or not guilty. If they do not, then I should dismiss the case. If they do, then it will go to the jury.

MR. JOHNSON: I mentioned the last time we met, Judge Moon, about the lack of flexibility and the rigid nature of this whole process. I mentioned, and I know that there hasn't been a conversation beyond this, that the system doesn't listen ever since my appeals and letters from 2004 through the current have gone unresponsive and unanswered.

The reason I say that is because I have a 9-year-old son and a 7-year-old daughter that have been without their father for some time and may be without their father for some time, and I find it unacceptable and intolerable that the opposition would never, from the very beginning, sit down and answer some simple, dignified questions about the nature of the tax system.

I'm not a party to any group or affiliation. I don't have a cache of weapons. I'm not some right-wing zealot. And, frankly, with all due candor to the opposition, Mr. Snipes made mistakes. I don't believe that the paperwork that's been received by the opposition reflects mistakes but a genuine intent to deal with Renee Mitchell to have her provide the setoff, settlement, and discharge of this matter, because there is a priority claim over the estate and the trust and this court case.

And I would ask for a final third time if you're prepared to provide the disposition, because, quite honestly, my understanding is that people's bonds are at stake here, that there could be a claim against people's bonds while in office looking at these issues.

I am genuinely seeking a resolution, which is why I sought the in camera -- which surprises me that you can't even do the "approach the bench" or in camera.

THE COURT: Well, this is a public trial, and the public has a right to it. And I don't know -- unless there's something of a -- some sort of obscene nature or something like that that it shouldn't be seen by the public, I don't -- there's just no way for the Court and the United States to conduct these trials in camera.

MR. JOHNSON: Do not attorneys and pro se litigants approach the bench often?

THE COURT: They do because it's inappropriate for the jury to hear what they're talking about. There's no jury here now. Everyone in the courtroom is an officer of the court. There's not even a spectator. Every person in the courtroom, as I observe now, are people who are on the payroll, and they're performing their legitimate function. And there's no way I could talk to you without the court reporter taking down what is being said.

MR. JOHNSON: Well, I guess in summation, then, my understanding is, is that the -- and I would ask you, do you take judicial notice of the fact that this case is in some form or fashion a trust and that there are securities involved in this case?

THE COURT: Well, the jury will be summonsed to try this case unless you waive the jury.

MR. JOHNSON: Sir, I'm asking you, do you take judicial notice of the fact that this court case is a trust and there are securities involved in this case?

THE COURT: I don't even understand what you're talking about, and I do not take judicial notice.

MR. JOHNSON: Okay. So --

THE COURT: Look, what it's about, this case, it's not against a trust. It's against you personally. Now, you know, if they prove -- don't prove that you violated the law but that John Doe did, then you go free. But the government -- a grand jury has indicted you. They found probable cause that the crimes alleged in the indictment took place and that you committed those crimes. Now, that's what will go before the jury, so ...

Anything else?

MR. JOHNSON: No, sir. I'd just like the record to reflect the fact that my understanding is that this is an implied constructive trust of some form, that this case has securities that's traded in it, and that every attempt has been made by private means through the IRS, ironically enough, to have them set offset on discharge, and if need be, my one petition would be that the Court would grant leave of this entire proceeding to have the IRS actually provide that disposition, because my understanding is they will.

I am incarcerated with the lack of the ability to petition the IRS -- and I believe it's under 15 U.S.C. 1692 -- to provide the verified assessment. If they are, in fact, a bookkeeping agency that has the ultimate liability and responsibility to balance the books, then there has been a claim against this case to the tune of $600 million.

And there has been no barter, which is the very nature of the 1099-B, sir, as you probably understand. And the OID shows the difference between the barter and the acquisition, with the C canceling the securities. The securities in this case are canceled, and if you would just grant leave to allow the IRS to do its job, the government would be paid. There's no reason for this case.

And, in fact, my understanding is that the express trust is -- it actually obviates this case. It's the operative law in this case at this point. The grantor's manifest intent is for the Court to provide the disposition and for the government to be made whole, and they have access.

THE COURT: Well, possibly, the situation would fit another -- if it's a civil matter, the law would be that you should have paid your taxes and then filed a case in the tax court, sued in the tax court to recover anything you paid if it was wrongfully assessed. And that's the procedure. It's not for -- this Court doesn't handle matters such as you're bringing up.

It would be a matter, probably, for the tax court. But I'm not here to give you legal advice. I mean, I'm just saying, maybe if you have some claim against the IRS, there's a tax court, but you probably should discuss that with a lawyer.

MR. JOHNSON: I have nothing further. I stand by my comments that I just read into the record. I have nothing further.

THE COURT: Are you going to be prepared for trial on --

What day is it, the 15th?

THE CLERK: (Nodding head up and down.)

THE COURT: On the 15th? Is it the 15th or --

THE CLERK: January 15th.

THE COURT: January 15th. And we'll have the jury here, and we'll proceed with the trial.

MR. JOHNSON: I stand by my comments that I've just entered into the record, sir.

THE COURT: All right. Mr. Cargill, I'm just -- I'm going to ask you, the last time we were here you stated your opinion that the defendant was aware of the

APPENDIX E – FEDERAL QUESTION #2

UNITED STATES DISTRICT COURT
WESTERN DISTRICT OF VIRGINIA

James Bowers Johnson Petitioner, v. UNITED STATES OF AMERICA DEPARTMENT OF JUSTICE DEPARTMENT OF THE TREASURY DEPARTMENT OF INTERNAL REVENUE INTERNAL REVENUE SERVICE Respondents,	)))))))))))	CIVIL ACTION: 7:15-cv-00067 FEDERAL QUESTION

FEDERAL QUESTION

COMES NOW petitioner, James Bowers Johnson, who, pursuant to 28 USC 1331 and Rule 5.1 of the Federal Rules of Civil Procedures, asks this Court of Equity a Federal Question arising under the Constitution, the Sixteenth Amendment and Title 26 of the United States Code, to wit:

> Are the earnings of private citizens subject to excise if they do not subscribe to federal social security benefits or have terminated their acceptance of the same and do not enjoy a federally excisable privilege?

Since Congress may not, "without apportionment, tax as income that which is not income within the 16th Amendment," Helvering v Edison Bros. Stores, 133 F 2d 575 (8th Cir. 1943) (See Eisner v Macomber 252 US 189 (1920), M.E. Blatt Co. v United States 305 US 267 (1938)) the "precise question at issue" Chevron U.S.A., Inc. v Natural Resources Defense Council, Inc. 467 US 837 (1984) is whether the enforcement of the tax code runs "counter to the fundamental law of the land" (16 Am Jur 2d, 177 Sec 256 (1979 ed)) for those who do not accept federally excisable benefits.

PARTIES

The parties to this action are:

Petitioner
James Bowers Johnson, 16665-084
Federal Satellite Low, Elkton
P.O. Box 10
Lisbon,Ohio 44432

Respondents
UNITED STATES OF AMERICA
c/o UNITED STATES ATTORNEY GENERAL
Department of Justice
950 Pennsylvania Ave N.W.
Washington D.C. 20530

and

DEPARTMENT OF THE TREASURY
1500 Pennsylvania Ave N.W.
Washington D.C. 20220

and

DEPARTMENT OF INTERNAL REVENUE
1111 Constitution Ave N.W.
Washington D.C. 20224

and

INTERNAL REVENUE SERVICE
1111 Constitution Ave N.W.
Washington D.C. 20224

FACTS

Tax on Federal Employees

Congress passed the Revenue Act of 1862 "...to provide Internal Revenue to support the Government and to pay interest on the Public Debt." Under this Act, employees of the Federal Government were liable to pay an excise on their salaries.

> ... there shall be levied, collected and paid on all salaries of officers, or payments to persons in the civil, military, naval or other employment of the United States, including senators and representatives and delegates in Congress... Sec 86

The Attorney General of the United States acknowledged the intent to tax "all civil officers except those Congress may not tax." 31 Op. Atty. Gen. 161, 1869

In 1894, Congress re-enacted the "income" tax with, once again, an excise upon "any person in the employ of the United States." There can be no doubt that prior to and subsequent to the Act of 1862, the "salaries" or earnings of private citizens were not subject to indirect tax by the Federal Government. Yet, under Art. 1, Sec. 8, Cl 17 of the Constitution, the government had plenary power to tax all within its domain. Those who worked for the Federal Government as a "privilege" (excise)(71 Am Jur 2d Sec 24) (See Flint v Stone Tracy Co. 220 US 107 (1911), United States v County of Allegheny 322 US 174 (1944)) were subject to the income tax. Noteworthy is that "the salaries and wages of states officials and employees were not subject to the income tax." 31 Op. Atty. Gen. 441, 1919. Congress was without the power to tax those outside the scope of federal taxation. (See United States v Bevans 16 US 366 (1818), McCulloch v Maryland 4 Wheat 316 (1819), Downes v Bidwell 182 US 244 (1901))

Tax on Income from Property

The Revenue Act of 1862 and subsequent Acts further provided for the collection of excises upon income "derived from any... other source whatever," which was congruent with the Supreme Court's decision in Hylton v United States 3 Dall 171 (1796). Congress, under Art. 1, Sec. 8, Cl. 1, may assess and collect taxes upon "income" (profits and gains) (See Stratton's Independence, Ltd. v Howbert 231 US 399 (1913), Doyle v Mitchell Bros. Co. 247 US 179 (1918), So. Pacific v Lowe 247 US 330 (1918), Eisner v Macomber 252 US 189 (1920), Merchants' Loan & Trust Co. v Smietanka 255 US 509 (1921)) from property, which was an indirect tax, and certainly not a direct tax, upon the property itself. (See Op. Atty. Gen. 218, 1877)

Constitutional Limits

There are two significant limitations to congressional taxing power. All indirect (excise) taxes must be uniform and direct taxes upon persons and property are subject to the rule of apportionment. Inherent with the nature of excises is that they are "voluntary." (See CJS Sec 92, 1029-1031) The engagement of an activity by volitional choice is the impetus that mandates the obligation to pay an excise. Conclusively, the taxing power of the Federal Government is comprehensive and that which is within its "lawful sphere" Downes supra, 289 and that which is introduced by its "permission." McCulloch supra, 429 The Attorney General underscored that Congress may levy an income tax unless prohibited by the Constitution. (See 31 Op. Atty. Gen. 475, 1919)

Precedent

In 1894, the Supreme Court issued a decision in Pollock v Farmers' Loan & Trust Co. 158 US 601 (1895) that disrupted the collection of taxes on income derived from property, a precedent that was

3

established by Hylton supra nearly 100 years earlier. With the high Court's mistake, Congress had to remedy the problem. This led to the passage of the Sixteenth Amendment, which granted no new taxing power to Congress than it already had. (See Stanton v Baltic Mining Co. 240 US 103 (1916), Peck & Co. v Lowe 247 US 165 (1918), Eisner v Macomber 252 US 189 (1920))

As reflected in the income tax debate (Cong. Rec. vol 44 p.3344, 1568-1570, 3377, 3900, 4067, 4105-4121, 4389-4441, vol. 45 p. 1694-1695, 2245-2247, 2359, 2450), Senator Brown noted that the Pollock decision abrogated congressional authority to tax tangible property, stocks, bonds, investments and the resultant income. As such, "from whatever source derived" had to be within congressional authority to tax. Cong Rec. 1569, 1697

Sovereignty

There can be no dispute that, prior to Pollock, Congress was unimpeded in its efforts to tax within the fullest extent of its powers granted by the Constitution. Noticeably absent, though, was an exaction upon the sovereignty of the several States or of the people. The Supreme Court, Congress and the People at the time understood that a man's earnings were not subject to federal exaction. For "...we know that our legislation is mostly in relation to property, concerning things, and not concerning persons. Id., 4392 The Attorney General reinforced this point stating that the Sixteenth Amendment

> ...removed the obstacle pointed out in the Pollock case, but did not change the law that were [sic] the source is not taxable neither is the income. 34 Op. Atty. Gen.275, 1924

4

The disclosure that not all sources were taxable reflects the historical context that some sources of "income" were sacrosanct and without the scope of Congress.

The sovereignty of the several States (See McCulloch supra, Farrington v Tennessee 95 US 679 (1877), Bailey v Drexel Furniture Co. 259 US 20 (1922), Hill v Wallace 259 US 44 (1922), Burnes Nat'l Bank v Duncan 265 US 17 (1924)) and the sovereignty of the people (See Yick Wo v Hopkins 118 US 356 (1886)) were beyond the reach of the Federal Government. The income tax amendment debate acknowledges the immutable truth that the "laws that govern persons" are "practically unchanged" Cong. Rec. 4392 from time immemorial.

Federal Excisable Privilege

Since the founding of America until the mid 1930s, America had a climate and understanding that the natural right to work (See Butchers' Union v Crescent City Co. 111 US 746 (1884), Allgeyer v Louisiana 165 US 578 (1897), Truax v Raich 239 US 33 (1915), Adams v Tanner 244 US 590 (1917), Meyer v Nebraska 260 US 390 (1923), Grosjean v American Dress Co. 297 US 233 (1936)) and to exchange one's efforts for earnings (Coppage v Kansas 236 US 1 (1915) was beyond exaction, unless by the rule of apportionment. It would be appropriate, then, to ask how Americans became subject to an excise upon their "salaries."

The Supreme Court answered this query in Charles C. Steward Machine v Davis 301 US 548 (1937) and Helvering v Davis 301 US 619 (1937), cases which became settled law and defined the excisable

5

nature of the federal benefits of social security and employment. Pointedly, upon voluntary acceptance of these federal privileges, (71 Am Jur 2d Sec 740) Americans became "taxpayers." Morse v United States 494 F 2d 876 (9th Cir. 1974) This realization was proved by the 1941 Report from Department of the Treasury, Division of Tax Research, "Collection at Source of Individual Normal Income Tax," which stated that as of 1936 only 3.9% of the population filed income tax returns, acknowledging that the income of most Americans was not subject to taxation. Notably, the federal Social Security Act was enacted in 1935.

Presumptive Liability

With the advent of the federal social security and employment benefits schemes, the earnings of Americans became excisable by voluntary participation. While the earnings were not the subject of the excise, they were the means of measuring the amount of the tax for the purpose of the excise. (See Cong Rec. 2580, March 27, 1943, p.2580, Federalist #21) Indisputably, those who subscribed to these federal benefits, whether done with full knowledge or not, created the presumption (Bailey v Alabama 219 US 219 (1911), Heiner v Donnan 285 US 312 (1932)) and prima facie evidence (Bailey v Alabama supra) of a legal income tax liability.

Rebuttal of Presumption

Logically, if an American did not voluntarily accept these federal privileges, he did not create an obligation. Moreover, if an American accepted these benefits but, subsequently, rescinded, repudiated, renounced, retracted or otherwise rejected them, he,

6

too, would no longer have an obligation. For example, if one wrote the Social Security Administration and Department of the Treasury of his deliberate intent to rescind his intent to the federal benefits, he would effectively rebut the presumption and any prima facie evidence of an income tax liability for the same. He would be as if he never entered the class subject to the jurisdiction of this congressional indirect taxing power in the first place. It is noteworthy that Charles Mullen, Associate Commissioner, Social Security Administration, stated that a social security number (SSN) is not required to live or work in the United States, but for "credit" for the "earnings for the work performed." (Exhibit A) Pointedly, an SSN is a prerequisite for the subscription of the privilege of social Security.

The very notion that the government may compel the acceptance or, upon acceptance, the continued use of a federal privilege, making the presumption conclusive, akin to a rule of substantive law, is incongruent with fundamental constitutional constraints. (See United States v Hill 123 us 681 (1887), Brushaber v Uhion Pacific R.R. Co. 240 US 1 (1916)) For not "every person" American Banana Co. v United Fruit Co. 213 US 347, 357 (1909)(See De Lima v Bidwell 182 US 1 (1901), Botta v Scanlon 288 F 2d 509 (2nd Cir.1961)) may be subject to federal benefits unless engaged on a voluntary basis. Conclusively, those who do not partake of federal privileges would not be classified as "taxpayers" within the scope of the Internal Revenue Code (IRC), which deals exclusively with indirect excises.

Form Over Substance

In 1916, Justice White, in his Brushaber decision, which reversed Pollock supra, opined that when an excise accomplished

> ...the result which the requirement as to apportionment of direct taxation was adopted to prevent... the duty would arise to disregard form and consider substance alone, and hence subject the tax to the regulation as to apportionment which otherwise as an excise would not apply to it. Brushaber supra, 17

White's wisdom echoed the Supreme Court's words in Hale v Henkel 201 US 43 (1906), decided a mere ten years earlier.

> The individual may stand upon his constitutional rights as a citizen. He is entitled to carry on his private business in his own way. His power to contract is unlimited. He owes no duty to the state since he receives nothing therefrom, beyond the protection of his life and property. His rights are such as existed by the law of the land long antecedent to the organization of the state, and can only be taken from him by due process of law, and in accordance with the Constitution. Id., 74

If there is any doubt as to the constraints upon Congress, Bailey v Alabama supra confirms that the legislative branch may not create by statutory presumption that which is prohibited by fundamental law. This sentiment was expressed in the income tax amendment debate. The "principle enunciated in the McCulloch case and Collector v Day" stressed that Congress did not have jurisdiction to control "state functions" or that of a "separate and individual sovereignty." Cong. Rec. p 1697 Moreover, congressional taxing power had to be "construed in the light of the objects, purpose and schemes of the Constitution as a whole." Id

Liability Under the Code

Any question as to the veracity of the foregoing representations

8

is confirmed by examining the tax code. The IRC corroborates that it is limited to the assessment and collection of excises from those who are liable for the same.

Only four parties are identified as liable within Subtitle A - "Income Taxes." The parties are partnerships (26 USC 701), partnerships seeking excess recapture credits (26 USC 704), foreign corporations (26 USC 884) and withholding agents for nonresident aliens and foreign corporations (26 USC 1461). There is another notable reference to an imposition of a tax within Substitle A, 26 USC 1, "Tax Imposed," which states, "There is hereby imposed upon the taxable income of..." The tax is not imposed upon a party. It is upon "taxable income."

Outside of Subtitle A, there is only one other reference to a party identified as "liable" for the income tax. In Subtitle C - "Employment Taxes and Collection of Income Taxes," the "employer," who withholds taxes on employees, is made liable under section 3403.

Taxable Income

The parties identified as liable under Subtitles A and C underscore that one does not have taxable income. (26 USC 1) if only because he is not involved in an excisable activity. If one is not liable, does the income tax apply?

The truth is revealed by the Attorney General who stated, if "the source is not taxable neither is the income." 34 Op. supra

It would be reasonable to surmise that if one has no "taxable income," he must be exempt.

9

Exempt Under the Constitution

There is historical context for the notion that "exempt" income is consistent with the limitations of congressional legislative authority. The corresponding tax regulations for the 1939 Code state

> Sec. 19.22(b)-1 Exemptions - Exclusions from gross income. Certain items of income specified in section 22(b) are exempt from tax and may be excluded from gross income. These items, however, are exempt only to the extent and in the amount specified. No other items are exempt from gross income except (1) those items of income which are, under the Constitution, not taxable by the Federal Government... [emphasis added]

The 1939 Code and regulations were replete with references to the fact that sources were exempt by the "Constitution," "fundamental law" or "limitations of the Sixteenth Amendment and federal taxing authority."

If only because the 1954 Code concerned "taxable income," these references were deleted. The 1939 Code was based upon "net income." Since the 1954 Code dealt with income that was ABLE TO BE TAXED - taxable - reference to the "Constitution" and "fundamental law" was not necessary. However, such deletions did not negate their legitimacy. The constraints of the Constitution upon Congress still prevailed.

Exempt Income

Given the clear attribution to sources that are without congressional authority, the obvious question must be asked: What income is exempt under the tax code? Section 861 of the code, "Income from sources from within the United States," and its corresponding regulation, 26 CFR 1.861-8T(d)(2)(ii) and (iii) address what is exempt.

> (ii) Exempt income and exempt asset defined. - (A) In general. For purposes of this section, the term exempt income means income that is, in whole or part, exempt, excluded or eliminated for federal income tax purposes.

> (iii) Income that is not considered tax exempt. The following items are not considered to be exempt, excluded or eliminated income and, thus, may have expenses, losses, or other deductions allocated and apportioned to them:

Section (iii) then lists the following as NOT exempt.

> (A) foreign taxpayer/foreign sales corporation
> (B) DISC/FSC and suppliers
> (C) possessions corporations
> (D) foreign earned income

Unbelievably, while section (ii) defines "exempt income," it does not identify sources that are exempt. Yet, section (iii) specifies what is NOT exempt. The reasonable legal conclusion must be that any other income, other than that which is not exempt, is "exempt, excluded or eliminated from the federal income tax." Thus, one who 1) does not have "taxable income" (26 USC 1), 2) is not engaged in any federally excisable privilege and 3) is not one of the parties identified as liable in Subtitles A and C must be without the scope of congressional indirect taxing power and, therefore, exempt.

Strict Construction

Given the language and construction of the code and regulations, it is important to note that tax laws must be strictly construed (See Billings v United States 232 US 261 (1914), United States v merriam 263 US 179 (1923)) and that any ambiguity must be resolved against the imposition of the tax (See TandyLeather Co. v United States 347 F 2d 693 (5th Cir. 1965)) Even the Attorney General concedes that the tax must be "clear and unambiguous." 30 Op. Atty. Gen. 273, 2014 Moreover, agency authority may not render an interpretation or application of the law that is "arbitrary, capricious or manifestly contrary to the statute." Chevron supra, 844 (See City of Arlington, Texas v FCC _ US _ 2013, Auer v Robbins 519 US 452 (1997))

What Sources are Taxable?

With the acknowledgement that sources of income are exempt, it is essential to understand what sources are taxable. Such a determination may validate what is cited as "not exempt" under (iii). As revealed in the income tax amendment debate, Congress knew it would receive no additional power with the passage of the Sixteenth Amendment. Furthermore, the terms "from whatever" in "from whatever source derived" did not broaden the classes subject to excise. Rather, the term has a confirming and defining effect. Thus, "from whatever source derived" is synonymous with "regardless of the source derived that is already ABLE TO BE TAXED - taxable - by the Federal Government under the Constitution, without regard to apportionment." There can be no doubt, then, that not all sources are taxable. For clarification, we need only look to the tax code.

Taxable Income

The IRC provides for "Taxable Income defined" (26 USC 63) which states, "taxable income means gross income minus deductions..."

12

Yet, what are sources of gross income? Section 861 only lists items of gross income. While "source" is still undefined, 861 refers to the regulations under 26 CFR 1.861-1 "Income from Sources within the United States." Parapraph (a) "Categories of Incomes" states

> Part 1... and the regulations... determine the sources of income for the purpose of the income tax. These sections explicitly allocate certain important sources of income to the United States...

Subparagraph (1) "Within the United States" explains, in part, "the taxable income from sources within the United States" and refers to 26 CFR 1.861-8, "Computation of taxable income from sources within the United States." The text of 1.861-8 explains that other sections "state in general terms how to determine taxable income... after gross income from sources within the United States has been determined." The very next portion cited in this laundry list of regulations reveals that "taxable income ... from specific sources" is referred to in paragraph (f)(1) as "operative sections."

Finally, under 26 CFR 1.861-8(f)(1), "Miscellaneous Matters," the "sources" identified as "taxable" is a list that is consistent with what is "not exempt" under 26 CFR 1.861-8T(d)(2)(iii).

> (i) foreign tax credit
> (iii) DISC and FSC taxable income
> (iv) Effectively connected income, nonresident alien individuals and foreign corporations in trade or business within the United States.
> (v) foreign base company income

The remainder of the list concerns foreign income and possessions of the United States.

13

Without Congressional Power

This brief and complicated foray into the tax code authenticates that "taxpayers" have an obligation to "sources" from which "taxable income" is "derived." If one has neither "taxable income" (26 USC 1) from a source within the scope of the indirect excise authority of Congress, nor an obligation under 26 USC 701, 704, 884, 1461 or 3403, and is not engaged in a federally excisable privilege, he must be without the purview of the IRC. As defined in 26 USC 7701(a)(14), a "taxpayer" "means any person subject to any internal revenue tax." Thus, if one has "income" "derived" from property, which must be a decision engaged on a "voluntary" basis, or opts for federal privileges, which must be a decision engaged on a voluntary basis, the indirect/excise tax must be paid.

The voluntary nature of securing a federal privilege is reflected within the income tax regulations 26 CFR 301.6109-1, "Identifying numbers," which acknowledges

> Individuals who... do not wish to participate in the benefits of the social security program...

Obviously, those who participate in social security become "taxpayers" liable for the corresponding excise.

Employer/Employee Relationship

Finally, within the context of acceptance of federal privileges, the distinction of the employer/employee is, according to past and current tax codes and regulations, a "legal relationship." (See Subchapter D "Collection of Income Tax at Source of Wages,"

14

sec. 1621, year 1943 and the current regulation under 26 CFR 31.: 3401 (c)) One's voluntary decision to accept the federal benefits of employment, predicated upon the completion of federal forms, consummates ~~on~~ one's designation within this "legal" classification.

This point returns us to the initial observation made at the beginning of this Federal Question. The Federal Government may tax those within the purview of the United States Government. Noteworthy is that in 1943, the definition of "employee" was a term that "specifically includes (See "noscitur a sociis" and "ejusdem generis" Black's Law Dictionary, 9th ed) (See Jarecki v G.D. Searle & Co. 367 US 303 (1961), Meese v Keene 481 US 465 (1987), Norfolk & Western R. Co. v Train Dispatchers 499 US 117 (1991), Gustafson v Alloyd Co. 513 US 561 (1995), Circuit City Stores v Adams 532 US 105 (2001)) officers and employees, whether elected or appointed, of the United States..." The current code lacks the term "specifically." Thus, title 26 USC 3401(c) states, in part, "... includes an officer, employee or elected official of the United States..." Conclusively, those who subscribe to the federal privileges of employment are deemed to be a member of this class. Conversely, those who do not voluntarily accept a federal privilege are without the liability of an "internal revenue tax" for the same, and must be exempt. They would not be a "taxpayer" within the intent of Congress. Those who are not in congressional taxing authority are exercising their sovereign and inalienable rights to the "fundamentals of life, liberty and the pursuit of happiness considered as individual possessions..." Yick Wo supra, 370

Federal Question

The Federal Question posed in this Civil Action must be answered in light of the "language, purpose and history" Southeastern College v Davis 442 US 397, 411 (1979) (See Chevron supra, City of Arlington supra) of the statute. Naturally, then, that which is beyond the sovereign power of Congress may only be reached by direct tax or not at all. The salaries and earnings of private citizens, who do not subscribe to excisable federal privileges, are protected by constitutional constraints. Such rights may not be breached by the interpretation or application of a "purely arbitrary power." Yick Wo supra, 367 (See Chevron supra, Auer supra)

CONCLUSION

Based upon the foregoing, may this Court of Equity affirm that an American's equitable rights may not be compromised when he either does not accept or terminates a federal privilege and, thus, its corresponding excise tax. The precise Federal Question posed by petitioner must be answered that

> The earnings of private citizens are not subject to excise if they do not subscribe to federal social security or employment benefits or have terminated their acceptance of the same and do not enjoy a federally excisable privilege.

WHEREFORE, for the reasons stated herein, petitioner moves this Court of Equity to decide accordingly.

Respectfully submitted,

original signed

James B. Johnson
Petitioner, Pro per

16

SOCIAL SECURITY

TEH2

[illegible] 23, 19[illegible]8

Dear Mr.

This is in response to your letter concerning the requirement and use of the Social Security number (SSN).

The Social Security Act does not require a person to have a Social Security number (SSN) to live and work in the United States, nor does it require an SSN simply for the purpose of having one. However, if someone works without an SSN, we cannot properly credit the earnings for the work performed.

Other laws require people to have and use SSNs for specific purposes. For example, the Internal Revenue Code (26 U.S.C. 6109 (a)) and applicable regulations (26 CFR 301.6109-1(d)) require an individual to get and use an SSN on tax documents and to furnish the number to any other person or institution (such as an employer or a bank) that is required to provide the Internal Revenue Service (IRS) information about payments to the individual. There are penalties for failure to do so. The IRS also requires employers to report SSNs with employees' earnings.

The requirements for including the SSN as the taxpayer identification number on individual tax returns and on tax reports made by employers, banks, and other financial institutions are set by law or regulations of the Department of the Treasury. Anyone who has questions or objections to providing an SSN for these purposes should contact the nearest Internal Revenue Service office.

Sincerely,

Charles H. Mullen
Associate Commissioner
Office of Public Inquiries

15,550.

THE COURT: All right.

(Pause.)

THE COURT: All right. He's going to give the instructions.

Call the jury back.

(Jury in at 4:45 p.m.)

THE COURT: All right. Members of the jury, I'll let you go at five o'clock, but I do think it is important we try to get a little -- as much in as possible.

All right.

Now that you have heard all of the evidence in the case, it becomes my duty to instruct you on the rules of law that you must follow and apply in arriving at your decision. You will follow and apply these rules of law after you have heard the final arguments of the lawyers for the parties.

You, as jurors, are judges of the facts. But in determining what actually happened in the case, that is, in reaching your decision as to the facts, it is your sworn duty to follow the law I am now in the process of defining for you.

And you must follow all of my instructions as a whole. You have no right to disregard or give special attention to any one instruction or to question the wisdom or correctness of any rule of law I may state to you. That is, you must not substitute or follow your own notion or opinion as to what the law is or ought to be. It is your duty to apply the law as I give it to you, regardless of the consequences.

By the same token, it is also your duty to base your verdict solely upon the testimony and evidence in the case, without prejudice or sympathy. That was the promise you made and the oath you took before being accepted by the parties as jurors in this case. And they have the right to expect nothing less.

The indictment or formal charge against a defendant is not evidence of guilt. Indeed, the defendant is presumed by the law to be innocent. The law does not require a defendant to prove his innocence or produce any evidence at all. And no inference whatever may be drawn from the election of a defendant -- Christ, that doesn't -- I'm sorry. That doesn't -- the defendant has obviously testified in this case, so we don't need to go into that, I don't think.

As stated earlier, it is your duty to determine the facts. And in so doing, you must consider only the evidence I have admitted in the case. The term "evidence" includes the sworn testimony of the witnesses and the exhibits admitted in the record.

Remember that any statements, objections, or argument made by the lawyers are not evidence in the case. The function of the lawyers is to point out those things that are most significant or most helpful to their side of the case, and in so doing call your attention to certain facts or inferences that might otherwise escape your notice. In the final analysis, however, it is your own recollection and interpretation of the evidence that controls in the case. What the lawyers say is not binding upon you.

Also during the course of the trial I occasionally made comments to the lawyers or asked questions of a witness or admonished a witness concerning the manner in which he or she should respond to the questions of counsel. Do not assume from anything I may have said that I have any opinion concerning any of the issues in the case. Except for my instructions to you on the law, you should disregard anything I may have said during the trial in arriving at your findings as to the facts.

So while you should consider only the evidence in the case, you are permitted to draw such reasonable inferences from the testimony and exhibits as you feel are justified in the light of common experience. In other words, you may make deductions and reach conclusions which reason and common sense lead you to draw from the facts which have been established by the testimony and evidence in the case.

You may also consider either direct or circumstantial evidence. Direct evidence is testimony of one who asserts actual knowledge of a fact, such as an eyewitness. Circumstantial evidence is proof of a chain of facts and circumstances indicating either guilt or innocence of the defendant. The law makes no distinction between the weight to be given to either direct or circumstantial evidence. It requires only that you weigh all of the evidence and be convinced of the defendant's guilt beyond a reasonable doubt before he can be convicted.

Now, I have said that you must consider all of the evidence. This does not mean, however, that you must accept all of the evidence as true or accurate.

You are the sole judges of the credibility or believability of each witness and the weight to be given to his or her testimony. In weighing the testimony of a witness, you should consider: one, his relationship to the government or to the defendant; his interest, if any, in the outcome of the case; his -- and I mean his or her manner of testifying; the witness's opportunity to observe or acquire knowledge concerning the facts about which the witness testified; the witness's candor, fairness, and intelligence; and the extent to which the witness has been supported or contradicted by other credible evidence. In short, you may accept or reject the testimony of any witness in whole or in part.

Also, the weight of the evidence is not necessarily determined by the number of witnesses testifying as to the existence or nonexistence of any fact. You may find that the testimony of a smaller number of witnesses as to any fact is more credible than the testimony of a larger number of the witnesses to the contrary.

A witness may be discredited or impeached by contradictory evidence, by a showing that he or she testified falsely concerning a material matter, or by evidence that at some other time the witness has said or done something or failed to say or do something which is inconsistent with the witness's present testimony.

If you believe that any witness has been so impeached, then it is your exclusive province to give the testimony of that witness such credibility or weight, if any, as you may think it deserves.

As I stated earlier, a defendant has a right not to testify. If he does testify, however, his testimony should be weighed and considered and his credibility determined in the same way as that of any other witness.

You will note that the indictment charges that the offense was committed on or about a certain date. The proof need not establish with certainty the exact date of the alleged offense. It is sufficient if the evidence in the case establishes beyond a reasonable doubt that the offense was committed on a date reasonably near the date alleged.

A separate crime or offense is charged in each count of the indictment. Each charge and the evidence pertaining to it should be considered separately. The fact that you may find the defendant guilty or not guilty as to one of the offenses charged should not control your verdict as to any other offense charged.

I caution you, members of the jury, that you are here to determine the guilt or innocence of the accused from the evidence in this case. The defendant is not on trial for any act or conduct or offense not alleged in the indictment. Neither are you called upon to return a verdict as to the guilt or innocence of any other person or persons not on trial as a defendant in this case.

Also, the punishment provided by law for the offense charged in the indictment is a matter exclusively within the proven of the court or judge and should never be considered by the jury in any way in arriving at an impartial verdict as to the guilt or innocence of the accused.

Count One of the indictment charges the defendant with violating section 7212(a) of the Internal Revenue Code -- section 7212(a) of the Internal Revenue Code which provides, in pertinent part, as follows: Title 26, United States Code, Section 7212(a) states in pertinent part that, "whoever corruptly obstructs or impedes or endeavors to obstruct or impede the due administration of this title" shall be guilty of an offense against the United States.

In order to sustain its burden of proof for the crime of obstructing the due administration of the Internal Revenue Code as alleged in Count One of the indictment, the government must prove the following elements beyond a reasonable doubt:

One, that during the time period stated in the indictment the Internal Revenue Service tried to ascertain, assess, compute, and collect federal income taxes, federal employment taxes, and penalties for the defendant;

Two, that the defendant knew that the Internal Revenue Service was attempting to duly administer the Internal Revenue Code; and

Three, that the defendant then corruptly obstructed, impeded, or endeavored to obstruct or impede the due administration of the Internal Revenue Code as detailed in the indictment.

To act corruptly, as that word is used in these instructions, means to act voluntarily and deliberately and for the purpose of improperly obstructing or impeding the due administration of the Internal Revenue Code.

A corrupt act is done with the intent to secure an unlawful advantage or benefit either for oneself or for another. Misrepresentation and fraud are examples of activities done with an intent to gain an improper benefit or advantage.

An endeavor is any effort or any act or attempt to effectuate an arrangement or to try to do something, the natural and probable consequences of which is to obstruct or impede the due administration of the Internal Revenue laws.

In order to sustain its burden of proof as to Count One of the indictment, it is not necessary for the government to prove that the defendant personally did every act constituting the offense charged. As a general rule, whatever any person is legally capable of doing himself he can do through another acting as his agent. So if the act or conduct of another is deliberately ordered or directed by the defendant or deliberately authorized or consented to by the defendant, then the law holds that defendant responsible for such acts or conduct just as if personally done by him.

United States Code section 7203 states in pertinent part that "any person required to make a return who willfully fails to make such return at the time or times required by law or regulation" shall be guilty of an offense against the United States.

In order to sustain its burden of proof for the

crime of willful failure to file a tax return, as charged in Counts Two, Three, and Four of the indictment, the government must prove the following essential elements beyond a reasonable doubt as to each count:

One, that the defendant was required by law or regulation to file a tax return concerning his income for the taxable year ending December 31, 2005, December 31, 2006, and December 31, 2007, respectively; two, that the defendant failed to file such a return or returns at the times required by law; and, three, that in failing to file a tax return the defendant acted willfully.

A person is required to file a federal income tax return for any calendar year in which he has gross income in excess of a certain amount. Gross income means the total of all income received before making any deductions allowed by law. Gross income includes the following: compensation for services, including fees, commissions, and similar items; gross income derived from business; three, gains derived from dealing in property; four, interest; five, rents; six, royalties; seven, dividends; eight, alimony or separate maintenance payments; nine, annuities; ten, income from life insurance and endowment contracts; 11, pensions; 12, income from discharge of indebtedness; 13, distributed share of partnership gross income; and 14, income in respect to a decedent; and 15, income from an interest in an estate or trust.

For the crime of willful failure to file a tax return, the government is not required to show that a tax is due and owing from the defendant. Nor is the government required to prove intent to evade or defeat any taxes.

A person is required to file a tax return if his gross income -- was required if his gross income for the calendar year 2005, 2006, or 2007 exceeded $14,600, $15,050, and $15,550 respectively, even though that person may be entitled to deductions from that income so that no tax is due.

Counts Two, Three, and Four of the indictment require that the defendant acted willfully. Willfulness requires that the government prove beyond a reasonable doubt that the law imposed a duty on the defendant; that the defendant knew of this duty; and that the defendant voluntarily and intentionally violated that duty.

The defendant's conduct is not willful if he acted through negligence, mistake, or due to a good faith misunderstanding of the requirements of the law.

I am going to stop at that point. It is five o'clock. And I can read the rest of the instructions tomorrow when we resume. It won't be so long.

But we'll recess now. And at your suggestion, which I think is right, we'll plan to start at 10:30 a.m.

And hopefully the streets were not so cold that there will be a lot of freezing. But it is going to be cold.

If you have any real -- any trouble, call and give us -- call -- I think you have the clerk's number -- and tell us if you are going to be delayed. I mean, we'll -- we can't do it without you, so we're not going to start without you.

So, anyway, we'll recess now. Do not discuss the case with anyone tonight. Do not allow anyone to discuss it with you. Do not read, hear, do any research, anything about the case.

So we'll see you in the morning.

We'll recess court.

(Jury out at 5:01 p.m.)

THE COURT: If you-all will look over the instructions in the morning before -- before 10:30 and let us know any changes you might -- you suggest.

MR. CARGILL: Can you scan them to us?

THE COURT: Sir?

MR. CARGILL: I was asking if the clerk would scan them to us.

THE LAW CLERK: I can send them to you.

THE COURT: Okay. Thank you all. We'll recess.

(Thereupon, at 5:02 p.m. these proceedings were recessed, to be reconvened on January 18, 2013, at

Appendix G – Government Response To 2255 Motion

UNITED STATES DISTRICT COURT
WESTERN DISTRICT OF VIRGINIA
LYNCHBURG DIVISION

JAMES BOWERS JOHNSON	:	
	:	
v.	:	**Case No. 6:12-CR-00015**
	:	
UNITED STATES OF AMERICA	:	

RESPONSE TO MOTION FOR RELIEF PURSUANT TO TITLE 28, UNITED STATES CODE SECTION 2255 AND MOTION TO DISMISS

COMES NOW, The United States of America, by its undersigned counsel, and responds to petitioner's motion for relief pursuant to Title 28, United States Code § 2255.

STATEMENT OF SUBJECT MATTER JURISDICTION

This Court has subject matter jurisdiction to consider this petition pursuant to Title 28, United States Code, § 2255(f)(3).

STATEMENT OF THE CASE

I. Procedural Background

a. Indictment

On April 5, 2012, a Federal Grand Jury for the Western District of Virginia returned an Indictment against the defendant, JAMES BOWERS JOHNSON, for four violations of the Internal Revenue Code. *United States v. Johnson*, 6:12-cr-00015, Doc. 1. Count One alleged that JOHNSON, beginning by at least January of 2001 and continuing through at least May of 2010, corruptly endeavored to obstruct, impede, or impair the due administration of the Internal Revenue Code, in violation of Title 26, United States Code, § 7212(a). Counts Two, Three and

1

Four alleged that JOHNSON willfully failed to file his personal income tax returns for the calendar years 2006, 2007, and 2008, in violation of Title 26, United States Code, § 7203.

b. Pre-Trial Appearances

JOHNSON appeared before U.S. Magistrate Judge James Welsh for his initial appearance on April 26, 2012. U.S. Magistrate Judge James Welsh appointed Andrea Harris, Assistant Federal Public Defender, as counsel. During the hearing, JOHNSON repeatedly challenged the authority of the Court and claimed that he was not the "Defendant." Based on JOHNSON'S repeated assertions that the Court lacked either subject matter or personal jurisdiction, U.S. Magistrate Judge Welsh determined that JOHNSON was not prepared to be arraigned at that time, and had not demonstrated a knowing and intelligent waiver of his right to counsel. Doc. 14, p. 15. On May 3, 2012, JOHNSON again appeared before U.S. Magistrate Judge Welsh and restated his objections to being identified as: James Bowers JOHNSON; Mr. JOHNSON; and the Defendant, claiming that each name was a misnomer. JOHNSON directed the Court to documents he had previously submitted to the Chief Judge of the Western District of Virginia and The United States Attorney for the Western District of Virginia. When asked if he would retain counsel, JOHNSON stated, "I'd like to invoke the Article III Court, superior court of record…where the common law decision applies." Doc. 22, pp. 2-3. U.S. Magistrate Judge Welsh determined that JOHNSON'S waiver effort to be ineffective and denied JOHNSON'S claim that the charges against him should be dismissed. *Id.*

On May 25, 2012, JOHNSON filed a handwritten *pro se* "Habeas Corpus Motion to Dismiss with Prejudice." Doc. 25. Upon reviewing the transcripts from the two previous hearings, and JOHNSON'S pro se motion to dismiss, the Honorable Judge Norman K. Moon ordered hearing to be held on June 8, 2012 to determine whether JOHNSON was competent to understand the nature and consequences of the proceedings against him and to assist properly in his defense. Doc. 26, p. 1. On May 29, 2012, Judge Moon dismissed JOHNSON'S *pro se* motion. Doc. 27. Judge Moon noted that JOHNSON'S motion to dismiss was not the appropriate mechanism for raising prospective defenses and that he may not file a pro se motion to dismiss the indictment while represented by counsel. Doc. 27, pp. 1-2. Judge Moon noted that U.S. Magistrate Judge Welsh correctly assigned JOHNSON counsel from the Office of the Federal Public Defender to represent him and that until a judicial officer found that JOHNSON had competently waived his right to counsel, he remained represented by appointed counsel and may not proceed *pro se*. Doc. 27, p. 2, citing *United States v. Young*, No. 06-710-02, 2008 WL 163045, at *3 (E.D. Pa. Jan 17, 2008) ("[A] criminal defendant has no right to 'hybrid' representation, that is, representation both pro se and by counsel in the same proceeding.") (citations omitted).

On June 13, 2012, JOHNSON appeared before Judge Moon for a competency hearing. Defense attorney Randy Cargill advised the Court that JOHNSON now accepted the representation of Assistant Federal Public Defenders Cargill and Harris. Judge Moon found that JOHNSON was competent and able to assist with trial preparation. Doc. 35. Judge Moon continued JOHNSON'S case until September 18, 2012. Doc. 44, pp. 1-2. On August 20, 2012, Judge Moon again continued JOHNSON'S case until January 15th, 2013. Doc. 49, p. 2.

On November 20, 2013, Judge Moon granted JOHNSON'S motion to proceed *pro se* and the District Court directed Assistant Federal Public Defenders Cargill and Harris to continue representation as "stand-by" counsel. Doc. 53. During a hearing on December 18, 2012, Judge Moon found that JOHNSON had violated the terms of his pretrial supervision, and revoked his bond. Doc. 75, p. 1. On January 2, 2013, Judge Moon denied the United States' motion for a competency hearing, and advised JOHNSON that if he wished to represent himself, he had to follow the rules of court.

c. JOHNSON'S Trial Before the Hon. Norman K. Moon

Trial began on January 15, 2013, with JOHNSON representing himself *pro se* until the conclusion of the government's examination of its first witness. At that point, JOHNSON requested that standby counsel be permitted to give an opening statement and represent him during the trial. Ex.1. Judge Moon then reappointed Assistant Federal Public Defenders Harris and Cargill. At the conclusion of a four-day jury trial, a jury convicted JOHNSON of all four charges on January 8, 2013.

d. Post-Conviction Motions

After trial, but before sentencing, JOHNSON again requested to proceed *pro se*. On March 28, 2013, a hearing was held on JOHNSON'S renewed motion to proceed *pro se*. Judge Moon granted JOHNSON'S motion allowing him to proceed *pro se* and once again appointed the Federal Public Defender's Office as "stand-by" counsel.

On April 8, 2013, JOHNSON filed hand-written motions to set aside the verdict and dismiss is case with prejudice. Doc. 147. In this filing, JOHNSON claimed that the IRS and "the Internal Revenue Code" lacked jurisdiction over him. Doc. 147, p. 1. On April 8, 2013, JOHNSON also filed a Motion for a New Trial With Outside Counsel. Doc. 145.

e. Sentencing & Contempt Charges

On April 11, 2013, the Honorable Norman K. Moon sentenced JOHNSON to 36 months on Count 1 of the indictment, and 12 months on each of Counts 2, 3, and 4, to be served concurrently with each other but consecutive to the term imposed in Count 1 and consecutive to any criminal contempt sentence. Doc. 151, p. 3. At the sentencing hearing, Judge Moon denied

JOHNSON'S *pro se* motions for a new trial pursuant to Rule 33 (Doc. 135), and motion for judgment of acquittal pursuant to Rule 29 (Doc. 147). At that point, JOHNSON questioned the jurisdiction of the Court, an issue that was raised in his motion for acquittal. Judge Moon informed JOHNSON that he had ruled on the jurisdiction issue, and that JOHNSON could appeal to the Court of Appeals for the Fourth Circuit. JOHNSON continued to press arguments, refused to sit down when instructed. He was informed by Judge Moon that he was defying the ruling of the Court, and that he would order standby counsel to take over if JOHNSON continued to act disruptively. JOHNSON asked Judge Moon to recuse himself and continued to argue.

Judge Moon *sua sponte* revoked JOHNSON'S pro se status, and re-appointed the Federal Public Defender. Following the government's argument regarding the presentencing report, JOHNSON stood up and accused the government of lying, and refused to sit when instructed. Judge Moon then summarily held JOHNSON in contempt of court and ordered that he be sentenced to 30 days imprisonment pursuant to Federal Rule of Criminal Procedure 42(b).

f. Appellate History

On April 15, 2013, JOHNSON, filed his notice of Appeal to the United States Court of Appeals for the Fourth Circuit with respect to the district court's Judgment, convicting him on all counts and sentencing him to 48 months of incarceration followed by a period of supervised release. On April 18, 2013, The United States Court of Appeals for the Fourth Circuit granted the motion of Assistant Federal Public Defenders Harris and Cargill to withdraw as counsel on appeal, who stated that their relationship with JOHNSON had deteriorated to an extent that effective representation of JOHNSON was no longer likely. *United States v. Johnson*, 571 F. App'x 205 (4th Cir. 2014). Paul Beers was appointed represent JOHNSON on appeal. Doc. 158.

On April 22, 2013, JOHNSON filed a Supplemental Notice of Appeal concerning the district court's Order holding him in criminal contempt. *Id.*

On appeal, JOHNSON argued that the district court abused its discretion by admitting evidence of other bad acts, that is, that he evaded his obligation to pay child support, and that the district court violated his Fifth Amendment by constructively amending Count One of the indictment. *Id.* In an unpublished, *per curiam* opinion, the Fourth Circuit affirmed JOHNSON'S conviction. The Court held that because the challenged evidence was relevant to JOHNSON'S mental state, the district court did not abuse its discretion in admitting it and did not commit plain error otherwise. *Id.* at 3. Additionally, because the district court's instructions to the jury did not broaden the bases for conviction beyond those charged in the indictment, the District Court did not constructively ament the indictment. *Id.*

JOHNSON timely filed a § 2255 motion on January 23, 2015 with this Court. Doc. 186-1, 6:12-cr-00015-NKM-RSB. On February 18, 2015, JOHNSON filed an amended Memorandum in Support. Doc. 189-1.

ARGUMENT

I. Summary of Argument

JOHNSON'S motion outlines four claims for relief, based on a claim of ineffective assistance of trial and appellate counsel. JOHNSON argues that trial and appellate counsel failed to investigate his "good faith belief and relevant law and failed to develop a strategy of defense to the alleged charges." Doc. 186-1, p. 7. JOHNSON contends that, (1) Trial and appellate counsel refused to argue the element of jurisdiction, (2) counsel failed to effectively argue the element of willfulness, (3) counsel failed to challenge the procedures used in grand jury selection, and (4) that counsel failed to move for a new trial. JOHNSON'S claims are meritless. In effort for a coherent discussion, the United States will address each argument in chronological order.

II. **Standard of Review**

28 U.S.C. § 2255 allows a prisoner in federal custody to challenge a sentence imposed in violation of the Constitution or laws of the United States. The Sixth Amendment guarantees criminal defendants the right to "reasonably effective" legal assistance. *Strickland v. Washington*, 466 U.S. 668, 687 (1984). The United States Supreme Court established a two-prong test for evaluating claims of ineffective assistance of counsel. *Id.* First, the defendant must show, considering all the circumstances, that counsel's performance fell below an objective standard of reasonableness. *Id.* at 689 (defendant must overcome presumption that, "under the circumstances, the challenged action might be considered sound trial strategy"). In evaluating counsel's performance, the court must be highly deferential to counsel's strategic decisions, avoiding the distorted effect of hindsight. *Id.* at 689. "This requires showing that counsel made errors so serious that counsel was not functioning as the 'counsel' guaranteed by the Sixth Amendment." Id. at 687. The determinative issue is not whether counsel was merely ineffective, but whether counsel was so manifestly ineffective that "defeat was snatched from the jaws of victory." *West v. Seabold*, 73 F.3d 81, 84 (6th Cir. 1996) (quoting United States v. Morrow, 977 F.2d 222, 229 (6th Cir. 1992)(*en banc*). In making this determination, there is a strong presumption that counsel's performance fell within the wide range of reasonable assistance. *Strickland*, 466 U.S. 668 at 689.

Second, the defendant must affirmatively prove prejudice, in that there is a reasonable probability that the outcome would have been different if not for the deficiency. *Id.* at 694. If a defendant fails to meet the burden of proving prejudice, the reviewing court need not even consider the performance prong. *Fields v. Attorney Gen. of Md.*, 956 F.2d 1290, 1297 (4th Cir. 1992).

III. <u>Trial and Appellate Counsel Correctly Determined that JOHNSON'S Jurisdictional Argument was Frivolous</u>

Although JOHNSON clearly benefitted from his rights as a United States Citizen, such as the presumption of innocence, a trial by a jury of his peers, a unanimous jury verdict, and representation during his trial and appeal by Court appointed tax payer funded counsel. Despite those factors, his first theory, couched within his ineffective assistance claim, is that the United States lacks jurisdiction, including jurisdiction to impose an income tax upon him. JOHNSON argues that his trial attorney's failure to argue that he had rebutted the "presumption that he was within the Government's purview for income taxes" constituted ineffective assistance of counsel. Doc. 186-1, p. 8.

JOHNSON contends that his argument was grounded in law and fact, and "given the legal significance of presumptions, failure to weigh the element of jurisdiction was not only ineffective, but ultimately, highly prejudicial." *Id.* p. 9. JOHNSON argues that he told defense counsel that he had developed a "good faith belief" that he had "knowingly and deliberately rebutted the prima facie evidence which established the nexus that he had a tax liability." *Id.* JOHNSON argues that after he admittedly stopped filing income tax returns in 1999, he "revoked and rescinded his signature and intent to the federal social security insurance scheme by written notification."[1] *Id.* at 37. JOHNSON argues that this written notification to the Social Security Administration and Secretary of the Treasury, "thereby rebutting the presumption that he was a 'taxpayer.'" *Id.* at 9. Additionally, JOHNSON argues that he sent written notice to the Secretary of the Treasury, "rebutting any presumption of any nexus with the Federal

---

[1] The IRS has directly stated that this argument is frivolous. *See* Rev. Rul. 2005-17, 2005-1 C.B. 823.

Government, which encompassed the relation of employment." *Id.* at 37. Because he "effectively rebutted any presumption held by the Government that he was liable for the federal income tax," JOHNSON argues that he is no longer within the jurisdiction of the United States for federal income and employment tax purposes. *Id.* at. 38.

The choice to not advance a frivolous argument was a sound trial strategy, and does not rise to the level of defective performance. Further, JOHNSON has offered no support for his argument that prejudice resulted beyond bare assertions. JOHNSON's argument is patently frivolous, and is "without merit and lack[s] factual and legal foundation." *Aldrich v Commissioner*, T.C. Memo. 2013-201, 106 T.C.M. (CCH) 192 (2013). Tax-protester arguments "are unlimited, may have little actual importance to those making them, have often already been answered, and are often patently frivolous." *Wnuck v. Commissioner*, 136 T.C. 498, 510-513 (2011). Courts often decline "to refute [frivolous] arguments with somber reasoning and copious citation of precedent; to do so might suggest that these arguments have some colorable merit." *Id.* (quoting *Crain v. Commissioner*, 737 F.2d 1417, 1417 (5th Cir. 1984).

The question of jurisdiction has been answered multiple times in this case, and always in favor of the Government. Although he made Harris, Cargill and Beers aware of his beliefs, JOHNSON argues that counsel "reflexively and categorically rejected the idea that the Government lacked jurisdiction." Doc. 186-1, p. 9.. The record reflects that JOHNSON himself attempted to raise this argument on many occasions, as discussed in the procedural history above.

On the first day of trial, JOHNSON made several motions on his own asking the Court for a proof of claim that he was in fact, the defendant, requesting the matter be transferred to a court of equity, and requesting to enter the case by special appearance as the grantor and beneficiary. *See generally* Exhibit 2. Before delivering an opening statement, JOHNSON stated, "I do note that it is perfectly permissible to question subject matter jurisdiction at this time. Is that not correct?" Exhibit 2, p. 7. Judge Moon responded, "Subject matter jurisdiction is not a problem in this case. I ruled the court has subject matter jurisdiction. We try these cases since 200 years before you were born. And so it is just a frivolous type of thing you are bringing up. I'm not going to have it anymore." *Id.* The Court denied each and every frivolous pre-trial motion made by JOHNSON.

Trial Counsel's failure to make a meritless argument does not amount to ineffective assistance. *United States v. Arena*, 180 F.3d 380, 396 (2d Cir. 1999). Although courts should not "conjure up tactical decisions an attorney could have made, but plainly did not," *Griffin v. Warden, Md. Correctional Adjustment Ctr.*, 970 F.2d 1355, 1358 (4th Cir. 1992), "[f]or judges to second-guess reasonable professional judgments and impose on appointed counsel a duty to raise every 'colorable' claim suggested by a client would disserve the very goal of vigorous and effective advocacy...." *Jones v. Barnes*, 463 U.S. 745, 754 (1983). Failure to raise a losing argument does not constitute ineffective assistance. *See Whitehead v. Cowan*, 263 F.3d 708, 731 (7th Cir. 2001). Attempts at trial to obscure the issues or interject frivolity are not the role of counsel. See *United States v. Collins*, 920 F.2d 619 (10th Cir. 1990). JOHNSON'S trial counsel was under no obligation to file or pursue frivolous arguments.

The right to effective assistance of counsel includes the right to effective assistance of appellate counsel. *Evitts v. Lucey*, 469 U.S. 387, 396 (1985). The omission of a specific issue from a filed appeal, even if the issue is non-frivolous, does not constitute ineffective assistance. *Jones v. Barnes*, 463 U.S. 745 at 754. Appellate counsel has no constitutional duty to raise every non-frivolous issue requested by defendant. *Id.* These standards apply to claims of ineffective assistance of appellate counsel raised in a motion under section 2255. *Ballard v. United States*, 400 F.3d 404, 407-08 (6th Cir. 2005). JOHNSON'S appellate counsel correctly determined not to raise such arguments at trial.

IV. JOHNSON'S Has Not Shown That His Counsel's Performance Prejudiced the Trial Outcome

In his amended motion, JOHNSON states that because of "defense counsel's timidity," and "scant knowledge of tax law…not only was petitioner denied effective assistance of counsel under the 6th Amendment, the entire trial process was adversely affected." Doc. 189-1, p. 2. JOHNSON'S attorneys were not ineffective for failing to make a frivolous argument because a failure to make a losing legal argument does not prejudice a defendant. *See Almond v. United States*, 854 F. Supp. 439, 446 (W.D. Va. 1994) (attorney's failure to make legal arguments that must fail did not prejudice petitioner).

Assuming arguendo that JOHNSON'S jurisdictional argument had even the slightest merit to it, JOHNSON presents no credible evidence that his lawyers did not understand the law or conduct requisite investigation. JOHNSON makes the baseless allegation that his trial attorneys did not "know much" about tax law, without presenting any evidence to support that claim or the claim. He then cites from *United States v. Burstenh*, 395 F.2d 296, 981 (5th Cir. 1969) in which Federal District Judge Harry Claiborne admitted while he was a federal judge, he knew nothing about federal tax law, and that "[w]e must note here, as a matter of judicial knowledge, that most lawyers only have scant knowledge of the tax laws." 395 F.2d 296, 981. Using this quote out of context, JOHNSON seems to argue that his lawyers were unqualified.

Rather, the record reflects that JOHNSON'S attorneys knew his jurisdictional argument was frivolous, and expressed it to him on multiple occasions. For example, in in a letter from Randy Cargill to JOHNSON, dated July 10, 2014, Cargill wrote,

> You have asked for the citation to the code of professional responsibility that governs a lawyer's responsibilities regarding asserting defenses or taking positions at odd with settled law. The provision is in Rule 3.3 of the Rules of Professional Conduct. Essentially, the Rule is that an attorney may not assert a position that he knows has no legal basis and which he cannot in good faith ask a court to adopt. In your case, we simply could not, consistent with our ethical obligations, argue that you were not subject to the jurisdiction of the court. Doc. 186-6, p. 11.

JOHNSON'S appellate counsel, Paul Beers, expressed similar views. In a letter dated August 19, 2013 from Paul Beers to JOHNSON, Beers enclosed the final draft of the Brief he filed in the United States Court of Appeals for the Fourth Circuit. In this letter, Beers told JOHNSON that the only claims he would raise on appeal were that, (1) that "The District Court abused its discretion under Rules 403 and 404 of the Federal Rules of Evidence by admitting evidence of [JOHNSON'S] child support arrearage"; and (2) that "The District Court violated the Fifth Amendment by constructively amending Count One of the Indictment." Doc. 186-5, p. 2. Beers specifically writes, that "[t]hese two issues are the only ones I find meritorious or colorable," and that he "read the motions and other pleadings [JOHNSON] filed in the district court," and "reviewed the legal arguments outlined in [JOHNSON'S] correspondence to me." *Id.* Beers notified JOHNSON that,

> I am constrained by ethical canons in writing appellate briefs to only raise those arguments which have merit. I cannot raise arguments which are not well grounded in law and fact. In my judgment, your challenges to the trial court's jurisdiction and arguments concerning the enforceability and or constitutionality of federal tax laws are not well grounded in law and fact. Therefore, I must decline to include arguments along those lines in our brief. Doc. 186-5, p. 3.

V. <u>Trial Counsel Appropriately Handled the Element of Willfulness</u>

In order to prove a violation of Section 7203, the government must prove that a defendant was a (1) Person required to file a return, (2) the defendant failed to file at the time required by law, and (3) the failure to file was willful. In his motion, JOHNSON admits to the first two elements of the statute, but challenges his counsel's representation in regards to the third element. JOHNSON argues that his trial attorneys failed to effectively counter the necessary element of willfulness, thus preventing the jury from understanding his state of mind and "propelled them to a determination of guilt." Doc. 186-1, p. 20. JOHNSON believes that had his "good faith belief" been offered to the jury, "counsel would have effectively eliminated the element of willfulness, which would have, invariably, led to a not guilty verdict." *Id.* This argument is without merit.

Willfulness has been described as the "intentional violation of a known legal duty." *United States v. Pomponio*, 429 U.S. 10 (1976); *United States v. Bishop*, 412 U.S. 346, 360 (1973); *United States v. Grumka*, 728 F.2d 794, 796 (6th Cir. 1984) and generally must be inferred from the Defendant's acts or conduct. *Spies v. United States*, 317 U.S. 492 (1943); *United States v. Schafer*, 580 F.2d 774, 781-82 (5th Cir. Page 6 of 13 Case 6:12-cr-00015-NKM Document 92 Filed 01/11/13 Page 6 of 13 Pageid#: 523 1978). The Government is not required to prove that the Defendant had a bad purpose. *United States v. Pomponio, supra.* Once the evidence establishes that the tax evasion motive played any role in a taxpayer's conduct, willfulness may be inferred even if the conduct also served another purpose. *Spies v. United States*, 317 U.S. at 499. Conduct that is of a willful nature has been found to include the following: a defendant's general attitude towards the reporting and payment of taxes. *See United States v. Hogan*, 861 F.2d 312 (1st Cir. 1970), *cert. denied*, 401 U.S. 911 (1971); *United States v. Stein*, 437 F.2d 775 (7th Cir.), *cert.denied*, 403 U.S. 905 (1971); *United States v. Taylor*, 305 F.2d 183, 185 (4th Cir.), *cert. denied*, 371 U.S. 894 (1962); a pattern of failing to report substantial income. *United States v. Skalicky*, 615F.2d 1117, 1120 (5th Cir.), *cert. denied*, 449 U.S. 832 (1980); prior and subsequent similar acts reasonably close to the prosecution years. *See*

United States v. Middleton, 246 F.3d 825, 836-837 (6th Cir. 2001); causing the books and records of one's business to be false and inaccurate. *See United States v. Bishop*, 264 F.3d 535, 553 (5th Cir. 2001); a defendant's general educational background can be considered as bearing on his or her ability to form willful intent. *United States v. Guidry*, 199 F.3d 1150, 1157-58 (10th Cir.1999) (willfulness inferred from defendant's expertise in accounting via her business degree and her work experience as comptroller of a company) *See United States v. Smith*, 890 F.2d 711, 715 (5th Cir. 1989).

At trial, the Government's theory was that JOHNSON acted willfully and in bad faith to enrich himself by concealing income from the IRS. Government's witnesses testified that Appellant established and used entities, such as limited liability companies and trusts, to evade his tax liability, as well as concealing his income and assets. Witnesses testified that JOHNSON directed tenants of his rental properties and customers of his phone card business to make payments to him with money orders issued to his various entities. The Government presented evidence that Appellant utilized a "warehouse bank" account called MYICIS that commingled customers' deposits. Depositors were issued money orders when withdrawing their funds, which made it nearly impossible to trace deposits and/or withdrawls.

The element of willfulness was challenged by counsel and through JOHNSON'S own testimony, and preserved for the record on appeal. In Affirming JOHNSON'S conviction, the Fourth Circuit noted upon reviewing the record that,

> Appellant's sole defense at trial was that he did not act with the requisite mens rea to be found guilty of obstructing the IRC or willfully failing to file tax returns, even though he concede that he had sufficient income to trigger the requirement to file tax returns in 2005, 2006, and 2007, and failed to do so. During his opening statement, Appellant's counsel told the jury that Appellant was a well-educated, family man, who believed in good faith, after much research on the issue, that the tax system was voluntary and did not apply to him." *United States v. Johnson*, 571 F. App'x 205 (4th Cir. 2014), at 5-6.

JOHNSON testified that through his involvement with these organizations and his own research, he came to believe that the IRC has been misapplied under the Constitution. The Fourth Circuit noted that JOHNSON testified that the Sixteenth Amendment did not apply to him, because he was outside of the jurisdiction of the United States, and that he testified in his belief that the tax system was voluntary. *Id.* On cross-examination, JOHNSON was asked, "And after reading all of that [tax protester] information, you developed a belief that in good faith you could – were not required to file tax returns?" Exhibit 3, p. 183. JOHNSON responded, "In good faith I belief that the tax code was – did not apply to me, that's correct." *Id.* At the close of trial, the District Court instructed the jury that good faith of the Defendant is a defense to the failure to file charges. Document 122, Pageid# 1625, Jury Instruction # 23. Despite his counsels' best efforts, the jury rejected the good faith defense and found JOHNSON guilty of Counts Two, Three and Four.

JOHNSON'S argument regarding the willfulness element is irrelevant to his conviction on Count One of the indictment. Count One, a felony, charged a violation of the omnibus clause of 26 U.S.C. § 7212(a), which prohibits corrupt or forcible endeavors to obstruct or impede the due administration of the Internal Revenue Code. The elements of the offense are that the defendant (1) in any way corruptly (2) endeavored (3) to obstruct or impede the due administration of the Internal Revenue Code. *United States v. Wilson*, 118 F.3d 228, 234 (4th Cir. 1997); *United States v. Bostain*, 59 F.3d 474, 476-77 (4th Cir. 1995). Since willfulness is not an element of the offense, good faith is not a defense.

JOHNSON'S contentions that his beliefs were held in good faith are further undermined by his own testimony at trial. JOHNSON'S testimony also supports the conclusion he made himself willfully blind to his tax obligations. On cross-examination, JOHNSON testified that he

15

firmly believed that he was not subject to taxation after consulting with various sources. JOHNSON was asked if he had read the Internal Revenue Code, and responded "I have read a lot of it, if not most of it." Exhibit 3, p. 183. When asked if he read Section 7203 or Section 7212(a) of the Internal Revenue Code, JOHNSON responded, "Yeah," and "Okay. I read that." *Id.*

JOHNSON also identified a letter he received from the IRS on August 30th, 2004, titled, "Response to Frivolous Arguments." *Id.* at 207. He acknowledged that the document sent in response to a letter he sent to the IRS. He testified that the document was "30, 40 pages" long, and that he had "looked at it." *Id.* at 206-7. When asked, "But you could parcel your way through the Internal Revenue Code, but not read something about frivolous tax filings?" JOHNSON responded, "I just admitted that I didn't probably read the whole thing, but I acknowledged it and looked at it." *Id.* at 207. When asked, "So by August 30th, 2004, you were advised that there were positions different than your position?" JOHNSON responded, "Yeah. And I knew most of those positions already within that document." *Id.* In response to JOHNSON'S admission that he hadn't really read the pamphlet, he was asked, "So you had already made up your mind as to what you were going to believe when this came out and you weren't going to look at any other side?" *Id.* at 211. JOHNSON responded, "My answer is that by '99, 2000, when I made the decision that the one thing that bound em to the liability of taxation was the Social Security trust account and that number, that I made a very courageous and uncommon decision to step into the wild and say, "I'm not going to file anymore." *Id.*

JOHNSON obviously spent enough effort acquainting himself with tax law materials to be able to give citations (however misguided) of statutes, regulations, and court opinions. But it seems clear that in that effort he must have studiously ignored the copious amount of available information that prove, definitively, that his beliefs are incorrect.

VI. JOHNSON Fails to Raise a Cognizable Claim about the Grand Jury and Individual Jurors

JOHNSON argues that he was denied the opportunity to challenge the grand jury and individual jurors, and defense counsel should have asserted this right. Because he never "received the opportunity to and defense counsel did not take advantage to challenge the grand jury or individual jurors," he "was deprived of substantial due process." Doc. 186-1, p. 29. Both claims are meritless.

The government or defendant may challenge a grand jury on the ground that it was not lawfully drawn, summoned, or selected, and may challenge an individual juror on the ground that the juror is not legally qualified. Fed. R. Crim. P. 6(b)(1). However, JOHNSON fails to make any allegations as to how the grand jury's selection or the procedures used were improper.

"The grand jury proceeding is accorded a presumption of regularity, which generally may be dispelled only upon particularized proof of irregularities in the grand jury process." *United States v. Mechanik,* 475 U.S. 66, 75 (1986) (O'Connor, J., concurring) (citing *United States v. Johnson,* 319 U.S. 503, 512-13 (1943)); *see also United States v. Buffington,* 815 F.2d 1292, 1304 (9th Cir. 1987) ("[T]he party challenging this presumption faces a heavy burden."). Absent special circumstances, those involved in the grand jury process "must not disclose a matter occurring before the grand jury." Fed. R. Crim. P. 6(e)(2). The foreperson must "record the number of jurors concurring in [the] indictment," but this record "may not be made public unless the court so orders." Fed. R. Crim. P. 6(c). JOHNSON could have petitioned this Court to disclose those records under Fed. R. Crim. P. 6(e)(3)(E) but failed to do so.

The indictment naming JOHNSON as a defendant is valid on its face. An indictment returned by a legally constituted and unbiased grand jury…if valid on its face, is enough to call for trial of the charges on the merits." *United States v. Mills,* 995 F.2d 480, 487 (4th Cir. 1983) (quoting Costello v. United States, 350 U.S. 359, 363 (1956)). JOHNSON alleges no bias or misconduct. He does not contest the document's authenticity. Each count of the indictment contains the specific elements of the offense charged. *See United States v. Wills*, 346 F.3d 476, 488-89 (4th Cir. 2003) (indictment that tracks language of statute defining offense and properly alleges each element "is valid on its face").

Assuming, arguendo, that JOHNSON was able to allege a procedural defect, the harmlessness of the error nonetheless justifies dismissing the claim. This Court "may not dismiss an indictment for errors in grand jury proceedings unless such errors prejudiced the defendant." *Mills*, 995 F.2d at 487 (quoting Bank of Nova Scotia v. United States, 487 U.S. 250, 254 (1988)); see also Fed. R. Crim. P. 42(a) ("Any error, defect, irregularity, or variance that does not affect substantial rights must be disregarded."). JOHNSON does not allege that the indictment failed to give him fair notice of the charges against him. The indictment fulfilled "the primary function of an indictment," namely, "to notify the defendant of the charges against him and provide a sufficient basis upon which the defendant can plead the defense of former jeopardy." *United States v. Higgs*, 353 F.3d 281, 306 (4th Cir. 2003).

JOHNSON'S claim as it relates to individual jurors is similarly without merit. He argues in an attached declaration that he "did not participate in voir dire, stating in front of potential jurors that he was not the defendant." Doc. 186-1, p. 48. JOHNSON'S statement indicates that he was present for voir dire, and given the opportunity to speak. He chose not to. As the record indicates, JOHNSON asked for counsel to be reappointed after the conclusion of the government's first witness. At this point, the jury had been selected, sworn, and trial had begun.

Further, JOHNSON has procedurally defaulted on this objection. A defendant is required to make any challenge to jury selection procedures before voir dire or within seven days after he discovered or should have discovered the grounds for the challenge. 28 U.S.C. § 1867(a).

VII. Failure to Move for a New Trial Pursuant to Rule 33 FRCP Does Not Constitute Ineffective Assistance of Counsel

Trial Counsel's decision to not move for a new trial under Rule 33 does not rise to ineffective assistance of counsel. JOHNSON argues that counsel deprived him of the right to request a new trial, "even after express instructions to do so." Doc. 186-1, p. 25. In fact, Cargill's decision to not file a motion for a new trial on behalf of JOHNSON was not a malicious act, but rather based on sound professional judgment.

At some point before January 30th, 2013, attorney Jay Nanavati, who never filed an appearance, was contacted regarding JOHNSON's case. In an email from Cargill to Nanavati, attached as an Exhibit to JOHNSON'S amended motion, Cargill wrote that he didn't think the motion for a new trial was a wise choice, even though he disagreed with the Court's admission of evidence of JOHNSON'S failure to pay child support, and his attempt to pay child support using a "bogus instrument." Doc. 189-2, p. 4. Cargill wrote that, "all in all, I think a new trial motion coming from us would be counterproductive."

A letter included in JOHNSON'S original motion supports the conclusion that Cargill's decision was one of sound professional judgment. The letter from Cargill to JOHNSON, dated March 18, 2013, reads,

> As to the motion for new trial: I recall that when we met on the deadline day for a new trial motion, you expressed a desire to file such a motion. There was some question about whether you were going to retain counsel and seek/follow the advice of retained counsel on the issue. Still, I think it's fair to assay that you wanted a motion to be filed. I did not file that motion because I did not believe there were valid grounds and because I felt that such a motion could be counterproductive in that it would amount to an attack on the impartiality on the Judge who soon will sentence you. I am still of that view, and as

> we discussed you may raise on direct appeal all claims of error that you would raise in a new trial motion. Doc. 196-6, p. 19.

JOHNSON rests this argument on a line from the email sent from Cargill to Nanavati on January 30th, 2013. In that e-mail, Cargill noted that he felt as if Judge Moon "unfairly insinuated himself into the trial in aggressively cross-examining [JOHNSON] and interrupting [Andrea Harris] while she was trying to direct examine [JOHNSON]. Doc. 189-2, p. 4. Cargill said that because JOHNSON had previously filed a retaliatory filing against Judge Moon,

> [O]ne could credibly argue that we should have moved for recusal. It would have been quite awkward as we weren't even brought back in it until after the first witness testified but I think I should have had the courage to raise this. To that point, [JOHNSON] would not even speak with us; he refused mail and even refused to come out of his cell to meet with me. Doc. 189-2, p. 4.

JOHNSON interprets this e-mail as evidence that Randy Cargill "lied, or if granted the benefit of the doubt, he took liberties with the truth to craft a retrospective representation so that he would appear as 'counsel' granted by the Sixth Amendment." Doc. 189-2, p. 4. JOHNSON alleges that Cargill was motivated to not argue a motion for a new trial "only because he regularly appeared before Judge Moon." *Id.* Cargill's decision to not file this motion, JOHNSON argues, "reflects his deficient and ineffective advocacy throughout the trial process." Doc. 189-1, p. 2. JOHNSON claims that this 'posture, born out of fear, reflects an indecisive, if not schizophrenic mindset." *Id.* at 3.

The Fourth Circuit generally is reluctant to second-guess a trial lawyer' tactical decisions. *Goodson v. United States*, 564 F.2d 1071, 1072 (4th Cir. 1977). Although courts should not "conjure up tactical decisions an attorney could have made, but plainly did not," *Griffin v. Warden, Md. Correctional Adjustment Ctr.*, 970 F.2d 1355, 1358 (4th Cir. 1992), "[f]or judges to second-guess reasonable professional judgments and impose on appointed counsel a duty to raise every 'colorable' claim suggested by a client would disserve the very goal of vigorous and effective advocacy...." *Jones v. Barnes*, 463 U.S. 745, 754 (1983).

JOHNSON has failed to show that even if Cargill had filed a motion for a new trial, that there is a reasonable probability that such motion would be granted, and the outcome of a subsequent trial would have been different. Cargill, after weighing the benefits and risks of filing such a motion, determined that it would be unsound strategy to do so. The issues that would provide the grounds to support a motion for a new trial were argued unsuccessfully prior to trial and to the Fourth Circuit, all to no avail.

CONCLUSION

The refutation of JOHNSON'S "frivolous anti-tax argument" by the IRS, District Court, and Court of Appeals for the Fourth Circuit has "fall[en] on deaf ears," as he "persists in making the same doomed argument." *Wnuck v. Commissioner*, 136 T.C. 498, 505 (2011). The United States respectfully requests that JOHNSON'S petition be denied, because "[w]e are confronted here with [a taxpayer] who [simply] refuses to accept the judgments of the courts." *Lonsdale v. United States*, 919 F.2d 1440, 1448 (10th Cir. 1990). Based upon the foregoing and the record before this Court, the United States of America respectfully requests that this Court deny

Petitioner's Motion for Relief under 28 U.S.C. § 2255, dismiss Petitioner's claims with prejudice, and strike this matter from the Court's docket.

Respectfully submitted,

ANTHONY GIORNO
Acting United States Attorney

By: s/ C. Patrick Hogeboom III
C. Patrick Hogeboom III
Assistant United States Attorney
WA Bar Number 16598
P.O. Box 1709
Roanoke, Virginia 24008

s/Julia Mayer
Julia Mayer
Third Year Law Student
Washington and Lee

APPENDIX H – REPLY TO GOVERNMENT RESPONSE

UNITED STATES DISTRICT COURT
WESTERN DISTRICT OF VIRGINIA

James Bowers Johnson Petitioner,	)	
v	)	Case No.: 6:12-cr-00015-NKM
UNITED STATES OF AMERICA Respondent,	)	

PETITIONER'S REPLY TO GOVERNMENT'S RESPONSE IN SUPPORT OF MOTION FOR RELIEF PURSUANT TO 28 USC 2255 AND SUMMARY JUDGMENT

James B. Johnson
Petitioner, Pro per

TABLE OF CONTENTS

TABLE OF POINTS AND AUTHORITIES

United States Supreme Court

American Banana Fruit Co. v United Fruit Co., 213 US 347 (1909) - 16

Auer v Robbins, 519 US 452 (1997) - 5, 12, 13, 16

Bowles v Seminole Rock, 325 US 410 (1945) - 5, 12

Brown v Gardner, 513 US 115 (1994) - 3, 4, 12

Casey v United States, 276 US 413 (1928) - 9

Charles C Steward Machine v Davis, 301 US 548 (1937) - 10

Chevron USA Inc. v Natural Resources Defense Council, 467 US 887 (1984) - 1, 4, 5, 12, 14, 15

Chicago v Morales, 527 US 41 (1999) - 7

City of Arlington v FCC, _ US _ (2013) - 9, 12, 13, 14, 15, 16

Clapper v Amnesty Int'l USA, _ US _ (2013) - 17

Cohens v Virginia, 6 Wheat 264

Decker v Northwest Envt'l Def Center, _ US _ (2013) - 13, 16

De Lima v Bidwell, 182 US 1 (1901) - 16

Downes v Bidwell, 182 US 244 (1901) - 4

Flint v Stone Tracy Co., 220 US 107 (1911) - 2, 14

Hawes v Georgia, 258 US 1 (1922) - 9

Helvering v Davis, 301 US 619 (1937) - 4, 12

Jones v Barnes, 463 US 745 (1983) - 6

Nat'l Cable & Telecomm v Brand X, 545 US 967 (2005) - 14

Rindskopf v United States, 105 US 418 (1882) - 9

Sosna v Iowa, 419 US 393 (1975) - 4

Southern Pacific Terminal Co. v ICC 219 US 498 (1911) - 4

Courts of Appeal

iii

PRELIMINARY STATEMENT

Petitioner respectfully submits this Reply to the government's response (GR) to his motion pursuant to 28 USC 2255, for an order to vacate, set aside or correct the sentence imposed.

INTRODUCTION

Petitioner's guilt or innocence is irrelevant; the validity and fairness of the proceeding are. (See United States v Kastenbaum 613 F 2d 86 (5th Cir. 1980)) Considering the "precise question at issue" Chevron USA Inc. v Natural Resources Defense Council Inc. 467 US 837, 842 (1984) - that petitioner rebutted the government's presumption and prima facie evidence that he was liable for specific excises and, therefore, the IRS acted ultra vires against one without its authority, with effective assistance of counsel, the court would have applied a correct interpretation of the statute (See Perry v Miner, U.S. Dist Lexis 20283 (2005 DC NJ) and argued against prosecution of non criminal conduct. Failure to recognize counsel's unwillingness to argue violation of the Constitution or laws of the United States and lack of court jurisdiction renders the 2255 process inadequate, especially since these elements could have been raised on appeal. (See Grimes v United States, 607 F 2d 6 (2nd Cir. 1979)) For petitioner supports his innocence and constitutional error, (See Gray v United States 385 Fed Appx 160 (3rd Cir. 2010)) which affords a remedy which is the substantial equivalent of the conventional writ of habeas corpus. (See United States v Anselmi, 207 F 2d 312 (3rd Cir. 1953)) Claim of error substantiates a lack of court jurisdiction (See Percan v United States, 294 F Supp 2d 505 (2nd Cir. 2003)) and demonstrates error of law and fact that constitutes fundamental defect.

1

The merit of petitioner's good faith belief is supported by James Bowers Johnson v United States of America, 7:15-cv-00067 (Exhibit 1) and James Bowers Johnson v United States of America, 7:15-cv-00076 (Exhibit 2)

ARGUMENT

Since 2000, especially since the IRS investigation began in 2004, (Exhibit 3) petitioner naively, but fervently, relied upon the Constitution to ensure his rights and government accountability. In 2009, when the IRS recommended he be prosecuted, petitioner wrote the Departments of Internal Revenue and Justice (Decl, 20) (Exhibit 4, 2) for the law that required him to file tax returns. Like agents Biggs and Pompei, (Decl, 16-18) the agencies never responded. With the government's refusal to communicate for nine years, (Decl 6, 7, 16-20) (Exhibit 3), suffering the loss of his marriage, family, home and livelihood, and facing almost certain incarceration, petitioner no longer relied upon the Constitution and was forced to seek other solutions. (Decl 22) As the executive branch acted with impunity, petitioner expected counsel to defend and the court to allow for the constitutional basis of his belief.

However, counsel disregarded that, under fundamental law, having rejected federal benefits, petitioner's "property which of itself considered is nontaxable." Flint v Stone Tracy Co. 220 US 107, 165 (1911) They also ignored that if the government believed petitioner was "potentially liable" Mórse v United States 494 F 2d 876, 880 (9th Cir. 1974) for specific excises, it had a responsibility to counter his rebuttal. Lack of a counter was grounds for counsel to attack the indictment and provide "for his defence." United States v Wade 388 US 218, 225 (1967)

2

THE GOVERNMENT"S RESPONSE

With its response, the government provided no evidence in the form of affidavits and ignored and failed to defeat petitioner's claims that counsel: 1) refused to argue the element of jurisdiction, 2) failed to effectively argue the element of willfulness and 3) failed to file a motion for a new trial. Moreover, the foregoing were not resolved with its conclusion that the "IRS, District Court and Court of Appeals" (GR pg 21) provided a refutation of a "frivolous anti-tax argument." Id.

To the contrary, the District Court "ruled" (GR pg. 10) on the claim of jurisdiction without any explanation of petitioner's belief. Absent competent counsel to argue petitioner's belief, a refutation by the court or government was never possible. The government now lobbies for the Court and its decision against "tax protester arguments." (GR p 9). The government contends that any argument in any tax case is frivolous and the defendant is a tax protester. This tact does not defeat petitioner's claim that counsel failed to challenge personal jurisdiction or argue the element of willfulness. Why? The Court did not have any of the facts or circumstances outside of the trial record that establish petitioner's belief.

If the government is not required to refute petitioner's belief based upon the Constitution, congressional intent or agency authority, it does not have to contend with an argument outside the legal culture and consciousness for "60 years" <u>Gardner</u> infra, overcome a statutory application that was "plainly wrong" <u>Universal Battery</u> infra, acknowledge counsel's failure to challenge making "criminal conduct which such law leaves untouched," <u>Standard Brewery</u> infra or defend

3

the IRS "defin[ing] the boundaries of constitutional application." Powers infra. Since counsel never pressed for the requisite "judicial interference" Gardner, the government now relies solely upon its thoughtless "tax protester" (GR p 9) theme.

Here is the rub. The government attacks petitioner as a tax protester precisely because defense counsel never argued the reason petitioner believed he was not liable. This reflects a performance that fell below an objective standard of reasonableness. Petitioner was prejudiced because counsel refused to accomplish what is quite elementary - investigate the merits of their client's belief. Had they done so, the government and the court would have had a responsibility to offer a refutation based upon the facts and law. Otherwise, "the precise question at issue" Chevron is "capable of repetition, yet evading review," Sosna v Iowa 419 US 393, 399 (1975) especially since there is "the necessity or propriety of deciding some question of law." Southern Pacific Terminal Co. v ICC 219 US 498, 516 (1911) That petitioner never posed a frivolous argument to the IRS is essential to the claim of ineffective assistance of counsel. Based upon only what they knew, counsel merely agreed with the government's position and attacked his belief as "crazy" (Decl 91) before the jury. Yet,

> ...when an act of any department is challenged because not warranted by the Constitution, the existence of the authority is to be ascertained by determining whether the power has been conferred by the Constitution. Downes v Bidwell 182 US 244, 288 (1901)

The import of a constitutional challenge is reflected in United States v Bostain 59 F 3d 474, 477 (4th Cir. 1995), in which defendant

> maintains that none of his actions constituted a violation of section 7212(a). Thus, he raises a question of

4

> statutory construction, disagreeing with the government's view of the scope of the language employed in describing the offense.

Bostain aptly expresses that with settled law (See Chevron supra, Auer infra and Seminole Rock infra) and the canons of ethics, counsel was obligated to challenge the agency's statutory construction for "the precise question at issue." Chevron

CLAIM IV - COUNSEL FAILED TO FILE A MOTION FOR A NEW TRIAL

The government contends that "Cargill's decision not to file a motion for a new trial was... sound professional judgment." (GR p 19) However, on 2/1/13, Cargill told petitioner that filing a motion would not be prejudicial, and that if denied, both the denied motion and trial could be appealed. (Decl 120) Cargill's position was validated when Nanavati, who spoke with Cargill, agreed in an email to Cargill that petitioner should "take a bite the apple (with an appeal being the second)." (See Dkt 189, Exhibit B) The government fails to overcome and purposely misrepresents petitioner's claim. Petitioner stated that Cargill "attempted to color," (Pet Mot p 25) cited or "took liberties with the truth" Id concerning his failure to file for a new trial. Now, curiously, the government gratuitously links petitioner's words with Cargill's email to Nanavati (GR p 20) However, this email was not offered in the 2255 motion. It was in the Motion to Amend.(Dkt 189) The evidence in the 2255 factually show that Cargill has an integrity issue. The email shows that he has a lack of courage that affected the new trial request. So why would the government not rely upon the merits of the 2255? The answer is that the 2255 shows Cargill has no credibility and

> that the tactical decision of counsel was unreasonable... that it amounted to a deprivation of an attorney who

5

> acted within the range of competence demanded of attorneys in criminal cases. Goodson v United States 564 F 2d 1071, 1072 (4th Cir. 1977) quoting McMann v Richardson 397 US 759 (1970)

Cargill fell short of the standard which "requires that he support his client's [request] to the best of his ability." [added] Jones v Barnes 463 US 745, 754 (1983) quoting Anders v California 386 US 738 (1967) There can be no doubt that counsel performed "in a professionally unreasonable manner." (Pet Mot p 25)

Petitioner's unrebutted testimony is that 1) Cargill himself stressed the need for a new trial, (Pet Mot p 26) 2) he was too timid to file the motion, Id. 3) Petitioner asked Cargill to file the motion, Id. 4) Cargill failed to file the motion Id. and 5) the rules and canons of ethics required him to do so.

The government did not refute that Cargill "labored under a conflict of interest," Strickland v Washington 466 US 668, 692 (1984) to the point that the conflict of interest affected his performance. Thus, "prejudice is presumed." Id. Moreover, the prejudice cited in the 2255 motion stands as claimed.

CLAIM II - COUNSEL FAILED TO EFFECTIVELY ARGUE THE ELEMENT OF WILLFULNESS

The government responds to petitioner's willfulness claim by misrepresenting the facts, just as it consistently misrepresents his belief. Contrary to the government's claim, petitioner did not admit "to the first two elements of the statute" (7203). (GR p 12-13) With adequate investigation, the government would have learned that petitioner asserted "counsel's failure to contest [all] three elements." (Pet Mot p 17) Did the government make a false presumption regarding petitioner's willfulness claim without conducting "the requisite investigation," (GR p 11) just as defense counsel

6

failed to investigate the fundamentals of petitioner's belief? Pointedly, failure to conduct the requisite investigation equals the failure to validate or invalidate the merits of a belief and does not reflect a lawyer's "best efforts." (GR p 15) So while the government failed to provide its "best efforts" concerning the willfulness claim, defense counsel failed to offer its best to defeat the element of willfulness.

Mens rea requires an actus reus;(See Chicago v Morales 527 US 41 (1999)) the lack of the latter precludes the former. Actus non facit reum, nisi mens sit rea - an act does not make a man guilty, unless he does so with intention. With petitioner's rebuttal, counsel was duty bound to argue an absence of actus reus and mens rea. There was a reason petitioner had no intent to violate the law - he believed that he was without its scope. One must have knowledge of facts that make conduct illegal, (See Staples v United States 511 US 600 (1994)) just as specific and general intent to commit a crime require "purpose" and "knowledge" respectively. United States v Bailey 444 US 394, 404 (1980) (See United States v Neiswender 590 F 2d 1269 (4th Cir. 1979))

Trial and appellate counsel's summary dismissal of the constitutional merits of petitioner's belief prevented them from understanding that he had no "purpose" or "knowledge" of a wrongful act. Their dismissal precluded their investigation of agency authority and congressional intent. (See Bostain supra) They rejected that petitioner had "good faith" (Neiswender supra) based upon "reasonable investigation," Id. and that his good faith "negates specific intent." South Atl Lmtd Ptrshp of Tenn v Reise 218 F 3d 518, 531 (4th Cir. 2002)

7

26 USC 7212(a) AND INTENT

The government asserts that willfulness is not an element of 26 USC 7212(a) and, therefore, good faith is not a defense. Had counsel argued their client's belief, they would have established that there was no willfulness and, therefore, no mens rea, because there was no actus reus. Thus, there could have been no willful violation of 7212(a). Intent is central to the 7212(a) offense.

> We have held that the term "corruptly," as used in the statute, forbids acts committed with the intent to secure an unlawful benefit for oneself of for another. United States v Wilson, 118 F 3d 228, 234 (4th Cir. 1997) (See Bostain supra, 479) [emphasis added]

Significantly, had counsel effectively argued petitioner's belief, they would have defeated an intent to corruptly violate 7212(a) and proved there was no actus reus. For petitioner, knowing that he was without congressional indirect excise authority,(Exhibit 1), could not have acted corruptly. Moreover, counsel could have argued that petitioner lived his life the same before, during and after the IRS criminal investigation. Given his belief, the IRS investigation had no bearing as to how he thought or acted. Ergo, petitioner sought no unlawful benefit. Since counsel were not prepared to defend him against circumstantial evidence that the government used to create a crime for conduct, which petitioner believed was not criminal, they prejudiced petitioner. They did not contest the evidence with his reasonable belief before the jury or court.

CLAIM I - COUNSEL FAILED TO EFFECTIVELY ARGUE JURISDICTION

The government's response to the element of jurisdiction reflects the same sentiment expressed by Cargill - it is "crazy" (Decl 91). Yet, the government does not state, defend or argue how or why petitioner is liable. Instead, it asserts that all Americans

8

are liable for an excise tax and any dissent is a "tax protester" argument,(GR p 9) case closed. Since defense counsel did the same, the court never learned why petitioner's belief is a question of jurisdiction and not a "frivolous anti-tax argument." (GR p 21) Pointedly, had defense counsel listened, they would have learned that the IRS exceeded the intent and powers of congress. Curiously, then, why didn't counsel for both the government and defense permit the court to understand that, for "the precise question at issue," Chevron the agency exceeded its authority and congressional intent with errant statutory construction? (See Bostrain supra)

Since "judicial review of most agency action instructs reviewing courts to decide 'all relevant questions of law' 5 USC 706," City of Arlington v FCC _ US _, _ (2013) counsel had the obligation to argue what was actually tried "200 years" ago (GR p 10) - the rebuttal of presumptions and prima facie evidence. (See Hawes v Georgia 258 US 1 (1922), Casey v United States 276 US 413 (1928), Rindskopf v United States 105 US 418 (1882)) For such tax cases, the Supreme Court

> 1) stated a presumption was "subject to explanation" Hawes, 5 2) acknowledged that defendants had "the burden of proving facts peculiarly within their knowledge" Casey, 418 and 3) noted "every material fact upon which his liability was asserted was open to contestation." Rindskopf, 422

Counsel should have argued the question of personal jurisdiction. The "strategy" that petitioner simply did not have the "requisite mens rea" (Exhibit 5 p 4), without including "explanation," "knowledge" and "every material fact," was deficient.

The Federal Government did not have the power to directly tax

9

a man's earnings two centuries ago[1] and does not now. Moreover, the excisable federal benefits/privileges of social security and employment were not settled (See Charles C. Steward Machine v Davis 301 US 548 (1937) and Helvering v Davis 301 US 619 (1937)) until some sixty years ago. Even the Department of the Treasury stated, "For 1936, taxable income tax returns filed represented only 3.9% of the population." (Collection at Source of the Individual Normal Income Tax, 1941). Americans became liable for the income tax by accepting federal social security benefits on a voluntary basis.

So, the government is incorrect on two points. Counsel was not "unqualified" (GR p 11) to investigate. Secondly, the question of jurisdiction was not "answered multiple times." (GR p 9) Rather, the court "ruled" (GR p 10) against a lack of "personal jurisdiction." (GR p 2) Without competent counsel, the court never understood that petitioner's belief was not frivolous, but reasonable.

It is important to note that the word "frivolous" (Exhibit 6) originated with Agent Biggs. In fact, counsel failed to weigh Kotmair's letters (Pet Mot, Exhibit C) to Agent Biggs from 08/04 - 10/04. Kotmair stated that he was qualified as power of attorney; Biggs disagreed.(Exhibit 6) Counsel did not reconcile that Kotmair was NOT "barred from representing or assisting others" (Exhibit 7, 4) before the IRS until December 2004. Kotmair was, therefore, qualified afterall and Biggs was beholden to respond. Even Biggs stated, "If... qualified... I was required to... deal with Mr. Kotmair... not... Mr. Johnson..." (Exhibit 8, 132) Biggs and the IRS deliberately hid behind questionable agency authority for not answering substantive questions from Kotmair and petitioner. This is a critical issue since even Biggs was not certain that petitioner even "had a filing requirement" (Exhibit 8 p 137) when questioned on direct. Biggs stated "the evidence... was a bit of a mixture." Id. Counsel neglected to consider the significance of Biggs' avoidance of Kotmair and petitioner's belief while under investigation; for, Biggs skirted the matter by labeling petitioner's "concerns" and "arguments" as "frivolous" and sending him a "Response to Frivolous Arguments" Id. pamphlet. Yet, petitioner never posed a frivolous argument. Moreover, counsel did not argue against the pro forma pamphlet or ask why Biggs simply did not answer Kotmair's or petitioner's question as to the law that required him to comply. Confronted with his belief, Biggs would have been certain as to whether petitioner had a liability or not. This mistake was prejudicial.

Now the government lambasts petitioner for not reading all of the pamphlet when 1) he never posed a frivolous argument, 2) already knew of such baseless positions and 3) was directed by Biggs specfically "to page 19." (Exhibit 6) The government then strains to connect not reading the pamphlet while chastising petitioner for making his "way through the Internal Revenue Code" (GR p 16) and then accusing him of not looking "at the other side." Id. Counsel failed to validate that reading the code and asking questions were looking at the other side and not reading about frivolous arguments was reasonable. Moreover, counsel did not argue that the government did not offer "the other side" for nine years,(Exhibit 3) while Biggs avoided accountability with Kotmair during his investigation. Unbelievably, the government denigrates petitioner for "acquainting himself" (GR p 16) with "statutes, regulations and court opinions"

11

and ignoring what had no application to his belief - frivolous arguments. This is how Biggs infected the government's case with its unmerited tax protester argument with no antidote from counsel.

SIGNIFICANCE OF CHEVRON

Counsel should have argued that the agency exceeded it authority. (See Chevron supra, Auer v Robbins 519 US 452 (1997), Bowles v Seminole Rock 325 US 410 (1945)) Since a tax statute must be expressed in "clear and unambiguous language" 30 Op Atty Gen 273, 7/15/1914, the agency "must give effect to... the intent of Congress." Chevron 843 Therefore, acts that are ultra vires cannot be from a "gap" or "ambiguity" Id. but from the agency's interpretation or application of the statutes or regulations. Had counsel investigated "whether the agency has gone beyond what Congress has permitted," Arlington _ or offered a "permissible construction of the statute," Chevron 843 they would have argued that "statutory text forecloses the agency's assertion of authority." Arlington

Administrative Construction 39 L Ed 2d 942 refers to an historical train of abuse of government taxing authority.

> St Paul M&M Co. v Phelps 137 US 528 (1890), United States v Standard Brewery Inc 251 US 210 (1920), Grand Trunk W.R. Co v United States 252 US 112 (1920), Universal Battery Co v United States 281 US 580 (1930), Lucas v American Code Co 280 US 445 (1931), Fawcus Machine V United States 282 US 375 (1931), Burnett v Chicago Portrait Co 285 US 1 (1932), Helvering v Powers 293 US 214 (1934), M.E. Blatt Co v United States 305 US 267 (1938), Estate of Sanford v Commissioner 308 US 39 (1939), Helvering v Sabine Transportation 318 US 306 (1943), United States v Midland-Ross Corp 381 US 54 (1945), Volkswagenwerk v Federal Maritime Co 390 US 261 (1968), Federal Maritime Co v Seatrain Lines Inc 411 US 726 (1973), Brown v Gardner 513 US 115 (1994), Judulang v Holder 565 US _ (2011)

Such precedent requires advocates to probe the "who, what, where and when of regulatory power: which subject matters may an agency

12

regulate and under what conditions?" Arlington Without this strategy, "administrative application of law is administrative formulation of law." Id. Under the "Chevron framework", Id. challenging whether the "agency's application of its authority" Id. permitted criminal charges against one without the subject matter of specific excises would have been reasonable. Auer is the same, since Auer is "Chevron... applied to regulations rather than statutes." Decker v Northwest Envt'l Def Center _ US _ (2013) Or "Seminole Rock addresses the further question whether the agency's interpretation is consistent with the regulation." Kentuckians for the Commonwealth v Rivenburgh 317 F 3d 425, 440 (4th Cir. 2002) With deference tests, counsel would have reconciled that the "agency's expansive constructiion of the extent of its own power... wrought a fundamental change in the regulatory scheme," Arlington - that is, the assessment and collection of excises from "taxpayers" engaged in specific activities or privileges, which includes social security and employment. Those who do not subscribe to such benefits are without the scheme.

To illustrate, it is those who voluntarily engage in tires who (26 USC 4071) would pay an excise until no longer engaged. Congress cannot statutorily presume jurisdiction and tax those without the scope of the statute and the IRS may not enforce what Congress never intended. Thus, charges for non criminal conduct, Standard Brewery supra unsubscribing to excisable benefits, was worthy of a vigorous defense. For, "without express purpose to disobey the law", United States v Ratzlaf 510 US 135, 141 (1994) the mens rea element (See 28 Op OLC 297 12/30/04; 2002 OLC Lexis 19, 8/1/02) may not be satisfied. Moreover, petitioner knew he did not violate the law. (See

13

United States v Manuso 42 F 3d 836, 837 (4th Cir 1994), United States v Cheek 498 US 192, 202 (1991))

SEPARATION OF POWERS

Given petitioner's rebuttal, jurisdiction was asserted by errant agency authority. Thus, "when Government acts in excess of its lawful power... liberty is at stake." United States v Bond _ US _ (2011) Ambiguities from agency interpretations of statutes or regulations violate the separation of powers doctrine. (See 16 Op OLC 136 9/1/92) For "there can be no liberty" 5 Op OLC 294 10/7/81 when an agency both writes and interprets a law. As such, rather than move the court to employ "traditional tools of statutory construction," Chevron fn 9 counsel allowed for the collusion and abuse of legislative, executive and judicial power. Counsel failed to ask whether "Congress had an intention on the precise question at issue, in which case, that intention is the law and must be given effect." Id. Thus, judicial construction of statutory terms would have invalidated government indiscretion. (See Nat'l Cable & Telecomm v Brand X 545 US 967, 1018 (2005))

The clarity of the term "taxpayer" 26 USC 7701 (a)(14) within the context of Art. 1, Sec. 8, Cl 1, a clearly defined power to collect "excises," Stone Tracy supra another clearly defined term, required a challenge to the "agency's determination of its own jurisdiction," Arlington as "arbitrary, capricious, or manifestly contrary to the statute." Chevron 844 Morse supra shows that the term "taxpayer" is clear and requires the court to "trump" Brand X the agency's construction and conform with congressional intent. For,

> ...agencies are not a law unto themselves. ...the last

14

> words in law belong to Congress and the Supreme Court. Home Concrete & Supply LLC v United States 634 F 3d 249, 259 (4th Cir. 2010)

An effective defense would have defeated "agency expertise" Id. and a corresponding "lack of accountability." Id.

THE COURT

Errant agency authority could only be addressed by the court. Without sound advocacy, the court sanctioned the agency's unfettered determination of the statute. It was vital, then, for counsel to move the court "to question... whether the agency has stayed within the bounds of its statutory authority," Arlington or if there was "an incorrect application" Id. and "assertion of authority" Id. of an agency's determination of "specific provisions." Id. So, "whether the court decided correctly is a question that has different consequences from the question whether it had power to decide at all." Id.

For example, the Chevron court stated, "the basic legal error... was to adopt a static judicial definition of the term stationary source," Id 842 that the statute was read "inflexibly," Id 864 and was "not a distinction that Congress ever articulated itself." Id. In Arlington, the court asked if the FCC exceeded "the bounds of its statutory authority."Id. In the instant case, counsel should have asked the court

> If the agency exceeded "the bounds of its statutory authority" of the regulatory scheme by assessing and collecting "income" and "employment" taxes from one who rebutted the presumption and prima facie evidence that he was a "taxpayer" engaged in federally excisable benefits.

Counsel did not assert unambiguous statutory terms or argue an "erroneous judgment" Arlington by all parties concerned, most im-

15

portantly, the court.

> We are not free to selectively apply Chevron deference to an agency's interpretation of a statute in some cases, but not in others. '[T]he meaning of words in a statute cannot change with the statute's application.' Patel v Napolitano 706 F 3d 370, 376 (4th Cir. 2012), United States v Santos 553 US 507, 522 (2008)

Thus, jurisdiction was arguable under Rule 12(b)(6) or, if needed, before the jury.

The tax statutes and IRS are not immune from scrutiny. "Vague regulations... maximiz[e] agency power" Decker supra and "the power to prescribe" Id. and interpret is not a new evil." Id. The court noted, Auer is a "dangerous permission slip for the arrogation of power." Id. Since Congress is limited to those within the subject matter jurisdiction of particular excises, counsel should have argued that the court did not have personam jurisdiction. The court, then, may not even unwittingly, by mistake or oversight, decide based upon "personal policy preferences" Arlington and foster what was legislatively, executively and judicially untenable.

ADVICE TO COUNSEL

Petitioner stressed separation of powers to counsel and that

* there is no obligation to a statute for those who "fall without its scope." De Lima v Bidwell 182 US 1 (1901) (Decl 33)
* revenue laws must be "directly traceable to the power granted to Congress by Sec 8, Art 1 of the Constitution..." United States v Hill 123 US 681, 686 (1887) Id.
* "every person" American Banana Fruit Co v United Fruit Co 213 US 347, 357 (1909) means only those "subject to such legislation." Id.
* when the court lacks jurisdiction, it would be "treason to the Constitution" Cohens v Virginia 6 Wheat 264, 404 to presume so.

Petitioner asserted that he had no tax liability, (See Botta v Scanlon 288 F 2d 504, 506 (2nd Cir. 1961)) a fact that would compel the

16

judiciary's "proper role in our system." Clapper v Amnesty Int'l USA _ US _ (2013) As such, use of deference tests was critical to move the court to decide "... whether an action taken by one of the other two branches of the Federal Government was unconstitutional." Id. Doing so would have negated willful intent by establishing errant agency authority.

NOVEL POSITIONS

Undeniably, under a self-imposed threat of sanctions (Decl 32, 43), counsel failed to investigate "novel positions of first impressions." United States v Nelson 885 F 2d 547, 550 (9th Cir. 1989) Since counsel must feel at "liberty to press all claims that could conceivably invalidate his client's conviction," Id. counsel's "willingness and ability to press forward with a claim of first impression" Id. was essential. If counsel had been willing and able, the court would have

1) respected an argument with information outside the trial record
2) decided that the agency's power was impermissible
3) decided that the court lacked personam jurisdiction, or
4) allowed counsel to argue all the facts and circumstances to the jury

Significantly, counsel knew that petitioner submitted a writ of habeas corpus before trial in which he asserted,

> The United States has no authority over [petitioner]... especially since formally revoking/rescinding any benefit claim to the federal social security insurance program in 2000, thus rebutting the presumption of being a United States employee. (Exhibit 9) [added]

With this foundation, counsel should have defeated the element of jurisdiction and willfulness. Yet, they asked no questions and did not investigate. Counsel's closed perspective precluded them from

17

accepting what even Chief Justice Rehnquist acknowledged.

> The applicant [for government benefits] who objects to submitting the information required retains the option to decline participation in the program... The Washington Star, 11/28/76, Stephens Lectures, University of Kansas Law School

Petitioner's novel position was easy to understand. By declining benefits that would require an excise tax on income, petitioner was, naturally, outside the jurisdiction of the agency and, therefore, not subject to the tax code or 20 CFR, "EMPLOYEES' BENEFITS."

CONCLUSION

With this reply to the government's response to petitioner's 2255 motion, the court may appreciate that he had neither a base motive nor the requisite specific intent to violate a law. Rather, petitioner had a grounded belief predicated upon constitutional and statutory constraints. Pointedly, his belief was not argued before the court. Counsel's fear of sanctions and of the court deterred them from not only investigating their client's belief and rebuttal, they did not argue that there was no actus reus and, therefore, no mens rea. For these and the reasons cited herein, the two prong test under Strickland has been satisified. "Counsel's representation fell below an objective standard of reasonableness." Strickland, 688 There is a "reasonable probability that, but for counsel's unprofessional errors, the outcome would have been different." Id, 703

1 " I am under no moral or other obligation to publish to the world, how much my Expences or my Incomes amount to yearly." President John Adams' Diary

18

WHEREFORE, for the reasons stated herein and as supported by the record, motion and exhibits filed herewith, petitioner moves this court for summary judgment on Claims I, II and IV, to vacate, set aside or correct the sentence, and in doing so, to set aside the jury's verdict and, thereafter, grant any relief the court deems just and equitable.

Respectfully,

J.B.J

James B. Johnson
Petitioner, Pro per

CERTIFICATE OF SERVICE AND DECLARATION IN COMPLIANCE WITH 28 USC 1747

Know all men by these presents:

I, James B. Johnson, do hereby declare under penalty of perjury that on the 22nd day of April, 2015, I sent via the established legal mail protocol at Federal Correctional Institution Elkton, the original of the foregoing Motion and Memorandum to the entity listed below:

United States District Court
210 Franklin Rd SW
Suite 540
Roanoke, VA 24011-2208

Witness my hand this 22nd day of April, 2015

Witness

J.B.J

Petitioner

19

UNITED STATES DISTRICT COURT
WESTERN DISTRICT OF VIRGINIA

James Bowers Johnson Petitioner, v. UNITED STATES OF AMERICA Respondent.	)))))))	Case No.: 6:12-cr-00015-NKM Supplemental Declaration

COMES NOW, petitioner, James B. Johnson, having full knowledge of the facts and who is competent to testify on the matters stated, does hereby submit this Supplemental Declaration in Support of the motion pursuant to 28 USC 2255 to vacate, set aside or correct the conviction and sentence by reason of ineffective assistance of counsel.

1. In his Declaration submitted 01/07/15, paragraph 21 was inadvertently omitted. It states:

> 21. When petitioner received notification in February 2009 that the IRS recommended to the Department of Justice (DOJ) that he be prosecuted, petitioner wrote a passionate letter to Mr. Salad at DOJ. Petitioner pleaded that Mr. Salad provide the law that required him to file a federal income tax return. Petitioner stated that he revoked and rescinded his intent to federal benefits of social security. He stated that his intent was to comply with all applicable tax laws. Mr. Salad never responded.

Petitioner further adds the following point.

> When petitioner met with defense counsel in Harrisonburg, Virginia, they disclosed a plea offer tendered by the Federal Government. When petitioner summarily rejected the plea and Harris asked if he wanted to know the details, petitioner replied negatively. Harris asked, "Are you trying to be a martyr?" Petitioner responded, "I am innocent."

Further Declarant sayeth not.

In accord with 28 USC 1746, I declare under penalty of perjury under the laws of the United States of America that the foregoing is true and correct. Executed this 22nd day of April, 2015.

J.B.J.
James B. Johnson

TIMELINE

	1992	1999	2000	2001	2002	2003	2004	2005	2006	2007	2008	2009	2010	2011	2012	2013	2014	2015
Petitioner actions	1	2	3				4	5	6						7	8		
Government/Defense actions/inactions			3				4	5	6						7	8		

1) Petitioner begins studies of law, taxes, gov't
2) files last federal income tax return
3) revokes/rescinds federal benefits, notifies SSA and DOT/SOS - gov't never counters rebuttal
4) Petitioner and Kotmair send letters/questions to agent Biggs - Biggs never answers, introduces "frivolous" argument langauge
5) Petitioner sends letters/questions to agent Pompei - Pompei never answers
6) Petitioner sends letters/questions to elected officials, IR Comm., IRS and DOJ - these agencies refuse to answer and most do not respond
7) Petitioner states constitutional good faith belief to counsel - counsel ignores belief as "frivolous" and never investigates; states to jury that client has a tax liability
8) Petitioner's questions and belief remain unanswered to this day, (Sosna v Iowa, 419 US 393 (1975))

Appendix I – Declaration, New Trial

(This Is A Continuation Of The Declaration In Appendix A As It Concerns The New Trial Motion)

120. Cargill met with Petitioner at the jail on 2/1/13, at which time Cargill stated that he believed there were grounds upon which to request a new trial. Yet, Cargill stated that he did not personally want to submit the motion. Cargill suggested that Petitioner have outside counsel file the request. Cargill stated that Judge Moon would not likely approve the motion if he submitted it, since he practiced in Moon's Court. Cargill went on to explain that filing a motion would not be prejudicial, that if the motion were denied, both the denied motion and trial could be appealed.

121. Petitioner had the name of a lawyer, Jay Nanavati, given to Petitioner by his sister some weeks earlier. After Petitioner explained Cargill's idea, Nanavati advised Petitioner to have Cargill submit the motion for a new trial. Nanavati contacted Cargill by phone, Petitioner by mail.

122. On 3/7/13, Harris met with Petitioner at the jail. Harris told Petitioner, only after he asked about the new trial request, that they never submitted the motion. Harris stated that they decided against this course; she said it would not be "strategically beneficial" for sentencing.

57

123. Petitioner could not believe her comments. He could not believe their failure to act. When Petitioner asked Harris to file the request, she stated that the deadline had passed. Then she rather flippantly and dismissively suggested that Petitioner could file for ineffective assistance of counsel.

124. Petitioner prepared his own "motion for a new trial with outside counsel" with an affidavit dated 3/14/13. (Exhibit P)

125. Cargill sent Petitioner a letter dated 3/18/13 and stated, "I recall that when we met on the deadline day for a new trial motion, you expressed a desire to file such a motion." He then stated," There was some question about whether you were going to retain counsel and seek/follow the advice of retained counsel on the issue." He continued with, "I did not believe there were valid grounds and because I felt that such a motion could be counterproductive in that it would amount to an attack on the impartiality of the Judge who will soon sentence you." (Exhibit Q) Petitioner immediately noted the apparent inconsistencies with Cargill's recollection and statements.

126. Cargill did not meet with Petitioner on the 4th - the "deadline day for a new trial motion." Cargill did not visit the jail on 2/4/13. He met with Petitioner on 2/1/13. This is evident given the note Petitioner sent to Cargill on 2/3/13, received by Cargill on 2/5/13, in which Petitioner requested that Cargill submit the new trial request. (Exhibit R)

127. Petitioner sent Cargill another handwritten note received on 2/11/13, stating, "I am confident you filed a motion." (Exhibit S) As disclosed by Petitioner's affidavit, (Exhibit P), paragraph 6, Petitioner stated that Cargill "encouraged me to contact [outside

counsel] and to notify Cargill no later than Monday the 4th, the final date to submit a notice of intent to file a motion for a new trial."

128. The question of Cargill supposedly meeting with Petitioner on the 4th, the "deadline day," is poignant, if only because Petitioner was not able to even contact Cargill. As revealed in paragraphs 7 through 14 of Petitioner's affidavit (Exhibit P) and note received by Cargill on 2/11/13 (Exhibit S), Petitioner went to extraordinary efforts to ensure that somehow someone would contact Cargill.

129. Contrary to Cargill's assertion, there never "was some question about whether you [Petitioner] were going to retain counsel and seek/follow the advice of retained counsel on the issue." (Exhibit Q) Cargill, alone, proffered the need to request a new trial and suggested outside counsel accomplish this act. Cargill was clear that the motion would likely be denied if he were to argue the merits. He believed that outside counsel would have a greater chance of prevailing. Petitioner's written note, received by Cargill on 2/5/13, contemporaneously reflects Cargill's reasoning and motivation. Petitioner states, "I agree with your assesment [reason for a new trial]." (Exhibit S) The advice for a new trial was already established by Cargill. Moreover, Petitioner then wrote, "I will try to reach Jay on Monday," thereby noting Cargill's advice to retain other counsel. There never was a question about Petitioner contacting another lawyer, if only because of Cargill's reluctance to submit the paperwork or argue the issue himself.

130. Cargill's comment in his 3/18/13 letter (Exhibit Q) that he did not file the motion "because I did not believe there were valid grounds..." is without any factual basis. Cargill is the only one

59

who suggested the motion for a new trial; for, he believed that the child support issue was highly prejudicial. He also acknowledged less important reasons a new trial should be granted. Petitioner memorialized those reasons in his affidavit. (Exhibit P)

131. Even if the new trial request was made for the child support issue alone, the very impetus of Cargill's recommendation, there were "valid grounds" from his perspective. Cargill's "valid grounds" served as the catalyst for the furious activity to reach outside counsel and follow-up with Cargill by Monday, the 4th, the "deadline day," so that the request would be preserved.

132. Outside counsel's involvement only reached the level of stating that Cargill should submit the motion and, if granted, he would consider handling the new trial. Consequently, if only because Petitioner was able to contact outside counsel did outside counsel send Cargill a text/email alerting him to follow his own advice and file on behalf of his own client.

133. At a minimum, referring back to the note received by Cargill on 2/5/13, Petitioner asked Cargill to "submit a motion for a new trial." Cargill knew that Petitioner would try to contact outside counsel by the 4th. Moreover, Cargill received express instructions from Petitioner to file. (Id.)

134. Petitioner did not consider a request for a new trial prior to Cargill's suggestion on 2/1/1/13. Petitioner had no understanding as to justification for doing so.

135. Cargill stated in his 3/18/13 letter that he "felt such a motion could be counterproductive" as "an attack on the impartiality of the Judge who soon will sentence you." (Exhibit Q) This observation is consistent with Harris' statement made on 3/7/13, when she told

60

Petitioner that filing would not have been "strategically beneficial" for sentencing. Defense counsel's recommendation for a new trial morphed into the polar opposite. A request for a new trial would prove to be injurious to Petitioner. Thus, such a request would be prejudicial to any defendant before any sentencing.

136. Petitioner mailed a request to Nanavati on 12/29/14 for a copy of the email/text sent to Cargill on or about 2/3/13.

FURTHER AFFIANT SAYETH NOT.
In accord with 28 USC 1746, I declare under penalty of perjury under the laws of the United States of America that the foregoing is true and correct.

Executed this 7th day of January, 2015.

James B. Johnson
Affiant/Petitioner

* Please note, while many court cases were given to counsel, the citations were not, which are provided herein for the convenience of the court.

** Please note the current transcript does not reflect the actual exchange. Petitioner has a separate transcript at home that is properly transcribed.

61

Appendix J – 2255 Motion, New Trial

(This Is A Continuation Of The 2255 Motion In Appendix B As It Concerns The New Trial Motion)

COUNSEL FAILED TO MOVE FOR A NEW TRIAL PURSUANT TO RULE 33 OF THE FEDERAL RULES OF CRIMINAL PROCEDURES

Under Rule 33(b)(2) of the Federal Rules of Criminal Procedures, a defendant has the right to file a "motion for a new trial grounded on any reason...[and] must be filed within 14 days after the verdict or finding of guilty." [brackets added] The Supreme Court stated,

> the core purpose of the counsel guarantee was to secure "Assistance" at trial, when the accused was confronted with both the intricacies of the law and the advocacy of the public prosecutor. United States v. Ash, 413 US 300, 309 (1973).

Legal counsel may deprive this right with a failure to provide adequate assistance. Counsel's ineffectiveness occurred with their unwillingness to file a motion for a new trial. In United States v Matthews, 239 Fed. Appx.

24

806, 807 (4th Cir. 2007), the defendant "claimed that after the sentencing hearing he asked his counsel to file a notice of appeal." In its opinion, the Court referred to United States v. Peak, 992 F. 2d 39, 41 (4th Cir. 1993).

> ...the Sixth Amendment obligates counsel to file an appeal when his client requests him to do so. Failure to note an appeal upon timely request constitutes ineffective assistance of counsel, regardless of the likelihood of success on the merits. Id at 42. Counsel who consults with the defendant and fails to follow the defendant's express instructions... performs in a professionally unreasonable manner. [emphasis added]

Counsel deprived Petitioner of the right to request a new trial, even after express instructions to do so. (Decl. 126, 127, 132, 133). Moreover, Cargill misrepresented the facts of what transpired, which raises the issue of credibility. With his 3/18/13 letter to Petitioner (Exhibit Q), Cargill reshaped his understanding of the events. Candidly, Cargill attempted to color the circumstances surrounding the timeline so that the "facts" obscured his neglect. In a word, Cargill lied; or, if granted the benefit of the doubt, he took liberties with the truth to craft a retrospective representation so that he would appear as "counsel" granted by the Sixth Amendment.

Cargill was clearly motivated not to argue the motion for a new trial (Decl. 120), only because he regularly appeared before Judge Moon (Decl. 120). Cargill conveniently reasoned that Moon would give outside counsel more credibility. Yet, such justification denigrates the Court. A fair and impartial Court would dignify the merits of a motion tendered by competent counsel, any counsel, public or private, inside or outside. To follow Cargill's reasoning, then, a pro se litigant's submission would be considered worthless. Cargill's reasoning and neglect can do nothing but establish prejudice. Consider that,

1) Cargill now denies ever suggesting the new trial request. (Decl. 129) (Exhibit Q)

25

2) Cargill reasoned for outside counsel to file the motion because the Court was less than impartial.

3) Cargill "recalls" (Decl. 129) (Exhibit Q) meeting on the "deadline day," while overlooking the email from outside counsel (Decl. 125) and Petitioner's notes, which establish meeting on 2/1/13. (Decl. 120, 126) (Exhibits R, S)

4) Given the urgency of the issue, if only for the immediacy of the deadline of 2/4/13, Cargill did not convey his failure to file until the 3/~~1~~7/13 meeting with Harris (Decl. 122) or Cargill's 3/18/13 letter (Decl. 125), both of which were 4 to 6 weeks after the fact!

5) Cargill couched his language in his 3/18/13 letter (Exhibit Q) with implications that: 1) the idea for a new trial originated with Petitioner and, 2) that Petitioner suggested securing outside counsel. Cargill's select prose artfully excludes any hint that he suggested: 1) the need to move for a new trial and, 2) that Petitioner contact outside counsel to accomplish this end.

6) Unbelievably and inconceivably, Cargill audaciously stated in his 3/18/13 letter that he "did not believe there were valid grounds" for a new trial. (Exhibit Q). This statement, which is wholly disingenuous, does not square with Cargill's ultimate decision that he "felt such a motion could be counterproductive" as "an attack on the impartiality of the Judge who soon will sentence you." Id. Logically, the latter reason not to submit a motion is inconsistent with the former. If Cargill believed there were "no valid grounds," there would have been no reason to submit what would have been "counterproductive."

7) Counsel's final justification was that the submission of a motion for new trial was not "strategically beneficial." (Decl. 135)

As reflected by the evidence, Cargill covered the landscape to excuse his outright failure to protect and defend his client's rights and best interests. Thus, we arrive at the crux of the matter. Cargill did not want to appear

26

appear before Judge Moon and risk any repercussions that might befall him, which is the same reason counsel failed to argue the element of jurisdiction in the first claim: Counsel sought to protect their own interests at the expense of the truth and their client's rights. When a Petitioner is able to show that counsel "labored under an actual conflict of interest" and that the conflict "adversely affected his [attorney's] performance," prejudice under the second prong of the Strickland test is presumed. Strickland, 692. The prejudice that resulted from counsel's neglect cannot be denied. Petitioner, without proper training and resources, was forced to submit an inferior request after the "deadline day" that lacked effective legal reasoning and corresponding prose. Counsel, on the other hand, could have offered a professional and balanced argument, highlighting what, in fact, counsel, in good faith believed - that the evidence concerning child support was extremely prejudicial and factored significantly in the jury's finding of guilt.

Pointedly, counsel could have tendered an argument that, if denied by the court, could have withstood scrutiny upon appeal. With competent counsel, in keeping with professional norms, they would have effectively secured the opportunity to prevail with a new trial by motion or by appeal to any denial. Failing to do so was prejudicial.

EVIDENTIARY HEARING

In determining whether to hold an evidentiary hearing in a post-conviction filing, 28 USC 2255 (b) is controlling. It is clear that Petitioner is not "entitled to no relief." Petitioner has established plausible claims of ineffective assistance of counsel, with detailed controverted issues of fact, supported by competent evidence. A hearing would permit proof that would entitle granting relief. Petitioner's claims are not "vague, conclusory or palpably incredible..." Raines v United States, 423 F 2d, 526, 531 (4th Cir. 1970) (citing Machibroda v United States, 368 US 487, 495 (1962)) However,

27

APPENDIX K – MOTION TO AMEND, NEW TRIAL

UNITED STATES DISTRICT COURT
WESTERN DISTRICT OF VIRGINIA

James Bowers Johnson	)	
	)	
	)	
v.	)	MOTION TO AMEND
	)	CASE NO. 6:12-cr-00015-1
	)	
UNITED STATES OF AMERICA	)	

COMES NOW petitioner, James Bowers Johnson, who submits this Motion to Amend the Motion to vacate, set aside or correct a sentence under 28 USC 2255. Please see attached Memorandum in Support and exhibits.

Respectfully,

James B. Johnson

Petitioner, Pro per

MEMORANDUM IN SUPPORT

STATEMENT OF FACTS

On 12/24/14 and 1/22/15, petitioner, by written correspondence, requested that attorney Jay Nanavati provide the email he sent to defense counsel, Randy Cargill, which conveyed petitioner's request that Cargill file a motion for a new trial. Nanavati responded on 2/3/15. (Exhibit A) This new evidence supports petitioner's claims asserted in his 2255 action.

ARGUMENT

Petitioner has the burden under Strickland v Washington 466 US 668 (1984) to demonstrate that "deficient performance prejudiced the defense," Id., 687 and that "but for counsel's unprofessional errors, the result would have been different." Id., 694 To this end, petitioner argued that defense counsel:

1) refused to argue the element of jurisdiction
2) failed to argue the element of willfulness
3) failed to exercise provisions of Rule 6, F.R.Crim.P.
4) failed to move for a new trial

In Cargill's response to Nanavati's question of 1/29/13, on 1/30/13, as to whether or not he intended to file a motion for a new trial, Cargill admitted there were grounds upon which one could "credibly argue" for the recusal of the judge. Cargill then stated, "i think i should have had the courage to raise this." (Exhibit A)

Petitioner stated in his 2255 Memorandum of Law (MOL) and underscores now that, but for defense counsel's "timidity" (MOL, pg 2) and "scant knowledge of tax law" (United States v Bursten 395 F 2d 976, 981 (5th Cir. 1968), not only was petitioner denied effective assistance of counsel under the 6th Amendment, the entire trial process was adversely affected. Pointedly, the greatest injury from counsel's fear was their failure to argue petitioner's good faith belief, which had a "constitutional basis." (MOL, 10)

2

Significantly, Cargill's admission that he lacked the courage for so serious a concern as the recusal of the judge and petitioner's good faith belief is as monumental as it is damning. Cargill's lack of courage of the recusal was equal to his fear of sanctions for arguing a good faith defense that was anything but "frivolous." Cargill's fear and subsequent failure to act on behalf of his client reflects his deficient and ineffective advocacy throughout the trial process.

The Supreme Court cited the American Bar Association on "Standards for Criminal Justice, Defense Function, Sec. 1.6 (Approved draft 1971), which states,

> [T]he duties of a lawyer to his client are to represent his legitimate interests and considerations of personal and professional advantage should not influence his advice or performance. Maness v Myers 419 US 449, n 16 (1975)

The Court then referred to the "introductory comments."

> A lawyer cannot be timorous in his representation. Courage and zeal in the defense of his client's interests are qualities without which one cannot fully perform as an advocate. [emphasis added] Id

This tone is reflected in Sacher v United States 343 US 1, 13 (1952).

> ...this Court... will unhesitatingly protect counsel in fearless, vigorous and effective performance of every duty pertaining to the office of the advocate on behalf of any person whatsoever.

Petitioner asserts that legal advocacy which is void of courage cannot equal the effective assistance of advocacy expected under the 6th Amendment. There can be little dispute that courage is equal, if not of greater importance, to knowledge. If counsel lacks either, he cannot ensure the best strategic or tactical interests of his client. Rather, absent fearless advocacy, "personal and professional advantage" Maness supra obstruct and deny any sacred duty owed.

Petitioner duly summarizes that, if only for lack of courage, counsel:

1) refused to investigate petitioner's good faith belief. Their personal fear of "sanctions" prevailed. Consequently, their timorous posture tainted their entire outlook from the earliest stages of the proceedings. Because they were fearful, petitioner had to, however inartfully and indelicately, attempt to argue the government's lack of jurisdiction.

2) was unwilling to explore and introduce "available mitigating evidence" Wong v Belmontes 558 US _ (2009). This posture belies their competence to research and argue "the precise question at issue." Chevron U.S.A. Inc. v Natural Resources Defense Council 467 US 837, 842 (1984)

3) was too intimidated to pursue a motion for a new trial, even with the valid reasons Cargill gave Nanavati. This posture, borne out of fear, reflects an indecisive, if not schizophrenic, mindset. For, Cargill waffled between not submitting a motion, to offering valid reasons, then suggesting the effort was "counterproductive" (Exhibit A), to stating the petitioner should have outside counsel file the motion (MOL, 26) and, finally, to ignoring petitioner's express directive to file as somehow "strategically beneficial" (MOL, 26). It was Cargill, afterall, who did not want to argue the motion before Judge Moon. (MOL, 27)

Clearly, based upon the foregoing concerns, defense counsel did not fulfill the "duties of a lawyer" Maness supra and represent their client's "legitimate interests." Id Why? Counsel suffered from a lack of courage.

Analagous to a three legged stool, an attorney's efforts represent courage, knowledge and competence. The absence of just one leg, courage, renders the stool dysfunctional. With the concession that they had "scant knowledge" Bursten supra of tax law, counsel's competence is inherently questionable. Counsel was without a stable foundation upon which to stand and, therefore, neglected to accomplish their prime directive - subject the prosecutor's case to "meaningful adversarial testing" United States v Cronic 466 US 648, 656 (1984). But for their self-imposed "conflict of interest" Id., fn 31 anchored in fear, petitioner's defense was relegated in importance to counsel's personal and professional advantage. Candidly, without the requisite courage, no attorney may overcome the lions and tigers and bears encountered during a

4

trial process. Cargill did not offer a "fearless, vigorous and effective performance of every duty" Maness [emphasis added] of his office as advocate. He lacked the courage.

This truth was proved with Nanavati's email of 2/4/13 (Exhibit B) in which he states that Cargill's client's intent is "that you file the motion for a new trial or a motion for an extension of time to file." Noteworthy, Cargill did not acknowledge this time sensitive issue until 2/8/13, three days after the deadline day. Moreover, contrary to professional courtesy, Cargill did NOT disclose that he did NOT file a motion, while stating he would "advise of any major developments." Instead, Cargill revealed his plan, for his personal and professional advantage, of asking for CLE credit had he worked with Nanavati. Meanwhile, petitioner did not learn of Cargill's failure to file a motion until 3/7/13, and only from his assistant, Andrea Harris.

CERTIFICATE OF SERVICE AND DECLARATION IN COMPLIANCE WITH 28 USC 1747

Know all men by these presents:

I, James Johnson, do hereby declare under penalty of perjury that on the ___th day of February, 2015, I sent via the established legal mail protocol at Federal Correctional Institute Elkton, the original of the foregoing motion to the person listed below:

United States District Court
western District of Virginia
Clerk of the Court
210 Franklin Rd SW, Ste 540
Roanoke, VA 24011-2208

Signed this ___ day of February 2015

James B. Johnson

5

APPENDIX L – BP-8 (COAT INCIDENT)

U.S. DEPARTMENT OF JUSTICE
Federal Bureau of Prisons

REQUEST FOR ADMINISTRATIVE REMEDY

Type or use ball-point pen. If attachments are needed, submit four copies. Additional instructions on reverse.

From: Johnson, James B. (LAST NAME, FIRST, MIDDLE INITIAL) 16665-084 (REG. NO.) GA (UNIT) FSL EEkton (INSTITUTION)

Part A- INMATE REQUEST - Request use of coat during inclement weather, request discernment and reasonable judgment of staff concerning adverse weather conditions. On 4/21/15, MArtin, R. (LT) met with me concerning the "Request for Administrative Remedy" submitted on 4/17/15. Martin was combative, accusatory and not even remotely in a professional demeaner that would reflect a good faith effort to resolve the comŧlaint, which reflects her rigid posture concerning the coat policy. Rather than discuss the issue, she accused me of not following directions. Forexample, she stated that I did not complete the "Date/Time" portion of the BP8, which is not myrespons-ibility. Martin's agenda could not be any more obvious - attack without the intent to resolve the issue at hand. Moreover, she stated that in addition to a "history" of not following directions, she said I lied to her about my circulation problem. While looking at my medical redcords, she said that I did not have an issue. i informed her that my family has a history that is not in the records, and said that I showed her my white fingers on 4/16 as proof that the cold affected me. Martin was unaffected. She noted my receipt of the Inmate Handbook, showed me a copy of the policy and explained that I could buy a poncho from commissary. To date MArtin is unfamiliar as to whether or what the coat policy is in the program statement. Meanwhile, she exercises arbitrary and aapricious power that equates to cruel and unusual punishment under the eighth amendment concerning the well-being of those in adverse weather conditions. Her response does not reflect that "good faith efforts were attempted to resolve the inmate's complaint." (See BP8) (see attached)

4/22/15
DATE

SIGNATURE OF REQUESTER

Part B- RESPONSE

This issue was informally resolved.

K. Hoover, Lieutenant

James B. Johnson
16665-084

DATE

WARDEN OR REGIONAL DIRECTOR

If dissatisfied with this response, you may appeal to the Regional Director. Your appeal must be received in the Regional Office within 20 calendar days of the date of this response.

ORIGINAL: RETURN TO INMATE

CASE NUMBER:

CASE NUMBER: 819462-F1

Part C- RECEIPT

Return to: LAST NAME, FIRST, MIDDLE INITIAL | REG. NO. | UNIT | INSTITUTION

SUBJECT:

4/30/15
DATE

RECIPIENT'S SIGNATURE (STAFF MEMBER)

USP LVN

BP-229(13)
APRIL 1982

Request for Administrative Remedy (continued)

MArtin is not concerned with the health of guilty men attempting to reform or innocent men fighting to leave an unjust system; her intent is to enforce the policy regardless. She even mentioned that I was lucky that she did not order all coats to laundry for cleaning and repair. Moreover, a poncho does not protect one from winter-like and stormy conditions, if one can afford to purchase such an item.

In Porter v Nussle 534 US 516 (2002), the Supreme Court stated that "an unwarranted assault by a corrections officer may be reflective of a systemic problem traceable to poor hiring practices, inadequate training, or insufficient supervision." The court also stated that "... prison authorities' interest in receiving prompt notice of and opportunity to take action against guard brutality is no less compelling than their interest in receiving notice and an opportunity to stop other types of staff wrongdoing." In Wilkins v Gaddy, 559 US _ (2010), the Court considered "The core judicial inquiry on an Eighth Amendment excessive force claim was whether force was applied in a good faith to maintain or restore discipline, or maliciously and sadistically cause harm." Appropriately, the court stated, "when prison officials maliciously and sadistically used force to cause harm, contemporary standards of decency were always violated, whether or not significant injury was evident." Martin's rigid enforcement belies those standards of decency.

Just as the track is closed in the winter, not for the cold, but for wind chill factors, just as the track is closed in the summer, not for the heat, but for wet bulb humidity readings, there is discernment involved regarding the health and well-being of inmates. On 4/16/15, it was cold, windy and raining. When I met with MArtin on 4/21, it was cold, windy and overcast. I wore my coat. Her reluctance to exercise reasonable judgment that 61 degrees is not really 61 reflects depraved indifference to a population that is older, using walkers, canes, wheel chairs etc as they stand in line for chow in less than temperate conditions. As stated in Preiser v Rodriguez 411 US 475 (1973), the court acknowledged "For... prisoners, eating, sleeping, dressing, washing, working and playing are all done under the watchful eye of the" BOP. Responses to an inmate's concern about his health, welfare and well-being are equally under that watchful eye.

Candidly, I am an innocent man fighting to get out of here. Arbitrary use of power runs counter to an effective administrative remedy process. Since I spend my time writing and typing legal work, the condition of my body and fingers is a prime concern. Notably, this is why I wear a coat and gloves in the housing unit. I am adversely affected by the cold on the inside, which is warmer than 60 degrees.

As stated in the BP8, I request that staff use discernment during inclement weather. This may require standards of deceny and compassion as opposed to a cold posture on already less than temperate days.

APPENDIX M – BP-8/BP-9 (COPY CARD INCIDENT)

U.S. DEPARTMENT OF JUSTICE
Federal Bureau of Prisons

REQUEST FOR ADMINISTRATIVE REMEDY

Type or use ball-point pen. If attachments are needed, submit four copies. Additional instructions on reverse.

From: Johnson, James B. — 16665-084 — 6A — FCI-Low, Elkton
LAST NAME, FIRST, MIDDLE INITIAL — REG. NO. — UNIT — INSTITUTION

Part A- INMATE REQUEST * This matter concerns deprivation of constitutional rights *
As a matter of record, I respectfully appeal the incident report and action for the following reasons:
1) The accusing "education" staff never found me in possession of another's copy card; rather, I simply told Mr. Sisson that I lost one. When the card was found and in Sisson's possession, I said that it belonged to Devine Harvin. However, I admitted that I had previously used the card. This admission was the ONLY basis for Ms. Stewart's unilateral and overzealous actions.

continued

6/25/2015 — *This is time sensitive.
DATE — SIGNATURE OF REQUESTER

Part B- RESPONSE

DATE — WARDEN OR REGIONAL DIRECTOR

If dissatisfied with this response, you may appeal to the Regional Director. Your appeal must be received in the Regional Office within 20 calendar days of the date of this response.

ORIGINAL: RETURN TO INMATE — CASE NUMBER: ____

CASE NUMBER: ____

Part C- RECEIPT

Return to: LAST NAME, FIRST, MIDDLE INITIAL — REG. NO. — UNIT — INSTITUTION

SUBJECT: ____

DATE — RECIPIENT'S SIGNATURE (STAFF MEMBER)

USP LVN — Printed on Recycled Paper — BP-229(13) APRIL 1982

2) Ms. Stewart and other staff routinely see and hear of inmates asking others for copy cards or to have others make copies. Staff see the "giving/receiving of value;" yet, they say and do nothing. Moreover, they see men performing legal work (research, typing, copying) for others. They see "writ-writers" re-searching and writing legal briefs for others. The Supreme Court, in Johnson v Avery, 393 US 483 (1969) recognized that the right of access to the courts included a right of legal assistance. The court went so far as to direct the California Department of Corrections, in Younger v Gilmore, 404 US 15 (1971), "to heed the Johnson decision and abandon a prison rule making it difficult for inmates to get legal help from writ-writers." The court cited Nolan v Scafati, 430 F 2d 548, 551 (CA 1970) which stated, "Johnson v Avery stand for the general proposition that an inmate's right of access to the court involves a corollary right to obtain some assistance in preparing his communication with the court." In Jones v North Carolina Prisoners' Union, 433 US 119 (1977), the Court acknowledged Johnson v Avery and "concluded that the rule prohibiting the use of 'writ-writers' from aiding fellow prisoners in preparing legal papers... was unconstitutional because of its impact on prisoners' right of access to the courts." This court stated that "By word and deed, then, we have repeatedly reaffirmed that'a policy of judicial restraint cannot encompass any failure to take cognizance of valid constitutional claims... when a prison regulation or practice offends a constitutional guarantee, federal courts will discharge their duty to protect constitutional rights." Ms. Stewart took it upon herself to deny my constitutional right to access the courts, by purposely targeting me and involving herself in a situation of which she had no part. Inmate Harvin, akin to a writ-writer, who provides services to the illiterate and indigent, was helping me "communicate" with the courts. Harvin gave me help in my "right of access to the court [which] involves some assistance in preparing [my] communication" with the court. Harvin attempted to help me "in preparing legal papers." Clearly, Stewart's decision to enforce a "prison regulation or practice that offends a constitutional guarantee" was arbitrary and capricious. Harvin even told Stewart that the copy card was used for legal work. I was prepared to copy my appellate brief (thanks to Harvin) and mailit with stamps from other inmates (a service a writ-writer would provide). I was to mail the brief that next morning to meet the deadline. Regardless of the obvious "giving/receiving of value" between inmates in the law library, the venue of writ-writers and legal efforts of so many, staff has done and does nothing. Why? Why did she now choose to holdme accountable for VERBALLY admitting to Mr. Sisson that I had another man's card for legal work? Why did Stewart involve herself in a matter to which she was not a party? Candidly, many of her statements in herreport were simply not true. These are concerns that led to an 8.5 for depriving me of a constitutional right and harassment. The Supreme Court in Porter v Nussle, 534 US 516 (2002) held that to sustain a claim of excessive force, a prisoner need not show significant injury. The court further explained that "...a specific incident may be symptomatic rather than aberrational. An unwarranted assault... may be reflective of a systemic problem traceable to poor hiring practices, inadequate training or insufficient supervision." Finally, the court said, "when prison officials maliciously... cause harm, contemporary standards of decency [are] always violated, whether or not significant injury was evident." I mention the foregoing because I am worried about a patternof harassment that affects my constitutional rights.

3) I met with LT Brinker on 6/24/15 and he said the report was "BS," that he was going to get rid of it and state that I did extra duty. Yet, when I read the report, I told him that it was filled with false testimony. As such, I could not agree. I said that Stewart was harassing me, as was evident by her passive aggressive behavior, and that unless she was held accountable, the problem might surface later. I decided to file an 8.5 on Stewart (see attached). However, had I known that I could get a copy of the incident report without Brinker processing it, I would have resolved the matter informallythat evening, as Harvin did. The frivolous report would not be a matter of record.

4) Please note that before he retired, I spoke directly with Unit Manager, Mr. Garcia, about the BOP providing copies and postage for legal work because of my frequent lack of funds. Garcia refused. As such, Ihave no choice but to rely upon the generosity of others. To illustrate, this response requires that I either type or write in pen. I would have to receive something of value to do either. So I borrowed a type writer ribbon to satisfy the requirement.

5) I respectfully request that the incident report be expunged. I request that staff (Stewart) receive training concerning the value of a man's right to access the courts, which would require that staff discern that there are scenarios that one man may in fact help another to manifest this right to communicate with the courts. I ask that staff not target one unnecessarily, especially in a venue like the law library, which is filled with men who are earnestly fighting for their rights and their eventual release, ultimately relying upon their coveted constitutional rights to access the courts, with or without the assistance of others.

Respectfully,

A couple of months ago, I and the man who works in the law library had a disagreement about the typewriters. The door to the education office was closed. Yet, Stewart opened the door and asked, "Are you bothering my law clerk?" I responded that I was having a private conversation with another man." She then threatened to ban me from the law library. Stewart injected herself into a situation that did not involve her.

On 6/24/15, at 11:15, I specifically asked Mr. Sisson if anyone turned in a copy card. He invited me in to look and yelled back to Stewart to ask if anyone turned in a copy card. She said "No." As I was leaving, Stewart said, "Who's asking?" I did not turn around or respond but heard he say, "Oh!"

At 11:40, with the library open, I asked the law clerk if anyone turned in a card. He said "Yes" and that Sisson had it. I walked back to the office and Sisson had a card in his hand and was looking at the computer screen. I said that if it was the card that it belonged to Devine Harvin. Sisson responded, "Oh, you had another inmate's card?" I said "yes." Rather than give me the card, he asked that I have Harvin get it directly from Sisson. I left and promptly explained to Harvin that he see Sisson without uniform, that Sisson was waiting.

By the time Harvin arrived, Stewart had paged him. I was now outside the door playing a guitar. When Harvin came out, he had a strange look and said, "You dealt with Mr. Sisson, right?" I agreed. Harvin replied that based upon what he just experienced, I could never have spoken with Stewart. I said that Stewart had nothing to do with with this issue, that I never dealt with her.

Harvin said that Stewart asked him why Johnson had his copy card, to which he responded that he was helping me copy legal work, that he was leaving next week. Harvin said that she replied that she was keeping thecard until further notice.

I explained to Harvin that Stewart had a problem with me, that the issue was not about the card or him, that men share cards frequently in the library in her presence. When I returned the guitar, the recreation staff said that Stewart came to retrieve my name and ID number.

Affidavit

Comes now James Johnson, of sound mind, having full knowledge of the facts, willingly, truthfully and without any mental reservation, who attests to the following, to wit:

1) On June 30, 2015, at 8:10 p.m., I went to the law library to speak with Mr. Sisson about the lost copy card issue of 6/24/15.
2) I asked Sisson how Stewart, not directly involved, came to be in control of the situation. He responded with a general answer that they work as a team.
3) I stressed that Stewart appears to have a problem with me. I further stated that I specifically spoke with him about the card on 6/24 and purposely avoided Stewart. Sisson confirmed that this is what I had done, that I only spoke with him.
4) I mentioned that when I returned to the law library after lunch, that he had the card and was looking for the name of the owner on the computer. Sisson agreed that this is what occurred.
5) I mentioned that Sisson had resolved the issue when he directed me to get the owner of the card, as he could not give me another man's card. Again, Sisson agreed that this was what had transpired and that the matter was resolved.
6) Yet, when I mentioned that something happened after I left to get Harvin, that Stewart must have directly involved herself, Sisson agreed. He said that she took the copy card and assumed control.
Further affiant sayeth naught.
I declare under penalty of perjury under the laws of the United States of America that the following is true and correct. Executed this 2nd day of July, 2015.

James Johnson

REQUEST FOR ADMINISTRATIVE REMEDY
PART B – RESPONSE

Johnson, James Bowers
Reg. No. 16665-084
Remedy I.D.: 827411-F2
Qtr: Unit GA

This is in response to your Request for Administrative Remedy receipted July 14, 2015, in which you appeal Incident Report No. 2730280. As grounds for your appeal, you contend staff did not find you in possession of another inmate's copy card. You request the incident report be expunged.

A review of your disciplinary record reveals you received an incident report on June 24, 2015, for violating Code 328, Giving/receiving money or anything of value to/from another inmate, or any person without staff authorization. On June 24, 2015, you asked education staff if they had located your commissary copy card of which you had lost. The card you lost was found a few minutes later in the education hallway; however, it had another inmate's registration number on it. The report indicates the other inmate admitted to giving you his copy card to use, and during the UDC hearing, you admitted he gave you his commissary copy card which you were in possession of, and subsequently dropped in the education hallway. The UDC based their decision you committed the prohibited act upon the reporting staff's, observation and your admittance you were in possession of another inmates copy card. The UDC sanctioned you to 15 days loss of commissary, suspended, pending 180 days clear institutional conduct.

Pursuant to Program Statement 5270.09, Inmate Discipline Program, the reviewing official for decisions by the UDC is the Warden. Upon appeal, the reviewing authority shall consider: (1) whether the UDC substantially complied with the regulation on inmate discipline; (2) whether the UDC based its decision on some facts, and if there was conflicting evidence, whether the decision was based on the greater weight of the evidence; and (3) whether an appropriate sanction was imposed according to the severity level of the prohibited act. Based on this information, the UDC hearing complied with regulations in accordance with the inmate discipline policy, and the sanctions imposed were commensurate with the offense.

Based on the above information, your Request for Administrative Remedy is denied.

If you are not satisfied with this response, you may appeal to the Regional Director, Bureau of Prisons, Northeast Region, U.S. Customs House, 7th Floor, 2nd and Chestnut Streets, Philadelphia, Pennsylvania, 19106, within 20 calendar days of the date of this response.

R. Hanson, Warden   8-4-15
Date

U.S. Department of Justice

Federal Bureau of Prisons

JR 8/7/15 JB.

Regional Administrative Remedy Appeal

Type or use ball-point pen. If attachments are needed, submit four copies. One copy of the completed BP-DIR-9 including any attachments must be submitted with this appeal.

From: Johnson, James B. (LAST NAME, FIRST, MIDDLE INITIAL) 16665-084 (REG. NO.) 6A (UNIT) FSL - Elkton (INSTITUTION)

Part A--REASON FOR APPEAL The warden, Mr. Hanson, did not, apparently, consider the merits of my argument. Candidly, I could not and should not have been charged for "giving/receiving anything of value" because I was merely receiving "writ-writer" assistance. The Supreme Court has acknowledged the role of other inmates who help others access the courts.

Equally important is that the incident report was the result of a BoP employee's deliberate harassment. This harassment charge was addressed with a BP-8 and a sworn affidavit and informally resolved. Had Ms Stewart inquired as to why Harvin was helping me, she would not have imposed "a prison regulation or practice [that] offends a constitutional guarantee," unless her intent was to harass me. Per my original request, please expunge this incident report.

8/8/15 (DATE) [signature] (SIGNATURE OF REQUESTER)

Part B--RESPONSE

See attached Response.

DATE REGIONAL DIRECTOR

If dissatisfied with this response, you may appeal to the General Counsel. Your appeal must be received in the General Counsel's Office within 30 calendar days of the date of this response.

ORIGINAL: RETURN TO INMATE CASE NUMBER: 827411-R1

Part C--RECEIPT

CASE NUMBER:

Return to: LAST NAME, FIRST, MIDDLE INITIAL REG. NO. UNIT INSTITUTION

SUBJECT:

USP LVN DATE Previous editions not usable SIGNATURE, RECIPIENT OF REGIONAL APPEAL BP-230(13) APRIL 1982

JOHNSON, James
Reg. No. 16665-084
Appeal No. 827411-R1
Page One

Part B - Response

You appeal the June 25, 2015, decision of the Unit Discipline Committee (UDC) at FCI Elkton finding you committed the prohibited act of Receiving Anything of Value from Another inmate, Code 328, Incident Report No. 2730280. You deny committing the prohibited act. You contend you were receiving "writ writer" assistance.

A review of your appeal reveals questions concerning the disciplinary process. Accordingly, this disciplinary action is being remanded for further review. You will be notified of the date and time of further proceedings if necessary. After further proceedings, you may appeal again to the Warden if you desire. Your appeal is partially granted.

Date: September 11, 2015

J. E. NORWOOD
Regional Director

BP-A0288
AUG 11
U.S. DEPARTMENT OF JUSTICE INCIDENT REPORT FORM Rehearing of Report #2736280 FEDERAL BUREAU OF PRISONS

Part I - Incident Report

1. Institution: **FSL ELKTON**

2. Inmate's Name	3. Register Number	4. Date Of Incident	5 Time
Johnson, James	16665-084	06/24/2015	11:30am

6. Place Of Incident	7. Assignment	8. Unit
FSL Education	Unit Orderly	GA

9. Incident Communicating:	10. Prohibited Act Code(s)
Giving,receiving anything of value to another inmate	328

11. Description Of Incident (Date: Time: Staff become aware of incident)

12. Typed Name/Signature/Title of Reporting Employee	13. Date and Time

14. Incident Report Delivered To Above Inmate By(Typed Name/Signature)	15. Date Incident Report Delivered	16.Time Incident Report Delivered

Part II - Committee Action

17. Comments Of Inmate To Committee Regarding Above Incident Inmate Johnson denies the charge. Attached is a copy of inmate Johnson's statement.

18. A. It is the finding of the committee that you:

____ Committed The Prohibited Act as charged.

X Did not Commit a Prohibited Act /Expunged

Committed Prohibited Act Codes(s)

B. NA The Committee is referring the Charge(s) to the DHO for further Hearing.

C. NA The Committee advised the inmate of its finding and of the right to file an appeal within 20 calendar days.

19. Committee Decision is Based on Specific Evidence as Follows: Based on further review of the incident report, the UDC expunged this incident report based on lack of evidence. This is a reversal of the initial UDC decision. No statement was obtained from inmate Calvin by the investigating Lieutenant to verify/solidify the charge. No card/or photocopy of said card was presented as evidence.

20. Committee action and/or recommendation if referred to DHO (Contingent upon DHO finding inmate committed prohibited act)

21. Date And Time Of Action 9/24/15 11:55am (The UDC Chairman's signature certifies who sat on the UDC and that the completed report accurately reflects the UDC proceedings.)

John Manuck | L. Shepas |
Chairman (Typed Name/Signature) | Member (Typed Name) | Member (Typed Name)

INSTRUCTIONS: All items outside heavy rule are for staff use only. Begin entries with the number 1 and work up. Entries not completed will be voided by staff.

DISTRIBUTE: Original-Central File record; COPY-1-DHO; COPY-2-Inmate After UDC Action; Copy 3-Inmate

PDF Prescribed by P5270 Replaces BP-S288.052 Of MAY 94

TRULINCS 16665084 - JOHNSON, JAMES BOWERS - Unit: ELK-G-A

FROM: 16665084
TO: Education
SUBJECT: ***Request to Staff*** JOHNSON, JAMES, Reg# 16665084, ELK-G-A
DATE: 09/01/2015 03:45:29 PM

To: Callahan
Inmate Work Assignment: PM Compound

I am James Johnson. I spoke with you about the copy card issue/Ms Lamb(Stewart) harassment in Mr. Mraulak's office.

As I fight the charge for "giving/receiving something of value" from another inmate, which is now at Region, appealled because the Warden upheld the punishment, I wanted to pass on an observaton.

Last week, Friday as I recall, Ms Stewart, who had repeatedly paged an inmate to education, with the express intent to return his lost copy card, came from her office into the law library. She told her law clerk about the lost card and gave it to him for his own personal benefit. Since the inmate never came to retrieve his rightful possession, as she factored thta perhaps she was not able to read the numbers on the back of the card correctly, the clerk was to be the beneficiary of the card.

I am not going to bother explaining the import of this act and the significance it means to me. I believe that you are fully capable to discern for yourself. Suffice it to say that something of value was exchanged, as was in my case.

My concern was the issue of harassment with Ms Lamb.

To his credit, the law clerk stated that perhaps he would leave it at the desk for men who needed to make copies and who were otherwise unable. He eventually, as I understand, gave it to a friend who put it to good use.

The punishment from my possession of a man's copy card, who left this institution a week later, may stand, which I will appeal until suit is filed in federal court, but the "injustice" of another warrantless indiscretion of a BOP official leaves regarding another copy card underscores that my initial reaction was appropriate.

Regards

APPENDIX N – ABA COMPLAINT

Inquiry Form

VIRGINIA STATE BAR

Mail to:
VIRGINIA STATE BAR
INTAKE OFFICE
1111 East Main Street, Suite 700
Richmond, Virginia 23219-3565
Telephone: (804) 775-0570

NOTE: Send in this form if you have concerns about a lawyer's conduct. Your inquiry might result in discipline to the lawyer. If you are seeking other remedies against the lawyer, you may need to seek legal advice from a lawyer in private practice. Also, the bar may require your further involvement in an investigation by asking you to be interviewed by a bar investigator and/or to participate at a hearing.

Please do not submit original documents to the bar. Instead, please preserve all original documents until your inquiry has been resolved.

YOUR NAME: X Mr. _ Mrs. _ Miss _ Ms.
James B. Johnson
first initial last

YOUR ADDRESS:
#16665-084
street
Federal Satellite Low
P.O. Box 10
city state zip code
Lisbon, Ohio 44432
e-mail

Daytime Telephone No.:
☐ home ( )
☐ work ( )
Other Telephone No. and times you can be reached:
☐ ( )
☐ ( )

LAWYER'S NAME:
Randy V. Cargill
first initial last

LAWYER'S ADDRESS:
Federal Public Defender
Western District of Virginia
lawyer's law firm, if known
210 1st Street, Suite 400
street address or P.O. Box
Roanoke, VA 24011
city state zip code

Lawyer's Telephone No.:
(540) 777-0880

LAWYER'S ACTIONS COMPLAINED OF:

1) Cargill did not file a motion for a new trial and, then, in retrospect ~~took liberties with the facts. (Exhibit A (pages 57-61), B (pages 24-27),~~ c, D, E, F and G) 2) Cargill did not have the"courage" (Exhibit F and G) ~~to ask the judge to recuse himself for the reasons Cargill indicated.~~ 3) Cargill did not investigate his client's reasonable good faith belief ~~as a reasonable defense, which precluded him from challenging the element~~ of jurisdiction (Exhibits A (pages 31-61) and B (pages 1-23))

(See attached)

(Continue on the back or a separate page if you need more space. Also, attach **copies** of any documents that help explain your inquiry.)

YOUR SIGNATURE: Original Signed DATE: May 29, 2015

FORM MUST BE SIGNED AND DATED

Turn this form over for more information we need from you to analyze your inquiry. ☛

I would like to be very clear about my objective for filing a complaint with the Virginia State Bar (ABA) against Randy Cargill. I believe there is a chronic problem within the legal profession that is rarely expressed and, in all probability, never reconciled. Prosecutors are not held to account for pursuing charges that should not have been tried. Conversely, defense lawyers are not held accountable for their failure to adequately defend their clients.

America is the most incarcerated country in the world. Surely, the ABA must realize that attorney competency and integrity are directly correlated to these high conviction and imprisonment rates. I believe Cargill's incompetency and lack of integrity are concrete reasons for my unjust conviction. My objective, therefore, is to effectively express what I believe should be a legitimate concern for the ABA: Cargill's actions and, more importantly, his inactions and lack of courage and integrity are directly attributable to his inferior advocacy.

Pointedly, if the ABA has "canons of ethics" behind which attorneys hide for their prudent decisions, then, those same canons should be applied to their negligence. For example, Cargill never steered from his "good faith" belief that to argue my good faith belief was a violation of the ABA's canons of ethics. Yet,

> The canons of ethics of the legal profession require a lawyer's "entire devotion to the interest of the client, warm zeal in the maintenance and defense of his rights and the exertion of his utmost and ability" to the end that nothing be taken or withheld from him, save the rules of law, legally applied. American Bar Association, Canons of Ethics, Canon 15, DuBoise v North Carolina, 225 F Supp 51, fn2 (4th Cir. 1964)

Since Cargill viewed my good faith belief as "frivolous" as soon as I expressed it, which foreclosed him even remotely satisfying the sentiment in DuBoise, he failed to reach the benchmark expected in the canons of ethics. Consequently, as stated in Sallie v North Carolina, 587 F 2d 636, 640 (4th Cir. 1978) con-

1

cerning what is fair,

> The standard does not require that representation be flawless only that all decisions materially affecting defendant's representation be the product of informed judgment, not neglect or ignorance.

Thus, we arrive at the conundrum that the canons pose. Cargill's dismissal of my belief as "frivolous," which allows him to comply with "the code of professional responsibility that governs a lawyer's responsibilities" (Exhibit H), excuses his adherence to the idea that "...there can be no restrictions upon the function of counsel in defending a criminal prosecution..." United States v Cronic, 466 US 648 n15 (1984)

Significantly, since Cargill was "defending" against tax charges, the ABA must give some credence "that most lawyers have only scant knowledge of tax laws." United States v Bursten, 395 F 2d 976, 981 (5th Cir. 1968) The relevance of this point is that, as established in United States v Cheek, 498 US 192 (1991), Cargill should have researched that, at a minimum,

> ... a good faith belief of legality, no matter how unreasonable, negates the statutory element of willfulness for tax evasion and failure to file a return, and that a jury must be allowed to consider evidence of such a belief. Snyder v United States, 897 F Süpp 241, 244 (4th Cir. 1995)

Given the Supreme Court's intent in Cheek concerning beliefs that may even be "unreasonable," one would reasonably expect that a lawyer would perform to his "utmost and ability" to defend a reasonable good faith belief. Such an effort by Cargill would have obviated his "neglect or ignorance."

Ineffective advocacy is no trifle matter. The defense of any criminal defendant merits the exaction of any and all advantages in a system that is, all too often, rigid and unforgiving. Even the Supreme Court acknowledged that the ABA canons of ethic "'are only guides' and do not establish the constitutional baseline for effective assistance of counsel." Rompilla v Beard, 545 US 374, 400 (2005), quoting Strickland v Washington 466 US 688 (1984)

Please understand that Cargill did NO research into my belief. Quite literally, once I expressed my good faith belief, he rejected it - case closed. In our private consultations, he said that I had a tax liability, that I owed the tax and eventually explained to the jury that it was "crazy" for me to believe otherwise. Given Cargill's own "good faith" that I had a liability, he never challenged the element of jurisdiction.

The Fourth District Court will, inevitably, grant Cargill a pass and state, as it relates to my 2255, that given the circumstances, his "strategy" was sound. Therefore, Cargill could not have been ineffective. Where does this leave the justice system and the ABA? Granting ineffective and timorous lawyers a reprieve is no different than federal agents and U.S. Attorneys securing convictions by fraud. Those who are unjustly convicted by fraud cannot hold agents accountable until the conviction is overturned! This is difficult to reconcile.

Is it unreasonable for one unschooled and unskilled in the "legal profession to surmise that the entire "system" (all its components - public and private) protects its own? I will also hazard a guess that, aside from "billing" indiscretions, such subjective complaints, as this one may be perceived, may not be viewed by the ABA with the severity it should be accorded. However, given the three concerns highlighted at the beginning of this complaint, perhaps the ABA will acknowledge a pattern that aptly depicts Cargill's negligence.

I will allow the exhibits to convey the facts and concerns. In the meantime, permit me to explain a very important point. Cargill acted out of self-preservation. Notably, Cargill's fear was reflected in his lack of "courage" to ask the judge to recuse himself. Cargill's fear of reprisal for filing and arguing for a new trial in a court in which he frequently appeared motivated him not to do so. Cargill's fear of sanctions for arguing a good faith belief

32

that he considered to be "frivolous" prevented him from defending his client's best interests. This pattern reflects a lack of integrity and credibility that would fail to satisfy a lawyer's obligations under the ABA's canons of ethics.

Perhaps it is fitting to make reference to the comments made to me by Cargill's assistant, Andrea Harris. On 3/7/13, as memorialized in my Declaration (Exhibit A, #123), she said, in response to their failure to file a motion for a new trial, that I could file for ineffective assistance of counsel. Such is the attitude of attorneys who are rarely held to account and, more importantly, they know they will not be held accountable. Harris' posture and comments are telling. So, I will ask the ABA if Cargill's repeated and collective failures to effectively employ fundamentals of the legal profession, to include the intangible virtues, unduly prejudice an expected standard of performance? And, does Cargill's struggle with the virtue of integrity compromise the ABA's standards?

I have had only one other reason to submit a concern to the ABA, which was in 1995 and involved Larry Lunn, who, based upon my complaint, was recommended for disbarrment before the Maine Supreme Court. Lunn suffered from a lack of integrity for "contemporaneous billing." I assure you that I view Cargill's lack of advocacy and integrity as far more egregious. I only ask that you consider the totality of his inaction, sourced in fear and questionable integrity, as justification to hold your profession to a higher standard. Clearly, Cargill did not provide the assistance of counsel guaranteed under the Sixth Amendment. At what baseline of measurement will The ABA account for the lack of due diligence expected of an attorney and shun the oft refrain that failure to do so was justified with an alternative "sound strategy?"

Respectfully,

James B. Johnson

4

Virginia State Bar

1111 East Main Street Suite 700
Richmond, Virginia 23219-3565
Telephone: (804) 775-0500

Fax: (804) 775-0597 TDD: (804) 775-0502

June 8, 2015

PERSONAL AND CONFIDENTIAL

James B. Johnson #16665-084
Federal Satellite Low
P.O. Box 10
Lisbon, OH 44432

Re: Your information about Randy Virlin Cargill

Dear Mr. Johnson:

The Virginia State Bar received your correspondence. The bar disciplines lawyers who violate the Virginia Rules of Professional Conduct. This office reviewed your correspondence to ascertain whether it described conduct that might violate a provision of the Rules.

We have determined that we will not take further action on your matter for the following reason(s): Mr. Cargill stated in his March 18, 2013 letter that he did not believe valid grounds existed to file a motion. The bar cannot compel your former counsel to file a motion for a new trial especially when the lawyer believes the motion is frivolous. A lawyer can be disciplined by the bar if he files a frivolous motion – as indicated by Mr. Cargill in his July 10, 2014 letter. I discern no misconduct.

Please note that the bar has limited authority and cannot address all situations through its disciplinary process. For more information about the bar's disciplinary process please visit our website at: www.vsb.org.

Very truly yours,

James C. Bodie

James C. Bodie
Intake Counsel

JCB/jhc

There is no formal appeal process if you disagree with our decision not to initiate a formal investigation. If you seek review of our decision, write us a brief letter stating facts supporting your inquiry. Be brief. Merely asking us to review the same material again is not helpful in evaluating your inquiry. We cannot receive this information by telephone. Mail your request to the address on the letterhead. Do not call this office for a status report. The review process may take several weeks. We will notify you in writing of our decision. Our limited resources do not allow us to review the same information numerous times. Normally, after reviewing your inquiry twice, we will not continue to communicate with you about the same inquiry.

APPENDIX O – CORRESPONDENCE TO/FROM CARGILL

NOTICE

James B. Johnson
16665-084
Federal Satellite Low, Elkton
P.O. Box 10
Lisbon, OH 44432

July 30, 2015

Mr. Randy V. Cargill
Federal Public Defender
210 1st Street, Ste. 400
Roanoke, VA 24011

Subject: Request for Agreement Concerning Facts about Legal Representation

Dear Mr. Cargill:

As you are likely aware, I submitted a 2255 Motion for criminal case, 6:12-cr-00015-NKM, James Bowers Johnson v UNITED STATES OF AMERICA. Noticeably absent from the Government's Response to my 2255 motion was any sworn affidavit from you. It is largely because the court is without your corroboration as to the facts outside the trial record that I send this correspondence. Your stipilation to the following statements as true will assist me in conveying to the court that the conviction and sentence were unjust and should be overturned.

Please agree to the attached as true and provide your signature as confirmation. Should you not agree with some of the statements, please refute each on a point by point basis by sworn affidavit. Lack of an acknowledgment to the statements within 30 days from the date of this letter will confirm your concession to the same as true.

Thank you for your prompt attention to this matter.

Sincerely, Original mailed 7/30/15

James B. Johnson

STIPULATION OF THE FACTS

I, Randy V. Cargill, do hereby affirm, by my initials next to each, that the statements offered by James B. Johnson are true, to wit:

__ True 1. Immediately after my arrest, I, proceeding pro se, argued that the federal government did not have personam jurisdiction.

__ True 2. Upon explaining my good faith belief, you reflexively condemned it as "frivolous," did not investigate its merits and stated that if you argued such a position, the court would impose sanctions.

__ True 3. In our pre-trial meetings, you prepared a defense argument with a position that I believed that I did not have a federal income tax liability, without explaining the basis for my good faith belief concerning jurisdiction.

__ True 4. In my writ of habeas corpus submitted to the court shortly after arraignment, I stated, "The United States has no authority over Johnson and he is without the geography and power of the same, especially since revoking/rescinding any benefit claim to the federal social insurance program in 2000, thus rebutting the presumption of being a United States employee."

__ True 5. In our pre-trial meetings, you learned that the Department of Internal Revenue, the Internal Revenue Service and the Department of Justice, from 2004-2009, failed to answer my question as to the law that obligated me to file a federal income tax return.

__ True 6. In our pre-trial meetings, you learned that Internal Revenue agent Robert Biggs never answered the questions of my power-of-attorney, John Kotmair, as to the legal authority by which Biggs presumed to act and the law that obligated me to file a federal income tax return.

__ True 7. In our pre-trial meetings, you learned that in 2000, I sent notification to the Social Security Administration that I revoked and rescinded my signature and intent to the federal privilege of social security insurance, which was the binding nexus that once obligated me to the federal income tax.

__ True 8. In our pre-trial meetings, you learned that in 2000, I sent notification to the Department of the Treasury stating that I no longer accepted or participated in the federal privilege of social security.

__ True 9. Based upon my termination of the federal benefit of social security, you knew, as a legal professional, that I effectively rebutted the presumption and prima facie evidence that I was liable to file a federal income tax return.

__ True 10. In our pre-trial meetings, you learned of my belief that, by terminating my participation in the federal benefit of social security, I was no longer obligated to the settled law of the United States Supreme Court (See Charles C. Steward Machine v Davis, 304 US 548 (1937) and Helvering v Davis, 304 US 619 (1937)) and, therefore, without the jurisdiction of the IRS and the federal government for income tax purposes.

__ True 11. In our pre-trial meetings, you learned that I believed the federal income tax and Internal Revenue Code are constitutional as applied to those who accept the federal benefit of social security.

__ True 12. In our pre-trial meetings, you learned that from 2004-1012, none of my elected representatives of Congress answered my query as to the law that obligated me to the federal income tax returns.

__ True 13. You knew that, at arraignment on May 3, 2012, I asked the court to rule on my "motion to quash and actually dismiss the defective claim for lack of jurisdiction."

__ True 14. In our pre-trial meetings, I explained to you that the federal income tax was an excise and, therefore, voluntary in nature, based upon one accepting the federal privilege for which the tax is owed, the federal benefit of social security.

__ True 15. In our pre-trial meetings, I explained to you that I entered the "relation of employment" without fully informed consent and while under the age of majority.

__ True 16. You refused to accept my belief as credible for fear of being sanctioned by the court. You did not investigate the merits of my good faith belief, that having rejected the federal benefit of social security, I rebutted the presumption that I was a "taxpayer" as defined in the tax code.

__ True 17. In our pre-trial meetings, you learned that I relied upon the determination of the Social Security Administration that a social security number is not required to live or work in the United States.

__ True 18. Even with the explanation of my good faith belief, you immediately disagreed and without investigation, stated "You are a U.S. person" as defined in the Internal Revenue Code.

__ True 19. In our pre-trial meetings, you refused to consider my explanation that the defense you intended to argue before the jury, which was the antithesis of my good faith belief, was a continuation of the government's fraud upon the court.

__ True 20. I raised the issue of jurisdiction at the initial hearing, throughout the trial process and through the end of the sentencing hearing.

__ True 21. You had a "good faith" (Exhibit A) belief that you could not argue my "good faith" belief because of the ABA canons of ethics.

__ True 22. I dispensed with your legal representation before trial because you would not argue my good faith belief.

__ True 23. You stated to the jury, "if the question in this case were whether he should have filed returns and whether he owes taxes to the federal government, the case would have been over, done. Of course he does."

__ True 24. You told the court that I "was required by law, regulations, to file tax returns in the specific years '05, '06 and '07. There's uncontroverted that he was."

___ True 25. You told the jury, "Mr. Johnson believes that the tax code doesn't apply to him and he still had no obligation to file a return. But, as a matter of law, as a matter of who is correct, we all know he should have filed returns, I mean, come on, he should have."

___ True 26. You stated the above to the jury without substantiating what law obligated me, while refusing to argue that I rebutted the presumption that I fell under the settled law that imposes this obligation.

___ True 27. Without giving the jury the explanation of my good faith defense, you openly questioned my belief that I wasn't "supposed to file. Is he right? No. It is crazy."

___ True 28. In our pre-trial meetings, you admitted that you had a lack of knowledge of tax law.

___ True 29. In my motion challenging jurisdiction and standing to sue, which was submitted after trial, you knew that I continued to argue that I was without the jurisdiction of the IRC, the federal government and, therefore, the court.

___ True 30. In the aforementioned motion, you knew that I stated that I was "not an 'employer' or an 'employee' and did not work for the federal government." That I, "having revoked and rescinded [my] signature and intent to the federal insurance social insurance scheme, may not be presumed to be a 'United States person'...within... [the] jurisdiction of the federal UNITED STATES government as defined by the IRC."

___ True 31. In the same motion, you knew that I stated, "Petitioner rebuts any presumption that he is within the jurisdiction of the federal government."

___ True 32. As a professional lawyer and as my legal advocate, you ignored and failed to assert the "settled law" of the Supreme Court, as stated in Cheek v United States, 498 US 192 (1991), as evidenced in Snyder v United States, 897 F Supp 241, 244 (4th Cir. 1995) "that a good faith belief of legality, no matter how unreasonable, negates the statutory element of willfulness... and that a jury must be allowed to consider evidence of such a belief."

___ True 33. As a professional lawyer and my legal advocate, you relied upon the settled law that I had a federal income tax obligation, while ignoring the settled law that I could have and did have a belief, no matter how unreasonable or not, that I did not have a federal income tax obligation.

I, Randy V. Cargill, hereby affirm that I have initialed to foregoing statements as true and, if not, I have provided a sworn affidavit rebutting those that are not true.

____
Randy V. Cargill

FEDERAL PUBLIC DEFENDER
WESTERN DISTRICT OF VIRGINIA
210 FRANKLIN ROAD, SW, ROOM 604
ROANOKE, VIRGINIA 24011
Telephone: (540) 777-0880
Fax: (540) 777-0890

Larry W. Shelton
Federal Public Defender

August 3, 2015

James Johnson
Reg. No. 16665-084
Federal Satelite Low, Elkton
P.O. Box 10
Lisbon, OH 44432

Re: United States v. James Johnson

Dear James:

I have your undated letter which I received today, August 3, 2015. I am glad to see that you are in a satellite facility and hope things are going well for you.

James, you are asking me to stipulate to a series of assertions that I simply do not recall in the way that you write. Yes, you asserted many theories over the course of our representing you. Few, to be candid, made any sense to me and none, which I will categorize under the rubric of sovereign citizen arguments, had any legal support. I and Andrea did tell you several times that these arguments have no legal basis and that we could not ethically pursue them.

I do hope that your remaining time passes quickly and I wish you the best.

Sincerely,

Randy V. Cargill
Assistant Federal Public Defender

SECOND NOTICE

James B. Johnson
16665-084
Federal Satellite Low, Elkton
P.O. Box 10
Lisbon, OH

August 15, 2015

Mr. Randy V. Cargill
Federal Public Defender
210 1st Street, Ste. 400
Roanoke, VA 24011

Subject SECOND NOTICE: Request for Agreement Concerning Facts about Legal Representation

Dear Mr. Cargill:

I am in receipt of your 8/3/15 letter, which was in response to my 7/30/15 letter (see attached). Given the immediacy of your reply, it appears as though you did not give my correspondence the attention it deserved. As stated in my first letter, the Court is without your corroboration of the facts outside the trial record. It is my hope and intention to exonerate myself with your agreement to facts that would confirm what the Court never heard. More importantly, your agreement will confirm evidence of my good faith belief that is in the record.

Mr. Cargill, the facts listed are very plain. They are not fraught with questionable interpretation, as you suggest by stating the words "recall in the way that [I] write." Moreover, the statements, some of which are confirmed by the record, are not based upon "many theories" but, a grounded good faith belief, a belief you considered to be "frivolous" and one you did not investigate. For example, statements 4 and 30 are two facts in the record that underscore the import of statements 5, 7, 10, 16, 21, 25 and 26. However, rather than attest to these facts, you defaulted to a practice employed during the trial. You agreed with the government's theory that I had a tax liability and even told the jury so. Now you refer to "sovereign citizen" arguments that I never offered as my good faith belief. This was language and such were theories used by the prosecution.

I have not relented in my claim of innocence and I intend to prevail. As such, your willingness to agree to very direct and incontrovertible facts will help me toward this end. I appeal to your sense of equity and I humbly ask you to nobly, if not heroically, admit that these simple statements are true. I respectfully ask that you concede that you were not without fault concerning my one good faith belief. Please consider that your agreement that you failed to employ the Supreme Court's wisdom in Cheek (see statements 33 and 34) will enable me to prevail in any current or post habeas corpus action.

I am asking you to consider that, as the Supreme Court stated in Wood v

Allen, 558 US _ (2010)

> a decision cannot be fairly characterized as "strategic" unless it is a conscious choice between two legitimate and rational alternatives. It must be born of deliberation and not happenstance, inattention or neglect.

Furthermore, the Court stated in Trevino v Thaler _ US _ (2013) that

> counsel's failure to investigate and present mitigating circumstances deprived defendant of effective assistance of counsel.

Perhaps you will afford me the latitude that your reflexive response to my good faith belief, born out of a lack of knowledge of tax law and your concern of sanctions were the cause for your failure to investigate.

This is a SECOND NOTICE requesting your agreement to the attached statements as true and your signature as confirmation. In the event that you do not agree with some of the statements, please refute each on a point by point basis, as you would write them, by sworn affidavit. Please do so within fourteen days from the date of this letter. Your failure to respond will signify your tacit acquiescence.

Thank you for your prompt attention to this matter.

Sincerely,

James B. Johnson

NOTICE OF FAULT

James B. Johnson
16665-084
Federal Satellite Low Elkton
P.O. Box 10
Lisbon, OH 44432

September 2, 2015

Mr. Randy V. Cargill
Federal Public Defender
210 1st Street, Ste. 400
Roanoke, VA 24011

Subject NOTICE OF FAULT - Request for Agreement Concerning Facts about Legal Representation

Dear Mr. Cargill:

This a NOTICE OF FAULT.

On two previous occasions, I sent you correspondence (Exhibits A & B) with a request that you agree to the STIPULATION OF FACTS provided. In the event that you did not agree with some of the facts, I requested that you refute each on a point by point basis by sworn affidavit. To date, you have failed to do so.

With this NOTICE OF FAULT, I have your tacit acquiescence to the STIPULATION OF FACTS.

Mr. Cargill, my efforts to prevail with any post conviction remedies will not succeed without your direct and specific response. Regrettably, the court will likely determine that your assistance of counsel was effective - without hearing from you. The Government - the very entity that prosecuted me, defended your assistance of counsel as effective; yet, it does not know of any information outside the trial record. How is the Government's defense of your assistance as effective reasonable or just? Will you remain disengaged while the court is without your confirmation of the facts outside the trial record, which would square with the facts in the record? Without your participation, the court will not receive valuable insight that would confirm my sworn testimony and refute the Government's unfounded claims.

Allow me to share with you two federal questions that I filed recently. (Exhibits C & D) As expressed to you in 2012, these questions are the essence of my good faith belief. If I can, as a layman, further pursue the merits of my own good faith belief, surely you as a competent attorney could have investigated these as well.

The irony is that once I am released, these questions will likely remain unanswered, and with the same good faith belief, I will potentially face the same criminal charges. Will you or any professional advocate still view my good faith belief as "frivolous" and offer only a perfunctory effort in my defense?

Please consider that your concession that your assistance of counsel vas not effective vould go a long vay to correcting an unjust conviction. I implore you to consider that your admission that you did not fully consider or investigate my good faith belief vill instruct the court and right an egregious vrong.

I respectfully ask you to respond to this NOTICE OF FAULT vithin seven Days.

Sincerely,

original signed

James Johnson

& mailed

9/2/15

Sent via certified mail # 7015 0640 0006 3638 4652

James B. Johnson
16665-084
Federal Satellite Low Elkton
P.O. Box 10
Lisbon, OH 44432

September 10, 2015

Mr. Randy Cargill
Federal Public Defender
210 1st Street, Ste 400
Roanoke, VA 24011

Subject: NOTICE OF DEFAULT - Request for Agreement Concerning Facts about Legal Representation

Dear Mr. Cargill:

This is a NOTICE OF DEFAULT.

On three separate occasions I sent you requests (see attached) for your agreement to the enclosed STIPULATIONS OF FACTS. You failed to do so. In the event that you did not agree with some or all of the facts, I requested that you refute each on a point by point basis by sworn affidavit. You failed to do so. You are in default.

I offered a good faith belief that would have likely defeated the charges for which I was convicted. As my legal counsel, not only did you reject my belief as "frivolous," you were not willing to investigate its merits. To demonstrate the soundness of my belief, I sent you copies of two Federal Questions that I recently filed into the court.

Given that I revoked the federal benefit of social security, your failure to investigate that there was no law that made me liable for the excise equaled the lack of specific performance of Agents Biggs and Pompei and my elected representatives in Congress to provide me the law. If the court refuses to compel the United States to answer these Federal Questions, all three branches will have refused to do so. This would be quite an indictment.

Suffice it to say, since the government did not ask you to refute any of my testimony in my 2255 Motion, I sought your agreement by administrative private process. With the likely denial of the habeas corpus petition, I intend to take your tacit acquiescence to the STIPULATION OF FACTS for a post 2255 remedy. Whether by 2241 or a writ of coram nobis, this silent concession may be helpful.

Sincerely,

original mailed 9/11/15

James B. Johnson

FEDERAL PUBLIC DEFENDER
WESTERN DISTRICT OF VIRGINIA
210 1st Street, Suite 400
ROANOKE, VIRGINIA 24011
Telephone: (540) 777-0880
Fax: (540) 777-0890

Larry W. Shelton
Federal Public Defender

September 11, 2015

James Johnson
Reg. # 16665-084
Federal Satelite Low
P.O. Box 10
Lisbon, OH 44432

Re: United States v. James Johnson

Dear James:

This responds to your letter of September 2, 2015. You are asking me to buy into these theories about the federal income tax that have been rejected by the courts for decades. You are in prison because you have acted on these rejected theories and I fear that you will just cycle in and out of prison until you finally accept that these theories are not valid. I am satisfied that your good faith defense was fairly presented at trial. I am sorry that the jury rejected the defense but do not believe there is anything I can do at this point to help you. Certainly, I would do so if I could.

I do wish you the best.

Sincerely,

Randy V. Cargill
Assistant Federal Public Defender

James B. Johnson
16665084
Federal Satellite Low Elkton
P.O. Box 10
Lisbon, OH 44432

August 24, 2015

Mr. Randy Cargill
Federal Public Defender
210 1st Street, Ste 400
Roanoke, VA 24011

Subject: Copies of Communications with U.S. Attorney

Dear Mr. Cargill:

I recently wrote you with a request for copies of any and all communications you had with the U.S. Attorney. I have not received a reply. Would you please provide me a copy of all letters, emails, faxes, etc., that were exchanged throughout the course of the government's case against me.

This information is essential for my post conviction remedies.

Thank you for your assistance.

Sincerely, original mailed 8/24/15

James Johnson

Appendix P – IRS Frivolous Tax Argument

THE TRUTH ABOUT FRIVOLOUS TAX ARGUMENTS

MARCH 4, 2013

20

3. Contention: Taxpayer is not a "person" as defined by the Internal Revenue Code, thus is not subject to the federal income tax laws.

Some individuals and groups maintain that they are not a "person" as defined by the Internal Revenue Code, and thus not subject to the federal income tax laws. This argument is based on a tortured misreading of the Code.

The Law: The Internal Revenue Code clearly defines "person" and sets forth which persons are subject to federal taxes. Section 7701(a)(14) defines "taxpayer" as any person subject to any internal revenue tax and section 7701(a)(1) defines "person" to include an individual, trust, estate, partnership, or corporation. Arguments that an individual is not a "person" within the meaning of the Internal Revenue Code have been uniformly rejected. A similar argument with respect to the term "individual" has also been rejected. The IRS warned taxpayers of the consequences of making this frivolous argument. Rev. Rul. 2007-22, 2007-1 C.B. 866.

Relevant Case Law:

United States v. Karlin, 785 F.2d 90, 91 (3d Cir. 1986), cert. denied, 480 U.S. 907 (1987) – the court affirmed Karlin's conviction for failure to file income tax returns and rejected his contention that he was "not a 'person' within meaning of 26 U.S.C. § 7203" as "frivolous and requir[ing] no discussion."

United States v. Studley, 783 F.2d 934, 937 n.3 (9th Cir. 1986) – in affirming a conviction for failure to file income tax returns, the court rejected the taxpayer's contention that she was not subject to federal tax laws because she was "an absolute, freeborn, and natural individual" and noted that "this argument has been consistently and thoroughly rejected by every branch of the government for decades."

Biermann v. Commissioner, 769 F.2d 707, 708 (11th Cir. 1985), reh'g denied, 775 F.2d 304 (11th Cir. 1985) – the court said the claim that Biermann was not "a person liable for taxes" was "patently frivolous," and given the Tax Court's warning to Biermann that his positions would never be sustained in any court, awarded the government double costs plus attorney's fees.

Smith v. Commissioner, T.C. Memo. 2000-290, 80 T.C.M. (CCH) 377, 378-89 (2000) – the court described the argument that Smith "is not a 'person liable' for tax" as frivolous, sustained failure to file penalties, and imposed a penalty for maintaining "frivolous and groundless positions."

Other Cases:

APPENDIX Q – LETTER TO SENATOR RAND PAUL AND THE JUDICIARY COMMITTEE

James B. Johnson
Federal Satellite Low, Elkton
P.O. Box 10
Lisbon, Ohio 44432

February 10, 2015

Senator Rand Paul
124 Russell Building
Washington, D.C. 20510

Dear Senator Paul:

Enclosed is a copy of a civil action in which I ask a Federal Question.

You may recall that I recently sent a copy of my "2255" in which I asserted that my defense attorneys refused to argue my good faith belief - that I rebutted the presumption and prima facie evidence that I was within the jurisdiction of the IRS for the "income" tax. They considered my argument to be "frivolous." Noteworthy is that this "Federal Question" invites the court to consider this very issue.

Sadly, while under investigation in 2004 and beyond, after sending requests to Congressman Wolf and Senators Allen, Warner (John), Warner (Mark) and Webb asking for the law that obligated me to file a tax return, none were willing to satisfy this simple request. Unbelievably, with an army of aides at their disposal, they simply passed my query to the IRS. These elected officials were satisfied with the agency's boilerplate responses that failed to answer with substance. This issue is a political football that is handed off to others to avoid accountability.

With respect to the "Federal Question," will the Department of Justice and Attorney General tender an objective response? Will the court address the question? Time will tell.

I am confident, however, that the question not posed is an invitation to remain ignorant. If the Federal Government and court neglect this interrogatory, we will know that all three branches of government have offered, with willful and deliberate indifference, the only response necessary - the question will not be addressed at all.

In the pursuit of liberty,
I am, sincerely,

James B. Johnson

cc:
Mr. Warner
Mr. Kaine
Mr. Wolf

James B. Johnson
REG. # 16665-084
Federal Satellite Low, Elkton
P.O. Box 10
Lisbon, Ohio 44432

April 26, 2015

Senator Chuck Grassley
Judiciary Committee
135 Hart Senate Office Building
Washington, D.C. 20510

Senator Patrick Leahy
Judiciary Committee
437 Russell Senate Office Building
Washington, D. C. 20510

Representative Bob Goodlatte
Judiciary Committee
2309 Rayburn House Office Building
Washington, D.C. 20515

Representative John Conyers
Judiciary Committee
2426 Rayburn House Office Building
Washington, D.C. 20515

Subject: Unjust Convictions

Dear Mr. Grassley, Mr. Leahy, Mr. Goodlatte and Mr. Conyers,

I am requesting that you consider a congressional inquiry as to why the unjustly incarcerated are without credible recourse to overturn wrongful convictions. This is a concern that does not receive the attention it deserves. If only for how the criminal and judicial systems are operated, there is no practical remedy for a man to have a fair appraisal of an unwarranted imprisonment. There are a number of factors that underscore why unjust convictions are irreversible:

1) As the most incarcerated country in the world, America, indisputably, has a culture to incarcerate within the criminal justice system, at all levels of government, to convict, even when "evidence" urges caution.
2) For decades, Attorneys General have warned against prosecutorial focus on the number of convictions for personal gain to the disadvantage of the public and truth.
3) Given the recent admission by the FBI of false testimony by agents in thousands of cases, investigatory authorities are a primary reason for unjust convictions.
4) Both private and public defense counsel are often ill prepared to adequatley defend their clients, while their performance is routinely sanctioned by the courts as competent "strategy."

5) The grand jury is a rubberstamp for questional charges by the government, for which jurors are unprepared to challenge.
6) Trial jurors are often uninformed and, therefore, entirely accepting of government charges and evidence.
7) The 28 USC 2255 (habea corpus) process is limited to claims of ineffective assistance of counsel.
8) Relief under 28 USC 1983 and other provisions against government officials for fraud are unavailable unless the conviction is overturned.

The foregoing indicators underscore the probability that the innocent are imprisoned without recourse.

This is the situation with Orlando Carter (438 Fed Appx 70 (6th Cir. 2012)). He is an innocent man who has spent the last five years fighting an unjust conviction. He was charged with bank fraud for a loan guaranty that never existed as a libility for himself or his business entities. His attorneys and those involved in the judicial process refused to consider the truth. So, after his wrongful conviction, Carter secured a certified financial forensic audit which proves his innocence. The auditor is prepared to testify as to exactly what the the U.S. Attorney and FBI ageny knew, and what his defense lawyers refused to investigate - Carter was NOT responsible for any loan guaranty with PNC Bank.

Regrettably, since Carter is unable to bring the certified audit before the court, he is unable to prove that the FBI pursued an investigation and the Department of Justice prosecuted a case they knew was meritless. This brings us back to the "culture" of the entire judicial system. Carter was punished even though there was no actus reus and, therefore, no mens rea.

Notably, before trial, the government offered Carter a plea for which he would have received probation, - no prison sentence. However, since he knew that he was innocent, he fought the charges. He received a fifteen year sentence! Carter was taken from his son who was only two months old. This is a tragedy. This dynamic of unjust convictions profoundly affects the American public.

The American people have a grave problem if only because Congress has a problem. Without a provision in the statutes or effective oversight that would prevent errant use of government authority, it is impossible to overturn a conviction predicated upon fraud by federal agents. Consequently, the innocent are without a remedy. This leads to a rather transparent conclusion - America is no longer free to those brave enough to contend with a system that seeks neither truth nor justice.

The only other relevant point to offer is that Carter is a black man who was unduly affected by Ohio politics that had a federal influence. House Speaker John Boehner, in relation to the government's case, is attributed with the question "What was that black man thinking?" Not unlike hotbeds of racial injustice by law enforcement so prevalent today, racial profiling in the fabricated financial crime in Carter's case is appalling. When does the injustice end?

As elected officials, especially as leaders of the Judiciary Committee, are you affected when an innocent person is freed from prison after decades under a wrongful conviction? What do you think when you learn that the FBI falsified testimony for use at trials? Will Congress ever weigh the improbability of those like Carter ever proving their innocence in a post conviction process? There is a credible inadequacy in the "justice" process that precludes an efficacious and timely resolution to convictions of the innocent. I implore you to resolve this unconscionable situation. There must be a way for those like Carter to exonerate and liberate themselves.

I, for one, am no longer willing to remain silent. While Mr. Carter does not know of this letter to your committee, I know that his five year old son pines away for his father's presence. I beseech you to truly appraise a judicial system that provides no remedy for the innocent who are wrongly convicted.

Sincerely,

Jmaes B. Johnson

Appendix R – Letter To Editor Of The Enquirer

James B. Johnson
16665-084
Federal Satellite Low, Elkton
P.O. Box 10
Lisbon, Ohio 44432

May 30, 2015

Letters to the Editor
The Enquirer
312 Elm Street
Cincinnati, OH 45202

Dear Editor:

Recent deaths at the hands of police in Ferguson, Columbus and Baltimore has America recoiling from the pernicious abuse of power that has persisted unabated for too long. As we attempt to appreciate that "law enforcement" is neither as we thought nor as it should be, police brutality is a clarion call to delve even further into the criminal justice system. Why? The view of a glacier above the water reveals only 10% of the ice - 90% is hidden below the surface.

America, rather ignominously, is the most incarcerated country in the world. The land of the free and home of the brave has 5% of the population, yet 25% of those imprisoned. Not only does this number reflect the subjugation of a supposedly peaceful, free and morally resolute people, it impugns all parties involved within the judicial process at all levels of government. Pointedly, if we extrapolate the significance of three deaths in as many months and cities, we must account for our anemic predisposition to wrongful convictions.

Those who have looked below the surface know that all components of the law enforcement apparatus are complicit with illegal investigations, arrests, prosecutions and sentences. Candidly, police actions are catalysts for the progression of questionable actions and decisions that remain hidden. The only impediments to our understanding the pervasiveness of this problem are our ignorance, apathy and disbelief.

Just as we did not appreciate the unconscionable police "blue line," which operates at the expense of society, we must consider that innocent Americans are sacrificed by officials who seek convictions at all costs. Otherwise, there is no other way to reconcile the number of Americans behind bars. Frankly, America is not any more immoral than any other country.

Regrettably, the devastation suffered by the unjustly incarcerated and their families is far removed from public awareness. Unlike the death of Freddie Gray, those unjustly imprisoned become statistics, without a face, absent a story and, therefore, void of a moral authority that clamors for the truth. No, they remain impotent within state and federal penal institutions - a "business" (often privatized) in need of bodies to fill billets for its bottomline. Sadly, the tragedy of prosecuting innocent Americans is not a prevalent issue in local communities, which precludes potential national engagement.

For example, we need only traverse from Baltimore to Butler County, Ohio to understand the implications of an unjust conviction predicated upon racial prejudice that reaches the highest levels of Congress. Father, husband, businessman and friend to many, Orlando Carter, is serving a 15 year federal sentence for a crime he did not commit. He has spent the last five years fighting to exonerate himself and return home to his wife and children.

The truth, which is largely unknown, was not and cannot now be heard by a court. Such is the nature of "American justice."Moreover, multiple parties, be it the FBI, Department of Justice, defense counsel, local and national politicians, PNC Bank, the court and more have shunned the truth. Individually and collectively, they are responsible for Carter's plight.

How is this possible? The answer is rather simple. When agents and agencies operate without accountability, often behind a "code" of mutual protection, with influential offices that act with legal immunity, the mosaic of power blends and blurs until the truth is obscured into insignificance. Rather, an altered reality is manifested, willed into existence, by a disjointed but discernibly collaborative effort by those with the license to fabricate and/or sanction what is false. In the end, fiction becomes fact. Invariably, these "facts" prevail to the detriment of truth, justice, the very integrity of society and the precious lives of those suffering from this cold and hard reality.

Attorneys General have warned for decades against prosecutorial abuse of discretion solely for convictions. Without accountability, without a legal construct that would foreclose unwarranted charges, the criminal justice system will permit the morphing of what should not be into what will be. This dynamic shields us from knowing what is beneath the surface. Instead, we reflexively accept what the "system" proffers as the "truth."

This is the rub in Carter's situation. He and his businesses did not have a $4 million loan guaranty with PNC Bank.Significantly, this alleged loan guaranty was contrived by the machinations of PNC Bank, FBI agent Gormley, Assistant U.S. Attorney Chema, the perversion of local Butler County politics, the undue, if only indirect, influence of House Speaker John Boehner, the cowardly ineptness of defense counsel and a court procedurally indifferent to its eventual receipt of a certified forensic financial audit that obviates any alleged pecuniary liability owed by Carter.

Ultimately, once the facts are fully vetted, the public will know that Carter is as true to his character and integrity now as he was before the government's shameful actions led to equally shameful charges. Furthermore, the public will learn that their dutiful servant, former Butler County Auditor, Kay Rogers, was not guilty of the crime to which she pled. People will soon understand the extent of local corruption that metasticized into a federal power play of egregious proportions.

In the meantime, until we appreciate the loss of "life" to America's jails and prisons, the real reasons for the convictions of our innocent brothers and sisters will remain unknown, which will further erode what was once hailed as American excellence.

If the tragedies of the recent past have awakened and inspired Americans to embrace civic engagement, perhaps they will heed the call to look beyond the 10% that is seen and root out the balance of an historical injustice. If we continue to proclaim our freedom with a court system that relies on the "finality" of convictions, without the possibility of reviewing government fraud to secure "guilty" verdicts, we are fighting a losing battle.

This is an important observation because Orlando Carter is the exception. He will not cease his fight for freedom, while most capitulate to a system that is without solutions. Perhaps this is the saving grace for the citizens of Butler County. They have in Carter a man who not only fights for his family, he fights for the people. He wakes everyday resolved to reveal the truth of a broken justice system to those who have no inkling of its failings. He seeks to remedy what will afflict his children if he does not arrest its overbearing tendencies.

The irony is that John Boehner asked prematurely and ill-advisedly, "What was that black man thinking?" The answer is simple. Carter was thinking and doing no differently than any honest and successful CEO who happens to be white, brown or black. Butler County citizens will learn that Carter, the man, is innocent and now contends for truth, justice and liberty. This is what morally grounded and principled men do. They do not surrender to what is inferior.

Carter will triumph; of this there is no doubt. His raison d'etre is beyond contestation. He will advocate for the greater good of all. May his actions and impeachable beliefs serve as a testimony to the greatness that is within all who prize freedom over self and truth over that which is convenient. May his resolve inspire us to tap into the 90% of our unseen capacity for change in a culture in dire need of warriors and champions.

Take note, Butler County, a lion will soon be uncaged and he will roar. He will roar for one reason alone. He has seen the 90% that is beneath the surface of what we naively believe to be a "justice" system. The lion will roar with a mighty purpose.

James B. Johnson

Appendix S – Motion To Amend, New Evidence

UNITED STATES DISTRICT COURT
WESTERN DISTRICT OF VIRGINIA

James Bowers Johnson Petitioner, v UNITED STATES OF AMERICA Respondent.	)))))))	Case No.: 6:15-cv-80797-NKM-RSB

MEMORANDUM OF LAW IN SUPPORT OF MOTION TO AMEND
2255 Motion under 2255 (f)(4)

James B. Johnson
Petitioner, Pro Se

TABLE OF CONTENTS

TABLE OF POINTS AND AUTHORITIES

UNITED STATES SUPREME COURT

ii

Procedural History

On April 5, 2012, a federal grand jury for the western district of Virginia issued an indictment against Petitioner for four violations of the Internal Revenue Code, one count under 26 USC 7212(a) and three counts under 26 USC 7203. After Petitioner's arrest, the initial hearing and arraignment, the trial began on January 15, 2013 and ended with a guilty verdict on January 18, 2013. Petitioner was sentenced on April 11, 2013 to 48 months. Petitioner filed a notice of appeal on April 15, 2013. The Fourth Circuit affirmed the district court decision (United States v Johnson, 571 F Appx 205 (4th Cir. 2014)). Petitioner timely filed his 2255 motion on January 23, 2015 (Dkt 186) and a motion to amend on February 18, 2015 (Dkt 189). The government offered its Response on April 3, 2015 (Dkt 194). Petitioner filed his Reply on April 22, 2015 (Dkt 198). Petitioner now files this motion to amend.

Introduction

This is an introductory abridgement of Petitioner's issue, designed to provide this court complete and concise factual and legal context to demonstrate that Petitioner's claim is commensurate with controlling law.

The Department of Internal Revenue (DIR) deliberately offered **perjured testimony** through its agent, to its sister agency, the Department of Justice (DOJ) and into this court. Consequently, without investigating thoroughly, the government's main witness, Internal Revenue agent Robert Biggs, testified falsely that John Kotmair was not qualified to serve as Power-of-Attorney (POA).

Petitioner has **newly-discovered evidence** which confirms that Kotmair's Representative Number was not revoked and that he was qualified to serve as POA. In a 10/6/15 response to Petitioner's FOIA request, the IRS confirmed that it has NO documentation of a revocation. (Exhibit C). Yet, a Fourth Circuit case[1] cites that, in 1993, the IRS revoked Kotmair's number. However, the court also acknowledged

[1]United States v Kotmair, 2006 U.S. Dist. LEXIS 96885, fn 6.

1

that Kotmair disputed any revocation on due process grounds[2]. The court then, quite logically, if not presumptiously, concluded that the number was revoked.[3] Yet, since the IRS cannot now confirm this act, credence must be granted that there was a lack of **due process** in 1993 and the revocation never occurred. Rather, the IRS simply established and furthered a **fraud**. The claim that the IRS revoked the number is even more suspect with another Fourth Circuit case[4] in which Kotmair prevailed, with the decision reflecting nothing about Kotmair's status being denied or revoked just three years earlier!

Similiar to the above cases, in the instant case, the court, defense and jury believed the claim that Kotmair was not qualified. So, what was actually **perjury, concealment, impeached testimony, misrepresentation** or a **lie**[5] was accepted as truth. Under Brady infra and its progeny, the prosecution is held liable for **knowingly** or by **constructive/imputed knowledge** suppressing information[6]. Since the prosecutor was aware of Biggs perjured testimony and the resulting **constitutional error**, the court must address the character of the evidence and not the character of the prosecutor.[7] With new evidence that is both **exculpatory** and **impeaching** and **withheld**, as well as being **material** to the point of **prejudice**, the court must reconcile that Petitioner was denied due process[8]. This new evidence reveals a controversy of such subtlety and significance that, but for Petitioner's **due diligence**[9], the court would not have known of the government's deliberate intent, to promote the fiction that Kotmair's number was revoked when it was not.

This raises the issue of witness **credibility**[10] and Biggs' impact on the jury. Since prosecutors foist the prestige of the government,[11] the prosecutor and an agent may easily taint[12] his role and testimony. This practice clouds the jurors' estimate of the witness and adversely affects its determination.[13]

2 Id.
3 Id.
4 Save-A-Patriot-Fellowship v United States, 962 F Supp 695 (1996)
5 Napue v Illinois, 360 US 264 (1959)
6 Odle v Calderon, 65 F Supp 2d 1065 (9th Cir. 1999)
7 United States v Agurs 427 US 97, 110 (1976)
8 Brady v Maryland, 373 US 83, 87 (1963)
9 McQuiggin v Perkins, __ US __ 2013

The impact from Biggs' testimony was realized simply because it was accepted as true,[14] destroyed any meaningful challenge to the government's case and projected false impressions to the jury.[15] With Biggs' perjury, Kotmair and Petitioner were portrayed as less than credible. With Biggs' reliance upon advice from his manager and counsel (Exhibit B) the IRS avoided Kotmair's substantive questions and concerns about Petitioner's belief and enabled Biggs to label Petitioner's concerns as "frivolous." This grand and deceptive design enabled the government to avoid Petitioner's rebuttal of its **presumption** and **prima facie evidence** that he was liable for the **excise** on **income**. Consequently, the jury, through presentation of **false evidence**,[16] perceived Petitioner's belief as "frivolous," without hearing Biggs' refutation of or agreement with that belief.

The government prosecuted Petitioner under a **false claim** or presumption that he had a filing requirement, knowing that Petitioner rejected the federal benefit of social security which once made him liable. Knowing that Petitioner rebutted the government's presumption and prima facie evidence, the IRS knew that any dialogue with Kotmair would have substantiated Petitioner's belief and diminished its claims. So, rather than overcome Petitioner's rebuttal before or during trial, the IRS avoided Kotmair and Petitioner's concerns. These tactics precluded the government from contesting a belief of merit before the jury and denied Petitioner a full expression of his argument. This was prejudicial.

Since the jurors were denied Petitioner's full argument and Biggs' testimony that would have been consistent with that belief, they could not understand that there never could have been any **mens rea** and, therefore, no **actus reus**, the

[10] United States v Bartko, 728 F 3d 327, (4th Cir. 2013)
[11] United States v Francis, 170 F 3d 546, 550, (6th Cir. 1999)
[12] Bartko supra, 335
[13] Napue supra, 269
[14] Bartko supra
[15] Id
[16] United States v Giglio, 405 US 150, 153 (1971)

3

very elements of the crime.[17] Because of the perceived knowledge, conduct and credibility[18] (prestige) of Biggs and the office of the prosecutor and the government's deceitful veil placed over the judicial process, Biggs' perjured testimony affected **reasonable doubt**. Moreover, since this court was unaware of the IRS deceit, it committed reversible error on two separate occasions by permitting an unconstitutional presumption.

Biggs' perjury defeated the search for truth,[19] when the judicial system aspires to protect the truth-finding process.[20] Since the truth was substituted with a lie, the court must provide a remedy for an accused who was treated unfairly.[21]

[17] Id.
[18] Id.
[19] Nix v Whiteside, 475 US 157, 166 (1986)
[20] United States v Rhynes, 206 F 3d 348, 369 (4th Cir. 1998)
[21] Brady supra, 86-87

4

ISSUE

PETITIONER HAS NEWLY-DISCOVERED EVIDENCE THAT THE GOVERNMENT'S MAIN WITNESS, AGENT ROBERT BIGGS, TESTIFIED FALSELY DURING TRIAL, WHICH IS A VIOLATION OF DUE PROCESS AND CONSTITUTIONAL ERROR THAT MERITS RELIEF UNDER 28 USC 2255(f)(4).

THE FACTS

In 2000, Petitioner revoked and rescinded his signature and intent, nunc pro tunc, to the federal social security insurance program, sent by certified mail to the Social Security Administration. Petitioner also sent this document to the Secretary of the Treasury, which served as his rebuttal of any presumption and prima facie evidence that he was liable for the federal excise on income. (Decl. 1, 2) When the government began a civil investigation into Petitioner's lack of tax return filings, he asked John Kotmair to serve as his Power-of-Attorney (POA). Kotmair immediately wrote to Agent Biggs for the laws that required Petitioner to file a return and gave Biggs the authority to investigate. (Decl. 3, 4) Rather than respond to Kotmair, Biggs sent Petitioner a letter stating that Kotmair did not qualify as POA. (Decl. 5) Kotmair responded that he did qualify and reasserted Petitioner's concern. Biggs refused to answer Kotmair; yet, based upon his letters, Biggs sent Petitioner a "Frivolous Arguments" pamphlet. (Decl. 6, 7, 8) Biggs then refused to respond to Kotmair's third letter, in which he asserted that Petitioner's concerns were not frivolous. (Id)

Petitioner, if only because Biggs failed to respond to Kotmair, wrote to Biggs, CID Agent Pompei, all of his elected representatives, Internal Revenue Commissioners Rossotti and Shulman, Mr. Salad at the Department of Justice and the IRS. Every agency and official refused to respond to Petitioner's queries, which were identical to Kotmair's. (See 2255 Decl. 18, 19, 20, 23 and Supp. Decl. to Petitioner's Reply brief, 1)

During the 2013 trial, Biggs testified that if Kotmair had been qualified, he would have been required to deal with him and not Petitioner. (Exhibit B) Biggs further testified that he was told by his manager and counsel that Kotmair was not qualified. (Id) Moreover, given the nature of Kotmair's concerns, Biggs testified that his manager and counsel advised him to send the frivolous arguments

6

pamphlet as the official IRS response. (Id) Biggs also testified, when asked if Petitioner had a tax liability, that "it was sort of a mixture." (Id)

Since Petitioner could not reconcile the IRS claim that Kotmair was not qualified as POA, after his 2255 submissions, he researched the issue. Petitioner searched the computer and confirmed that Kotmair was not barred from serving as POA until the court issued an injunction in 2007. (Decl. 13) In August 2015, Petitioner requested through the FOIA that the IRS provide any documents that confirmed the date that the agency revoked Kotmair's Representative Number. (Decl. 14) The IRS responded on 10/6/15 that it was unable to locate any documents that complied with Petitioner's request. (Decl. 15) Petitioner then discovered that in 2006 (U.S. Dist LEXIS, 98665 (4th Cir.)), Kotmair was notified in 1993 that his number was revoked. However, this footnote revealed that Kotmair disputed any revocation on "due process" grounds. (Decl. 16) Petitioner then discovered a case (Save-A-Patriot-Fellowship v United States, 962 F Supp 695 (1996)) which revealed NO hint of any revocation of Kotmair's number. (Decl. 17) Finally, Petitioner found no revocation protocol within the code or regulations for Circular 230, 10.7(c)(1)(iv) or any of the qualifications claimed by Kotmair.

THE LAW AND ARGUMENT

Standard

Under 28 USC 2255(f)(4), Brady supra and its progeny, Petitioner offers newly-discovered evidence which proves a violation of due process under the Fifth Amendment and constitutional error in the instant case. There are three components to a Brady violation: 1) the evidence is favorable to the accused, 2) the evidence was suppressed and 3) prejudice ensued. (See Strickler v Greene 527 US 263, 281-282 (1999).

Newly-discovered evidence

The IRS FOIA Division responded (Exhibit C) to Petitioner's request

7

(Exhibit A) stating that it could not locate any documents which proved the agency revoked Kotmair's Representative Number. This new evidence contradicts the record and Biggs' testimony. Moreover, Fourth Circuit case history (footnotes 1 & 2) suggests that the number was not revoked on due process grounds. The fact that the IRS has no proof of a revocation substantiates the due process claim. Biggs testified falsely. Furthermore, the new evidence was suppressed. The foregoing establishes the first two Brady components. The following argument establishes prejudice.

<u>Biggs' False Testimony</u>

In conflict with the new evidence, Biggs testified to two critical elements.

1) Kotmair was not qualified

> I notified our counsel and my manager... and asked if Mr. Kotmair could represent... Mr. Johnson... if he was qualified to do that, then I was required to then respond to Mr. Kotmair and not deal with Mr. Johnson directly. The information came back from the manager and counsel that Mr. Kotmair did not qualify... as power of attorney. (Exhibit B)

2) Kotmair's concerns were "frivolous"

> And they also advised me that the IRS has published a response to frivolous arguments and I should attach that, because Mr. Kotmair's, you know letter, did raise some issues, that would have been the official response to it. (Id.)

His superiors precluded Biggs and the IRS from answering credible concerns from a qualified POA. Consequently, failure to address what was "frivolous" in 2004 precluded Biggs from doing so at trial. Since Biggs <u>believed</u> the information of his two superiors (See <u>United States v Price</u>, 722 F 2d 88 (5th Cir. 1983)), this hearsay bolstered his testimony before the jury. Like <u>Price</u>, in the instant case, the jury depended upon Biggs for the determination of alleged material facts, the very "truth of the evidence." Id at 90 This is reversible error.

A mere survey of Kotmair's letters (Exhibit A) reveals why the IRS prevented Biggs from responding.

Furthermore, it appears... that you are claiming that Mr. and Mrs.

8

> Johnson are personally subject to (or liable for) the tax at issue. However, you make this claim in such a general way that it is impossible to determine any statutory basis for it. This is precisely why they have repeatedly requested that the Internal Revenue Service provide the statute which makes them liable for the tax you allege they owe... If you would provide such statute... then no further correspondence would be necessary. (Id)

And he stated

> In regards to the "Tax Form 1040,"... please be aware that Mr. Johnson has determined that he does not have a requirement to file for the years at issue. Therefore, if you have determined that he does have such a requirement, in spite of his determination to the contrary, then please cite your authority to make such a determination and forward any documents or other information upon which you base your determination. (Id.)

When the prosecutor asked Biggs, "What part of [Kotmair's letters] was considered to be frivolous by - the arguments made?" [brackets added] Biggs testified, "It is the <u>advice</u> I got from counsel." (Id.) [emphasis added] Biggs' blind acceptance of the advice of his superiors was the extent of his investigation into Kotmair's status and Petitioner's concerns. Biggs' perfunctory effort is significant since he could not determine if Petitioner even had a liability to file returns. When asked, "What did you determine in regards to whether or not [Petitioner] had a filing requirement from the records you obtained?" Biggs testified, "And the evidence that I had seen was a bit of a mixture." (Id.) Yet, by investigating Kotmair's letters, Biggs would have contended with Petitioner's rebuttal of the government's presumption that he had a liability. (See <u>Romano</u> infra, <u>Casey</u>, infra, <u>Hayes</u> infra and <u>Rindskopf</u> infra) and heeded Kotmair's admonition to stay within Biggs' own authority (See <u>Federal Crop Ins. Corp. v Merrill</u>, 332 US 380, 384 (1974)) Rather than respect Kotmair's warning, Biggs became a willing pawn for an agency that had an interest in the prosecution. (See <u>United States v Wood</u>, 57 F 3d 733 (9th Cir. 1995))

<u>No Meaningful Challenge Denied Exculpatory Evidence</u>

Because of Biggs' false testimony, the IRS ensured that the government's failure to overcome Petitioner's rebuttal was not argued before the jury.

9

Had this truth been aired, the jury would have learned what the government intended to avoid and deny - Petitioner's rebuttal and reasonable belief or his sincere intent to know of his liability, any of which would have resolved the civil investigation. With adequate investigation, Biggs would have

1) contended with Petitioner's rejection of the federal benefit of social security as the reason he was no longer subject to the federal tax (excise) on income
2) overcome Petitioner's rebuttal of the government's presumption and prima facie evidence that he was liable to file tax returns
3) arrived at a conclusion that was not a "mixture," but one of certainty - that Petitioner was not one within the class subject to the federal income tax

The IRS purposely and severely limited Petitioner from introducing evidence that would have exonerated him. This development suggests that "it is upon such subtle factors as the possible interest in the witness in testifying falsely." Napue 269 The IRS knew "the natural consequences of [its] acts." Ungar v Sarafite 376 US 575, 578 (1964) [brackets added]

> Newly-discovered evidence, however, may go so directly to the interest of the prosecution that if his testimony was essential to the prosecution a new trial should be awarded in which the interest of the witness may be shown. United States v McCoy, 478 F 2d 846, 847 (4th Cir. 1973)

Credibility of the Witness

Hiding behind the prestige of the government and his role as an agent (See Francis supra 550), Biggs's false testimony tainted Bartko supra 334 (See Napue 269), the jury's judgment, while denigrating Petitioner's credibility. The Fourth Circuit states,

> ... proof that a witness perjured himself... is no different from discovery of new evidence which impeaches the integrity of the records supporting the judgment from which relief is sought. Chrysler Corp. v Superior Dodge Inc. 1979 83 F.R. D. 179, fn 6 (D. Md. 1979)

The Supreme Court stated,

> The jury's estimate of the truthfulness and reliability of a given witness may well be determinative of guilt or innocence... Napue 269

Clearly, when a witness offers false testimony that is uncorroborated, it

10

weighs heavily for a conviction. Biggs' credibility was critical and unchallenged, which made suppression of the perjured information material to guilt.

False Impressions

The prosecution capitalized on the government's and Biggs' credibility, while using the prestige of its office to create false impressions. Bartko supra (See United States v Gillon, 704 F 3d 284 (4th Cir. 2012), United States v Colton 231 F 3d 890 (4th Cir. 2010)) Moreover since Biggs was not challenged since 2004, the jury believed the government's presumption that Petitioner was liable for a specific excise. This was a false impression. Also, by avoiding its obligation to overcome Petitioner's rebuttal, the government created the false impression that it had no such requirement. Without the jury hearing and understanding the antithesis of these false impressions, the jurors would believe that whatever Biggs avoided since 2004 was frivolous, which is yet another false impression. The false impressions, then, deserved challenges that would have compelled Biggs' agreement or disagreement before the jury.

Denial of Full Presentation

False impressions served one overarching goal; they denied Petitioner the ability to offer a full presentation of his argument. This is critical in one fundamental regard. Without a full argument, the jury never heard Biggs contend with the entirety of Petitioner's legitimate, lawful and reasonable belief. This fact is noteworthy since Petitioner asked Biggs to "supply me the information requested by Mr. Kotmair in his letters." (Exhibit A) Pointedly, this was an invitation for Biggs and the government to disregard the issue of Kotmair's lack qualification to serve as POA and to respond directly to Petitioner. Biggs remained silent. His unresponsiveness more than suggests that Kotmair's status was a false front. The agency's intent was to deny answers that would otherwise have revealed Petitioner's position. This tactic diminished reasonable doubt. Jurors

11

will not understand what is incomplete. Consequently, when reasonable doubt was marginalized, the jury did not understand why there could have been no mens rea and no actus reus. The IRS acted with depraved indifference that was

> designed specifically to subvert the fact-finding process by defeating full presentation of the adversary's case. See United States v Throckmorton, 98 US 1 at 65-66, Superior Dodge supra.

Petitioner's "federal constitutional right to have a meaningful opportunity to present a complete defense," Holmes v South Carolina, 547 US 319 (2006) (See Crane v Kentucky 476 US 683, 690 (1986), Clark v Arizona 548 US 735 (2006), California v Trombetta 467 US 479 (1984)) which is grounded in the Fifth and Sixth Amendments due process and compulsory process or confrontation clauses, was violated.

The Court was Misled

With its proforma response to what the IRS treated as a typical tax protestor case, the government evaded responsibility to overcome Petitioner's rebuttal. This failure, accomplished through fraud, adversely affected this court. As with its sister court in 2006 (See footnote 1), this court accepted the IRS assertion that Kotmair was not qualified and that Petitioner's belief was frivolous. However, as Petitioner stated in his Reply to the Government's Response to his 2255 motion (Dkt 198), the court has power to review application of federal law during adjudication as means to guard against what is unconstitutional enforcement of laws and regulations. The Due Process Clause mandates such review as "the essentials of due process and fair treatment" RE WINSHIP 397 US 358, 359 (1970) and to prevent manifest injustice. Quite significantly, with the government's concealment and Biggs' perjury, this court was misled to the point of permitting an unconstitutional presumption (See Yates v Evatt 500 US 391, 404 (1991), Connecticut v Johnson 460 US 73 (1983) and Sandstrom v Montana 442 US 510 (1979) or an irrebuttable presumption. This was error.

12

The federal government (IRS) had a responsibility to overcome Petitioner's rebuttal of its presumption of liability. As reflected in United States v Romano 382 US 136, 139 (1965) (See Leary v United States 395 US 6 (1965) and United States v Gainey 380 US 63 (1965)) the court acknowledged that presumption was allowable "only if the defendant failed to explain... to the satisfaction of the jury." Id at 143 Inevitably, the constitutionality of legislation depends upon "the rationality of the connection 'between the facts proved and the ultimate facts presumed.'" Id at 139 quoting Gainey supra.

In Casey v United States 276 US 413 (1928), the court opined that

> It is consistent with all constitutional protections of accused men to throw on them the proving of facts peculiarly within their knowledge... at 418

Constitutional protections are safeguards to allow the accused to prevail with the facts. In Hayes v Georgia 258 US 1 (1922) that court stated

> It is not arbitrary for the State to act upon the presumption and erect it into knowledge; not peremptory of course, but subject to explanation, and affording the means of explanation. at 3 [emphasis added]

Significantly, the court advised against the presumption being "strained" Id. upon the defendant. Without question, presumptions regarding excise matters are not irrebuttable. In United States v Rindskopf 105 US 418 (1882), the court stated that with

> a prima facie case of liability... If not impeached, it was sufficient to justify a recovery, but every material fact upon which... liability was asserted was open to contestation. at 422 [emphasis added]

Rindskopf had the liberty to rebut and, if in the right, defeat the assessment.

The point cannot be any more transparent. The IRS had a legal responsibility to overcome Petitioner's rebuttal of a tax liability. And, if anything, Petitioner had the right to rebut the IRS presumption in a court of law without contending with an unconstitutional presumption or a presumption that was not rebuttable. The IRS violated fundamental law when it sought to enforce what even

13

Congress may not do. This is why the agency enforced its presumption without not only overcoming, but by hiding Petitioner's rebuttal from the jury. This reckless posture continued for nine years, as Petitioner relied upon the Constitution as the rule of law, and into the trial. Rather than satisfy proper agency authority (See Romano, Casey, Hayes, Rindskopf supra), with its false representations beginning in 2004, the government's ploy denied Petitioner of recourse and remedies sourced in fundamental law.

This argument may be expressed differently. The government's refusal to overcome Petitioner's rebuttal destroyed Petitioner's presumption of innocence. Presumption of innocence endures - as with a rebuttal of an excise liability - until overcome by proof to the contrary. (See United States v Fleischman 339 US 349, 363 (1950)) The government's posture defeated the premise that "the law invests the defendant with a presumption of good character." Michelson v United States 335 US 469, 475 (1948)

While a court is not expected to substitute its judgment for an agency, when the agency's authority is arbitrary, unconstitutional and ultra vires, the court must intervene. Unfortunately, this court, as with the court in 2006 (See footnote 1), believed the IRS claims (indictment) and Biggs' false testimony. Consequently, this court never allowed for the prevention of what was an unconstitutional presumption. This was error.

Regrettably, though, based upon the IRS deception, this court committed a separate error before the trial began. The confluence of the factors that led to the basis of the agency's lie and Biggs' false testimony culminated in an indictment. This was enough to adversely influence this court. Significantly, while in solitary confinement, Petitioner submitted a timely Habeas Corpus writ, demanding his release. (Dkt 25, #9) Petitioner contended that "The United States has no authority over [Petitioner]... since formally revoking/rescinding any

14

benefit claim to the federal social insurance program in 2000, thus rebutting the [government's] presumption." Id Rather than consider and grant this motion, this court denied it (Dkt 27). This prima facie claim never received the judicial discernment it deserved. The court accepted the IRS presumption that Petititoner was liable to file tax returns without accounting for Petitioner's rebuttal of that very presumption. This court's refusal to weigh this Habeas Corpus claim, regardless of the disputed assertion that Petitioner had counsel, was error.

The Prosecutor

As a spokesman for the government (See Giglio supra 154), the prosecutor is obligated to the ABA Standards of Criminal Justice, §11-4.3(a) (3rd Ed 1996), for all material and information from those who participate in the investigation. (See United States v Zuno-Arce 44 F 3d 1420, 1427 (9th Cir. 1995)) The prosecutor violates due process when he knowingly uses false testimony.

> The individual prosecutor has a duty to learn of any favorable evidence known to others acting on the government's behalf in the case... Kyles v Whitley 514 US 419, 437 (1994)

The court went on to state,

> ... the prosecutor's responsibility for failing to disclose known favorable evidence rising to a material level of importance is inescapable. Id at 438

The Ninth Cirucit addressed the matter by stating

> Given the manifest reason to question the veracity of the prosecution's witness, the Constitution required a prompt pretrial investigation of the integrity of the government's evidence before the witnesses were called to the stand. Commonwealth of Northern Mariana Islands v Bowie, 243 F 3d 1109, 1123 (9th Cir. 2000)

This is no small matter.

> The prosecutor is "deemed to have knowledge of and access to anything in the custody or control of any federal agency participating in the same investigation of the defendant". Calderon supra 1072

As stated in Giglio "suppression of material evidence justifies a new trial irrespective of the good faith or bad faith of the prosecution." Id at 154 (See Cone v Bell 556 US

15

_ (2009))

Given that agencies may, have and do suppress information from the prosecution, this court must conclude that the IRS knew that Kotmair was qualified and that his concerns were not "frivolous." This court must consider that the same culture encompasses prosecutors who intentional use false testimony to secure convictions. Moreover, it is not enough to suggest that any sister agency would accept the IRS "facts" as true, with belief that the IRS, another sister agency, conducted an adequate investigation. (See Appalachian Power Co. v EPA _ US _ (2001))

The same holds for a sister court. Any court may rest upon the judicial finding of another court, especially one in the same district, as true. Such a dynamic - the trust of sister entities - easily facilitates the suppression of information. However, as reflected in Munchinski v Wilson, 2011 U.S. Dist. LEXIS 86665 (W.D. Pa., 2011), when evidence is suppressed by some agent (agency) of the prosecution's investigating team, which results in constitutional error, the court must acknowledge the character of the evidence. The reason is simple. The prosecutor has contructive or implied knowledge (See United States v Endicott, 869 F 2d 452, 456 (9th Cir. 1989)) in at least two ways: 1) when investigative agencies are involved in the prosecution (See Whitley supra 437-438) and 2) these same agencies are interested in the prosecution. Woods supra

The prosecutor has a solemn and vital duty to ensure the interest of justice. He "is legally charged with responsibility for information uncovered in civil investigations that he may be required to disclose in criminal cases that he prosecutes." United States v Reyes, 577 F 3d 1060, 1078 (9th Cir. 2009)

With the government's civil investigation, Hogeboom knew that Petitioner relied upon Kotmair for answers that would have resolved the matter or, in the event the investigation became criminal, Petitioner would have had information,

16

vith documented correspondence between Kotmair and Biggs, that proved Petitioner's intent to comply with the lav or the government's failure to overcome Petitioner's rebuttal. This never happened - which Hogeboom knew. In accordance with the Department of Justice Mission Statement "to ensure fair and impartial administration of justice for all Americans", the federal prosecutor has a sacred duty not to impede the truth. Reyes, 1077 "The government cannot with its right hand say it has nothing while its left holds what is of value." Wood supra 737 Hogeboom compromised his sacred duty; he knew what was in both hands.

The Jury

The jury's judgment was tainted because of Biggs' perjury and Hogeboom's failure to disclose what was in the possession of the prosecutor's investigative team. As a result, the jurors were without the knowledge that 1) Petitioner rebutted the government's presumption and 2) the government never overcame it. The jurors did not hear and learn that Biggs never reconciled that Petitioner could not be liable based upon his rejection of the federal benefit of social security, for which the excise on income is assessed. The jurors only knew that the government considered Petitioner's (Kotmair's) questions to be frivolous and that Biggs did not have to respond. Consequently, the jurors did not learn that even Congress lacked constitutional power to tax one who is without the class liable for a specific excise. The jurors, therefore, were led to an irrebuttable or unconstitutional presumption. With the government's deliberate fraud, it evaded a responsibility to afford the jury a full and untainted representation of all the facts. Significantly, then, there is the ever present concern that reasonable doubt in the juror's minds was sorely affected by the "knowledge" and credibility of the prosecution's key witness. The jurors were given false impressions that served as the means for sequential false impressions that vanquished reasonable doubt.

17

It is beyond dispute that the government ruse was devilishly crafted to withhold evidence and arguments that would have defeated its case before the jury, while denying opposing arguments that were grounded in fundamental law and supported by prima facie evidence. Noteworthy is that the ruse was accomplished by preying upon the prejudices of jurors that Petitioner should do as any American - comply without question or challenge for something that is PRESUMED to be an automatic legal liability, the filing of federal tax returns. Because Petitioner asked a question, the government acted deceitfully, absolutely and unfairly with the intent to secure an advantage with the jury.

> It reasonably follows that if the omitted evidence creates a reasonable doubt that did not otherwise exist, constitutional error has been committed. Agurs supra 112

The disclosure of the new evidence or the correction of Biggs' false testimony could have produced a different jury verdict.

The Court

This court was unaware of the IRS deception and nondisclosure of this new evidence. In fact, this court, if only because the prosecution failed to reveal what was prejudicial, had no reason to question the truthfulness of the government's key witness. This court must now reconcile the impact of Biggs' perjury and the compromising IRS scheme.

> Disclosure of evidence is pertinent to accused's preparation for trial. United States v Avellino, 136 F 3d 249, 255 (2nd Cir. 1992)

as well as to the court's adjudicative role. This court must account for the fact that

> A petitioner shows "cause" when the reason for his failure to develop facts in... court was the... suppression of relevant evidence. Wolfe v Clarke, 691 F 3d 410, 420 (4th Cir. 2012)

Finally, this court must consider the impact of Biggs' credibility upon the jury and the weight of the prestige of the prosecutor as a whole.

18

> When the reliability of a witness may be determinative of an accused's guilt or innocence, the nondisclosure of evidence that affects credibility is denial of due process. Hillman v Hinkle, 114 F Supp 2d 497, 502 (4th Cir. 2000) (See Giglio supra)

With the creation of false impressions, which affected reasonable doubt, the trial was unfair. A tainted conviction is grounds for post conviction relief. This court must conclude that fundamental fairness was denied. The government's "expert" witness was not effectively challenged because of his lies. Plainly stated, unlike the previously referenced sister court in 2006, which had a choice between the government's representation that Kotmair's number was revoked or that it was not revoked for at least due process grounds, this court should accept that Kotmair was qualified. Why? The IRS, the very agency that was investigating Petitioner, cannot prove that the number was revoked. This court must reject the agency's claim that Petitioner's questions were **"frivolous"** - a claim that appeared plausible only because it was a part of the planned perjury. The knowing use of perjured testimony constitutes a denial of due process because such a "deliberate deception of the court and jury" is "inconsistent with the rudimentary demands of justice." Mooney v Holohan 294 US 103, 112 (1935) This conviction "must be set aside [since] there is a reasonable likelihood that false testimony... affected the judgment of the jury. Agurs 103 [brackets added]

Conclusion

Wherefore, in the context that pro se pleadings must be construed and treated literally under whatever rules or law appropriate for relief (See Haines v Kerner, 404 US 519 (1972), Boag v McDougall, 454 US 364 (1982)), Petitioner respectfully asks this court to find that Petitioner has established cause and prejudice and to provide for an evidentiary hearing and appropriate relief. Petitioner also asks that this court have the opposition show cause why this relief should not be granted.

Respectfully,

James B. Johnson
Petitioner, Pro se

19

CERTIFICATE OF SERVICE

I herety certify that on this 5th day of November 2015, I mailed the enclosed Motion under 28 USC 2255(f)(4), Motion for Issuance of Subpoena and Motion fo the appointment of counsel in the established legal mail protocol at Federal Correctional Institution Elkton to the District Court in Roanoke, Virginia.

James B. Johnson
Petitioner, Pro se

20

John Kotmair's letters may be found in Exhibit C of the 2255 Motion.

Ex A

Case 6:12-cr-00015-NKM Document 127-5 Filed 01/18/13 Page 10 of 29 Pageid#: 1774

DEPARTMENT OF THE TREASURY
INTERNAL REVENUE SERVICE
Washington, D.C. 20224

SMALL BUSINESS/SELF-EMPLOYED DIVISION

August 30, 2004

ROBERT A. BIGGS
Revenue Agent,
Badge # 54-01418
Phone # 304-263-5901 Ext 115

Internal Revenue Service
SB/SE: Area 6: Char 4
55 Meridian Parkway
Suite 107
Martinsburg, WV 25401

James Johnson
219 Jefferson St
Winchester, VA 22601

Dear Mr. Johnson

I have received a Privacy Act Release form and Power of Attorney, from Mr. John B. Kotmair, Please be advised that under Circular No. 230 at 10.7 (c) (1) (iv) Mr. Johns B. Kotmair does not qualify as your Power of Attorney for Federal Income Tax purposes.

Please refer to Internal Revenue Service Publication 3498 regarding Representation. If you would like to some one else represent you, please provide me with one of the following:
A completed Form 2848, Power of Attorney and Declaration of Representative
Form 8821, tax information Authorization
For your convenience please find attached form 2848.

In Mr. Kotmair's letter dated August 24, 2004 a number of concerns were raised, please find enclosed a copy of Response to Frivolous Arguments, I encourage you to read all of this document, please pay special attention to page 19 of this document.

Mr. Johnson, Federal tax laws are passed by Congress and signed by the President. The Internal Revenue Service is responsible for administrating federal tax laws fairly and ensuring that taxpayers comply with the laws. We do not have authority to change the tax laws.

The Internal Revenue Service strives to collect the proper amount of revenues at the least cost to the public, and in a manner that warrants the highest degree of public confidence in our integrity, efficiency, and fairness. In accomplishing this, we continually strive to help taxpayers resolve legitimate account problems as effectively as possible. While tax collection is not a popular function of government, it clearly is a necessary one. Without it all other functions would eventually cease.

2SAR-1-0525

2SAR-1-0525

-780-

Exhibits

A - Kotmair/Biggs/Petitioner Letters

B - Transcripts

C - Newly-Discovered Evidence

D - Petitioner's Declaration

Ex A

There are people who encourage others to deliberately violate our nation's tax laws. It would be unfortunate if you were to rely on their opinions. These persons take legal statements out of context and claim that they are not subject to tax laws. Many offer advice that is false and misleading, hoping to encourage others to join them. Generally, their advice isn't free. Taxpayers who purchase this kind of information often wind up paying more in taxes, interest, and penalties than they would have paid simply by filing correct tax returns. Some may subject themselves to criminal penalties, including fines and possible imprisonment.

Federal courts have consistently ruled against the arguments you have made. Therefore, we will not respond to future correspondence concerning these issues.

Sincerely yours,

RAB

Robert A. Biggs
Internal Revenue Agent

Enclosure:

Copy of John B Kotmir letter dated August 24, 2004
Form 2848 Power of Attorney and Declaration of representative
IRS Pub 3498
Copy of Response to Frivolous Arguments

2SAR-1-0526

2SAR-1-0526

EX A

Certified Mail #_7004 0750 0000 4570 3994

James Johnson
219 Jefferson Street
Winchester, VA 22601

November 1, 2004

Robert A. Biggs, Revenue Agent
Internal Revenue Service
55 Meridian Parkway, Suite 107
Martinsburg, WV 25401

RE: Your letter of October 1, 2004, requesting I call your office to set a date and time for a meeting regarding years 2000 through 2003.

Dear Mr. Biggs:

I am in receipt of your letter, referenced above, in which you state "I have not received a phone call from you as requested."

In fact, your letter of September 27, 2004 stated, "please call me on or before October 8, 2004." Why did you send a follow-up letter on October 1st? The time frame for your request had not yet elapsed.

Nevertheless, it appears that the purpose for your writing on October 4th was to attach a Form 4564, "Information Document Request," apparently to request documents you wanted me to bring to a proposed meeting.

However, as you surely are aware by now, I have already responded to your requests via my Power of Attorney, Mr. John Kotmair. His letter, dated October 1, 2004, stated, among other things, that I have determined that I do not have a requirement to file for the years at issue. He also advised you that no one has given me notice, pursuant to IRC Section 6001, to keep any records pertaining to any tax years.

Furthermore, it appears that your Form 4564, including such items as a "[c]opies of all bank statements" and "[a] list of all trusts in which you were involved," etc., goes far beyond the scope of any documents which could possibly be necessary to establish a requirement to file.

GOVERNMENT EXHIBIT 5-8 6:12CR15-1

Page 1 of 2

2SAR-1-0546

2SAR-1-0546

-796-

In conclusion, unless and until you supply me with the information requested by Mr. Kotmair in his letters of August 24th and October 1st; information that support your actions, I will be unable to attend this or any future scheduled meetings.

Sincerely,

James Johnson

Enclosures: Copy of your letter of October 1, 2004.

2SAR-1-0547

2SAR-1-0547

Ex B

BIGGS - DIRECT

BY MR. HOGEBOOM:
Q. Now, on this particular document it says it is being done pursuant to a power of attorney?
A. Yes.
Q. Prior to August 24th of 2004, had you talked to either James Johnson or Diane Johnson?
A. I came to their house to give them the letters that I had prepared for them, prior to this letter that I received from Mr. Kotmair.
Q. And had you had any contact with Mr. Kotmair?
A. No, I had not.
Q. Did you ever have any contact with Mr. Kotmair?
A. Other than this letter and subsequent letters that he wrote?
Q. Yes.
A. No.
Q. Now, attached to this letter is a power of attorney and a -- had you ever heard of the fiduciary of Save-A-Patriot Fellowship?
A. I had not when I first received this, no.
Q. And you had other correspondence from Mr. Kotmair?
A. Yes, after that.
Q. Now, let me hand you up Government's Exhibit 5-3 and ask if you can identify that particular document.
A. Yes. This is a letter that I can identify.

-130-

Q. Okay. Would you tell the jury what that letter is.
A. After receiving Mr. Kotmair's response to me, then I wrote a response to Mr. Johnson.
Q. Okay.
MR. HOGEBOOM: Your Honor, at this time I would move for the admission of Government's Exhibit 5-3.
THE COURT: It will be admitted.
(Government's Exhibit No. 5-3 was marked for identification and received in evidence.)
BY MR. HOGEBOOM:
Q. Now, your --
MR. HOGEBOOM: And if I may publish it, Your Honor, to the jury?
THE COURT: Yes, sir.
BY MR. HOGEBOOM:
Q. Your letter is directed to Mr. Johnson, not Mr. Kotmair; is that correct?
A. That's correct.
Q. Okay. And you refer to certain IRS publications. And what was the purpose of that reference to the publications?
A. Are you referring to the paragraph there in Mr. Kotmair's letter of August 24th?
Q. Yes.
A. Can I have a second to reread that? It has been a number of years now.

Yes. The -- after receiving Mr. Kotmair's letter to me, I notified our counsel and my manager down in Charleston and asked them if Mr. Kotmair could represent -- did he qualify to represent Mr. Johnson. If he had've -- if he was qualified to do that, then I was required to then respond to Mr. Kotmair and deal with Mr. Kotmair, and to not deal with Mr. Johnson directly.

The information came back from the manager and counsel that Mr. Kotmair did not qualify to represent Mr. Johnson as power of attorney. And they also advised me that the IRS has published a response to frivolous arguments and I should attach that, because Mr. Kotmair's, you know, letter did raise some issues, and that would have been the official IRS response to it.

Q. And what was the -- if you recall, what part of it was considered to be frivolous by -- the arguments being made?

A. The part of the IRS response or the part --

Q. Yes, the IRS considered to be frivolous.

A. The -- I'm sorry. You mean Mr. Kotmair's frivolous --

Q. Yes, Mr. Kotmair's.

A. I would have to read back. It is the advice I got from counsel.

Q. Now, do you know whether or not Mr. Johnson received that letter?

A. I don't recall off the top of my head if I sent that

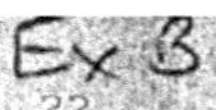

certified mail or not.
Q. Let me hand you Government's Exhibit 5-4 and ask if you can identify that document.
A. Oh, yeah. This is a document that I received from Mr. Kotmair again, after the letter I sent to Mr. Johnson.
MR. HOGEBOOM: Your Honor, I move for the admission of Government's Exhibit 5-4 and ask that it be published.
THE COURT: It will be admitted and you may publish.
(Government's Exhibit No. 5-4 was marked for identification and received in evidence.)
BY MR. HOGEBOOM:
Q. And, in fact, if you look at the letter that you received, doesn't it reference the prior letter that I had showed you?
A. Yes, it does.
Q. Okay. And then, in particular, this section there, did you find that to be somewhat unique, beginning "Finally"?
A. It was unusual to me, yes.
Q. Had you ever received that type of response before?
A. No, I had not.
Q. When you talked to counsel, was there anything that you were doing outside of what you had determined to be your authority?
A. Oh, absolutely not, no.

Ex C

James B. Johnson
16665-084
Federal Satellite Lov Elkton
P.O. Box 10
Lisbon, OH 44432

August 19, 2015

IRS FOIA Request
Stop 211
P.O. Box 621506
Atlanta, GA 30362-3006

Subject: FOIA REQUEST

To Whom it May Concern:

I am requesting, in accord with the Freedom of Information Act, all documents pertaining to the termination date of Representative Number: 2605-47815R, for John B. Kotmair, Jr., Save-A-Patriot Fellowship, with a recorded address of P.O. Box 91, Westminster, MD 21158.

The Department of Internal Revenue issued the above number to the aforementioned person and entity, who, pursuant to 26 CFR 301.6103(c)-1, 26 CFR 601.502(a), 26 cfr 601.502(b)(5)(ii) and Treasury Circular No. 230, §10.7(c)(1)(iv), represented Citizens as their Power-of-Attorney. The documents that I am requesting should clearly indicate the date that the Department of Internal Revenue revoked this number, which is supposedly in December 2004.

Please forward the requested documents to the address listed above. I understand that I will be billed for any excess copies pursuant to FOIA guidelines.

Sincerely,

James B. Johnson

original mailed 8/20/15 to stop 93A as well

Ex C

PRIVACY, GOVERNMENTAL LIAISON AND DISCLOSURE

DEPARTMENT OF THE TREASURY
INTERNAL REVENUE SERVICE
WASHINGTON, DC 20224

October 6, 2015

James B. Johnson
16665-084
P.O. Box 10
Lisbon, OH 44432

Dear Mr. Johnson:

I am responding to your Freedom of Information Act (FOIA) request dated August 19, 2015 that we received on August 25, 2015.

You asked for copies of documents that clearly indicate the date that the Department of Internal Revenue revoked Representative Number 2605-47815R. I found no documents specifically responsive to your request.

I have enclosed Notice 393 explaining your appeal rights.

If you have any questions please call Disclosure Specialist Denise E Hensley ID # 1000197063, at 859-669-4048 or write to: Internal Revenue Service, Centralized Processing Unit – Stop 93A, PO Box 621506, Atlanta, GA 30362. Please refer to case number F15238-0106.

Sincerely,

Bruce Hayes

Bruce Hayes
Disclosure Manager
Disclosure Office 5

Enclosure
Notice 393

UNITED STATES DISTRICT COURT
WESTERN DISTRICT OF VIRGINIA

James Bovers Johnson Petitioner, v UNITED STATES OF AMERICA Respondent.	)))))))	 Case No.: 6:15-cv-80797-NKM-RSB Declaration of James Bovers Johnson

COMES NOW, Petitioner, James Bovers Johnson, having full knowledge of the facts, who hereby submits this Declaration in support of the Motion pursuant to 28 USC 2255(f)(4).

PETITIONER HAS NEWLY-DISCOVERED EVIDENCE THAT THE GOVERNMENT'S MAIN WITNESS, AGENT ROBERT BIGGS, TESTIFIED FALSELY DURING TRIAL, WHICH IS A VIOLATION OF DUE PROCESS AND CONSTITUTIONAL ERROR THAT MERITS RELIEF UNDER 28 USC 2255(f)(4).

1. By written notification to the Social Security Administration, in 2000, Petitioner revoked and rescinded his signature and intent to the federal social insurance program, and sent confirmation of the same to the Secretary of the Treasury as a rebuttal of the government's presumption and prima facie evidence that Petitioner was a taxpayer liable for the federal income tax.

2. In 2004, Department of Internal Revenue Agent Robert Biggs began a civil investigation into Petitioner's lack of federal tax return filings.

3. Petitioner appointed John B. Kotmair as his Power of Attorney (POA).

4. John Kotmair sent an 8/24/04 letter to Biggs and stated that he was qualified to represent Petitioner under Representative Number 2605-4781R, in accord with 26 CFR 301.6103(c)-1, 26 CFR 601.502(a), 26 CFR 601.502(b)(5)(ii) and Treasury Circular 230 at 10.7(c)(1)(iv). (Exhibit A)

5. Biggs replied directly to Petitioner on 8/30/04 that Kotmair was not qualified as POA under Circular 230, 10.7(c)(1)(iv). (Exhibit A)

6. Kotmair responded to Biggs' letter by stating that he was qualified. (Exhibit A)

7. Biggs never replied to any of the questions or concerns expressed in Kotmair's first, second or third (10/1/04) letters. (Exhibit A)

8. Yet, because of the content in Kotmair's letters, Biggs sent Petitioner the IRS "Frivolous Arguments" pamphlet.

9. During the criminal trial, Biggs testified that had Kotmair been qualified as POA, Biggs would have been required to communicate with Kotmair, not Petitioner.

10. Biggs further testified that his manager and counsel advised him that Kotmair was not qualified to serve as POA. (Exhibit B)

11. Biggs testified that his manager and counsel advised him to send Petitioner the "Frivolous Arguments" pamphlet as the IRS official response to Kotmair. (Exhibit B)

12. When Biggs was asked on direct if Petitioner had a filing requirement, he said that the evidence he had seen "was a bit of a mixture." (Exhibit B)

13. Petitioner, after submission of his 2255 Motion, Motion to Amend and Reply to the government's response, decided to use his extra time to conduct and initial search to determine when Kotmair's Representative Number was revoked. He learned that the court issued an injunction against Kotmair in 2007. (234 Fed. Appx 65, 4th Cir. 2007)

14. In August 2015, Petitioner sent a FOIA request to the IRS for any documents that showed the date that the agency revoked Kotmair's number. (Exhibit C)

15. The IRS responded on 10/6/15 that the agency was not able to locate any documents that confirmed the revocation of Kotmair's number. (Exhibit C)

16. Petitioner searched again and read the court's decision of 11/29/2006, from the Fourth Circuit (U.S. Dist. LEXIS 96885), in particular, footnote 6. Petitioner learned that the IRS notified Kotmair as early 1993 that his number was revoked and that the court also acknowledged that Kotmair contested the revocation for "due process" reasons.

17. Petitioner found an even earlier case, 962 F. Supp 695, Save-A-Patriot-Fellowship v United States, (4th Cir. 1996), which indicated no revocation at all.

In accord with 28 USC 1746, I declare under penalty of perjury that under the laws of the United States of America that the foregoing is true and correct.

James B. Johnson

APPENDIX T – CARGILL LETTER, KOTMAIR NEW EVIDENCE

James Johnson
112 West Pall Mall Street
Winchester, VA 22601

April 19, 2016

Randy Cargill
210 First Street, SW Suite 400
Roanoke, VA 24011

Dear Mr. Cargill:

Enclosed is a brief I submitted to the Court of Appeals. I am respectfully asking that you carefully read this document.

I specifically recall that there was a pre-trial hearing with Judge Moon in which you and the court discussed the meaning of "United States citizen." I do not have the transcripts, but as you can see, definitions and status are central to the application of the "Code." Please consider that any party who fails or neglects to reconcile such a fundamental issue is either willingly advancing what is untrue into court or so ignorant as to the law that what is untrue is granted access and acceptance.

Mr. Cargill, I have not relented in my belief that I am innocent and was and am outside the jurisdiction of the IRS, as established by their own codes and regulations. Consequently, the court never had jurisdiction. At a minimum, my good faith belief, based upon the CODES and REGULATIONS, was a grounded and reasonable belief that should have been argued.

Please consider making an appeal to the district court or the court of appeals that had you understood my belief, a belief that was not unreasonable, you would have argued an alternative strategy. I implore you to favorably consider this request.

Sincerely,

APPENDIX U – DECLARATORY JUDGMENT REQUEST

UNITED STATES DISTRICT COURT
WESTERN DISTRICT OF VIRGINIA

James Bowers Johnson Petitioner, v United States of America Respondent.	)))))))	Case No.: 6:15-cv-80797-NKM-RSB ISSUANCE OF DECLARATORY JUDGMENT

COMES NOW, Petitioner, James Bowers Johnson, who repectfully requests that this court issue a Declaratory Judgment pursuant to Fed. R. Civ. P. 57 and 26 USC 2201.

The grounds for this request/action are: the government made specific reference to Internal Revenue Ruling 2005-17, 2005-1 C.B. 823 (Doc 194, p 8) as the agency's determination that Petitioner's revocation of the federal benefit was a "frivolous" (Id) argument.

In order for this court to render a decision concerning Petitioner's 2255 Motion (Doc 186), this Declaratory Judgment is warranted. A Declaratory Judgment will resolve a controversy that exists within the record.

MEMORANDUM IN SUPPORT

FACTS:

Government's Assertion

The government states in its Response (Doc 194) to Petitioner's 2255 Motion

> Johnson contends that his argument was grounded in law and fact... [and] revoked and rescinded his signature and intent to the federal social security insurance scheme by written notification.[1]

Notably, the government placed a footnote, to wit:

> [1]The IRS has directly stated that this argument is frivolous. See Rev. Rul. 2005-17, 2005-1 C.B. 823

The government admits that after filing his 1999 income tax return (Id), Petitioner, by written notification to the Social Security Administration and the Secretary of Treasury, revoked the federal benefit of social security. Yet, it was not until 2015 that the government argued into the record a refutation

1

of Petitioner's actions and beliefs with the 2005 Internal Revenue Ruling. Previously, the IRS and the government simply labeled Petitioner's belief as frivolous without substantiation.

The controversy is transparent:

1) In 2000, Petitioner ceased his participation in the federal social security insurance program - a non frivolous belief at the time.
2) The IRS initiated a civil and criminal investigation in 2004 and, shortly thereafter, declared Petitioner's/Kotmair's written queries as frivolous and with no justification.
3) In 2004, because of Petitioner's questions, Agent Biggs sent Petitioner a "Frivolous Arguments" pamphlet, which did not and could not contain the government's frivolous argument cited in its 2005 Revenue Ruling.
4) From 2000 into 2005, the IRS never responded to Petitioner's concerns or belief with a substantial response or rebuttal.
5) Now, in 2015, the government wields its 2005 Revenue Ruling as grounds to ensure the finality of a conviction, when authorities, heretofore, never referred to this ruling.

Why didn't the IRS or government raise this counterargument to Petitioner's belief previously? A controversy centers upon 1) whether or not the Revenue Ruling has a retroactive effect, 2) if retroactivity was allowed , whether or not the enforcement was harsh and 3) if the Revenue Ruling escapes the scrutiny that a "Chevron-style deference" warrants. Dominion infra

LAW AND ARGUMENT

Court Discretion

This court has the discretion to grant a Declaratory Judgment, Van Buskirk v United States, 2011 U.S. Dist. LEXIS 89259 (4th Cir) which "is an additional remedy for use..." when "federal courts already have jurisdiction." Davis v Bantz, 2015 U.S. Dist. LEXIS 56535 (4th Cir.) According to United States v Belt, 2011 U.S. Dist. LEXIS 81548 (4th Cir.) this court may issue a Declaratory Judgment since 1) "the complaint alleges an 'actual controversy' between the parties of 'sufficient immediacy and reality to warrant issuance of a Declaratory Judgment,'" 2) this court "possesses an independent basis for jurisdiction over the parties" and 3) this is "not an abuse of its discretion in its exercise of juris-

2

diction." quoting Volvo Const. Equip. N. Am. v CLM Equip. Co. 386 F 3d 581, 592 (4th Cir. 2004) Significantly, "a district court will not abuse its discretion in issuing a Declaratory Judgment if doing so 'will serve as a useful purpose in clarifying and settling the legal relations in issue' and 'will terminate and afford relief from the uncertainty, insecurity and controversy giving rise to the proceeding.'" quoting Aetna Cas. & Sur. Co. v Quarles, 92 F 2d 321, 325 (4th Cir. 1937)

Revenue Rulings

The courts have stated that Revenue Rulings are:

1) "not binding upon the courts" Pender v Bank Am. Corp., 756 F Supp 2d 674 (4th Cir. 2010)
2) "do not have force of law" 2004 U.S. Dist. LEXIS 6894, Talton v I.H. Caffey Distrib. Co. (4th Cir.)
3) "are nothing more than the position of a party and they are afforded little or no weight as authority." Tiddy v United States, 762 F Supp 122 (4th Cir. 1991)
4) are "entitled to considerably less deference than an agency's properly promulgated regulations." Black & Decker Corp. v United States, 436 F 3d 431, 440 (4th Cir. 2005)
5) as the court stated in Dominion Resources Inc. v United States, 219 F 3d 359, 366 (2000) "agency opinion letters are entitled to 'respect' but 'do not warrant Chevron-style deference.'" (See Christensen v Harris County 529 US 576 (2000))

Retroactivity

In Norfolk Southern Corp. v Commissioner, 140 F 3d 240, 247 (4th Cir. 1997), the court recognized that "review of the Commissioner's decision to apply revenue rulings on a retroactive basis is for abuse of discretion." (See Baker v United States, 748 F 2d 1465, 1467 (11th Cir. 1984) (holding that "although courts presume prospective application, they review retroactive application for abuse of discretion.") The court then questioned "whether under all the circumstances, retroactive application is warranted." Id. Appropriately, in Baker supra, the court concluded that although "retroactivity is presumptively permissible, in each case the reviewing court must determine whether under all circumstances, retroactive application is warranted." [emphasis added]

3

Intended or Unintended Consequences

While the prosecutor in the instant case refers to Revenue Ruling 2005-17, he makes no reference to its retroactive effect, if any. Notably, in Farmers' & Merchants' Bank v United States, 476 F 2d 406, 409 (4th Cir. 1973) the court cites that

> The Government attempts to salve its determination by embracing the discretion of the Secretary of Treasury by U.S.C. 7805 as follows:
>
> ... (b) Retroactivity of regulations and rulings. The Secretary or his delegate may prescribe the extent, if any, to which any ruling or regulation relating to Internal Revenue laws shall be applied with retroactive effect. [emphasis added]

The courts are cautious when deferring to agency interpretation, especially considering retroactivity and its impact. In Reynolds Metals Co. v United States, 389 F Supp 2d 692 (4th Cir. 2005) "the court was especially cautious with Revenue Ruling 2004-17 because of its issuance during the pendency of Reynold's complaint." [emphasis added] Retroactivity against Petitioner is of greater import because he changed his status with respect to the federal government by a past act. Consequently, it is suspect whether the agency's ruling, issued years after Petitioner's revocation, may influence this act. Pointedly, the government never attempted to reconcile its ruling with a Citizen who lawfully and effectively terminated his obligation for receipt of a federal benefit. Moreover, had the court been aware of these circumstances, it would have been especially cautious given the criminal charges and the consequences of enforcement.

In Tiddy v United States, 1992 U.S. App LEXIS 3979 (4th Cir. 2004), the court's language is even more severe, recognizing that "retroactive application of [a]... Revenue Ruling... would be 'unduly harsh.'" The court denied the government's claim in Tiddy. In the instant case, if only because the IRS could not regard Petitioner's decisions and actions as frivolous in 2004, the application of its 2005 Revenue Ruling was not only harsh but morally depraved. Petitioner should never have been charged, much less found guilty for what was not criminal

4

or frivolous just a year earlier.

Properly Promulgated Regulations

The Court in Black & Decker supra stated that "an agency's properly promulgated regulations" are given greater emphasis than revenue rulings. Significantly, there are no promulgated regulations for 26 USC 7203 and 7212, the crimes for which Petitioner was charged and convicted. In Calif. Bankers Assoc. v Shultz, 416 US 21, 26 (1974), the court stated that an

> Act's civil and criminal penalties attach only upon violation of regulations promulgated by the Secretary; if the Secretary were to do nothing, the Act itself would impose no penalties on anyone...

The court went on to state

> The Government urges that since only those who violate these regulations may incur civil or criminal penalties, it is the actual regulation issued by the Secretary of the Treasury and not the broad authorizing language of the statute" Id, 44

that may be enforced. In the instant case, the government enforcement of its 2005 Revenue Ruling when there are no regulations for the crimes charged is problematic

Moreover, since Petitioner revoked the federal benefit of social security in 2000, he may not be presumed liable for a tax when his status is one within a class that is without congressional constitutional taxing authority. As such, Petitioner may not be one of "every person" liable in any statute or promulgated and implementing regulation for the income tax - a taxpayer. The government may not ignore the underlying constitutional challenge attendant with Petitioner's revocation, especially in light of congressional intent concerning a statute's "history and purpose," Reynolds supra as reflected in the congressional record. For, the significance of the revocation of a federal benefit is not, ultimately, about the receipt or rejection of the benefit and any resulting tax, it is about the status of a Citizen and the constraints of congressional power under the Federal Constitution.

The Precise Question at Issue

In his 2255 Motion (Doc 186) and Reply to the government's Response (Doc

194), Petitioner fully developed that the government's failure to contest his act and belief was a failure to answer "the precise question at issue" (Id pp 12-14) As stated in Dominion supra 366, Petitioner's belief warranted a "Chevron-style deference" rather than a capricious retroactive enforcement of a Revenue Ruling. By dismissing Petitioner's belief as violative of an agency's "opinion letter," the government avoided and the court did not hear an issue to the scale of a first impression or an underlying constitutional claim. The government's use of its revenue ruling was limited and orchestrated by design. The IRS and government did not want the precise question at issue addressed. So, just as in Tiddy v United States, 1992 U.S. App LEXIS 3979 (4th Cir.) "The bald assertion by the IRS" was not favorably considered because it was "insufficient," (Id) we see that the IRS avoided any and all accountability concerning Petitioner's revocation. Furthermore, as with Tiddy, in this case, the IRS did not contend "with an issue of material fact" (Id) within the meaning of the tax code and failed to dignify congressional intent and the statute's history and purpose. Ultimately, the government avoided the review of a question of statutory interpretation that challenged congressional jurisdiction over a Citizen who was without congressional constitutional taxing authority. Such scrutiny is significant considering that

> criminal statutes "are to be strictly construed and should not be interpreted to extend criminal liability beyond that which Congress has 'plainly and unmistakenly' proscribed." United States v Hylton, 701 F 3d 959, 966 (4th Cir. 2012)

The court went further and stated,

> In light of the serious consequences flowing from a criminal conviction the rule of strict construction rests on the principle that no [Citizen] shall be held criminally responsible for conduct which he could not reasonably understand to be proscribed. Id. quoting United States v Lanier, 520 US 259, 265-66 (1997) [brackets added]

Role of the Prosecutor

A prosecutor "is not an ordinary party to a controversy, but of a sovereign whose obligation... in a criminal prosecution is not that it shall win a case,

6

but that justice shall be done." Berger v United States, 295 US 78, 88 (1935) Moreover, "It is as much his duty to refrain from a wrongful conviction as it is to use every legitimate means to bring about a just one." (Id.) Given the merits of Petitioner's request, since the government must concede that the 2005 Revenue Ruling did NOT exist at the time the IRS began its civil and criminal investigations, the prosecutor's support of a Declaratory Judgment under the circumstances would be a matter of course.

Any attempt to now superimpose a 2005 Revenue Ruling upon one who decided and acted in good faith that his belief was legal and lawful for the previous five years is inconsistent with the ends of justice. This is particularly true since Hogeboom knew that the civil and criminal investigations began before the issuance of the Revenue Ruling. He had to, therefore, know that Petitioner did not act and could not have acted with willful intent to commit a crime. It can hardly be considered fair for the IRS, during a criminal investigation, to deem a Citizen's good faith belief as "frivolous" at a period of time when the agency itself had not deemed Petitioner's belief to be frivolous. That the IRS rejected Petitioner's belief as frivolous in 2004, without responding to Petitioner's questions for the agency's own understanding and clarification, and without establishing its own ruling, confirms that the agency never considered the MERITS of Petitioner's questions, concerns and belief in the first instance. To the contrary, the agency simply issued a proforma non-response to a legitimate challenge and sent an unresponsive "frivolous arguments" pamphlet to summarily dismiss the matter.

However, assuming, arguendo, that the 2005 Revenue Ruling had any retroactive application, or the agency presumptively applied the ruling to an already active criminal investigation, this court must now consider that such action was and is still "unduly harsh." Tiddy supra. In the instant case, the IRS exerted criminal enforcement authority against a lawful good faith belief before it issued

7

a Revenue Ruling that determined that very belief to be "frivolous." Now the prosecution wants to assert in its current argument that the 2005 Revenue Ruling justifies sustaining the current conviction.

No Resolution

The tragedy in this case is that the IRS never addressed the merits of Petitioner's good faith belief and actions before the issuance of its ruling. Moreover, the government never answered or contended with his belief during the trial. Instead, Petitioner's belief was resoundingly determined to be frivolous, which precluded any adversarial testing of IRS decisions or the government's argument.

Avoidance of a Constitutional Claim

If an agency can refuse to answer questions or overcome a rebuttal of its presumption that one has a tax liability, simply because it may now rely upon a ruling issued after the fact, and a prosecutor may avoid a contest of a constitutional belief based upon that investigating ageny's unresponsiveness, undoubtedly, that belief, that constitutional claim, will never be tested in a court of law and justice will be denied. With such a dynamic in the instant case, Petitioner never received and will not receive substantive answers to equally substantive queries based upon his lawful and grounded belief, regardless of the date of any Internal Revenue Ruling.

Controversy

A controversy exists. The government suggests that Petitioner's belief was frivolous in 2000 when the IRS did not rule that such a belief was frivolous until 2005.

Independent Basis

This court, with jurisdiction over the pending Motion to Amend and the existing 2255 Motion, has an independent basis over the parties and action.

8

Proper Use of Discretion

The issuance of a Declaratory Judgment concerning this controversy is not an abuse of discretion. To the contrary, it would be proper and would serve the ends of justice for this court to do so.

A Pro Se Litigant's Earnest Plea

Behind the guise of discretion, the government does not have to nor does it respond to Citizen actions, questions or beliefs. While the courts often sanction this exercise of discretion, the toll of unwarranted unresponsiveness is difficult to reconcile. Consequently, although Petitioner may have adequately argued that a Declaratory Judgment is warranted, perhaps, if only because he is without the benefit of experienced and competent legal counsel, who would shape and conclude this action more effectively, Petitioner will expend his efforts to further plead this matter in the interest of justice.

A Closed Loop

Enforcement of the Internal Revenue Code today may be described as a closed loop, from which one may not leave. The harsh reality is that the IRS presumes one is a "taxpayer" and liable for the federal income tax. This presumption is based upon one's 1) acceptance of the federal benefit of social security, 2) entering "the relation of employment" (See Doc. 186 p 7) and 3) filing the first 1040 form (See Doc. 186 p 7) Based upon the government's representation, prior to the 2005 Internal Revenue Ruling, the revocation of the federal benefit of social security was not "frivolous." Ostensibly, one could cease participation in social security and volitionally change one's status from a "taxpayer" to one who is NOT a taxpayer. The decision to revoke the benefit of social security is no different than choosing not to participate in any other activity subject to excise or rejecting any other federal benefit. For example, the federal government may not compel one to either accept social security or manufacture tires,

9

both of which are excisable. The government may not direct one to accept or reject food stamps if he qualifies. Such a position would be extra-constitutional or ultra vires. If such a power were presumed to be consistent with fundamental law, the presumption would be subject to challenge as a constitutional claim. Petitioner asserts a constituional challenge that warrants Chevron-style scrutiny in the instant case.

Since Petitioner revoked the federal benefit of social security in 2000, the very activity/privilege that made him liable for the income tax, (See Doc 186 p 7 - re: Charles C Steward Machine v Davis, 302 US 548 (1937) and Helvering v Davis, 301 US 619 (1937)) he alone severed the nexus that made him liable to file a tax return. He alone changed his status by written notification to the Secretary of the Treasury. Petitioner was no longer bound within THE CLOSED LOOP.

By foreclosing one's option to revoke or otherwise reject a federal benefit, in this case, social security, (refer to Internal Revenue Ruling 2005-17, 2005-1 C.B. 823) the government effectively traps one within the "system," with the permanent designation or status of "taxpayer." Even more significantly, the government limits one to "adequate remedies" (See Lloyd v Agents for Internal Revenue Service, 1999 U.S. Dist. Dist. LEXIS 12814) that are applicable for taxpayers only, namely, 26 USC 6212, 6213, 7422 and, by default, filing suit in court. These adequate remedies take years and cost potentially thousands and tens of thousands of dollars for competent counsel, with little to no likelihood of satisfaction.

In Lloyd, the defendant sought a "determination letter" from the IRS for her verified status for tax purposes. The court ruled that the IRS was under no obligation to issue such a letter. Left with "adequate remedies," (Id) according to the court, Lloyd had no recourse to exit the closed loop - if that was her intent. The IRS, with its provisions in place, and exercise of discretion, effectively assured that she would remain a "taxpayer."

Aside from the request for a determination letter and the remedies available within the tax code, is there a practical way to change one's status from a "taxpayer" to one who is not a taxpayer? The simple answer is "No." Conclusively, then, this rather austere dynamic poses significant legal and constitutional concerns that are not likely to be addressed, especially when the IRS and the Department of Justice exercise discretion to avoid a credible response.

Let's suppose for a moment that Petitioner did not revoke the federal benefit of social security until 2006. With its 2005 Revenue Ruling, the agency would have easily cited its determination that such an act was "frivolous." However, this does not preclude a constitutional challenge in the spirit of Chevron. Yet, in all probability, Petitioner would have been forced to use the same remedies cited in Lloyd or faced criminal action, with no effective provision for ending his acceptance of the social security benefit and becoming one who is not a taxpayer.

Now, if we consider Petitioner's current circumstances, he clearly revoked the federal benefit in 2000, notified the Secretary of the Treasury of his rebuttal of the government's presumption and prima facie evidence and change in status. As a result, Petitioner impliedly demonstrated his good faith that he did not act willfully, had no mens rea and could not be perceived as committing an actus reus, for he was not a taxpayer liable for the income tax.

Sadly, the government not only seeks to maintain the finality of a criminal conviction, it seeks to bring Petitioner back into the closed loop that must be WITHOUT effective constitutional constraints.

Petitioner's belief is NOT predicated upon his right and ability to revoke the federal benefit of social security, or any federal benefit for that matter, it is predicated upon the underlying constitutional premise/claim that the IRS

11

and government, the "United States," may not exercise an authority that Congress does not possess, because it is not an authority that is not afforded under fundamental law. Congress may no sooner tax a Citizen without a class subject to a specific excise than compel one to remain within a class subject to excise. Not only did Petitioner revoke the federal benefit of social security prior to Revenue Ruling 2005-17, which defeats any willfulness or criminal intent, Petitioner asserts that the government escapes all accountability to his Chevron-styled claim, a claim that trumps the belated CRIMINAL enforcement for a crime that was never committed.

Resolution

Given the IRS' and prosecution's extensive reliance upon Agent Biggs' perjured testimony (See Motion to Amend dated 11/5/15) that 1) Petitioner avoided communicating with the IRS and 2) the "Frivolous Arguments" pamphlet, which could not have included the 2005-17 Revenue Ruling, Petitioner's request for a Declaratory Judgment takes on greater importance. Consequently, Petitioner's constitutional claim, which was avoided by the Biggs, the IRS and, therefore, the prosecution, is equally heightened. For, the government contends that Petitioner's belief and exercise of a right to end his participation in the federal social security program in 2000 was "frivolous," while the IRS did not determine that such an act was "frivolous" until 2005.

Conclusion

Since courts look to the prospective application of Revenue Rulings, while, in "each case" Baker supra, "under all the circumstances" Norfolk supra, review retroactivity for undue harshness (See Tiddy supra), based upon the facts, law and argument, Petitioner asks this court to issue a Declaratory Judgment, whereby the court declares that the year the civil and criminal investigations began, Petitioner's belief was not deemed "frivolous" by the IRS.

Respectfully,

James B. Johnson

12

Appendix V – Motion To Reconsider, Federal Question

UNITED STATES DISTRICT COURT
WESTERN DISTRICT OF VIRGINIA

James Bowers Johnson Petitioner,	)	
v	)	Case No: 7:15-cv-00067 and 7:15-cv-00076 Motion to Reconsider
UNITED STATES OF AMERICA Respondent.	)	

COMES NOW, petitioner, James Bowers Johnson, in accord with Rule 59 of the F.R. Civ. P. with this Motion to Reconsider and the attached supporting affidavit. Petitioner offers no new material and offers clarification and support for the specific intent of said Motion.

On May 8, 2015, this Court rightly entered a MEMORANDUM OPINION that petitioner failed to establish standing. Secondly, the Court indicated that it may not issue advisory opinions.

Beginning with the latter, petitioner did not and does not seek an advisory opinion. Rather, he requests that the court compel the Department of Justice (DOJ) to answer the instant federal questions and adjudicate any dispute.

In furtherance of this request, petitioner hereby establishes standing.

Memorandum in Support

> The district courts shall have original jurisdiction of all civil actions under the Constitution, laws, or treaties of the United States. 28 USC 1331

However, the Supreme Court requires that a litigant have standing. (See Warth v Seldin 422 US 490 (1975)) In Valley Forge Christian College v Americans United for Separation of Church and State, Inc. 454 US 464, 472 (1982), the Supreme Court declared that in order to challenge conduct that violates federal law, the party must suffer "actual or threatened injury" traceable to the "challenged action," with redress upon a "favorable decision." Moreover, the party's standing must be affected by "statute or constitutional guarantee."

Association of Data Processing Service Organizations, Inc. v Camp 397 US 150, 153 (1978)

As determined in Schlesinger v Reservists Committee to Stop the War 418 US 208 (1974), the potential injury-in-fact is the salient component which underscores the merits that the challenged action is unlawful and requires judicial oversight. (See Simon v Eastern Kentucky Welfare Rights Organization 426 US 26 (1976), Gollust v Mendell 501 US 115 (1991), Metropolitan Washington Airports Authority v Citizens for Abatement of Aircraft Noise Inc. 501 US 252 (1991), Northeastern Fla Chapter of Associated Gen. Contractors v Jacksonville 508 US 656 (1993), Raines v Byrd 521 US 811 (1997), Int'l Primate Protection League v Administrators of Tulane Educational Fund 500 US 72 (1991)

As stated in Lujan v Defenders of Wildlife 504 US 555, 559-560 (1992), the "Constitution's central mechanism of separation of powers" is to ensure that the executive appropriately apply legislative intent for which the Court may resolve disputes and, thereby, obviate any threatened injury-in-fact.

Since the Departments of Justice and Treasury means of enforcement may precipitate claims of "injunctive relief and power to review decisions and actions of federal agencies," Parkview Corp. v Dept of Army Corps of Engineers 490 F Supp 1278 (1980 ED Wis) nonstatutory review of agency action under 28 USC § 1331, if equitable, obviates sovereign immunity, (See Jaffee v United States (1979) CA3 NJ 592 F 2d 712) especially since action taken by an agent/agency in a sovereign's name is claimed to be unconstitutional. (See Johnson v Hoffman (1977 ED Mo) 424 F Supp 490) Such disputes (federal questions) are "appropriately resolved through the judicial process" Whitmore v Arkansas 495 US 149, 155 (1990) and establish standing with and through a threatened injury.

Petitioner contends that he cannot be a "taxpayer" subject to the federal income (excise) tax, for, he is not within the class that is within congressional authority for the federal privilege/benefit of social security. Consequently, executive enforcement of tax statutes and regulations that is unconstitutional and, therefore, ultra vires, presents a credible threat of injury. Rightfully, then, petitioner has standing under 28 USC § 1331 and the court has jurisdiction; as these federal questions challenge the interpretation of a federal act and action. (See Calderon v Ashmus 523 US 740, 744 (1998) Critically, petitioner's "course of action" is predicated upon a "right or immunity created by the Constitution or laws of the United States" Gully v First Nat'l Bank 299 US 109, 112 (1936) and "that it will be supported if the Constitution or laws of the United States are given one construction or effect, and defeated if they receive another." Id. Conclusively, these federal questions involve a dispute or controversy respecting the validity, construction or effect of such a law, upon the determination of which the result depends." Id 114

Petitioner seeks relief on grounds that the interpretation and application of tax statutes and regulations and the subsequent controversy of jurisdiction of agency enforcement of what is in fact not a crime - failure of a private citizen who does not enjoy the federal benefit of social security to pay the corresponding "excise" tax. Therefore, petitioner asserts that the implementation of tax statutes and regulations by the Departments of Justice and Treasury may be pre-empted with proper interpretation of those very statutes and regulations.

As such, petitioner's federal questions, submitted with standing, with the knowledge that petitioner cannot be liable for a specific excise tax, asserts that, aside from this course of action, he is without a remedy. (See Shalala v Illinois Council on Long Term Care 529 US 1 (2000) Absent a response from the Attorney General, petitioner is faced with an "exceptional situation" that is capable of repetition, yet evading review, whereby he will be subjected to errant agency authority that is inconsistent with congressional intent and constitutional constraints. (See Los Angeles v Lyons 461 US 95, 109 (1983))

The consequences of inappropriate agency actions will result in potential criminal investigation, prosecution, imprisonment, fines and penalties. Indisputably, petitioner would benefit from the Court's facilitation in a tangible manner that would halt "the continuing and intolerant burden... on his conscience, and his constitutional rights." Valley Forge supra 510

For the reasons set forth, petitioner has established standing to pursue the federal questions. Petitioner respectfully requests the Court to dignify this standing by asking the Department of Justice to respond accordingly.

Respectfully,

James B. Johnson
Petitioner

original signed 5/21/15 mailed 5/21/15

4

UNITED STATES DISTRICT COURT
WESTERN DISTRICT OF VIRGINIA

James Bowers Johnson Petitioner, v UNITED STATES OF AMERICA Respondent.	)))))))	7:15-cv-00067 and 7:15-cv-00076 Affidavit of James Bowers Johnson

COMES NOW, Affiant, James Bowers Johnson, of the age of majority and sound mind, with firsthand knowledge of the facts, who truthfully attests, to wit:

1) In 2000, by written notification to the Social Security Administration and the Secretary of the Treasury, affiant revoked and rescinded his signature and participation, nunc pro tunc, in the federally excisable privilege of social security.

2) In 2009, affiant asked the Department of Justice (DOJ) for the law that required the filing of a federal income tax return for the payment of an "excise" on his earnings, if he no longer engaged in the federal social security insurance scheme. The DOJ never responded.

3) Affiant believes that adverse action, be it an investigation or prosecution, by the Federal Government for failure to file a tax return and pay an "excise" from his labor/earnings is inevitable, even though he no longer enjoys the federal benefit of social security. Whatever action taken will result in a loss to affiant, whether economic or not.

4) Affiant believes that his only recourse is to pose the federal questions under 28 USC § 1331 and ask the district court to request responses from the United States Attorney General.

5) Affiant believes that failure of the DOJ to respond will permit unconstitutional agency action under the federal statutes, adversely affecting rights and

constitutional guarantees, which threatens affiant with injury-in-fact.

Further affiant sayeth naught.

In accord with 28 USC 1746, I declare under penalty of perjury under the laws of the United States of America that the foregoing is true and correct.

Executed this ____ day of May, 2015

Signed 5/20/15 mailed 5/21/15

James B. Johnson, Affiant

APPENDIX W – JUDGE MOON'S DENIAL OF 2255 MOTION

IN THE UNITED STATES DISTRICT COURT
FOR THE WESTERN DISTRICT OF VIRGINIA
LYNCHBURG DIVISION

UNITED STATES OF AMERICA	)	**Criminal Case No. 6:12cr00015**
	)	
v.	)	**2255 MEMORANDUM OPINION**
	)	
JAMES BOWERS JOHNSON,	)	**By: Norman K. Moon**
Petitioner.	)	**United States District Judge**

Petitioner James Bowers Johnson, a federal inmate proceeding *pro se*, filed this motion to vacate, set aside, or correct sentence, pursuant to 28 U.S.C. § 2255, challenging his 48-month sentence following his conviction on four counts of violating the Internal Revenue Code. Johnson claims that trial and appellate counsel provided ineffective assistance by refusing to dispute the court's jurisdiction over him, failing to argue that he did not act willfully when he failed to file tax returns, failing to challenge the grand and petite jury procedures and refusing to make a motion for a new trial. He filed a motion to amend seeking to provide additional evidence that counsel provided ineffective assistance of counsel, which was granted. The government filed a motion to dismiss and Johnson responded. He then filed an additional motion to amend arguing that newly discovered evidence establishes that the government presented perjured testimony at trial. Accordingly, this matter is ripe for consideration. I conclude that Johnson's ineffective assistance of counsel claims fail to meet the exacting standard set forth in *Strickland v. Washington*, 466 U.S. 668, 669 (1984). I also conclude that his claimed due process violation based on the presentation of perjured testimony is futile. *United States v. Pittman*, 209 F.3d 314, 317 (4th Cir. 2000). Therefore, I will grant the government's motion to dismiss.

I.

On April 5, 2012, a grand jury returned a four Count indictment against Johnson. Count One alleged that Johnson obstructed, impeded or impaired the due administration of the Internal Revenue Code, in violation of 26 U.S.C. § 7212(a). Counts Two, Three and Four alleged that Johnson willfully failed to file his personal income tax returns in 2006, 2007 and 2008, respectively, in violation of 26 U.S.C. § 7203.

On April 26, 2012, Johnson appeared before United States Magistrate Judge James G. Welsh for an initial appearance. At the hearing, Johnson insisted that he was "not the defendant" and that the court did not have jurisdiction over him. (Initial Appearance Trans. at 3, 10, ECF No. 14). Magistrate Judge Welsh appointed counsel to represent Johnson because he never clearly answered whether he wanted to represent himself and thus did not unequivocally waive his right to counsel. (*Id.* at 10-11). Magistrate Judge Welsh concluded that Johnson was not prepared to be arraigned because he stated he did not understand either the charges against him or his rights. (*Id.* at 14-15). Johnson then filed a *pro se* "Habeas Corpus Motion to Dismiss with Prejudice." (Habeas Motion, ECF No. 25). I dismissed this motion, concluding that it was not the appropriate means by which to raise defenses to the charges against him and more fundamentally, that because he was represented he could not successfully file *pro se* motions. (Order at 1-2, ECF No. 27).

On June 13, 2012, I held a competency hearing and determined that Johnson was able to understand the proceedings against him and assist properly in his defense. (ECF 35). Johnson stated that he was willing to accept representation from appointed counsel. (ECF 35). However, Johnson later changed his mind about accepting representation. At a November 20, 2012 status

2

hearing, following careful questioning, I concluded that Johnson willingly waived his right to counsel. (ECF 53). I directed appointed counsel to remain as standby counsel. (*Id.*).

On January 15, 2013, a jury trial began with Johnson representing himself. After the government's first witness testified, Johnson requested representation. (Trial Trans. at 4320, ECF No. 168). I granted his request and appointed counsel assumed Johnson's representation. (*Id.*). At the conclusion of a four-day trial, the jury found Johnson guilty on all four charges. (ECF 120).

After the trial, Johnson made some attempts to retain counsel. (Mot. To Amend at 3, ECF 189-2). He also requested that his appointed counsel file a motion for a new trial. (New Trial Motion at 6, ECF 145). Appointed counsel did not file the motion. (*Id.*). Before sentencing, Johnson again requested to represent himself as he was unsatisfied with his representation. (ECF 137). On March 28, 2013, I held a hearing and granted Johnson's request but asked appointed counsel to remain as standby counsel. (ECF 139, 141). I also allowed Johnson to file a new trial motion, even though the deadline to do so had passed. (ECF 141). Fed. R. Crim. P. 33 (requiring that a motion for a new trial be filed within 14 days after the verdict). Johnson then filed a motion for a new trial. (ECF 145). He also filed a motion to set aside the verdict and dismiss the case with prejudice claiming that he is not a United States citizen and does not fall within the jurisdiction of the Internal Revenue Service (IRS). (Motion at 3, ECF 147).

On April 11, 2013, I held a sentencing hearing and orally denied Johnson's motions for a new trial and to set aside the verdict. (Sent. Trans. at 3-7, ECF 172). Johnson then challenged the court's jurisdiction over him. (*Id.* at 7.). He refused to follow court procedure, continually interrupted me, and refused to discuss anything other than his jurisdictional argument. (*Id.* at 8-

3

10). I warned Johnson that I would reappoint standby counsel if he was unable to follow court procedure. (*Id.* at 8-9.). When Johnson did not heed the warning, I revoked his *pro se* status and ordered standby counsel to represent him for sentencing.

I sentenced Johnson to a term of 48-months' imprisonment: 36 months on Count One and 12 months on each of Counts Two, Three, and Four, to be served concurrently, but consecutive to the term imposed in Count One. (Judgment at 3, ECF 151).

On April 15, 2013, Johnson filed a Notice of Appeal to the United States Court of Appeals for the Fourth Circuit. (ECF 153). On April 18, 2013, the Fourth Circuit granted a motion by appointed counsel to withdraw as counsel on appeal and appointed a different attorney to represent Johnson. (ECF 158). The Fourth Circuit affirmed Johnson's conviction. *United States v. Johnson*, 571 F. App'x 205 (4th Cir. 2014). He did not file a petition for a writ of certiorari.

On January 23, 2015, Johnson filed the instant § 2255 motion. (ECF 186). He filed a motion to amend on February 18, 2015, seeking to supplement his ineffective assistance of counsel claims, which was granted. (ECF 189, 193). The government filed a motion to dismiss and Johnson responded. (ECF 194, 198). On November 9, 2015, Johnson filed another motion to amend, asserting a claim that the government presented perjured testimony at trial. (ECF 205).

II.

To state a viable claim for relief under § 2255, a petitioner must prove: (1) that his sentence was "imposed in violation of the Constitution or laws of the United States;" (2) that "the court was without jurisdiction to impose such a sentence;" or (3) that "the sentence was in excess of the maximum authorized by law, or is otherwise subject to collateral attack." 28

4

U.S.C. § 2255. Johnson bears the burden of proving grounds for a collateral attack by a preponderance of the evidence. *Jacobs v. United States*, 350 F.2d 571, 574 (4th Cir. 1965).

III.

Johnson claims that counsel provided ineffective assistance by: (1) refusing to investigate and develop the argument that he was not within the jurisdiction of the United States for income tax purposes because he did not "voluntarily" agree to be taxed (Mem. at 4883, ECF 186); (2) refusing to argue that he did not act willfully in violating the Internal Revenue Code because he honestly believed that he was exempt (Mem. at 4891, ECF 186); (3) failing to challenge the empanelling of the grand and petit juries (Mem. at 4899, ECF 186); and (4) failing to move for a new trial (Mem. at 4900, ECF 186). He also argues in his second motion to amend that the government offered perjured testimony from Internal Revenue Agent Robert Biggs who testified at trial that Johnson's mentor, John Kotmair, was not qualified to act as a power of attorney for Johnson. (Amend. Mem. at 5248, ECF 205). Johnson's ineffective assistance of counsel claims are meritless and must be dismissed and his request to file a second motion to amend denied.

A. Ineffective Assistance of Counsel

In order to establish a viable claim of ineffective assistance of counsel, a defendant must satisfy a two-prong analysis: he must show both that counsel's performance fell below an objective standard of reasonableness and that he was prejudiced by counsel's alleged deficient performance. *Strickland*, 466 U.S. at 669. When considering the reasonableness prong of *Strickland*, courts apply a "strong presumption that counsel's conduct falls within the wide range of reasonable professional assistance." *Id.* at 689; *see also Gray v. Branker*, 529 F.3d 220, 228-29 (4th Cir. 2008). Counsel's performance is judged "on the facts of the particular case," and assessed "from counsel's perspective at the time." *Id.*

5

To satisfy the prejudice prong of *Stickland*, a defendant must show that there is a reasonable probability that, but for counsel's unprofessional error, the outcome of the proceeding would have been different. *Id.* at 694. "A reasonable probability is a probability sufficient to undermine confidence in the outcome." *Id.*

Johnson's claims of ineffective assistance of counsel do not satisfy *Strickland's* stringent requirements. Johnson first claims that both his trial and appellate counsel provided deficient representation because they refused to develop Johnson's theory that he did not fall within the jurisdiction of the United States for income tax purposes. (Mem. at 4879, ECF 186). The crux of Johnson's argument appears to be that he is not a "taxpayer" because federal income taxes are excise taxes, and therefore "voluntary." (Mem. at 4879, ECF 186). He argues that he opted out of this responsibility by sending letters to the Social Security Administration and the Treasury stating that he would not be "accept[ing] federal social security and employment benefits." (*Id.*).

It is well settled that all workers earning income in this country are subject to federal income taxation. *See, e.g., Lovell v. United States*, 755 F.2d 517, 519 (7th Cir. 1984) ("All individuals, natural or unnatural, must pay federal income tax on their wages. . . ."). Moreover, "the debate over whether the income tax is an excise tax or a direct tax is irrelevant to the obligation of citizens to pay taxes and file returns." *United States v. Melton*, 86 F.3d 1153, 1996 WL 271468, at *2, 1996 U.S. App. LEXIS 11683, at * 8 (4th Cir. May 22, 1996) (unpublished). Accordingly, this argument is frivolous and Johnson's lawyers could not ethically raise it. *See, e.g., Jones v. Barnes*, 463 U.S. 745, (1983) (noting that counsel must exercise their professional judgment in determining which issues to raise before the court); *Evans v. Thompson*, 881 F.2d 117, 124 (4th Cir. 1989).

6

Johnson conceded at trial that he lived and worked in Virginia and made enough income to trigger income tax responsibilities. (Trial Trans. at 24; ECF 171). As Johnson's lawyers explained to him, the Model Rules of Professional Conduct do not allow a lawyer to raise a frivolous argument before the court. (Mot.Exh., ECF 186-5 at 5028; 186-6 at 5044, 5046.); Model Rules of Prof'l Conduct r. 3.3 (Am. Bar Ass'n 2013). Because they were constrained by the professional cannon of ethics to raise only non-frivolous arguments, counsels' conduct was not deficient.[1] *See generally Wheat v. United States*, 486 U.S. 153, 160 (1988) (noting that the American Bar Association's Model Code of Professional Responsibility and its Model Rules of Professional Conduct impose limitations on the conduct of lawyers to ensure that "criminal trials are conducted within the ethical standards of the profession. . . .").

Johnson's second claim of ineffective assistance of counsel is that his trial counsel failed to argue "the element of willfulness" for Counts Two, Three and Four, charging him with failing to file income tax returns. (Mem. at 4891, ECF 186). Section 7203, which criminalizes tax return violations, requires that a defendant "willfully fail[]" to pay taxes in order to be found guilty. 26 U.S.C. § 7203.

Johnson's argument, however, is belied by the record. Defense counsel, in his opening statement, noted that if a taxpayer "believes in good faith that he or she is not obligated to file taxes, then—if you reach that conclusion, that undercuts the notion that that person has willfully failed to file" income tax returns. (Trial Trans. at 15, ECF 178). Johnson's lawyer went on to distill the entire trial for those charges down to a question of whether Johnson acted willfully: "And so that's what it comes down to: good faith. Did he act in good faith? Did he act

[1] Moreover, Johnson raised this jurisdictional issue before the court. While Johnson was representing himself during his trial, he questioned the court's subject matter jurisdiction. (Trial Trans. at 7, ECF 168). I reminded Johnson that courts have been hearing these types of cases for hundreds of years and that jurisdiction was well established. *Id.* Johnson also testified during his case-in-chief. He explained that it was his understanding based on the Constitution and Supreme Court precedent that "I'm outside of the jurisdiction of the U.S. as far as not living or working in the U.S." so that the tax code did not apply to him. (Trial Trans. at 4641-42, ECF 170).

willfully?" *Id.* Johnson also took the stand and testified that he did a lot of research and reading about the Internal Revenue Code and developed an honest belief that it did not apply to him: "In good faith I believe that the tax code was—did not apply to me. . . ." (Trial Trans. at 4668, ECF 170). Finally, during closing argument, defense counsel again argued that "the government has to show that Mr. Johnson willfully did these things. . . ." (Trial Trans. at 28, ECF 171). In fact, Johnson's counsel focused almost exclusively on how Johnson did not act willfully in refusing to file tax returns. *Id.*

It is the province of the jury to determine credibility issues. *United States v. Lowe*, 65 F.3d 1137, 1142 (4th Cir. 1995) ("Credibility determinations are within the sole province of the jury. . . .). Defense counsel raised and the jury considered and ultimately rejected Johnson's willfulness argument. Because the record establishes that Johnson's counsel did, in fact, raise a willfulness argument, he has not shown that counsel failed to address the issue and therefore that his representation fell below "an objective standard of reasonableness." *Strickland*, 466 U.S. 687-91.

Johnson asserts, in his third ineffective assistance of counsel claim, that defense counsel should have challenged the empanelling of the grand jury and individual jurors during the voir dire process. (Mem. at 5899, ECF186). Grand jury proceedings are presumed to have been legally empanelled without specific evidence to the contrary. *See United States v. Mechanik*, 475 U.S. 66, 75 (1986) (O'Connor, J. concurring) ("[T]he grand jury proceeding is accorded a presumption of regularity, which generally may be dispelled only upon particularized proof of irregularities in the grand jury process."). Johnson has failed to allege any type of impropriety with regard to the grand jury. Without "particularized proof" this allegation must fail. *Id.*

Similarly, in order to make a viable challenge to the petit jury, a defendant must establish a prima facie showing of impropriety with regard to jury selection. *Snyder v. Louisiana*, 552 U.S. 472, 476-77 (2008). As with the grand jury, Johnson fails to allege any bias or misconduct. Because Johnson cannot point to any specific instances of misconduct, this argument also lacks merit. Moreover, during the empaneling of the petit jury, Johnson was representing himself. He had the opportunity to make challenges. He did not. By exercising his constitutional right to present his own defense, Johnson necessarily waived his constitutional right to be represented by counsel. *See Faretta v. California*, 422 U.S. 806, 834 (1975). A defendant cannot waive his right to counsel and then complain about the quality of his own defense. *Id.* at 834 n.46; *United States v. Singleton*, 107 F.3d 1091, 1101 (4th Cir. 1997). Johnson has therefore failed to establish that his counsel provided deficient representation.

In his fourth and final ineffective assistance of counsel claim, Johnson asserts that his counsel failed to move for a new trial following his guilty verdict, even though Johnson explicitly asked him to do so. (Mem. at 4900, ECF186). There was some confusion about who would represent Johnson on appeal, because he was in the process of attempting to obtain counsel. (New Trial Motion, ECF 145 at 6). It appears that appointed counsel made a strategic decision not to file a motion for a new trial. (New Trial Motion, ECF 145 at 6). *See also Strickland*, 466 U.S. at 690-91 ("Mere errors of judgment and tactical mistakes by counsel do not constitute ineffective assistance, and the court may not second-guess the strategic decisions of counsel and order a new trial simply because another defense attorney, with the benefit of hindsight, might have taken a different course.").

But even assuming, *arguendo*, that appointed counsel's failure to make a motion for a new trial when directed to do so is analogous to failing to file an appeal, and therefore erroneous,

Johnson cannot establish prejudice. *See generally United States v. Peak*, 992 F.2d 39 (4th Cir. 1993) (holding that trial counsel's failure to file a notice of appeal when requested by defendant to do so is a *per se* deprivation of the Sixth Amendment right to counsel). This is because once Johnson alerted the court to fact that he was having trouble communicating with his appointed counsel who had not filed a motion for a new trial, I allowed Johnson to file the motion, out-of-time, on his own behalf. (ECF 141). He promptly did so. (ECF 145). I considered his motion for a new trial on the merits and denied it. (Sent. Trans. at 3, ECF 172). In his motion for a new trial, Johnson raised two issues that I addressed: (1) whether I erred by interrupting him and counsel during the trial. (New Trial Motion at 3, ECF 145). I carefully reviewed each of these claims and determined that the child support evidence was more probative than prejudicial especially in light of Johnson's personal testimony that he had done everything he could to care for his children. (Sent. Trans. at 4, ECF 172). With regard to the interruptions, I determined that they were limited and helped facilitate the smooth running of the trial. *Id.* at 6-7. Johnson does not claim that there were additional issues that would have been raised had counsel filed the motion for a new trial.

Because his motion for a new trial was adjudicated on the merits, Johnson cannot establish that his counsel's failure to file the motion on his behalf prejudiced him in any way. Accordingly, he cannot satisfy the requirements of *Strickland*.

B. Perjury Claim

After filing his § 2255 motion, his first motion to amend, and his response in opposition to the government's motion to dismiss, Johnson filed a second motion to amend, raising a new issue. Johnson asserts that that the government presented perjured testimony at trial. (ECF 205). Rule 15(a) of the Federal Rules of Civil Procedure provides that after a responsive pleading is

10

served, a party seeking to amend the original pleading must seek either the written consent of the opposing party or leave of court. Fed.R.Civ.P. 15(a)(2). Leave of court to amend "shall be given freely, absent bad faith, undue prejudice to the opposing party, or futility of amendment." *Pittman*, 209 F.3d at 317.

Johnson's request for leaved to amend his § 2255 motion to include a perjury claim would be futile. It is well established that a conviction obtained partly on the basis of evidence the prosecution knew to be false violates a defendant's due process rights. *See Napue v. Illinois*, 360 U.S. 264, 269 (1959). To establish such a violation, a defendant must show (i) that the testimony was perjured, (ii) that the prosecution knew or should have known of the perjury, and (iii) that the testimony was material to the conviction. *See Chavis v. North Carolina*, 637 F.2d 213, 222 (4th Cir.1980).

Johnson has not satisfied the first requirement for establishing a perjury claim because he has not shown that the government presented false testimony. Johnson takes issue with the testimony of former Internal Revenue Agent, Robert Biggs, who stated that the IRS determined that John Kotmair was not qualified to represent Johnson through a power-of-attorney while it was investigating Johnson. (Amend. Mem. at 5241, ECF 205). Biggs testified that he sent two letters to Johnson notifying him that his tax returns were being investigated. (Trial Trans. at 4282, ECF 168). Biggs stated that he then received a letter in response from John Kotmair with an attached power of attorney, stating that Kotmair was going to represent Johnson. (*Id.* at 4285.). Biggs testified that he contacted his managers who told him that Kotmair was not qualified to represent Johnson, and so Biggs continued to send correspondences to Johnson rather than Kotmair. (*Id.*).

Johnson argues that Biggs presented perjured testimony because Kotmair was, in fact, qualified to act as his power of attorney. Johnson claims that Kotmair had a valid "representation number" and so should have been allowed to represent him before the IRS. (Amend. Mem. at 5242, ECF 205). The gravamen of his argument is that Biggs' managers were mistaken in their belief that Kotmair could not act as a power of attorney, so Biggs' testimony at trial to that effect was a lie.

Johnson's argument fails because he has presented no evidence that Biggs' testimony was false. Biggs' recitation of events regarding his communications with Johnson and Kotmair appears to be accurate. Johnson takes issue with the decision, made by Biggs' managers in August of 2004, that Kotmair was unqualified to represent Johnson before the IRS. Yet even assuming that this decision was improperly made, Biggs testified truthfully about his role in the investigation. True statements cannot give rise to a perjury charge. *Bronston v. United States*, 409, U.S. 352, 362 (1973); *United States v. Earp*, 812 F.2d 917, 919 (4th Cir. 1987). Amendment of his § 2255 motion would therefore be futile. *Pittman*, 209 F.3d at 317. Accordingly, I deny his motion to amend.[2]

---

[2] Johnson's amendment would also be futile because the request to amend was untimely filed after the end of the statute of limitations period provided in § 2255(f). A petition under § 2255 must be filed within one year after the latest date on which (1) the judgment against the defendant became final; (2) any impediment to making the motion that was created by the government and violates the Constitution or laws of the United States was removed; (3) the Supreme Court first recognized the right the defendant claims, provided that the right applies retroactively to cases on collateral review; or (4) the facts supporting the defendant's claim could have been discovered by exercising due diligence. 28 U.S.C. § 2255(f). When a cause of action is barred by an applicable statute of limitations, amendment is futile and an amendment based on such a cause of action can be denied. *Keller v. Prince George's County*, 923 F.2d 30, 33 (4th Cir.1991). The Fourth Circuit's judgment in Johnson's case became final on May 12, 2014. The time to file a petition for a writ of certiorari ended, and Johnson's conviction became final, on August 10, 2014. *See Clay v. United States*, 537 U.S. 522, 524–25 (2003). Johnson did not file a second amendment to his § 2255 motion until November 9, 2015, more than a year after his conviction became final. Johnson's perjury claim does not relate to any of the claims made in his original § 2255 motion, and therefore is not entitled to relation back under Rule 15(c). *See Mayle v. Felix*, 545 U.S. 644, 664 (2005); *Pittman*, 209 F.3d at 317. Finally, although Johnson claims that his perjury claim involves newly discovered evidence, Kotmair's qualification to represent Johnson before the IRS is a fact that could have been discovered before trial.

APPENDIX X – CERTIFICATE OF APPEALABILITY AND SUPPLEMENTAL BRIEF

In The
United States Court of Appeals
For the Fourth Circuit

James Bowers Johnson
Plaintiff – Appellant

v.

UNITED STATES OF AMERICA
Appellee

ON APPEAL FROM THE UNITED STATES DISTRICT COURT
FOR THE WESTERN DISTRICT OF VIRGINIA

INFORMAL BRIEF OF APPELLANT
IN RESPONSE TO MEMORANDUM OPINION
DENYING PETITIONER'S MOTION UNDER 28 USC 2255

CASE NO. 16-6244
RE: UNITED STATES v James B. Johnson
6:12-cr-00015-NKM-RSB-1, 6:15-cv-80797-NKM-RSB

James B. Johnson
112 West Pall Mall Street
Winchester, Virginia [22601]

Appellant

STATEMENT OF SUBJECT MATTER APPELLATE JURISDICTION

The United States District Court for the Western District Court of Virginia exercised subject matter jurisdiction over Peritioner's Habeas Corpus Motion under 28 USC 2255. On the 7th of January 2016 the Court issued its MEMORANDUM OPINION denying the claim. Petitioner now files this INFORMAL BRIEF and seeks a Certificate of Appealability. The United States Court of Appeals for the Fourth Circuit has jurisdiction to hear this matter.

TIMELINESS

The informal brief was sent by certified mail on April 4, 2016.

CERTIFICATE OF APPEALABILITY

The District Court did not grant a Certificate of Appealability.

ISSUES

1. The Court Erred Concerning Petitioner's Ineffective Assistance of Counsel Claim for Failure to Challenge Jurisdiction

The gavamen of this INFORMAL BRIEF rests upon the District Court's statements that Petitioner must prove "that his sentence was 'imposed in violation of the Constitution or laws of the United States;' (2) that "the Court was without jurisdiction to impose such a sentence..."" (MEMORANDUM OPINION (M.O.), p. 4) However, the Court overlooked that without defense counsel arguing the element of jurisdiction, neither of the Court's points would be proved during the trial process or the 2255 post conviction remedy. Rather, the Court relied upon "the record" that does not contain a proper juridictional claim. Why? Defense counsel never raised it. This was ineffective assistance of counsel. The Court erred.

With counsel's failure to research and argue Petitoner's good faith belief, the Court now ignores Petitioner's argument of ineffective assistance of counsel (Dkt 186, pgs 3- 15), (Id., Declaration, 6-11, 24, 28-54, 63, 65, 66, 89-91) For Petitioner argues that counsel, at a minimum, should have raised jurisdiction under Rule 12, which would have been fundamental advocacy.

For defense counsel to simply PRESUME that the Government and the Court had jurisdiction was gross error. Petitioner's sworn and unrebutted Declaration (Dkt 186) establishes that defense counsel pursued their own PRESUMPTION - to the benefit of the Government, - that Petitioner was a "taxpayer" with an obligation to file. (Dkt 186, P. 18-20, Decl., 63, 65, 66, 89-91) Consequently, counsel did not bother to investigate why Petitioner was WITHOUT congressional indirect exaction for the federal income tax. If a jurisdictional claim is not made by defense and proved by the plaintiff, jurisdiction is NOT addressed; rather, it is presumed that the court has subject matter and in personam jurisdiction, (Dkt 186, p. 18-21) which is fatal to the fairness of the trial process.

In Matthew A. Fogel v. UNITED STATES of America, 2001 WL 306496 (S.D Cal.), a case in which the Government sought a dismissal, the Court stated under Section 1, "Subject Matter Jurisdiction," A. "Standard of Review,"

> Under Federal Rule of Civil Procedure 12(b)(1), a motion to dismiss for lack of subject matter jurisdiction may be properly granted if the plaintiff does not meet its burden in establishing that the court has such jurisdiction. Because federal courts are courts of limited jurisdiction, the plaintiff must demonstrate that the court has been authorized to preside over the case either by statute or the constitution. See Willy v. Coastal Corp., 503 U.S. 131, 136-137 (1992). Whenever it appears that the court lacks subject matter jurisdiction, the court is obligated to dismiss the action. Fed.R.Civ.P. 12(h)(3). In a suit against the United States, a 12(b)(l) motion is proper when sovereign immunity has not been waived. See McCarthy v. United States, 850 F .2d 558, 560 (9th Cir. 1988). "[A] waiver cannot be implied but must be unequivocally expressed." United States v. King, 395 U.S. 1,4 (1969) (emphasis added)

In paragraph B, "Analysis," the Court stated,

> The government's motion to dismiss for lack of subject matter jurisdiction must be granted pursuant to 28 U.S.C. § 2201 (a), which expressly declares an exception to federal court jurisdiction in controversies "with respect to Federal taxes" when the plaintiff requests declaratory relief. See Hughes v. United States, 953 F.2d 531, 536-37 (9th Cir.1991) (where the real issue in the case is whether the plaintiff must pay taxes, the court lacks subject matter jurisdiction under § 2201). Because Plaintiff has requested a declaratory judgment finding that he is a "non-taxpayer" and is not required to file taxes in the United States, this Court lacks subject matter jurisdiction and is obligated to grant the United States' motion to dismiss. (emphasis added)

Contrary to the action taken in Fogel, rather than attack the Government's jurisdictional claim, rather than challenge subject matter or in personam jurisdiction, defense counsel simply said that Petitioner's belief was "frivolous." (Dkt 186, Decl. 31, 32, 43, Dkt 198, p. 10-11) Considering Fogel, it is clear that defense counsel had the frivolous belief. But for defense counsel's antipathy toward a legitimate jurisdictional claim, the Court decided during the trial process, as it now decides, that it had jurisdiction. Why would the Court decide any differently without an argument to the contrary? It would not; so it did not.

Without the requisite due diligence, counsel did not determine that Petitioner's good faith belief was actually REASONABLE. Counsel was never in a position to argue that since the Government did not have jurisdiction, the Court could not have jurisdiction. Yet, with adequate understanding of the statutes and regulations and case law, counsel would have realized that they did not know what Petitioner knew, and what they knew was plainly wrong. Even the Supreme Court stated that a belief may be unreasonable, but sincerely held. (See United States v Cheek, 498 US 192 (1991) and Snyder v United States, 897 F. Supp 241, 244 (4th Cir. 1995)) Regrettably, it was defense counsel's unreasonable belief, and not Petitioner's reasonable one, that assured his unjust conviction and imprisonment and perpetuates the Court's reluctance to decide differently.

The Supreme Court, in Scheuer v Rhodes, 416 US 232, 236 (1974) states,

> When a federal court reviews the sufficiency of a complaint, the issue is not whether a plaintiff will ultimately prevail but whether the claimant is entitled to offer evidence to supprt the claims. Indeed it may appear on the face of the pleadings that a recovery is very remote and unlikely but that is not the test.
>
> In passing on a motion to dismiss, whether on the ground of lack of jurisdiction over the subject matter or for failure to state a cause of action, the allegations of the complaint should be construed favorably to the pleader.

Since the Government was without power to level charges (in violation of the Constitution), the Court could not possibly have had jurisdiction. Consequently, defense counsel was beholden to challenge jurisdiction under Rule 12(b)(2) (Motions That May Be Made at Any Time. A motion that the court lacks jurisdiction may be made at any time while the case is pending.) or consider a similar action to Declaratory Judgment under 26 USC and the raising of a Federal Question (28 USC 1331). Failure to challenge jurisdiction by whatever means was ineffective assistance of counsel.

Revocation of Election

Petitioner's Revocation of Election, 26 USC 6013(g)(4)(A), (See Exhibit 1) is the same action that Petitioner took in 2000. It is this act that defense counsel flatly refused to dignify as other than frivolous. Rather than investigate, counsel limited their "strategy" to what they understood. (Dkt 186, Decl 63, 65, 66, 89-91) As a result, they only foresaw sanctions (Id., 106, 108, 110, 111) for arguing what was otherwise a belief grounded in law and fact. The argument that Petitioner revoked an election to any federal benefit that previously obligated him to the federal income, social security and employment tax would have denied the Court the possibility of hearing the case. Petitioner would have been exonerated without a trial. Like Foley, the Court would have concluded that it did not have jurisdiction. Why? Because defense counsel would have raised jurisdiction and the Government would not have been able to prove it.

Petitioner's revocation of any federal benefit and election is significant in light of the Court's recent denial. For, the sentence was in violation of the Constitution or laws of the United States and the Court was without jurisdiction. This would have been proved had defense counsel learned and argued that:

1. Congress may not tax by indirect or direct means unless it has Constitutional authority. Congress does not have absolute taxing power over the Citizens of the several States. (Appendix D, Exhibit 1) Since Petitioner was able to prove that he was without congressional authority, and defense counsel did not make the argument, the conviction and sentence imposed were in violation of the Constitution and laws of the United States. Furthermore, since Petitioner was not liable for the tax, like Fogel, the Court could never have had jurisdiction.

2. Congress must provide an exit to legislative Acts that are not otherwise mandatory upon the people of the several States. Constitutional and legislative exit provisions, such as the exemption or election from the federal income tax system, are established by statutes and regulations (i.e., 26

USC 6013(g)(4)(A)). (Appendix B, Exhibit 1) Since Petitioner executed this exit provision, defense counsel was beholden to argue the same before the Court.

3. There is no implementing regulation for 26 USC 7203, the statute governing "Willful Failure to File Return," (Appendix G, Exhibit 1) which renders it unenforceable in the several States. It is, however, fully enforceable in the UNITED STATES – the District of Columbia and its territories and possessions. (Appendix D, Exhibit 1) Congress has plenary power over venues that it (the United States) controls and nonresident alien individuals who elect to be treated as U.S. Resident aliens within the United States. As such, the lack of implementing regulations for 26 USC 7203 is immaterial. Since Petitioner revoked his election to be treated as a U.S resident, he was without congressional authority and his "status" and, therefore, jurisdiction should have been argued before the court.

4. That Congress may not tax what is without its jurisdiction is supported by Department of the Treasury acknowledgement, whereby payment of the federal income tax is an "Estate and Gift Tax." (Appendix F, Exhibit 1) This includes the W-2 "Wage and Tax Statement," W-4 "Employee's Withholding Certificate" and 1099 designations. (Id.) With this insight, defense counsel could not have ignored that a "gift" or a "bequest" cannot be mandatory, especially when it is terminated or revoked. Petitioner revoked and terminated the obligation for the payment of what is a "gift."

5. Based upon its own statutes and regulations, the Government never had jurisdiction over Petitioner. (Appendix B, Exhibit 1) With an sound appreciation for the statues and regulations, counsel would have argued that the Governemnt (IRS) was beholden to comply with all revocations and Petitoner's changed "status." The point cannot be any more transparent. Based upon the statutes, with or without implementing regulations, defense counsel ignored a legal and lawful jurisdictional basis for Petitioner's actions and belief. Consequently, when all parties involved in the trial process PRESUMED that Petitioner was within the jurisdiction of the Government and, therefore, the Court, especially when there was ample proof the Government did not have jurisdiction, justice was not achieved - a conviction was imposed in violation of the Constitution and without the Court's jurisdiction.

The Court's MEMORANDUM OPINION

The impact of defense counsel's abject failure to apprise the Court of Petitioner's established belief compromised the fairness of the judicial process. For the Court still concludes that Petitioner "did not 'voluntarily' agree to be taxed," (M.O. p. 5) which is not even relevant given that defense counsel only argued that Petitioner simply **believed** that he did not owe taxes. At a minimum, counsel was obligated to inform the Court as to why Petitioner held that belief. The Court's assessment that Petitioner did not agree to be taxed is inconsistent with Petitioner's prior acts; he revoked any former election to be "subject" to any given tax. It cannot be denied that defense counsel's frivolous and incompete argument, which the Court now relies upon as "the record," was a discredit to the Court and to Petitoner. The Court never knew the truth.

The Court went further by stating that Petitioner's "argument **appears** to be that he is not a 'taxpayer' because federal income taxes are excise taxes, and therefore "voluntary.'" (Id., p.6) (emphasis added) Had defense counsel made the proper jurisdictional argument in the first place, the Court would never have been in a position to draw a conclusion based upon appearances. To the contrary, with effective assistance of counsel, the Court, with assurance, would have required that the Government prove jurisdiction, at no pecuniary risk (sanctions) to counsel.

The Court now gratuitously argues, "It is well settled that all workers earning income in this country are subject to federal income taxation." (Id.) Unfortunately, the Court is making an argument that is not germane to Petitioner's ineffective assistance of counsel claim. The Court's legal justification for what it believes is Petitioner's "status" as a "worker" is equally dismissive of any ineffective assistance contention. The same is true regarding the Court's reference that "the debate over whether the income tax is an excise or a direct tax is irrelevant to the obligation of citizens to pay taxes and file returns." (Id.) Since Petitioner did not debate the question as to whether the tax was direct versus indirect, especially since the Petitioner asserted that the Internal Revenue Code is constitutional and addresses only indirect taxes, (Dkt 186, Decl. 10, 11, 103) the statement deflects the real argument, whether Petitioner was a "citizen" with an "obligation," a jurisdictional claim that counsel did not argue. Since defense counsel never made the jurisdictional argument, the Court exercises its license to argue that Petitioner was a "taxpayer" and, therefore, "subject" to the tax.

The Court then states, "All individuals... must pay federal income taxes on their wages." (M.O. p. 6.) Yet, in the face of agency regulations and supporting documentation that one may NOT be liable for the federal income tax, (Appendix B, Exhibit 1) the Court's "well settled" notion must be limited ONLY to "workers" who "are subject to federal income taxation." For, "All individuals... must pay federal income taxes on their wages..." would be true ONLY for ALL INDIVIDUALS who have WAGES subject to the federal income tax. Those who are NOT one of ALL would have a valid jurisdictional claim that the Government is without jurisdiction. It would stand to reason that the Court would make the same presumption as defense counsel BECAUSE counsel did not challenge jurisdiction. Meanwhile, quite significantly, Petitioner "refused to discuss anything other than his jurisdictional argument." (M.O., p 3) (Dkt 186, Decl. 27-29, 94, 95, 97, 100-102, Dkt 198, p.4) Why would an innocent man, fully aware of his action and the law, not discuss anything other than jurisdiction. Given the persistence of Petitoner's jurisdicitonal claim from arrest until now, it is unreasonable for the Court to grant counsel a pass for not arguing what was NOT frivolous.

The Court's unwillingness to weigh counsel's failure to research and argue Petitioner's jurisdictional claim speaks to a larger concern – whether it is the intent of all parties involved in the legal system to avoid and evade the jurisdictional argument at all costs. There are jurisdictional claims that, when made, must be pursued. Fogel underscores that defense counsel failed.

To further substantiate that defense counsel provided ineffective assistance, and to underscore that the Court's refusal to accept testimony outside the trial record, Petitioner offers the following references. Had defense counsel served as professional legal advocates, rather than blind followers of what they presumed to be a legal obligation, they would have realized that:

1. The "United States" is limited and specific to the "territory" under direct congressional control.

A. As stated in Federalist Papers 1-5,

... the United States has an indefinite discretion to make requisitions for men and money; but they have no authority to raise either, by regulations extending to the individual citizens of America. (emphasis added)

B. There are those who are subject to the jurisdiction of the United States. As reflected in 8 USC 1401, "Nationals and citizens of the United States at birth,"

(a) a person born in the United States and subject to the jurisdiction thereof.

C. 3C Am Jur 2d Section 2689 – "Who is born in the United States and subject to the United States jurisdiction" states,

A person is born subject to the jurisdiction of the United States, for acquiring citizenship at birth, if his or her birth occurs in territory over which the United States is sovereign...

D. Congress identified the jurisdiction of the United States in the Sixty-Third Congress, Session 1, 1913, Ch. 16, 1913, page 177, Section 2 – ACT OF CONGRESS, October 3, 1913, Sixteenth Amendment,

That the word "State" or "United States" when used in this section shall be construed to include any Territory, Alaska, the District of Columbia, Puerto Rico, and the Philippines Islands, when construction is necessary to carry out its provisions. (emphasis added)

2. In the context of the limited scope of the "United States," the definition of certain classes is paramount. The terms "nonresident alien individuals," "U.S. resident," "U.S. person," and "taxpayer" have specific definitions and reflect a "status" that depends upon whether they fall within the jurisdiction of the "United States." Of particular note is the term "nonresident alien individual."

A. 26 USC 7701(b)(1)(B) "Nonresident alien"

An individual is a nonresident alien if such individual is neither a citizen of the United States nor a resident of the United States.

B. IRS FORM 8233 states,

Note: Definitions of terms: 1. United States defined at 26 7408(d) means the District of Columbia; 2. Nonresident alien individual defined at 26 USC 7701(b)(1)(B) and 26 CFR 1.871-1(b)(4) to mean **those born in the 50 states**. (emphasis added)

C. According to the Federal Retirement Thrift Investment Board,

A nonresident alien is an individual who is neither a U.S. Citizen nor a resident of the United States (emphasis added)

3. Significantly, since the "United States" may tax only within the limitations of the Constitution, the definition of "trade or business" is essential. "Trade or business" is limited in scope to the jurisdiction of the UNITED STATES and does not apply to certain people.

A. 26 USC 7701(a)(26) "Trade or Business"

The term "trade or business" includes [consists of to the exclusion of all other terms] the performance of the functions of a public office. [Public offices are created by the US Congress for IRC purposes] [emphasis and brackets added]

4. Nonresident alien individuals may not have a federal income tax liability.

26 CFR 1.871-1 "Classification and Manner of Taxing Alien Individuals" states,

(b) Classes of nonresident aliens – (1) In general. For purposes of the income tax, nonresident alien individuals are divided into the following three classes: (i) Nonresident alien individuals who at no time during the taxable year are engaged in a trade or business in the United States... (emphasis added)

5. Notably, the designation of what sources of income may be taxed by the "United States" is a jurisdictional limitation to those involved in a "trade or business," which may or may not involve a nonresident alien.

A. 26 USC 861(a) "Gross income from sources within United States"

The following items of gross income shall be treated as income from sources within the United States:

(3) Personal Services – Compensation for labor or personal services performed in the United States; except that compensation for labor or services performed in the United States shall not be deemed to be income from sources within the United States if -

(C) the compensation is for labor or services performed as an employee of or under contract with – (i) a nonresident alien... not engaged in trade or business within the United States (emphasis added)

B. According to the Yale Law Review,

Commensurate with the practical limitations upon the Bureau of Internal Revenue's ability to collect moneys assessed, federal jurisdiction to tax incomes in a given case is theoretically predicated upon a taxpayer's connection with the United States in at least one of three ways: (1) by citizenship, (2) by residence, or (3) by source of income. Since by definition the taxation of nonresident aliens must always rest upon the last basis alone, an **in personam jurisdiction may not be claimed, as it may of citizens and resident aliens**, which would enable levy upon earnings from all sources whether foreign or domestic, but only an authority in rem to tax income originating in this country. (emphasis added)

6. Nonresident alien individuals may not be liable for the federal income tax.

A. 26 USC 871 "Tax on Nonresident Alien Individuals" states,

A nonresident alien individual engaged in trade or business within the United States during the taxable year shall be taxable as provided in section 1 or 55 on his taxable income which is effectively connected with the conduct of a trade or business within the United States. (emphasis added)

B. 26 CFR 1.871-1(a) "Classification and manner of taxing alien individuals."

... **Nonresident alien individuals are taxable only on certain income** from sources within and without the United States which is effectively **connected** for the taxable year **with the conduct of a trade or business in the United States.** (emphasis added)

C. According to the Federal Retirement Thrift Investment Board,

a nonresident alien participant who never worked for the U.S. Government in the United States will not be liable for U.S. Income tax. (emphasis added)

7. There are those who are not required to have a social security number, specifically nonresident aliens, and there are those nonresident aliens who are treated as "residents" under 26 USC 6013 who have a social security number.

A. 26 CFR 301.6109-1 "Identifying Numbers"

(b)(2) Foreign Persons. The provisions of paragrapph (b)(1) of this section regarding the furnishing of one's own number shall apply to the following foreign persons -

(iii) A nonresident alien **treated as a resident** under section 6013(g) or (h) (emphasis added)

The regulation continues with

B. (d) Obtaining a taxpayer identifying number

(4) Coordination of taxpayer identifying numbers -

(i) ... The individual can use the social security number for all tax purposes under this title, even though the individual is, or later becomes, a nonresident alien individual. (emphasis added)

and

C. (g) Special rules for taxpayer identifying numbers issued to foreign persons

(1) General rule - (i) Social security number. A social security number is generally identified in the records and database of the Internal Revenue Service as **a number belonging to a U.S. Citizen or resident alien individual. A person may establish a different status for the number by providing proof of foreign status with the Internal Revenue Service** under such procedures as the Internal Revenue Service may prescribe, including the use of a form as the Internal Revenue Service may specify. **Upon accepting an individual as a nonresident alien individual, the Internal Revenue Service will assign this status to the individual's social security number.** (emphasis added)

(iii) IRS individual taxpayer number. An IRS individual taxpayer identification number is generally identified in the records and database of the Internal Revenue Service as a number belonging to a nonresident alien individual. If the Internal Revenue Service determines at the time of application or subsequently, that an individual is not a nonresident alien individual, the Internal Revenue Service may require that the individual apply for a social security number. If a social security number is not available, the Internal Revenue Service may accept that the individual use an IRS individual taxpayer identification number, which the Internal Revenue Service will identify as a number belonging to a U.S. resident alien. (emphasis added)

(2) Change of foreign status. Once a taxpayer identifying number is identified in the records and database of the Internal Revenue Service as a number belonging to a U.S. or foreign person, the status of the number is permanent until the circumstances of the taxpayer change. A taxpayer whose status changes (for example, **a nonresident alien individual with a social security number becomes a U.S. resident alien**) must notify the Internal Revenue Service of the change of status under such procedures as the Internal Revenue Service shall prescribe, including the use of a form as the Internal Revenue Service may specify.

8. Congressional statutes are enforceable within the several States only if there are implementing regulations published in the Federal Register.

A. 26 CFR 601.702 – Publication, public inspection, and specific requests for records.

B. 5 USC 552 Public Information; agency rules, opinions, orders, records, and proceedings

C. 26 USC – Subtitle F – Enforcement Regulations (There is no implementing regulation for 26 USC 7203)

D. National Archives, letter, May 16, 1994 states,

Our records indicate that the Internal Revenue Service has not incorporated by reference in the Federal Register (as that term is defined in the Federal Register system) a requirement to make an income tax return. (emphasis added)

9. Given the foregoing evidence that one may not be required to file a federal income tax return or be subject to the "United States" as a "U.S. person," "taxpayer" or "U.S. Resident," the following

citation confirms the need for defense lawyers to raise a jurisdictional claim at the appropriate time and in the proper venue, especially since there may be no implementing regulation and Congress is not required to cite its authority.

A. American Law Division, Congressional Research Service, The Library of Congress, letter dated September 22, 1995 states,

Among these powers, Congress has been granted the authority to exercise exclusive jurisdiction over the District of Columbia. It should be noted, however, that there is no similar clause in the Constitution that gives Congress authority to exercise jurisdiction over the states.

When Congress passes a law, there is no requirement under the Constitution that the Congress identify the nature or source of its authority. ...Consequently, **legal analysis evaluating the constitutional basis** would need to be done on a case by case basis. Occasionally, arguments are made in federal courts that Congress has acted outside of the scope of its constitutional authority in passing a piece of legislation. In these cases, the constitutional basis for a particular piece of legislation may address the issue of which Congressional powers are the basis for the legislation. (emphasis added)

10. IRS Forms and Instructions reflect that some are not obligated to pay the federal income tax.

A. IRS Form 8233 "Exemption From Withholding on Compensation for Personal Services of a Nonresident Alien Individual" asks "Who Should Use This Form?"

If you are a nonresident alien individual who is receiving...

compensation for independent personal services not deemed as income from sources within the United States or

compensation for dependent personal services not deemed as income from sources in the United States. (emphasis added)

B. IRS FORM 8233 also states,

Note: Definitions of terms: 1. United States defined at 26 USC 7408(d) means the District of Columbia; 2. Nonresident alien individual defined at 26 USC 7701(b)(1)(B) and 26 CFR 1.871-1(b)(4) to mean **those born in the 50 states**. (emphasis added)

C. Instructions for Form 8233 state,

Definitions
Nonresident Alien
If you are an alien individual (that is, an individual who is not a U.S. Citizen), specific rules apply to determine if you are a resident or nonresident alien for tax purposes. Generally,

> you are a resident alien if you meet either the "green card test" or the "substantial presence test" for the calendar year. <u>Any person not meeting either test is generally a nonresident alien</u>. (emphasis added)
>
> U.S. Person
> For purposes of this form, **<u>a U.S. Person is a U.S. Citizen or resident alien</u>**. (emphasis added)
>
> D. IRS Form W-8Ben states,
>
> Do NOT use this form if:
>
> You are NOT an individual living/working in the 50 states
> You are a U.S. Citizen or other U.S. Person, including a resident alien individual

The foregoing references are not all encompassing and clearly indicate that defense counsel did not provide effective assistance. Counsel did not rebut the presumption that the Court had jurisdiction. Ultimately, it must be reconciled that Petitioner could not have been within the jurisdiction fo the United States District Court. Consider that the Supreme Court stated,

> The United States District Court is not a true United States court established under article 3 of the Constitution to administer the judicial power of the United States therein conveyed. It is created by virtue of the sovereign congressional faculty, granted under article 4, 3, of that instrument, of making all needful rules and regulations respecting the territory belonging to the United States. The resemblance of its jurisdiction to that of true United States courts, in offering an opportunity to nonresidents of resorting to a tribunal not subject to local influence, does not change its character as a mere territorial court. Balzac v Porto Rico, 258 US 298 (1922)

Based upon the foregoing, Petitioner's good faith belief - that he was without the jurisdiction of the United States - was a credible and worthy jurisdictional argument. Petitioner established for counsel that he is a not resident within the "United States," which prohibited him from classification as a "U.S. Resident," "U.S. person" or "taxpayer" subject to any federal income or excise tax. Petitioner did not have income effectively connected with a "trade or business." Petitioner revoked social security and employment benefits. He revoked his election to be treated as a U.S person or U.S resident. (Dkt 186, Decl. 6, 7) Consequently, the United States Government and the IRS did not have authority for what even Congress was prohibited from doing. The Court, then, did not have subject matter or in personam jurisdiction. Now, there is no doubt that Congress may subject all Americans who elect, under 26 USC 6013(g), to be classified as U.S. Residents, which would place them within the District of Columbia, and the jurisdiction of the United States District Courts. As such, the lack of implementing regulations would be immaterial. With Petitioner's acts of revocation, he was, undoubtedly, not one of ALL subject to this legitimate, legal and lawful federal income tax and the corresponding jurisdiction.

The Record and Unrebutted Testimony

In order to prove that defense counsel's advocacy was ineffective, in that they did not research Petitioner's belief and ask the court to require that the Government prove jurisdiction, this Court of Appeals need only weigh the conclusions defense counsel offered to Petitioner after the trial.

> Your claim that you were not a "taxpayer" or "U.S. citizen" have been deemed frivolous. ... This does not mean that... you misunderstood the law differently (or that you had a good faith, but mistaken, belief about what the law meant, it just means that a lawyer could not argue that your interpretation of the law was correct... (Dkt 186, Decl 115)

And

> An attorney may not assert a position he knows has no legal basis and which he cannot in good faith ask the court to adopt. (Id., 116)

In contrast to the foregoing statutes, regulations and evidence, counsel's continued ignorance and belief is quite stark. There can be no doubt that defense counsel's reliance upon the ABA Canons of Ethics to prevent sanctions for arguing what was "frivolous," was without merit. In light of the law and facts, they should have researched and understood Petitioner's belief and rebuttal of the Government's presumption and prima facie evidence. Defense counsel had a professional responsibility to Petitioner to argue that the Court reconcile a legitimate jurisdictional claim.

With the District Court's admonition that the sentence must be in violation of the Constitution or laws of the United States and it was without jurisdiction, may this Court of Appeals consider that:

Petitioner:
- revoked his status as a "taxpayer" and all federal benefits (Id., 6-8, 12, 24)
- believed the income tax was constitutional (Id., 10)
- challenged jurisdiction (Id., 27, 29, 37, 56, 57, 60, 82, 93, 95-97, 98)
- believed he was not a "U.S person" or "taxpayer" as defined in the tax code (Id., 12, 24, 36, 37)
- was not able to explain the nature of the "United States" and its limited authority (Id., 83, 85)

and

Defense Counsel:
- stated that we all have to pay income tax (Id., 28)
- stated that Petitioner was liable for the income tax (Id., 31, 34)
- stated they would be sanctioned for arguing jurisdiction (Id., 32, 35, 43)
- stated that Petitioner was a "U.S. person" (Id., 45, 46-48)
- refused to consider that the Government had limited jurisdiction (Id., 50)
- argued before the court that Petitioner believed the income tax was "voluntary" (Id., 60)
- told the jury, "Of course he is required to file tax returns." (Id., 66)
- told the Court there was "uncontroverted evidence" Petitioner was required to file returns (Id., 89)
- told the jury that

> Mr. Johnson still believes that the tax code doesn't apply to him and he still had no obligation to file a return. **But, as a matter of law,** as a matter of who is correct, we all

know he should have filed returns, I mean, come on, he should have." (emphasis added)

and

Is he right? No. It is crazy." (Id., 90, 91)

Noteworthy, the Court not only sanctioned defense counsel's failure to investigate the proper exercise of the Government's taxing authority as it related to Petitioner, but accepted the Government's use of IRS Revenue Ruling 2005-17, 2005-1 C.B. 823. (Dkt 194, RESPONSE TO MOTION FOR RELIEF PURSUANT TO TITLE 28, page 8.) By accepting the Government's assertion that the IRS Revenue Ruling refuted Petitioner's belief, the Court gave the IRS Revenue Ruling undue merit. Revenue Rulings have no weight in law and are merely opinions that should withstand judicial scrutiny. Revenue Ruling 2005-17 was issued, conveniently for the IRS, AFTER the criminal investigation began and it certainly did not withstand judicial vetting at any point during the trial process. In addition to their failure to research Petitioner's good faith belief, defense counsel failed to research the basis of the Government's position. Consequently, Petitioner's reasonable good faith belief was not dignified the same as the Court's fluid acceptance of the government's untested 2005-17 Revenue Ruling. Because defense counsel erred, the Court erred.

2. <u>The District Court Rejected Newly Discovered Evidence</u>

The District Court rejected Petitioner's amendment to his 2255 Motion based upon discovery of new evidence. Rather than accepting Petitioner's claim under 28 USC 2255(f)(4), the Court prevented it under (f)(1). This was error.

28 USC 2255 - Federal custody; remedies on motion attacking sentence

(f) A 1-year period of limitation shall apply to a motion under this section. The limitation period shall run from the latest of—

(1) the date on which the judgment of conviction becomes final;

(2) the date on which the impediment to making a motion created by governmental action in violation of the Constitution or laws of the United States is removed, if the movant was prevented from making a motion by such governmental action;

(3) the date on which the right asserted was initially recognized by the Supreme Court, if that right has been newly recognized by the Supreme Court and made retroactively applicable to cases on collateral review; or

(4) the date on which the facts supporting the claim or claims presented could have been discovered through the exercise of due diligence.

Petitioner discovered the new evidence in the spirit of (f)(4), which was "the latest of" as stipulated by the statute. Petitioner offered a complete explanation as to how this evidence met this provision. By dismissing the amendment under (f)(1), the Court rejected a valid concern about false testimony that was prejudicial.

Moreover, it was disingenuous to give Internal Revenue Agent Robert Biggs a pass on his failure to investigate the qualifications of John Kotmair, Petitioner's power of attorney (not MENTOR as unjustly characterized by the Court), especially in light of the fact that Biggs simply **believed** the information from his superiors. (See United States v Price, 722 F 2d 88 (5th Cir. 1983))

Given the prestige of the Government and the perceived "credibility" of an Internal Revenue Agent, false testimony before the jury was harmful. Proper judicial review of the newly discovered evidence and review of questionable testimony was warranted. The Motion to Amend should have been granted. The District Court erred.

3. Defense Failed to Prove Lack of Willfulness

The Court ignored Petitioner's claim that defense counsel failed to argue willfulness. Counsel failed because they refused to investigate why he was not willful. What counsel did argue before the jury was ONLY that Petitioner believed that he was not liable. Like an empty and meaningless mantra,

> He believed! He truly, truly believed! We won't explain why he believed as he did, but just know, ladies and gentlemen of the jury, he believed the tax code did not apply to him.

This shallow approach, which is supposedly seasoned legal advocacy, guaranteed a conviction and sentence for crimes Petitioner did not commit. Had defense counsel investigated, they would have argued the very reasons why Petitioner had no mens rea, because they would have learned that there could have been no actus reus. (Dkt 198, p. 6-10) Counsel should have argued WHY Petitioner believed as he did.

Defense counsel could not see that there was no actus reus by virtue of the fact that they did not accept that Petitioner made the revocations necessary to negate liability for any federal excise. With the proper understanding, counsel would have been forearmed with the knowledge that Americans are able to elect NOT to be within congressional taxing authority and, therefore, not liable for the federal income tax. Counsel would have learned that Americans are NOT required to have a social security number to live and work in the United States. With the facts and documentation, defense counsel would have realized that they had EVERY reason to do battle with a jurisdictional argument. Counsel would have reasonably asked the Court to require that the Government prove jurisdiction.

Because defense counsel presumed that Petitioner was a "taxpayer" and liable to file tax returns (Dkt 186, p. 10), they did not investigate and argue his reasonable good faith belief. This flawed approach permitted their presumption that Petitioner was culpable, which permitted the Court to presume that Petitioner was within its jurisdiction. (Id., p. 19-21) Since the Court presumed that it had subject matter and in personam jurisdiction the Government moved forward with its presumption. Presumptions reigned supreme throughout the trial process, almost by design, as if there was an unspoken collaboration, whereby each party avoided the topic of jurisdiction.

Petitioner believed then and believes this very day that he is without the congressional excise authority and, therefore, the court's jurisdiction. Moreover, the Government has yet to respond to Petitioner's rebuttal of its presumption and prima facie evidence. This means that this issue is capable of repetition, yet evading review. (Dkt 198, p.4) Since defense counsel did not argue jurisdiction, as in Foley supra, the question of the Government's and Court's jurisdiction remains unchallenged and, therefore, unresolved.

6. Additional Issues Not Certified For Review by the District Court

A. Petitioner's Testimony Stands Unrefuted

The Government did not rebut Petitioner's sworn declaration. (Dkt. 186) Specifically, the Government's Response (Dkt 194) offers no refutation by defense counsel of Petitioner's sworn testimony. Petitioner's declaration offers facts and truth as to what occurred outside the trial record. Without a rebuttal, his testimony stands uncontested. The District Court should have relied upon Petitioner's unrebutted testimony as to the facts of the matter outside the trial record, testimony that substantiates the claim of a violation of a constitutional magnitude - ineffective assistance of counsel, as well as proof that the sentence was imposed outside the Constitution and laws of the United States and that the Court did not have jurisdiction. To dismiss the only testimony offered during the post conviction proceeding, especially as it relates to information that only Petitioner and defense counsel could offer, was error.

C. Petitioner Denied Access to the Case File and Correspondence Between Defense Counsel and the United States Attorney

Throughout the 2255 process, Petitioner made requests of former defense counsel, the United States Attorney and the District Court for the correspondence between defense counsel and the United States Attorney. Defense attorney Randy Cargill stated in writing that he would help if able, but he refused this simple request. The U.S. Attorney did not respond to Petitioner's request for the correspondence. Finally, the Court denied Petitioner's subpoena requests to gain access to the defense case file and correspondence between the opposing parties. It is telling that the Court sanctioned defense counsel's "strategy" that Petitioner was a "taxpayer" and within the Government's taxing power, but would not allow Petitioner access to documents and material that may have information which contradicts that "strategy." The Court erred.

D. The District Court Denied Petitioner's Call for EQUITY

During the proceedings, Petitioner invoked the Court of Equity (Dkt 186, Decl. 57) and asked the Court to apply maxims of equity, particularly as it related to Petitioner's property – his body. Petitioner even submitted a Bill in Equity (Id.) and asked for the dismissal of the charges and to be released. The Court denied these efforts. While Petitioner is not schooled in law or the Court's rules and procedures, the call for Equity was fundamental, equal to the submission to the Writ of Habeas Corpus (Id., 46) , which was denied simply because the Court ruled that Petitioner was represented by counsel. The Court's denial of Equity and the Writ of Habeas Corpus, especially when both were invoked within the challenge of jurisdiction, was error. The Supreme Court stated,

> officers... who threaten and are about to commence proceedings, either of a civil or

criminal nature, to enforce against parties by an unconstitutional act, violating the Federal Constitution may be enjoined by a Federal court of equity from such action. Home Teleph & Teleg., v Los Angeles, 227 US 278, 293 (1913)

Since Petitioner was without congressional power for the act charged, there was a violation of the Constitution and Equity was appropriately invoked.

7. Relief Requested

For the foregoing reasons, Petitioner requests that this Court grant a Certificate of Appealability and any relief deemed appropriate to effectively overturn this conviction. If this Court should consider it worthy, Petitioner moves the Court to immediately overturn the conviction and sentence and to SEAL the case. Petitioner is innocent of the charges and has suffered the loss of four years of his life, not to mention the destruction of his family and marriage. Petitioner hereby forgives those who exercised indiscretion that has led to this travesty. Moreover, Petitioner declares by waiver

from the beginning, with God as my witness, I, as a true man of God, acknowledge all blessings from God, repent all transgressions against God and waive all claims without God.

Respectfully Submitted,

James B. Johnson

Certificate of Service

Petitioner certifies that he mailed this Informal Brief to the Court of Appeals of the Fourth Circuit on this _____ day of April, 2016 and because of costs, did not mail a copy to the opposition.

____

James B. Johnson, Petitioner

In The
United States Court of Appeals
For the Fourth Circuit

James Bowers Johnson
Appellant

v.

UNITED STATES OF AMERICA
APPELLEE

SUPPLEMENTAL MEMORANDUM IN SUPPORT OF APPELLANT'S INFORMAL BRIEF SUBMITTED APRIL 4, 2016

CASE NO. 16-6244
RE: UNITED STATES v James B. Johnson
6:12-cr-00015-NKM-RSB-1, 6:15-cv-80797-NKM-RSB

James B. Johnson
112 West Pall Mall Street
Winchester, Virginia [22601]

Appellant

SUPPLEMENTAL MEMORANDUM IN SUPPORT

Petitioner submitted an INFORMAL BRIEF to this Court of Appeals on April 4, 2016. He also filed a Motion for an Extension in hopes of receiving documentation confirming that John Kotmair was not unqualified to serve as his Power of Attorney in 2004 and that Biggs' trial testimony in 2013 was false. This Court of Appeals granted the Motion. Petitioner, having received the additional documentation, submits this Supplemental Memorandum in Support of his INFORMAL BRIEF.

TIMELINESS

This Supplemental Memorandum in Support is timely and was filed on April 19, 2016.

ISSUE

The District Court Ignored Petitioner's Argument And Grounds For Relief That Agent Biggs Testified Falsely When Stating John Kotmair Was Not Qualified To Serve As Power of Attorney In 2004

In his Motion to Amend (Dkt 205) the 2255 Petition (Dkt 186) based upon newly discovered evidence under 28 USC 2255(f)(4), Petitioner argued that the IRS used false information (Dkt 205, pg. 1) to prevent Agent Biggs from responding to John Kotmair's questions in 2004 and addressing matters of law and jurisdiction during the 2013 trial. Biggs' trial testimony, which he may not have known was false, if only because he did not properly investigate, (See Federal Crop Ins v Merrill, 332 US 380, 384 (1906) and United States v Price, 722 F 2d 88 (5th Cir. 1983)) originated with his manager and counsel. (Id., p. 6) In short, these two functionaries orchestrated and furthered a corporate lie and used Agent Biggs to deny and defy justice.

Biggs' manager and counsel relied upon a dubious 1994 IRS determination that Kotmair was ineligible (Exhibits E, F) to serve as Petitioner's Power of Attorney (POA). This was by design; for the agency (manager and counsel) sought to avoid what was NOT frivolous – a request for the law that made Petitioner liable to the federal income tax and Biggs' delegated authority to demand information from Petitioner. (Dkt. 186, Exhibit C)

Even after the agency prevented Biggs from answering Kotmair in 2004, Petitioner asked Biggs to respond directly to him with the answers to Kotmair's questions. Biggs never did. (Dkt 205, p. 11) Biggs' refusal is proof that the IRS NEVER intended to account for a valid legal and jurisdictional claim, whether Kotmair was qualified or not. It was the nature of Kotmair's questions and the subsequent answers the agency sought to avoid. The IRS claim that Kotmair was ineligibile was a false front and Biggs was a mere stooge.

Petitioner's Motion to Amend (Dkt. 205) established how and why Biggs' false testimony was prejudicial and the reasons relief should have been granted. Petitioner highlighted that, if only for the agency's unilateral determination that Kotmair was ineligible, the court was deceived and, consequently, committed reversible error on two separate occasions. (Id., pgs. 12 and 14)

Now the District Court states that Petitioner must show Biggs' testimony was perjured, the prosecution knew or should have known of the perjury and that the testimony was material to the conviction. (MEMORANDUM OPINION, p. 11) Yet, the Court ignored Petitioner's argument that both Biggs and the U.S. Attorney may have been oblivious to the macro scheme employed by the IRS. The Court also could have recognized that had Biggs and Hogeboom done their due diligence (Dkt 205, pgs. 10, 11, 15-17), they would have realized that Kotmair was qualified.

Consider that, with material from UNITED STATES OF AMERICA v. John Baptitst Kotmair, Jr., Civil No. WMN05CV1297, which goes beyond the newly discovered evidence (Dkt 205, Exhibit C),

1) The IRS gave Kotmair a Representative Number in 1990. (Exhibit B #16, C, D)

2) Kotmair used the number for over four years to represent members of his organization, without objection by the IRS or violation by Kotmair. (Exhibits B # 16-18, C, D, E)

3) In 1994, the IRS unilaterally decided that Kotmair was ineligible because he did not represent those "described in Section 10.7" of Circular 230. (Exhibits A, B, C, E, L, N, Q, S)

4) Mr. Kotmair responded that Section 10.7 of Circular 230 was met and that he was an officer of an organization comprised of members. (Exhibits C, F, N)

5) The District Court determined that the Fellowship was an "organization" with "members" (Exhibit M) and an "unincorporated association." (Exhibit R, pgs. 72,73)

6) Kotmair said, "But I still have the right to represent people and power of attorney as the circular says," with the response, "I understand that. I understand exactly." (Exhibit C pgs. 29, 30)

7) In violation of Circular 230, the IRS never resolved Kotmair's dispute of a due process concern or provide for Kotmair's remedies under the law. (Exhibits A p.12, B, C, F, N)

In light of the foregoing, it is noteworthy that the District Court stated

> The gravamen of [Petitioner's] argument is that Biggs' managers were mistaken in their belief that Kotmair could not act as a power of attorney, so Biggs' testimony at trial was a lie. (MEMORANDUM OPINION, p. 12) [brackets added]

Based upon the above seven elements, Petitioner's argument cannot fail (Id.) Moreover, the District Court's reference that Biggs' "recitation" (Id.) "appears" (Id.) to be "accurate" (Id.) must fail. What APPEARS and what IS are two separate distinctions. For Kotmair's Representative Number was not revoked. Consequently, the expression of what **appears** to be true in a court of law **is** of prime concern, whether those responsible for the expression of what is **"true"** are unaware that they are perpetuating a fraud. This Court of Appeals must conclude, then, that Biggs' (a mere messenger) untruthful statements give rise to a perjury claim. (Id.)

With the IRS' maligned decision in 1994 that Kotmair was ineligible to serve as POA, the agency effectively prevented one who understands the law and regulations from holding the IRS accountable for the proper interpretation and application of the law and regulations for "members"

(Exhibit F) of an "organization" (Id.), of which Kotmair was an officer (Id.). It should be no surprise, then, that the IRS "stonewalled" (Exhibits A, p. 12, F, G, H, I, J, K, N, O, P) Kotmair's request for a hearing since 1994, which allowed the agency to repeat its false refrain that he was not eligible to represent Petitioner in 2004.

Since the IRS did not dignify Kotmair's request for an administrative hearing and no third party (administrative law judge or court) held the IRS accountable to valid questions, or prevent the agency from enforcing laws and regulations against those who were not taxpayers, the IRS, through agents like Biggs, exercised agency authority without a governor. This is nothing less than the absence of any checks and balance upon an unaccountable executive agency. If the IRS is not accountable to questions about its enforcement of the law and regulations, to include a supposed revocation of a Representative Number, it is not accountable to the law and regulations. Rather, it is a law unto itself; and all parties that support the agency's indiscretions are complicit in a conspiracy. As a result, the property of men is not proptected and that very property is subjected to wrongful attack. Regarding Proprietors of Charles River Bridge v. Proprietors of Warren Bridge, 36 US 420 (1837), this Court must acknowledge that

> ... "No man shall be taken," "no man shall be desseised," without due process of law, is a principle taken from magna charta, infused into all our state constitutions, and is made inviolable by the federal government, by the amendments to the constitution."

The impact of the IRS' claim that Kotmair was not qualified is transparent. Petitioner never received answers to what was not frivolous in 2004, which would have negated a criminal trial in 2013. (Id., pgs. 9, 10) Moreover, if Biggs answered Kotmair's and Petitioner's questions in 2004, Petitioner would have had testimony and admissions that would have proved beneficial at trial and prevented his unjust incarceration. (Id., 12-14) Moreover, Biggs and the prosecuting attorney would not have been able to hide behind the prestige of the government or create the resulting false impression that unduly tainted the jury. (Id., 10, 11). If only because of the IRS ruse that Kotmair was ineligible, Biggs became not only the agency's witting or unwitting pawn for the IRS avoidance scheme, but the purveyor of material that suggested Kotmair's concerns were "frivolous" (Id., p. 3, 9), which fostered the presumption that Petitioner was within the agency's jurisdiction.

The IRS strategy is a marvelously effective ploy only when the courts underwrite the belief that the agency's determination is correct – that Kotmair was ineligible. Regrettably, the courts in the western district have summarily accepted that Kotmair's Representative Number was revoked (Dkt. 205, fn 1, fn 4) without accounting for the agency's failure to conduct an administrative hearing, in the interests of due process, under Title 31 CFR, Circular No. 230. (Exhibit S) By ignoring the agency's failure to grant a hearing from the date it was requested, the courts sanctioned the agency's scheme to avoid accountability to the tax laws and regulations.

Petitioner's Motion to Amend (Dkt. 205) is a compelling argument in favor of relief under 28 USC 2255(f)(4), not (f)(1), and he moves this Court of Appeals to acknowledge the entire Motion and the District Court's error in its MEMORANDUM OPINION and to grant relief as deemed appropriate.

Respectfully,

BIBLIOGRAPHY

- Ballentine's Law Dictionary, 3rd Edition
- Bouvier's Law Dictionary, 6th Edition
- Black, Henry Campbell. Black's Law Dictionary, 6th Edition
- Garner, Bryan A., Ed. Black's Law Dictionary, 9th Edition
- Garner, Bryan A., Ed. Black's Law Dictionary, 10th Edition
- Gibson, Henry. A Treatise on Suits in Chancery, Gaut-Ogden Co., 1907
- Hugo, Victor. Les Miserables, Signet Classic, by Penguin Group, 1997
- Merriam Webster's Dictionary and Thesaurus, Merriam-Webster, 2007
- Powell, Lynn. Framing Innocence, The New Press, 2010

- American Jurisprudence
- California Government Code
- Code of Federal Regulations
- Congressional Globe, 37th Congress, 2nd Session
- Congressional Rec. 1913
- Congressional Rec. 1916
- Congressional Rec. 1943
- Constitution of the United States
- Cooley, Const. Lim 7th Ed. 680
- United States. Federal Rules of Criminal Procedure
- United States. Federal Rules of Civil Procedures
- United States. Louisiana Civil Code
- United States. Oklahoma Statutes
- United States. Salary Tax Act of 1939
- United States. United States Code

- District Court Cases (6:12-00015-NKM (2013)
- Federal Court of Appeals Cases
- Supreme Court of Indiana Case Law
- Supreme Court of Maine Case Law
- United States Supreme Court Case Law

- Foster, Roger. A Treatise on the Federal Income Tax under the Act of 1913
- Kerik, Bernard. U.S. Criminal Justice System in Dire Need of Repair, 2011
- "On Trial: Evidence Gathering." The Wall Street Journal, November 2013, p. A3
- Treasury, Department of. Division of Tax Research. Collection at Source of Individual Normal Income Tax (1941)
- Zaritsky, Howard. Some Constitutional Questions Regarding the Federal Income Tax Laws, 1979 Report No. 80-19A
- Adams, John. "Argument in Defense of the Soldiers in the Boston Massacre Trials." Dec. 1770. 9 May 2016 <http://www.quotationspage.com/quote/3235.html>

- Barone, Michael. "Obama forfeits trust by not enforcing Obamacare." Washington Examiner. 10 July 2013. 11 May 2016 <http://www.washingtonexaminer.com/obama-forfeits-trust-by-not-enforcing-obamacare/article/2532884>
- "Bureau of Justice Statistics Bulletin." 5May 2016 <http://www.bjs.gov/content/pub/pdf/p2581.pdf>
- "Criminalizing Everyone." Washington Times. 5 October 2009. 5 May 2016 <http://www.washingtontimes.com/news/2009/oct/05/criminalizing-everyone/?page=all>
- Cryer, Tommy. "Motion to Dismiss"5 May 2016 <http://wethepeoplefoundation.org/MISC/Cryer/CRYER--MotiontoDismiss.pdf>
- Dale, Helle. "The American Experiment." 5 July 2007. 5 May 2016 <http://www.heritage.org/research/commentary/2007/07/the-american-experiment>
- 10 May 2016 <https://www.goodreads.com/quotes/860090-the-study-of-human-institutions-is-always-a-search-for>
- 12 May 2016 < https://www.goodreads.com/author/quotes/17142.Edmund_Burke>
- Grossman, Andrew. "The Unlikely Orchid Smuggler: A Case Study in Overcriminalization." 27 July 2009. 5 May 2016 <www.heritage.org/research/reports/2009/07/the-unlikely-orchid-smuggler-a-case-study-in-overcriminalization>."
- 10 May 2016 <http://www.goodreads.com/quotes/234863-the-study-of-history-is-a-powerful-antidote-to-contemporary>
- "Incarceration in the United States." 5 May 2016 <https://en.wikipedia.org/wiki/Incarceration in the United States>
- 5 May 2016 <http://legal-dictionary.thefreedictionary.com/Uniform+Commercial+Code>
- Madison, James. "The Federalist No. 62" Independent Journal. 27 Feb. 1788. 9 May 2016 <http://www.constitution.org/fed/federa62.htm>
- Malkin, Michelle. "America's Sociopath Fetish." 12 July 13. 10 May 2016 <http://michellemalkin.com/2013/07/12/americas-sociopath-fetish/>
- Malkin, Michelle. "America's Sociopath Fetish." 12 July 13. 5 May 2016 <http://www.realclearpolitics.com/articles/2013/07/12/americas_sociopath_fetish__119171.html>
- "Meet the Federal Prisoners About to be Released." The Marshall Project. 9 Oct. 2015. 11 May 2016 <https://www.themarshallproject.org/2015/10/09/meet-the-federal-prisoners-about-to-be-released#.OuWDLcMzN>
- Obituary. "On This Day." 6 Jan. 1933. 9 May 2016 <http://www.nytimes.com/learning/general/onthisday/bday/0704.html>
- Ponnuru, Ramesh. "ObamaCare: Inconvenient Truths." Fox News.10 July 2013. 11 May 2016 <http://nation.foxnews.com/2013/07/10/obamacare-inconvenient-truths>
- 9 May 2016 <http://quotes.liberty-tree.ca/quotes_by/jean-francois+revel>
- Rotunda, Ronald. "On the health-care mandate, Obama reaches beyond the law." The Washington Post. 18 July 2013. 10 May 2016 <https://www.washingtonpost.com/opinions/on-the-health-care-mandate-obama-

reaches-beyond-the-law/2013/07/18/d442aefc-efb4-11e2-a1f9-ea873b7e0424_story.html>

- Sowell, Thomas. "Is This Still America?"16 July 2013. 9 May 2016 <http://www.nationalreview.com/article/353502/still-america-thomas-sowell>
- Sullum, Jacob. "Why George Zimmerman Should Be Acquitted." 10 July 2013. 9 May 2016 <http://reason.com/archives/2013/07/10/why-george-zimmerman-should-be-acquitted>
- 5 May 2016 <www.theodore-roosevelt.com/trsorbonnespeech.html>
- "United States incarceration rate." 5 May 2016 <https://en.wikipedia.org/wiki/United_States_incarceration_rate>
- 10 May 2016 <http://www.tsowell.com/quotes.html>

About the Author

A native of the Commonwealth of Virginia, James Bowers Johnson grew up in the Shenandoah Valley. He has four children: Cory, Heather, Timothy, and Emma.

Mr. Johnson was graduated from the Virginia Military Institute in 1987 with a Bachelor of Arts degree in English and French. He was a Distinguished Military Graduate with a Regular Army commission in the United States Army and served four years in the field of Military Intelligence. Upon completion of his military service, he committed himself to extensive research into the Constitution, law, government, taxation, and banking. He subsequently revoked any prior election of any federal status and benefits.

After suffering the travesty that is a "tax trial" in the "American Justice" system, Mr. Johnson served another four-year tour of duty for his country in a federal prison for a crime he never committed. He continues to fight the conviction in the federal courts.

Mr. Johnson is available for speaking engagements and book signings. He may be contacted at: intruthandhonor@protonmail.com.

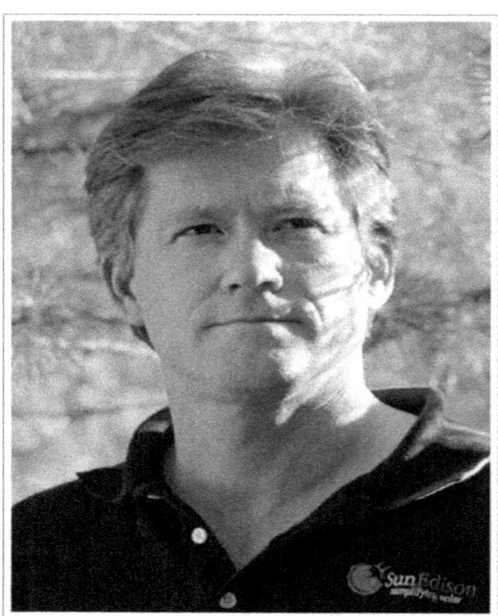

James Bowers Johnson

If you are studying tax law and the federal income tax system, please be cautious as to the philosophies and leaders you follow. If you want insight and a full understanding of Mr. Johnson's experience, to include trial records, contact him. Don't be less than informed. Be wise and purposeful. Fear not!

www.ingramcontent.com/pod-product-compliance
Lightning Source LLC
Chambersburg PA
CBHW081209220326
41598CB00037B/6726

* 9 7 8 0 9 9 7 9 5 4 2 0 3 *